Accession no.
36167115

KT-476-690

Health Psychology

WITHDRAWN

"Jane Ogden manages to write in an uncomplicated manner but without doing injustice to the complexities of the theories and research being described. She provides good historical and societal contexts for the different strands of research, so students can appreciate the relevance of Health Psychology in and for the real world."

Roger Ingham, Professor of Health and Community Psychology,
University of Southampton,UK

"This 5th edition of *Health Psychology* represents an even more attractive book than the previous editions. The new figures and images illustrate the text and students are provided with clear, up-to-date and accessible information on the major theoretical and empirical issues in health psychology. There are five new chapters and the one on health promotion is particularly impressive. The book now seems suited not only to health psychology students but also for those in allied professions such as physiotherapists, nurses, dieticians, physicians and medical students."

Ad A. Kaptein, Professor of Medical Psychology,
Leiden University Medical Centre, the Netherlands

"Jane Ogden's *Health Psychology* is an impressive introduction to the field. The book is suitable for students of all backgrounds wishing to gain a comprehensive introduction to the exciting field of health psychology. The chapters are clearly organized and integrate the latest international research findings into an easy to read and well illustrated textbook."

Keith J. Petrie, Professor of Health Psychology,
Department of Psychological Medicine, University of Auckland

"This thought-provoking book is in tune with students' questions about health psychology and places the student at the centre of knowledge dissemination."

Dr. Catherine Sykes, Team Leader, Health Psychology,
City University, London, UK

"Jane Ogden's *Health Psychology* is a smart and readable textbook that should appeal to both instructors and students of health psychology. Its overall structure is intuitively appealing and progresses from health beliefs to factors associated with becoming ill to the actual state of being ill. New to this edition is a wonderful chapter on the demographics of health and health behaviours. Using a number of striking graphs, Ogden highlights the disparities in health by geography, social class, and gender. The book's greatest appeal, however, is its focus on the major ideas in health psychology. The reader is not bombarded with subtleties of dozens of studies; rather the broader theories are emphasized. Whether you come to health psychology with a background in social, clinical, physiological, or other specialization, you will find this to be a compelling book."

James W. Pennebaker, Regents Centennial Professor of Psychology,
University of Texas at Austin, USA

Health
Psychology

Fifth Edition

Jane Ogden

LIS LIBRARY

Date	Fund
26/11/12	nm-Riv ✓

Order No
2360822

University of Chester

WITHDRAWN

Mc Graw Hill   Open University Press

London   Boston   Burr Ridge, IL   Dubuque, IA   Madison, WI   New York   San Francisco
St. Louis   Bangkok   Bogotá   Caracas   Kuala Lumpur   Lisbon   Madrid   Mexico City
Milan   Montreal   New Delhi   Santiago   Seoul   Singapore   Sydney   Taipei   Toronto

Open University Press
McGraw-Hill Education
McGraw-Hill House
Shoppenhangers Road
Maidenhead
Berkshire
England
SL6 2QL

email: enquiries@openup.co.uk
world wide web: www.openup.co.uk

and Two Penn Plaza, New York, NY 10121-2289, USA

First published 2012

Copyright © Jane Ogden 2012

All rights reserved. Except for the quotation of short passages for the purposes of criticism and
review, no part of this publication may be reproduced, stored in a retrieval system, or transmitted,
in any form or by any means, electronic, mechanical, photocopying, recording or otherwise,
without the prior written permission of the publisher or a licence from the Copyright Licensing
Agency Limited. Details of such licences (for reprographic reproduction) may be obtained from
the Copyright Licensing Agency Ltd of Saffron House, 6-10 Kirby Street, London, EC1N 8TS.

A catalogue record of this book is available from the British Library

ISBN-13: 978 0 335 243839 (pb)
ISBN-10: 0 335 243835 (pb)

Library of Congress Cataloging-in-Publication Data
CIP data applied for

Senior Commissioning Editor: Monika Lee
Editorial Assistant: Richard Townrow
Senior Marketing Manager: Kevin Watt
Senior Product Manager: Bryony Skelton
Senior Production Editor: James Bishop

Typeset by SR Nova Pvt. Ltd, Bangalore, India
Printed by Markono Print Media Pte Ltd

Fictitious names of companies, products, people, characters and/or data that may be used herein
(in case studies or in examples) are not intended to represent any real individual, company,
product or event.

The McGraw-Hill Companies

Brief table of contents

Detailed table of contents

List of figures and tables

FIGURES

TABLES

List of abbreviations

ADL	activity of daily living
AIDS	acquired immune deficiency syndrome
APT	adaptive pacing therapy; adjuvant psychological therapy
AVE	abstinence violation effect
BDI	Beck depression inventory
BMI	body mass index
BSE	breast self-examination
CAD	coronary artery disease
CBSM	cognitive behavioural stress management
CBT	cognitive behavioural therapy
CHD	coronary heart disease
CIN	cervical intraepithelial neoplasia
CMV	cytomegalovirus
COPD	chronic obstructive pulmonary disease
CR	conditioned response
CS	conditioned stimulus
D&C	dilatation and curettage
DAFNE	dose adjustment for normal eating
DEBQ	Dutch Eating Behaviour Questionnaire
ERPC	evacuation of the retained products of conception
FAP	familial adenomatous polyposis
FH	familial hypercholesterolaemia
GAS	general adaptation syndrome
GCT	gate control theory
GHQ	General Health Questionnaire
GSR	galvanic skin response
HAART	highly active anti-retroviral therapy
HADS	hospital anxiety and depression scale
HAPA	health action process approach
HBM	health belief model
HPA	hypothalamic-pituitary-adrenocorticol
HRT	hormone replacement therapy
IPA	interpretative phenomenological analysis
IPQ	illness perception questionnaire
IPQR	revised version of illness perception questionnaire
LISRES	life stressors and social resources inventory
MAT	medication adherence training
MHLC	multidimensional health locus of control
MI	motivational interviewing, myocardial infarction
MPQ	McGill Pain Questionnaire
MACS	Multi Centre AIDS Cohort Study
NHP	Nottingham Health Profile
NHS	National Health Service
NKCC	natural killer cell cytotoxicity
OCD	obsessive compulsive disorder
PDA	personal digital assistant
PFSQ	parental feeding style questionnaire
PMT	protection motivation theory
PNI	psychoneuroimmunology

PSE	present state examination
PSS	perceived stress scale
PTSD	post-traumatic stress disorder
SEIQoL	schedule for the individual quality of life
SES	socioeconomic status
SEU	subjective expected utility
SIP	Sickness Impact Profile
SLQ	Silver Lining Questionnaire
SOS	Swedish Obese Subjects study
SRE	Schedule of Recent Experiences
SRRS	social readjustment rating scale
STD	sexually transmitted disease
TOP	termination of pregnancy
TPB	theory of planned behaviour
TRA	theory of reasoned action
UR	unconditioned response
US	unconditional stimulus
WHO	World Health Organization
WRAP	Women, Risk and AIDS Project

Preface to the fifth edition

WHY I FIRST WROTE THIS BOOK

I first wrote this book in 1995 after several years of teaching my own course in health psychology. The texts I recommended to my students were by US authors and this was reflected in their focus on US research and US health care provision. In addition, they tended to be driven by examples rather than by theories or models, which made them difficult to turn into lectures (from my perspective) or to use for essays or revision (from my students' perspective). I decided to write my own book to solve some of these problems. I wanted to supplement US work with that from my colleagues in the UK, the rest of Europe, New Zealand and Australia. I also wanted to emphasize theory and to write the book in a way that would be useful. I hope that the first four editions have succeeded.

AIMS OF THIS NEW FIFTH EDITION

Over time a book starts to look dated. This fifth edition feels to me like a completely new book as I have rewritten, restructured, updated and added new sections and whole new chapters. In particular I have made the following changes.

- **A new structure**: the book is now organized into five parts: 1) The context of health psychology; 2) Health beliefs, behaviour and behaviour change; 3) Becoming ill; 4) Being ill; and 5) Reflecting on health psychology. These parts highlight a continuum model of health and illness and the chapters now cover theory and research along this continuum as we move from being healthy through to being ill.

- **The focus on health psychology**: I have now expanded my description of the focus on health psychology in the introductory chapter and have not only described how our discipline draws upon the biopsychosocial model but also how it sees health and illness as being on a continuum, how it strives to explain individual variability and how it focuses on both the direct and indirect pathways between psychological factors and health.

- **Health inequalities**: Chapter 2 is new and highlights variation in health and illness in terms of geographical location, time, social class and gender. I have described possible explanations for this variation in terms of medical interventions (e.g. vaccinations, access to skilled health professionals), environmental factors (e.g. sanitation, clean drinking water, town planning) and behaviour (e.g. smoking, diet and exercise). The chapter then describes how health psychology tends to focus on the role of behaviour.

- **Individual behaviours**: the book still contains separate chapters on addictive behaviours, eating behaviour, exercise and sex but these have been rewritten to reflect recent research and the areas that are currently the focus of health psychology.

- **Addictive behaviours**: Chapter 4 focuses on smoking and alcohol consumption but for this edition I have added sections on caffeine use and exercise dependence to illustrate how disease and social learning theories of addiction can be applied to addictions which involve the intake of a drug (e.g. caffeine) and those which are behaviourally based (e.g. exercise dependence).

- **Health promotion**: the biggest development in health psychology since this book was first published is the shift in emphasis from *predicting* behaviour to *changing* behaviour. This edition contains a new Chapter 8 which describes a wide range of key behaviour change theories and strategies and provides useful details and practical examples of how they can be used in practice. Some examples include cognitive behaviour therapy, motivational interviewing, incentives, mass media interventions and interventions using new technologies such as laptops and mobile phones. I hope this chapter will be useful for anyone needing a thorough overview of this vast literature.

- **Coping and social support**: I have extended these sections in Chapters 9 and 11 and have provided more up-to-date research, details of measurement issues and their impact upon health outcomes.

- **Access to health care**: the next main change in health psychology is the emphasis on patient populations rather than just healthy people (and students!). The new Chapter 10 reflects this shift towards health psychology in practice and explores the role of psychological theory and methods in the health care setting. It focuses on why people seek help (or delay), how screening encourages help-seeking before symptoms have started, communication between the health professional and the patient and the factors which predict adherence.
- **Chronic illness**: there are many chronic illnesses and health psychology is relevant to them all. In this edition I have still focused in Chapters 14 and 15 on HIV/AIDS, cancer, coronary heart disease and obesity but have attempted to highlight how all our research is relevant to a multitude of other chronic conditions such as diabetes, chronic fatigue syndrome and asthma.
- **Men's health**: in the last edition I included a chapter on women's health. This edition now includes a new chapter on men's health (Chapter 17). In this I have explored gender differences in life expectancy and causes of mortality and then described how these can be explained for men in terms of health-related, risky and help-seeking behaviours. Further, I have explored why men behave in the ways they do in terms of their health beliefs, social norms of masculinity and emotional expression. Finally, this chapter evaluates these factors in the context of three case studies: prostate cancer, suicide and coronary heart disease.
- **Critical health psychology**: students are often told to be 'more critical' in their thinking and writing, but often lecturers are unclear as to how this can be achieved. I have rewritten the final chapter to highlight the kinds of questions that can be asked about health psychology as a means to develop a more critical perspective. This chapter describes how to be critical and how to analyse theory, methods, measurement tools and the discipline as a whole, and draws together the 'Some problems with . . .' boxes and the 'Assumptions in health psychology' sections that are in each chapter. This final chapter then concludes with a description of critical health psychology and presents some options for further reading.
- **Additional sections**: I have added many new sections throughout the book to reflect recent approaches. Examples include post-traumatic stress symptoms, exercise and chronic fatigue syndrome, post-traumatic growth and benefit finding, visualization and illness cognitions, and the response shift. I have also placed more emphasis on measurement and described the ways in which constructs and behaviours such as exercise, exercise dependence, coping, social support, eating behaviour and illness cognition can be assessed.
- **The use of figures and images**: the book is now much more visual and I have used far more figures and images throughout. The aim is to bring health psychology to life and to emphasize how psychological factors are relevant to our daily existence whether we are healthy or not.

This edition still contains a number of familiar features:

- **'Some problems with . . .'** This is a short box that appears in each chapter, asking students to consider some of the issues surrounding research in a particular area of health psychology. For example, Chapter 3 considers some problems with health beliefs research. In this case, how do we know that asking people about health beliefs doesn't change the way they think? Is it possible that beliefs that predict and explain behaviour are different to those that change behaviour? And so on. The aim of including these examples is to encourage students to develop an awareness of some common pitfalls of research in health psychology and to engage them in challenging, evaluating and analysing the integrity of their own research and those of other academics in the field. The issues highlighted in these boxes are discussed further in Chapter 19.
- **Focus on research examples**. I have changed most of the focus on research sections and have included studies which are either classics in their area or which use original methods or measurements. For additional research papers see either the further reading sections at the end of each chapter or my *Essential Readings in Health Psychology* (see p. xxviii), which contains the original texts plus commentaries.

- **Further reading and review questions**. Finally, as you would expect from a new edition, there is a full update throughout, including new data and figures where appropriate, updated further reading sections featuring new and recent publications, a comprehensively updated list of references and new questions at the end of the chapters for use either in class as discussion points or as an aid to student learning.
- **An Online Learning Centre website** accompanies this edition with useful materials for students of health psychology and their lecturers, including PowerPoint presentations, artwork and more.

For more information about the new edition's features, see the 'Guided tour' on pages xxxiii–iv, which leads you through the elements common to each chapter.

THE STRUCTURE OF THE FIFTH EDITION

Health psychology focuses on a biopsychosocial perspective – health and illness as a continuum, the indirect and direct pathways between psychology and health and variability. This book has been organized to reflect this continuum model of health and illness in the organization of its five new parts. Each chapter within this structure highlights a biopsychosocial perspective, explores the indirect and direct pathways and assesses a multitude of variables in explaining variability.

PART 1: THE CONTEXT OF HEALTH PSYCHOLOGY

Chapter 1 explores the main perspectives of health psychology and outlines the aims and structure of this book. Chapter 2 provides the broader context for health psychology and focuses on health inequalities. This chapter illustrates how health and illness vary according to factors such as gender, age, time and geographical location. It then explores possible explanations for this variation with a focus on medical progress, environmental factors and the role of behaviour. The chapter then describes how health psychology tends to emphasize the role of behaviour as an explanation for health inequalities.

PART 2: HEALTH BELIEFS, BEHAVIOUR AND BEHAVIOUR CHANGE

Central to understanding health and illness is the role of beliefs and behaviour. Chapter 3 describes a number of theories of health beliefs and then outlines the key models of health beliefs such as the stages of change model, the health belief model and the theory of planned behaviour. Central to the focus on health beliefs is the argument that behaviours can be best understood, predicted and changed if and when we can describe a person's health beliefs. Chapters 4–7 then focus on individual behaviours and describe theories and research which have explored why people do or do not behave in healthy ways. The key behaviours addressed are smoking, drinking and other addictions (Chapter 4), eating behaviour (Chapter 5), exercise (Chapter 6) and sex (Chapter 7). The last chapter in Part 2 then addresses health promotion and theories of behaviour change and explores the ways in which interventions have been developed to encourage people to become more healthy. This is a vast literature and Chapter 8 highlights behaviour change strategies such as cognitive behavioural therapy, motivational interviewing, the use of fear appeals, the role of the mass media and the use of new technologies such as the internet and mobile phones.

PART 3: BECOMING ILL

The next stage along the continuum from health to illness addresses the early factors involved when becoming ill. Chapter 9 describes illness cognitions and ways in which people perceive symptoms and develop representations of their illness. It then addresses theories of coping with illness and the role of both illness cognitions and coping in predicting patient health outcomes. Chapter 10 then explores the ways in which individuals come into contact with the health care system. First it examines the mechanisms involved in help-seeking, such as symptom perception and the costs and benefits of visiting a doctor. Next it describes the research on screening, whereby people are drawn into health care even in the absence of any symptoms. Theories and research related to communication in the consultation, with an emphasis on decision-making and how health professionals develop a diagnosis are then discussed. Finally, the chapter explores the issues relating to adherence and how psychological factors such as illness and health beliefs predict whether or not a patient behaves in the way recommended by the health care team. Chapters 11 and 12 then describe theories of stress and the ways in which stress can cause illness. Chapter 12 also explores the roles of coping, social support, control and personality variables in moderating the link between stress and illness and describes the impact of stress on both physiology and behaviour.

PART 4: BEING ILL

Following along the continuum is the next stage: being ill. The key issues surrounding being ill are addressed in Part 4. Chapter 13 describes theories of pain and approaches to pain management. It also highlights the important role of the placebo effect and the possible mechanisms behind this process. Chapters 14 and 15 then focus on specific chronic illnesses and assess how the many psychological constructs and theories addressed in the book so far relate to the onset, progression and outcomes of HIV, cancer (Chapter 14), obesity and coronary heart disease (Chapter 15). These chapters also discuss how the key psychological factors such as health beliefs and behaviours, illness cognitions, adherence, coping and social support also relate to all other chronic conditions such as asthma, diabetes and arthritis. Part 4 then explores women's health issues such as miscarriage, pregnancy and termination (Chapter 16) and men's health (Chapter 17) with a focus on men's behaviour, beliefs, the social norms of masculinity and emotional expression. Finally, Chapter 18 examines the role of health status and quality of life in patient outcomes and the ways in which these constructs have been conceptualized and measured.

PART 5: REFLECTING ON HEALTH PSYCHOLOGY

This final part takes a broad overview of the all material covered in the book so far and Chapter 19 highlights the ways in which we can think critically about all aspects of health psychology with a focus on theory, methods, measurement and the discipline as a whole.

Also available: *Essential Readings in Health Psychology*

Essential Readings in Health Psychology **edited by Jane Ogden**

ISBN: 9780335211388 (Softback) 9780335211395 (Hardback)

Available from www.mcgraw-hill.co.uk

Jane Ogden has also produced a reader in health psychology, containing 29 papers that employ different theories and methods and offer a more in-depth approach to the discipline. Covering the breadth of topics dealt with in this textbook, the reader aims to provide a range of good case examples of health psychology work. By reading them, students of psychology should gain a greater insight into what health psychology research can (and cannot) achieve. Throughout, the papers are framed by editorial discussions of their context, meaning and contribution to health psychology as a whole.

This textbook has provided the structure for choosing the papers in the reader. The papers have been grouped into five parts, covering the context of health psychology, health behaviours, health care, stress and health, and chronic illness. The reader can therefore be used as an adjunct to this textbook to provide more detail than that covered in a more general introductory text such as this one. In fact some of the papers selected for the reader are referenced in the textbook in brief in the 'Focus on research' boxes.

The structure of the reader also follows the key areas highlighted by the British Psychological Society as central to health psychology and as such would be an ideal resource for any undergraduate or postgraduate course, presenting good examples of key theories, models and methods. It could also provide the starting point for a reading list to accompany an undergraduate or postgraduate course, or the papers could be used to focus a seminar discussion or a journal club. In addition, the papers are published in their entirety, including their reference lists, so they can be used to develop reading lists and recommend further reading. Below is the list of papers in *Essential Readings in Health Psychology*.

SECTION 1: THE CONTEXT OF HEALTH PSYCHOLOGY

Mokdad, A.H., Marks, J.S., Stroup, D.F. and Gerberding, J.L. (2004) Actual causes of death in the United States, 2000, *JAMA*, 10(29): 1238–45.

Kaplan, R.M. (1990) Behaviour as the central outcome in health care, *American Psychologist*, 45: 1211–20.

SECTION 2: HEALTH BEHAVIOURS

Sutton, S. (1998) Predicting and explaining intentions and behaviour: how well are we doing? *Journal of Applied Social Psychology*, 28: 1317–38.

Ogden, J. (2003) Some problems with social cognition models: a pragmatic and conceptual analysis, *Health Psychology*, 22(4): 424–8.

West, R. (2005) Time for a change: putting the Transtheoretical (Stages of Change) model to rest, *Addiction*, 100: 1036–9.

Armitage, C.J. (2005) Can the Theory of Planned Behaviour predict the maintenance of physical activity? *Health Psychology*, 24(3): 235–45.

Murgraff, V., White, D. and Phillips, K. (1999) An application of protection motivation theory to riskier single occasion drinking, *Psychology and Health*, 14: 339–50.

DiClemente, C.C., Prochaska, J.O., Fairhurst, S.K. et al. (1991) The process of smoking cessation: an analysis of precontemplation, contemplation, and preparation stages of change, *Journal of Consulting and Clinical Psychology*, 59: 295–304.

Wardle, J. and Beales, S. (1988) Control and loss of control over eating: an experimental investigation, *Journal of Abnormal Psychology*, 97: 35–40.

Woodcock, A., Stenner, K. and Ingham, R. (1992) Young people talking about HIV and AIDS: interpretations of personal risk of infection, *Health Education Research: Theory and Practice*, 7: 229–34.

Aiken, L.S., West, S.G., Woodward, C.K., Reno, R.R. and Reynolds, K.D. (1994) Increasing screening mammography in asymptomatic women: evaluation of a second generation, theory based program, *Health Psychology*, 13: 526–38.

Gollwitzer, P.M. and Sheeran, P. (2006) Implementation intentions and goal achievement: a meta-analysis of effects and processes, *Advances in Experimental Social Psychology*, 38: 69–119.

SECTION 3: HEALTH CARE

Roter, D.L., Steward, M., Putnam, S.M. et al. (1997) Communication pattern of primary care physicians, *Journal of the American Medical Association*, 277: 350–6.

Mead, N. and Bower, P. (2000) Patient centredness: a conceptual framework and review of empirical literature, *Social Science and Medicine*, 51: 1087–110.

Marteau, T.M., Senior, V., Humphries, S.E. et al. (2004) Psychological impact of genetic testing for familial hypercholesterolemia within a previously aware population: a randomized controlled trial, *American Journal of Medical Genetics*, 128(A): 285–93.

Horne, R. and Weinman, J. (2002) Self regulation and self management in asthma: exploring the role of illness perceptions and treatment beliefs in explaining non adherence to preventer medication, *Psychology and Health*, 17: 17–32.

Simpson, S.H., Eurich, D.T., Majumdar, S.R., Padwal, R.S., Tsuyuki, R.T., Varney, J. and Johnson, J.A. (2006) A meta-analysis of the association between adherence to drug therapy and mortality, *British Medical Journal*, July 1, 333(7557): 15.

SECTION 4: STRESS AND HEALTH

Everson, S.A., Lynch, J.W., Chesney, M.A. et al. (1997) Interaction of workplace demands and cardiovascular reactivity in progression of carotid atherosclerosis: population based study, *British Medical Journal*, 314: 553–8.

Pereira, D.B., Antoni, M.H., Danielson, A. et al. (2003) Life stress and cervical squamous intraepithelial lesions in women with human papillomavirus and human immunodeficiency virus, *Psychosomatic Medicine*, 65(1): 1–8.

Ebrecht, M., Hextall, J., Kirtley, L.G., Taylor, A., Dyson, M. and Weinman, J. (2004) Perceived stress and cortisol levels predict speed of wound healing in healthy male adults, *Psychoneuroendocrinology*, 29: 798–809.

Pennebaker, J.W. (1997) Writing about emotional experiences as a therapeutic process, *Psychological Science*, 8(3): 162–6.

Petrie, K.J., Booth, R.J. and Pennebaker, J.W. (1998) The immunological effects of thought suppression, *Journal of Personality and Social Psychology*, 75: 1264–72.

SECTION 5: CHRONIC ILLNESS

Eccleston, C., Morley, S., Williams, A., Yorke, L. and Mastroyannopoulou, K. (2002) Systematic review of randomised controlled trials of psychological therapy for chronic pain in children and adolescents with a subset meta-analysis of pain relief, *Pain*, 99(1–2): 157–65.

Smith, J.A. and Osborn, M. (2007) Pain as an assault on the self: an interpretative phenomenological analysis of the psychological impact of chronic benign low back pain, *Psychology and Health*, 22: 517–34.

Taylor, S.E. (1983) Adjustment to threatening events: a theory of cognitive adaptation, *American Psychologist*, 38: 1161–73.

Petrie, K.J., Cameron, L.D., Ellis, C.J., Buick, D. and Weinman, J. (2002) Changing illness perceptions after myocardial infarction: an early intervention randomized controlled trial. *Psychosomatic Medicine*, 64: 580–6.

Antoni, M.H., Carrico, A.W., Duran, R.E. et al. (2006) Randomized clinical trial of cognitive behavioral stress management on human immunodeficiency virus viral load in gay men treated with highly active anti retroviral therapy, *Psychosomatic Medicine*, 68: 143–51.

Ogden, J., Clementi, C. and Aylwin, S. (2006) The impact of obesity surgery and the paradox of control: a qualitative study, *Psychology and Health*, 21(2): 273–93.

Rapkin, B.D. and Schwartz, C.E. (2004) Towards a theoretical model of quality of life appraisal: Implications of findings from studies of response shift, *Health and Quality of Life Outcomes*, 2: 14.

If you wish to use the reader as a supplementary text alongside this textbook, we have listed here the papers from the reader in relation to the parts of this book.

Part 1 The context of health psychology	Kaplan, R.M. (1990) Mokdad, A.H. et al. (2004)
Part 2 Health beliefs, behaviour and behaviour change	Aiken, L.S. et al. (1994) Armitage, C.J. (2005) DiClemente, C.C. et al. (1991) Gollwitzer, P.M. and Sheeran, P. (2006) Kaplan, R.M. (1990) Mokdad, A.H. et al. (2004) Murgraff, V. et al. (1999) Ogden, J. (2003) Simpson S.H. et al. (2006) Sutton, S. (1998) Wardle, J. and Beales, S. (1988) West, R. (2005) Woodcock, A. et al. (1992)
Part 3 Becoming ill	Antoni, M.H. et al. (2006) Ebrecht, M. et al. (2004) Everson, et al. (1997) Horne, R. and Weinman, J. (2002) Marteau, T.M. et al. (2004) Mead, N. and Bower, P. (2000) Pennebaker, J.W. (1997) Pereira, D.B. et al. (2003) Petrie, K.J. et al. (1998) Petrie, K.J. et al. (2002) Roter, D.L. et al. (1997) Simpson S.H. et al. (2006) Taylor, S.E. (1983)
Part 4 Being ill	Antoni, M.H. et al. (2006) Eccleston, C. et al. (2002) Everson, S.A. et al. (1997) Ogden, J. et al. (2006) Pereira, D.B. et al. (2003) Petrie, K.J. et al. (1998) Petrie, K.J. et al. (2002) Rapkin, B.D. and Schwartz, C.E. (2004) Simpson S.H. et al. (2006) Smith, J.A. (2008) Taylor, S.E. (1983) Woodcock, A. et al. (1992)
Part 5 Reflecting on health psychology	All papers relate to this chapter

Guided tour

CHAPTER OVERVIEW

This chapter offers a broad introduction to the discipline
history of health psychology and highlights differences b
biomedical model. It then describes the focus of health p
health and illness as being on a continuum, the direct and
and health and the emphasis on explaining variability. N
psychology and the future of our discipline. Finally, this
describes how the book is structured.

Chapter Content

The title page for each chapter lists all the main
headings within that chapter for quick and easy
reference to specific topics.

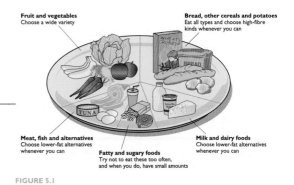

Fruit and vegetables
Choose a wide variety

Bread, other cereals and potatoes
Eat all types and choose high-fibre
kinds whenever you can

Meat, fish and alternatives
Choose lower-fat alternatives
whenever you can

Fatty and sugary foods
Try not to eat these too often,
and when you do, have small amounts

Milk and dairy foods
Choose lower-fat alternatives
whenever you can

FIGURE 5.1
The balance of good health

Figures and Tables

Clear and well-represented tables and figures
throughout the book provide up-to-date information and data in a clear and easy-to-read format.

FOCUS ON RESEARCH 4.1: TEST

**Using aversive images to enhance healthy food choices: an ev:
Prestwich and Marteau, 2011).**

Central to a developmental model of eating behavior is the role
associative learning. From this perspective we learn which foods
of other cues or stimuli in our environment. For example, we mig
corn with a trip to the cinema and so these foods become conside
make negative pairings which is why food aversions develop a
being made to drink warm lumpy milk at school put a generation
first to explicitly use a conditioning paradigm to explore whet
unhealthy consequences can reduce participants preferences for
both implicit and explicit attitudes.

METHOD

Sample: 134 staff and students from a London University were
Design: The study used a randomized control trial and partici
control or experimental conditions.
Intervention: Participants were asked to watch a slide show fea
in random order: chocolate, biscuits, cake, crisps and a ran
each snack image was followed by a 1 second image of one of
consequences of unhealthy eating (eg. Obesity in men, obesi
one image of heart surgery). For those in the control conditi

Focus on Research

Boxes that include both recent and classic
research studies in health psychology, explaining
the background, methodology, results and
conclusion of the work.

Problems with . . .

This feature encourages you to pause for thought
and reflect on health psychology research. Each
box highlights some concerns with collecting,
evaluating and validating research and includes
three or more potential problems to consider.

BOX 4.1 Some Problems With . . . Eat

Below are some problems with research in this area that you may wi

1 Measuring behaviour is always difficult. Measuring eating behavi
up of many different components, happens at many different time
suring it either by self-report, observation or in the laboratory c:
change the ways in which people eat.

2 Much research uses healthy eating as the outcome variable by tryi
a better diet. However, trying to define what is a healthy diet and
very problematic.

CONCLUSION

The study illustrates that food preferences can be learned
change implicit attitudes and actual behavior. These res
development of food preferences and eating behavior
intervention.

Conclusion

A wrap-up of the main themes to emerge from
the chapter and a useful revision tool to recap
the material in a topic area.

Questions

Short questions to test your understanding and
encourage you to consider some of the issues
raised in the chapter. A useful means of assessing your comprehension and progress.

QUESTIONS

1 How might parents influence their children's eati
2 How do our beliefs about food influence what we
3 What are the problems with the developmental an
4 Dieting causes overeating. Discuss.

FOR DISCUSSION

Think of someone you know who has successfully changed
eaten less, cut out chocolate). What factors contributed tow

For discussion

A discussion point for a seminar or group
work, or to form the basis of an essay.

ASSUMPTIONS IN HEALTH PSY

The research on smoking and alcohol highlights some of the a

1 *Mind–body dualism.* Theories of addictions and addictive
or physiological processes. This separation is reflected in th
the social learning perspectives. Therefore, although some
mind (e.g. cue exposure) and body (e.g. nicotine replacem
of the individual.

Assumptions in Health Psychology

A section that explains some of the basic assumptions made in health psychology of which you
should be aware when reading the material.

FURTHER READING

Ogden, J. (2010) *The Psychology of Eating: From Healthy*
    Blackwell.
This book provides a detailed map of research relating to
and addresses questions such as 'Why do so many people
unhappy with their body shape?', 'What are the causes of o
ders?'. It is written in a similar style to this textbook.

Grogan, S. (2008). *Body Image: Understanding Body Diss*
    ed. London: Routledge.

Further Reading

A list of useful essays, articles, books and
research which can take your study further.
A good starting point for your research for
essays or assignments.

Glossary

At the end of the text there is a brief glossary of
the commonly used terms in health psychology
methodology.

Methodology glossary

B

Between-subjects design: this involves making comparisons between different groups of subjects; for example,
males versus females, those who have been offered a
health-related intervention versus those who have not.

C

Case-control design: this involves taking a group of subjects who show a particular characteristic (e.g. lung cancer – the dependent variable), selecting a control group
without the characteristic (e.g. no lung cancer) and retrospectively examining these two groups for the factors that
may have caused this characteristic (e.g. did those with
lung cancer smoke more than those without?).

Q

Qualitative study: this involves
interviews in order to collect da
tive data is a way of describi
interpretations and behaviours
ject group without making gene
tion as a whole. It is believed th
more able to access the subje
taminating the data with the re
tions. Qualitative data are desc
and categories.

Quantitative study: this involve
form of numbers using method
naires and experiments. Quant

Technology to enhance learning and teaching

Visit www.mcgraw-hill.co.uk/textbooks/ogden today

Online Learning Centre (OLC)

After completing each chapter, log on to the supporting Online Learning Centre website. Take advantage of the study tools offered to reinforce the material you have read in the text, and to develop your knowledge in a fun and effective way.

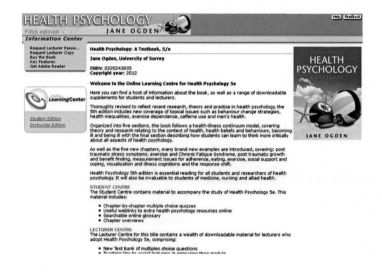

Resources for students include:

- *Chapter-by-chapter multiple choice quizzes*
- *Useful weblinks to extra health psychology resources online*
- *Searchable online glossary*
- *Chapter overviews*

Also available for lecturers:

- *New Test Bank of multiple choice questions*
- *Teaching tips to assist lecturers in preparing their module*
- *PowerPoint presentations for use in class or as handouts*
- *Artwork from the text*
- *Suggested essay questions to help prepare assessments and exams*

Visit **www.mcgraw-hill.co.uk/textbooks/ogden** today

Custom publishing solutions

Let us help make our **content** your **solution**

At McGraw-Hill Education our aim is to help the lecturer find the most suitable content for their needs and the most appropriate way to deliver the content for their students. Our **Custom Publishing Solutions** offer the ideal combination of content delivered in the way which suits lecturer and students the best. The idea behind our Custom Publishing programme is that via a database of over 2 million pages called Primis (www.primisonline.com) the lecturer can select just the material they wish to deliver to their students.

Lecturers can select chapters from:

- textbooks
- professional books
- case books – Harvard Articles, Insead, Ivey, Darden, Thunderbird and BusinessWeek
- Taking Sides – debate materials

Across the following imprints:

- McGraw-Hill Education
- Open University Press
- Harvard Business School Press
- US and European material

www.mcgrawhillcreate.com

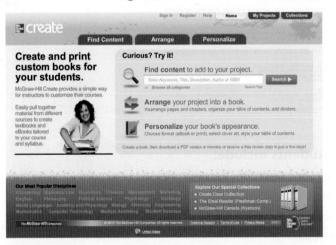

There is also the option to include material authored by lecturers in the custom product – this does not necessarily have to be in English.

We will take care of everything from start to finish in the process of developing and delivering a custom product to ensure that lecturers and students receive exactly the material needed in the most suitable way.

With a Custom Publishing Solution, students enjoy the best selection of material deemed to be the most suitable for learning everything they need for their courses – something of real value to support their learning. Teachers are able to use exactly the material they want, in the way they want, to support their teaching on the course.

Please contact your local McGraw-Hill representative with any questions or alternatively contact Warren Eels **e:** warren_eels@mcgraw-hill.com.

Make the grade

Improve your grades!

20% off any Study Skills book!

Our Study Skills books are packed with practical advice and tips that are easy to put into practice and will really improve the way you study. Our books will help you:

- Improve your grades
- Avoid plagiarism
- Save time
- Develop new skills
- Write confidently
- Undertake research projects
- Sail through exams
- Find the perfect job

Special offer!

As a valued customer, buy online and receive 20% off any of our Study Skills books by entering the promo code **BRILLIANT**

www.openup.co.uk/studyskills

Acknowledgements

My thanks again go to my students and research assistants and to my colleagues over the years for their comments, feedback and research input. I am particularly grateful to Amelia Hollywood for helping me find some of the figures and to Harry and Ellie for giving me that work–life balance and for being a wonderful source of meaning and fun. This fifth edition has been a huge task and for the past few months my children have had to manage somewhat stricter bedtimes!

The publishers would also like to thank the reviewers who commented on the previous edition and gave their time and expertise to provide helpful and constructive feedback. Their advice and suggestions were extremely helpful in shaping the fifth edition. The reviewers were:

Sheila Bonas, University of Leicester

Rachel Cook, Anglia Ruskin University

Lucy Flitton, University of Chester

Mary Ivers, University College Dublin

Jack James, National University of Ireland, Galway

Aled Jones, Swansea University

Devinder Rana, Birmingham City University

Michelle Tytherleigh, University of Chester

Finally, every effort has been made to contact copyright holders to secure permission to republish material in this textbook, and to include correct acknowledgements where required. The publishers would be happy to hear from any copyright holders whom it has not been possible for us to contact.

All photographs are © Jane Ogden unless otherwise stated.

PART ONE
The Context of Health Psychology

© Hybert Design

1 Introduction to Health Psychology

© Mauro Scarone Vezzoso/iStock

CHAPTER OVERVIEW

This chapter offers a broad introduction to the discipline of health psychology. First it provides a brief history of health psychology and highlights differences between health psychology and a more traditional biomedical model. It then describes the focus of health psychology in terms of a biopsychosocial model, health and illness as being on a continuum, the direct and indirect pathways between psychological factors and health and the emphasis on explaining variability. Next the chapter explores the aims of health psychology and the future of our discipline. Finally, this chapter outlines the aims of this textbook and describes how the book is structured.

THE BACKGROUND TO HEALTH PSYCHOLOGY

During the nineteenth century, modern medicine was established. 'Man' (the nineteenth-century term) was studied using dissection, physical investigations and medical examinations. Darwin's thesis, *The Origin of Species*, was published in 1856 and described the theory of evolution. This revolutionary theory identified a place for man within nature and suggested that we are part of nature, that we developed from nature and that we are biological beings. This was in accord with the biomedical model of medicine, which studied man in the same way that other members of the natural world had been studied in earlier years. This model described human beings as having a biological identity in common with all other biological beings.

WHAT IS THE BIOMEDICAL MODEL?

The biomedical model of medicine can be understood in terms of its answers to the following questions:

- *What causes illness?* According to the biomedical model of medicine, diseases either come from outside the body, invade the body and cause physical changes within the body, or originate as internal involuntary physical changes. Such diseases may be caused by several factors such as chemical imbalances, bacteria, viruses and genetic predisposition.

- *Who is responsible for illness?* Because illness is seen as arising from biological changes beyond their control, individuals are not seen as responsible for their illness. They are regarded as victims of some external force causing internal changes.

- *How should illness be treated?* The biomedical model regards treatment in terms of vaccination, surgery, chemotherapy and radiotherapy, all of which aim to change the physical state of the body.

- *Who is responsible for treatment?* The responsibility for treatment rests with the medical profession.

- *What is the relationship between health and illness?* Within the biomedical model, health and illness are seen as qualitatively different – you are either healthy or ill, there is no continuum between the two.

- *What is the relationship between the mind and the body?* According to the biomedical model of medicine, the mind and body function independently of each other. This is comparable to a traditional dualistic model of the mind–body split. From this perspective, the mind is incapable of influencing physical matter and the mind and body are defined as separate entities. The mind is seen as abstract and relating to feelings and thoughts, and the body is seen in terms of physical matter such as skin, muscles, bones, brain and organs. Changes in the physical matter are regarded as independent of changes in state of mind.

- *What is the role of psychology in health and illness?* Within traditional biomedicine, illness may have psychological consequences, but not psychological causes. For example, cancer may cause unhappiness but mood is not seen as related to either the onset or progression of the cancer.

THE TWENTIETH CENTURY

Throughout the twentieth century there were challenges to some of the underlying assumptions of biomedicine which emphasized an increasing role for psychology in health and a changing model of the relationship between the mind and body.

PSYCHOSOMATIC MEDICINE

The earliest challenge to the biomedical model was psychosomatic medicine. This was developed at the beginning of the twentieth century in response to Freud's analysis of the relationship between the mind and physical illness. At the turn of the century, Freud described a condition called 'hysterical paralysis', whereby patients presented with paralysed limbs with no obvious physical cause and in a pattern that did not reflect the organization of nerves. Freud argued that this condition was an indication of the individual's state of mind and that repressed experiences and feelings were expressed in terms of a physical problem. This explanation indicated an interaction between mind and body and suggested that psychological factors may not only be consequences of illness but may contribute to its cause.

BEHAVIOURAL MEDICINE

A further discipline that challenged the biomedical model of health was behavioural medicine, which has been described by Schwartz and Weiss (1977) as being an amalgam of elements from the behavioural science disciplines (psychology, sociology, health education) and which focuses on health care, treatment and illness prevention. Behavioural medicine was also described by Pomerleau and Brady (1979) as consisting of methods derived from the experimental analysis of behaviour, such as behaviour therapy and behaviour modification, and involved in the evaluation, treatment and prevention of physical disease or physiological dysfunction (e.g. essential hypertension, addictive behaviours and obesity). It has also been emphasized that psychological problems such as neurosis and psychosis are not within behavioural medicine unless they contribute to the development of illness. Behavioural medicine therefore included psychology in the study of health and departed from traditional biomedical views of health by not only focusing on treatment, but also focusing on prevention and intervention. In addition, behavioural medicine challenged the traditional separation of the mind and the body.

WHAT IS HEALTH PSYCHOLOGY?

Health psychology is probably the most recent development in this process of including psychology in an understanding of health. It was described by Matarazzo as 'the aggregate of the specific educational, scientific and professional contribution of the discipline of psychology to the promotion and maintenance of health, the promotion and treatment of illness and related dysfunction' (1980: 815). Health psychology again challenges the mind–body split by suggesting a role for the mind in both the cause and treatment of illness, but differs from psychosomatic medicine and behavioural medicine in that research within health psychology is more specific to the discipline of psychology.

Recommended health behaviour can be encouraged by community

SOURCE: © wavebreakmedia/iStock

Health psychology can be understood in terms of the same questions that were asked of the biomedical model:

- *What causes illness?* Health psychology suggests that human beings should be seen as complex systems and that illness is caused by a multitude of factors and not by a single causal factor. Health psychology therefore attempts to move away from a simple linear model of health and claims that illness can be caused by a combination of biological (e.g. a virus), psychological (e.g. behaviours, beliefs), and social (e.g. employment) factors.

- *Who is responsible for illness?* Because illness is regarded as a result of a combination of factors, the individual is no longer simply seen as a passive victim. For example, the recognition of a role for behaviour in the cause of illness means that the individual may be held responsible for their health and illness.

- *How should illness be treated?* According to health psychology, the whole person should be treated, not just the physical changes that have taken place. This can take the form of behaviour change, encouraging changes in beliefs and coping strategies, and compliance with medical recommendations.

- *Who is responsible for treatment?* Because the whole person is treated, not just their physical illness, the patient is therefore in part responsible for their treatment. This may take the form of responsibility to take medication and/or responsibility to change their beliefs and behaviour. They are not seen as a victim.

- *What is the relationship between health and illness?* From this perspective, health and illness are not qualitatively different, but exist on a continuum. Rather than being either healthy or ill, individuals progress along this continuum from health to illness and back again.

- *What is the relationship between the mind and the body?* The twentieth century saw a challenge to the traditional separation of mind and body suggested by a dualistic model of health and illness, with an increasing focus on an interaction between the mind and the body. This shift in perspective is reflected in the development of a holistic or a whole-person approach to health. Health psychology therefore maintains that the mind and body interact.

- *What is the role of psychology in health and illness?* Health psychology regards psychological factors not only as possible consequences of illness but as contributing to it at all stages along the continuum from healthy through to being ill.

THE FOCUS OF HEALTH PSYCHOLOGY

Health psychology draws upon four key perspectives in its analysis of health and illness. These are the biopsychosocial model of health, health as a continuum, the direct and indirect pathways between psychology and health, and a focus on variability. These will now be described.

THE BIOPSYCHOSOCIAL MODEL

The biopsychosocial model was developed by Engel (1977; see Figure 1.1) and represented an attempt to integrate the psychological (the 'psycho') and the environmental (the 'social') into the

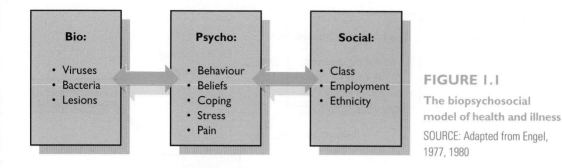

FIGURE 1.1

The biopsychosocial model of health and illness

SOURCE: Adapted from Engel, 1977, 1980

traditional biomedical (the 'bio') model of health as follows: (1) the *bio* contributing factors included genetics, viruses, bacteria and structural defects; (2) the *psycho* aspects of health and illness were described in terms of cognitions (e.g. expectations of health), emotions (e.g. fear of treatment) and behaviours (e.g. smoking, diet, exercise or alcohol consumption); (3) the *social* aspects of health were described in terms of social norms of behaviour (e.g. the social norm of smoking or not smoking), pressures to change behaviour (e.g. peer group expectations, parental pressure), social values on health (e.g. whether health was regarded as a good or a bad thing), social class and ethnicity.

HEALTH AS A CONTINUUM

Health psychology emphasizes health and illness as being on a continuum and explores the ways in which psychological factors impact health at all stages. Therefore, psychology is involved in illness onset (e.g. beliefs and behaviours such as smoking, diet and stress), help-seeking (e.g. symptom perception, illness cognitions, doctor – patient communication), illness adaptation (e.g. coping, behaviour change, social support, pain perception), illness progression (e.g. stress, behaviour change) and health outcomes (e.g. quality of life, longevity). This perspective is illustrated in Figure 1.2.

THE RELATIONSHIP BETWEEN PSYCHOLOGY AND HEALTH

Health psychologists consider both a direct and indirect pathway between psychology and health. The direct pathway is reflected in the physiological literature and is illustrated by research

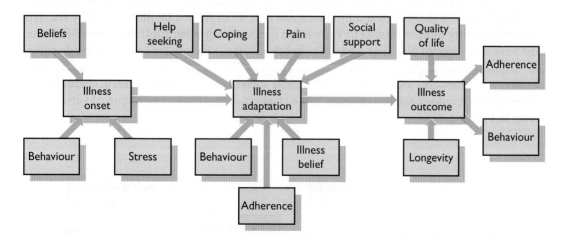

FIGURE 1.2

Health as a continuum and psychology throughout the course of life

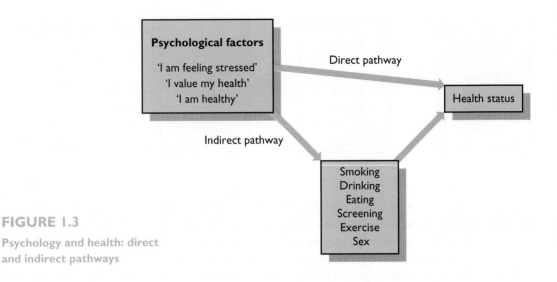

FIGURE 1.3

Psychology and health: direct
and indirect pathways

exploring the impact of stress on illnesses such as coronary heart disease and cancer. From this perspective, the way a person experiences their life ('I am feeling stressed') has a direct impact upon their body which can change their health status. The indirect pathway is reflected more in the behavioural literature and is illustrated by research exploring smoking, diet, exercise and sexual behaviour. From this perspective, the way a person thinks ('I am feeling stressed') influences their behaviour ('I will have a cigarette') which in turn can impact upon their health. The direct and indirect pathways are illustrated in Figure 1.3.

A FOCUS ON VARIABILITY

Health and illness vary along a number of domains including geographical location, time, social class and gender (see Chapter 2). Health psychology explores this variability with a focus on the role of behaviour. However, there is also variability between *people* and this is also the focus of health psychology. For example, two people might both know that smoking is bad for them but only one stops smoking. Similarly, two people might find a lump in their breast but only one goes to the doctor. Further, two people might both have a heart attack but while one has another attack in six months' time, the other is perfectly healthy and back to work within a month. This variability indicates that health and illness cannot only be explained by illness severity (i.e. type of cancer, severity of heart attack) or knowledge (i.e. smoking is harmful), but that other factors must have a key role to play. For a health psychologist these factors are central to the discipline and include a wide range of psychological variables such as cognitions, emotions, expectations, learning, peer pressure, social norms, coping and social support. These constructs are the nuts and bolts of psychology and are covered in the chapters in this book. The notion of variability is shown in Figure 1.4.

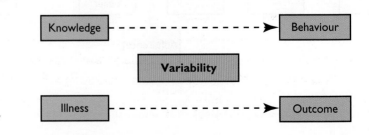

FIGURE 1.4

The notion of variability

WHAT ARE THE AIMS OF HEALTH PSYCHOLOGY?

Health psychology emphasizes the role of psychological factors in the cause, progression and consequences of health and illness. The aims of health psychology can be divided into (1) understanding, explaining, developing and testing theory, and (2) putting this theory into practice.

1 *Health psychology aims to understand, explain, develop and test theory by:*

  a Evaluating the role of behaviour in the aetiology of illness. For example:
  - Coronary heart disease is related to behaviours such as smoking, food intake and lack of exercise.
  - Many cancers are related to behaviours such as diet, smoking, alcohol and failure to attend for screening or health check-ups.
  - A stroke is related to smoking, cholesterol and high blood pressure.
  - An often overlooked cause of death is accidents. These may be related to alcohol consumption, drugs and careless driving.

  b Predicting unhealthy behaviours. For example:
  - Smoking, alcohol consumption and high fat diets are related to beliefs.
  - Beliefs about health and illness can be used to predict behaviour.

  c Evaluating the interaction between psychology and physiology. For example:
  - The experience of stress relates to appraisal, coping and social support.
  - Stress leads to physiological changes which can trigger or exacerbate illness.
  - Pain perception can be exacerbated by anxiety and reduced by distraction.

  d Understanding the role of psychology in the experience of illness. For example:
  - Understanding the psychological consequences of illness could help to alleviate symptoms such as pain, nausea and vomiting.
  - Understanding the psychological consequences of illness could help alleviate psychological symptoms such as anxiety and depression.

  e Evaluating the role of psychology in the treatment of illness. For example:
  - If psychological factors are important in the cause of illness, they may also have a role in its treatment.
  - Changing behaviour and reducing stress could reduce the chances of a further heart attack.
  - Treatment of the psychological consequences of illness may have an impact on longevity.

2 *Health psychology also aims to put theory into practice. This can be implemented by:*

  a Promoting healthy behaviour. For example:
  - Understanding the role of behaviour in illness can allow unhealthy behaviours to be targeted.
  - Understanding the beliefs that predict behaviours can allow these beliefs to be targeted.
  - Understanding beliefs can help these beliefs to be changed.

  b Preventing illness. For example:
  - Changing beliefs and behaviour could prevent illness onset.
  - Modifying stress could reduce the risk of a heart attack.
  - Behavioural interventions during illness (e.g. stopping smoking after a heart attack) may prevent further illness.

Illness can be prevented by reducing stress

SOURCE: © acilo/iStock

- Training health professionals to improve their communication skills and to carry out interventions may help to prevent illness.

WHAT IS THE FUTURE OF HEALTH PSYCHOLOGY?

Health psychology is an expanding area in the UK, across Europe, in Australia and New Zealand and in the USA. For many students this involves taking a health psychology course as part of their psychology degree. For some students health psychology plays a part of their studies for other allied disciplines, such as medicine, nursing, health studies and dentistry. However, in addition to studying health psychology at this preliminary level, an increasing number of students carry out higher degrees in health psychology as a means to develop their careers within this field. This has resulted in a range of debates about the future of health psychology and the possible roles for a health psychologist. To date these debates have highlighted three possible career pathways: the clinical health psychologist, the professional health psychologist, and the academic health psychologist.

THE CLINICAL HEALTH PSYCHOLOGIST

A clinical health psychologist has been defined as someone who merges 'clinical psychology with its focus on the assessment and treatment of individuals in distress . . . and the content field of health psychology' (Belar and Deardorff 1995). In order to practise as a clinical health psychologist, it is generally accepted that someone would first gain training as a clinical psychologist and then later acquire an expertise in health psychology, which would involve an understanding of the theories and methods of health psychology and their application to the health care setting. A trained clinical health psychologist would tend to work within the field of physical health, including stress and pain management, rehabilitation for patients with chronic illnesses (e.g. cancer, HIV or cardiovascular disease) or the development of interventions for problems such as spinal cord injury and disfiguring surgery.

THE PROFESSIONAL HEALTH PSYCHOLOGIST

A professional health psychologist is someone who is trained to an acceptable standard in health psychology and works as a health psychologist. Within the UK, the term 'health psychologist' is now used and is managed by the Health Professions Council. Across Europe, Australasia and the USA, the term 'professional health psychologist' or simply 'health psychologist' is used (Marks et al. 1998). Although still being considered by a range of committees, it is now generally agreed that a professional health psychologist should have competence in three areas: research, teaching and consultancy. In addition, they should be able to show a suitable knowledge base of academic health psychology, normally by completing a higher degree in health psychology. Having demonstrated that they meet the required standards, a professional health psychologist could work as an academic within the higher education system, within the health promotion setting, within schools or industry, and/or within the health service. The work could include research, teaching and the development and evaluation of interventions to reduce risk-related behaviour.

THE ACADEMIC HEALTH PSYCHOLOGIST

An academic health psychologist usually has a first degree in psychology and then completes a masters in health psychology and a PhD in a health psychology-related area. For example, they may focus their PhD on obesity, stress, coronary heart disease or behaviour change. They will then enter the pathway for an academic health psychologist by getting a post-doctoral position or a lectureship at a university. The pathway in the UK involves the progression from lecturer, to senior lecturer, to reader and then professor (although in many countries the terms 'assistant professor', 'associate professor' and 'full professor' are used). The career of an academic involves teaching at all levels (undergraduate and postgraduate), project supervision for students, carrying out research, writing books and research articles in peer review journals and presenting work at conferences. Most academics also have an administrative role such as managing the examination process or directing the teaching programmes for undergraduate or postgraduate students.

WHAT ARE THE AIMS OF THIS BOOK?

Health psychology is an expanding area in terms of teaching, research and practice. Health psychology *teaching* occurs at both the undergraduate and postgraduate level and is experienced by both mainstream psychology students and those studying other health-related subjects. Health psychology *research* also takes many forms. Undergraduates are often expected to produce research projects as part of their assessment, and academic staff and research teams carry out research to develop and test theories and to explore new areas. Such research often feeds directly into *practice*, with intervention programmes aiming to change the factors identified by research. This book aims to provide a comprehensive introduction to the main topics of health psychology. The book will focus on psychological theory supported by research. In addition, how these theories can be turned into practice will also be described. The book is now supported by a comprehensive website which includes teaching aids such as lectures and assessments.

A NOTE ON THEORY AND HEALTH PSYCHOLOGY

Health psychology draws upon a range of psychological perspectives for its theories. For example, it uses learning theory with its emphasis on associations and modelling, social cognition theories with their emphasis on beliefs and attitudes, stage theories with their focus on change and progression, decision-making theory highlighting a cost–benefit analysis and the role of hypothesis testing and physiological theories with their interest in biological processes and their links with health. Further, it utilizes many key psychological concepts such as stereotyping, self-identity, risk perception, self-efficacy and addiction. This book describes many of these theories and explores how they have been used to explain health status and health-related behaviours. Some of these theories have been used across all aspects of health psychology such as social cognition models, stage theories and the self-regulation model. These theories are therefore described in detail in Chapters 3 and 9. In contrast, other theories and constructs have tended to be used to study specific behaviours. These are therefore described within each specific chapter. However, as cross-fertilization is often the making of good research, many of these theories could also be applied to other areas.

A NOTE ON METHODOLOGY AND HEALTH PSYCHOLOGY

Health psychology also uses a range of methodologies. It uses quantitative methods in the form of surveys, randomized control trials, experiments and case control studies. It also uses qualitative methods such as interviews and focus groups and researchers analyse their data using approaches such as discourse analysis, interpretative phenomenological analysis and grounded theory. A separate chapter on methodology has not been included as there are many comprehensive texts that cover methods in detail (see further reading at the end of this chapter). The aim of this book is to illustrate this range of methods and approaches to data analysis through the choice of examples described throughout each chapter.

A NOTE ON REFERENCING

This is now the fifth edition of this book and I am now 45. For me, 'recent research' means about 1990, but I am aware that many of the students reading this book were not born then. This edition has therefore been completely revised and updated throughout. I have not, however, removed *all* earlier references in favour of more recent ones for two reasons. Firstly, some of the key theories used in health psychology were developed in the 1980s and 1990s. I have retained these original references throughout. Secondly, many of the studies testing these theories were carried out in the 1990s. Therefore I have also retained some of these as, although many more studies may have been done in recent years, testing the same theories using the same populations and methods, it feels unjust to use the more recent less original papers rather than the earlier original ones.

A COMPLETE COURSE IN HEALTH PSYCHOLOGY

This book takes the format of a complete course in health psychology. Each chapter could be used as the basis for a lecture and/or reading for a lecture and consists of the following features:

- A chapter overview, which outlines the aims of the chapter.
- A set of questions for seminar discussion or essay titles.
- Recommendations for further reading.
- Diagrams to illustrate the models and theories discussed within the text.
- A 'focus on research' section, which aims to illustrate three aspects of health psychology: (1) 'testing a theory', which examines how a theory can be turned into a research project with a description of the background, methods used (including details of measures), results and conclusions for each paper chosen; (2) 'putting theory into practice', which examines how a theory can be used to develop an intervention; and (3) 'the experience of ...', which presents studies addressing the patient's experience. Each 'focus on research' section takes one specific paper that has been chosen as a good illustration of either theory testing or practical implications.
- A 'some problems with ...' section which describes some of the main methodological and conceptual problems for each area of research.
- An 'assumptions in health psychology' section, which examines some of the assumptions that underlie both the research and practice in health psychology, such as the role of methodology and the relationship between the mind and body. These problems and assumptions are addressed together in Chapter 19.

In addition, there is a glossary at the end of the book, which describes terms within health psychology relating to methodology.

TO CONCLUDE

Health psychology explores how a number of psychological factors impact upon health and illness and emphasizes four perspectives: a biopsychosocial perspective, health, and illness and as being on a continuum, the direct and indirect pathways between psychology and health, and the problem of variability. This book covers the breadth of health psychology and can be used as the basis for a complete course for students at both undergraduate and postgraduate levels and for those both within psychology and in other allied disciplines such as nutritionists, nurses, doctors and dieticians.

QUESTIONS

1 To what extent does health psychology challenge the assumptions of the biomedical model of health and illness?
2 Why do health psychologists consider health and illness to be on a continuum?
3 Is the biopsychosocial model a useful perspective?
4 What problems are there with dividing up the pathways into indirect and direct pathways?
5 What factors could explain variability between people in terms of their behaviour and health outcomes?
6 To what extent does health psychology enable the whole person to be studied?
7 Design a research study to illustrate the impact of the bio, psycho and social processes in an illness of your choice.

FOR DISCUSSION

Consider the last time you were ill (e.g. flu, headache, cold, etc.). Discuss the extent to which factors other than biological ones may have contributed to your illness.

FURTHER READING

Aboud, F.E. (1998) *Health Psychology in Global Perspective*. London: Sage.
This book emphasizes the cross-cultural aspects of health psychology and locates behaviour and beliefs within the cultural context.

Kaplan, R.M. (1990) Behaviour as the central outcome in health care, *American Psychologist*, 45: 1211–20.
This paper provides an interesting discussion about the aims of health psychology and suggests that rather than focusing on biological outcomes, such as longevity and cell pathology, researchers should aim to change behaviour and should therefore evaluate the success of any interventions on the basis of whether this aim has been achieved.

Kaptein, A. and Weinman, J. (eds) (2010) *Health Psychology*, 2nd edn. Oxford: BPS Blackwell.
This edited collection provides further detailed description and analysis of a range of areas central to health psychology.

Michie, S. and Abraham, C. (eds) (2004) *Health Psychology in Practice*. Oxford: Blackwell.
This edited collection provides a detailed account of the competencies and skills required to be a chartered health psychologist in the UK. However, the information is also relevant internationally to anyone interested in pursuing a career in health psychology.

Ogden, J. (2007) *Essential Readings in Health Psychology*. Maidenhead: Open University Press.
This is my reader which consists of 29 papers I have selected as good illustrations of theory, research, methodology or debate. The book also contains a discussion of each paper and a justification for its inclusion.

RESEARCH METHODS

Bowling, A. and Ebrahim, S. (2005) *Handbook of Health Research Methods: Investigation, Measurement and Analysis.* Buckingham: Open University Press.
This provides an excellent overview of quantitative and qualitative methods including systematic reviews, surveys, questionnaire design, modelling and trials. Its focus is on health research.

Breakwell, G., Hammond, S., Fife-Schaw, C. and Smith, J.A. (eds) (2006) *Research Methods in Psychology*, 3rd edn. London: Sage.
This edited book provides a thorough and accessible overview of a range of different qualitative and quantitative research methods specific to psychology.

Brocki, J.M. and Wearden, A.J. (2006) A critical evaluation of the use of Interpretive Phenomenological Analysis (IPA) in health psychology, *Psychology and Health*, 21: 87–108.
This provides a thorough overview of the research using IPA in health psychology and presents some interesting criticisms.

Jenkinson, C. (2002) *Assessment and Evaluation of Health and Medical Care.* Buckingham: Open University Press.
This is an accessible and detailed account of a range of quantitative research designs including cohort studies, trials and case control studies.

Lyons, E. and Coyle, A. (eds) (2007) *Analyzing Qualitative Data in Psychology.* London: Sage.
This book provides an excellent overview of four different qualitative approaches (IPA, grounded theory, narrative analysis, discourse analysis) and then explores how they can be used and the extent to which they produce different or similar accounts of the data.

Smith, J.A. (2003) *Qualitative Psychology: A Practical Guide to Research Methods.* London: Sage.
This offers a very clear hands-on guide to the different qualitative approaches and is extremely good at showing how to carry out qualitative research in practice.

Willig, C. (2001) *Introducing Qualitative Research in Psychology: Adventures in Theory and Method.* Buckingham: Open University Press.
An extremely well-written and clear guide to the different qualitative approaches whih offers an accessible overview of their similarities and differences in terms of epistemology and method.

 Visit the website at www.openup.co.uk/ogden for additional resources on Chapter 1 to help you with your study, such as multiple choice questions, weblinks and a searchable online glossary.

2 Health Inequalities

© jameslee1/Fotolia

CHAPTER OVERVIEW

Health and illness are not constants but differ across a number of variables including geographical location, time, socioeconomic status (SES) and gender. This is sometimes called the social patterning of health, health inequalities or health variation. This chapter describes evidence for this variation and gives examples across a number of different health problems. It then explores possible explanations for this variation in terms of medical interventions, environmental factors and behaviour. Whereas medicine and sociology focus on the role of medical interventions and the environment, health psychology acknowledges the role of these first two explanations but tends to focus on behaviour. This chapter then explores the role of behaviour and health.

HEALTH INEQUALITIES

Due to the internet and the publication of online reports there is now a huge volume of data available from respected bodies such as the World Health Organization (WHO) and the Office for National Statistics (ONS), health charities such as British Heart Foundation (BHF), Cancer Research UK (CRUK), the British Diabetes Association (BDA) and the American Cancer Society (ACS) as well as academic groups such as the European Heart Network. These data provide insights into health inequalities across the world and within individual countries, and evidence generally indicates that the diseases people are diagnosed with and whether or not they die from them vary according to four key dimensions: geographical location; time; SES and gender. Time (i.e. changes throughout history) will not be explored independently as most available data includes this dimension in its analyses. Please read the following as a useful preliminary insight into the notion of variation and health inequalities, but do not expect it to be an exhaustive or systematic analysis of this vast database.

GEOGRAPHICAL LOCATION

It is clear that the prevalence of a range of diseases and their mortality rates vary both between and within countries. For example, worldwide death rates in 2006 are shown in Figure 2.1 per 1,000 population. The figure illustrates huge variations across the world, with the highest death rates being in Sub-Saharan Africa, Afghanistan, Russia and Eastern Europe.

Childhood mortality rates also vary by geographical area. For example, data from the WHO shown in Figure 2.2 illustrate that the highest child mortality rates are in Africa, the Eastern Mediterranean region and South-East Asian region with the lowest rates being in Europe and the Americas. The graph also shows changes in child mortality between 1990 and 2008 and indicates that mortality has fallen universally.

There are also geographical differences in specific diseases. For example, the global prevalence of HIV in 2009 is shown in Figure 2.3, which shows that the highest rates were in Sub-Saharan Africa and Russia.

Health and illness also vary within continents. For example, Figure 2.4 illustrates incident rates of lung cancer across Europe in 2008. These data indicate that the highest rates were in Hungary, Poland, Estonia and Belgium and that the lowest rate was in Sweden. The graph also shows that lung cancer is consistently higher in men than in women. Gender differences are described later in this section.

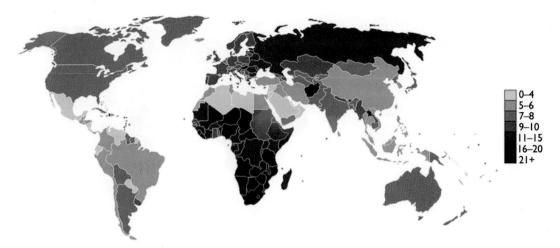

FIGURE 2.1

Death rates by geographical area worldwide in 2006 per 1,000 population

SOURCE: CIA Factbook 2006; Wikimedia Commons 2011

Finally, there is also geographical variation within countries. For example, Figure 2.5 illustrates how mortality rates in people aged under 75 vary across England. It can be seen that mortality rates from all causes are higher in northern England than southern England and even vary within London, with the highest rates being in East London.

These illustrations are just a snapshot of the available data, but they illustrate how mortality and disease prevalence rates vary by geographical location in terms of broad WHO region, continent, country and even within a capital city.

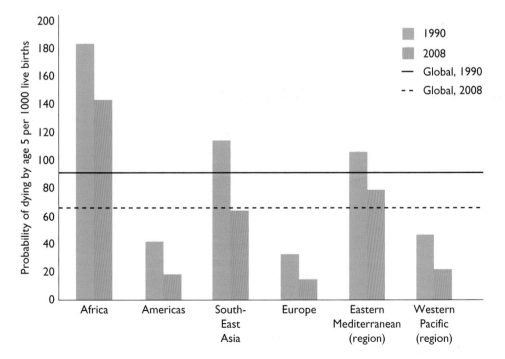

FIGURE 2.2

Child mortality rates by WHO region (1990 and 2008)

SOURCE: WHO *World Health Statistics 2010*, www.who.int/whosis/whostat/EN_WHS10_Full.pdf

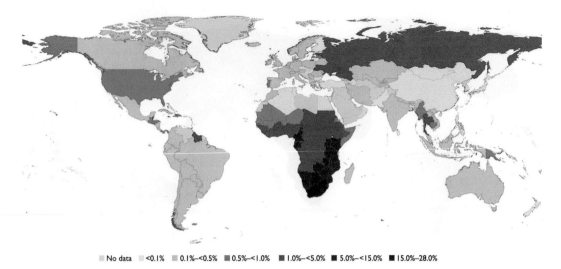

No data   <0.1%   0.1%–<0.5%   0.5%–<1.0%   1.0%–<5.0%   5.0%–<15.0%   15.0%–28.0%

FIGURE 2.3

Global prevalence of HIV, 2009

SOURCE: *UNAIDS Report on the Global AIDS epidemic 2010*, www.unaids.org/globalreport/Global_report.htm

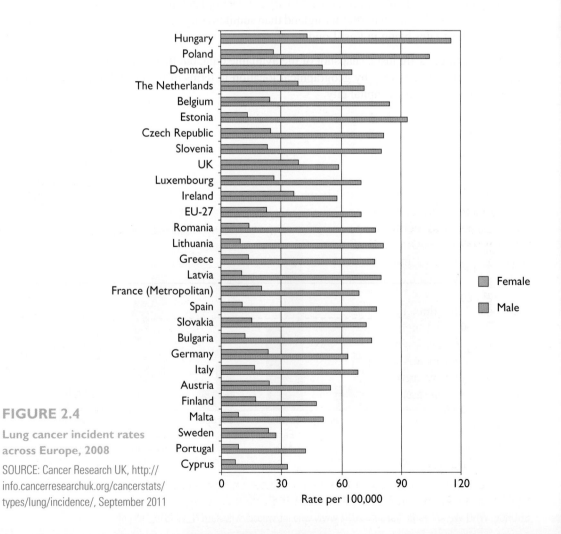

FIGURE 2.4

Lung cancer incident rates
across Europe, 2008

SOURCE: Cancer Research UK, http://
info.cancerresearchuk.org/cancerstats/
types/lung/incidence/, September 2011

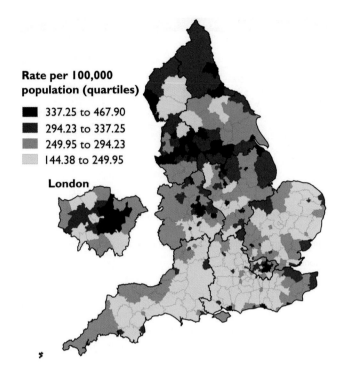

Rate per 100,000
population (quartiles)

■ 337.25 to 467.90
■ 294.23 to 337.25
■ 249.95 to 294.23
☐ 144.38 to 249.95

London

FIGURE 2.5

Mortality rates in people under 75 by local health authority across England

SOURCE: National Centre for Health Outcomes Development, *Compendium of Clinical and Health Indicators*, Contains Ordnance Survey Data © Crown copyright and database right 2011

SOCIOECONOMIC STATUS

Social class can be defined in terms of economic situation (income or deprivation) or educational status, or even as subjective social class whereby people identify themselves as being working class, middle class or upper class. For the purposes of this chapter the term socioeconomic status (SES) will be used. Whatever definition is used, a consistent relationship emerges between SES, health, illness and mortality. For example, the WHO has classified the countries of the world into three income groups: low income, middle income and high income, and has explored the relationship with premature mortality (i.e. < 75). These data are shown in Figure 2.6 and demonstrate a clear gradient by income group, with deaths by communicable disease, perinatal conditions and nutritional deficiencies decreasing as income increases and non-communicable conditions (e.g. cancer, coronary heart disease – CHD, diabetes)

What difference does homelessness or low income make to people's health situation?

SOURCE: © Mikael Damkier/iStock

increasing as income increases. Interestingly, death by injury is highest in the middle income group.

The prevalence of individual illnesses also varies by SES. For example, variation of obesity in the UK is shown in Figure 2.7. These data indicate that for women there is a clear relationship

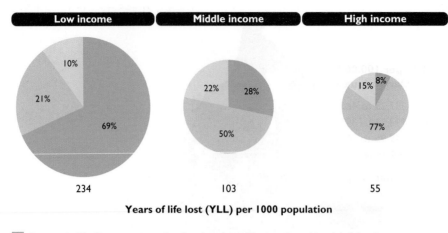

| Low income | Middle income | High income |

234   103   55

Years of life lost (YLL) per 1000 population

■ Communicable diseases, maternal and perinatal conditions and nutritional deficiencies
■ Noncommunicable conditions
■ Injuries

FIGURE 2.6

Premature mortality (i.e. < 75 years) worldwide by country income group, 2004

SOURCE: WHO *World Health Statistics 2010*, www.who.int/whosis/whostat/EN_WHS10_Full.pdf

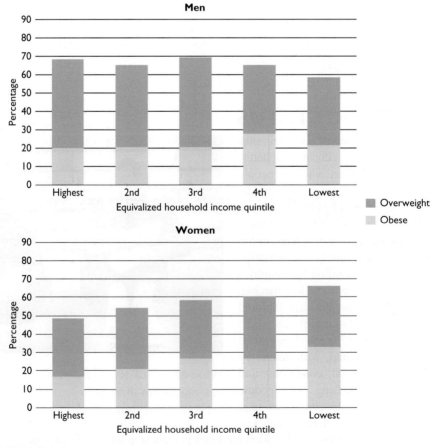

FIGURE 2.7

Prevalence of overweight and obesity by household income and sex, 2009

SOURCE: copyright © 2010, re-used with the permission of The Health and Social Care Information Centre, all rights reserved

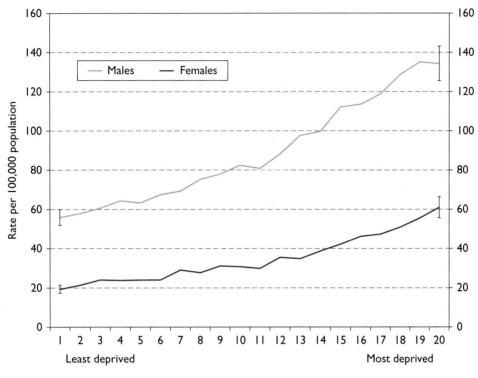

FIGURE 2.8

Incidence rates of lung cancer by deprivation category, England and Wales, 1993

SOURCE: Cancer Research UK, http://info.cancerresearchuk.org/cancerstats/types/lung/incidence/, September 2011

between income and both overweight and obesity, with body weight increasing as income decreases. The pattern for men is less clear-cut with the highest rate of overweight being in the middle income group and the highest rate of obesity being in the second to lowest income group.

Lung cancer rates can also be seen to vary by SES as measured by deprivation category (see Figure 2.8). These data indicate a clear relationship between an increase in deprivation and an increase in lung cancer in England and Wales. This gradient can be seen for both men and women although rates in men are much higher.

Finally, rates of diabetes also vary by SES (see Figure 2.9). These data show a similar pattern to obesity, with a linear relationship between income and diabetes in women, but with men in the middle income group showing the highest rates.

The data therefore show variation in mortality rates, causes of mortality and specific illness by SES, with those in the lower income groups having consistently poorer health than those in the higher income groups. Overall, there are three consistent findings concerning the relationship between SES and health as follows (see Marmot and Wilkinson 2005). As SES increases (however measured) there is:

- An improvement in mortality rates, disease progression and life expectancy.
- A reduction in infant mortality, chronic disease and psychiatric morbidity.
- An increase in self-reported mental and physical health.

Furthermore, it is interesting to note that these relationships show a gradient effect rather than a threshold effect as the association is linear, with an increase in SES being directly related to an increase in health status.

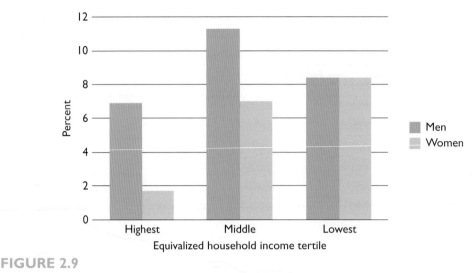

FIGURE 2.9

Prevalence of diabetes by household income and sex, England and Wales, 2009

SOURCE: Copyright © 2010, re-used with the permission of The Health and Social Care Information Centre, all rights reserved

GENDER

The third clear source of variation in health and illness is gender. The data shown already illustrate gender differences in diabetes, obesity and lung cancer. It is also established that women tend to live longer than men and at present the average life expectancy for women in the UK is 81.9 years and for men 77.7 years (from birth). Life expectancy for men and women and over time is shown in Figure 2.10 which shows an increase for both men and women since 1980, that women live longer than men but that the gap between men and women is gradually closing.

In 1996, MacIntyre et al. carried out an analysis of two British data sets to explore gender differences in common physical symptoms and a range of illnesses. They reported that although there were no consistent gender differences for illnesses such as hernia, respiratory disorders, asthma and epilepsy, or for symptoms relating to eyes, ears, colds, flu, palpitations or coughs, there were several consistent differences between men and women. Gender differences in illness are shown in Figure 2.11. MacIntyre et al. also explored gender differences in physical symptoms and the results are shown in Figure 2.12. In general, women seem to get more symptoms and illnesses than men and yet live longer. Interestingly, although men die younger, they have less contact with health care services, are less likely to have seen their general practitioner (GP) in the past 12 months, have fewer hospital admissions and are less likely to have a screening test or a general health check (DH 2001; Bayram et al. 2003; Eurostat 2007). However, men are about four times more likely to die from suicide than women (see Chapters 16 and 17 for a detailed discussion on women's and men's health issues).

Going strong at 98: women generally live longer than men

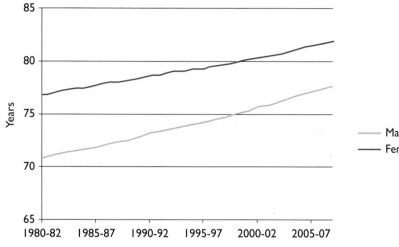

FIGURE 2.10

Life expectancy in men and women, 1980–2007

SOURCE: Office for National Statistics, statistics.gov.uk

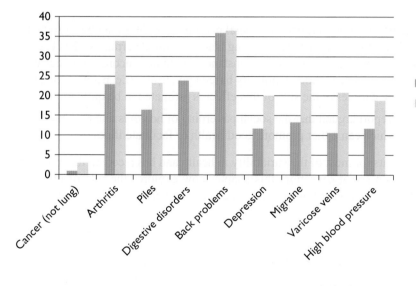

FIGURE 2.11

Gender differences in a range of illnesses

SOURCE: adapted from MacIntyre et al. (1996)

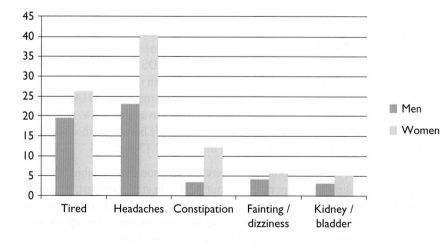

FIGURE 2.12

Gender differences in physical symptoms

SOURCE: adapted from MacIntyre et al. (1996)

In summary, health, illness, mortality and symptoms vary by geographical location, time, SES and gender. This variation can be understood from a number of different theoretical, disciplinary and political perspectives. The most commonly used explanations focus on the role of medical interventions, environmental factors and behaviour in explaining inequalities in health and illness. These will now be explored.

EXPLAINING VARIABILITY IN HEALTH AND ILLNESS

In 1980 the Black Report was produced in the UK by the Department of Health (DH) working group on health inequalities to explore the possible explanations for variability by SES. Although focusing on the variability due to SES the explanations are also relevant to differences by geographical location and gender. The report described three possible explanations as follows:

- *Artefact.* It was argued that the relationship between SES and health may simply be an artefact of how these two constructs are measured. However, it is generally now accepted that the relationship is too robust across measures and countries to be simply a matter of measurement error.

- *Social selection.* The Black Report argued that social patterning by SES may be a product of social selection and that rather than SES determining health, health determines SES, because those with better health improve their social circumstances including income and education. Although there is some evidence for social mobility based upon health (i.e. people who are ill can't work and therefore earn less), the size of this effect is estimated to be quite moderate.

- *Social causation.* The report argued that the social patterning of health is due to a number of key social conditions which can either promote good health or facilitate illness.

This third explanation accounts for most of the variability in health and has received the most support. In line with the focus on social causation, this chapter now explores the role of three key social conditions as explanations of health inequalities: medical interventions, environmental factors and behavior.

MEDICAL INTERVENTIONS

From a medical perspective, variations in health and illness are explained with a focus on the success or failure of medical interventions and the availability of health care. Research indicates wide variations in health care provision and access, particularly by geographical area in terms of the types and costs of medicines, the training and expertise of health care professionals, the distances needed to travel to access health care and the availability of free health care versus the need for health insurance. A good example of the impact of medical interventions is that of HIV/AIDS. In the western world HIV/AIDS is now considered a chronic illness with many people living with the HIV virus having a normal life expectancy. This change has been attributed to the antiretroviral medication HAART (see Chapter 14). In Sub-Saharan Africa, however, where HAART is far less available, HIV/AIDS still shows the pattern of an acute terminal illness. Differences in life expectancy between those with and without AIDS in non-African and African countries are shown in Figures 2.13 and 2.14.

These figures illustrate that in non-African countries where medication is available, the life expectancy of a person with AIDS is similar to a person without AIDS. In stark contrast, however, in African countries where medication is not so easily accessible, a huge gap exists between the life expectancy of these two populations: medical intervention directly impacts upon the life expectancy of people with this condition, translating it from an acute to a chronic disorder.

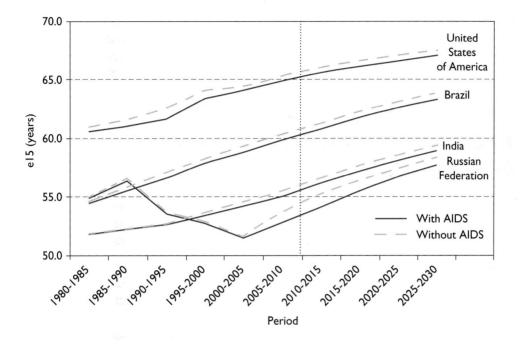

FIGURE 2.13

Life expectancy at age 15 with & without AIDS in selected non-African countries, 1980–2030

SOURCE: Bongaarts et al. (2009)

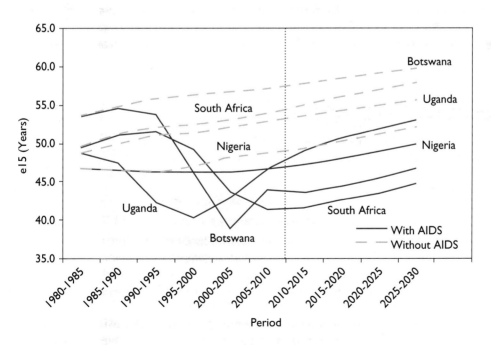

FIGURE 2.14

Life expectancy at age 15 with & without AIDS in selected African countries, 1980–2030

SOURCE: Bongaarts et al. (2009)

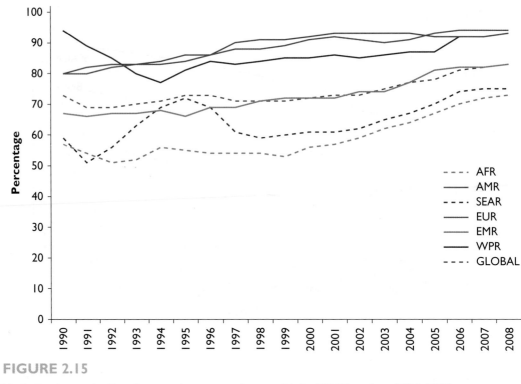

FIGURE 2.15

Variation in vaccination for measles among 1-year-olds by WHO region, 1990–2008

SOURCE: WHO, *World Health Statistics 2010*, www.who.int/whosis/whostat/EN_WHS10_Full.pdf

There is also worldwide variation in vaccinations for illnesses such as measles. Figure 2.15 shows vaccination for measles by WHO region and indicates changes over time since 1990. The highest rates are in Europe and America while the lowest are in Africa and the eastern Mediterranean region. Such variation will obviously impact upon the health of any given population.

Child mortality rates vary by geographical region (see Figure 2.2, p. 17). One possible reason is the presence of a skilled health professional at the birth. This does not happen universally, however, and in the WHO African and South-East Asian regions less than 50 per cent of women received skilled care during childbirth in 2008 (see Figure 2.16).

The availability and use of medicines may therefore explain some of the variation in health and illness. The impact of medicine on health and illness is not, however, always this clear, particularly in the developed world. In his book *The Role of Medicine*, Thomas McKeown (1979) examined the impact of medicine on health since the seventeenth century. In particular, he evaluated the widely held assumptions about medicine's achievements and the role of medicine in reducing the prevalence and incidence of infectious illnesses, such as tuberculosis, pneumonia, measles, influenza, diphtheria, smallpox and whooping cough. McKeown argued that the commonly held view was that the decline in illnesses, such as tuberculosis, measles, smallpox and whooping cough, was related to medical interventions such as chemotherapy and vaccinations – for example, that antibiotics were responsible for the decline in illnesses such as pneumonia and influenza. He showed, however, that the reduction in such illnesses was already underway before the development of the relevant medical interventions. This is illustrated in Figure 2.17 (for tuberculosis). McKeown therefore claimed that the decline in infectious diseases seen throughout the past three centuries is best understood not in terms of medical intervention, but in terms of social and environmental factors. He argued that:

The influences which led to [the] predominance [of infectious diseases] from the time of the first agricultural revolution 10,000 years ago were insufficient food, environmental

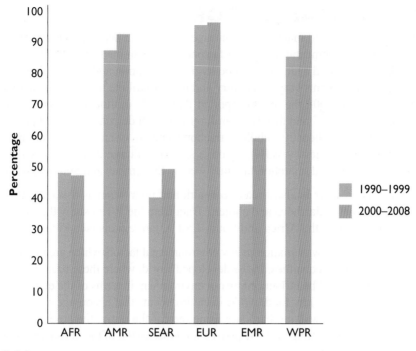

FIGURE 2.16

Births attended by a skilled health professional by WHO region, 1990–2008

SOURCE: WHO, *World Health Statistics 2010*, www.who.int/whosis/whostat/EN_WHS10_Full.pdf

hazards and excessive numbers and the measures which led to their decline from the time of the modern Agricultural and Industrial revolutions were predictably improved nutrition, better hygiene and contraception.

(McKeown 1979: 117)

Health, illness and mortality vary by geographical location, gender and SES. Some of this variation, particularly in geographical location, can be explained by medical interventions in terms of the availability of medicines and vaccinations and free access to health care. Even within specific countries it is possible that gender differences may also relate to medical interventions, with men being less likely to attend for health check-ups or screening than women. However, an alternative analysis focuses on the role of the environment.

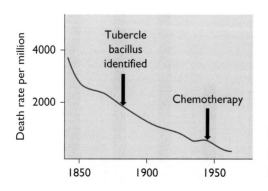

FIGURE 2.17

Decline in mortality from tuberculosis

SOURCE: Adapted from McKeown (1979)

ENVIRONMENTAL FACTORS

According to McKeown (1979) much of the improvement seen in health and mortality in the developed world is due to environmental and social factors rather than medical interventions. Such environmental factors include food availability, food hygiene, sanitation and sewage facilities, and clean water. These basic requirements vary by country and may contribute to health inequalities. In terms of sanitation facilities, in 2008 the WHO reported that 2,600 million worldwide were not using 'improved sanitation facilities' and that 1,100 million were still defecating in the open, which raises the risk of worm infestation, hepatitis, cholera, trachoma and environmental contamination. The use of improved sanitation facilities by WHO region is shown in Figure 2.18, which indicates that the lowest rates of use of improved sanitation facilities were in the African and South-East Asian regions.

The state of drinking water is also linked to health and poor water is associated with illnesses such as vomiting, sickness, diarrhoea and cholera. Data from the WHO show that the lowest levels of safe drinking water are in the Africa and South-East Asian regions (see Figure 2.19).

All these data therefore shows variation in key environmental factors which are linked to health and may help to explain health inequalities. In the developed world, where these basic requirements tend to be met, our health may still be influenced by our environment in terms of the quality of food available, easy access to fast unhealthy food, working environments that encourage a sedentary lifestyle, town planning which makes walking hard and using the car the norm, the absence of walkways or cycle paths and poor street lighting (see Chapter 15 for a discussion of the obesogenic environment).

In an attempt to explain variations in health by geographical location, time and gender, research points to a role for environmental factors both in terms of basic standards of hygiene and the more micro structures of the world we live in. Both medical and environmental perspectives provide powerful explanations for why health is not a constant and for the health inequalities shown above. They are particularly effective at explaining geographical differences around the world as many developing countries remain without access to skilled health care, medicines and a basic level of sanitation and water. A third explanation of this variability, however, focuses on the role of behaviour and argues that even when medicines are available, or when healthy food is on offer, or when cycle paths are built, such medical and environmental factors will only impact on health if and

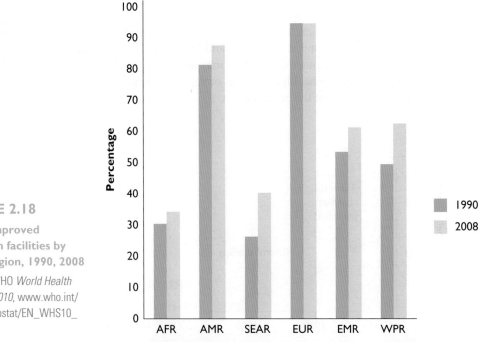

FIGURE 2.18

Use of improved sanitation facilities by WHO region, 1990, 2008

SOURCE: WHO *World Health Statistics 2010*, www.who.int/whosis/whostat/EN_WHS10_Full.pdf: 19

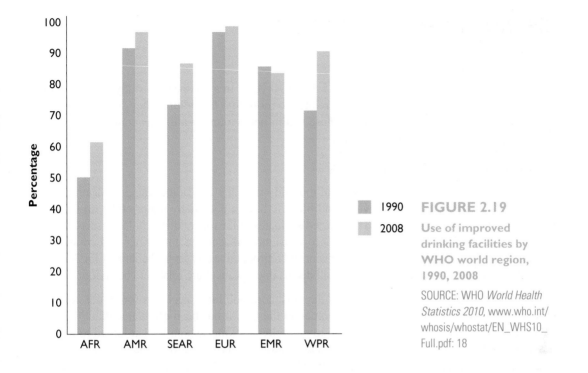

FIGURE 2.19

Use of improved drinking facilities by WHO world region, 1990, 2008

SOURCE: WHO *World Health Statistics 2010*, www.who.int/whosis/whostat/EN_WHS10_Full.pdf: 18

when individuals behave in a more or less healthy way. Accordingly, medication for HIV/AIDS may well be available in the western world but it only works if a person chooses to take it. Further, people in the developed countries may have better access to health care and cleaner water but if they choose to smoke and lead sedentary lives then some of this health gain will be undermined by unhealthy lifestyles – in other words, the way people behave.

BEHAVIOUR

McKeown (1979) examined health and illness throughout the twentieth century and argued that contemporary illness is caused by 'influences ... which the individual determines by his own behaviour (smoking, eating, exercise, and the like)' (p. 118). More recent data support this emphasis on chronic illnesses which are related to behaviour. For example, in 2008 Allender et al. published data on the most common causes of death across Europe (including the UK) and concluded that cardiovascular diseases and cancer account for 64 per cent of male and 71 per cent or female deaths (Allender et al. 2008a, 2008b). Similar figures are also found in the USA where cardiovascular diseases and cancer accounted for 56 pet cent of deaths in men and 55 per cent of deaths in women (National Center for Health Statistics 2009).

BEHAVIOUR AND LONGEVITY

The role of behaviour has also been highlighted by the work of Belloc and Breslow and their colleagues (Belloc and Breslow 1972; Breslow and Enstrom 1980) who examined the relationship between mortality rates and behaviour among 7,000 people as part of the Alameda County study in the USA, which began in 1965. They concluded from their original correlational analysis that seven behaviours were related to positive health status. These behaviours were:

1 Sleeping 7–8 hours a day.

2 Having breakfast every day.

3 Not smoking.

4 Rarely eating between meals.

5   Being near or at prescribed weight.

6   Having moderate or no use of alcohol.

7   Taking regular exercise.

Their large sample was followed up over 5.5 and 10 years in a prospective study and the authors reported that these seven behaviours were related to mortality. In addition, they suggested for people aged over 75 who carried out all of these health behaviours, health was comparable to those aged 35–44 who followed less than three.

BEHAVIOUR AND MORTALITY

It has also been suggested that 50 per cent of mortality from the 10 leading causes of death is due to behaviour. This indicates that behaviour and lifestyle have a potentially major effect on longevity. Early research by Doll and Peto (1981) reported estimates of the role of different factors as causes for all cancer deaths. They estimated that tobacco consumption accounts for 30 per cent of all cancer deaths, alcohol for 3 per cent, diet for 35 per cent and reproductive and sexual behaviour for 7 per cent. Accordingly, approximately 75 per cent of all deaths due to cancer are related to behaviour.

More specifically, lung cancer, which is the most common form, accounts for 36 per cent of all cancer deaths in men and 15 per cent in women in the UK. It has been calculated that 90 per cent of all lung cancer mortality is attributable to cigarette smoking, which is also linked to other illnesses such as cancers of the bladder, pancreas, mouth, larynx and oesophagus and CHD. The impact of smoking on mortality was shown by McKeown when he examined changes in life expectancies in males from 1838 to 1970. His data are shown in Figure 2.20 which indicates that the increase in life expectancy shown in non-smokers is much reduced in smokers. The relationship between mortality and behaviour is also illustrated by bowel cancer which is linked to behaviours such as a diet high in total fat, high in meat and low in fibre.

In 2004, Mokdad et al. also explored the role of health behaviour in illness and mortality. Their analysis was based upon studies which had identified a link between risk behaviours such as smoking, diet, activity, alcohol consumption, car crashes and sexual behaviour and the deaths of 2.4 million people who had died in the year 2000 in the USA. They then developed an estimate of how many of the disease-related deaths could be accounted for by a particular behaviour and multiplied this by the data on actual causes of deaths in 2000. For example, from the literature they estimated what proportion of deaths by cancer could be accounted for by diet. They then multiplied this estimate by the number of people who actually died from cancer in the year 2000. Then, by collating these figures they arrived at the total number of deaths (regardless of disease) attributable to each behaviour. The

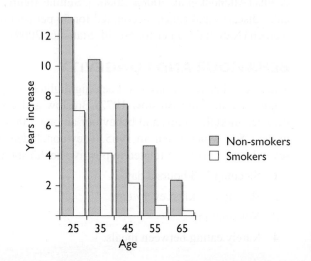

FIGURE 2.20

The effect of smoking on increase in expectation of life: males, 1838–1970

SOURCE: Adapted from McKeown (1979)

results from this analysis showed that the percentage of deaths caused by behaviours were as follows: tobacco: 18.1 per cent; diet and inactivity: 16.6 per cent; alcohol: 3.5 per cent; motor vehicle: 1.8 per cent; firearms: 1.2 per cent; sexual behaviour: 0.8 per cent; illicit drug use: 0.7 per cent. In 2008, data from a study in England also illustrated the impact of behavior on mortality. Khaw et al. (2008) carried out a longitudinal study over 11 years of 20,244 men and women and concluded that death from all causes, cancer and cardiovascular disease was related to four health behaviours: smoking, not being physically active, drinking more than moderate amounts of alcohol and not eating five or more portions of fruit and vegetables per day. This study therefore again supported the link between behaviour and mortality. In addition, it supports the role of a healthy lifestyle as mortality was predicted by the combined impact of these four behaviours, not just individual behaviours.

The relationship between behaviour and mortality can also be illustrated by the longevity of people in different countries. For example, in the USA and the UK, only 3 people out of every 100,000 live to be over 100. However, in Georgia, among the Abkhazians, 400 out of every 100,000 live to be over 100, and the oldest recorded Abkhazian was 170 (although this is obviously problematic in terms of the validity of any written records in the early 1800s). Weg (1983) examined the longevity of the Abkhazians and suggested that, relative to that in other countries, it is due to a combination of biological, lifestyle and social factors including:

- Genetics.
- Maintaining vigorous work roles and habits.
- A diet low in saturated fat and meat and high in fruit and vegetables.
- No alcohol or nicotine.
- High levels of social support.
- Low reported stress levels.

Analysis of this group of people suggests that health behaviours may be related to longevity and are therefore worthy of study. However, such cross-sectional studies are problematic to interpret, particularly in terms of the direction of causality: does the lifestyle of the Abkhazians cause their longevity or is it a product of it?

Research therefore points to a role for behaviour in explaining health, illness and mortality, particularly in the developed world where the most common problems are chronic illness such as cancer, CHD, obesity and diabetes, which have strong links to behaviour.

TO CONCLUDE

Data indicate that health, illness and mortality vary along a number of dimensions including geographical location, time, SES and gender. Overall, it would seem that the developing countries have poorer health than developed countries, that better health is related to increased income and that although women have more symptoms and illnesses than men, they tend to live longer. Such variation can be explained using a number of different perspectives. A medical perspective emphasizes the role of access to health care, skilled professionals and the use of the medical interventions; an environmental perspective emphasizes sanitation, clean drinking water and the structural factors that influence our daily lives; and a behavioural perspective argues that most mortality in the developed world is nowadays due to chronic conditions such as cancer, CHD and obesity and that these are strongly associated with health-related behaviours. Although health psychology as a discipline acknowledges the role of all these perspectives, its main focus tends to be on behaviour and the ways in which our behaviour influences illness in terms of its onset (e.g. smoking, diet), help-seeking (e.g. symptom perception, illness cognitions), illness management (e.g. coping, adherence to medication, behaviour change), illness progression (e.g. behaviour change, coping) and health outcomes (e.g. quality of life, longevity).

QUESTIONS

1 In what ways do health and illness vary?
2 What factors could account for this variation?
3 What evidence is there for the role of behaviour in explaining some of this variation?
4 How could governments reduce health inequalities?
5 Why do you think health psychology tends to focus on behaviour as the main explanation for health inequalities?

FOR DISCUSSION

Have you been on holiday to another country? Consider any differences between that country and your own (e.g. access to health care, transport, sanitation, diet, levels of exercise, etc.) and think about how these differences might explain any differences in patterns of health and illness.

FURTHER READING

The literature in health inequalities consists of large-scale studies illustrating the existence of variations according to factors such as gender, ethnic group, age, SES and geographical location. These tend to come from epidemiology and public health medicine and can be found in the medical journals such as *The Lancet*, the *Journal of the American Medical Association* (*JAMA*) and the *British Medical Journal (BMJ)*. The literature also involves theoretical analyses of such variation and this tends to come from a more sociological perspective. This list provides some suggestions for further reading from both these perspectives.

EPIDEMIOLOGY

Marmot, M. (2010) *Fair Society, Healthy Lives: A Strategic Review of Health Inequalities in England Post-2010*. London: The Stationery Office, www.marmotreview.org/AssetLibrary/pdfs/Reports/FairSocietyHealthyLives.pdf.

Professor Michael Marmot is an expert on health inequalities and has carried out numerous empirical studies and reviews of the existing data and literature. This is the most recent summary of the evidence for health inequalities in England, contains a wealth of data and analysis and presents a way forward for the reduction of health inequalities.

Mokdad, A.H., Marks, J.S., Stroup, D.F. and Gerberding, J.L. (2004) Actual causes of death in the United States, 2000, *JAMA*, 291(10): 1238–45.

This paper presents an analysis of mortality data in the USA and calculates the relationship between health related-behaviours (e.g. diet, smoking, alcohol, etc.) and causes of death. It is surprisingly easy to follow and is a good insight into how epidemiologists work and think.

SOCIOLOGY/SOCIAL EPIDEMIOLOGY

Annandale, E. and Hunt, K. (eds) (2001) *Gender Inequalities in Health*. Buckingham: Open University Press.

Ellen Annandale is a sociologist and has written extensively on gender and health. This book provides an interesting review of the literature relating to gender and health inequalities.

Bartley, M. (2004) *Health Inequalities: An Introduction to Concepts, Theories and Methods*. Oxford: Polity Press.

A very well-written and accessible book that provides a useful overview of the health inequalities literature. It also describes the different theoretical perspectives that have been taken to explain health inequalities with a focus on behavioural, psychosocial, material and life-course approaches.

Wilkinson, R. and Pickett, K. (2009) *The Spirit Level: Why More Equal Societies Almost Always Do Better*. London: Allen Lane.

Richard Wilkinson is a social epidemiologist and wrote a book in 1996 called *Unhealthy Societies: The Affliction of Inequalities*, in which he argued that although health inequalities can be explained by factors such as SES, deprivation and access to health care, it is the existence of unequal distribution of wealth within societies which causes most health and social problems. This is his most recent book and it elaborates upon this argument and provides evidence to indicate that more equal societies with less difference between the rich and poor have better health and fewer social problems, such as violence and drug addiction, than societies in which the gap is greater. Wilkinson argues that this is the case even when absolute levels of deprivation within a country are accounted for. His argument has not gone unchallenged and has generated much debate within the health inequalities world (see Lynch and Davey Smith 2002; Lynch et al. 2004). Nevertheless it is good to be aware of his position and how it fits into this literature.

Young, F.W. (2004) Socioeconomic status and health: the problem of explanation and a sociological solution, *Social Theory and Health*, 2: 123–41.

An interesting sociological paper which provides a good insight into the nature of the problem and then offers a sociologically orientated explanation. It is a useful insight into how sociologists think about theory and provides a stimulating introduction to more psychological analyses.

 Visit the website at www.openup.co.uk/ogden for additional resources on Chapter 2 to help you with your study, such as multiple choice questions, weblinks and a searchable online glossary.

PART TWO
Health Beliefs, Behaviour and Behaviour Change

© Joshua Hodge Photography/iStock

3 Health Beliefs

© wavebreakmedia/iStock

CHAPTER OVERVIEW

Chapter 2 described how variations in health and illness can in part be explained in terms of changes in behaviour-related illnesses, such as coronary heart disease (CHD), cancers and HIV. This chapter explores what health behaviours are and the extent to which they can be predicted by health beliefs, with a focus on attributions, risk perception, motivation and self efficacy. The chapter then describes a number of key stage models and social cognition models which are often used to predict health behaviours. It explores problems with these models and describes studies that address the gap between behavioural intentions and actual behaviour, and focuses on the ways these models have been extended and integrated.

WHAT ARE HEALTH BEHAVIOURS?

Kasl and Cobb (1966) defined three types of health-related behaviour. They suggested that:

- A *health behaviour* was a behaviour aimed to prevent disease (e.g. eating a healthy diet).
- An *illness behaviour* was a behaviour aimed to seek remedy (e.g. going to the doctor).
- A *sick role behaviour* was any activity aimed at getting well (e.g. taking prescribed medication, resting).

Health behaviours were further defined by Matarazzo (1984) in terms of either:

- *Health-impairing habits*, which he called 'behavioural pathogens' (e.g. smoking, eating a high fat diet), or
- *Health protective behaviours*, which he defined as 'behavioural immunogens' (e.g. attending a health check).

In short, Matarazzo distinguished between those behaviours that have a negative effect (the behavioural pathogens, such as smoking, eating foods high in fat, drinking large amounts of alcohol) and those behaviours that may have a positive effect (the behavioural immunogens, such as tooth brushing, wearing seat belts, seeking health information, having regular check-ups, sleeping an adequate number of hours per night).

Generally health behaviours are regarded as behaviours that are related to the health status of the individual.

PREDICTING HEALTH BEHAVIOURS: THE ROLE OF HEALTH BELIEFS

Chapter 2 described how health behaviours are important in predicting mortality and the longevity of individuals. Health promotion and health education perspectives tend to emphasize the role of knowledge in predicting health behaviours and aim to change behaviour by improving what people know. In line with this, some studies indicate that knowledge does play a role in how we behave. For example, Rimer et al. (1991) reported that knowledge about breast cancer is related to having regular mammograms and several studies have also indicated a positive correlation between knowledge about breast self-examination (BSE) and breast cancer (Lashley 1987; Champion 1990). One study manipulated knowledge about pap tests for cervical cancer by showing subjects an informative videotape and reported that the resulting increased knowledge was related to future healthy behaviour (O'Brien and Lee 1990). Within health psychology, however, most research has emphasized health beliefs as the key predictors of behaviour as in general it is believed that know-ledge alone cannot predict or change behaviour and that we need to understand the ways in which people *think* about their behaviour. This chapter describes four key approaches to health beliefs:

- Attribution theory (and the related notion of health locus of control)
- Risk perception which has been explored in terms of unrealistic optimism, risk compensation and self-affirmation theory
- Motivation and self-determination theory
- Self-efficacy.

It then explores how different beliefs have been combined to form structured models in terms of stage theories and social cognition models. A health belief is simply any belief that is related to health.

ATTRIBUTION THEORY

The origins of attribution theory can be found in the work of Heider (1958), who argued that indi-viduals are motivated to see their social world as predictable and controllable – i.e. there is a need to understand causality. Kelley (1971) developed these original ideas and proposed a clearly defined attribution theory suggesting that attributions about causality were structured according to causal schemata made up of the following criteria:

- *Distinctiveness:* the attribution about the cause of a behaviour is specific to the individual carrying out the behaviour.
- *Consensus:* the attribution about the cause of a behaviour would be shared by others.
- *Consistency over time:* the same attribution about causality would be made at any other time.
- *Consistency over modality:* the same attribution would be made in a different situation.

Kelley argued that attributions are made according to these different criteria and that the type of attribution made (e.g. high distinctiveness, low consensus, low consistency over time, low consist-ency over modality) determines the extent to which the cause of a behaviour is regarded as a product of a characteristic internal to the individual or external to them (i.e. the environment or situation).

Since its original formulation, attribution theory has been developed extensively and differentia-tions have been made between self-attributions (i.e. attributions about one's own behaviour) and other attributions (i.e. attributions made about the behaviour of others). In addition, the dimensions of attribution have been redefined as follows:

- *Internal versus external* (e.g. my failure to get a job is due to my poor performance in the interview versus the interviewer's prejudice).
- *Stable versus unstable* (e.g. the cause of my failure to get a job will always be around versus was specific to that one event).
- *Global versus specific* (e.g. the cause of my failure to get a job influences other areas of my life versus only influenced this specific job interview).
- *Controllable versus uncontrollable* (e.g. the cause of my failure to get a job was controllable by me versus was uncontrollable by me).

Brickman et al. (1982) have also distinguished between attributions made about the causes of a problem and attributions made about the possible solution. For example, they claimed that whereas an alcoholic may believe that he is responsible for becoming an alcoholic due to his lack of will-power (an attribution for the cause), he may believe that the medical profession is responsible for making him well again (an attribution for the solution). Attribution theory has many similarities to the self-regulation model described in Chapter 9 in the context of illness cognitions.

ATTRIBUTIONS FOR HEALTH-RELATED BEHAVIOURS

Attribution theory has been applied to the study of health and health-related behaviour. Herzlich (1973) interviewed 80 people about the general causes of health and illness and found that health is regarded as internal to the individual and illness is seen as something that comes into the body from the external world.

More specifically, attributions about illness may be related to behaviours. For example, Bradley (1985) examined patients' attributions for responsibility for their diabetes and reported that perceived control over illness ('is the diabetes controllable by me or a powerful other?') influenced the choice of treatment by these patients. Patients could choose (1) an insulin pump (a small mechanical device attached to the skin, which provides a continuous flow of insulin); (2) intense conventional treatment; or (3) a continuation of daily injections. The results indicated that the patients who chose an insulin pump showed decreased control over their diabetes and increased control attributed to powerful doctors. Therefore, if an individual attributed their illness externally and felt that they personally were not responsible for it, they were more likely to choose the insulin pump and were more likely to hand over responsibility to the doctors.

HEALTH LOCUS OF CONTROL

The internal versus external dimension of attribution theory has been specifically applied to health in terms of the concept of a *health locus of control*. Individuals differ as to whether they tend to regard events as controllable by them (an internal locus of control) or uncontrollable by them (an external locus of control). Wallston and Wallston (1982) developed a measure of the health locus of control which evaluates whether an individual regards their health as controllable by them (e.g. 'I am directly responsible for my health'), whether they believe their health is not controllable by them and in the hands of fate (e.g. 'whether I am well or not is a matter of luck'), or whether they regard their health as under the control of powerful others (e.g. 'I can only do what my doctor tells me to do'). Health locus of control has been shown to be related to whether an individual changes their behaviour (e.g. gives up smoking) or adheres to recommendations made by their doctor (see Norman and Bennett 1995 for a review). In addition, it has also been shown to relate to the kind of communication style people require from health professionals. For example, if a doctor encourages an individual who is generally *external* to change their lifestyle, the individual is unlikely to comply as they do not deem themselves responsible for their health (see e.g. Weiss and Larson 1990). Furthermore, in a study of young people with diabetes, whereas an internal locus of control related to seeing the benefits of adhering to a self-care regimen for diabetes as outweighing the costs, a belief in powerful others was associated with a lower perception of the risks associated with the disease (Gillibrand and Stevenson 2006).

Although the concept of a health locus of control is intuitively interesting, there are several problems with it:

- Is the health locus of control a state or a trait (am I always internal)?
- Is it possible to be both external and internal?
- Is going to the doctor for help external (the doctor is a powerful other who can make me well) or internal (I am determining my health status by searching out appropriate intervention)?

RISK PERCEPTION

One key health belief that people hold relates to their perception of risk and their sense of whether or not they are susceptible to any given health problem. For example, people may believe that because their grandmother smoked all her life and didn't die until she was 85, they are not at risk from lung cancer if they smoke. In contrast, others may overestimate their risk of illness, believing that obesity runs in their family and that there is little they can do to prevent themselves from becoming overweight. Perceptions of risk have been studied within three frameworks: unrealistic optimism, risk compensation and self-affirmation theory.

UNREALISTIC OPTIMISM

Weinstein (1983) suggested that one of the reasons that people continue to practise unhealthy behaviours is due to inaccurate perceptions of risk and susceptibility – their *unrealistic optimism*. He asked subjects to examine a list of health problems and to state 'compared to other people of your age and sex, what are your chances of getting [the problem] – greater than, about the same, or less than theirs?' The results of the study showed that most subjects believed that they were less likely to get the health problem. Weinstein called this phenomenon unrealistic optimism as he argued that not everyone can be less likely to contract an illness. Weinstein described four cognitive factors that contribute to unrealistic optimism: (1) lack of personal experience with the problem; (2) the belief that the problem is preventable by individual action; (3) the belief that if the problem has not yet appeared, it will not appear in the future; and (4) the belief that the problem is infrequent. These factors suggest that perception of own risk is not a rational process.

In an attempt to explain why individuals' assessment of their risk may go wrong, and why people are unrealistically optimistic, Weinstein argued that individuals show *selective focus*. He claimed that individuals ignore their own risk-increasing behaviour ('I may not always practise safe sex but that's not important') and focus primarily on their risk-reducing behaviour ('but at least I don't inject drugs'). He also argues that this selectivity is compounded by egocentrism: individuals tend to ignore others' risk-decreasing behaviour ('my friends all practise safe sex but that's irrelevant'). Therefore an individual may be unrealistically optimistic if they focus on the times they use condoms when assessing their own risk and ignore the times they do not and, in addition, focus on the times that others around them do not practise safe sex and ignore the times that they do.

In one study, subjects were required to focus on either their risk-increasing ('unsafe sex') or their risk-decreasing ('safe sex') behaviour. The effect of this on their unrealistic optimism for risk of HIV was examined (Hoppe and Ogden 1996). Heterosexual subjects were asked to complete a questionnaire concerning their beliefs about HIV and their sexual behaviour. Subjects were allocated to either the risk-increasing or risk-decreasing condition. Subjects in the risk-increasing condition were asked to complete questions such as 'since being sexually active how often have you asked about your partners' HIV status?' It was assumed that only a few subjects would be able to answer that they had done this frequently, thus making them feel more at risk. Subjects in the risk-decreasing condition were asked questions such as 'since being sexually active how often have you tried to select your partners carefully?' It was believed that most subjects would answer that they did this, making them feel less at risk. The results showed that focusing on risk-decreasing factors increased optimism by increasing perceptions of others' risk. Therefore, by encouraging the subjects to focus on their own healthy behaviour ('I select my partners carefully'), they felt more unrealistically optimistic and rated themselves as less at risk compared with those whom they perceived as being more at risk.

RISK COMPENSATION

Risk perception has also been understood within the framework of risk compensation. People are exposed to often competing desires and motivations. For example, they may like eating cake but want to be thin. Some individuals opt for an extremely healthy approach to life and ensure that all their behaviours are protective and that the only desires they give in to are the healthy ones. Many, however, show risk compensation and believe that 'I can smoke because I go to the gym at the weekend' or 'I can eat chocolate because I play tennis'. From this perspective people believe that one set of risky behaviours can be neutralized or compensated for by another.

Risk compensation: believing one healthy behaviour can compensate for an unhealthy one

SOURCE: © Lightkeeper/Dreamstime

Such beliefs have been studied by Rabiau et al. (2006) who developed the compensatory health beliefs model and argued that such beliefs may explain why people don't always adhere to dietary or exercise programmes. Similarly, Radtke et al. (2010) developed a scale to assess compensatory beliefs in the context of adolescent smoking and concluded that more compensatory health beliefs about smoking predicted a lower readiness to stop smoking. They argued that smokers are often in a state of cognitive dissonance (e.g. 'I want to be healthy' *but* 'I know smoking is unhealthy') and that compensatory health beliefs may be a mechanism for them to resolve this dissonance.

SELF-AFFIRMATION THEORY

Central to unrealistic optimism and risk compensation is the notion of risk perception and the proposal that individuals can process risk information in ways that enable them to continue their unhealthy behaviour. An example of this is smokers' ability to continue to smoke even when the words 'smoking kills' are written on their packet of cigarettes. In fact research suggests that those least persuaded by risk data are often those most at risk and that they can either ignore unwelcome information or find reasons for rejecting it (Sherman et al. 2000; Jacks and Cameron 2003). Recently, however, it has been suggested that self-affirmation may help reduce the tendency to resist threat information (Harris and Upton 2009). Self-affirmation theory suggests that people are motivated to protect their sense of self-integrity and their sense of themselves as being 'adaptively and morally adequate' (Steele 1988). Therefore, if presented with information that threatens their sense of self, they behave defensively and either ignore or reject it. However, if given the opportunity to self-affirm in another domain of their lives, then their need to become defensive is reduced. For example, if a smoker thinks that they are a sensible person, when confronted with a message that says that smoking is not sensible, their integrity is threatened and they behave defensively by blocking the information. If given the chance, however, to think about another area in which they are sensible, then they are less likely to become defensive about the anti-smoking message. A series of studies have tested the impact of self-affirmation on the processing of information about the link between alcohol and breast cancer in young women and smoking in young and adult smokers (Harris and Napper 2005; Harris et al. 2006; Armitage et al. 2008). In the first study, young women who were drinking above the recommended limit were randomized either to the self-affirmation condition or the control condition (Harris and Napper 2005). Those in the self-affirmation condition were asked to write about their most important value and why it was important to them. All were then given a health message about the links between excessive alcohol intake and breast cancer. The results showed that those who had self-affirmed were more accepting of the health message. In a similar study, smokers were asked to study four images depicting the dangers of smoking and half underwent a self-affirmation task. These results also showed that those who had self-affirmed rated the images as more threatening and reported higher levels of self-efficacy and intentions to stop smoking (Harris et al. 2006). Similar results were also found for adult smokers when presented with a government anti-smoking leaflet and given the chance to self-affirm (Armitage et al. 2008). Harris and Upton (2009) carried out a review of existing research on self-affirmation and concluded that although people can deny and block the risks associated with their behaviour, this defensive process is reduced if they are encouraged to self-affirm, thereby increasing their acceptance of unwelcome risk information. They also concluded that self-affirmation is particularly effective in those most at risk with people even showing changes in their intentions to carry out unhealthy behaviours in the future. This approach has implications for a wide range of health-related behaviours and the development of more effective interventions to change behaviour (see Chapter 8 for health promotion and behaviour change interventions).

MOTIVATION AND SELF-DETERMINATION THEORY

The motivation to carry out a behaviour is a core construct in a lot of research exploring health behaviour and it is widely accepted that an individual needs to be motivated to either start a new behaviour or change an existing one. The notion of motivation can be found either implicitly or explicitly in most models of health behaviour but plays a central role in self-determination theory (SDT) (Deci and Ryan 1985, 2000). SDT focuses on the reasons or motives that regulate behaviour and distinguishes between two kinds of motivation. First it describes autonomous motivations which relate to engaging in behaviours that fulfil personally relevant goals such as eating nice food or talking to friends. This is also referred to as *intrinsic motivation* and tends to make the person feel satisfied or rewarded. Deci and Ryan (1985, 2000) argue that such autonomous motivations satisfy three basic needs: autonomy ('I can manage my own behaviour'), competence ('I can master my environment') and relatedness ('I can develop close relationships with others'). Autonomous motivations tend to be associated with a sense of well-being and the persistence of health-related behaviours. Second it describes *controlled motivations* which are driven by external factors such as the need to please friends, and are also referred to as *extrinsic motivations*. These controlled motivations tend to make the person feel less personally satisfied and are linked with the avoidance of health behaviours.

SELF-EFFICACY

The notion of self-efficacy was first developed by Bandura in 1977 and then expanded as part of his social learning theory which has been used extensively to explain a range of behaviours from aggression and parenting to eating and exercise. Self-efficacy is 'the belief in one's capabilities to organize and execute the sources of action required to manage prospective situations' (Bandura 1986) and is very closely related to feeling confident in one's ability to engage in any given behaviour. Therefore stopping smoking would be related by the belief 'I am confident I can stop smoking' and eating more vegetables would be predicted by 'I can eat more vegetables in the future'.

In summary, there are a number of key factors which have been linked with health beliefs. Attribution theory and the health locus of control emphasize attributions for causality and control whereas unrealistic optimism, risk compensation and self-affirmation focus on perceptions of susceptibility and risk. Further, research has also explored the role of motivations and self-efficacy. These different aspects of health beliefs have been integrated into structured models of health beliefs and behaviour. Some of these models are considered to be *stage models* while others are known as *social cognition models*. These will now be described.

STAGE MODELS

Some models of health beliefs and health behaviour consider individuals to be at different ordered *stages* and describe how they move through these stages as they change their behaviour. A stage model is deemed to have four basic properties (Weinstein et al. 1998):

1 *A classification system to define the different stages:* each stage is therefore labelled and defined.
2 *Ordering of stages:* people pass through each stage in a predictable order, although they may not all reach the end-point, and some may pass backwards through the stages.

3 *People within the same stage face similar barriers:* in particular each stage is characterized by a similar set of barriers that prevent people from moving to the next stage.

4 *People from different stages face different barriers:* this means that each stage comes with a different set of barriers.

Stage models of behaviour can be found across a number of areas within psychology including models of child development, stages of grief and bereavement and the stages of adjustment to a serious illness or accident. The two-stage models most relevant to health psychology are the *stages of change model* (SOC) and the *health action process approach* (HAPA).

THE STAGES OF CHANGE MODEL

The transtheoretical model of behaviour change was originally developed by Prochaska and DiClemente (1982) as a synthesis of 18 therapies describing the processes involved in eliciting and maintaining change. It is now more commonly known as the stages of change model SOC Prochaska and DiClemente examined these different therapeutic approaches for common processes and suggested a new model of behaviour change.

Components of the SOC

The stages of change model is based upon the following stages:

1 *Pre-contemplation:* not intending to make any changes.
2 *Contemplation:* considering a change.
3 *Preparation:* making small changes.
4 *Action:* actively engaging in a new behaviour.
5 *Maintenance:* sustaining the change over time.

These stages, however, do not always occur in a linear fashion (simply moving from 1 to 5), and the theory describes behaviour change as dynamic and not 'all or nothing'. For example, an individual may move to the preparation stage and then back to the contemplation stage several times before progressing to the action stage. Furthermore, even when an individual has reached the maintenance stage, they may slip back to the contemplation stage over time.

The model also examines how the individual weighs up the costs and benefits of a particular behaviour, which is referred to as *decisional balance.* In particular, its authors argue that individuals at different stages of change will differentially focus on either the costs of a behaviour (e.g. 'stopping smoking will make me anxious in company') or the benefits of the behaviour (e.g. 'stopping smoking will improve my health'). For example, a smoker at the action stage ('I have stopped smoking') and the maintenance stage ('for four months') tends to focus on the favourable and positive feature of their behaviour ('I feel healthier because I have stopped smoking'), whereas smokers in the pre-contemplation stage tend to focus on the negative features of the behaviour ('it will make me anxious'). Central to any stage model is the position that the stages are qualitatively different to each other. For the SOC this means that the decisional balance of a person at the preparation change (for example) would be different to the decisional balance of someone at the action stage.

Using the SOC

If applied to smoking cessation, the model would suggest the following set of beliefs and behaviours at the different stages:

1 *Pre-contemplation:* 'I am happy being a smoker and intend to continue smoking'.
2 *Contemplation:* 'I have been coughing a lot recently, perhaps I should think about stopping smoking'.

3 *Preparation:* 'I will stop going to the pub and will buy lower tar cigarettes'.

4 *Action:* 'I have stopped smoking'.

5 *Maintenance:* 'I have stopped smoking for four months now'.

This individual, however, may well move back at times to believing that they will continue to smoke and may relapse (known as the *revolving door schema*). The SOC is illustrated in **Focus on Research 4.1** (p. 88).

Support for the SOC

The SOC has been applied to several health-related behaviours, such as smoking, alcohol use, exercise and screening behaviour (e.g. DiClemente et al. 1991; Cox et al. 2003; Armitage 2009). It is also increasingly used as a basis to develop interventions that are tailored to the particular stage of the specific person concerned. For example, a smoker who has been identified as being at the preparation stage would receive a different intervention to one who was at the contemplation stage. Marshall and Biddle (2001) and Rosen (2000) have carried out meta-analyses of the use of the model to understand a range of health-related behaviours. In general their conclusions indicate that the SOC can be used in research to explore changes in health behaviours and that some differences in decisional balance appear to exist between people classified as being at different stages. However, their analyses also revealed many inconsistencies in the data and the SOC has been subjected to many criticisms.

LIBRARY, UNIVERSITY OF CHESTER

Criticisms of the SOC

The SOC has recently been criticized for the following reasons (Weinstein et al. 1998; Sutton 2000, 2002a, 2005; West 2006):

- It is difficult to determine whether behaviour change occurs according to stages or along a continuum. Researchers describe the difference between linear patterns between stages which are not consistent with a stage model and discontinuity patterns which are consistent.

- The absence of qualitative differences between stages could either be due to the absence of stages or because the stages have not been correctly assessed and identified.

- Changes between stages may happen so quickly as to make the stages unimportant.

- Interventions that have been based on the SOC may work because the individual believes that they are receiving special attention, rather than because of the effectiveness of the model per se.

- Most studies based on the SOC use cross-sectional designs to examine differences between different people at different stages of change. Such designs do not allow conclusions to be drawn about the role of different causal factors at the different stages (i.e. people at the preparation stage are driven forward by different factors than those at the contemplation stage). Experimental and longitudinal studies are needed for any conclusions about causality to be valid.

- The concept of a 'stage' is not a simple one as it includes many variables: current behaviour, quit attempts, intention to change and time since quitting. Perhaps these variables should be measured separately.

- The model focuses on conscious decision-making and planning processes. Further, it assumes that people make coherent and stable plans.

- Using the model may be no better than simply asking people, 'Do you have any plans to try to . . . ?' or 'Do you want to . . . ?'.

THE HEALTH ACTION PROCESS APPROACH (HAPA)

The HAPA (see Figure 3.1) is another stage model of health beliefs and health behaviour and was developed by Schwarzer (1992) following his review of the literature, which highlighted the need to include a *temporal* element in the understanding of beliefs and behaviour. In addition, it emphasized the importance of self-efficacy as a determinant of both behavioural intentions and self-reports of behaviour. The HAPA includes several elements from the social cognition models (see pp. 48–55) and attempts to predict both behavioural intentions and actual behaviour.

Components of the HAPA

The main novel component of the HAPA is the distinction between a decision-making/motivational stage and an action/maintenance stage. Therefore the model adds a temporal and process factor to understanding the relationship between beliefs and behaviour and suggests that individuals initially decide whether or not to carry out a behaviour (the *motivation* stage), and then make plans to initiate and maintain this behaviour (the *action* phase).

According to the HAPA, the motivation stage is made up of the following components:

- *Self-efficacy* (e.g. 'I am confident that I can stop smoking').
- *Outcome expectancies* (e.g. 'stopping smoking will improve my health'), which has a subset of *social outcome expectancies* (e.g. 'other people want me to stop smoking and if I stop smoking I will gain their approval').
- *Threat appraisal*, which is composed of beliefs about the severity of an illness and perceptions of individual vulnerability.

According to the HAPA the end result of the process is an intention to act.

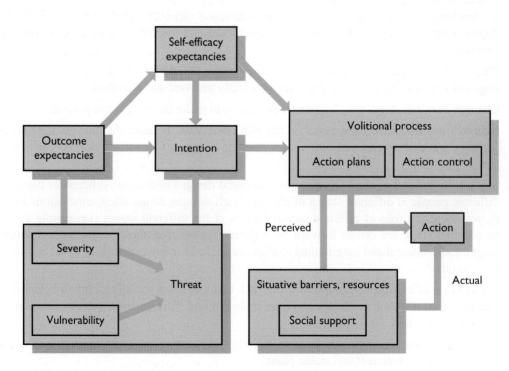

FIGURE 3.1

The health action process approach

The action stage is composed of cognitive (volitional), situational and behavioural factors. The integration of these factors determines the extent to which a behaviour is initiated and maintained via these self-regulatory processes. The cognitive factor is made up of action plans (e.g. 'if offered a cigarette when I am trying not to smoke I will imagine what the tar would do to my lungs') and action control (e.g. 'I can survive being offered a cigarette by reminding myself that I am a non-smoker'). These two cognitive factors determine the individual's determination of will. The situational factor consists of social support (e.g. the existence of friends who encourage non-smoking) and the absence of situational barriers (e.g. financial support to join an exercise club).

Schwarzer (1992) argued that the HAPA bridges the gap between intentions and behaviour and emphasizes self-efficacy, both in terms of developing the intention to act and also implicitly in terms of the cognitive stage of the action stage, whereby self-efficacy promotes and maintains action plans and action control, therefore contributing to the maintenance of the action. He maintained that the HAPA enables specific predictions to be made about causality and also describes a process of beliefs whereby behaviour is the result of a series of processes.

Support for the HAPA

The individual components of the HAPA have been tested, providing some support for the model. In particular, Schwarzer (1992) claimed that self-efficacy was consistently the best predictor of behavioural intentions and behaviour change for a variety of behaviours such as the intention to use dental floss, frequency of flossing, effective use of contraception, BSE, drug addicts' intentions to use clean needles, intentions to quit smoking and intentions to adhere to weight loss programmes and exercise (e.g. Beck and Lund 1981; Seydel et al. 1990). Research also indicates that the model, and in particular the element of self efficacy, predicted BSE in a large sample of German women (Luszczynska and Scwarzer 2003).

BOX 3.1 Some Problems with ... Health Beliefs Research

Below are some problems with research in this area that you may wish to consider.

1 Asking people about their health beliefs may not be a benign process; it may actually change the way they think.

2 We study health beliefs as a means to understand and change behaviour. It is possible that the beliefs that predict and explain behaviour are different to those that change behaviour.

3 Much research in this field relies upon self-report measures of behaviour. These may not always be accurate. However, objective measures may not always be possible to obtain.

4 Much research in this area relies upon cross-sectional designs which assess beliefs and behaviours at the same time. Conclusions are then made about the ways in which beliefs predict behaviour. It is possible, however, that behaviours predict or cause beliefs. Even longitudinal designs cannot entirely get around this problem. Only experimental designs can really allow conclusions about causality to be made.

5 There are many factors that may influence how a person behaves which cannot be captured by any individual model (e.g. what happened on the bus as they were intending to go to the doctor; what happened to them in the pub as they were intending not to smoke). There will always be variance that remains unexplained.

6 Trying to explain as much variance as possible can make the research too focused and too far removed from the interesting psychological questions (i.e. I can predict quite well what you are about to do in one minute's time in a specified place but am I really interested in that?).

Criticisms of the HAPA

The following questions arise when assessing the value of the HAPA in predicting health behaviours: are individuals conscious processors of information? And what role do social and environmental factors play? The social cognition models attempt to address the problem of the social world in their measures of normative beliefs. However, such measures only access the individual's cognitions about their social world. These will now be considered.

SOCIAL COGNITION MODELS

Stage models focus on the movement between stages as an individual changes their behaviour. Social cognition models examine the predictors and precursors to health behaviours and take a continuum approach to behaviour and behaviour change. They draw upon subjective expected utility theory (SEU) (Edwards 1954), which suggests that behaviour results from weighing up the costs and benefits of any given action and emphasizes how individuals are rational information processors. Social cognition models are also based upon social cognition theory which was developed by Bandura (1977, 1986) and suggests that behaviour is governed by expectancies, incentives and social cognitions. Expectancies include:

- *Situation outcome expectancies:* the expectancy that a behaviour may be dangerous (e.g. 'smoking can cause lung cancer').
- *Outcome expectancies:* the expectancy that a behaviour can reduce the harm to health (e.g. 'stopping smoking can reduce the chances of lung cancer').
- *Self-efficacy expectancies:* the expectancy that the individual is capable of carrying out the desired behaviour (e.g. 'I can stop smoking if I want to').

The concept of *incentives* suggests that a behaviour is governed by its consequences. For example, smoking behaviour may be reinforced by the experience of reduced anxiety, having a cervical smear may be reinforced by a feeling of reassurance after a negative result.

Social cognitions are a central component of social cognition models and reflect the *individual's representations of their social world*. Accordingly, social cognition models attempt to place the individual within the context both of other people and the broader social world, although the extent to which this is achieved varies between models. The main models currently in use within health psychology are the health belief model (HBM), protection motivation theory (PMT) and the theory of planned behaviour (TPB).

THE HEALTH BELIEF MODEL

The HBM (see Figure 3.2) was developed initially by Rosenstock (1966) and further by Becker and colleagues throughout the 1970s and 1980s in order to predict preventive health behaviours and also the behavioural response to treatment in acutely and chronically ill patients. However, over recent years, the HBM has been used to predict a wide variety of health-related behaviours.

Components of the HBM

The HBM predicts that behaviour is a result of a set of core beliefs, which have been redefined over the years. The original core beliefs are the individual's perception of:

- Susceptibility to illness (e.g. 'my chances of getting lung cancer are high').
- The severity of the illness (e.g. 'lung cancer is a serious illness').
- The costs involved in carrying out the behaviour (e.g. 'stopping smoking will make me irritable').

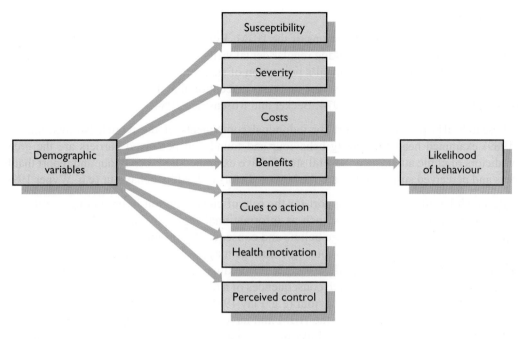

FIGURE 3.2

Basics of the health belief model

- The benefits involved in carrying out the behaviour (e.g. 'stopping smoking will save me money'; 'smoking is cool'.
- Cues to action, which may be internal (e.g. the symptom of breathlessness), or external (e.g. information in the form of health education leaflets).

The HBM suggests that these core beliefs should be used to predict *the likelihood that a behaviour will occur*. In response to criticisms the HBM has been revised to add the construct 'health motivation' to reflect an individual's readiness to be concerned about health matters (e.g. 'I am concerned that smoking might damage my health'). Becker and Rosenstock (1987) also suggested that perceived control (e.g. 'I am confident that I can stop smoking') should be added to the model.

People weigh up the costs and benefits of a health behaviour: 'smoking is cool' may be a perceived benefit

SOURCE: © Claudia Dewald/iStock

Using the HBM

If applied to a health-related behaviour such as screening for cervical cancer, the HBM predicts regular screening if an individual perceives that she is highly susceptible to cancer of the cervix, that cervical cancer is a severe health threat, that the benefits of regular screening are high, and that the costs of such action are comparatively low. This will also be true if she is subjected to cues to action that are external, such as a leaflet in the doctor's waiting room, or internal, such as a symptom perceived to be related to cervical cancer (whether correct or not), such as pain or irritation. When using the new amended HBM, the model would also predict that a woman would attend for screening if she is confident that she can do so and if she is motivated to maintain her health.

Support for the HBM

Several studies support the predictions of the HBM. Research indicates that dietary compliance, safe sex, having vaccinations, making regular dental visits and taking part in regular exercise programmes are related to the individual's perception of susceptibility to the related health problem, to their belief that the problem is severe and their perception that the benefits of preventive action outweigh the costs (e.g. Becker 1974; Becker and Rosenstock 1984).

Research also provides support for individual components of the model. Norman and Fitter (1989) examined health screening behaviour and found that perceived barriers are the greatest predictors of clinic attendance. Several studies have examined BSE behaviour and report that barriers and perceived susceptibility are the best predictors of healthy behaviour (e.g. Wyper 1990).

Research has also provided support for the role of cues to action in predicting health behaviours, in particular external cues such as informational input. In fact, health promotion uses such informational input to change beliefs and consequently promote future healthy behaviour. Information in the form of fear-arousing warnings may change attitudes and health behaviour in such areas as dental health, safe driving and smoking (e.g. Sutton and Hallett 1989). General information regarding the negative consequences of a behaviour is also used both in the prevention and cessation of smoking behaviour (e.g. Flay 1985). To date, two large-scale reviews have been carried out on studies using the HBM and have shown some support for some but not all of its components and at times the links between beliefs and behaviour within the model have been very small (Harrison et al. 1992; see Abraham and Sheeran 2005 for a thorough analysis of HBM data).

Criticisms of the HBM

The HBM has been criticized for these conflicting results. It has also been criticized for several other weaknesses, including the following:

- Its focus on the conscious processing of information (e.g. is tooth-brushing really determined by weighing up the pros and cons?).
- Its emphasis on the individual (e.g. what role does the social and economic environment play?).
- The interrelationship between the different core beliefs (e.g. how should these be measured and how should they be related to each other? Is the model linear or multifactorial?).
- The absence of a role for emotional factors such as fear and denial.
- The fact that alternative factors may predict health behaviour, such as outcome expectancy and self-efficacy (Seydel et al. 1990; Schwarzer 1992).
- Its static approach to health beliefs. Schwarzer (1992) suggests that within the HBM, beliefs are described as occurring simultaneously with no room for change, development or process.
- The fact that health-related behaviour is due to the perception of symptoms rather than the individual factors as suggested by the HBM (Leventhal et al. 1985).

Although there is much contradiction in the literature surrounding the HBM, research has used aspects of this model to predict screening for hypertension, screening for cervical cancer, genetic screening, exercise behaviour, decreased alcohol use, changes in diet and smoking cessation.

PROTECTION MOTIVATION THEORY (PMT)

Rogers (1975, 1985) developed the PMT (see Figure 3.3), which expanded the HBM to include additional factors. The main contribution of PMT over the HBM was the addition of fear and an attempt to include an emotional component into the understanding of health behaviours.

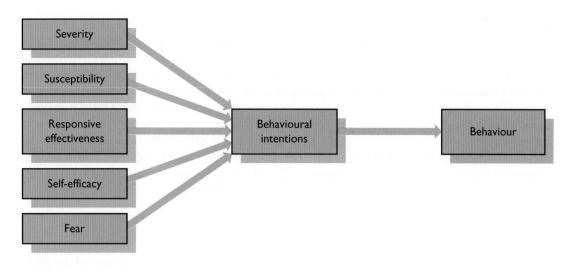

FIGURE 3.3
Basics of protection motivation theory

Components of PMT

PMT describes health behaviours as a product of five components:

1 Severity (e.g. 'bowel cancer is a serious illness').
2 Susceptibility (e.g. 'my chances of getting bowel cancer are high').
3 Response effectiveness (e.g. 'changing my diet would improve my health').
4 Self-efficacy (e.g. 'I am confident that I can change my diet').
5 Fear (e.g. an emotional response: 'I am scared of getting cancer').

These components predict *behavioural intentions* (e.g. 'I intend to change my behaviour'), which are related to behaviour. PMT describes severity, susceptibility and fear as relating to *threat appraisal* (i.e. appraising to outside threat) and response effectiveness and self-efficacy as relating to *coping appraisal* (i.e. appraising the individual themselves). According to PMT, there are two types of sources of information – environmental (e.g. verbal persuasion, observational learning) and intrapersonal (e.g. prior experience). This information influences the five components of PMT (self-efficacy, response effectiveness, severity, susceptibility, fear), which then elicit either an 'adaptive' coping response (i.e. behavioural intention) or a 'maladaptive' coping response (e.g. avoidance, denial).

Using the PMT

If applied to dietary change, PMT would make the following predictions: information about the role of a high fat diet in CHD would increase fear, increase the individual's perception of how serious CHD is (perceived severity) and increase their belief that they are likely to have a heart attack (perceived susceptibility/susceptibility). If the individual also felt confident that they could change their diet (self-efficacy) and that this change would have beneficial consequences (response effectiveness), they would report high intentions to change their behaviour (behavioural intentions). This would be seen as an adaptive coping response to the information.

Support for the PMT

Rippetoe and Rogers (1987) gave women information about breast cancer and examined the effect of this information on the components of PMT and their relationship to the women's intentions to practise BSE. The results showed that the best predictors of intentions to practise BSE were response effectiveness, severity and self-efficacy. In a further study, the effects of persuasive appeals for increasing exercise on intentions to exercise were evaluated using the components of PMT. The results showed that susceptibility and self-efficacy predicted exercise intentions but that none of the variables was related to self-reports of actual behaviour. Norman et al. (2003) also used PMT to predict children's adherence to wearing an eye patch. Parents of children diagnosed with eye problems completed a baseline questionnaire concerning their beliefs and a follow-up questionnaire after two months describing the child's level of adherence. The results showed that perceived susceptibility and response costs were significant predictors of adherence. Similarly, Plotnikoff et al. (2010) used PMT to predict physical activity in adults with type 1 diabetes and reported that self-efficacy and severity were good predictors of intention, although perceived vulnerability was not. Furthermore, similar results were found for predicting activity in a large sample of healthy adults (Plotnikoff et al. 2009).

Criticisms of PMT

PMT has been less widely criticized than the HBM; however, many of the criticisms of the HBM also relate to PMT. For example, PMT assumes that individuals are conscious information processors; it does not account for habitual behaviours, nor does it include a role for social and environmental factors.

REASONED ACTION AND PLANNED BEHAVIOUR (TRA AND TPB)

The theory of reasoned action (TRA) (see Figure 3.4) has been extensively used to examine predictors of behaviours and was central to the debate within social psychology concerning the relationship between attitudes and behaviour (Fishbein 1967; Fishbein and Ajzen 1975). The TRA emphasized a central role for social cognitions in the form of subjective norms (the individual's beliefs about their social world) and included both beliefs and evaluations of these beliefs (both factors constituting the individual's attitudes). The TRA was therefore an important model as it placed the individual within the social context and in addition suggested a role for *value*, which was in contrast to the traditional more rational approach to behaviour. The theory of planned behaviour (TPB) (see Figure 3.5) was developed by Ajzen and colleagues (Ajzen and Madden 1986; Ajzen

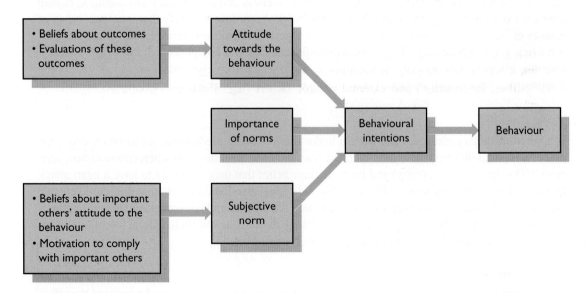

FIGURE 3.4

Basics of the theory of reasoned action

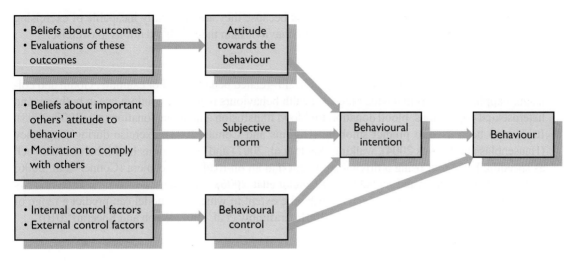

FIGURE 3.5

Basics of the theory of planned behaviour

1988) and represented a progression from the TRA. Where the TRA had added subjective norms to previous models, the TPB added both subjective norms and a measure of *behavioural control*. Both models also emphasize behavioural intentions as an important precursor to actual behaviour.

Components of the TPB

The TPB emphasizes *behavioural intentions* as the outcome of a combination of several beliefs. The theory proposes that intentions should be conceptualized as 'plans of action in pursuit of behavioural goals' (Ajzen and Madden 1986) and are a result of the following beliefs:

- *Attitude towards a behaviour*, which is composed of either a positive or negative evaluation of a particular behaviour and beliefs about the outcome of the behaviour (e.g. 'exercising is fun and will improve my health').
- *Subjective norm*, which is composed of the perception of social norms and pressures to perform a behaviour, and an evaluation of whether the individual is motivated to comply with this pressure (e.g. 'people who are important to me will approve if I lose weight and I want their approval').
- *Perceived behavioural control*, which is composed of a belief that the individual can carry out a particular behaviour based upon a consideration of internal control factors (e.g. skills, abilities, information) and external control factors (e.g. obstacles, opportunities), both of which relate to past behaviour.

According to the TPB, these three factors predict behavioural intentions, which are then linked to behaviour. The TPB also states that perceived behavioural control can have a direct effect on behaviour without the mediating effect of behavioural intentions.

Using the TPB

If applied to alcohol consumption, the TPB would make the following predictions: if an individual believed that reducing their alcohol intake would make their life more productive and be beneficial to their health (attitude to the behaviour), and believed that the important people in their life wanted them to cut down (subjective norm), and in addition believed that they were capable of drinking less alcohol due to their past behaviour and evaluation of internal and external control factors (high behavioural control), then this would predict high intentions to reduce alcohol intake (behavioural intentions). The model also predicts that perceived behavioural control can predict behaviour without the influence of intentions. For example, if perceived behavioural control reflects actual control, a belief that the individual would not be able to exercise because they are physically incapable of exercising would be a better predictor of their exercising behaviour than their high intentions to exercise.

Support for the TPB

The TPB has been used to assess a variety of health-related behaviours. For example, Godin and colleagues applied the TPB to a wide range of health behaviours including condom use in both gay and heterosexual populations, blood donation for blood transfusion and organ donation (e.g. 2007; 2008). It has also been used to predict smoking (Higgins and Conner 2003), exercise during pregnancy (Hausenblas and Downs 2004), walking (Scott et al. 2007) and less obvious health behaviours such as speeding behaviour using a driving simulator and an on-road speed camera (Conner et al. 2006) and deliberate self-harm and suicidality (O'Connor et al. 2006). There have now been several reviews and meta-analyses of the TPB which describe the extent to which this model can predict a range of health behaviours (Armitage and Conner 2001; Trafimow et al. 2002; Webb and Sheeran 2010).

Criticisms of the TPB

In contrast to the HBM and the PMT, the model attempts to address the problem of social and environmental factors (in the form of normative beliefs). It also includes a role for past behaviour within the measure of perceived behavioural control. The TPB has also been subjected to criticisms in terms of its constructs, the methods used to test the theory and the extent to which it can predict behaviour. These criticisms have generally been made for all social cognition models and will now be described.

PROBLEMS WITH SOCIAL COGNITION MODELS

Social cognition models provide a structured approach to understanding health beliefs and the prediction of health behaviours and offer a framework for designing questionnaires and developing interventions. Over recent years, however, several papers have been published criticizing these models. These problems can be categorized as conceptual, methodological and predictive.

CONCEPTUAL PROBLEMS

Some researchers have pointed to some conceptual problems with the models in terms of their variables and their ability to inform us about the world. These problems are as follows:

- Each model is made up of different concepts such as perceived behavioural control, behavioural intentions, perceived vulnerability and attitudes. Norman and Conner (1996) have argued that there is some overlap between these variables and Armitage and Conner (2000) have argued for a 'consensus' approach to studying health behaviour, whereby key constructs are integrated across models (see p. 61 for integrated models).
- The models describe associations between variables which assume causality. For example, the TPB describes attitude as causing behavioural intention. Sutton (2002a) argues that these associations are causally ambiguous and cannot be concluded unless experimental methods are used. Similarly, Smedslund (2000) criticized the models for their logical construction and said that assumptions about association are flawed.
- A theory should enable the collection of data which can either lead to that theory being supported or rejected. Ogden (2003) carried out an analysis of studies using the HBM, TRA, PMT and TPB over a four-year period and concluded that the models cannot be rejected as caveats can always be offered to perpetuate the belief that the model has been supported.
- Research should generate truths which are true by observation and require an empirical test (e.g. smoking causes heart disease) rather than by definition (i.e. heart disease causes narrowing of the arteries). Ogden (2003) concluded from her analysis than much research using the models produces statements that are true by definition (i.e. 'I am certain that I will use a condom therefore I intend to use a condom'). She argues that the findings are therefore tautological.

- Research should inform us about the world rather than create the world. Ogden (2003) argues that questionnaires that ask people questions such as 'Do you think the female condom decreases sexual pleasure for a man?' may change the way in which people think rather than get them to just describe their thoughts. This is similar to changes in mood following mood checklists, and the ability of diaries to change behaviour. Much research has now explored this possibility within the framework of the 'mere measurement effect' and 'measurement reactivity' and illustrates that the simple process or measuring can change cognitions, emotion and behaviour across a number of areas including blood donation and cervical screening attendance (e.g. Godin et al. 2008b, 2010; French and Sutton 2010).

METHODOLOGICAL PROBLEMS

Research using models such as the TPB, TRA and HBM often uses cross-sectional designs involving questionnaires which are analysed using multiple regression analysis or structural equation modelling. Researchers have highlighted some problems with this approach.

- Cross-sectional research can only show associations rather than causality. To solve this, prospective studies are used which separate the independent and dependent variables by time. Sutton (2002a) argues that both these designs are problematic and do not allow inferences about causality to be made. He suggests that randomized experimental designs are the best solution to this problem.

- Hankins et al. (2000) provide some detailed guidelines on how data using the TRA and TPB should be analysed and state that much research uses inappropriate analysis. They point out that if multiple regression analysis is used, adjusted $R2$ should be the measure of explained variance, that residuals should be assessed and that semi-partial correlations should be used to assess the unique contribution of each variable. They also state that 'structural equation modelling' might be a better approach as this makes explicit the assumptions of the models.

- Much psychological research does not involve a sample size calculation or a consideration of the power of the study. Hankins et al. (2000) argue that research using social cognition models should do this if the results are to be meaningful.

- Darker and French (2009) carried out a think-aloud study of a questionnaire based upon the TPB to explore how people made sense of the different items. On average the results showed around 16 problems with the 52 questions, indicating that research participants may not always interpret questions in the ways intended by the researchers.

- The TRA involves a generalized measure of attitude which is reflected in the interaction between 'expectancy beliefs' about the likelihood of the given behaviour leading to particular consequences, and evaluations about the desirability of these consequences. For example, an attitude to smoking is made up of the belief 'smoking will lead to lung cancer' and the belief 'lung cancer is unpleasant'. This is calculated by multiplying one belief with the other to create a 'multiplicative composite'. This is called the 'expectancy value' belief. In subsequent analysis this new variable is simply correlated with other variables. French and Hankins (2003) argue that this is problematic as the correlation between a multiplicative composite and other variables requires a ratio scale with a true zero. As with other psychological constructs, the 'expectancy value belief has no true zero, only an arbitrary was chosen by the researcher'. Therefore they argue that the expectancy value belief should not be used.

PREDICTIVE PROBLEMS

Models such as the TRA, TPB, HBM and PMT are designed to predict behavioural intentions and actual behaviour. However, two main observations have been made. First, it has been suggested that these models are not that successful at predicting behavioural intentions. For example, Sutton (1998a) argued that studies using social cognition models only manage to predict between 40 and 50 per cent of the variance in behavioural intentions. Therefore, up to 50 per cent of the variance remains unexplained. Secondly, it has been observed that such models are even less effective at predicting actual behaviour. Sutton (1998a) also argued that studies using these models only predict 19–38 per cent of the variance in behaviour. In 2010, Webb and Sheeran carried out an extensive meta-analysis of the TPB and concluded that while diet and physical activity were the better predicted behaviours (23.9 and 21.2 per cent respectively), others such as risk, safer sex and abstinence from drugs were only poorly predicted by TPB variables (between 13.8 and 15.3 per cent of the variance explained). Some of this failure to predict behaviour may be due to the behaviour being beyond the control of the individual concerned. For example, 'I intend to study at university' may not be translated into 'I am studying at university' due to economic or educational factors. Further, 'I intend to eat healthily' may not be translated into 'I am eating healthily' due to the absence of healthy food. In such instances, the correlation between intentions and behaviour would be zero. However, for most behaviours the correlation between intentions and behaviour is not zero but small, suggesting that the individual does have some control over the behaviour.

These predictive problems with the models have been addressed in three ways. First, it has been argued that they should be expanded to incorporate new cognitions. Secondly, research has explored the intention–behaviour gap and ways in which this gap can be minimized. Thirdly, it has been argued that due to the overlap between the models they should be integrated to produce versions that are both less repetitive and more inclusive (and therefore more predictive). These three amendments to the models will now be explored.

EXPANDING THE MODELS BY ADDING NEW COGNITIONS

In order to improve the effectiveness of the models, researchers have argued for the addition of a range of different variables.

EXPANDED NORMS

The TRA and the TPB include measures of social pressures to behave in a particular way – the subjective norms variable. However, it has been suggested that they should also assess other forms of norms. For example, the intention to carry out behaviours that have an ethical or moral dimension such as donating blood, donating organs for transplant, committing driving offences or eating genetically produced food may result from not only general social norms but also moral norms. Some research has shown the usefulness of including a moral norms variable. For example, Godin et al. (2005a) analysed six data sets relating to smoking, driving over the speed limit, exercising and applying precautions when taking blood. The results showed that people were more likely to carry out the behaviour if their intentions to perform the behaviour were in line with their moral norms. In addition, however, this role for moral norms was only present when people construed the behaviour in moral terms. The concept of social norms has also been expanded to include 'descriptive norms' which reflect the person's perception of whether other people carry out the behaviour (i.e. 'Do you think doctors eat healthily?'), 'injunctive norms' which reflect that other people might approve or disapprove of the behaviour (e.g. Povey et al. 2000) and group and image norms in the context of sun safety in Australia (White et al. 2008 see **Focus on Research 3.1**). One study even included the impact of the norms of future friends on adolescents' smoking behaviour and reported that smoking was not only influenced by the behaviour of existing friends but also by the behaviour of those whom people would like to be their friends in the future (Mercken et al. 2011).

FOCUS ON RESEARCH 3.1: PREDICTING SUN SAFETY

Using the TPB to predict young people's sun safety in Australia (White et al. 2008).

BACKGROUND

Many studies using social cognition models use cross-sectional designs and can therefore only make conclusions about the association between variables. They also often use student samples. This study has an impressive sample size involving both students and employees and uses a prospective design to assess whether the TPB can predict sun safety behaviour at a two-week follow-up. It includes additional measures of social influences to reflect the social nature of sun protection behaviour. The data were collected in Australia between March and May when the daily mean temperature ranged from 18–27°C.

METHODOLOGY

Sample

The baseline sample consisted of 693 female and 441 male (total n = 1,134) students and employees aged between 12–20 years recruited from school, university and further education. By two-week follow-up the sample had reduced to 734 participants.

Design

The study used a prospective design with measures collected at baseline and after two weeks.

Measures

Participants completed measures of the core TPB variables as follows:

1 **Intention** (e.g. '*It is likely that I will perform sun protective behaviours every time I go in the sun for more than 10 minutes in the next two weeks*').

2 **Attitude** (e.g. '*Performing sun protective behaviour every time I go in the sun for more than 10 minutes during the next two weeks would be: pleasant/unpleasant; good/bad*').

3 **Subjective norm** (e.g. '*Most people who are important to me would want me to perform sun protective behaviours every time I go out in the sun for more than 10 minutes in the next two weeks*').

4 **Perceived behavioural control** (e.g. '*If I wanted to, it would be easy for me to perform sun protective behaviours every time I go out in the sun for more than 10 minutes in the next two weeks*').

5 **Past behaviour** (e.g. '*Think about the past two weeks: how often did you perform sun protective behaviour every time you went out in the sun for more than 10 minutes?*').

In addition, participants completed measures of social influence as follows:

1 **Group norm** (e.g. '*Think about your friends. What percentage of them do you think would perform sun protective behaviours every time they go out in the sun for more than 10 minutes during the next fortnight?*').

2 **Image norm** (e.g. '*Young celebrities and movie stars always seem to have a tan*').

At two weeks follow-up all participants completed the following:

1 **Reported behaviour** (i.e. '*In the past two weeks how often did you peform sun protective behaviour when you went out in the sun for more than 10 minutes?*').

All scales were rated on seven-point Likert scales.

RESULTS

The data were analysed to predict behavioural intentions and actual behaviour at follow-up.

1 **Predicting behavioural intentions.** The results showed that standard TPB variables (attitude, subjective norm, perceived behavioural control) significantly predicted 25 per cent of the variance of behavioural intentions and that group norms accounted for an additional 11 per cent. Overall, the best predictors in order were group norm, perceived behavioural control, subjective norm and attitude. Image norm was not predictive.

2 **Predicting actual behaviour after two weeks.** At follow-up participants reported spending an average of 14.49 hours per week in the sun and described sun protective behaviours such as wearing a hat (74 per cent), using sun-screen (62 per cent), wearing sunglasses (35 per cent), seeking shade (33 per cent) and wearing protective clothing such as a long-sleeved shirt (18 per cent). The results showed that baseline measures of behavioural intention and perceived behavioural control predicted actual behaviour accounting for 25 per cent of the variance. Social influence variables only added 2 per cent of variance to this model. Overall, when all variables were in the model, sun protective behaviour was predicted by behavioural intentions and group norm. When past behaviour was also added into the model, the results indicated that past behaviour and intentions were the best predictors (not group norm).

CONCLUSION

The results from this study indicate that the TPB variables are good predictors of behavioural intentions and that the best predictors of actual behaviour are past behaviour and behavioural intentions. Further, the results show that although group norm does predict behaviour, this effect disappears when past behaviour is added.

AFFECTIVE BELIEFS

Although PMT explicitly includes a role for emotion in the form of fear, one of the central criticisms of social cognition models is that they do not adequately account for the role of *affect* (e.g. Manstead and Parker 1995). To address this, some researchers have argued for the inclusion of affect into the models. Because of the ways in which the beliefs are elicited and measured for social cognition research, researchers have addressed this problem by including affective beliefs. For example, while beliefs that a behaviour is healthy, harmful, safe or useful can be considered instrumental beliefs, those that describe a behaviour as enjoyable, pleasurable, worrying or depressing reflect affective beliefs (Manstead and Parker 1995). Lawton et al. (2006) recently explored the relative contribution of instrumental and affective beliefs in predicting driving above the speed limit and smoking in adolescents. The results showed that negative affective beliefs were the best predictors of observed speeding and that positive and negative affective beliefs were the best predictors of smoking. Furthermore, Lawton et al. (2009) explored the role of both cognitive and affective beliefs in predicting 14 different health-promoting and health risk behaviours at one month follow-up. The results showed that affective beliefs were significant predictors of all 14 behaviours and significantly better predictors than cognitive beliefs for six behaviours. A related construct 'affective judgement' has also been found to be a good predictor of physical activity (Rhodes et al. 2010).

ANTICIPATED REGRET

An alternative approach to emotion has taken the form of anticipated emotions, particularly anticipated regret. For example, the intention to practise safer sex – 'I intend to use a condom' – may be predicted by the anticipated feeling 'if I do not use a condom I will feel guilty'. Some research has shown that anticipated regret is important for predicting behavioural intentions (Richard and van der Pligt 1991). Similarly, Conner et al. (2006) reported that anticipated regret was significantly related both to the intentions to start smoking and actual smoking in a group of adolescents.

SELF-IDENTITY

Another variable which has been presented as a means to improve the extent social cognition models can predict behavioural intentions and behaviour is self-identity. It has been argued that individuals will only intend to carry out a behaviour if that behaviour fits with their own image of themselves. For example, the identity 'I am a healthy eater' should relate to the intention to eat healthily. Further, the identity 'I am a fit person' should relate to the intention to carry out exercise. Some research has supported the usefulness of this variable (Sparks et al. 1992). However, Norman and Conner (1996) suggested that this variable may also only have limited relevance.

AMBIVALENCE

Most models contain a measure of attitude towards the behaviour which conceptualizes individuals as holding either positive or negative views towards a given object. Some studies, however, have also explored the role of ambivalence in predicting behaviour (Thompson et al. 1995) which has been defined in a variety of different ways. For example, Breckler (1994) defined it as 'a conflict aroused by competing evaluative predispositions' and Emmons (1996) defined it as 'an approach – avoidance conflict – wanting but at the same time not wanting the same goal object'. Sparks et al. (2001) incorporated the concept of ambivalence into the TPB and assessed whether it predicted meat or chocolate consumption. A total of 325 volunteers completed a questionnaire including a measure of ambivalence assessed in terms of the mean of both positive and negative evaluations (e.g. 'how positive is chocolate' and 'how negative is chocolate') and then subtracting this mean from the absolute difference between the two evaluations (i.e. 'total positive minus total negative'). This computation provides a score that reflects the balance between positive and negative feelings. The results showed that the relationship between attitude and intention was weaker in those participants with higher ambivalence. This implies that holding both positive and negative attitudes to a food makes it less likely that the overall attitude will be translated into an intention to eat it.

PERSONALITY

There is much research in psychology that emphasizes the role of personality in predicting health and health-related behaviours (Vollrath and Toergersen 2002). In the main, personality research reflects a more stable, trait-like approach to the individual than much cognitive work and covers a range of personality traits such as the 'big five' which are agreeableness, conscientiousness, emotional stability, extraversion and intellect. These aspects of personality have been shown to be associated with a range of health behaviours such as smoking and diet (Bogg and Roberts 2004). Ingledew and Ferguson (2006) explored the role of personality alongside motivation in predicting safer sex in university students and concluded that the traits of agreeableness and conscientiousness predicted safer sex and this effect occurred due to the impact of these personality traits upon an individual's motivation.

THE INTENTION–BEHAVIOUR GAP

Social cognition research assesses behavioural intentions as a means to predict behaviour. The link between intentions and behaviour, however, is not always that straightforward and research has highlighted the problem of the intention–behaviour gap. Psychologists have addressed this problem in two ways: (1) past behaviour has been used as a direct predictor of behaviour; and (2) variables that bridge the intention–behaviour gap have been studied.

THE ROLE OF PAST BEHAVIOUR AND HABIT

Most research assumes that cognitions predict behavioural intentions, which in turn predict behaviour. This is in line with the shift from 'I think, therefore I intend to do, therefore I do'. It is possible, however, that behaviour is not predicted by cognitions but by behaviour. From this perspective, individuals are more likely to eat healthily tomorrow if they ate healthily today. They are also more likely to go to the doctor for a cervical smear if they have done so in the past. Research suggests that such past behaviour can account for about 13 per cent of future behaviour (Conner and Armitage 1998) and predicts behaviours such as cycle helmet use (Quine et al. 1998), BSE (Hodgkins and Orbell 1998), bringing up condom use (Yzer et al. 2001), wearing an eye patch (Norman et al. 2003), attendance at health checks (Norman and Conner 1993) and breakfast consumption (Wong and Mullan 2009). In addition, past behaviour may itself predict cognitions that then predict behaviour (Gerrard et al. 1996).

So how does past behaviour influence future behaviour? Ouellette and Wood (1998) identified two possible routes. First, they argued that past behaviour may influence future behaviour indirectly through a conscious change in cognitions – for example, 'I had breakfast yesterday and it made me realize that I had more energy so I will have breakfast again today'. Such a route is more common for behaviours which are infrequent as they offer a new experience. Secondly, they argued for a role of habit with future behaviour occurring after past behaviour in a more automatic way, with very little effort or conscious processing. This route is more likely to be taken for frequently-occurring behaviours which offer no new experience. In line with this second route, Verplanken and colleagues (e.g. Verplanken et al. 1994; Verplanken and Aarts 1999) have explored ways to measure habit strength, and research indicates a role for habit in explaining a number of behaviours such as travel mode (Verplanken et al. 1994), condom use (Trafimow 2000) and people's use of information (Aarts et al. 1998).

BRIDGING THE INTENTION–BEHAVIOUR GAP

The second approach to address the limited way in which research has predicted behaviour has been to suggest variables that may bridge the gap between intentions to behave and actual behaviour. In particular, some research has highlighted the role of plans for action, health goals commitment, action control and trying as a means to tap into the kinds of cognitions that may be responsible for the translation of intentions into behaviour (Schwarzer 1992; Bagozzi 1993; Luszczynska and Schwarzer 2003; Sniehotta et al. 2005). Most research, however, has focused on Gollwitzer's (1993) notion of implementation intentions, which are a simple form of action plans. According to Gollwitzer, carrying out an intention involves the development of specific plans as to what an individual will do given a specific set of environmental factors. Therefore, implementation intentions describe the 'what' and the 'when' of a particular behaviour. For example, the intention 'I intend to stop smoking' will be more likely to be translated into 'I have stopped smoking' if the individual makes the implementation intention 'I intend to stop smoking tomorrow at 12.00 when I have finished my last packet'. Further, 'I intend to eat healthily' is more likely to be translated into 'I am eating healthily' if the implementation intention 'I will start to eat healthily by having an apple tomorrow lunchtime' is made. Some experimental research has shown that encouraging individuals to make implementation intentions can actually increase the correlation between intentions and behaviour for behaviours such as adolescent smoking (Conner and Higgins 2010), fruit consumption (Armitage 2007a), exercise (Brickell et al. 2006), taking a vitamin C pill (Sheeran and Orbell 1998) and reducing dietary fat (Armitage 2004). Gollwitzer and Sheeran (2006) carried out a meta-analysis of 94 independent tests of the impact of implementation intentions on a range of behavioural goals including eating a low fat diet, using public transport, exercise and a range of personal goals. The results from this analysis indicated that implementation intentions had a medium to large effect on goal attainment and the analysis provides some insights into the processes involved in this approach. The use of implementation intentions is also supported by the goal-setting approach of cognitive behavioural therapy (CBT). Therefore, by tapping into variables such as implementation intentions it is argued that the models may become better predictors of actual behaviour.

INTEGRATING THE MODELS

The final development that has taken place over recent years in an attempt to improve the effectiveness of the different models of health behaviour is a call for an integration of the models to form one definitive model that consists of the most useful cognitions and can be used to predict (and change) most health behaviours. The most notable model has been called the 'major theorist's model' as it emerged out of a workshop attended by many of the most prominent researchers within psychology (e.g. Becker, Fishbein, Bandura and Kanfer). Through discussion they identified eight key variables which they believed should account for most of the variance in any given (deliberative) behaviour (Fishbein et al. 2001). These were divided into those that directly impact upon behaviour (e.g. environmental constraints, intention, skills) and those that relate to the intention (e.g. self-discrepancy, advantages/disadvantages, social pressure, self-efficacy, emotional reaction). Conner and Norman (2005) make some interesting comments about the model and suggest that although it is logical and includes some of the key constructs from existing models, it also includes new constructs that remain untested or for which evidence indicates they are not very predictive (e.g. self-discrepancy) and omits other variables which have been shown to be effective (e.g. risk perception, perception of severity). Further, they note that the model remains untested and that it still contains an unexplained gap between intentions and behaviour.

Research has also tested the effectiveness of integrating models in other ways. For example, Lippke and Plotnikoff (2009) integrated PMT with the SOC as a means to predict exercise and concluded that PMT variables functioned differently at the different stages of the SOC and that this was a useful way to examine behaviour. Further, Jacobs et al. (2011) explored the usefulness of integrating the TPB with STD in the context of diet and physical activity. In 2009 Hagger and Chatzisarantis carried out a meta-analysis of the integration of these two perspectives and concluded that this was a partially (but not totally) useful way forward.

Although the idea of integrating models makes common sense as there is substantial overlap between the different approaches, there are some problems:

- Models which are small and focused can be tested in research and used to develop interventions *but* may miss important other variables.
- Larger models that are more inclusive may miss out less but are more unwieldy to use in both research and practice.
- Theories and models are often the work of individuals who have invested a large part of their career in their development. They may be reluctant to have their model subsumed within someone else's model.
- There will always remain variance in any behaviour that cannot be explained by any model however refined, expanded or integrated, as any number of unexpected events (internal or external) may happen at any time to dislodge the individual from their path towards any given behaviour.

TO CONCLUDE

The role of health beliefs in predicting health-related behaviours has become increasingly salient with the recent changes in causes of mortality. Some studies have explored constructs such as attributions, health locus of control, unrealistic optimism, risk compensation, self-affirmation theory and self-efficacy. Psychologists have also developed models to integrate these different beliefs and to predict health behaviours such as stage models (SOC, HAPA) and social cognition models (HBM, PMT, TPB). These models consider individuals to be processors of information and vary in the extent to which they address the individual's cognitions about their social world. The models can be used to predict health behaviours quantitatively and have implications for developing methods to promote change.

QUESTIONS

1　Why is it important to explain and predict health-related behaviours?
2　Discuss the contribution of attribution theory to understanding health behaviours.
3　Health beliefs predict health behaviours. Discuss with reference to two models.
4　Discuss the role of the social world in understanding health behaviours.
5　Human beings are rational information processors. Discuss.
6　Discuss the argument that changing an individual's beliefs would improve their health.
7　Discuss some of the problems with the stage models of health behaviour.
8　Discuss some of the problems with the social cognition models of health behaviour.
9　Describe the ways in which researchers have tried to improve models of health behaviour.

FOR DISCUSSION

Consider one of your regular health-related behaviours (e.g. smoking, what you eat for breakfast, how much you sleep, any recent check-ups you have had). Discuss how your health beliefs relate to this behaviour.

ASSUMPTIONS IN HEALTH PSYCHOLOGY

Research into health beliefs highlights some of the assumptions in health psychology:

1　*Human beings as rational information processors*. Many models of health beliefs assume that behaviour is a consequence of a series of rational stages that can be measured. For example, it is assumed that the individual weighs up the pros and cons of a behaviour, assesses the seriousness of a potentially dangerous illness and then decides how to act. This may not be the case for all behaviours. Even though some of the social cognition models include past behaviour (as a measure of habit), they still assume some degree of rationality.

2 *Cognitions as separate from each other.* The different models compartmentalize different cognitions (perceptions of severity, susceptibility, outcome expectancy, intentions) as if they are discrete and separate entities. However, this separation may only be an artefact of asking questions relating to these different cognitions. For example, an individual may not perceive susceptibility (e.g. 'I am at risk from HIV') as separate to self-efficacy (e.g. 'I am confident that I can control my sexual behaviour and avoid HIV') until they are asked specific questions about these factors.

3 *Cognitions as separate from methodology.* In the same way that models assume that cognitions are separate from each other, they also assume that they exist independent of methodology. However, interview and questionnaire questions may actually *create* these cognitions.

4 *Cognitions without a context.* Models of health beliefs and health behaviours tend to examine an individual's cognitions out of context. This context could either be the context of another individual or the wider social context. Some of the models incorporate measures of the individual's representations of their social context (e.g. social norms, peer group norms), but this context is always accessed via the individual's cognitions

FURTHER READING

Conner, M. and Norman, P. (eds) (2005) *Predicting Health Behaviour*, 2nd edn. Buckingham: Open University Press.
This book provides an excellent overview of the different models, the studies that have been carried out using them and the new developments in this area. Each chapter is written by an expert in each model, yet the book still has a clear narrative that is often missing from edited books.

Webb, T.L. and Sheeran, P. (2006) Does changing behavioural intentions engender behaviour change? A meta-analysis of the experimental evidence, *Psychological Bulletin*, 132: 249–68.
This paper presents a meta-analysis of the research exploring the links between intentions and behaviour. It is useful in itself but also provides an excellent source of references.

Woodcock, A., Stenner, K. and Ingham, R. (1992) Young people talking about HIV and AIDS: interpretations of personal risk of infection, *Health Education Research: Theory and Practice*, 7: 229–47.
This paper is now getting quite old but I have always used it to illustrate a qualitative approach to health beliefs and it is a good example of how to present qualitative data.

Visit the website at www.openup.co.uk/ogden for additional resources on Chapter 3 to help you with your study, such as multiple choice questions, weblinks and a searchable online glossary.

4 Addictive Behaviours

© Lauri Patterson/iStock

CHAPTER OVERVIEW

Within health psychology, smoking and alcohol use tend to be studied using the social cognition models which are described in Chapter 3 while interventions tend to be based upon a number of theories which are described in Chapter 8. This chapter presents research and theories that are specific to more 'addictive' types of behaviour and should be read alongside the chapters on health behaviours in general (Chapters 5, 6, 7). This chapter examines the prevalence of smoking and alcohol consumption and evaluates the health consequences of these behaviours. The history of theories of addictive behaviours and the shift from a disease model of addictions to the social learning theory perspective is then described. The chapter then illustrates the disease and social learning perspectives through two examples: caffeine, which is the most commonly used drug across all societies, and exercise dependence, showing how a healthy behaviour can become excessive and potentially detrimental. The chapter also examines the four stages of substance use from initiation and maintenance to cessation and relapse, and discusses these stages in the context of the different models of addictive behaviour. Finally, it concludes with an assessment of the similarities and differences between behaviours and describes two models – excessive appetites theory and prime theory – which take a cross-addictive perspective.

WHO SMOKES?

Worldwide data show that in developed countries about 35 per cent of men and 22 per cent of women smoke, whereas in developing countries about 50 per cent of men and 9 per cent of women smoke (National Statistics 2005). China has the highest percentage of male smokers at about 300 million. This is equivalent to the entire US population. In the UK the overall prevalence of smoking has decreased in men from 52 per cent in 1974, to 30 per cent in 1990, and down to 26 per cent in 2004. In women it has decreased from 41 per cent in 1970, to 29 per cent in 1990 and to 23 per cent in 2004. In terms of amount smoked, in the UK 27 per cent of male smokers and 24 per cent of female smokers reported smoking more than 20 cigarettes per day in 2009, and overall men reported smoking one cigarette more than women, with the mean amount for men being 13.6 and for women 12.6. However, the data also showed that, although women smoke fewer cigarettes than men, fewer women than men are giving up. This decrease in smoking behaviour follows a trend for an overall decline, as shown in Figure 4.1.

In 2009, the highest prevalence of smoking was in those aged between 20 and 34. In addition, those aged over 55 smoked more heavily than younger age groups, particularly older men. These data are shown in Figure 4.2. Smoking also varies by social class and income. In 2009, although men generally smoked more than women across all income ranges, the number of people who smoked in the lowest income quintile was more than three times the number of people who smoked in the highest income quartile. These data are shown in Figure 4.3. Furthermore, evidence indicates that the decline in smoking in those performing routine/manual jobs has been slower than for those in non-routine/non-manual jobs. This is shown in Figure 4.4.

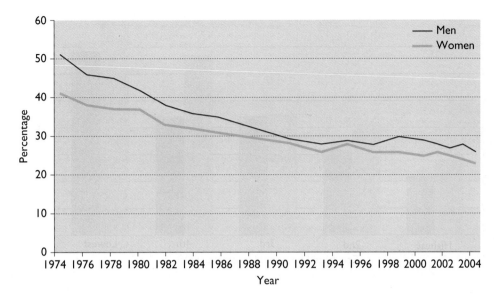

FIGURE 4.1

Changes in smoking, 1974–2004

SOURCE: Adapted from OPCS (2004)

In general, data about smoking behaviour suggest the following about smokers:

- Smoking behaviour is on the decline, but this decrease is greater in men than in women.
- Smokers tend to be in the unskilled manual group.
- Smokers tend to earn less than non-smokers.
- There has been a dramatic reduction in the number of smokers using middle-tar cigarettes.
- Two-thirds of smokers report wanting to give up smoking.
- The majority of smokers (58 per cent) say that it would be fairly/very difficult to go without smoking for a whole day.

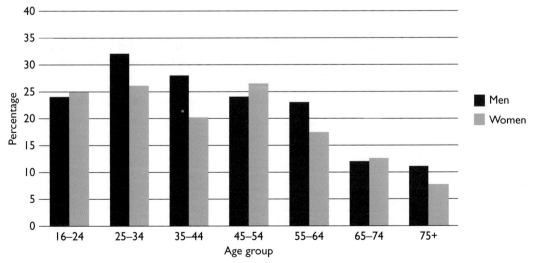

FIGURE 4.2

Amount smoked by age and sex, 2009

SOURCE: Copyright © 2011, re-used with the permission of The Health and Social Care Information Centre, all rights reserved

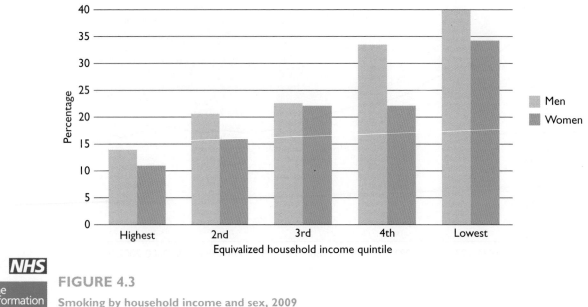

NHS
The
Information
Centre
for health and social care

FIGURE 4.3

Smoking by household income and sex, 2009

SOURCE: Copyright © 2011, re-used with the permission of The Health and Social Care Information Centre, all rights reserved

WHO DRINKS?

In 2009 in the UK around 89 per cent of men and 83 per cent of women had drunk alcohol in the last year. Men were more likely to have drunk alcohol is the past week (72 per cent) compared to women (56 per cent) and were also more likely to have drunk on five or more days throughout the week (22 per cent men; 12 per cent women). These data are shown in Figure 4.5.

Research also shows that alcohol intake varies with social class as measured by income. For example, men and women from the highest income quintile were more likely to have drunk alcohol in the previous week (86 per cent men; 72 per cent women) compared to those in the lowest income

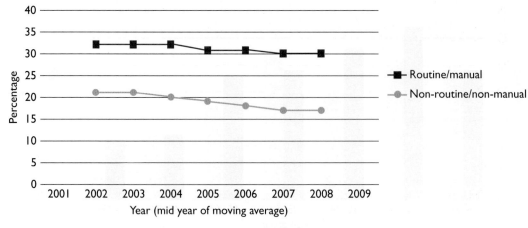

NHS
The
Information
Centre
for health and social care

FIGURE 4.4

Changes in smoking by type of job, 2009

SOURCE: Copyright © 2011, re-used with the permission of The Health and Social Care Information Centre, all rights reserved

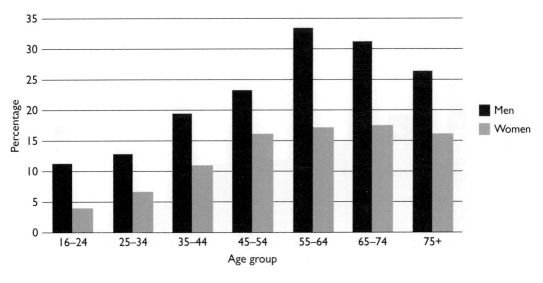

FIGURE 4.5

Sex and age differences in drinking on five days or more in the past week, 2009

SOURCE: Copyright © 2011, re-used with the permission of The Health and Social Care Information Centre, all rights reserved

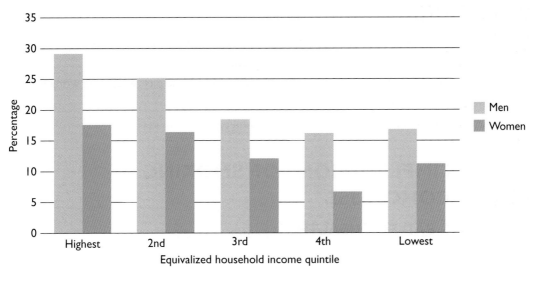

FIGURE 4.6

Sex and income differences for drinking on five days or more in the past week, 2009

SOURCE: Copyright © 2011, re-used with the permission of The Health and Social Care Information Centre, all rights reserved

quintile (54 per cent men; 47 per cent woman). In addition, men, in particular, from the highest income quintile were more likely to have drunk on five days or more in the past week compared to other income groups. These data are shown in Figure 4.6. Studies have also explored the prevalence of binge drinking and show that drinking more than twice the recommended amount on any given day is highest in men, particularly those aged 16–24. There is no sex difference in the 25–34 age range. This is shown in Figure 4.7.

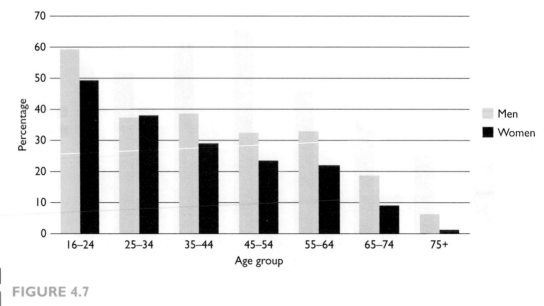

...

FIGURE 4.7

Binge drinking by age and sex, 2009

SOURCE: Copyright © 2011, re-used with the permission of The Health and Social Care Information Centre, all rights reserved

The data on alcohol intake shows the following:

- The large majority of the adult population has drunk alcohol in the past year.
- Men are more likely to drink alcohol than women.
- Men are more likely to have drunk on five or more days in the past week than women.
- Men aged 16–24 drink the most.
- There are no sex differences in the 24–35 age range.

HEALTH IMPLICATIONS OF SMOKING AND ALCOHOL USE

IS SMOKING BAD FOR HEALTH?

Negative Effects

Doll and Hill (1954) reported that smoking cigarettes was related to lung cancer. Since then, smoking has also been implicated in coronary heart disease (CHD) and a multitude of other cancers such as throat, stomach and bowel. In addition, the increase in life expectancy over the past 150 years is considerably less for smokers than for non-smokers (see Chapter 2). The risks of smoking were made explicit in a book by Peto et al. (1994), who stated that of 1,000 20-year-olds in the UK who smoke cigarettes regularly, about 1 will be murdered, 6 will die from traffic accidents, 250 will die from cigarettes in middle age (35–69) and another 250 will die from smoking in old age (70 and over). In industrialized countries smoking is the leading cause of loss of healthy life years. The average smoker dies 8 years early and starts to suffer disability 12 years early, while a quarter of smokers who fail to stop die an average of 23 years early (West and Shiffman 2004). Worldwide it is estimated that 4 million deaths per year are attributable to smoking. In the USA, an estimated 443,000 people die each year from smoking-related diseases (Center for Disease Control 2008). In

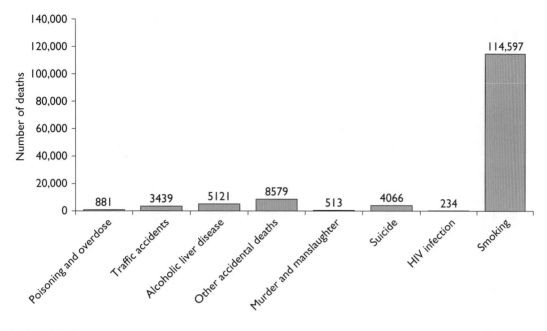

FIGURE 4.8

Deaths attributable to smoking in the US in 2008

the UK the number is about 106,000 (Twigg et al. 2004). The number of deaths by smoking is shown in Figure 4.8.

A review of the literature concluded that smoking may also interfere with recovery following surgery and that a longer period of smoking cessation prior to having an operation is associated with a reduction in the number of complications following surgery (Theadom and Cropley 2006; see Chapter 12 for a discussion of wound healing and psychoneuroimmunology). Smoking in adolescence has also been found to have more immediate effects and is linked with shortness of breath, asthma, higher blood pressure and an increased number of respiratory tract infections (American Lung Association 2002a, 2002b). There has also been an interest in passive smoking and research suggests an association between passive smoking and lung cancer in adults, and respiratory ill health in children (US Environmental Protection Agency 1992).

Positive Effects

There are very few positive health effects of cigarette smoking. It has been suggested that smokers report positive mood effects from smoking and that smoking can help individuals to cope with difficult circumstances (Graham 1987).

IS ALCOHOL CONSUMPTION BAD FOR HEALTH?

Negative Effects

Alcohol consumption has many negative effects on health. For example, alcoholism increases the chance of disorders such as liver cirrhosis, cancers (e.g. pancreas and liver), hypertension and memory deficits (White et al. 2002). Alcohol also increases the chances of harm through car accidents, non-traffic accidents, accidental falls, violence and unsafe sex (see e.g. Corbin and Fromme 2002). In terms of its impact on mortality, data from the UK show that the number of alcohol-related deaths has increased from 6.9 per 100,000 in 1991 to 13.0 in 2004 and that the number of deaths has more than doubled from 4,144 in 1991 to 8,380 in 2004. Data also shows that

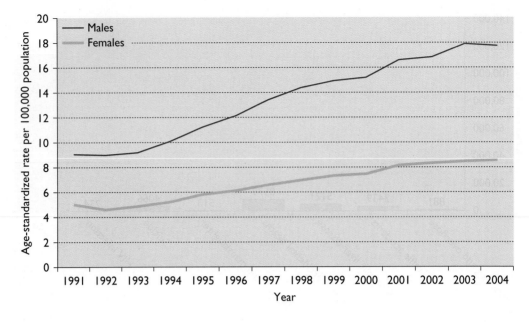

FIGURE 4.9
Alcohol-related deaths in the UK, 1991–2004

death rates are higher for men than for women and that this gap has widened over recent years. This data is shown in Figure 4.9.

Positive Effects

Alcohol may also have a positive effect on health. In a longitudinal study, Friedman and Kimball (1986) reported that light and moderate drinkers had lower morbidity and mortality rates than both non-drinkers and heavy drinkers. They argued that alcohol consumption reduces CHD via the following mechanisms: (1) a reduction in the production of catecholamines when stressed; (2) the protection of blood vessels from cholesterol; (3) a reduction in blood pressure; (4) self-therapy; and (5) a short-term coping strategy. The results from the *General Household Survey* (OPCS 1992) also showed some benefits of alcohol consumption with the reported prevalence of ill health being higher among non-drinkers than among drinkers. Although these data have been well received (particularly by red wine drinkers) it has been suggested that the apparent positive effects of alcohol on health may be an artefact of poor health in the non-drinkers who have stopped drinking due to health problems.

In an attempt to understand why people smoke and drink, much health psychology research has drawn upon the social cognition models described in Chapter 3. However, there is a vast addiction literature which has also been applied to smoking and drinking. These models are also relevant to all other potentially addictive behaviours such as caffeine drinking, drug-taking, gambling, food addiction and even sex addiction (see Orford 2002 for an excellent cross-addictive behaviour perspective). Addiction theories will now be explored. Exercise dependence and caffeine drinking are covered in detail later.

WHAT IS AN ADDICTION?

Many theories have been developed to explain addictions and addictive behaviours, including moral models which regard an addiction as the result of weakness and a lack of moral fibre;

biomedical models which see an addiction as a disease; and social learning theories which regard addictive behaviours as behaviours that are learned according to the rules of learning theory. The multitude of terms that exist and are used with respect to behaviours such as smoking and alcohol are indicative of these different theoretical perspectives and in addition illustrate the tautological nature of the definitions. For example:

- *An addict:* someone who 'has no control over their behaviour', 'lacks moral fibre', 'uses a maladaptive coping mechanism', 'has an addictive behaviour'.
- *An addiction:* 'a need for a drug', 'the use of a substance that is psychologically and physiologically addictive', 'showing tolerance and withdrawal'.
- *Dependency:* 'showing psychological and physiological withdrawal'.
- *Drug:* 'an addictive substance', 'a substance that causes dependency', 'any medical substance'.

These different definitions indicate the relationship between terminology and theory. For example, concepts of 'control', 'withdrawal' and 'tolerance' are indicative of a biomedical view of addictions. Concepts such as 'lacking moral fibre' suggest a moral model of addictions, and 'maladaptive coping mechanism' suggests a social learning perspective. In addition, the terms illustrate how difficult it is to use one term without using another, with the risk that the definitions become tautologies.

Many questions have been asked about different addictive behaviours, including the following:

- What causes someone to start smoking?
- What causes drinking behaviour to become a problem?
- Why can some people just smoke socially while others need to smoke first thing in the morning?
- Is it possible for an alcoholic to return to normal drinking?
- Do addictions run in families?

Questions about the causes of an addiction can be answered according to the different theoretical perspectives that have been developed over the past 300 years to explain and predict addictions, including the moral model, the first disease concept, the second disease concept and social learning theory. These different theories, their development and how they relate to attitudes to different substances will now be examined.

HISTORICAL CHANGES IN ATTITUDE AND THEORETICAL APPROACH

Theory is often viewed as independent of changes in social attitudes. However, parallels can be seen between changes in theoretical perspective over the past 300 years and contemporary attitudes. These parallels will be discussed in terms of alcohol use.

THE SEVENTEENTH CENTURY AND THE MORAL MODEL OF ADDICTIONS

During the seventeenth century, alcohol was generally held in high esteem by society. It was regarded as safer than water, nutritious, and the innkeeper was valued as a central figure in the community. In addition, at this time humans were considered to be separate from Nature, in terms of possessing a soul and a will and being responsible for their own behaviour. Animals' behaviour was seen as resulting from biological drives, whereas the behaviour of humans was seen to be a result of their own free choice. Accordingly, alcohol consumption was considered an acceptable behaviour, but excessive alcohol use was regarded as a result of free choice and personal responsibility. Alcoholism was therefore seen as a behaviour that deserved punishment, not treatment; alcoholics were regarded as choosing to behave excessively. This model of addiction was called the *moral model*. This perspective is similar to the arguments espoused by Thomas Szasz in the 1960s concerning the treatment versus punishment of mentally ill individuals and his distinction between being 'mad' or 'bad'. Szasz (1961) suggested that to label someone 'mad', and to treat them, removed the central facet of humanity, namely personal responsibility. He proposed that holding individuals responsible for their behaviour gave them back their sense of responsibility even if this resulted in them being seen as 'bad'. Similarly, the moral model of addictions considered alcoholics to have chosen to behave excessively and therefore be deserving of punishment (acknowledging their responsibility), not treatment (denying their responsibility). In effect, contemporary social attitudes were reflected in contemporary theory.

THE NINETEENTH CENTURY AND THE FIRST DISEASE CONCEPT

During the nineteenth century, attitudes towards addictions, and in particular alcohol, changed. The temperance movement was developed and spread the word about the evils of drink. Alcohol was regarded as a powerful and destructive substance and alcoholics were seen as its victims. This perspective is also reflected in prohibition and the banning of alcohol consumption in the USA. During this time, the *first disease concept* of addiction was developed. This was the earliest form of a biomedical approach to addiction and regarded alcoholism as an illness. Within this model, the focus for the illness was the substance. Alcohol was seen as an addictive substance, and alcoholics were viewed as passively succumbing to its influence. The first disease concept regarded the substance as the problem and called for the treatment of excessive drinkers. Again, social attitudes to addiction were reflected in the development of theory.

THE TWENTIETH CENTURY AND THE SECOND DISEASE CONCEPT

Attitudes towards addiction changed again at the beginning of the twentieth century. The USA learned quickly that banning alcohol consumption was more problematic than expected, and governments across the western world realized that they could financially benefit from alcohol sales. In parallel, attitudes towards human behaviour were changing and a more liberal, laissez-faire attitude became dominant. Likewise, theories of addiction reflected these shifts. The *second disease concept* of addiction was developed, which no longer saw the substance as the problem but pointed the finger at those individuals who became addicted. In this perspective, the small minority of those who consumed alcohol to excess were seen as having a problem, but for the rest of society alcohol consumption returned to a position of an acceptable social habit. This perspective legitimized the sale of alcohol, recognized the resulting government benefits and emphasized the treatment of addicted individuals. Alcoholism was regarded as an illness developed by certain people who therefore needed support and treatment. In the second disease perspective there are three different arguments: (1) pre-existing physical abnormalities; (2) pre-existing psychological abnormalities; and (3) acquired dependency theory. All of these have a similar model of addiction in that they:

- Regard addictions as discrete entities (you are either an addict or not an addict).
- Regard an addiction as an illness.
- Focus on the individual as the problem.
- Regard the addiction as irreversible.
- Emphasize treatment.
- Emphasize treatment through total abstinence.

PROBLEMS WITH A DISEASE MODEL OF ADDICTION

Although many researchers still emphasize a disease model of addiction, there are several problems with this perspective:

- The disease model encourages treatment through lifelong abstinence. However, lifelong abstinence is very rare and may be difficult to achieve.
- The model does not incorporate relapse into its concept of treatment. However, this 'all or nothing' perspective may actually promote relapse through encouraging individuals to set unreasonable targets of abstinence and by establishing the self-fulfilling prophecy of 'once a drunk, always a drunk'.
- The description of controlled drinking, which suggested that alcoholics can return to 'normal drinking' patterns (Davies 1962; Sobel and Sobel 1978), challenged the central ideas of the disease model. The phenomenon of controlled drinking indicated that perhaps an addiction was not irreversible and that abstinence might not be the only treatment goal.

THE 1970S AND ONWARDS: SOCIAL LEARNING THEORY

In the latter part of the twentieth century attitudes towards addictions changed again. With the development of behaviourism, learning theory and a belief that behaviour was shaped by an interaction with both the environment and other individuals, the belief that excessive behaviour and addictions were illnesses began to be challenged. Since the 1970s, behaviours such as smoking, drinking and drug-taking have been increasingly described within the context of all other behaviours. In the same way that theories of aggression shifted from a biological cause (aggression as an instinct) to social causes (aggression as a response to the environment/upbringing), addictions were also seen as learned behaviours. In this perspective, the term 'addictive behaviour' replaced 'addictions' and such behaviours were regarded as a consequence of learning processes. This shift challenged the concepts of addictions, addict, illness and disease; however, the theories still emphasized treatment. The social learning perspective differs from the disease model of addiction in several ways:

- Addictive behaviours are seen as acquired habits, which are learned according to the rules of social learning theory.
- Addictive behaviours can be unlearned; they are not irreversible.
- Addictive behaviours lie along a continuum; they are not discrete entities.
- Addictive behaviours are no different from other behaviours.
- Treatment approaches involve either total abstinence or relearning 'normal' behaviour patterns.

THE PROCESSES INVOLVED IN LEARNING AN ADDICTIVE BEHAVIOUR

From a social learning perspective, addictive behaviours are learned according to the following processes: (1) classical conditioning; (2) operant conditioning; (3) observational learning; and (4) cognitive processes.

CLASSICAL CONDITIONING

The rules of classical conditioning state that behaviours are acquired through the processes of associative learning. For example, an unconditioned stimulus (US, e.g. going to the pub) may elicit an unconditioned response (UR, e.g. feeling relaxed). If the unconditioned stimulus is associated with a conditioned stimulus (CS, e.g. a drink), then eventually this will elicit the conditioned response (CR, e.g. feeling relaxed). Classical conditioning may also result in two addictive behaviours such as smoking and drinking being linked together. This process of classical conditioning can happen as follows:

The unconditioned stimulus and the unconditioned response:

- going to the pub + feeling relaxed
- (US) + (UR)

Pairing the unconditioned stimulus and the conditioned stimulus:

- going to the pub + a drink
- (US) + (CS)

The conditioned stimulus and the conditioned response:

- a drink + feeling relaxed
- (CS) + (CR)

Therefore the conditioned stimulus now elicits the conditioned response.

Smoking and drinking alcohol can become associated with each other through classical conditioning

What Factors Can Pair with the Conditioned Stimulus?

Two types of factor can pair with the conditioned stimulus: *external* (e.g. the pub) and *internal* (e.g. mood) cues. In terms of a potentially addictive behaviour, smoking cigarettes may be associated with external cues (e.g. seeing someone else smoking, being with particular friends), or with internal cues (e.g. anxiety, depression or happiness). It has been argued that a pairing with an internal cue is more problematic because these cues cannot be avoided. In addition, internal cues also raise the problem of *generalization*. Generalization occurs when the withdrawal symptoms from a period of abstinence from an addictive behaviour act as cues for further behaviour. For example, if an individual has paired feeling anxious with smoking, their withdrawal symptoms may be interpreted as anxiety and therefore elicit further smoking behaviour; the behaviour provides relief from its own withdrawal symptoms.

OPERANT CONDITIONING

The rules of operant conditioning state that the probability of behaviour occurring is increased if it is either *positively reinforced* by the presence of a positive event, or *negatively reinforced* by the absence or removal of a negative event. In terms of an addictive behaviour such as smoking, the probability of smoking will be increased by feelings of social acceptance, confidence and control (the positive reinforcer) and removal of withdrawal symptoms (the negative reinforcer).

OBSERVATIONAL LEARNING/MODELLING

Behaviours are also learned by observing significant others carrying them out. For example, parental smoking, an association between smoking and attractiveness/thinness, and the observation of alcohol consumption as a risk-taking behaviour may contribute to the acquisition of the behaviour.

COGNITIVE FACTORS

Factors such as self-image, problem-solving behaviour, coping mechanisms and attributions also contribute to the acquisition of an addictive behaviour.

INTEGRATING DISEASE AND SOCIAL LEARNING PERSPECTIVES

Researchers often polarize a disease and a social learning perspective of addiction. For example, while some researchers argue that smoking is entirely due to the addictive properties of nicotine, others argue that it is a learned behaviour. However, implicit within each approach is the alternative explanation. For example, while a disease model may emphasize acquired tolerance following smoking or drinking behaviour and therefore draws upon a disease perspective, it implicitly uses a social learning approach to explain why some people start smoking/drinking in the first place and why only some continue to the extent that they develop acquired tolerance. People need exposure and reinforcement to make the smoking or drinking enough to develop tolerance. The concept of tolerance may be a disease model concept but it relies upon some degree of social learning theory for it to operate. Likewise, people might smoke an increasing number of cigarettes because they have learned that smoking relieves withdrawal symptoms. However, while this form of association is derived from a social learning perspective, it implicitly uses a disease perspective in that it requires the existence of physical withdrawal symptoms. Therefore most researchers draw upon both disease and social learning perspectives. Sometimes this interaction between the two forms of model is made explicit and the researchers acknowledge that they believe both sources of influence are important. However, at times this interaction is only implicit. The role of a disease model and a social learning model is explored here with two case studies. The first is on caffeine (see Box 4.1), which highlights the addictive nature of a common drug and its impact upon health, and the second is on exercise dependence (see Box 4.2), which reflects the addictive nature of a behaviour. West (2006) offers a new synthetic model of addiction that brings together a range of medical and psychological constructs including compulsion, self-control, habit and motivational states as a means to understand why people become addicted in the first place and how and why they sometimes manage to change their behaviour (see p. 98).

BOX 4.1 Caffeine: The Most Widely Consumed Psychoactive Substance in History

(This information was taken from the work of Jack James, who is the world expert in this field. Please see references such as James 2004, 2010; James and Rogers 2005; James and Keane 2007 for more detail.)

Caffeine is a psychoactive substance that causes physical changes in the body. It is also central to much social behaviour, and coffee and tea form the basis for many interactions with friends and family as well as offering a means to punctuate a busy working day.

Coffee drinking is central to many social interactions

Caffeine illustrates the ways in which a substance can be harmful and is in line with other forms of drug addiction. It also illustrates how all addictive behaviours have some form of learning processes implicit in them. This case study will describe what caffeine is and it how it affects our bodies. It will then describe the impact of caffeine on performance and mood and physical health.

Caffeine and Its Use

Caffeine, otherwise known as 1,3,7-trimethylxanthine, first became widely available after European colonization in the seventeenth and eighteenth centuries. It is mostly consumed through tea, coffee, soft drinks or energy drinks, but is also present in chocolate and some painkillers. For most people, their first exposure occurs while still in the womb as caffeine can cross the placenta. Use continues in childhood through the intake of soft drinks and then consolidates in adolescents and early adulthood. After this time patterns of intake tend to stabilize and continue throughout life. Worldwide, more than 80 per cent of people consume caffeine daily and its use is universal regardless of age, gender, geography and culture, far outweighing any other drug including nicotine, alcohol, cannabis or cocaine. Caffeine has a strong social role in that it forms the rationale and centrepiece for many social interactions. It is also a psychoactive drug that affects how we function. Once ingested, caffeine is quickly distributed around the body and is cleared from the stomach within about 20 minutes, reaching peak blood levels within 40–60 minutes. It has a half-life of about five hours in adults, which means that a daily intake of three or four cups will stay at active levels for most of a person's waking day. Caffeine is addictive in that repeated use results in physical dependence leading to behavioural, physiological and subjective withdrawal symptoms such as sleepiness, lethargy, headaches and reduction in psychomotor performance, including concentration and reaction time. Caffeine use has two important implications for health. First, people are motivated to use caffeine through expected benefits to performance and mood. Second, research highlights many detrimental effects on physical health.

Performance and Mood

Those who consume caffeine tend to hold two key expectancies of how the drug will affect them. First, they believe that caffeine enhances their mood, and second they believe it increases their performance, particularly by keeping them awake. Research has explored these expected effects to see if they are real. Some studies have compared consumers vs non-consumers and pre- and post-consumption, but such approaches have methodological problems. James and colleagues (James and Rogers 2005; James et al. 2005) have employed more powerful experimental designs with double-blinding and a placebo control. The results from these studies offer substantial support for the withdrawal reversal hypothesis: that caffeine does indeed improve performance and mood *but* only in relation to the impact of overnight abstinence from caffeine which has caused an initial deficit. Accordingly, if people didn't drink caffeine in the first place, then there would be no deficit to rectify by drinking more. In fact, in a recent study of academic achievement, James et al. (2010) explored the impact of caffeine use in 7,377 Icelandic adolescents and concluded that achievement deficits that would usually have been attributed to smoking and alcohol use were in fact accounted for by caffeine intake. In addition, the results indicated that this might be because caffeine also causes daytime sleepiness which in turn affects academic achievement. From this evidence it would seem that caffeine is not a psychostimulant as is often believed and only has cognitive and mood benefits in those experiencing withdrawal.

Cardiovascular Disease and Blood Pressure

The second main area of research relates to the impact of caffeine on physical health, particularly in relation to cardiovascular disease. Evidence for this comes from the acute and chronic effects of caffeine on blood pressure and epidemiological data on caffeine use and cardiovascular disease. Blood pressure has direct implications for cardiovascular disease, stroke and heart attacks and research conclusively shows that caffeine increases blood pressure acutely in both men and women of all ages with either no prior health problems or hypertension (James 1997). Increases tend to be between 5 to 15mm Hg systolic and 5 to 10mm Hg diastolic for an average daily intake. In addition, this increase adds to that caused by other factors such as smoking and stress. Research also indicates that, over time, rather than developing tolerance to caffeine, the acute effects of caffeine on blood pressure persist. There also appear to be chronic effects of caffeine on blood pressure although evidence for this is less conclusive.

Epidemiological Data

More than 100 large epidemiological studies have also explored links between caffeine and health at a population rather than an individual level and generally the conclusion is that caffeine is bad for cardiovascular function. There are, however, some problems with these studies, including the measurement of caffeine use which has resulted in some conflicting findings. Some authors have argued that these conflicts indicate that caffeine is not harmful, whereas others argue that this is due to measurement error and that the effects on health may be even larger than found in the research literature (James 2011). Similarly, epidemiological studies have also explored links between caffeine and population blood pressure levels. Again there are inconsistencies in the literature. However, it seems clear that people do not show tolerance to caffeine and therefore repeated use results in repeated episodes of raised blood pressure which, overall, causes population increases in blood pressure which in turn impacts negatively upon health.

Other Aspects of Health

Generally there are mixed results for the impact of caffeine on a range of cancers, although in the laboratory setting it has been shown to be carcinogenic under some conditions. More convincing evidence relates caffeine use to miscarriage, lower birth weight and some adverse reactions with some medicines.

Caffeine Drinking as an Addictive Behaviour

Caffeine clearly has psychoactive properties and acts as a drug on our bodies. People are motivated to use caffeine for its effects on their performance and mood, but research indicates that these benefits are in fact just compensating for the negative effects of withdrawal symptoms. However, caffeine drinking is also a learned behaviour as people associate coffee with social interactions, as an excuse for conversation ('going out for coffee') or with the end of a meal. They also hold positive outcome expectancies on the basis of their previous experiences. Caffeine drinking is therefore learned in all the ways that other behaviours are learned: through associative learning, reinforcement and modelling. Caffeine is a good example of an addictive drug that also involves a strong social learning component in its maintenance and cessation.

BOX 4.2 Exercise Dependence: When is There Too Much of a Good Thing?

Smoking and alcohol use (and caffeine, heroine, cannabis, etc.) illustrate addictive behaviours which involve a combination of physical responses to a drug (e.g. nicotine) and the consequences of a learned behaviour (e.g. social drinking with friends). Over recent years researchers have also recognized that people can become 'addicted' to behaviours which do not involve the intake of any external drug. For example, there are now literatures on shopping addiction ('shopaholics'), gambling addiction, sex addiction, food addiction and exercise dependence (see Orford 2002 for an excellent overview). A disease model of such addictions would argue that the behaviours become addictive because they generate endorphins which create a sense of arousal and pleasure. From a social learning perspective, however, it would be argued that these behaviours become excessive because they are reinforced by factors such as mood, social interaction, changes in body shape and financial gain, and are paired with cues such as friends, the pub, stress and relief from stress, which become triggers for subsequent behaviour. There is an alternative perspective which says they are not addictive behaviours at all, but this purely depends upon the definition of addiction being used (see pp. 72–3). This case study will focus on exercise dependence as an example of a behaviourally triggered addiction which has consequences for an individual's well-being. Exercise dependence is described in terms of its definition, possible causes and impact on the individual.

Defining Exercise Dependence

Early articles examined the concept of 'exercise addiction', discussed positive versus negative exercise addiction and deliberated over whether excessive exercise was harmful. The term 'exercise addiction' was later replaced by others such as 'obligatory running' (Coen and Ogles 1993), 'compulsive running' (Nash 1987), 'morbid exercising' (Chalmers et al. 1985) and 'exercise dependence' (Veale 1987). Several measures have been developed in an attempt to assess this behaviour, with some being specific to certain forms of exercise, including the 'Feelings About Running Scale' (Carmack and Martens 1979) and the 'Running Addiction Scale' (Chapman and Castro 1990), and others being more generic, such as the Obligatory Exercise Questionnaire (Pasman and Thompson, 1988) and the Exercise Dependence Questionnaire (Ogden et al. 1997).

In general, exercise dependence relates to the disease perspective:

- **Tolerance:** 'I need to do more and more to get the same effects'.
- **Withdrawal symptoms:** 'If I don't exercise I feel dreadful'.

And to the social learning perspective:

- **Feeling out of control:** 'I live to exercise'; 'I have to exercise'.
- **Interference with social life:** 'I cancel seeing my friends so I can exercise'.
- **Interference with family life:** 'My family complain I exercise too much'.
- **Interference with work:** 'My exercise makes me tired at work'.
- **Stereotypical behaviour:** 'I must not miss an exercise session'.
- **Excessive behaviour:** 'I exercise more than most people I know'.

Hence, exercise dependence (or whichever term is used) describes excessive exercise which impacts upon a person's life and reflects a feeling of being out of control. As with all definitions of addictive behaviours this is problematic as it assumes that there *is* a normal life (i.e. work, family, friends) and that a behaviour that interferes with this is harmful. Furthermore, it is quite possible that a person who exercises excessively feels perfectly in control of their behaviour as long as their life enables them to exercise to the level that they need. The definition of 'excessive' is also flawed because it depends upon social norms and a model of how we *should* distribute our time.

Causes of Exercise Dependence

There are several possible explanations as to why people can become addicted to exercise which can be understood in terms of the disease and social learning perspectives.

Disease Model

- **Tolerance:** people become tolerant to their level of exercise and therefore need to exercise more to achieve the same benefits.
- **Withdrawal symptoms:** exercise improves mood and generates a sense of arousal. After a period of time, however, this state deteriorates and the individual experiences a sense of withdrawal. They therefore exercise to reverse the withdrawal process (similar to caffeine, see Box 4.1).
- **Endorphins:** exercise generates endorphins in the brain which create a sense of euphoria ('joggers' high') but endorphins then decay, leaving the person wanting that feeling again.

Social Learning Model

- **Feeling out of control:** exercise can make people feel more in control of their lives and similarities have often been drawn with eating disorders. For example, if a person feels out of control of their relationships or their career, they may find satisfaction in being able to control how much they exercise.
- **Reinforcement:** exercise has many positive consequences (some of which are fairly immediate) such as improved mood, stress reduction, improved body shape and body image, and increased energy. These can become reinforcing for the behaviour with the individual exercising more as a means to experience these benefits. Changes in body shape are also frequently reinforced through the compliments of others.
- **Modelling:** social learning may also encourage excessive exercise if people start to socialize in groups of other excessive exercisers (e.g. body-building clubs, jogging clubs, rowing clubs, etc.).
- **Associative learning:** excessive exercise can be learned through association with a range of cues such as social groups (e.g. jogging clubs, gyms), being in the fresh air, feeling stressed, feeling unattractive and feeling fat. These internal and external factors can become cues for further exercise behaviour.

Consequences of Exercise Dependence

Regular exercise may result in physiological and psychological benefits and is recommended for both the prevention and treatment of physical disorders such as CHD, hypertension and obesity, and psychological problems such as depression and anxiety (see Chapters 6, 15). When taken to excess, however, exercise may be harmful. For example, people with exercise dependence often have physical injuries associated with their behaviour (e.g. problems with knees, ankles, feet and back) and rather than rest to allow these injuries to recover may continue to exercise, thereby exacerbating their problems. Excessive exercise may also have negative effects on interpersonal relationships– for example, becoming an absent parent or neglecting family/partner responsibilities. Finally, although exercise improves mood for most people, excessive exercise may be detrimental to depression and anxiety in the longer term if a person becomes overly dependent on exercise to manage their well-being (Orford 2002).

Exercise dependence is an example of how a behaviour can become excessive and therefore 'addictive'. It also shows how even a behaviourally-generated addiction can be explained through both disease and social learning perspectives. Parallel processes may well be involved for other problem behaviours such as shopping, gambling and sex addiction.

BOX 4.3 Some Problems with . . . Addiction Research

Below are some problems with research in this area that you may wish to consider.

1   There are very different theoretical perspectives on addictive behaviours which colour research in terms of theory, methods and interpretation. For example, those from a medical perspective emphasize the addictive nature of the drug while those from a behavioural perspective emphasize the behaviour. At times these two perspectives contradict each other but mostly the two camps publish in different journals and do not really communicate. This can lead to polarizing our understanding of these behaviours.

2   Most measures of smoking and alcohol are self-report. This can be problematic as people may under-report their behaviour in order to seem healthier than they are. There are some more objective measures available such as cotinine levels. However, these involve more commitment by both the researcher and the subject. In addition, measuring these behaviours may change them as any form of measurement can make people more aware of their behaviour.

3   The factors that explain smoking and alcohol use are many and complex. Related theories are therefore complex and often difficult to operationalize. Simpler theories are easier to operationalize but may miss many of the variables that predict these behaviours. There therefore always needs to be a trade-off between comprehensiveness and usefulness.

THE STAGES OF SUBSTANCE USE

Research into addictive behaviours has defined four stages of substance use: (1) initiation; (2) maintenance; (3) cessation; and (4) relapse. These four stages will now be examined in detail for smoking and alcohol use and are illustrated in Figure 4.10.

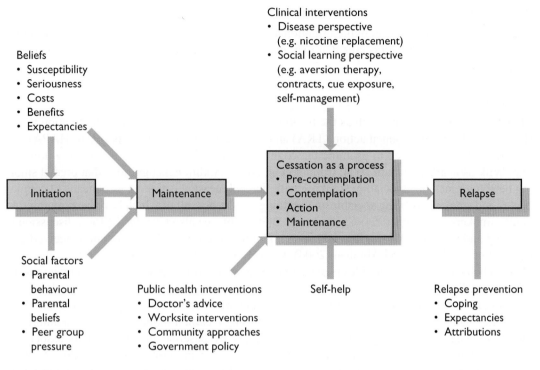

FIGURE 4.10

The stages of substance use

STAGES 1 AND 2: INITIATING AND MAINTAINING AN ADDICTIVE BEHAVIOUR

SMOKING INITIATION AND MAINTENANCE

As noted above, in 1954, Doll and Hill indicated that smoking was predictive of lung cancer. Over 50 years later, approximately 30 per cent of the adult population still smoke even though most of them are aware of the related health risks. In fact, research exploring whether smokers appreciate the risks of smoking in comparison with the risks of murder and traffic accidents showed that smokers were accurate in their perception of the risks and showed similar ratings of risk to both ex-smokers and those who had never smoked (Sutton 1998b). The early health promotion campaigns focused mainly on the determinants of smoking in adult men, but over recent years there has been an increasing interest in smoking in children and adolescents. Most children/adolescents try a puff of a cigarette. It is therefore difficult to distinguish between actual initiation and maintenance of smoking behaviour. Accordingly, these stages will be considered together.

Smoking in Children

Doll and Peto (1981) reported that people whose smoking is initiated in childhood have an increased chance of lung cancer compared with those who start smoking later on in life. This is particularly significant as most adult smokers start the habit in childhood and very few people start smoking regularly after the age of 19 or 20 (Charlton 1992). Further, the younger people start, the more likely they are to become an adult smoker (Chassin et al. 1990). In the USA, smoking in adolescents fell from 30 to 22 per cent between 1999 and 2003 but has remained at this level since. In the UK, 0.5 per cent of 11-year-olds are regular smokers but this rises to 14 per cent by 15 years of age (Center for Disease Control 2008; Fuller 2009).

Psychological Predictors of Smoking Initiation

In an attempt to understand smoking initiation and maintenance, researchers have searched for the psychological and social processes that may promote smoking behaviour with a focus on cognitions and social norms.

Cognitions

Models of health behaviour such as the health belief model (HBM), protection motivation theory (PMT), the theory of reasoned action (TRA) and the health action process approach (HAPA) (see Chapter 3) have been used to examine the cognitive factors that contribute to smoking initiation (e.g. Wilkinson and Abraham 2004; Connor et al. 2006). Additional cognitions that predict smoking behaviour include associating smoking with fun and pleasure, smoking as a means of calming nerves and smoking as being sociable and building confidence, all of which have been reported by young smokers (Charlton 1984; Charlton and Blair 1989; see also Chapter 12 for a discussion of smoking and stress reduction). Research also highlights a role for self-esteem and perceived ease of smoking (Wilkinson and Abraham 2004). Conner et al. (2006b) explored the role of theory of planned behaviour (TPB) variables (see Chapter 3) as well as anticipated regret and intention stability in predicting smoking initiation in adolescents aged between 11 and 12. Non-smoking adolescents (n = 675) completed measures at baseline and then were followed up after nine months to see if they had tried smoking, which was assessed using a carbon monoxide breath monitor. The results showed that smoking initiation was predicted by baseline intentions. This association between intentions and behaviour was only present, however, in those who did not express regret about starting smoking at baseline and who showed stable intentions. In terms of maintenance of smoking, Lawton et al. (2009) explored the relative role of cognitive attitudes (e.g. 'smoking is harmful') and affective attitudes (e.g. 'smoking is enjoyable') in predicting smoking at one month follow-up and concluded that affective attitudes had a direct impact upon behaviour (regardless of intentions), and that this might be a useful variable to target in interventions.

Social Norms

Much research focuses on the individual and takes them out of their social context. Interactions with the social world help to create and develop a child's beliefs and behaviour. In Britain, there have been five longitudinal studies that have identified elements of the child's social world that are predictive of smoking behaviour (Murray et al. 1984; McNeil et al. 1988; Charlton and Blair 1989; Gillies and Galt 1990; Goddard 1990). The main factor that predicts smoking is parental smoking, with reports that children are twice as likely to smoke if their parents smoke (Lader and Matheson 1991). In addition, parents' attitudes to smoking also influence their offspring's behaviour. For example, if a child perceives the parents as being strongly against smoking, he or she is up to seven times less likely to be a smoker (Murray et al. 1984). The next most important influence on smoking is peer group pressure. Mercken et al. (2011) explored the beliefs and behaviours of 1,475 Dutch adolescents and concluded that their smoking behaviour was predicted by parental, sibling and friend smoking. In addition, even those people that they would like to be friends with in the future influenced whether or not they smoked in the present. Similarly, studies in the USA have examined the relationship between peer group identity and tobacco use. The results showed that individuals who are identified by themselves and others as being problem-prone, doing poorly at school, rarely involved in school sports, high in risk-taking behaviour such as alcohol and drug use, and with low self-esteem, were more likely to have smoked (Mosbach and Leventhal 1988; Sussman et al. 1990). Research also shows an impact of an individual's wider social context. For example, a Cancer Research Campaign study in 1991 found that smoking prevalence was lower in schools that had a 'no smoking' policy, particularly if this policy included staff as well as students. Further, Helweg-Larsen et al. (2010) carried out a qualitative study of smokers from Denmark (where smoking is accepted) and the USA (where it is not) as a means to explore the role of an individual's cultural background. The results showed that although all smokers were aware of the risks of their behaviour, the Danes were more likely to minimize these risks. In addition, although all smokers also said that they had been the target for moralized attitudes from others, the Danes were more rejecting of these views.

In summary, social factors such as the behaviour and beliefs of parents and peers, and the wider social context influence the beliefs and behaviours of children. Using interviews with low-income women with preschool children, Graham (1987) further explored the contextual factors that may maintain smoking behaviour. She argued that although smoking is seen by researchers as unhealthy and something to be prevented, the women in her study regarded smoking as central to their attempts to 'reconcile health keeping and housekeeping when their reserves of emotional and physical energy may be seriously depleted' (1987: 55). She stated that smoking works to promote these women's sense of well-being and to help them cope with caring. She reported that smoking can be seen as 'the only activity they do, just for themselves'. Smoking is therefore a product not only of beliefs but also an individual's social world.

ALCOHOL INITIATION AND MAINTENANCE

Most people try alcohol at some time in their lives, with about 90 per cent of all adults having drunk alcohol in the past year. Some do describe themselves as lifelong abstainers (OPCS 1994) and the most common reasons for never drinking alcohol are religion and not liking it. Therefore, rather than examining predictors of drinking 'ever' or 'occasionally', this section examines which factors predict developing a problem with drinking. Research has focused on cognitive factors, affect and social factors.

Cognition and Affect

The tension-reduction hypothesis (Cappell and Greeley 1987) suggests that individuals may develop a drink problem because alcohol reduces tension and anxiety. Tension creates a heightened state of arousal and alcohol reduces this state, which perpetuates further drinking behaviour. However, it has been suggested that it is not the *actual* effects of alcohol use that promote drinking but the *expected* effects (George and Marlatt 1983). Therefore, because a small amount of alcohol may have positive effects, people assume that these positive effects will continue with increased use. This perspective is in line with the social learning model of addictive behaviours and emphasizes the role of reinforcement and cognitions. Studies have also focused on cognitions using social cognition models (see Chapter 3). For example, Norman and Conner (2006) used the TPB to predict binge drinking in undergraduate students and included a measure of past binge drinking as a means to measure habit. The results showed that the best predictors of intentions to binge drink at one week follow-up were attitude, self-efficacy and lower perceived control, and that intentions and self-efficacy in turn predicted actual behaviour. Furthermore, past behaviour also predicted both intentions and behaviour, showing an important role for habit in alcohol use.

Social Factors

Many of the social factors that relate to smoking behaviour are also predictive of alcohol consumption. For example, parental drinking is predictive of problem drinking in children. According to a disease model of addictions, it could be argued that this reflects the genetic predisposition to develop an addictive behaviour. However, parental drinking may be influential through 'social hereditary factors', with children being exposed to drinking behaviour and learning this behaviour from their parents (Orford and Velleman 1991). In addition, peer group alcohol use and abuse also predict drinking behaviour, as does being someone who is sensation-seeking, with a tendency to be aggressive and having a history of getting into trouble with authority. Johnston and White (2003) used the TPB to predict binge drinking in students. However, given the social nature of binge drinking, they focused on the role of norms. Using a longitudinal design, 289 undergraduate students completed a questionnaire concerning their beliefs with follow-up collected about reported binge drinking. The results showed an important role for norms, particularly if the norms were of a behaviourally relevant reference group with which the student strongly identified.

STAGE 3: CEASING AN ADDICTIVE BEHAVIOUR

Because of the potential health consequences of both smoking and alcohol consumption, research has examined different means to help smokers and drinkers quit their behaviour. (Much of this research can be understood in terms of the strategies for behaviour change described in Chapter 8.) Cessation of an addictive behaviour can be examined in terms of the *processes* involved in cessation and the *interventions* designed to motivate individuals to quit their behaviour.

THE PROCESS OF CESSATION

Most research to date has conceptualized cessation as the result of a slow process of cognitive shifts. In contrast, recent research has emphasized a more unplanned approach to cessation. These two approaches will now be considered.

Cessation as a Slow Process

Much research emphasizes the 'drip, drip' approach to cessation and the development of behavioural intentions or plans (see Chapters 3, 8). Such approaches include the use of social cognition models, implementation intentions and a stages of change approach.

Social Cognition Models

Research has used social cognition models (see Chapter 3) to examine the predictors of both intentions to stop smoking and successful smoking cessation. For example, Norman et al. (1999) examined the usefulness of the TPB at predicting intention to quit smoking and making a quit attempt in a group of smokers attending health promotion clinics in primary care. The results showed that the best predictors of intentions to quit were perceived behavioural control (e.g. 'How much control do you feel you have over not smoking over the next six months?') and perceived susceptibility (e.g. 'How likely do you think it might be that you will develop any of the following problems in the future if you continue to smoke?'). At follow-up, the best predictors of making a quit attempt were intentions at baseline (e.g. 'How likely is it that you will not smoke during the next six months?') and the number of previous quit attempts. Other similar studies report a role for individual cognitions such as perceptions of susceptibility, past cessation attempts and perceived behavioural control as predictors of smoking behaviour (Giannetti et al. 1985; Godin et al. 1992). Further, an extended TPB including descriptive norms and affective attitudes has been shown to be a good predictor of cessation (Rise et al. 2008). In addition TPB has been used as a framework to explore smoking cessation in a range of populations, including following a worksite ban (Borland et al. 1991), pregnant women, and the general population (Godin et al. 1992).

Implementation Intentions

Implementation intention research highlights the development of plans (Gollwitzer 1993) and has been used to promote changes in both smoking and alcohol use. For example, Conner and Higgins (2010) randomly allocated adolescents (aged 11–12) to receive either an implementation intention intervention (i.e. planning how, where and when they could refuse to smoke) or a self-efficacy intervention (i.e. planning how to refuse to smoke in increasingly difficult situations). They were then followed up for up to 24 months. The results showed that the implementation intention intervention was most effective at reducing adolescent smoking by two years. Similarly, Armitage

(2008, 2009) concluded from his experimental studies that implementation intentions could also reduce both smoking and alcohol intake by one month.

Stages of Change

The stages of change model (SOC) focuses on the gradual progression through a series of stages (Prochaska and DiClemente 1982). In particular, Prochaska and DiClemente (1984) adapted their SOC to examine cessation of addictive behaviours. This model highlighted the processes involved in the transition from a smoker to a non-smoker and from a drinker to a non-drinker. They argued that cessation involves a shift across five basic stages:

1 *Pre-contemplation:* defined as not seriously considering quitting.
2 *Contemplation:* having some thoughts about quitting.
3 *Preparation:* seriously considering quitting.
4 *Action:* initial behaviour change.
5 *Maintenance:* maintaining behaviour change for a period of time.

Prochaska and DiClemente maintain that individuals do not progress through these stages in a straightforward and linear fashion but may switch backwards and forwards (e.g. from pre-contemplation to contemplation and back to pre-contemplation again). They call this 'the revolving door' schema and emphasize the dynamic nature of cessation. This model of change has been tested to provide evidence for the different stages for smokers and outpatient alcoholics (DiClemente and Prochaska 1982, 1985; DiClemente and Hughes 1990), and for the relationship between stage of change for smoking cessation and self-efficacy. In addition, it has formed the basis of several interventions to promote smoking cessation. In a very early study by the model's authors, DiClemente et al. (1991) examined the relationship between stage of change and attempts to quit smoking and actual cessation at one- and six-month follow-ups. The authors categorized smokers into either pre-contemplators or contemplators and examined their smoking behaviour at follow-up. They further classified the contemplators into either contemplators (those who were smoking, seriously considering quitting within the next six months, but not within the next 30 days) or those in the preparation stage (those who were seriously considering quitting smoking within the next 30 days). The results showed that those in the preparation stage of change were more likely to have made a quit attempt at both one and six months, that they had made more quit attempts and were more likely to be not smoking at the follow-ups. This study is described in detail in **Focus on Research 4.1** (p. 88). Aveyard et al. (2006) also used the SOC to promote smoking cessation in pregnant women and concluded that a stage-matched intervention was more effective at moving women forward a stage than a non-stage-matched intervention. However, this was only for those in the preparation stage rather than the pre-contemplation or contemplation stages as suggested by the model (see Chapter 3 for a critique of the stages of change model).

Cessation as Unplanned

In contrast to this 'drip, drip' approach to cessation West (2006; West and Sohal 2006) has argued that sometimes cessation of an addictive behaviour can be unplanned. In a large-scale cross-sectional survey of smokers who had made at least one quit attempt (n = 918) and ex-smokers (n = 996) the researchers asked participants to describe whether they had made a serious quit attempt ('By serious attempt I mean you decided that you would try to make sure you never smoked another cigarette'). Those who had tried were then asked to describe the extent to which their attempt had been planned (ranging from 'I did not plan the quit attempt in advance' to 'I planned the quit attempt a few months beforehand') (West and Sohal 2006). The results showed that almost half (48.6 per cent) of the attempts had been made *without* planning. In addition the results showed that unplanned attempts were more likely to last for at least six months (65.4 per cent) compared to planned attempts (42.3 per cent). These results remained even when age, sex and social class were controlled for. These findings are in contrast to much of the research described earlier which emphasizes the role of plans and stages.

FOCUS ON RESEARCH 4.1: STAGES OF SMOKING CESSATION

A study to examine the stages of change in predicting smoking cessation (DiClemente et al. 1991).

Traditionally addictive behaviours were viewed as 'either/or' behaviours. Therefore smokers were considered either smokers, ex-smokers or non-smokers. However, DiClemente and Prochaska (1982) developed their transtheoretical model of change to examine the stages of change in addictive behaviours. This is a classic study which examined the validity of the SOC and assessed the relationship between stage of change and smoking cessation.

BACKGROUND

The original SOC describes the following stages:

- *Pre-contemplation:* not seriously considering quitting in the next six months.
- *Contemplation:* considering quitting in the next six months.
- *Action:* making behavioural changes.
- *Maintenance:* maintaining these changes.

The model is described as dynamic, not linear, with individuals moving backwards and forwards across the stages. In this study, the authors categorized those in the contemplation stage as either contemplators (not considering quitting in the next 30 days) or those in the preparation stage (planning to quit in the next 30 days).

METHODOLOGY

Subjects

A total of 1,466 subjects were recruited for a minimum intervention smoking-cessation programme from Texas and Rhode Island. The majority of the subjects were white, female, had started smoking at about 16 and smoked on average 29 cigarettes a day.

Design

The subjects completed a set of measures at baseline and were followed up at one and six months.

Measures

The subjects completed the following set of measures:

- *Smoking abstinence self-efficacy* (DiClemente et al. 1985), which measures the smokers' confidence that they would not smoke in 20 challenging situations.
- *Perceived stress scale* (Cohen et al. 1985), which measures how much perceived stress the individual has experienced in the last month.
- *Fagerstrom Tolerance Questionnaire* which measures physical tolerance to nicotine.
- *Smoking decisional balance scale* (Velicer et al. 1985), which measures the perceived pros and cons of smoking.
- *Smoking processes-of-change scale* (DiClemente and Prochaska 1985), which measures the individual's stage of change. According to this scale, subjects were defined as pre-contemplators (n = 166), contemplators (n = 794) and those in the preparation stage (n = 506).
- *Demographic data*, including age, gender, education and smoking history.

RESULTS

The results were first analysed to examine baseline difference between the three subject groups. They showed that those in the preparation stage smoked less, were less addicted, had higher self-efficacy, rated the pros of smoking as less and the costs of smoking as more, and had made more prior quitting attempts than the other two groups. The results were then analysed to examine the relationship between stage of change and smoking cessation. At both one and six months, the subjects in the preparation stage had made more quit attempts and were more likely to be not smoking.

CONCLUSION

The results provide support for the SOC of smoking cessation and suggest that it is a useful tool for predicting successful outcome of any smoking-cessation intervention.

INTERVENTIONS TO PROMOTE CESSATION

Interventions to promote cessation can be described as: (1) clinical interventions, which are aimed at the individual; (2) self-help movements; or (3) public health interventions, which are aimed at populations. Many of these interventions draw upon the behaviour change strategies described in Chapter 8.

CLINICAL INTERVENTIONS: PROMOTING INDIVIDUAL CHANGE

Clinical interventions often take the form of group or individual treatment programmes based in hospitals or universities, requiring regular attendance over a 6- or 12-week period. These interventions use a combination of approaches that reflect the different disease and social learning theory models of addiction and are provided for those individuals who seek help.

Disease Perspectives on Cessation

In the most recent disease models of addiction, nicotine and alcohol are seen as addictive and the individual who is addicted is seen as having acquired tolerance and dependency to the substance. Accordingly, cessation programmes offer ways for the individual to reduce this dependency. For example, *nicotine fading* procedures encourage smokers to gradually switch to brands of low nicotine cigarettes and gradually to smoke fewer cigarettes. It is believed that when the smoker is ready to quit completely, their addiction to nicotine will be small enough to minimize any withdrawal symptoms. Although there is no evidence to support the effectiveness of nicotine fading on its own, it has been shown to be useful alongside other methods such as relapse prevention (see e.g. Brown et al. 1984).

Nicotine replacement procedures also emphasize an individual's addiction and dependency on nicotine. Nowadays a number of different nicotine replacement therapies (NRTs) have become available such as nicotine chewing gum, patches that are applied to the skin, nasal sprays, inhalers and tablets. They vary in their accessibility (with some needing a prescription and some being sold over the counter) and different approaches work for different people. The evidence indicates that, compared to placebo, they increase cessation rates by 5 per cent at six months and that if used with behavioural support this rises to 10 per cent (West and Stapleton 2008). Treating excessive drinking from a disease perspective involves aiming for total abstinence as there is no suitable substitute for alcohol.

Social Learning Perspectives on Cessation

Social learning theory emphasizes learning an addictive behaviour through processes such as operant conditioning (rewards and punishments), classical conditioning (associations with internal/external cues), observational learning and cognitions. Therefore cessation procedures emphasize these processes in an attempt to help smokers and excessive drinkers stop their behaviour. These cessation procedures include: aversion therapies, contingency contracting, cue exposure, self-management techniques and multi-perspective cessation clinics.

1 *Aversion therapies* aim to punish smoking and drinking rather than rewarding it. Early methodologies used crude techniques such as electric shocks whereby each time the individual smoked a puff of a cigarette or drank some alcohol, they would receive a mild electric shock. However, this approach was found to be ineffective for both smoking and drinking (e.g. Wilson 1978), the main reason being that it is difficult to transfer behaviours that have been learnt in the laboratory to the real world. In an attempt to transfer this approach to the real world, alcoholics are sometimes given a drug called Antabuse, which induces vomiting whenever alcohol is consumed. This therefore encourages the alcoholic to associate drinking with being sick. This has been shown to be more effective than electric shocks (Lang and Marlatt 1982), but requires the individual to take the drug and also ignores the multitude of reasons behind their drink problem. Imaginal aversion techniques have been used for smokers and encourage the smoker to imagine the negative consequences of smoking, such as being sick (rather than actually experiencing them). However, imaginal techniques seem to add nothing to other behavioural treatments (Lichtenstein and Brown 1983). Rapid smoking is a more successful form of aversion therapy (Danaher 1977) and aims to make the actual process of smoking unpleasant. Smokers are required to sit in a closed room and take a puff every six seconds until it becomes so unpleasant they cannot smoke any more. Although there is some evidence to support rapid smoking as a smoking cessation technique, it has obvious side-effects, including increased blood carbon monoxide levels and heart rates. Other aversion therapies include focused smoking, which involves smokers concentrating on all the negative experiences of smoking, and smoke-holding, which involves smokers holding smoke in their mouths for a period of time and again thinking about the unpleasant sensations. Smoke-holding has been shown to be more successful at promoting cessation than focused smoking and does not have the side-effects of rapid smoking (Walker and Franzini 1985).

2 *Contingency contracting* procedures also aim to punish smoking and drinking and to reward abstinence. Smokers and drinkers are asked to make a contract with either a therapist, a friend or partner and to establish a set of rewards/punishments which are contingent on their smoking/drinking cessation. For example, money may be deposited with the therapist and only returned when they have stopped smoking/drinking for a given period of time. They are therefore rewarding abstinence. Schwartz (1987) analysed a series of contingency contracting studies for smoking cessation from 1967 to 1985 and concluded that this procedure seems to be successful in promoting initial cessation but once the contract was finished, or the money returned, relapse was high. In a study of alcoholics, 20 severe alcoholics who had been arrested for drunkenness were offered employment, health care, counselling, food and clothing if they remained sober (Miller 1975). The results showed that those with the contracts were arrested less, employed more, and were more often sober according to unannounced blood alcohol checks than those who were given these 'rewards' non-contingently. However, whether such changes in behaviour would persist over time is unclear. In addition, this perspective is reminiscent of a more punitive moral model of addictions.

3 *Cue exposure procedures* focus on the environmental factors that have become associated with smoking and drinking. For example, if an individual always smokes when they drink alcohol, alcohol will become a strong external cue to smoke and vice versa. Cue exposure techniques gradually expose the individual to different cues and encourage them to develop coping strategies to deal with them. This procedure aims to extinguish the response to the cues over time and is opposite to cue avoidance procedures, which encourage individuals not to go to the places where they may feel the urge to smoke or drink. Cue exposure highlights some of the problems with inpatient detoxification approaches to alcoholism whereby the alcoholic is hospitalized for a length of time until they have reduced the alcohol from their system. Such an approach aims to

reduce the alcoholic's physiological need for alcohol by keeping them away from alcohol during their withdrawal symptoms. However, being in hospital does not teach the alcoholic how to deal with the cues to drink. It means that they avoid these cues, rather than being exposed to them.

4 *Self-management procedures* use a variety of behavioural techniques to promote smoking and drinking cessation in individuals and may be carried out under professional guidance. Such procedures involve self-monitoring (keeping a record of own smoking/drinking behaviour), becoming aware of the causes of smoking/drinking (What makes me smoke? Where do I smoke? Where do I drink?), and becoming aware of the consequences of smoking/drinking (Does it make me feel better? What do I expect from smoking/drinking?). However, used on their own, self-management techniques do not appear to be more successful than other interventions (Hall et al. 1990).

Multi-Perspective Cessation Clinics

The many different types of intervention approaches for cessation are often integrated in multi-perspective cessation clinics which use a combination of aversion therapies, contingency contracting, cue exposure and self-management.

For smoking cessation this multi-perspective approach often incorporates disease model-based interventions such as NRT. Lando (1977) developed an integrated model of smoking cessation, which has served as a model for subsequent clinics. His approach included the following procedures:

- Six sessions of rapid smoking for 25 minutes for one week.
- Doubled daily smoking rate outside the clinic for one week.
- Onset of smoking cessation.
- Identifying problems encountered when attempting to stop smoking.
- Developing ways to deal with these problems.
- Self-reward contracts for cessation success (e.g. buying something new).
- Self-punishment contracts for smoking (e.g. give money to a friend/therapist).

Lando's model has been evaluated and research suggested a 76 per cent abstinence rate at six months (Lando 1977) and 46 per cent at 12 months (Lando and McGovern 1982), which was higher than the control group's abstinence rates. Killen et al. (1984) developed Lando's approach but used smoke-holding rather than rapid smoking, and added nicotine chewing gum into the programme. Their results showed similarly high abstinence rates to the study by Lando.

Multi-perspective approaches have also been developed for the treatment of alcohol use and include an integration of the aforementioned approaches and also an emphasis on drinking as a coping strategy. They sometimes also include the use of medical management with drugs such as opiate anagonists which help reduce craving or Antabuse which causes nausea or sickness if the person consumes alcohol. Drinking is therefore not simply seen as an unwanted behaviour that should stop but as a behaviour that serves a function in the alcoholic's life. Such approaches include the following.

- Assessing the drinking behaviour both in terms of the degree of the problem (e.g. frequency and amount drunk) and the factors that determine the drinking (e.g. What function does the drinking serve? When does the urge to drink increase/decrease? What is the motivation to change? Do the individual's family/friends support their desire to change?).
- Self-monitoring (e.g. When do I drink?).
- Developing new coping strategies (e.g. relaxation, stress management).
- Cue exposure (e.g. learning to cope with high-risk situations).

Multi-perspective approaches are often regarded as skills training approaches as they encourage individuals to develop the relevant skills needed to change their behaviour.

SELF-HELP MOVEMENTS

Although clinical and public health interventions have proliferated over the past few decades, up to 90 per cent of ex-smokers report having stopped without any formal help (Fiore et al. 1990). Lichtenstein and Glasgow (1992) reviewed the literature on self-help quitting and reported that success rates tend to be about 10–20 per cent at one-year follow-up and 3–5 per cent for continued cessation. The literature suggests that lighter smokers are more likely to be successful at self-quitting than heavy smokers and that minimal interventions, such as follow-up telephone calls, can improve this success. Research also suggests that smokers are more likely to quit if they receive support from their partners and if their partners also stop smoking (Cohen and Lichtenstein 1990) and that partner support is particularly relevant for women trying to give up smoking during pregnancy (e.g. Appleton and Pharoah 1998). However, although many ex-smokers report that 'I did it on my own', it is important not to discount their exposure to the multitude of health education messages received via television, radio or leaflets.

PUBLIC HEALTH INTERVENTIONS: PROMOTING CESSATION IN POPULATIONS

Public health interventions aim to promote behaviour change in populations and have become increasingly popular over recent years. Such interventions are aimed at all individuals, not just those who seek help. For smoking cessation, they take the form of doctor's advice, worksite interventions, community-wide approaches and government interventions. For drinking behaviour, most public health interventions take the form of government interventions.

1 *Doctor's advice.* Approximately 70 per cent of smokers will visit a doctor at some point each year. Research suggests that the recommendation from a doctor, who is considered a credible source of information, can be quite successful in promoting smoking cessation. In a classic study carried out in five general practices in London (Russell et al. 1979), smokers visiting their general practitioner (GP) over a four-week period were allocated to one of four groups: (1) follow-up only; (2) questionnaire about their smoking behaviour and follow-up; (3) doctor's advice to stop smoking, questionnaire about their smoking behaviour and follow-up; and (4) doctor's advice to stop smoking, leaflet giving tips on how to stop and follow-up. All subjects were followed up at 1 and 12 months. The results showed at one-year follow-up that 3.3 per cent of those who had simply been told to stop smoking were still abstinent, and 5.1 per cent of those who were told to stop and had received a leaflet showed successful cessation. This was in comparison to 0.3 per cent in the group that had received follow-up only and 1.6 per cent in the group that had received the questionnaire and follow-up. Although these changes are quite small, if all GPs recommended that their smokers stopped smoking, this would produce half a million ex-smokers within a year in the UK. Research also suggests that the effectiveness of doctors' advice may be increased if they are trained in patient-centred counselling techniques (Wilson et al. 1988). Minimum interventions for smoking cessation by health professionals are also illustrated by the results of the OXCHECK and Family Heart Study results (Muir et al. 1994; Wood et al. 1994), which are described in Chapter 10.

2 *Worksite interventions.* Over the past decade there has been an increasing interest in developing worksite-based smoking cessation interventions. These take the form of either a company adopting a no-smoking policy and/or establishing work-based health promotion programmes. Worksite interventions have the benefit of reaching many individuals who would not consider attending a hospital or a university-based clinic. In addition, the large number of people involved presents the opportunity for group motivation and social support. Furthermore, such interventions may have implications for reducing passive smoking at work, which may be a risk factor for CHD. Research into the effectiveness of no-smoking policies has produced conflicting results, with some studies reporting an overall reduction in the number of cigarettes smoked for up to 12 months (e.g. Biener et al. 1989) and others suggesting that smoking outside work hours compensates for any

reduced smoking at the workplace (e.g. Gomel et al. 1993). In two Australian studies, public service workers were surveyed following smoking bans in 44 government office buildings about their attitudes to the ban immediately after the ban and after six months. The results suggested that although immediately after the ban many smokers felt inconvenienced, these attitudes improved at six months with both smokers and non-smokers recognizing the benefits of the ban. However, only 2 per cent stopped smoking during this period (Borland et al. 1990). Many countries nowadays have worksite bans since the national smoking bans were introduced. Although these appear to contribute to the reduction in smoking in these countries, some people compensate by smoking more in non-work time while others smoke outside their buildings. Further, these bans were implemented at a time when public attitudes towards smoking were changing, so whether a reduction is smoking reflects the ban or such attitudes is unknown.

3 *Community-based programmes*. Large community-based programmes have been established as a means of promoting smoking cessation in large groups of individuals. Such programmes aim to reach those who would not attend clinics and to use group motivation and social support in a similar way to worksite interventions. Early community-based programmes were part of the drive to reduce CHD. In the Stanford Five City Project, the experimental groups received intensive face-to-face instruction on how to stop smoking and in addition were exposed to media information regarding smoking cessation. The results showed a 13 per cent reduction in smoking rates compared with the control group (Farquhar et al. 1990). In the North Karelia Project, individuals in the target community received an intensive educational campaign and were compared with those in a neighbouring community who were not exposed to the campaign. The results from this programme showed a 10 per cent reduction in smoking in men in North Karelia compared with men in the control region. In addition, the results also showed a 24 per cent decline in cardiovascular deaths, a rate twice that of the rest of the country (Puska et al. 1985). Other community-based programmes include the Australia North Coast Study, which resulted in a 15 per cent reduction in smoking over three years, and the Swiss National Research Programme, which resulted in an 8 per cent reduction over three years (Egger et al. 1983; Autorengruppe Nationales Forschungsprogramm 1984).

4 *Government interventions*. An additional means to promote both smoking cessation and healthy drinking is to encourage governments to intervene. Such interventions can take several forms:

- *Restricting/banning advertising*. According to social learning theory, we learn to smoke and drink by associating smoking and drinking with attractive characteristics, such as 'It will help me relax', 'It makes me look sophisticated', 'It makes me look sexy', 'It is risky'. Advertising aims to access and promote these beliefs in order to encourage smoking and drinking. Implementing a ban/restriction on advertising would remove this source of beliefs. In the UK, cigarette advertising was banned in 2003.

- *Increasing the cost*. Research indicates a relationship between the cost of cigarettes and alcohol and their consumption. Increasing the price of cigarettes and alcohol could promote smoking and drinking cessation and deter the initiation of these behaviours, particularly among children. According to models of health beliefs, this would contribute to the perceived costs of the behaviours and the perceived benefits of behaviour change. This relates to the notion of financial incentives which is described in Chapter 8.

- *Banning smoking in public places*. Smoking is already restricted to specific places in many countries. In 2007 the smoking ban came into force in the UK and now smoking is restricted either to outdoors or private places. Similar bans are in place in the USA, Ireland and Italy. A world map of smoking bans is shown in Figure 4.11. A wider ban on smoking may promote smoking cessation. According to social learning theory, this would result in the cues to smoking (e.g. restaurants, bars) becoming eventually disassociated from smoking. However, it is possible that this would simply result in compensatory smoking in other places as illustrated by some of the research on worksite no-smoking policies.

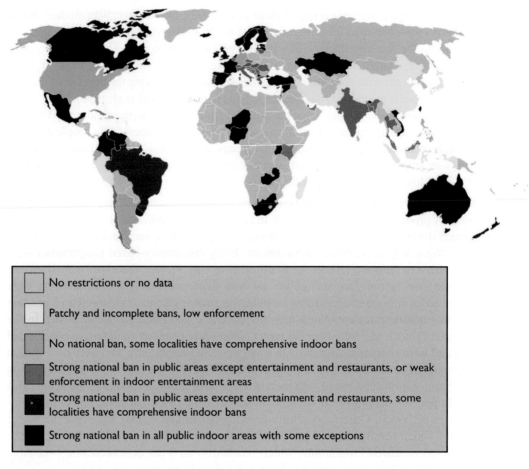

FIGURE 4.11

A world map of smoking bans, June 2011

SOURCE: CIA Factbook (2006) on Wikimedia Commons (2011)

- *Banning cigarette smoking and alcohol drinking.* Governments could opt to ban cigarettes and alcohol completely (although they would forego the large revenues they currently receive from advertising and sales). Such a move might result in a reduction in these behaviours. In fact the smoking bans in Ireland and in some states in the USA have resulted in a range of positive outcomes such as a reduction in smoking per se and even a decline in patients admitted to hospital for heart attacks.

EVIDENCE FOR CESSATION APPROACHES

There have recently been systematic reviews evaluating the relative effectiveness of different approaches to cessation for both smoking and alcohol use.

SMOKING

Recent reviews of the evidence for smoking cessation indicate that the most effective interventions (as shown by randomized controlled trials) are NRTs, self-help interventions, telephone and face-to-face behavioural counselling and individual behavioural counselling. The factors that may make these approaches more effective are social support, multiple treatment sessions, tailored information and appropriately trained counsellors (West and Stapleton 2008; Shahab and McEwen 2009; Shahab and Fidler 2010). In line with attempts to change other forms of behaviour (see Chapter 8) the evidence seems to suggest the more support there is from more people over more time, the more effective the interventions are.

ALCOHOL USE

There have also been several reviews of programmes for alcohol use disorders which have covered a wide range of therapies, behaviour intervention strategies and forms of medical management. The most comprehensive of these is the Mesa Grande project (Miller and Wilbourne 2002) which was updated by Raistrick et al. in 2006. The results from these reviews indicate that the most effective psychologically-based approaches (based on trials using a control group) are brief interventions, social skills training, behaviour contracting, behavioural marital therapy, case management and the community reinforcement approach. Two medical treatments also emerged as effective (opiate antagonists and acamprosate). The methods which seemed to be least effective were those designed to educate, confront, shock or foster insight into the nature and causes of alcoholism.

STAGE 4: RELAPSE

Although many people are successful at initially stopping smoking and changing their drinking behaviour, relapse rates are high. For example, nearly half of those smokers who make a quit attempt return to smoking within the year (National Statistics 2005). Interestingly, the pattern for relapse is consistent across a number of different addictive behaviours, with high rates initially tapering off over a year. This relapse pattern is shown in Figure 4.12.

In 1985, Marlatt and Gordon developed a relapse prevention model of addictions to address the processes involved in successful and unsuccessful cessation of any given addictive behaviour. This approach challenged some of the aspects of a disease model of addictions by emphasizing how addictive behaviours could be unlearned and arguing that believing in an abstinence-only model and that 'one drink = a drunk' is a self-fulfilling prophecy. This model is described in detail in Chapter 8. The key novel component is the focus on the transition from a lapse, which entails a minor slip (e.g. a cigarette, a couple of drinks), and a relapse, which entails a return to former

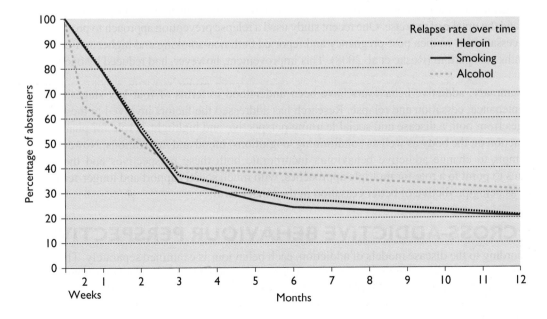

FIGURE 4.12

Relapse curves for individuals treated for heroin, smoking and alcohol addiction

behaviour (e.g. smoking 20 cigarettes, getting drunk). Marlatt and Gordon examined the processes involved in the progression from abstinence to lapse to relapse and called this the abstinence violation effect (AVE). The AVE occurs as follows:

- *Abstinence:* the individual sets abstinence as their target behaviour.
- *High-risk situation:* lowered mood, being in a drinking environment, being offered a cigarette, are all high-risk situations.
- *Coping behaviour:* if they can cope effectively, then abstinence will be maintained. If not, then the person will lapse.
- *Positive outcome expectancies:* Successful coping is helped by negative outcome expectancies (e.g. getting drunk will make me feel sick) but hindered by positive outcome expectancies (e.g. smoking will make me feel less anxious).
- *Self-efficacy:* successful coping is also helped by high levels of self-efficacy.
- *Lapse:* the initial lapse happens.
- *Full-blown relapse:* the lapse is then turned into a full-blown relapse (smoking a packet of cigarettes, getting drunk) if the following happens:
  - the lapse is attributed to the self (e.g. 'I am useless, it's my fault');
  - feeling guilt and self-blame;
  - this internal attribution lowers self-efficacy.
- *Abstinence returns:* the lapse returns to abstinence if the following happens:
  - the lapse is attributed to the external world (e.g. the situation, the presence of others);
  - guilt and self-blame are reduced;
  - self-efficacy remains high.

Relapse prevention approaches therefore focus on how individuals can help manage high-risk situations through developing effective coping strategies and using external attributions, and emphasize that although people will lapse at times, this does not inevitably have to lead to a full-blown relapse. Relapse prevention techniques are used as stand-alone interventions but also incorporated into the management of a wide range of problems, from addictive behaviours to the promotion of healthy eating and the uptake of exercise. One recent study used a relapse prevention approach to promote smoking cessation in women post-pregnancy and reported both non-smoking and higher self-efficacy six months post partum (Roske et al. 2008). This improvement, however, had reduced by one year.

In summary, addictive behaviours have been understood in terms of four key stages: initiation, maintenance, cessation and relapse. Research has addressed the factors involved in these different stages from both a disease and social learning perspective and highlights a role for pharmacological action on the body as well as conditioning, cognitions, mood and motivations. Nowadays, most attempts to change addictive behaviours incorporate both these perspectives and the evidence seems to point to a role for multiple approaches, with much social support and longer-term follow-ups as being predictive of better cessation in the longer term.

A CROSS-ADDICTIVE BEHAVIOUR PERSPECTIVE

According to the disease models of addiction, each behaviour is examined separately. Therefore an addiction to cigarettes is seen as separate and different to an addiction to alcohol as they are based upon a different substance with different effects on the body. From a social learning perspective, however, it is possible to examine similarities between behaviours and throughout this chapter many commonalities can be seen in terms of initiation, maintenance, cessation and relapse, and the role of conditioning, cognitions, mood and motivation. Furthermore, these factors are not only relevant to smoking, alcohol and caffeine use but also to other addictions such as exercise, sex, gambling and eating. Such an approach reflects a cross-addictive behaviours perspective and two models using this are now described.

EXCESSIVE APPETITES THEORY

Orford's (2002) book, *Excessive Appetites*, describes the ways in which any appetitive behaviour, such as gambling, eating, sex or exercise can become so excessive as to ruin people's lives. His complex model, called *excessive appetites theory*, was then further refined in terms of the ways in which some core addictions can emerge out of behaviours which are often ordinary and unproblematic. The following is a simplified version of his model.

- *Appetitive consumption:* appetitive behaviours are those which feel good, and Orford identifies core addictions as drinking, gambling, drug-taking, eating, exercise and sex. The model uses the term *appetitive consumption* rather than addiction.

- *Behaviour as rewarding:* all appetitive behaviours cause emotional rewards such as pleasure, fun or arousal or have positive consequences such as feeling relaxed, less stressed and more socially at ease. This reinforces the behaviour whether it be a drug-based pleasure or the consequences of a behaviour, and can engender feelings of necessity and lack of control.

- *Deterrents and restraints:* the model argues that although they are rewarding, most appetitive behaviours are limited by a set of barriers. For example, excessive alcohol use causes headaches, sickness, inability to get to work and a sense of being drunk that some people don't like. These deterrents and restraints would usually limit a behaviour. When these are reduced, however, the behaviour spills over like a river flooding its banks.

- *Methods of escalation:* Orford proposes two ways in which casual behaviour escalates into an excessive behaviour:
  - *low proportionate effect:* this reflects the notions of choice and self-control and describes how a behaviour will escalate if the incentives are perceived as great and the restraints to stop are perceived as weak;
  - *strong attachments:* the individual develops a strong attachment to the behaviour through reinforcements and this is exacerbated by increasing generalized anxiety and a reduction in the normal restrictions that limit the behaviour.

- *Social norms:* people are more likely to show excessive behaviour if their peer group also does the same. As people develop excessive behaviours, they also change peer groups to be with similar people with similar levels of behaviour.

- *AVE:* in line with relapse prevention (see p. 95) Orford argues that escalation is also exacerbated by the AVE and feelings of guilt, self-blame and internal attributions for lapses.

- *Social response to addiction:* once behaviours become excessive they have social consequences such as frustration and upset from others, breakdown of relationships, loss of employment, loss of property, loss of money (gambling) and secrecy. This gives rise to a secondary form of emotional cycles as the individual tries to compensate for these social consequences (e.g. gambling more to regain lost money; becoming more isolated and secretive to hide behaviour).

- *Conflict:* the strong attachment to the behaviour, due to high incentives and reinforcements and low deterrents and restraints in the context of the negative social response to addiction, causes conflict. This conflict may be a motivation to change. Orford calls this 'motivation for self-liberation'. It may, however, exacerbate feelings of anxiety which heighten the individual's attachment to the appetitive behaviour even more.

This model is relevant to a wide range of potential addictive behaviours whether they be drug- or behaviourally-based. It draws upon social learning perspectives on addictive behaviours with its emphasis on reinforcements, social norms, AVE and restraints, but it also allows for a disease element in terms of drug effects. The model is complex, however, and it is therefore difficult to operationalize and test. But it is hard to think of examples of addictive behaviour that cannot be accounted for by this approach.

PRIME THEORY

In 2006, West developed an alternative model of addictive behaviours that could also be applied to all drug-based and behaviourally-based addictions. This was called PRIME theory and was based upon a motivational model which could capture both conscious choice processes and non-conscious motivational systems, as well as classical and operant conditioning processes. The model is illustrated in Figure 4.13.

PRIME stands for the following aspects of the model:

P – plans (conscious mental representations of future actions plus commitment).

R – responses (starting, stopping or modifying actions)

I – impulses/inhibitory forces (can be experienced as urges)

M – motives (can be experienced as desires)

E – evaluations (evaluative beliefs)

These aspects influence addictive behaviours in the following ways. In terms of alcohol dependence, an individual who is emotionally vulnerable, who feels relief when drinking and lives within a social context where it is normal to drink heavily, will be more likely to drink to excess. Even if they do not respond well to the negative effects of alcohol, their problem will continue because, in terms of PRIME theory, this drinking behaviour will then be maintained through their impulses ('I need a drink'), emotional states ('I am anxious'), motives ('I want a drink') and evaluations ('drinking will make me feel better') which in turn make it unlikely they will make plans to change or stop their behaviour.

West's PRIME theory focuses more on the maintenance of an addictive behaviour rather than its uptake. It also highlights ways in which therapy could intervene by reducing impulses (e.g. NRT, alcohol reduction medication, methodone); changing evaluations (e.g. focusing on the negative

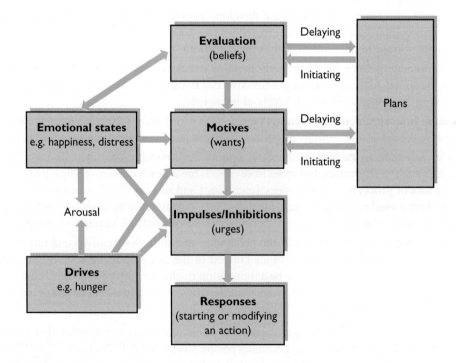

FIGURE 4.13

PRIME theory of addiction

SOURCE: Adapted from West (2006)

consequences of a behaviour); changing emotional states (e.g. cognitive behavioural therapy – CBT – relaxation, counselling) or challenging motives (e.g. reframing the craving for a drink as the need for something more healthy – exercise, social support, etc.).

Although most research focuses on specific behaviours such as smoking *or* alcohol use *or* drug-taking, there are many similarities across behaviours in terms of factors relating to initiation, maintenance, cessation and relapse. These two cross-addiction behaviour models explore some of these similarities and also highlight how individuals may show excessive behaviours for both drug-based and behaviourally-based addictions.

TO CONCLUDE

Smoking and alcohol consumption both have negative effects on health and yet are common behaviours. There are many different theories to explain why people smoke or drink and how they can be encouraged to adopt healthier behaviours. This chapter examined the different models of addiction, including the moral model, the disease models and the social learning perspective. It then examined the stages of substance use from initiation and maintenance (involving psychological factors, such as beliefs and expectancies, and social factors, such as parental and peer group behaviour), to cessation (involving clinical perspectives, self-help methods and public health interventions) or relapse. The chapter also focused on caffeine use as a case study of a commonly used drug which also serves a social function, and on the addictive potential of exercise. Finally, the chapter examined a cross-behavioural perspective with a focus on two models which highlight similarities between behaviours and the ways in which many ordinary and unproblematic behaviours can become excessive if the conditions are right.

QUESTIONS

1 Could we become addicted to anything?
2 Discuss the role of learning in the initiation and maintenance of an addictive behaviour.
3 Smoking is an addiction to nicotine. Discuss.
4 Discuss the role of health beliefs in the initiation of smoking behaviour.
5 Discuss the role of withdrawal reversal effects in the maintenance of an addictive behaviour.
6 It is the government's responsibility to prevent smoking. Discuss.
7 Lung cancer from smoking is a self-inflicted disease. Discuss.
8 To what extent are addictions governed by similar processes?
9 We have known for a half a century that smoking causes lung cancer. Why do people still continue to smoke?

FOR DISCUSSION

Have you ever tried a puff of a cigarette? If so, consider the reasons that you did or did not become a smoker. If you have never even tried a cigarette, discuss the possible reasons for this.

ASSUMPTIONS IN HEALTH PSYCHOLOGY

The research on smoking and alcohol highlights some of the assumptions in health psychology.

1 *Mind–body dualism*. Theories of addictions and addictive behaviour emphasize either the psychological or physiological processes. This separation is reflected in the differences between the disease models and the social learning perspectives. Therefore, although some of the treatment perspectives emphasize both mind (e.g. cue exposure) and body (e.g. nicotine replacement), they are still seen as distinct components of the individual.

2 *Changes in theory represent improvement*. It is often assumed that the most recent theoretical perspective is an improvement on previous theories. In terms of addictive behaviours, the moral model is seen as more naïve than the disease model, which is more naïve than a social learning theory perspective. However, perhaps these different models also illustrate different (and not necessarily better) ways of explaining behaviour and of describing the individual. Therefore, to see an individual who drinks a great deal as to blame and as being responsible for his or her behaviour (the moral model) reflects a different model of the individual than an explanation that describes a physiological predisposition (the second disease model) or learning the behaviour via reinforcement.

FURTHER READING

Heather, N. and Robertson, D. (1989) *Problem Drinking*. Oxford: Oxford University Press.
Examines the different theories of addictive behaviours and in particular outlines the contribution of social learning theory.

Marlatt, G.A. and Gordon, J.R. (1985) *Relapse Prevention*. New York: Guilford Press.
Provides a detailed analysis and background to relapse prevention and applies this approach to a variety of addictive behaviours. Chapter 1 is a particularly useful overview.

Orford, J. (2002) *Excessive Appetites: A Psychological View of Addictions*, 2nd edn. Chichester: John Wiley.
Illustrates the extent to which different addictive behaviours share common variables in both their initiation and maintenance and discusses the interrelationship between physiological and psychological factors.

West, R. (2005) Time for a change: putting the transtheoretical (stages of change) model to rest, *Addiction*, 100: 1036–9.
Presents a critique of the SOC and suggests that there are better ways of understanding addictive behaviours. It is accompanied by a series of papers which join in the debate including a response by the authors of the SOC.

West, R. (2006) *Theory of Addiction*. Oxford: Blackwell.
An interesting and comprehensive book which describes existing theories of addiction and offers a new synthetic model of addiction which combines a range of psychological processes.

West, R. and Shiffman, S. (2003) *Smoking Cessation*. Oxford: Health Press.
A very clearly written, accessible book which describes physiological and psychosocial reasons for smoking and provides an excellent account of smoking-cessation strategies.

Visit the website at www.openup.co.uk/ogden for additional resources on Chapter 4 to help you with your study, such as multiple choice questions, weblinks and a searchable online glossary.

5 Eating Behaviour

©braitvision/iStock

CHAPTER OVERVIEW

This chapter first examines what constitutes a healthy diet, the links between diet and health and who does and does not eat healthily. Three main psychological perspectives which have been used to study food intake are then described. First, the chapter describes developmental models of eating behaviour with their focus on exposure, social learning and associative learning. Second, it examines cognitive theories with their emphasis on motivation and social cognition models. Third, it explores the emphasis on weight concern and the role of body dissatisfaction and restrained eating.

WHAT IS A HEALTHY DIET?

The nature of a good diet has changed dramatically over the years. In 1824 *The Family Oracle of Good Health* published in the UK recommended that young ladies should eat the following at breakfast: 'plain biscuit (not bread), broiled beef steaks or mutton chops, under done without any fat and half a pint of bottled ale, the genuine Scots ale is the best', or if this was too strong it suggested 'one small breakfast cup . . . of good strong tea or of coffee – weak tea or coffee is always bad for the nerves as well as the complexion'. Dinner is later described as similar to breakfast with 'no vegetables, boiled meat, no made dishes being permitted much less fruit, sweet things or pastry . . . the steaks and chops must always be the chief part of your food'. Similarly in the 1840s Dr Kitchener recommended in his diet book a lunch of 'a bit of roasted poultry, a basin of good beef tea, eggs poached . . . a sandwich – stale bread – and half a pint of good home brewed beer' (cited in Burnett 1989: 69). Nowadays, there is, however, a consensus among nutritionists as to what constitutes a healthy diet (DH 1991a). Food can be considered in terms of its basic constituents: carbohydrate, protein and fat. Descriptions of healthy eating tend to describe food in terms of broader food groups and make recommendations as to the relative consumption of each of these groups. Current recommendations are as follows and illustrated in Figure 5.1.

- *Fruit and vegetables:* a wide variety of fruit and vegetables should be eaten and preferably five or more servings should be eaten per day.
- *Bread, pasta, other cereals and potatoes:* plenty of complex carbohydrate foods should be eaten, preferably those high in fibre.
- *Meat, fish and alternatives:* moderate amounts of meat, fish and alternatives should be eaten and it is recommended that the low-fat varieties are chosen.
- *Milk and dairy products:* these should be eaten in moderation and the low-fat alternatives should be chosen where possible.
- *Fatty and sugary foods:* food such as crisps, sweets and sugary drinks should be eaten infrequently and in small amounts.

Other recommendations for a healthy diet include a moderate intake of alcohol (a maximum of 3–4 units per day for men and 2–3 units per day for women), the consumption of fluoridated water where possible, a limited salt intake of 6g per day, eating unsaturated fats from olive oil and oily fish rather than saturated fats from butter and margarine, and consuming complex carbohydrates (e.g. bread and pasta) rather than simple carbohydrates (e.g. sugar). It is also recommended that men aged between 19 and 59 require 2,550 calories per day and that similarly aged women require 1,920 calories per day although this depends upon body size and degree of physical activity (DH 1995).

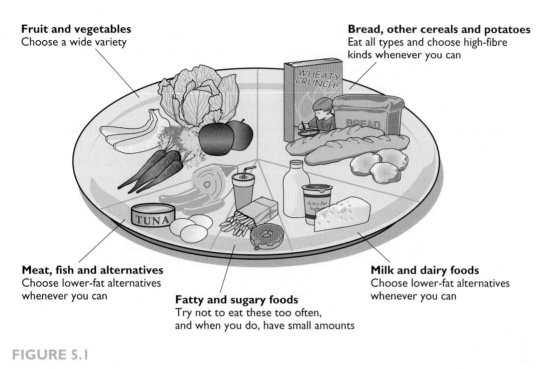

Fruit and vegetables
Choose a wide variety

Bread, other cereals and potatoes
Eat all types and choose high-fibre
kinds whenever you can

Meat, fish and alternatives
Choose lower-fat alternatives
whenever you can

Fatty and sugary foods
Try not to eat these too often,
and when you do, have small amounts

Milk and dairy foods
Choose lower-fat alternatives
whenever you can

FIGURE 5.1

The balance of good health

HOW DOES DIET AFFECT HEALTH?

Diet is linked to health in two ways: by influencing the onset of illness and as part of treatment and management once illness has been diagnosed.

DIET AND ILLNESS ONSET

Diet affects health through an individual's weight in terms of the development of eating disorders or obesity. Eating disorders are linked to physical problems such as heart irregularities, heart attacks, stunted growth, osteoporosis and reproduction. Obesity is linked to diabetes, heart disease and some forms of cancer (see Chapter 15). In addition, some research suggests a direct link between diet and illnesses such as heart disease, cancer and diabetes (see Chapters 14 and 15). Much research has addressed the role of diet in health and, although at times controversial, studies suggest that foods such as fruit and vegetables, oily fish and oat fibre can be protective while salt and saturated fats can facilitate poor health.

DIET AND TREATING ILLNESS

Diet also has a role to play in treating illness once diagnosed. Obese patients are mainly managed through dietary-based interventions (see Chapter 15). Patients diagnosed with angina, heart disease or following a heart attack are also recommended to change their lifestyle with particular emphasis on stopping smoking, increasing their physical activity and adopting a healthy diet (see Chapter 15). Dietary change is also central to the management of both type 1 and type 2 diabetes. At times this aims to produce weight loss as a 10 per cent decrease in weight has been shown to result in improved glucose metabolism (Wing et al. 1987). Dietary interventions are also used to improve the self-management of diabetes and aim to encourage diabetic patients to adhere to a more healthy diet.

WHO EATS A HEALTHY DIET?

A healthy diet therefore consists of high carbohydrate and low fat intake and links have been found between diet and both the onset of illnesses and their effective management. However, research indicates that many people across the world do not eat according to these recommendations. Research has explored the diets of children, adults and the elderly.

- *Children:* data on children's diets in the western world do not match the recommendations for a healthy diet, and children have been shown to eat too much fat and too few fruit and vegetables (USDA 1999). Therefore dietary recommendations aimed at the western world in the main emphasize a reduction in food intake and the avoidance of becoming overweight. For the majority of the developing world, however, undereating remains a problem, resulting in physical and cognitive problems and poor resistance to illness due to lowered intakes of both energy and micronutrients. The World Health Organization (WHO) indicates that 174 million children under the age of 5 in the developing world are malnourished and show low weight for age and that 230 million are stunted in their growth. Further, the WHO estimates that 54 per cent of childhood mortality is caused by malnutrition, particularly related to a deficit of protein and energy consumption. Such malnutrition is the highest in South Asia which is estimated to be five times higher than in the western hemisphere, followed by Africa, then Latin America.

- *Adults:* research has also explored the diets of young adults. One large-scale study carried out between 1989–90 and 1991–2 examined the eating behaviour of 16,000 male and female students aged between 18 and 24 from 21 European countries (Wardle et al. 1997). The results suggest that the prevalence of these fairly basic healthy eating practices was low in this large sample of young adults. In terms of gender differences, the results showed that the women in this sample reported more healthy eating practices than the men. The results also provided insights into the different dietary practices across the different European countries. Overall, there was most variability between countries in terms of eating fibre, red meat, fruit and salt. Fat consumption seemed to vary the least. Countries such

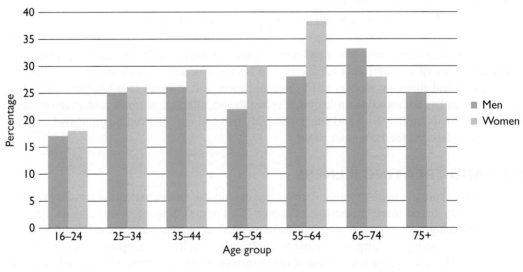

FIGURE 5.2

Daily intakes of five or more portions of fruit and vegetables by age and sex

SOURCE: Copyright © 2011, re-used with the permission of The Health and Social Care Information Centre, all rights reserved

as Sweden, Norway, The Netherlands and Denmark ate the most fibre, while Italy, Hungary, Poland and Belgium ate the least. Mediterranean countries such as Italy, Portugal and Spain ate the most fruit and England and Scotland ate the least. Further, Belgium and Portugal made least attempts to limit red meat while Greece, Austria, Norway and Iceland made more attempts. Finally, salt consumption was highest in Poland and Portugal and lowest in Sweden, Finland and Iceland.

- *The elderly:* research exploring the diets of the elderly indicates that although many younger and non-institutionalized members of this group have satisfactory diets, many elderly people, particularly the older elderly, report diets that are deficient in vitamins, too low in energy and have poor nutrient content.

In the UK a large-scale survey explored the consumption of fruit and vegetables and the types of fruit and vegetables by age, sex and social class as measured by household income. The results showed that overall the average daily intake of fruit and vegetables was higher in women, with age differences showing lower intakes in the youngest and oldest groups (see Figure 5.2). The survey also explored fruit and vegetable intake by social class as measured by household income and showed a linear relationship between income and fruit and vegetable intake, with intake being the highest in the highest income quartile and lowest in the lowest income quartile. This pattern was fairly similar for men and women (see Figure 5.3).

In addition the survey also explored the types of fruit and vegetables consumed and showed that the most common across all income groups were fresh fruit and vegetables and the least common was dried fruit. This pattern was fairly similar for men and women and by income groups, although those in the highest income quintile tended to eat more of each type of fruit and vegetable than those in the lower income quintile (see Figure 5.4 on p. 106).

Research indicates that many people do not eat according to current recommendations. Much research has explored why people eat what they do and chapter describes developmental models, cognitive models and the role of weight concern in understanding eating behaviour (see Figure 5.5 on p. 107).

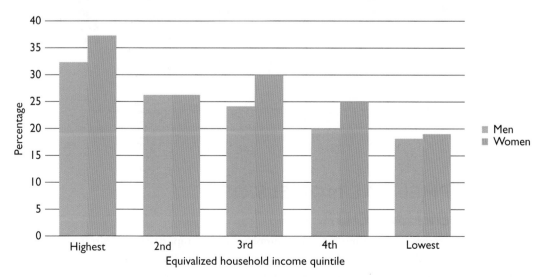

FIGURE 5.3

Daily intake of five or more portions of fruit and vegetables by sex and household income

SOURCE: Copyright © 2011, re-used with the permission of The Health and Social Care Information Centre, all rights reserved

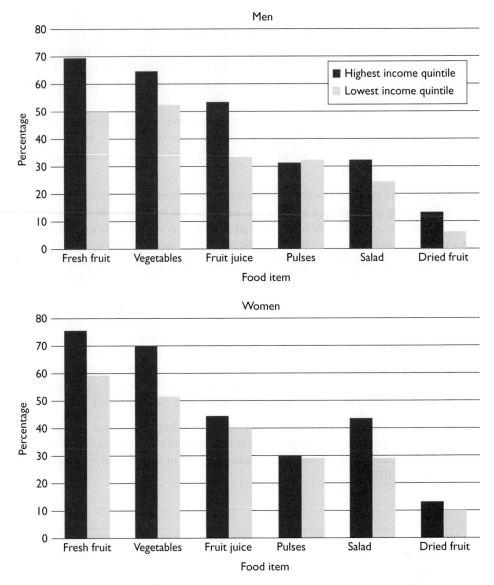

FIGURE 5.4

Consumption of different types of fruit and vegetables by income group and sex

SOURCE: Copyright © 2011, re-used with the permission of The Health and Social Care Information Centre, all rights reserved

DEVELOPMENTAL MODELS OF EATING BEHAVIOUR

A developmental approach to eating behaviour emphasizes the importance of learning and experience and focuses on the development of food preferences in childhood. An early pioneer of this research was Davis (1928), who carried out studies of infants and young children living in a paediatrics ward in the USA for several months. The work was conducted at a time when current feeding policies endorsed a very restricted feeding regime and Davis was interested to examine infants' responses to a self-selected diet. She explored whether there was an 'instinctive means of handling . . . the problem of optimal nutrition'. The children were offered a variety of 10 to 12 healthy

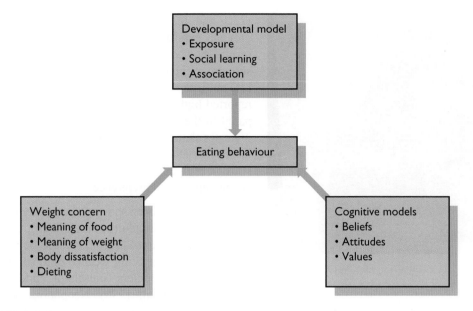

FIGURE 5.5

A developmental, cognitive and weight concern model of eating behaviour

foods prepared without sugar, salt or seasoning and were free to eat whatever they chose. Her detailed reports from this study showed that the children were able to select a diet consistent with growth and health and were free from any feeding problems. The results from this study generated a theory of 'the wisdom of the body' which emphasized the body's innate food preferences. In line with this, Davis concluded from her data that children have an innate regulatory mechanism and are able to select a healthy diet. She also, however, emphasized that they could only do so as long as healthy food was available and argued that the children's food preferences changed over time and were modified by experience. Birch (1989), who has extensively studied the developmental aspects of eating behaviour, interpreted Davis's data to suggest that what was innate was the 'ability to learn about the consequences of eating [and] to learn to associate food cues with the consequences of ingestion in order to control food intake'. Birch therefore emphasized the role of learning and described a developmental systems perspective (e.g. Birch 1999; Anzman et al. 2010; Birch and Anzman 2010). In line with this analysis, the development of food preferences can be understood in terms of exposure, social learning and associative learning.

EXPOSURE

Human beings need to consume a variety of foods in order to have a balanced diet and yet show fear and avoidance of novel foodstuffs called *neophobia*. This has been called the 'omnivore's paradox' (Rozin 1976). Young children will therefore show neophobic responses to food but must come to accept and eat foods that may originally appear as threatening. Research has shown that mere exposure to novel foods can change children's preferences. For example, Birch and Marlin (1982) gave 2-year-old children novel foods over a six-week period. One food was presented 20 times, one 10 times, one 5 times while one remained novel. The results showed a direct relationship between exposure and food preference and indicated that a minimum of about 8 to 10 exposures was necessary before preferences began to shift significantly. However, research also indicates that the impact of exposure to new foods is accumulative: if more and more new foods are added to a diet, they take less exposures before they become acceptable (Williams et al. 2008). Wardle et al. (2003) carried a trial which involved identifying a least preferred vegetable in children aged 2–6

Simple exposure can help children prefer healthy foods

years and then assigning them to one of three groups: exposure, information or control. The results showed that after 14 days those in the exposure group, involving daily exposure to the vegetable, ate more of the vegetable in a taste test and reported higher ratings of liking and ranking compared to the other two groups. Similarly, research indicates that children can identify and are willing to taste vegetables if their parents purchase them (Busick et al. 2008). Simple exposure can therefore change intake and preference.

Neophobia has been shown to be greater in males than females (both adults and children), to run in families (Hursti and Sjoden 1997), to be minimal in infants who are being weaned onto solid foods but greater in toddlers, preschool children and adults (Birch et al. 1998). Neophobia is sometimes called being a 'picky eater' or a 'fussy eater' and can be measured using a questionnaire (MacNicol et al. 2003).

One hypothesized explanation for the impact of exposure is the 'learned safety' view (Kalat and Rozin 1973) which suggests that preference increases because eating the food has not resulted in any negative consequences. This suggestion has been supported by studies that exposed children either to just the sight of food or to both the sight and taste of food. The results showed that looking at novel foods was not sufficient to increase preference and that tasting was necessary (Birch et al. 1987). It would seem, however, that these negative consequences must occur within a short period of time after tasting the food as telling children that a novel food is 'good for you' has no impact on neophobia whereas telling them that it will *taste* good does (Pliner and Loewen 1997). The exposure hypothesis is also supported by evidence indicating that neophobia reduces with age (Birch 1989).

SOCIAL LEARNING

Social learning describes the impact of observing other people's behaviour on one's own behaviour and is sometimes referred to as 'modelling' or 'observational learning'. This has been explored in terms of peers, parents and the media.

Peers

An early study explored the impact of 'social suggestion' on children's eating behaviours and arranged to have children observe a series of role models engaging in eating behaviours different to their own (Duncker 1938). The models chosen were other children, an unknown adult and a fictional hero. The results showed a greater change in the child's food preference if the model was an older child, a friend or the fictional hero. The unknown adult had no impact on food preferences. In another study, peer modelling was used to change children's preference for vegetables (Birch 1980). The target children were placed at lunch for four consecutive days next to other children who preferred a different vegetable to themselves (peas versus carrots). By the end of the study the children showed a shift in their vegetable preference which persisted at a follow-up assessment several weeks later. Similarly, Salvy et al. (2008) asked children to play a sorting task while exposed to cookies either on their own, with an unfamiliar peer or a sibling, and reported that the consumption of cookies was highest in those who sat with their sibling. Furthermore, overweight girls have been found to eat more when sitting with another overweight girl than with one of normal weight (Salvy et al. 2007). The impact of social learning has also been shown in an intervention study designed to change children's eating behaviour using video-based peer modelling (Lowe et al. 1998). This series of studies used video material of 'food dudes', who were older children enthusiastically consuming refused food, which was shown to children with a history of food refusal. The results showed that exposure to the 'food dudes' significantly changed the children's food preferences and specifically increased their consumption of fruit and vegetables. Food preferences therefore change through watching others eat.

Parents

Parental attitudes to food and eating behaviours are also central to the process of social learning. For example, research indicates that adolescents are more likely to eat breakfast if their parents do (Pearson et al. 2009) and that emotional eating is

Social eating: food preferences can change as a result of watching others eat

concordant between adolescents and their parents (Snoek et al. 2007). Klesges et al. (1991) showed that children selected different foods when they were being watched by their parents compared to when they were not, and Olivera et al. (1992) reported a correlation between mothers' and children's food intakes for most nutrients in preschool children, and suggested targeting parents to try to improve children's diets. Likewise, Contento et al. (1993) found a relationship between mothers' health motivation and the quality of children's diets, and Brown and Ogden (2004) reported consistent correlations between parents and their children in terms of snack food intake, eating motivations and body dissatisfaction. Parental behaviour and attitudes are therefore central to the process of social learning with research highlighting a positive association between parents' and children's diets.

There is, however, some evidence that mothers and children are not always in line with each other. For example, Wardle (1995) reported that mothers rated health as more important for their children than for themselves. Alderson and Ogden (1999) similarly reported that whereas mothers were more motivated by calories, cost, time and availability for themselves, they rated nutrition and long-term health as more important for their children. In addition, mothers may also differentiate between themselves and their children in their choices of food. For example, Alderson and Ogden (1999) indicated that mothers fed their children more of the less healthy dairy products, breads, cereals and potatoes and fewer of the healthy equivalents to these foods than they ate themselves. Furthermore, this differentiation was greater in dieting mothers, suggesting that mothers who restrain their own food intake may feed their children more of the foods that they are denying themselves. A relationship between maternal dieting and eating behaviour is also supported by a study of 197 families with pre-pubescent girls by Birch and Fisher (2000). This study concluded that the best predictors of the daughter's eating behaviour were the mother's level of dietary restraint and the mother's perceptions of the risk of her daughter becoming overweight. In summary, parental behaviours and attitudes may influence those of their children through the mechanisms of social learning. This association, however, may not always be straightforward with parents differentiating between themselves and their children both in terms of food-related motivations and eating behaviour.

The Media

Radnitz et al. (2009) analysed the nutritional content of food on television aimed at children under 5 and showed that unhealthy foods were given almost twice as much air time and were shown as valued significantly more than healthy foods. The role of social learning is also shown by the impact of television and food advertising. Halford et al. (2004) used an experimental design to evaluate the impact of exposure to food-related adverts. Lean, overweight and obese children were shown a series of food and non-food-related adverts and their snack food intake was then measured in a controlled environment. The results showed that overall the obese children recognized more of the food adverts than the other children and that the degree of recognition correlated with the amount of food consumed. Furthermore, all children ate more after exposure to the food adverts than the non-food adverts. Similarly, King and Hill (2008) showed children adverts for healthy or less healthy foods and measured their hunger, food choice and product recall. No effects were found for hunger or food choice but children could remember more of the less healthy than the healthy foods.

In summary, social learning factors are central to choices about food. This includes significant others in the immediate environment, particularly peers, parents and the media, which offer new information, present role models and illustrate behaviour and attitudes that can be observed and incorporated into the individual's own behavioural repertoire.

ASSOCIATIVE LEARNING

Associative learning refers to the impact of contingent factors on behaviour. At times these contingent factors can be considered reinforcers in line with operant conditioning. In terms of eating behaviour, research has explored the impact of pairing food cues with aspects of the environment. In particular, food has been paired with a reward, used as the reward and paired with physiological consequences. Research has also explored the relationship between control and food.

Rewarding Eating Behaviour

Some research has examined the effect of rewarding eating behaviour as in 'if you eat your vegetables I will be pleased with you'. For example, Birch et al. (1980) gave children food in association with positive adult attention compared with more neutral situations. This was shown to increase food preference. Similarly an intervention study using videos to change eating behaviour reported that rewarding vegetable consumption increased that behaviour (Lowe et al. 1998). Further, an intervention introduced a 'kids' choice' school lunch programme whereby children were given tokens for eating fruit or vegetables which could be later traded in for prizes. The results showed that preference and consumption increased at two weeks after the programme (Hendy et al. 2005). However, by seven months, when the programme had finished, levels had returned to baseline. One recent experimental study explored the impact of pairing images of snack foods with potential negative health consequences such as obesity or an unhealthy heart (Hollands et al. 2011; see **Focus on Research 5.1**). The results showed that not only did the pairing result in more negative implicit attitudes to the snacks but it also reduced intake in a behavioural choice task which offered snacks or fruit. Rewarding food choice can therefore encourage healthy eating either by positively reinforcing healthy foods or negatively reinforcing unhealthy ones.

Food as the Reward

Other research has explored the impact of using food as a reward. For these studies gaining access to the food is contingent upon another behaviour, as in 'if you are well behaved you can have a biscuit'. Birch et al. (1980) presented children with foods either as a reward, as a snack or in a non-social situation (the control). The results showed that food acceptance increased if the foods were presented as a reward but that the more neutral conditions had no effect. This suggests that using food as a reward increases the preference for that food.

The relationship between food and rewards, however, appears to be more complicated than this. In one study, children were offered their preferred fruit juice as a means to be allowed to play in an attractive play area (Birch et al. 1982). The results showed that using the juice as a means to get the

FOCUS ON RESEARCH 5.1: USING AVERSIVE IMAGES TO AFFECT FOOD CHOICE

Using aversive images to enhance healthy food choices: an evaluative conditioning approach (Hollands et al. 2011).

Central to a developmental model of eating behaviour is the role of conditioning on food preferences through associative learning. From this perspective we learn which foods to like or dislike by pairing them with a range of other cues or stimuli in our environment. For example, we might associate ice creams with holidays or popcorn with a trip to the cinema, and so these foods become considered 'treats' and therefore taste better. We also make negative pairings, which is why food aversions develop after an experience of food poisoning or why being made to drink warm lumpy milk at school put a generation of people off milk-drinking. This study was the first to explicitly use a conditioning paradigm to explore whether pairing images of unhealthy foods with unhealthy consequences can reduce participants' preferences for those foods. In addition the study focused on both implicit and explicit attitudes.

METHODOLOGY

Sample

A total of 134 staff and students from a London university were recruited into the study.

Design

The study used a randomized control trial and participants were randomly allocated to either the control or experimental conditions.

Intervention

Participants were asked to watch a slideshow featuring 100 images of snacks (five snack images in random order: chocolate, biscuits, cake, crisps and a range). For those in the experimental condition each snack image was followed by a one-second image of one of five aversive images relating to the unhealthy consequences of unhealthy eating (e.g. obesity in men, obesity in women, two images of arterial disease, one image of heart surgery). For those in the control condition, a blank screen was presented instead.

Measures

Measures were collected pre and post intervention. Pre-intervention involved a baseline measure of implicit attitudes using the Implicit Attitude Task (IAT) which asks participants to sort words using sort keys. For this study participants had to sort fruit words (e.g. apple, banana) and snack words (e.g. chocolate, biscuits) into two groups: pleasant (represented by rainbow, happy, smile) or unpleasant (represented by pain, death, sickness). Post-intervention, explicit attitudes were assessed using Likert scales ranging from healthy/not at all healthy; enjoyable/not at all enjoyable; unpleasant/not at all unpleasant; good/not at all good).

Behaviour

Participants were asked to make two choices of food between fruit and snack products as rewards for their participation.

RESULTS

The results showed that those in the intervention group reported more negative implicit attitudes on the IAT towards the energy-dense snacks and were more likely to choose fruit rather than snacks as their reward. There was no effect on explicit attitudes.

CONCLUSION

The study illustrates that food preferences can be learned by association and that conditioning can be used to change implicit attitudes and actual behaviour. These results have implications for understanding both the development of food preferences and eating behaviour and how these could be changed via a simple intervention.

reward reduced the preference for the juice. Similarly, Lepper et al. (1982) told children stories about children eating imaginary foods called 'hupe' and 'hule' in which the child in the story could only eat one if he or she had finished the other. The results showed that the food that was used as the reward became the most preferred one, which has been supported by similar studies (see Birch 1999). These examples are analogous to saying, 'if you eat your vegetables you can eat your pudding'. Although parents use this approach to encourage their children to eat vegetables, the evidence indicates that this may be increasing their children's preference for pudding even further as pairing two foods results in the 'reward' food being seen as more positive than the 'access' food. As concluded by Birch, 'although these practices can induce children to eat more vegetables in the short run, evidence from our research suggests that in the long run parental control attempts may have negative effects on the quality of children's diets by reducing their preferences for those foods' (1999: 10).

Not all researchers, however, agree with this conclusion. Dowey (1996) reviewed the literature examining food and rewards and argued that the conflicting evidence may relate to methodological differences between studies and that studies designed to change food preference should be conducted in real-life situations, should measure outcomes over time and not just at one time point, should involve clear instructions to the children and should measure actual food intake, not just the child's stated preference. The intervention study described earlier incorporated these methodological considerations into its design (Lowe et al. 1998) and concluded that food preferences could be improved by offering rewards for food consumption as long as the 'symbolic context' of reward delivery was positive and did not indicate that 'eating the target foods was a low value activity' (Lowe et al. 1998: 78). As long as the child cannot think that 'I am being offered a reward to eat my vegetables, therefore vegetables must be an intrinsically negative thing', then rewards may work.

Food and Control

The associations between food and rewards highlight a role for parental control over eating behaviour. Some research has addressed the impact of control as studies indicate that parents often believe that restricting access to food and forbidding children to eat food are good strategies to improve food preferences (Casey and Rozin 1989). Birch (1999) reviewed the evidence for the impact of imposing any form of parental control over food intake and argued that it is not only the use of foods as rewards that can have a negative effect on children's food preferences but also attempts to limit a child's access to foods. She concluded from her review that 'child feeding strategies that restrict children's access to snack foods actually make the restricted foods more attractive' (1999: 11). For example, when food is made freely available, children will choose more of the restricted than the unrestricted foods, particularly when the mother is not present (Fisher and Birch 1999; Fisher et al. 2000). From this perspective parental control would seem to have a detrimental impact upon a child's eating behaviour. In contrast, however, some studies suggest that parental control may actually reduce weight and improve eating behaviour. For example, Wardle et al. (2002: 453) suggested that 'lack of control of food intake [rather than higher control] might contribute to the emergence of differences in weight'. Similarly, Brown and Ogden (2004) reported that greater parental control was associated with higher intakes of healthy snack foods. Furthermore, other studies indicate that parental control may have no impact in some populations (Constanzo and Woody 1985). There are several possible explanations for these conflicting results. First, the studies have been carried out using different populations in different countries. Second, the studies have used different measures, with Birch et al. (2001) using the child feeding questionnaire which operationalizes control in terms of monitoring, restriction and pressure to eat, and Wardle et al. (2002) using the Parental Feeding Style Questionnaire (PFSQ) which operationalizes control in terms of restriction and items such as 'I control how many snacks my child should have'. Third, and related to the above, these contradictory results may reflect the contradictory nature of parental control, with parental control being a more complex construct than acknowledged by any of the existing measures. Ogden et al. (2006c) explored this third possibility and examined the effect of differentiating between 'overt control' which can be detected by the child (e.g. being firm about how much your child should eat) and 'covert control' which cannot be detected by the child (e.g. not buying unhealthy foods and bringing them into the house). The results showed that these different forms of control differently predicted snack food intake and that, while higher covert control was related to decreased intake of unhealthy snacks, higher overt control predicted an increased intake of healthy snacks. Similar results were also found in another sample of parents with small children (Brownet et al. 2008) indicating that while some forms of control may well be detrimental to a child's diet, others may be beneficial. In particular, controlling the child's environment in terms of what food is brought into the house or which cafés and restaurants they visit may encourage healthy eating without having the rebound effect of more obvious forms of control. The role of covert control is further supported by evidence that children eat according to the amount on their plate and that the best predictor of the amount consumed is the amount served, suggesting that parents can successfully control their children's diets (Mrdjenovic and Levitsky 2005).

Food and Physiological Consequences

Studies have also explored the association between food cues and physiological responses to food intake. There is a wealth of literature illustrating the acquisition of food aversions following negative gastrointestinal consequences (e.g. Garcia et al. 1974). For example, an aversion to shellfish can be triggered after one case of stomach upset following the consumption of mussels. Research has also explored pairing food cues with the sense of satiety which follows their consumption. One early study of infants showed that by about 40 days of age infants adjusted their consumption of milk depending upon the calorific density of the drink they were given (Formon 1974). Similarly, children can adjust their food intake according to the flavour of foods if certain flavours have been consistently paired with a given calorific density (Birch and Deysher 1986).

PROBLEMS WITH A DEVELOPMENTAL MODEL

A developmental approach to eating behaviour provides detailed evidence on how food preferences are learned in childhood. This perspective emphasizes the role of learning and places the individual within an environment that is rich in cues and reinforcers. Such an analysis also allows for a moderate interaction between learning and physiology. However, there are some problems with this perspective as follows.

- Much of the research carried out within this perspective has taken place within the laboratory as a means to provide a controlled environment. Although this methodology enables alternative explanations to be excluded, the extent to which the results would generalize to a more naturalistic setting remains unclear.

- A developmental model explores the meaning of food in terms of food as a reward, food as a means to gain a reward, food as status, food as pleasant and food as aversive. However, food has a much more diverse set of meanings which are not incorporated into this model. For example, food can mean power, sexuality, religion and culture.

- Once eaten, food is incorporated into the body and can change body size. This is also loaded with a complex set of meanings such as attractiveness, control, lethargy and success. A developmental model does not address the meanings of the body.

- A developmental model includes a role for cognitions because some of the meanings of food, including reward and aversion, are considered to motivate behaviour. These cognitions remain implicit, however, and are not explicitly described.

In sum, developmental models of eating behaviour highlight a central role for learning. From this perspective, eating behaviour is influenced by exposure which can reduce neophobia, social learning through the observation of important others and associative learning as food cues can be paired with aspects of the environment and the physiological consequences of eating.

COGNITIVE MODELS OF EATING BEHAVIOUR

A cognitive approach to eating behaviour focuses on an individual's cognitions and has explored the extent to which cognitions predict and explain behaviour. Most research using cognitive approach has drawn upon social cognition models. These models have been applied to eating behaviour both as a means to predict eating behaviour and as central to interventions to change eating behaviour. This chapter section focuses on research using the theory of reasoned action (TRA) and the theory of planned behaviour (TPB) as these have most commonly been applied to aspects of eating behaviour (see Chapter 3 for details).

USING THE TRA AND TPB

Some research using a social cognitive approach to eating behaviour has focused on predicting the intentions to consume specific foods. For example, research has explored the extent to which cognitions relate to the intentions to eat biscuits and wholemeal bread (Sparks et al. 1992), skimmed milk (Raats et al. 1995), organic food (Arvola et al. 2008) and fish (Verbeke and Vackier 2005). Much research suggests that behavioural intentions are not particularly good predictors of behaviour per se which has generated work exploring the intention–behaviour gap (Gollwitzer 1993; Sutton 1998a). Therefore, studies have also used the TRA and TPB to explore the cognitive predictors of actual behaviour. For example, Shepherd and Stockley (1985) used the TRA to predict fat intake and reported that attitude was a better predictor than subjective norms. Similarly, attitudes have also been found to be the best predictor of table salt use (Shepherd and Farleigh 1986), eating in fast-food restaurants (Axelson et al. 1983), the frequency of consuming low-fat milk (Shepherd 1988) and healthy eating conceptualized as high levels of fibre, fruit and vegetables and low levels of fat (Povey et al. 2000). Research has also pointed to the role of perceived behavioural control in predicting behaviour particularly in relation to weight loss (Schifter and Ajzen 1985) and healthy eating (Povey et al. 2000). In addition, studies highlight the importance of past behaviour and habit in predicting a number of different aspects of eating including seafood consumption, having breakfast and the intake of sweetened drinks (e.g. Honkanenet et al. 2005; Wong and Mullan 2009). The social norms component of these models has consistently failed to predict eating behaviour.

Research from a cognitive perspective has also developed a number of interventions to change and improve diet. For example, Jacobs et al. (2011) used the TPB and self-determination theory, Gratton et al. (2007) used the TPB together with a motivational intervention and implementation intentions, and Armitage (2007a) and Keller and Abraham (2005) used an implementation intention intervention. The results generally show that such interventions can change dietary behaviour in the short term but that these changes may not always persist in the longer term (see Chapter 8 for a description of behaviour change interventions).

PROBLEMS WITH A COGNITIVE MODEL

A cognitive model of eating behaviour highlights the role of cognitions that makes explicit the cognitions which remain only implicit within a developmental perspective. It provides a useful framework for studying these cognitions and highlights their impact upon behaviour. However, there are some problems with this approach.

- Most research carried out within a cognitive perspective uses quantitative methods and devises questionnaires based upon existing models. This approach means that the cognitions being examined are chosen by the researcher rather than offered by the person being researched. It is possible that many important cognitions are missed which are central to understanding eating behaviour.

- Although focusing on cognitions, those incorporated by the models are limited and ignore the wealth of meanings associated with food and body size.

- Research from a cognitive perspective assumes that behaviour is a consequence of rational thought and ignores the role of affect. Emotions such as fear (of weight gain, of illness), pleasure (over a success which deserves a treat) and guilt (about overeating) might contribute towards eating behaviour.

- Some cognitive models incorporate the views of others in the form of the construct 'subjective norm'. This does not adequately address the central role that others play in a behaviour as social as eating.

- At times the cognitive models appear tautological in that the independent variables do not seem conceptually separate from the dependent variables they are being used to predict. For example, is the cognition 'I am confident I can eat fruit and vegetables' really distinct from the cognition 'I intend to eat fruit and vegetables'?

- Although the cognitive models have been applied extensively to behaviour, their ability to predict actual behaviour remains poor, leaving a large amount of variance to be explained by undefined factors.

In sum, from a social cognitive perspective, eating behaviour can be understood and predicted by measuring an individual's cognitions about food. The research in this area points to a consistently important role for attitudes towards a food (e.g. 'I think eating a healthy meal is enjoyable') and a role for an individual's beliefs about behavioural control (e.g. 'How confident are you that you could eat a healthy diet?'). There is also some evidence that ambivalence may moderate the association between attitude and intention and that implementation intentions can change behaviour. However, there is no evidence for either social norms or other hypothesized variables. Such an approach ignores the role of a range of other cognitions, particularly those relating to the meaning of food and the meaning of size, and at times the associations between variables is weak, leaving much of the variance in eating behaviour unexplained.

BOX 5.1 Some Problems with . . . Eating Research

Below are some problems with research in this area that you may wish to consider.

1 Measuring behaviour is always difficult. Measuring eating behaviour is particularly difficult as it is made up of many different components, happens at many different times and in different places. Further, measuring it either by self-report, observation or in the laboratory can both be inaccurate and can actually change the ways in which people eat.

2 Much research uses healthy eating as the outcome variable by trying to predict healthy eating or promote a better diet. However, trying to define what is a healthy diet and what foods are either 'good' or 'bad' is very problematic.

3 There are very different models and theories of eating behaviour which take different perspectives and emphasize different variables. How these fit together or can be integrated is unclear.

A WEIGHT CONCERN MODEL OF EATING BEHAVIOUR
THE MEANING OF FOOD AND WEIGHT

So far this chapter has explored developmental and cognitive models of eating behaviour. Developmental models emphasize the role of learning and association and cognitive models emphasize the role of attitudes and beliefs. However, food is associated with many meanings such as a treat, a celebration, the forbidden fruit, a family get-together, being a good mother and being a good child. Furthermore, once eaten, food can change the body's weight and shape, which is also associated with meanings such as attractiveness, control and success (Ogden 2010). As a result of these meanings, many women, in particular, show weight concern in the form of body dissatisfaction, which often results in dieting.

BODY DISSATISFACTION

Body dissatisfaction comes in many forms (see Grogan 2008 for a review of the literature on body dissatisfaction). It has been described as follows.

Distorted Body Size Estimation

Some research has conceptualized body dissatisfaction in terms of a *distorted body size estimation* and a perception that the body is larger than it really is. This can be measured by asking people to adjust the distance between two light beams to match the width of different aspects of their body (Slade and Russell 1973), by asking participants to mark either ends of a life-size piece of paper (Gleghorn et al. 1987), to adjust the horizontal dimensions on either a television or video image of themselves (Freeman et al. 1984), or to change the dimensions on a distorting mirror (Brodie et al. 1989). This research has consistently shown that individuals with clinically defined eating disorders show greater perceptual distortion than non-clinical subjects. However, the research has also shown that the vast majority of women, with or without an eating disorder, think that they are fatter than they actually are.

Discrepancy between Ideal versus Perceived Reality

Some research has emphasized a discrepancy between *perceptions of reality versus those of an ideal*, without a comparison to the individual's actual size as objectively measured by the

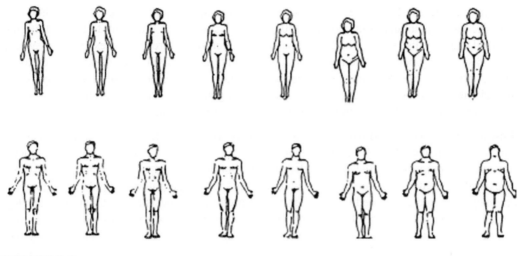

FIGURE 5.6

Measuring body dissatisfaction – which one would you prefer to be?

researcher. This research has tended to use whole-body silhouette pictures of varying sizes whereby the subject is asked to state which one is closest to how they look now and which one best illustrates how they would like to look. It has consistently been shown that most girls and women would like to be thinner than they are and most males would like to be either the same or larger (see Figure 5.6).

Negative Feelings about the Body

The final and most frequent way in which body dissatisfaction is understood is simply in terms of *negative feelings* and cognitions towards the body. This has been assessed using questionnaires such as the Body Shape Questionnaire (Cooper et al. 1987), the Body Areas Satisfaction Scale (Brown et al. 1990) and the body dissatisfaction subscale of the Eating Disorders Inventory (Garner 1991). These questionnaires ask questions such as 'Do you worry about parts of your body being too big?', 'Do you worry about your thighs spreading out when you sit down?' and 'Does being with thin women make you feel conscious of your weight?'

Body dissatisfaction can be conceptualized as either a discrepancy between individuals' perception of their body size and their real body size, a discrepancy between their perception of their actual size and their ideal size, or simply as feelings of discontent with the body's size and shape. However, whichever conceptualization is used and whichever measurement tool is chosen to operationalize body dissatisfaction, it seems clear that it is a common phenomenon and certainly not one that is limited to those few individuals with clinically defined eating disorders. So who shows body dissatisfaction?

THE PREVALENCE OF BODY DISSATISFACTION

The prevalence of body dissatisfaction has been explored in terms of a wide range of demographics including sexuality, gender, age, ethnic group and cultural differences (see Grogan 2008 for a review). This section focuses on differences between men and women.

Women

Concerns about weight and shape are conventionally associated with women. Fallon and Rozin (1985) asked 227 female students in the USA to rate their current figure and ideal figure using body silhouettes, and showed that in general women wanted to be thinner than they thought they were. Similarly, Tiggemann and Pennington (1990) asked 52 students in Australia to repeat this study and found that they also showed body dissatisfaction. Overall, research indicates that many women show a discrepancy between their real and ideal weight, have actively dieted during the past six months, participate in organized weight loss programmes, prefer to be thinner and engage in both safe and dangerous food-restriction strategies (see Grogan 2008). This research also shows that women are more likely to show these aspects of body dissatisfaction than men.

Research has also explored which parts of their body women are dissatisfied with. For example, Furnham and Greaves (1994) asked 55 British women to rate a range of body parts and reported that women were most dissatisfied with their thighs, buttocks and hips. Ogden and Taylor (2000) also examined women's dissatisfaction with body parts using computer-manipulated photographs from magazines and concluded that women would prefer their chests to be larger and their legs, stomachs, bottoms and overall body shape to be smaller. The majority of women seem to show body dissatisfaction, particularly with their stomach, hips, thighs and bottoms. They show greater dissatisfaction than men, and such gender differences are apparent in children aged 12 to 13 years (Wardle and Beales 1988) and even as young as 9 years (Hill et al. 1994).

Men

When compared to women, men's body dissatisfaction appears to be lower, but men also show body dissatisfaction. Cash et al. (1986) concluded from their survey that 34 per cent of men were dissatisfied with the way they looked and that 41 per cent were dissatisfied with their weight. Similarly, Tiggemann et al. (2008) asked 200 heterosexual men in Australia to rate multiple aspects of their bodies using an online survey. They concluded that men were primarily worried about their penis size, body weight and height and that their overall self-esteem was related to their satisfaction with their weight, muscularity, height and penis size. Ogden and Taylor (2000) used real photographs and reported that in general men would prefer their arms, chests and shoulders to be larger and their stomachs and overall body to be smaller. Overall, research indicates that some men do diet, are aware of cultural norms of male attractiveness, are concerned with physical attractiveness, upper body strength, and physical condition, and report a preferred size which is different to their perceived shape (see e.g. Grogan 2008).

Overall, research indicates that body dissatisfaction is common. In general, individuals with eating disorders show greater body dissatisfaction than those without, dieters show greater body dissatisfaction than non-dieters and women in general show greater body dissatisfaction than men, although men still show dissatisfaction with the way they look. So what causes this problem?

CAUSES OF BODY DISSATISFACTION

Much research has looked at the role of the media and the family.

The Media

The most commonly-held belief in both the lay and academic communities is that body dissatisfaction for women is a response to representations of thin women in the media. Magazines, newspapers, television, films and even novels predominantly use images of thin women. These women may be advertising body-size related items such as food and clothes or neutral items such as vacuum cleaners and wallpaper, but they are always thin. Alternatively, they may be characters in a story or simply passers-by to illustrate the real world, but this real world is always represented by thinness. Whatever their role and wherever their existence, women used by the media are generally thin, and we are therefore led to believe that thinness is not only the desired norm but also *the* norm. When, on those rare occasions, a fatter woman appears, she is usually there making a statement about being fat (fat comedians make jokes about chocolate cake and fat actresses are either evil or unhappy), not simply as a normal woman. Research has addressed whether these representations make women dissatisfied with their bodies, how the process works and whether interventions can make people less influenced by what they see in the media.

Some empirical research has directly explored the association between media presentations of women and experiences of body dissatisfaction. For example, using correlational designs research shows an association between the frequency of reading popular magazines and the importance placed on the images used in such magazines, and factors such as body dissatisfaction, drive for thinness and pathological eating (e.g. Harrison and Cantor 1997; Tiggemann and McGill 2004). Similarly, McCabe and Ricciardelli (2001) reported that greater exposure to television and magazines had a greater impact upon adolescent girls, and Field et al. (1999) concluded from their survey of young girls that the majority stated that magazine images of women influenced their idea of the perfect shape and that nearly a half wanted to lose weight because of the images they saw in magazines.

Other research has used experimental designs and has explored the impact of showing women magazine images of the 'ideal body shape'. Using this approach research suggests that acute exposure to media images for only a few minutes increases body size distortion in those with anorexia, bulimia and pregnant women compared to neutral images (Waller et al. 1992; Hamilton and Waller 1993). Such exposure can also make women report a significant increase in their body dissatisfaction (see Figure 5.7) (Ogden and Mundray 1996; Halliwell and Dittmar 2004; see Groesz et al. 2002 for a review).

Social comparison theory provides an explanation for why media images may cause body dissatisfaction (Martin and Kennedy 1993). Upward social comparisons occur when an individual compares themselves to someone perceived to be socially better than them. If a discrepancy is perceived between the individual and the comparison figure, the individual will be motivated to make personal alterations in order to progress towards the comparison standard. Models in the media signify the societal ideal, so are subsequently used as comparison figures. Upward social comparisons reveal a discrepancy between their self and the media causing a self-discrepancy, which in turn may increase body dissatisfaction (Harrison and Cantor 1997; Posavac and Posavac 2002). Not all women exposed to such media images, however, show body dissatisfaction and research also highlights *internalization* (Stice et al. 1994; Stormer and Thompson 1996). Body dissatisfaction may therefore be exacerbated by media images of the 'perfect woman' if a woman internalizes these ideals and makes favourable upward comparisons to these images. Accordingly, if internalization and upward comparisons could be prevented, might then body dissatisfaction may not transpire. Interventions have been designed for this purpose.

Body dissatisfaction is therefore common particularly among women and the media would seem to have a major role in both its development and perpetuation. Some researchers have argued that women could be taught to be more critical of the methods used by the media as a means to minimize its impact (Oliver 2001). In line with this, Stormer and Thompson (1996) developed an educational intervention concerning the methods used by the media to manipulate images, making them more 'ideal', and reported improvements in young women's body image and decreased internalization of the ideal image. Similarly, Thompson and Heinberg (1999) developed an intervention to show how images of beauty are created using techniques such as airbrushing and computer-generated images and reported decreases in weight-related anxiety. Ogden and Sherwood (2008) explored whether the impact of exposure to media images of thin or fatter women could be minimized if participants were shown the extent to which airbrushing can change how women look. Participants were therefore shown images of either thin or fatter women and then those in the intervention group were also shown an intervention based upon a website which shows how airbrushing can improve complexion, make waists narrower and breasts larger (see Figure 5.8). The results showed that in line with previous research, seeing the thin images made women more critical of their bodies. However, this effect was much reduced if they had been taught about the

Please now study the following photographs and rate on a scale of 1–10, in the boxes below, how attractive you think the person is : 1 = not at all, 10 = very attractive. Then place a tick next to the one you would most like to be

FIGURE 5.7

Acute exposure to thin images

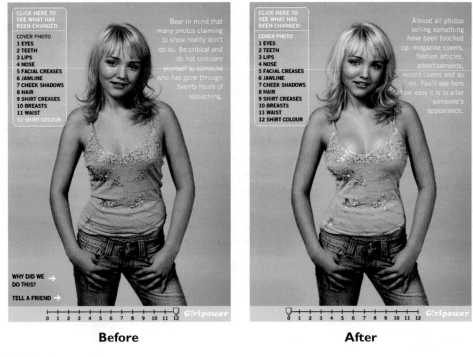

Before   **After**

FIGURE 5.8

The power of airbrushing (before and after)

SOURCE: Forsman and Bodenfors, http://demo.fb.se/e/girlpower/retouch

power of airbrushing. Therefore, although women may be influenced by the media, it would seem that they can also be taught to be more critical of the images it provides.

The Family

Research has also focused on the impact of the family on predicting body dissatisfaction in terms of associations between mothers' and daughters' body dissatisfaction and the mother–daughter relationship. Studies have highlighted a role for the mother and suggested that mothers who are dissatisfied with their own bodies communicate this to their daughters, which results in the daughters' own body dissatisfaction. For example, Hall and Brown (1982) reported that mothers of girls with anorexia show greater body dissatisfaction than mothers of non-disordered girls. Likewise, Steiger et al. (1994) found a direct correspondence between mothers' and daughters' levels of weight concern, and Hill et al. (1990) reported a link between mothers' and daughters' degree of dietary restraint. However, research examining concordance between mothers and daughters has not always produced consistent results. For example, Attie and Brooks-Gunn (1989) reported that mothers' levels of compulsive eating and body image could not predict these factors in their daughters. Likewise, Ogden and Elder (1998) reported discordance between mothers' and daughters' weight concern in both Asian and white families.

Some research has also explored the nature of the mother–daughter relationship. For example, Crisp et al. (1980) argued that undefined boundaries within the family and the existence of an enmeshed relationship between mother and daughter may be important factors. Likewise, Smith et al. (1995) suggested that a close relationship between mother and daughter may result in an enmeshed relationship and problems with separation in adolescence. Further, Minuchin et al. (1978) argued that although optimum autonomy does not mean breaking all bonds between mother and daughter, mother–daughter relationships that permit poor autonomy for both parties may be predictive of future psychopathology. Further, Bruch (1974) argued that anorexia may be a result of a child's struggle to develop her own self-identity within a mother–daughter dynamic that limits the daughter's autonomy. Some authors have also examined the relationship between autonomy, enmeshment and intimacy. For example, Smith et al. (1995) argued that an increased recognition of autonomy within the mother–daughter relationship corresponds with a decrease in enmeshment and a resulting increase in intimacy. Further, it is suggested that such intimacy may be reflected in a reduction in conflict and subsequent psychological problems (Smith et al. 1995). One study directly explored whether the mother–daughter relationship was important in terms of a 'modelling hypothesis' (i.e. the mother is body dissatisfied and therefore so is the daughter) or an 'interactive hypothesis' (i.e. it is the relationship itself between mother and daughter that is important). The study examined both the mothers' and the daughters' own levels of body dissatisfaction and the nature of the relationship between mother and daughter (Ogden and Steward 2000). The results showed no support for the modelling hypothesis but suggested that a relationship in which mothers did not believe in either their own or their daughter's autonomy and rated projection as important was more likely to result in daughters who were dissatisfied with their bodies.

Body dissatisfaction is common and may come from the media through internalization and social comparisons and the family, particularly mother–daughter relationships. The most common consequences of body dissatisfaction are dieting and an attempt to change body size through eating less.

DIETING

The weight concern of eating behaviour includes a role for body dissatisfaction as described above. Research indicates that feeling critical of how you look consistently relates to dieting which in turn influences eating behaviour. The term 'restrained eating' has become increasingly synonymous with dieting, and restraint theory was developed as a framework to explore this behaviour. Restrained eating is measured using scales such as the Restraint Scale (Heatherton et al. 1988), the restrained eating section of the Dutch Eating Behaviour Questionnaire (van Strien et al., 1986) and the dietary restraint section of the Three Factor Eating Questionnaire (Stunkard and Messick 1985). These self-report measures ask questions such as 'How often are you dieting?', 'How conscious are you of what you are eating?', 'Do you try to eat less at mealtimes than you would like to eat?', and 'Do you take your weight into account with what you eat?' Restraint theory (e.g. Herman and Mack 1975; Herman and Polivy 1984) was developed to evaluate the causes and consequences of dieting (referred to as restrained eating) and suggests that dieters show signs of both undereating and overeating.

Dieting and Undereating

Restrained eating aims to reduce food intake and several studies have found that at times this aim is successful. Thompson et al. (1988) used a preload/taste test methodology to examine restrained eaters' eating behaviour. This experimental method involves giving subjects either a high calorie preload (e.g. a high calorie milk shake, a chocolate bar) or a low calorie preload (e.g. a cracker). After eating/drinking the preload, subjects are asked to take part in a taste test. This involves asking subjects to rate a series of different foods (e.g. biscuits, snacks, ice cream) for a variety of different qualities, including saltiness, preference and sweetness. The subjects are left alone for a set amount of time to rate the foods and then the amount they have eaten is weighed (the subjects do not know that this will happen). The aim of the preload/taste test method is to measure food intake in a controlled environment (the laboratory) and to examine the effect of preloading on participants' eating behaviour. Thompson and colleagues reported that in this experimental situation the restrained eaters consumed fewer calories than the unrestrained eaters after both the low and high preloads. Some studies also show that dieters eat the same as unrestrained eaters (e.g. Sysko et al. 2007). Restrained eaters aim to eat less and are sometimes successful. At other times these attempts may be ineffective but at least they do not do harm (see Chapter 15 for a discussion of dieting and obesity management).

Dieting and Overeating

Several studies have suggested that higher levels of restrained eating are related to increased food intake. For example, the original study by Herman and Mack (1975) used a preload/taste test paradigm, and involved giving groups of dieters and non-dieters either a high calorie preload or a low calorie preload. The results are illustrated in Figure 5.9 and indicated that, whereas the non-dieters showed compensatory regulatory behaviour, and ate less at the taste test after the high calorie preload, the dieters consumed more in the taste test if they had had the high calorie preload than if they had had the low calorie preload. This has been called 'disinhibition', 'counter regulation' or 'the what the hell effect' and has been identified as characteristic of overeating in restrained eaters (Herman and Mack 1975).

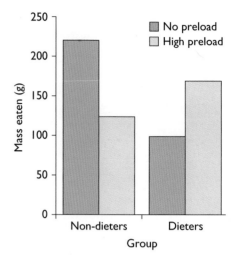

FIGURE 5.9

Overeating in dieters in the laboratory

SOURCE: Adapted from Herman and Mack (1975)

This form of disinhibition or the 'what the hell' effect illustrates overeating in response to a high calorie preload. Disinhibition in general has been defined as 'eating more as a result of the loosening of restraints in response to emotional distress, intoxication or preloading' (Herman and Polivy 1989: 342) and its definition paved the way for a wealth of research examining the role of restraint in predicting overeating behaviour.

CAUSES OF OVEREATING

Research has explored possible mechanisms for the overeating shown by restrained eaters. These are described below and include the causal model of overeating, the boundary model of overeating, cognitive shifts, mood modification, denial, overeating as relapse and the central role for control.

The Causal Analysis of Overeating

The causal analysis of eating behaviour was first described by Herman and Polivy (Herman and Mack 1975; Polivy and Herman 1983; Herman and Polivy 1988). They suggested that dieting and bingeing were causally linked and that 'restraint not only precedes overeating but contributes to it causally' (Polivy and Herman 1983). This suggests that attempting not to eat paradoxically increases the probability of overeating – the specific behaviour that dieters are attempting to avoid. The causal analysis of restraint represented a new approach to eating behaviour and the prediction that restraint actually caused overeating was an interesting reappraisal of the situation. Wardle (1980) further developed this analysis and Wardle and Beales (1988) experimentally tested the causal analysis of overeating. They randomly assigned 27 obese women to either a diet group, an exercise group or a no-treatment control group for seven weeks. At weeks four and six all subjects took part in a laboratory session designed to assess their food intake. The results showed that subjects in the diet condition ate more than both the exercise and the control group, supporting a causal link between dieting and overeating. From this analysis the overeating shown by dieters is actually caused by attempts at dieting.

The Boundary Model of Overeating

In an attempt to explain how dieting causes overeating, Herman and Polivy (1984) developed the 'boundary model', which represented an integration of physiological and cognitive perspectives on food intake. The model is illustrated in Figure 5.10.

According to the model, food intake is motivated by a physiologically determined hunger boundary and deterred by a physiologically determined satiety boundary. In addition, the boundary model suggests that the food intake of restrained eaters is regulated by a cognitively determined 'diet boundary'. It indicates that dieters attempt to replace physiological control with cognitive control

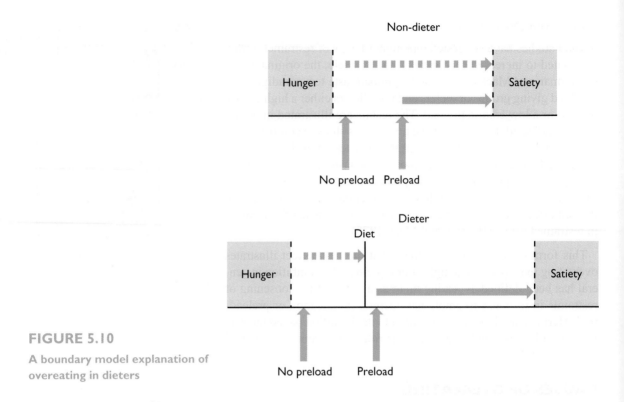

FIGURE 5.10

A boundary model explanation of
overeating in dieters

which represents 'the dieter's selected imposed quota for consumption on a given occasion'
(Herman and Polivy 1984: 149). Herman and Polivy described how, after a low calorie preload, the
dieter can maintain her diet goal for the immediate future since food intake remains within the
limits set by the 'diet boundary'. However, after the dieter has crossed the diet boundary (i.e. eaten
something 'not allowed'), they will consume food ad lib until the pressures of the satiety boundary
are activated. The boundary model proposes a form of dual regulation, with food intake limited
either by the diet boundary or the satiety boundary.

Cognitive Shifts

The overeating found in dieters has also been understood in terms of shifts in the individual's cognitive set. Primarily this has been described in terms of a breakdown in the dieter's self-control
reflecting a 'motivational collapse' and a state of giving in to the overpowering drives to eat (Polivy
and Herman 1983). Ogden and Wardle (1991) analysed the cognitive set of the disinhibited dieter
and suggested that such a collapse in self-control reflected a passive model of overeating and that
the 'what the hell' effect as described by Herman and Polivy (1984) contained elements of passiv-
ity in terms of factors such as 'giving in' and 'resignation'. In particular, interviews with restrained
and unrestrained eaters revealed that many restrained eaters reported passive cognitions after a
high calorie preload, including thoughts such as 'I'm going to give in to any urges I've got' and 'I
can't be bothered, it's too much effort to stop eating' (Ogden and Wardle 1991).

An alternative model of overeating contended that overeating reflected an active decision to
overeat, and Ogden and Wardle (1991) argued that implicit within the 'what the hell' effect was an
active reaction against the diet. This hypothesis was tested using a preload/taste test paradigm and
cognitions were assessed using rating scales, interviews and the 'Stroop task' which is a cognitive
test of selective attention. The results from two studies indicated that dieters responded to high
calorie foods with an increase in an active state of mind characterized by cognitions such as 'rebellious', 'challenging' and 'defiant' and thoughts such as 'I don't care now, I'm just going to stuff
my face' (Ogden and Wardle 1991; Ogden and Greville 1993). It was argued that, rather than

simply passively giving in to an overwhelming desire to eat, as suggested by other models, the overeater may actively *decide* to overeat as a form of rebellion against self-imposed food restrictions. This rebellious state of mind has also been described by obese binge eaters who report bingeing as 'a way to unleash resentment' (Loro and Orleans 1981).

Mood Modification

Dieters overeat in response to lowered mood and researchers have argued that disinhibitory behaviour enables the individual to mask their negative mood with the temporary heightened mood caused by eating. This has been called the 'masking hypothesis' and has been tested by empirical studies. For example, Polivy and Herman (1999) told female subjects that they had either passed or failed a cognitive task and then gave them food either *ad libitum* or in small controlled amounts. The results in part supported the masking hypothesis as the dieters who ate *ad libitum* attributed more of their distress to their eating behaviour than to the task failure. The authors argued that dieters may overeat as a way of shifting responsibility for their negative mood from uncontrollable aspects of their lives to their eating behaviour. This mood modification theory of overeating has been further supported by research indicating that dieters eat more than non-dieters when anxious, regardless of the palatability of the food (Polivy et al. 1994). Overeating is therefore functional for dieters as it masks dysphoria and this function is not influenced by the sensory aspects of eating.

The Role of Denial

Cognitive research illustrates that thought suppression and thought control can have the paradoxical effect of making the thoughts that the individual is trying to suppress more salient (Wenzlaff and Wegner 2000). This has been called the 'theory of ironic processes of mental control' (Wegner 1994). For example, in an early study participants were asked to try not to think of a white bear but to ring a bell if they did (Wegner et al. 1987). The results showed that those who were trying not to think about the bear thought about the bear more frequently than those who were told to think about it. Similar results have been found for thinking about sex (Wegner et al. 1999), thinking about mood (Wegner et al. 1993) and thinking about a stigma (Smart and Wegner 1999). A decision not to eat specific foods or to eat less is central to the dieter's cognitive set. Therefore, as soon as food is denied it simultaneously becomes forbidden which translates into eating which undermines any attempts at weight loss. Boon et al. (2002) directly applied the theory of ironic processes of thought control to dieting and overeating. They used a factorial design and a standard preload taste test paradigm. Restrained and unrestrained eaters were given a preload that they were told was either high or low in calories and then were either distracted or not distracted. Their food intake was then measured in a taste test. The results showed that the restrained eaters ate particularly more than the unrestrained eaters in the high calorie condition if they were distracted. The authors argued that this lends support to the theory of ironic processes as the restrained eaters have a limited cognitive capacity, and when this capacity is 'filled' up by the distraction their preoccupation with food can be translated into eating. In a similar vein, Soetens et al. (2006) used an experimental design to explore the impact of trying to suppress eating-related thoughts on subsequent thoughts about eating. The sample was divided into restrained and unrestrained eaters; the restrained eaters were then divided into those who were either high or low on disinhibition. The results showed that the disinhibited restrained eaters (i.e. those who try to eat less but often overeat) used more thought suppression than the other groups. The results also showed that this group had a rebound effect following the thought suppression task. This means that restrained eaters who tend to overeat try to suppress thoughts about food more often, but if they do, they think about food more often afterwards.

Overeating as a Relapse

Parallels exist between the undereating and overeating of the restrained eater and the behaviour of the relapsing smoker or alcoholic. The traditional biomedical perspective of addictive behaviours

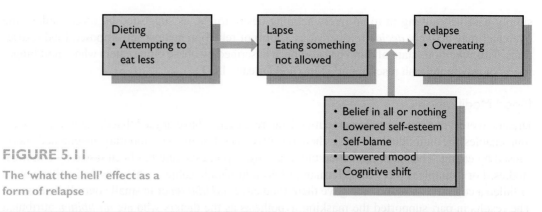

FIGURE 5.11

The 'what the hell' effect as a
form of relapse

viewed addictions as being irreversible and out of the individual's control (see Chapter 4). It has
been argued that this perspective encourages the belief that the behaviour is either 'all or nothing',
and that this belief is responsible for the high relapse rate shown by both alcoholics and smokers
(Marlatt and Gordon 1985). Thus the abstaining alcoholic believes in either total abstention or
relapse, which itself may promote the progression from lapse to full-blown relapse. In the case of
the restrained eater, it is possible that they too believe in the 'all or nothing' theory of excess which
promotes the shift from a high calorie lapse to the 'what the hell' response characterized by disinhibition. This is similar to the abstinence violation effect (AVE) (described in Chapters 4 and 8).
This transition from lapse to relapse and the associated changes in mood and cognitions is illustrated in Figure 5.11.

These parallels have been supported by research suggesting that both excessive eating and alcohol use can be triggered by high-risk situations and low mood (Brownell et al. 1986b). In addition,
the transition from lapse to relapse in both alcohol and eating behaviour has been found to be
related to the internal attributions (e.g. 'I am to blame') for the original lapse (e.g. Ogden and
Wardle 1990). In particular, researchers exploring relapses in addictive behaviours have identified
the AVE which describes the transition from a lapse (one drink) to a relapse (becoming drunk) as
involving cognitive dissonance (e.g. 'I am trying not to drink but I have just had a drink'), internal
attributions (e.g. 'It is my fault') and guilt (e.g. 'I am a useless person') (Marlatt and Gordon 1985).
These factors find reflection in the overeating shown by dieters (Ogden and Wardle 1990).

The Role of Control

Dieting is linked to overeating and many different mechanisms have been described to explain this
process. Central to these is the role of control. For example, control is challenged by a high-risk situation, undermined by lowered mood or cognitive shifts and problems with control are exacerbated by
internal attributions – a rebound effect against denial. These processes are illustrated in Figure 5.12.

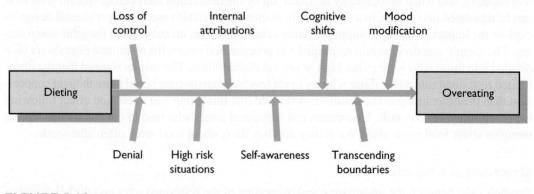

FIGURE 5.12

From dieting to overeating

Dieting and Weight Loss

Dieting is associated with periods of overeating. Research indicates that this is sometimes translated into weight fluctuations. Although dieters aim to lose weight by attempting to restrict their food intake, this aim is only sometimes achieved. Heatherton et al. (1991) reported that restrained eaters show both under- and overeating and that this behaviour results in weight fluctuations but not actual weight loss. Thus actual weight loss is limited by compensatory overeating. Heatherton et al. (1988: 20) argued that 'the restrained eater who is exclusively restrained . . . is not representative of restrained eaters in general, whereas the restrained eater who occasionally splurges is'. Ogden (1993) examined the concept of restraint as assessed by a variety of measures and found that high scorers on measures of restraint were characterized by both successful and failed restriction, suggesting that restrained eating is best characterized as an intention which is only sporadically realized. Therefore 'to diet' is probably best understood as 'attempting to lose weight but not doing so' and 'attempting to eat less which often results in eating more'.

THE ROLE OF DIETING IN MOOD AND COGNITIVE CHANGES

A classic study by Keys et al. (1950) suggested that overeating is not the only possible consequence of restricting food intake. The study involved 36 healthy non-dieting men who were conscientious objectors from the Korean War. They received a carefully controlled daily food intake of approximately half their normal intake for a period of 12 weeks, and consequently lost 25 per cent of their original body weight. Keys stated that they developed a preoccupation with food, often resulting in hoarding or stealing it. They showed an inability to concentrate and mood changes, with depression and apathy being common. At the end of the period of dieting, the men were allowed to eat freely. They often ate continuously and reported loss of control over their eating behaviour, sometimes resulting in binge eating. The authors concluded that these effects were probably due to the restriction of their diet. To examine the effects of dieting without extreme weight loss, Warren and Cooper (1988) carried out a controlled study for a two-week period and found that food restriction resulted in increased preoccupation with food. In a further study, Ogden (1995a) monitored the effects of self-imposed dieting over a six-week period and reported increased depression and preoccupation with food. These results suggest that dieting can have several negative consequences and that these changes are possibly involved in causing overeating.

FOCUS ON RESEARCH 5.2: OVEREATING AS A REBELLION

A study to examine the cognitive changes to preloading using self-report and the Stroop task (Ogden and Greville 1993).

The aim of this study was to examine changes in cognitive state in dieters and non-dieters following the consumption of a 'forbidden food'. The study used both self-report measures and the Stroop task to examine these changes. Self-report measures provide some insights into an individual's state of mind, but are open to factors such as denial and expectancy effects. The Stroop task, however, also aims to access an individual's cognitions but without these problems. The Stroop task is a useful cognitive tool which can be applied to study a range of behaviours and beliefs other than eating.

BACKGROUND

Dieters have been shown to overeat following a high calorie preload. This behaviour has been called disinhibition or the 'what the hell' effect. The boundary model of overeating suggests that the preload forces the dieters to cross their diet boundary and consequently overeat. It has been suggested that this overeating may be related to lowered mood (either as a result of the preload or independently) and/or changes in their cognitive state. This study aimed to examine shifts in cognitive state following the consumption of a 'forbidden food' using self-report measures and the Stroop task.

METHODOLOGY

Subjects

A total of 56 female subjects from a London university took part in the study and were categorized as either restrained eaters or unrestrained eaters according to their scores on the restrained eating section of the Dutch Eating Behaviour Questionnaire (van Strien et al. 1986). They ranged in age from 19 to 25 years and were of average weight.

Design

The subjects were randomly allocated to one of two conditions (low calorie preload versus high calorie preload) and completed a set of rating scales and the Stroop tasks before and after the preload.

Procedure

After completing the rating scales and the Stroop tasks, the subjects were given either a high calorie preload (a chocolate bar) or a low calorie preload (a cream cracker). Subjects then completed the ratings scales and Stroop tasks again.

Measures

The following measures were completed before and after the preload:

1 *Stroop tasks.* The original Stroop task (Stroop 1935) involved a repeated set of colour names (e.g. 'green', 'red', 'blue', 'black') written on a card in different colour inks (e.g. green, red, blue, black). Subjects were asked to name the colour of the ink (not the word itself). For example, if the word 'green' was written in blue ink, the subject should say 'blue'. The time to complete the task was recorded and it was argued that a longer time indicated greater interference of the meaning of the word. Research has used the Stroop task to examine anxiety, phobias and post-traumatic stress disorder using words such as 'fear', 'anxiety' and 'panic' instead of names of colours. Subjects are still asked to name the colour of the ink and it has been suggested that longer times infer that the words are more relevant to the individual's concerns. For example, an anxious subject would take longer to colour name anxiety-related words than a non-anxious one. The present study used an adaptation of the Stroop task to examine: (1) 'food' words; (2) 'body shape' words and words relating to the individual; and (3) cognitive state, in order to assess the effect of preloading on the subjects' processing of these words.

    • Food Stroop: the subjects were asked to colour name a set of food-related words (e.g. dinner, cake, sugar), which were compared with a set of neutral words matched for word length and frequency (e.g. record, powder, boot).

    • Body shape Stroop: the subjects colour named body shape words (e.g. chest, fat, thigh) and matched neutral words (e.g. crowd, grass, rust).

    • Cognitive state: items were included to examine two types of cognitive state, which were hypothesized to trigger overeating. These were a 'passive cognitive state' (e.g. submit, quit, abandon) representing 'giving in to the overpowering drive to eat' and an 'active cognitive state' (e.g. rebellious, defiant, challenging) representing overeating as an active decision to rebel against self-imposed restraint.

2 *Rating scales.* The subjects also completed the following set of rating scales:

- Motivational state: the subjects completed ratings of their hunger and fullness using visual analogue scales ('not at all hungry/full' to 'as hungry/full as I've ever been').

- Mood: anxiety and depression were measured using the profile of mood state checklist (McNair et al. 1971).

- Cognitive state: the active and passive cognitive states were measured using a checklist of relevant items.

RESULTS

The results for the Stroop tasks were analysed by creating a pure reaction time (experimental words – matched control words) and then by assessing the effect of condition (low preload versus high preload) on the change in the reaction time from before the preload to after the preload. The results showed that the dieters responded to the high calorie preload with increases in 'rebelliousness', as measured by the active cognitive state Stroop, increases in preoccupation with body shape and increases in the preoccupation with food, as indicated by retarded reaction times on these tasks compared with the non-dieters, and the dieters' responses to the low calorie preload. The results also suggested that the dieters showed an increase in rebelliousness as measured by the rating scales.

CONCLUSION

The results suggest that overeating in dieters in response to preloading may be related to increased feelings of rebelliousness ('what the hell, I'm going to eat whatever I want'), increased concern with body shape and increased preoccupation with food. These results indicate that diet-breaking behaviour shown by normal-weight dieters, the obese on weight-reduction programmes and bulimics may relate to an active decision to overeat and suggest that perhaps self-imposed limits ('I'm going to eat less') may activate a desire to rebel against these limits.

Restraint theory therefore suggests that:

- Dieters aim to eat less as a means to lose weight and change their body shape. At times this aim is achieved and they successfully manage to restrict their food intake. Dieters therefore sometimes show undereating. Sometimes they eat the same as non-dieters.

- Dieters, however, also show episodes of overeating, particularly in response to triggers such as high calorie preloads, anxiety or smoking abstinence.

- This overeating can be understood in terms of the transgression of boundaries, shifts in cognitive set, mood modification, a response to denial, a lapse or changes in self-control. Increasing or promoting dieting can result in an increased preoccupation with food, increased depression and, paradoxically, increased eating behaviour.

The dieter's aim to eat less and consequently to lose weight is rarely achieved and this failure may be a product of changes that occur as a direct response to imposing a cognitive structure upon eating behaviour. Dieting is also related to changes in weight in terms of weight variability, the development of eating disorders and the onset and progression of obesity (see Chapter 15 for the links between dieting and obesity).

PROBLEMS WITH A WEIGHT CONCERN MODEL

Although a weight concern model of eating and restraint theory has generated a wealth of research and provided an insight into overeating behaviour, there are several problems with this theory.

- Central to the boundary model is the traditional dualistic division between mind and body. The concept of separate biological and psychological boundaries suggests that the physical and psychological are separate entities which interact.
- Restraint theory relies on a belief in the association between food restriction and overeating. However, although dieters, bulimics and bingeing anorexics report episodes of overeating, restricting anorexics cannot be accounted for by restraint theory. If attempting not to eat results in overeating, how do anorexics manage to starve themselves?
- If attempting not to eat something results in eating it, how do vegetarians manage never to eat meat?

TO CONCLUDE

Although notions of what constitutes a healthy diet have changed over time, currently the consensus states that a healthy diet should be high in carbohydrate and low in fat. Diet is related to health in terms of promoting good health and managing illness. This chapter has explored three core approaches which have been used to understand eating behaviour. Developmental models emphasize the importance of learning by association and reward, cognitive models emphasize the role of beliefs and attitudes, and weight concern research highlights the impact of body dissatisfaction and dieting on food intake.

QUESTIONS

1 How might parents influence their children's eating behaviour?
2 How do our beliefs about food influence what we eat?
3 What are the problems with the developmental and cognitive models of eating behaviour?
4 Dieting causes overeating. Discuss.
5 How could a parent limit their child's intake of unhealthy foods without making those foods 'forbidden fruit'?
6 To what extent is our food intake governed by taste?

FOR DISCUSSION

Think of someone you know who has successfully changed their eating behaviour (e.g. become a vegetarian, eaten less, cut out chocolate). What factors contributed towards their success?

FURTHER READING

Grogan, S. (2008) *Body Image: Understanding Body Dissatisfaction in Men, Women and Children*, 2nd edn. London: Routledge.
An accessible and comprehensive book that reviews the vast literature on body image in a useful and interesting way.

Ogden, J. (2010) *The Psychology of Eating: From Healthy to Disordered Behaviour*, 2nd edn. Oxford: Blackwell.
This book provides a detailed map of research relating to eating behaviour, obesity and eating disorders and addresses questions such as 'Why do so many people not eat a healthy diet?', 'Why do women feel unhappy with their body shape?', 'What are the causes of obesity?' and 'Why do people develop eating disorders?'. It is written in a similar style to this textbook.

Rumsey, N. and Harcourt, D. (2005) *The Psychology of Appearance*. Maidenhead: Open University Press.
This is an excellent book that reviews issues of body image and appearance concerns. Some of this relates to eating and weight-related issues but it also presents research on disfigurement following injury or illness or the experiences of those born with a visible difference. It therefore takes a much broader perspective on body image than the current chapter in a clearly written way.

 Visit the website at www.openup.co.uk/ogden for additional resources on Chapter 5 to help you with your study, such as multiple choice questions, weblinks and a searchable online glossary.

6 Exercise

© Chris Schmidt/iStock

CHAPTER OVERVIEW

Over the past few decades, there has been an increasing interest in the role of exercise in promoting health. This chapter examines the development of the contemporary interest in exercise and describes definitions of exercise, physical activity and fitness. The chapter next examines who exercises and then describes the physical and psychological benefits of exercise. The predictors of uptake and maintenance of exercise are then described and finally the chapter presents interventions designed to increase exercise uptake at both an individual and social/political level.

DEVELOPING THE CONTEMPORARY CONCERN WITH EXERCISE BEHAVIOUR

Until the 1960s exercise was done by the young and talented and the emphasis was on excellence. The Olympics, Wimbledon tennis and football leagues were for those individuals who were the best at their game and who strove to win. At this time, the focus was on high levels of physical fitness for the elite. However, at the beginning of the 1960s there was a shift in perspective. The 'Sport for All' initiative developed by the Council of Europe, the creation of a Minister for Sport and the launching of the Sports Council suggested a move towards exercise for everyone. Local councils were encouraged to build swimming pools, sports centres and golf courses. Although these initiatives included everyone, however, the emphasis was still on high levels of fitness and the recommended levels of exercise were intensive. The 'no pain, no gain' philosophy abounded. More recently, however, there has been an additional shift. Exercise is no longer for the elite, nor does it have to be at intensive and often impossible levels. Government initiatives such as 'Look After Yourself', 'Feeling Great' and 'Fun Runs' encourage everyone to be involved at a manageable level. In addition, the emphasis is no longer on fitness, but on both physical and psychological health. Contemporary messages promote moderate exercise for everyone to improve general (physical and psychological) well-being. There is also an increasing recognition that exercise that can be included in a person's daily life may be the way to create maximum health benefits. The most sedentary members of the population are more likely to make and sustain smaller changes in lifestyle such as walking, cycling and stair use rather than the more dramatic changes required by the uptake of rigorous exercise programmes. Interventions are therefore designed to make people more active and do more exercise. In addition, the emphasis is now also on making people less sedentary.

WHAT IS EXERCISE?

Aspects of exercise have been defined in different ways according to intention, outcome and location.

1 *Intention.* Some researchers have differentiated between different types of behaviour in terms of the individual's intentions. For example, Caspersen et al. (1985) distinguished between physical activity and exercise. *Physical activity* has been defined as 'any bodily movement produced by skeletal muscles which results in energy expenditure'. This perspective emphasizes the physical and biological changes that happen both automatically and through intention. *Exercise* has been defined as 'planned, structured and repetitive bodily movement done to improve or maintain one or more components of physical fitness'. This perspective emphasizes the physical and biological changes that happen as a result of intentional movements.

2   *Outcome.* Distinctions have also been made in terms of the outcome of the behaviour. For example, Blair et al. (1992) differentiated between physical exercise that improves fitness and physical exercise that improves health. This distinction illustrates a shift in emphasis from intensive exercise resulting in cardiovascular fitness to moderate exercise resulting in mild changes in health status. It also illustrates a shift towards using a definition of health that includes both biological and psychological changes.

3   *Location.* Distinctions have been made in terms of location. For example, Paffenbarger and Hale (1975) differentiated between *occupational activity*, which was performed as part of an individual's daily work, and *leisure activity*, which was carried out in the individual's leisure time.

These definitions are not mutually exclusive and illustrate the different ways that exercise has been conceptualized. Most research nowadays uses the term 'exercise' to reflect discrete episodes of activity (e.g. running, going to the gym, playing sport) and 'physical activity' to describe all levels of non-sedentary behaviour.

MEASURING EXERCISE

As with all health-related behaviour, measuring exercise is not simple as all methods have their strengths and limitations. Subjective self-report measures ask people to record how much exercise they do using either retrospective questionnaires (e.g. 'over the past week', 'in an average week') or daily diaries. They ask about specific activities ('climbing stairs, walking, playing sport') or target a specific intensity of exercise ('exercise to raise your heart rate' or 'until you feel breathless'). They may also ask about the location of exercise ('at your work' or 'in your leisure time'). Such subjective measures are useful for large-scale surveys but are liable to error due to problems with recall bias, social desirability and individual variability in the interpretation of the terms (e.g. 'feeling breathless'). Other studies therefore use more objective measures of exercise such as pedometers and heart rate monitors. These produce more detailed physiological data and are good for small-scale studies. However, they are not feasible for large-scale surveys. In addition, they may well change exercise behaviour as participants are aware that they are being monitored. Finally, some studies involve laboratory measures of exercise by bringing people into the laboratory to use exercise bikes or treadmills. These obviously produce reliable objective data but cannot be used on a large scale and also have limited ecological validity as the laboratory setting is controlled but unlike real life. As an alternative solution, some studies measure sedentary behaviour as a means to measure the converse to exercise. This can be done through questions about TV viewing, computer use or car use and is very useful for larger-scale studies, particularly with children. But again, this approach is problematic because a very active person (lots of exercise in the evenings) could also be very sedentary during the day.

CURRENT RECOMMENDATIONS

Recommendations for exercise have changed over time and vary between countries depending upon how sedentary a culture is and what is deemed to be a reasonable, yet beneficial, level. It is therefore no use recommending that a sedentary population do one hour per day of heart-rate raising exercise as this will simply make people give up. However, recommending too little will have no health benefits. The current UK Department of Health (DH) recommendations (DH 2004) suggest at least five sessions of exercise a week, which reflects current healthy eating guidelines (see Chapter 5). The DH recommends:

* *Adults:* five or more days a week should include at least 30 minutes of at least moderate intensity physical activity.
* *Children:* every day should include at least 60 minutes of at least moderate intensity physical activity with at least two sessions including activities to improve bone health, muscle strength and flexibility.

Another simple target that has been used, particularly in Australia, followed on from the increased availability of pedometers and recommended 10,000 steps per day. This is a clear target, which can be clearly assessed and some evidence indicates that just wearing a pedometer and/or getting feedback from a pedometer can increase walking (Rooney et al. 2003; Stovitz et al. 2005). However, the UK National Institute for Health and Clinical Excellence (NICE) suggest that there is insufficient evidence on the effectiveness of pedometers to make any clear recommendations.

WHO EXERCISES?

The Healthy People 2000 programmes in the USA show that only 23 per cent of adults engage in light to moderate physical activity five times per week and up to a third remain completely sedentary across all industrialized countries. The results of a survey in 2003 in which men and women in the UK were asked about their exercise behaviour over the past 12 months are shown in Figure 6.1. They suggest that the five most common forms of exercise are walking (46 per cent), swimming (35 per cent), keep fit/yoga (22 per cent), cycling (19 per cent) and snooker/pool/billiards (17 per cent). Overall, 75 per cent of adults had taken part in some sport/game/physical activity in the past 12 months but men were generally more likely to have done so than women. Activity generally decreased with age.

A large survey in the UK in 2010 also asked about exercise but this time the data were explored in terms of occupational activities (i.e. sitting or standing, walking around, climbing stairs or ladders, lifting or carrying loads) or non-occupational activities (i.e. heavy housework or walking). The results for men and women for occupational activities are shown in Figure 6.2 and demonstrate that the most common activity was sitting or standing and the least common was lifting or carrying loads. The only main difference between men and women was that men spent more time carrying loads than women.

The data from this survey were also analysed to explore differences in non-occupational activities and the results are shown in Figure 6.3. This graph also looks at changes over the life span. The results show that both men and women get less active in terms of non-occupational activities as they get older and that while men are more active than women in the 16–24, 25–34 and 75+ age bands, there are only marginal sex differences in the middle age bands. It is important to note that this is

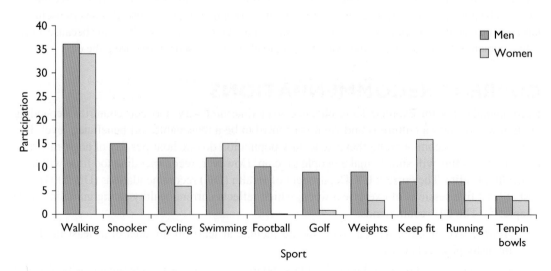

FIGURE 6.1

Participation in sport in the past 12 months (2003)

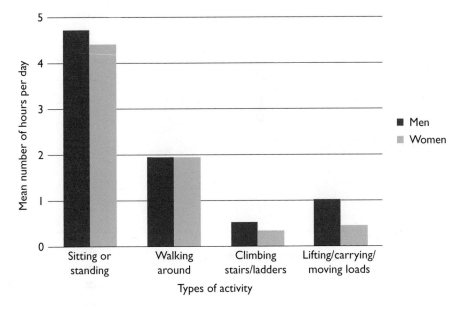

FIGURE 6.2

Occupational activities by sex

SOURCE: Copyright © 2011, re-used with the permission of The Health and Social Care Information Centre, all rights reserved

cross-sectional data and therefore age differences do not necessarily reflect changes over time but could indicate cohort effects, with those who are older now coming from a more sedentary history than those who are younger. Only longitudinal data can accurately tell us changes over time.

As noted above, current daily recommendations for physical activity in the UK are 30 minutes or more of moderate or vigorous activity on at least five days per week. Research has also explored

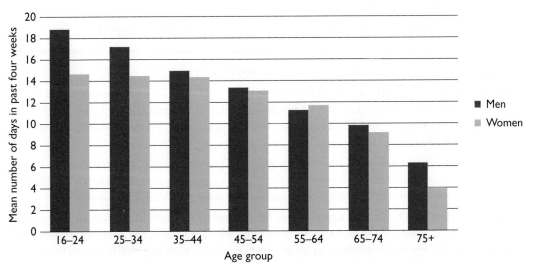

FIGURE 6.3

Non-occupational activity by sex and age

SOURCE: Copyright © 2011, re-used with the permission of The Health and Social Care Information Centre, all rights reserved

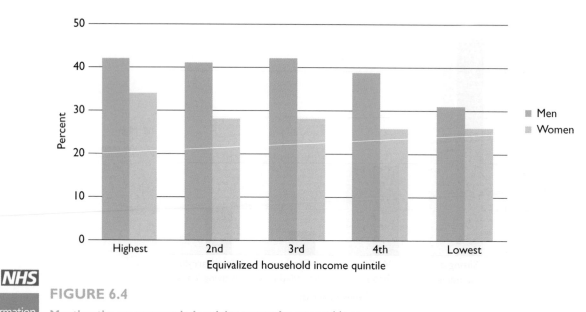

NHS

The
Information
Centre

for health and social care

FIGURE 6.4

Meeting the recommended activity target by sex and income

SOURCE: Copyright © 2011, re-used with the permission of The Health and Social Care Information Centre, all rights reserved

whether or not people reach this target. Figure 6.4 shows the data by sex and income quintile. The results show that only 40 per cent or less of the population reach this target across all income groups but that men are more likely to meet it than women and that those in the lowest income quintile are least active.

Measuring exercise or physical activity is difficult as people tend not to remember small tasks such as walking up stairs or moving around their house or workplace and it is quite possible for two people to spend the same amount of time on any given activity but for one to use up much more energy than

---

BOX 6.1 Some Problems with . . . Exercise Research

Below are some problems with research in this area that you may wish to consider.

1 Measuring exercise behaviour is difficult as some exercise takes the form of structured, organized activity such as sport, whereas some takes the form of behaviour which is integrated in a person's daily life such as walking and stair climbing. Self-report measures may be inaccurate and more objective measures (e.g. monitors) may actually change behaviour.

2 Exercise can promote both psychological (e.g. well-being) and physiological (e.g. heart rate) changes. Working out how these changes interact is complicated. Further, combining research is made difficult as some studies focus on psychological outcomes while others rely upon physiological outcomes.

3 Exercise is mostly studied as a behaviour that is under the control of the individual, that is, we explore whether a person's beliefs, emotions or motivations determine whether or not they exercise. However, it is also a behaviour that is very much determined by the environment, which may not be controllable. For example, structural factors such as safe paths, street lighting, free access to sports centres and town planning may have an enormous impact upon activity levels. Research needs to incorporate such factors into the models used.

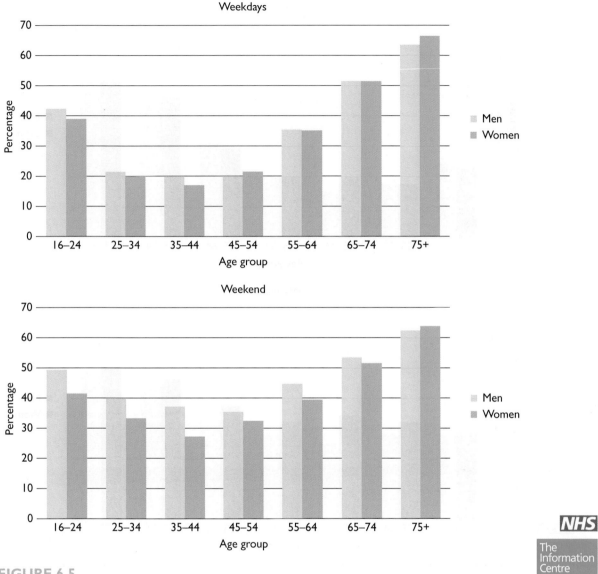

FIGURE 6.5

Being sedentary by age and sex on weekdays and at the weekend

SOURCE: Copyright © 2011, re-used with the permission of The Health and Social Care Information Centre, all rights reserved

the other. An alternative approach is is to ask people how sedentary they are and in the UK this was done in terms of watching TV and being sedentary in general. Figure 6.5 shows the data for men and women across the life span on weekdays and at weekends. The results from this analysis show a U-shaped curve with people being most sedentary in the youngest age band (16–24) and the oldest age bands (65–74, 75+). The results show only minimal sex differences for weekday activity but men tended to be more sedentary at the weekend. In terms of TV watching, these data are shown in Figure 6.6. The results show a more linear relationship between age and TV watching with men in the middle bands (35–44, 45–54, 55–64) watching more TV than women, particularly at weekends.

Overall, data seem to indicate that the majority of people do not meet the recommended targets for activity, that generally people get more sedentary and less active as they get older and that men are more active than women particularly when young, but watch more TV than women as they get older.

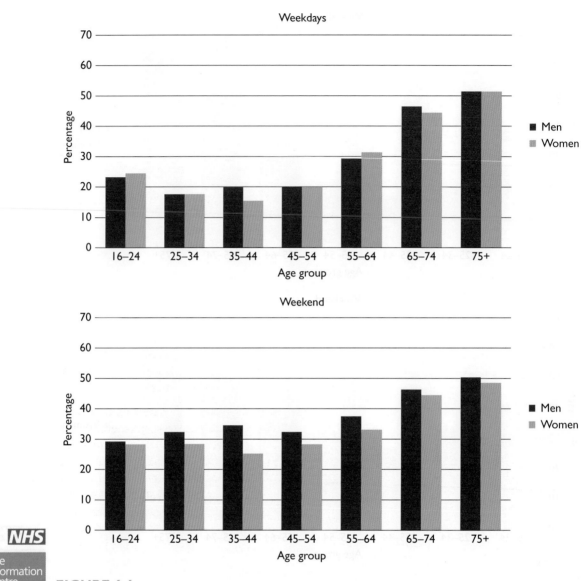

FIGURE 6.6

Watching TV on weekdays and at the weekend by age and sex

SOURCE: Copyright © 2011, re-used with the permission of The Health and Social Care Information Centre, all rights reserved

WHY EXERCISE?

Research has examined the physical and psychological benefits of exercise.

THE PHYSICAL BENEFITS

Physical activity has been shown to improve health in terms of longevity and a number of chronic illnesses, particularly through a reduction in cardiovascular disease. It also improves subjective health status and recent evidence indicates that it is an effective treatment approach for chronic fatigue syndrome (CFS).

Longevity

Paffenbarger et al. (1986) examined the relationship between weekly energy expenditure and longevity for a group of 16,936 Harvard alumni aged 35 to 70. They reported the results from a longitudinal

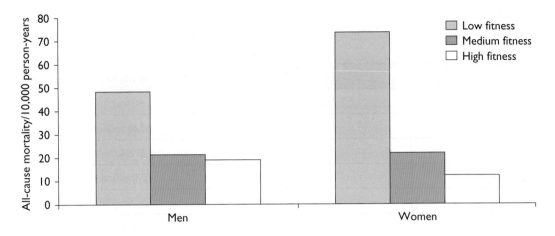

FIGURE 6.7

Mortality and fitness levels in individuals with a BMI > 25.4

SOURCE: Adapted from Blair (1993)

study which suggested that individuals with a weekly energy expenditure of more than 2,000kcal on exercise reported as walking, stair climbing and sports lived for 2.5 years longer on average than those with an energy expenditure of less than 500kcal per week on these activities.

Blair has also carried out much research in this area and has argued that increases in fitness and physical activity can result in significant reductions in the relative risk of disease and mortality (see e.g. Blair et al. 1989; 1996). Blair et al. (1989) examined the role of generalized physical fitness and health status in 10,224 men and 3,120 women for eight years and reported that physical fitness was related to a decrease in both mortality rates (all cause) and coronary heart disease (CHD). Blair has also explored the relationship between fatness and fitness and the data from one study are shown in Figure 6.7. This study indicated that overweight men and women who showed low fitness scores had a high risk of all-cause mortality. Those overweight individuals, however, who showed either medium fitness scores or high fitness scores showed a substantial reduction in this risk. Fitness was therefore protective against the effects of fatness.

Chronic Illness

In 2004 the DH completed a report exploring the evidence for physical activity as a cause or prevention for physical health problems. The conclusions are summarized in Table 6.1 and indicate that increased physical activity would seem to prevent many physical illnesses. The report also explored physical activity as a treatment for physical illness and the conclusions were less clear. It would seem that there is medium evidence for a moderate effect of physical activity for treating CHD, peripheral vascular disease, obesity/overweight and osteoarthritis and strong evidence for a strong effect for lower back pain. However there was insufficient data or only weak evidence for the remaining conditions.

Exercise may influence physical health in the following ways:

1 Increased muscular activity protects the cardiovascular system by stimulating the muscles that support the heart.

2 Increased exercise may increase the electrical activity of the heart.

3 Increased exercise may increase an individual's resistance to ventricular fibrillation.

4 Exercise may be protective against other risk factors for CHD (e.g. obesity, hypertension).

TABLE 6.1 PHYSICAL ACTIVITY AS A CAUSE OR PREVENTION OF PHYSICAL HEALTH PROBLEMS

Physical illness	Level of evidence	Impact of physical activity
CHD	High	Strong
Stroke: occlusive	High	Moderate
Stroke: haemorrhagic	Medium	Weak
Obesity/overweight	Medium	Moderate
Type 2 diabetes	High	Strong
Osteoporosis	High	Strong
Lower back pain	Medium	Weak
Colon cancer	High	Strong
Rectal cancer	Medium	No effect
Breast cancer	High	Moderate
Lung cancer	Low	Moderate
Prostate cancer	Medium	Equivocal
Endometrial	Low	Weak

Source: Department of Health (2004)

5 Exercise helps the laying down of calcium in the bones to prevent bone thinning.
6 Exercise strengthens muscles, improving body posture and thereby reducing back pain.
7 Exercise may improve immune functioning.
8 Exercise may help smoking cessation thereby reducing the risks of smoking-related diseases.

Self-Rated Health

Research has also addressed the impact of activity on subjective health. For example, Parkes (2006) carried out a large-scale longitudinal study of 314 industry employees to explore the role of both job activity and leisure activity on self-rated health (SRH) at five years follow-up. The results showed that an interaction between both job activity and leisure activity at baseline predicted follow-up SRH, indicating that the more active people were at the start of the study, the higher they rated their health at the end. Individually, however, leisure activity at baseline was only predictive of higher SRH in younger participants. In addition, active and strenuous jobs were predictive of lower SRH although the author argued that this could be due to the confounding effect of adverse work conditions.

Treatment for CFS

Exercise is used to manage obesity and in rehabilitation programmes for people with CHD (see Chapter 15). It is also used in varying degrees of intensity to help treat a number of other health problems such as back pain, injury, constipation, headaches and diabetes. One area that has received much interest over recent years is the use of exercise in the treatment of CFS. CFS is characterized by chronic disabling fatigue in the absence of any alternative diagnosis and prognosis is poor if it not treated. The preferred treatment approach by patient groups is called adaptive pacing therapy (APT) which sees CFS patients as having a finite and reduced amount of energy (an envelope) which must be carefully used. Therefore APT encourages patients to limit their activity so as not to exhaust their energy supplies, to detect early warning signs as to when they might be becoming fatigued and to plan regular rest and relaxation and limit demands placed upon them. However, current NICE guidelines recommend cognitive behavioural therapy (CBT) (see Chapter 8) and graded exercise therapy (GET), despite the fact that patient groups report that these approaches can be harmful. GET is based on the idea that people with CFS have become 'deconditioned' and intolerant to exercise and they therefore need to build up their strength and improve their energy levels through exercise. The treatment involves an identification of baseline levels and negotiated, incremental increases in activity levels, usually through walking. A recent large-scale randomized trial explored the impact of interventions based on either CBT, APT and GET compared to specialist medical care, alone or with the other treatments (White et al. 2011). The main outcome variables were fatigue and physical function and the results showed that after one year, compared to APT, both CBT and GET were associated with less fatigue and better physical function. Of the 641 patients, only 9 showed adverse reactions which were equally spread across the different groups. The authors conclude that both CBT and GET can be added to standard medical care to improve fatigue and that these treatments are both effective and safe. This provides support for a deconditioning rather than an envelope model of CFS and indicates that exercise can help reduce fatigue.

Exercise therefore influences longevity, mortality, chronic illnesses and subjective health status. It is also used as a treatment for many chronic and acute conditions and recently has been shown to be effective in the treatment of CFS.

THE PSYCHOLOGICAL BENEFITS

Research indicates that exercise may improve psychological well-being in terms of depression, positive and negative mood, responses to stress, body image and smoking withdrawal.

Depression

Research using correlational designs suggests an association between the amount of exercise carried out by an individual and their level of depression. Many of the reviews of this association have stressed the correlational nature of the research and the inherent problems in determining causality (e.g. Morgan and O'Connor 1988). However, McDonald and Hodgdon (1991) carried out a meta-analysis of both the correlational and experimental research into the association between depression and exercise and concluded that aerobic exercise was related to a decrease in depression and that this effect was greatest in those with higher levels of initial depressive symptoms. In an attempt to clarify the problem of causality, McCann and Holmes (1984) carried out an experimental study to evaluate the effect of manipulating exercise levels on depression. Forty-three female students who scored higher than the cut-off point on the Beck Depression Inventory (BDI) were randomly allocated to one of three groups: (1) aerobic exercise group (one hour of exercise, twice a week for 10 weeks); (2) placebo group (relaxation); (3) no treatment. After five weeks, the results showed a significant reduction in depressive symptomatology in the exercise group compared with the other two subject groups, supporting the relationship between exercise and depression and suggesting a causal link between these two variables, that is, increased exercise resulted in a reduction in depression. However, the authors report that subsequent exercise had no further effects.

Positive and Negative Mood

Research has also explored the impact of exercise on mood in general in terms of positive and negative mood and feelings of pleasure.

Exercise can enhance mood and create feelings of pleasure

Hall et al. (2002) used an experimental design to explore the relationship between exercise and affect with 30 volunteers rating their affective state every minute as they ran on a treadmill. The results showed improvements in affect from baseline to follow-up which supports previous research suggesting that exercise is beneficial. However, the results also showed a brief deterioration in mood mid-exercise. The authors suggest that although prolonged exercise may improve mood, this dip in mood may explain why people fail to adhere to exercise programmes. Lind et al. (2008) also explored the impact of exercise on mood but differentiated between exercise at a desired level of intensity and that which exceeded this level. In their experimental study 25 middle-aged sedentary women took part in two treadmill sessions. For one they selected the desired speed and for one the speed was raised 10 per cent above the level selected. They then rated their pleasure. The results showed that pleasure ratings were stable for the selected speed but decreased in the raised speed condition. The researchers argued that new exercisers may experience displeasure if they are pushed too far and that this might explain non-adherence to exercise regimens. Parfitt et al. (2006) also explored the impact of exercise intensity on affect but focused on levels that were either self-selected or above or below the anaerobic threshold. Twelve participants took part in the three conditions in randomized order and the results showed that affective ratings during exercise were lowest in the above anaerobic threshold compared to the self-selected or below anaerobic threshold. This again suggests that pushing people too far may be a deterrent to exercise and that self-selected levels may be the most effective way to promote continued physical activity.

Response to Stress

Exercise has been presented as a mediating factor for the stress response (see Chapters 11 and 12). Exercise may influence stress either by changing an individual's appraisal of a potentially stressful event by distraction or diversion (e.g. 'This situation could be stressful but if I exercise I will not have to think about it') or may act as a potential coping strategy to be activated once an event has been appraised as stressful (e.g. 'Although the situation is stressful, I shall now exercise to take my mind off things').

Body Image and Self-Esteem

It has also been suggested that exercise may enhance an individual's psychological well-being by improving body image and self-esteem. Many studies have been carried on the links between body image and exercise and in 2006 Hausenblas and Fallon carried out a meta-analysis of the results. They identified 121 studies using either cross-sectional designs (i.e. exercisers versus non-exercisers), experimental designs (i.e. before and after an exercise intervention compared to a control group) or cohort studies (i.e. before and after exercise). Overall, the results indicated small effect sizes indicating a moderate impact of exercise. However, exercisers had a more positive body image than non-exercisers, exercise resulted in improved body image compared to a control group and body image improved from before to after exercise. There are many possible explanations for this effect including the impact of exercise on mood (which in turn influences body image), changes in actual body shape and size and changes in energy levels (see pp. 142–3 for a discussion of exercise and fatigue).

Smoking Withdrawal

Many people experience withdrawal symptoms such as agitation, irritability and restlessness when they have stopped smoking, even for just a few hours. Some research has explored the effectiveness of exercise at reducing withdrawal symptoms following smoking cessation. For example, Ussher et al. (2001) explored the impact of a 10-minute period of exercise of moderate intensity on withdrawal symptoms caused by an overnight period of smoking cessation. The results showed that those who had exercised reported a significant reduction in withdrawal symptoms while exercising which lasted up to 15 minutes post-exercise. In a similar vein, Daniel et al. (2006) examined the impact of either light intensity or moderate intensity exercise and reported that only moderate intensity exercise reduced withdrawal symptoms. As a means to explore why exercise might have this effect, the researchers compared exercise with a cognitive distraction task to see whether the benefits of exercise were due to exercise per se or just the process of doing something to take one's mind off smoking. The results showed that exercise was still more effective when compared to the distraction task. In addition, this effect was not just due to the impact of exercise on mood.

The DH (2004) carried out a review of the impact of physical activity on both the prevention and treatment of psychological problems. This report concluded that generally there was only weak or insufficient data for physical activity as a cause/prevention for psychological problems such as clinical depression, mental well-being or social well-being. The report also indicated that there was medium level of evidence for a moderate impact of physical activity as a treatment for clinical depression and mental well-being in general.

FOCUS ON RESEARCH 6.1: EXERCISE AND MOOD

A study to examine the effects of exercise on mood (Steptoe et al. 1993).

This study examined the relationship between exercise and mood. Many studies in this area are cross-sectional or longitudinal in their design. Because of the experimental design, the results allow some conclusions to be made about the direction of causality.

BACKGROUND

Exercise is believed to be important for a healthy life. However, as with many health-related behaviours, adherence to health promotion recommendations may be more motivated by short-term immediate effects (e.g. feeling good) than the potential changes in the long term (e.g. living longer). Therefore, understanding the immediate effects of exercise on mood has obvious implications for encouraging individuals to take regular exercise. Steptoe et al. (1993) examined changes in mood, mental vigour and exhilaration in sportsmen and inactive men following maximal, moderate and minimal exercise.

METHODOLOGY

Subjects

The subjects were 36 male amateur athletes who were regularly involved in a variety of sports and exercised for more than 30 minutes at least three times per week, and 36 inactive men who exercised for less than 30 minutes per week.

Design

All subjects took part in two exercise sessions and completed measures of mood before and after each exercise session. This study was therefore experimental in design and involved repeated measures.

Procedure

At session 1, all subjects completed a set of profile questionnaires (background physical and psychological measures) and took part in a maximal exercise session on a cycle ergonometer. Maximal exercise was determined by oxygen uptake. At session 2, subjects were randomly allocated to 20 minutes of either maximal, moderate or minimal exercise. All subjects completed ratings of mood before exercise, 2 minutes after exercise and after 30 minutes of recovery.

Measures

The subjects rated items relating to tension/anxiety, mental vigour, depression/dejection, exhilaration and perceived exertion before and after each exercise session. In addition, all subjects completed measures of (1) personality and (2) trait anxiety once only at the beginning of the first session.

RESULTS

The results were analysed to examine the effect of the differing degrees of exercise on changes in mood in the sportsmen and the inactive men. The results showed that only the sportsmen reported decreases in tension/anxiety after the maximal exercise. However, *all* subjects reported increased exhilaration and increased mental vigour 2 minutes after both the maximal and moderate exercise compared with the minimal condition, and in addition the increase in exhilaration was maintained after the 30 minutes of recovery.

CONCLUSION

The authors concluded that both maximal and moderate exercise results in beneficial changes in both mental vigour and exhilaration in both sportsmen and inactive men and suggest that 'exercise leads to positive mood changes even among people who are unaccustomed to physical exertion'. They also suggest that greater attention to the immediate effects of exercise may improve adherence to exercise programmes.

WHAT FACTORS PREDICT EXERCISE?

Because of the potential benefits of exercise, research has evaluated which factors are related to exercise behaviour. The determinants of exercise can be categorized as demographic, social, cognitive and emotional (see Figure 6.8).

DEMOGRAPHIC DETERMINANTS

Dishman (1982) reported that non-modifiable factors such as age, education, smoking, ease of access to facilities, body fat/weight and self-motivation were good predictors of exercise. The results of a prospective study indicated that the best predictors of exercise behaviour were low body fat, low weight and high self-motivation (Dishman and Gettman 1980). King et al. (1992) evaluated the factors predicting being active in leisure time. They described the profile of an active individual as younger, better educated, more affluent and more likely to be male. However, it is possible that other individuals (less affluent/less educated) may be more active at work. Research has also examined ethnic differences in predicting exercise behaviour. Several studies indicate that blacks are less active than whites, that black women are especially less active and that these differences persist even when income and education are controlled (e.g. Shea et al. 1992).

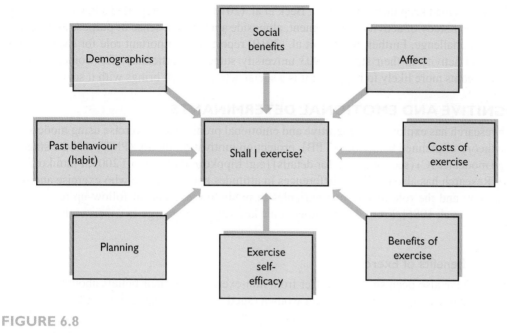

FIGURE 6.8
Predictors of exercise

SOCIAL DETERMINANTS

Research examining the predictors of exercise behaviour consistently suggests that the main factors motivating exercise are the beliefs that it is enjoyable and provides social contact. In a cross-sectional study examining the differences in attitude between joggers and non-joggers, the non-joggers reported beliefs that exercise required too much discipline, too much time, that they did not believe in the positive effects of jogging and a lower belief that significant others valued regular jogging (Riddle 1980). Similarly, Hardy and Grogan (2009) carried out a qualitative study to explore the reasons for exercising in older adults (aged 52–87) and concluded that although they exercised to prevent a decline in their health status, other key factors included the role of other

Social contact and fun encourage exercise

people who helped keep them motivated. Beck et al. (2010) likewise reported a key role for social factors in their study of activity in retirement, alongside a need for a sense of purpose and a source of personal challenge. Further, Molloy et al. (2010) reported an important role for social support for physical activity in their study of 903 university students, particularly for women. Exercise therefore seems more likely to happen if it is a social activity which brings with it social benefits.

COGNITIVE AND EMOTIONAL DETERMINANTS

Much research has explored the cognitive and emotional predictors of exercise using models such as the theory of planned behaviour (TPB), protection motivation theory (PMT) and the stages of change model (SOC) (see Chapter 3 for details) (e.g. Lippke and Plotnikoff 2009; Plotnikoff et al. 2009). Research has also explored differences in attitudes between those who exercise and those who do not, and the role of baseline variables in predicting exercise at follow-up (e.g. Riddle, 1980; Sallis et al. 1986). From these studies some key variables emerge as consistently predictive of exercise.

Costs and Benefits of Exercise

Exercisers have also been shown to differ from non-exercisers in their beliefs about the benefits of exercise. For example, a study of older women (aged 60–89) indicated that exercisers reported a higher rating for the health value of exercise, reported greater enjoyment of exercise, rated their discomfort from exercise as lower and perceived exercise programmes to be more easily available than non-exercisers (Paxton et al. 1997). Hausenblas et al. (2001) argued that it is not only the benefits of exercise that promote the activity but also the barriers to exercise that prevent uptake. They developed a questionnaire entitled the Temptation to Not Exercise Scale which measured two forms of barrier: 'affect' and 'competing demands'. Subjects are asked to rate a series of answers following the statement 'Please indicate how tempted you are not to exercise in the following situations . . .'. The answers include 'when I am angry' and 'when I am satisfied' to reflect 'affect', and 'when I feel lazy' and 'when I am busy' to reflect competing interests. The authors argue that such temptations are central to understanding exercise uptake and should be used alongside the SOC. Using a stages of change framework, Marcus et al. (1992) examined the relationship between the pros and cons of exercise and stage of change in 778 men and women. The pros and cons of exercise and decisional balance (pros versus cons) were related to exercise adoption and higher ratings of pros were found in those individuals closer to the maintenance stage of behaviour. This suggests that encouraging individuals to focus on the pros of exercise may increase the transition from thinking about exercising to actually doing it. Cropley et al. (2003) used a reasoning task to assess beliefs about the pros and cons of exercise and asked people to list 'as many advantages/disadvantages of taking part in exercise' as they could. They then explored how accessible these beliefs were by timing how long it took for people to think of their first pro or con and then assessed how many pros and cons could be generated in 60 seconds. Participants were then divided according to whether they were pre-contemplators or maintainers. The results showed that pre-contemplators could think of more cons than pros and that maintainers could think of more pros than cons. In addition, the pre-contemplators were quicker to think of their first pro reason. The authors concluded that while maintainers can think of lots of benefits of exercise, the pre-contemplators may not exercise because they can't think of any reason to do so.

Self-Efficacy

Exercise self-efficacy consistently emerges as a good predictor of exercise. For example, in an early study, Sallis et al. (1986) indicated that exercise self-efficacy, attitudes to exercise and health knowledge were the best predictors of initiation and maintenance of vigorous/moderate exercise for one year. Jonas et al. (1993) followed up 100 men and women and reported the best predictors of intentions to participate in exercise programmes and actual participation were attitudes to continued participation, perceived social norms and perceived behavioural control (similar to self-efficacy). Similarly, Sniehotta et al. (2005) used a longitudinal design to explore physical activity in 307 cardiac rehabilitation patients and concluded that self-efficacy was an important mediator between intentions to exercise and actual exercise at four months follow-up. Further, Lippke and Plotnikoff (2009) and Plotnikoff et al. (2009) concluded that self-efficacy was a key predictor in their longitudinal study of Canadian adults.

Past Behaviour and Habit

Much exercise is habitual and Norman and Smith (1995) found that, although most of the TPB variables were related to exercise, the best predictor of future behaviour was past behaviour. Similarly, Brickell et al. (2006) used a TPB framework to explore past behaviour and spontaneous implementation intentions to predict physical activity over a three-week period. The results showed that past behaviour predicted future behaviour. However, this was reduced if participants generated implementation intentions in the interim. Further, implementation intentions only predicted future behaviour in those who showed low levels of activity in the past. Therefore, past behaviour predicts future behaviour (i.e. we are creatures of habit), but implementation intentions can help break this pattern in those who haven't done much exercise before. This links in with research on planning.

Planning

In line with much research on bridging the intention–behaviour gap (see Chapter 3), research has addressed the role of planning and implementation intentions in predicting and promoting exercise and consistently shows that both spontaneous (i.e. made by the participant unprompted) and researcher-prompted plans to do exercise (e.g. 'I will walk up the stairs at work tomorrow') are good predictors of physical activity (Sniehotta et al. 2005; Scholz et al. 2008; Molloy et al. 2010).

Value on Health

Although many individuals exercise for reasons other than health, a MORI poll in 1984 suggested that the second main correlate of exercising is a belief that health and fitness are important (MORI 1984). In support of this is the aforementioned study by Riddle (1980) in which non-joggers reported a lower value on good health than joggers.

Affect

Many theories of health behaviours, including physical activity, have been criticized for focusing on cognitions and ignoring emotion. One version of emotion that has been studied is the construct 'affective judgement' which relates to feelings such as pleasure, enjoyment or feeling happy. Rhodes et al. (2009) carried out a review and meta-analysis and concluded that 83 out of the 85 correlational studies reviewed showed a significant relationship between affective judgements and physical activity that was consistent regardless of sample, measures used or the quality of the study.

The relationship between cognitions and physical activity is not always consistent, however. For example, Hardeman et al. (2011) carried out a study in primary care of 252 sedentary adults at risk of type 2 diabetes and reported that TPB variables failed to predict either absolute brisk walking or an increase in brisk walking by 12 months follow-up. Similarly, Scott et al. (2007) explored the role of TPB variables in predicting walking while wearing a pedometer and concluded that although the variables predicted intentions to walk, they did not predict actual walking as measured by the pedometer.

The use of TPB to predict exercise is discussed further in **Focus on Research 6.2.**

FOCUS ON RESEARCH 6.2: PREDICTING EXERCISE

A study using the TPB to predict exercise (Armitage 2005).

This study used a prospective design to explore the role of TPB variables in predicting actual participation in physical activity over a 12-week period. This is an interesting study as it tracks behaviour change over time and uses an objective measure of actual behaviour as its outcome variable.

BACKGROUND

Research shows that, although exercise is linked with improved psychological and physical health, many people remain inactive. Furthermore, although some people may start an exercise routine, maintenance of this routine remains poor. The present study focused on the development of exercise habits over a 12-week period and explored whether the TPB variables predicted behavioural intentions and actual behaviour and also assessed the time at which habits were established and when relapse rates started to diminish.

METHODOLOGY

Design

The study used a prospective design with measures taken at baseline and after 12 weeks. Behaviour was measured objectively throughout the study.

Sample

Ninety-four participants were recruited through a private gym in the south of England. They were aged between 16 and 65, split in terms of men and women and had never attended this particular gym before the onset of the study.

Measures

At baseline all participants completed measures of the following variables: attitudes, subjective norm, perceived behavioural control, behavioural intentions. These were all assessed using seven-point Likert scales. Self-reported behaviour was measured using the question 'How often have you participated in regular physical activity in the last three months?' Actual attendance at the gym was monitored on a weekly basis by using the computer records of membership swipe cards.

Data Analysis

The data were analysed in the following ways:

- *The role of TPB variable in predicting behaviour.* Because of the repeated measures nature of the data (i.e. baseline and follow-up and all the intervening assessments of actual behaviour), the data were analysed using repeatable events survival analysis. This enabled the results to be analysed to assess the role of the TPB variables in predicting lapses in exercise behaviour.
- *The development of habits.* The results were also analysed to explore the impact of past behaviour on future behaviour as a means to assess the development of habits. This was done using Helmert contrasts and repeated measures analysis. This enabled the association between past behaviour and actual behaviour to be determined and an assessment of when past behaviour stopped influencing future behaviour. This second form of analysis was done so that the formation of habits could be assessed in terms of when the habit was created and when the habit was stopped.

RESULTS

The results showed that baseline levels of perceived behavioural control predicted both behavioural intentions and actual behaviour. The results also showed that stable exercise habits developed in the first five weeks of the study. This meant that those who had not developed these habits tended to stop exercising by this time point, whereas those who had developed these habits were very unlikely to stop exercising by the end of the 12-week period. Further, the results showed that successful exercising behaviour in the past enhanced participants' perceptions of behavioural control.

CONCLUSION

The author concludes that the perceived behavioural control component of the TPB predicts exercise behaviour in the longer term. Further, the results show that once exercise habits have been established (i.e. past behaviour reliably predicts actual present behaviour), then they are less likely to extinguish and that the establishment of habits enhances perceptions of control over behaviour.

IMPROVING EXERCISE BEHAVIOUR

Given the physical and psychological benefits of exercise and based upon our understanding of the predictors of exercise uptake and maintenance, research has also addressed ways in which people can be encouraged to exercise more. This has involved social and political changes and the use of behavioural strategies to encourage exercise.

SOCIAL AND POLITICAL FACTORS

An increased reliance on technology and reduced daily activity in paid and domestic work has resulted in an increase in the number of people having relatively sedentary lifestyles (see Figures 6.5 and 6.6 above). In addition, a shift towards a belief that exercise is good for an individual's well-being and is relevant for everyone has set the scene for social and political changes in terms of emphasizing exercise. Since the late 1960s many government initiatives have aimed to promote sport and exercise including:

- Initiatives such as 'Sport for All', 'fun runs' and targets for council facilities, such as swimming pools and sports centres.
- Rethinking town planning to make walking easier and the introduction of street lighting and cycle paths.
- Charging more for car use in residential areas and encouraging the use of public transport, cycling or walking.
- Limiting the use of lifts or escalators to those who cannot use the stairs.
- Some cities now have bikes available that can be hired and used as and when they are needed.

Some of these approaches encourage exercise through the use of sports facilities. Many, however, attempt to make small changes to people's daily lives that can be sustainable such as walking or changing a person's usual mode of transport. Evidence for the effectiveness of these approaches is still forthcoming but any effort to make people less sedentary and more active in their daily lives would predictably be of benefit.

EXERCISE PRESCRIPTION SCHEMES

One recent approach to increasing exercise uptake is the exercise prescription scheme whereby GPs refer targeted patients for exercise. This could take the form of vouchers for free access to the local leisure centre, an exercise routine with a health and fitness adviser or recommendations from a health and fitness adviser to follow a home-based exercise programme, such as walking.

STAIR CLIMBING

An alternative and simpler approach involves the promotion of stair rather than escalator or lift use. Interventions to promote stair use are cheap and can target a large population. In addition, they can target the most sedentary members of the population who are least likely to adopt more structured forms of exercise. This is in line with calls to promote changes in exercise behaviour which can be incorporated into everyday life (Dunn et al. 1998). Research also indicates that stair climbing can lead to weight loss, improved fitness and energy expenditure and reduced risk of osteoporosis in women (e.g. Boreham et al. 2000). Some research has therefore attempted to increase stair use. For example, motivational posters between stairs and escalators or lifts have been shown to increase stair walking (e.g. Andersen et al. 1998; Kerr et al. 2001). In a more detailed study, Kerr et al. (2001) explored what characteristics of poster prompts were most effective and whether this varied according to message, gender and setting. The results showed that larger posters were more effective at promoting stair use, that effectiveness was not related overall to whether the message emphasized time and health (i.e. 'stay healthy, save time, use the stairs') or just health (i.e. 'stay healthy, use the stairs'), but that whereas the message including time was more effective for women in a train station, it was more effective for men when presented at a shopping centre.

BEHAVIOURAL STRATEGIES

Many behavioural strategies are available for the promotion of exercise in both healthy and unhealthy populations (see Chapter 8). These include those derived from learning theory (e.g. modelling, reinforcement, incentives) and social cognition theory (e.g. planning, implementation intentions) and have taken place in the community, via the mass media (e.g. advertising campaigns, TV, billboards) or using new technologies (e.g. texts, email). Most interventions utilize a number of different approaches and over the past few years there have been a series of key systematic reviews of the evidence for promoting exercise (Dishman et al. 1998; Marcus et al. 1998; Tudor-Locke et al. 2001; Rubak et al. 2005; Eakin et al. 2007). These highlight several factors as effective in promoting exercise as follows.

Social Support

Research indicates that local support groups, 'buddy' systems, walking groups and exercise contracts can promote exercise (Kahn et al. 2002).

Learning and Social Cognition Strategies

Planning, goal-setting, self-reward schemes, relapse prevention and tailoring interventions to the need of the individual can be effective approaches (Sniehotta et al. 2006; Conner et al. 2010).

Self-Monitoring

The use of pedometers is a simple and easy to use form of self-monitoring and may promote exercise. As noted earlier, Australia encourages a 10,000 steps a day target, but although evidence shows that wearing a pedometer can increase walking (Rooney et al. 2003), it has been argued that this is too low for children and too high for sedentary adults (Tudor-Locke et al. 2001).

School-based Interventions

Evidence shows that simply increasing time spent on physical exercise at school can increase activity without damaging academic achievement. However, whether or not this influences activity outside school remains unclear (Kahn et al. 2002). In addition, changing the structure of school playgrounds and the introduction of extra equipment can also increase activity (Stratton et al. 2008).

Work-based Interventions

Work-based interventions are a useful way to target large numbers of the population, improve the well-being of a workforce and promote social support. However, although those involved report improvements in absenteeism and productivity, reviews indicate no significant improvements in fitness or physical activity (Dishman et al. 1998; Engbers et al. 2005).

Mass Media Campaigns

Social marketing approaches have been used to change exercise behaviour via TV, billboards and magazines. Reviews show that although people can recall the messages, they have little impact on actual behaviour (Finlay and Faulkner 2005; Marcus et al. 2009).

New Technologies

Mobile phones, laptops, smartphones and the internet all provide new opportunities to prompt healthier behaviour. Although evidence in this area is still in its infancy there is some promising evidence that this approach might be effective for encouraging activity both through texts, websites and telephoning (Eakin et al. 2007; Vandelanotte et al. 2007; Sirriyeh Lawton and Ward 2010).

EXERCISE ADHERENCE AND RELAPSE

Research has examined which variables predict relapse and drop-out rates from exercise programmes. Dishman et al. (1985) examined factors that predicted relapse rates and indicated that relapse was highest among blue-collar workers, smokers and those who believe that exercise is an effort, and lowest in those who report a history of past participation, those with high self-motivation, those who have the support of a spouse, those who report having the available time, those who have access to exercise facilities, and those who report a belief in the value of good health. Further, using a SOC approach, Ingledew et al. (1998) explored which factors were important for the transition between the earlier stages of adoption and the later stages of continued behaviour and concluded that continued exercise was predicted by intrinsic motives, specifically enjoyment. These factors are very similar to those that relate to both the initiation and maintenance of exercise behaviour and also highlight those which could be targeted by interventions.

TO CONCLUDE

As we become an increasingly sedentary society, there has been an increased emphasis on understanding and promoting exercise. This chapter has covered the benefits of exercise, the predictors of exercise and the ways in which people can be encouraged to become more active. Overall, research indicates that increased physical activity prevents illnesses such as cardiovascular disease, obesity and osteoporosis and causes positive changes in well-being and mood. Exercise is also a useful treatment approach for many psychological and physical health problems. There are many predictors of the uptake of exercise but most important seem to be perceptions of social benefits, minimal costs, expected effects on mood and well-being and high self-efficacy. A similar pattern of factors can also be seen for interventions to improve exercise. Further, social and political changes can also promote exercise by increasing facilities, encouraging stair use and making walking and cycling safer forms of transport.

QUESTIONS

1 Why is exercise difficult to define and measure?
2 Exercise has both psychological and physical benefits. Discuss.
3 To what extent can we predict exercise behaviour?
4 How can psychological theories be used to promote exercise behaviour?
5 Making people more active is easier than getting them to exercise. Discuss.
6 Exercise behaviour has to be an integrated part of people's lives. Discuss.
7 Describe a possible research project designed to predict attendance at an exercise class.

FOR DISCUSSION

Consider your own exercise behaviour and discuss the extent to which your health beliefs are contributing factors.

ASSUMPTIONS IN HEALTH PSYCHOLOGY

The exercise literature illustrates some of the assumptions central to health psychology:

1 *The mind–body problem.* Research into exercise maintains the mind–body split. This is illustrated in the discussion of the benefits of exercise (physical and psychological) and the reasons for exercising (e.g. health and fitness versus enjoyment).

2 *Data exist independently of the methodology used.* If different sets of cognitions are measured according to the different models, do these beliefs exist prior to the subject being asked about them (e.g. the question 'Do you think health is important?' primes the subject to think about health as having a value)? Methodology is seen as objective, and not interacting with the 'data'.

FURTHER READING

Biddle, S.J.H., Fox, K.R. and Boutcher, S.H. (eds) (2000) *Physical Activity and Psychological Wellbeing.*
    London: Routledge.
This book provides a description of the research exploring the links between exercise and aspects of mental health including emotion, mood, self-esteem, self-perception, depression, stress and cognitive performance.

Biddle, S.J.H. and Mutrie, N. (2008) *Psychology of Physical Activity: Determinants, Wellbeing and Interventions* 2nd edn. London: Routledge.
An excellent book that provides a thorough and expert guide to the literature of physical activity.

Dishman, R.K. (1982) Compliance/adherence in health-related exercise, *Health Psychology*, 1: 237–67.
This is an early classic paper that examines the literature on factors predicting exercise behaviour.

Faulkner, G.E.J. and Taylor, A.H. (eds) (2005) *Exercise, Health and Mental Health.* London: Routledge.
A comprehensive edited collection of chapters that cover the impact of exercise on a range of physical health problems including cancer, heart failure, HIV and schizophrenia. It provides a good summary of the existing research and a useful summary chapter at the end.

 Visit the website at www.openup.co.uk/ogden for additional resources on Chapter 6 to help you with your study, such as multiple choice questions, weblinks and a searchable online glossary.

7 Sex

© Gene Chutka/iStock

> ## CHAPTER OVERVIEW
>
> This chapter first provides a brief history of the literature on sex, including early discussions of biology and sex for reproduction, debates about sexual pleasure and the work of Kinsey and the Hite Reports, sex as a risk behaviour in the context of pregnancy avoidance and sexually transmitted diseases (STDs), HIV and AIDS and a recent focus on sexual health as being more than just the absence of disease but as a state of physical, emotional and social well-being. The chapter then explores psychological research within these different perspectives including predicting contraception use, a focus on condoms in the context of HIV, sex as an interaction and the role of negotiation, perceptions of risk and susceptibility, sex education from both the government and at school, power relations between sexual partners and the social norms of the gay community.

A BRIEF HISTORY OF THE LITERATURE ON SEX

SEX AS BIOLOGICAL, FOR REPRODUCTION

Prior to the nineteenth century, sexual behaviour was regarded as a religious or spiritual concern and guidance came from religious leaders. However, from the beginning of the 1800s sexuality and sexual behaviour became a focus for scientific study. Doctors and scientists took over the responsibility for teaching about sex and it was subsequently studied within medicine and biological sciences. Sex was viewed as a biological function alongside eating and drinking.

During the nineteenth century, much was written about sexual behaviour. Attempts were made to develop criteria to describe sexual normality and abnormality. Generally behaviours linked to reproduction were seen as normal and those such as masturbation and homosexuality as abnormal. This is illustrated by the Victorian concern with sexual morality, movements proclaiming sexual puritanism and attempts to control prostitution. Sex was seen as a biological drive that needed to be expressed but which should be expressed within the limitations of its function: reproduction.

SEX AS BIOLOGICAL, FOR PLEASURE

From the beginning of the twentieth century, there was a shift in perspective. Although sex was still seen as biological, the emphasis was now on sexual behaviour rather than on outcome (reproduction). This involved a study of sexual desire, sexual pleasure and orgasms. It resulted in a burgeoning literature on sex therapy and manuals on how to develop a good sex life. This emphasis is illustrated by the classic survey carried out by Kinsey in the 1940s and 1950s, the research programmes developed by Masters and Johnson in the 1960s and the Hite Reports on sexuality in the 1970s and 1980s.

The Kinsey Report

Kinsey interviewed and analysed data from 12,000 white Americans and his attempts to challenge some of the contemporary concerns with deviance were credited with causing 'a wave of sexual hysteria' (e.g. Kinsey et al. 1948). He developed his analysis of sexual behaviour within models of biological reductionism and argued that sex was natural and therefore healthy. Kinsey argued that the sexual drive was a biological force and the expression of this drive to attain pleasure was not only acceptable but desirable. He challenged some of the contemporary concerns with premarital sex and argued that as animals do not get married, there could be no difference between marital and premarital sex. He emphasized similarities between the sexual behaviour of men and women and argued that if scientific study could promote healthy sex lives, then this could improve the quality of marriages and reduce divorce rates. His research suggested that a variety of sexual outlets were acceptable and emphasized the role of sexual pleasure involving both sexual intercourse and masturbation for men and women.

Masters and Johnson

This emphasis on the activity of sex is also illustrated by the work of Masters and Johnson in the 1960s. They used a variety of experimental laboratory techniques to examine over 10,000 male and female orgasms in 694 white middle-class heterosexuals (e.g. Masters and Johnson 1966). They recorded bodily contractions, secretions, pulse rates and tissue colour changes and described the sexual response cycle in terms of the following phases: (1) excitement; (2) plateau; (3) orgasm; and (4) resolution. They emphasized similarities between men and women and argued that stable marriages depended on satisfactory sex. According to Masters and Johnson, sexual pleasure could be improved by education and sex therapy and again their research suggested that masturbation was an essential component of sexuality – sex was for pleasure, not for reproduction.

The Hite Reports

Shere Hite (1976, 1981, 1987) published the results from her 20 years of research in her reports on female and male sexuality. Her research also illustrates the shift from the outcome of sex to sex as an activity. Hite's main claim is that 'most women (70 per cent) do not orgasm as a result of intercourse', but she suggests that they can learn to increase clitoral stimulation during intercourse to improve their sexual enjoyment. She describes her data in terms of women's dislike of penetrative sex ('Perhaps it could be said that many women might be rather indifferent to intercourse if it were not for feelings towards a particular man') and discusses sex within the context of pleasure, not reproduction. Segal (1994) has criticized Hite's interpretation of the data and argues that the women in Hite's studies appear to enjoy penetration (with or without orgasm). Although this is in contradiction to Hite's own conclusion, the emphasis is still on sex as an activity.

SEX AS A RISK TO HEALTH

In the late twentieth century there was an additional shift in the literature on sex. Although research still emphasized sex as an activity, this activity was viewed as increasingly risky and dangerous. As a consequence, sex was discussed in terms of health promotion, health education and self-protection. This shift has resulted in a psychological literature on sex as a risk both in terms of pregnancy avoidance and in the context of STDs/HIV preventive behaviour.

SEX AND WELL-BEING

Since the turn of the twenty-first century there has been an additional shift in the ways in which sex is conceptualized. Although much work still continues to explore how to prevent unwanted pregnancy or STDs, sexual research has begun to incorporate a notion of the benefits of sex, not just the costs. There has therefore been an increasing interest in sex as pleasure, masturbation, fantasy and the role of a sexual life within a more holistic view of the individual. This is reflected in the World Health Organization (WHO) definition in 2002: 'Sexual health is a state of physical, emotional, mental and social well being related to sexuality; it is not merely the absence of disease.'

This approach is also reflected in Robinson et al.'s (2002) all-inclusive sexual health model which locates sex within the context of physical and mental health, relationships and culture. Although this was developed within the context of HIV prevention it has implications for thinking about sexual behaviour across all domains of any individual's life. The model is illustrated in Figure 7.1.

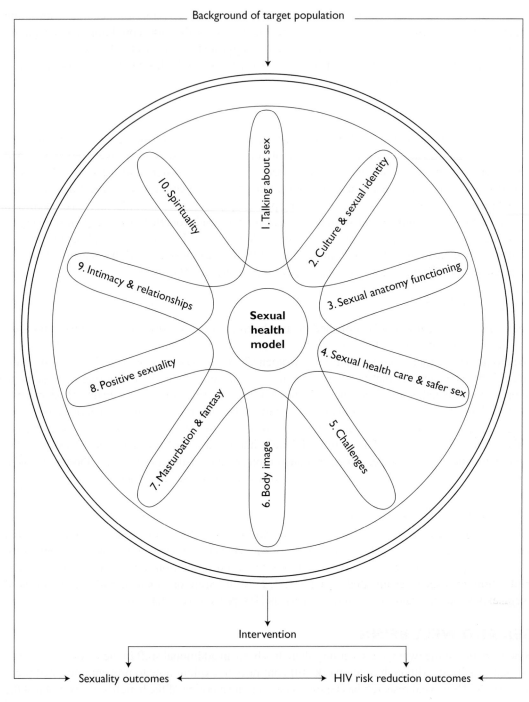

FIGURE 7.1

The sexual health model

SOURCE: Robinson et al. (2002), reproduced by permission of Oxford University Press

IN SUMMARY

Early literature emphasized sex as a biological process and the focus was on reproduction. From the start of the twentieth century, however, sex was no longer described as a biological means to an end but as an activity in itself. Discussions of 'good sex', orgasms and sexual pleasure emphasized sex as action; however, even as an activity sex remained predominantly biological. Kinsey regarded sex as a drive that was natural and healthy, Masters and Johnson developed means to measure and improve the sexual experience by examining physiological changes and Hite explained pleasure with descriptions of physical stimulation. By the end of the twentieth century, however, discussions had shifted towards a more negative model of sex with the emphasis being on risk and danger and a focus on pregnancy avoidance and STDs, particularly in the light of HIV/AIDS. Nowadays a new shift is occurring towards a more integrated model of sex in terms of well-being which includes not only a sense of physical health but also one of pleasure and a sense that sexuality and sexual behaviour are central to how people feel about themselves.

Over the past few decades these different perspectives have generated a number of different strands of research. These include an analysis of contraception use for pregnancy avoidance, condom use in the context of HIV and STDs, sex as an interaction and the role of negotiation, the complexities of risk perception, sex education from the government and schools, power relations between men and women and the social norms of the gay community. These will now be described.

CONTRACEPTIVE USE FOR PREGNANCY AVOIDANCE

The focus on sex as a risk resulted in a literature on contraception use and pregnancy avoidance. Research on the termination of pregnancy is described in Chapter 16. Psychologists have developed models in order to describe and predict this behaviour. Some of these models are described in detail in Chapter 3, and Chapter 8 includes a discussion of the development of behaviour change interventions. This section explores definitions of contraception use, who uses contraception and a number of key factors which predict the use of contraceptives.

WHAT IS CONTRACEPTIVE USE?

Researchers have used several different classifications of contraception in an attempt to predict contraceptive use. For example, contraception has been characterized as:

- Coitus independent (the pill, injection) or coitus dependent (the condom).
- Reliable (the pill, condom) or unreliable (rhythm method).
- Female controlled (the pill, coil) or male controlled (the condom).
- Prescription based (the pill, coil, injection) or prescription independent (the condom).

In addition, different measures of actual behaviour have been used when predicting contraceptive use:

- At first ever intercourse.
- At most recent intercourse.
- At last serious intercourse.
- At last casual intercourse.

WHO USES CONTRACEPTION?

The National Survey of Sexual Attitudes and Lifestyles (Wellings et al. 1994) examined the sexual behaviour of nearly 20,000 men and women across Britain. This produced a wealth of data about factors such as age at first intercourse, homosexuality, attitudes to sexual behaviours and contraception use. For example, Figure 7.2 shows the proportion of respondents who used no contraception at first intercourse. These results suggest that the younger someone is when they first have sex (either male or female), the less likely they are to use contraception.

The results from this survey also show what kinds of contraception people use at first intercourse. The data for men and women aged 16–24 years are shown in Figure 7.3 and suggest that the condom

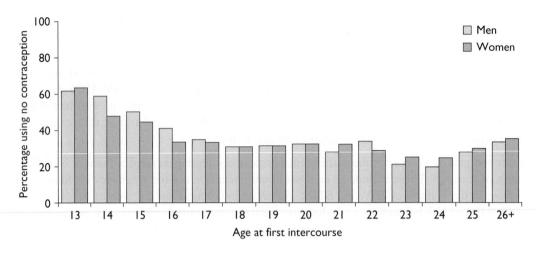

FIGURE 7.2

Percentage using no contraception at first intercourse, by age at first intercourse

SOURCE: Adapted from Wellings et al. (1994)

is the most popular form of contraception; however, many respondents in this age group reported using no contraception, or unreliable methods, such as withdrawal or the safe period.

In 2008/9 the Office for National Statistics published data on condom and pill use in women under 50 and these are shown in Figure 7.4. The results show that whereas the pill is the preferred mode of contraception for women in their early twenties and thirties, women in their early forties are more likely to use the male condom. However, the data from a survey in the US published in 2005 indicate that the numbers of young girls who were sexually active but not using any form of

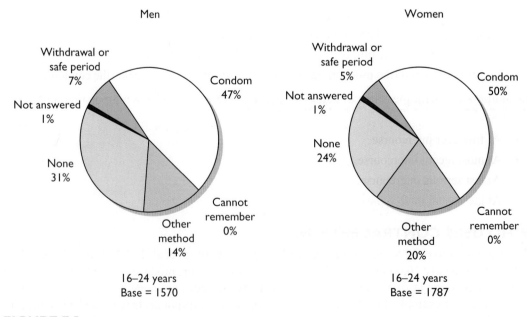

FIGURE 7.3

Contraception use at first intercourse in those aged 16–24

SOURCE: Adapted from Wellings et al. (1994)

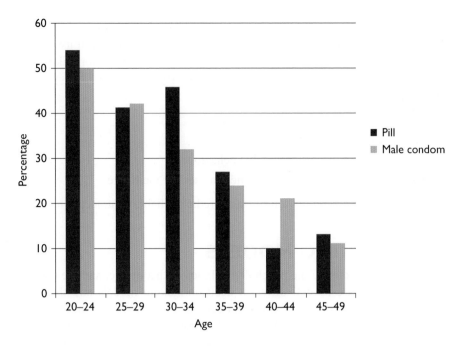

FIGURE 7.4
Percentage of women using the pill or male condom by age
SOURCE: Office for National Statistics (2008/9)

contraception were as follows: 15–19 years, 19 per cent; 20–24 years, 9 per cent; 25–29, 6 per cent (The Henry J. Kaiser Family Foundation 2005). Further, Mosher et al. (2004) calculated that 1.43 million women could be at risk of unplanned pregnancy in the USA, with the highest risk groups being sexually active Hispanic and black women.

Sheeran et al. (1991) analysed the literature on contraceptive use and suggested that models used to examine contraceptive use for pregnancy avoidance can be described as either *developmental models* or *decision-making models*. Some key models will now be described.

DEVELOPMENTAL MODELS

Developmental models emphasize contraception use as involving a series of stages. They suggest that the progress through these stages is related to sexual experience and an increasing role for sexuality in the individual's self-concept. Therefore they describe the transition through the different stages but do not attempt to analyse the cognitions that may promote this transition.

LINDEMANN'S THREE-STAGE THEORY

Lindemann (1977) developed the three-stage theory of contraception use, which suggests that the likelihood of an individual using contraception increases as they progress through the three stages:

1 *Natural stage:* at this stage intercourse is relatively unplanned, and the individual does not regard themselves as sexual. Therefore contraception use is unlikely.

2 *Peer prescription stage:* at this stage the individual seeks contraceptive advice from friends, sexual intercourse is more frequent and most contraception involves less effective methods.

3 *Expert stage:* at this stage, the individual has incorporated sexuality into their self-concept and will seek professional advice and plan contraceptive use.

RAINS'S MODEL

This model was developed by Rains (1971) and again places contraception use within the context of sexuality and self-concept. It suggests that contraception use is more likely to occur at a stage when the individual believes that sexual activity is 'right for them'. This process involves the following four stages:

1   Falling in love: this provides a rationale for sex.
2   Having an exclusive, long-term relationship.
3   Sexual intercourse becomes an acceptable behaviour.
4   Individuals accept themselves as sexual and plan sex for the future.

According to this model, reaching the fourth stage predicts reliable contraception use.

DECISION-MAKING MODELS

Decision-making models examine the psychological factors that predict and are the precursors to contraception use. There are several different decision-making models and they vary in their emphasis on individual cognitions (e.g. costs and benefits of contraception use) and the extent to which they place these cognitions within the specific context of the relationship (e.g. the interaction, seriousness of relationship, frequency of sexual intercourse in the relationship) and the broader social context (e.g. peer norms, social attitudes).

SUBJECTIVE EXPECTED UTILITY THEORY

Most decision-making models of behaviour are based on subjective expected utility theory (SEU) (Edwards 1954). SEU predicts that individuals make subjective estimates of the possible costs and benefits of any particular behaviour and, based on this assessment, make a decision as to which behaviour results in the least costs and the most benefits (material, social and psychological). It therefore characterizes behaviour as rational. Luker (1975) examined SEU in the context of contraceptive use and argued that individuals weigh up the costs and benefits of pregnancy against the costs and benefits of contraception. Sheeran et al. (1991) argued that this approach was important as it undermined the belief that contraception has no costs for women and pregnancy has no benefits. SEU is predominantly individualistic with its focus on cognitions and the role of both the relationship and social contexts is minimal.

THE HEALTH BELIEF MODEL

Lowe and Radius (1982) developed the health belief model (HBM) (see Chapter 3) specifically to predict contraception and aimed to examine individual cognitions within both the context of the relationship and broader social norms. They added the following variables:

- Self-esteem.
- Interpersonal skills.
- Knowledge about sex and contraception.
- Attitudes to sex and contraception.
- Previous sexual, contraceptive and pregnancy experiences.
- Peer norms.
- Relationship status.
- Substance use prior to sex.

The HBM has been used to predict contraception use (e.g. Winfield and Whaley 2002) and although this model still examines cognitions, it includes measures of the individuals' cognitions about their social world.

THE SEXUAL BEHAVIOUR SEQUENCE MODEL

This model was developed by Byrne and Byrne (1977) and adds sexual arousal and emotional responses to sex to the factors included in the theory of reasoned action (TRA) (see Chapter 3 for details). Sexual arousal refers to how aroused an individual is at the time of making a decision about contraception. Emotional responses to sex describe a personality trait that Byrne et al. (1977) defined as either *erotophilia* (finding sexual cues pleasurable) or *erotophobia* (finding sexual cues aversive). According to the sexual behaviour sequence model, decisions about contraception are made in the context of both rational information processing and emotions. This model attempts to add a degree of emotions and social norms (from the TRA) to the individual's cognitions. The TRA and amended versions of this model have been used to predict aspects of sexual behaviour including condom use and contraception use (e.g. Albarracin et al. 2001; Muoz-Silva et al. 2007).

HEROLD AND MCNAMEE'S MODEL

Herold and McNamee's (1982) model is made up of the following variables: (1) parental and peer group norms for acceptance of premarital intercourse; (2) number of lifetime sexual partners; (3) guilt about intercourse and attitudes to contraception; (4) involvement with current partner; (5) partner's influence to use contraception; and (6) frequency of intercourse. This model differs from other models of contraception use as it includes details of the relationship. It places contraception use both within the general context of social norms and also within the context of the relationship.

IN SUMMARY

These decision-making models regard contraceptive use as resulting from an analysis of the relevant variables. However, they vary in the extent to which they attempt to place the individual's cognitive state within a broader context, both of the relationship and the social world.

INTEGRATING DEVELOPMENTAL AND DECISION-MAKING APPROACHES TO CONTRACEPTIVE USE

Developmental models emphasize behaviour and describe reliable contraception use as the end product of a transition through a series of stages. These models do not examine the psychological factors which may speed up or delay this transition. In contrast, decision-making models emphasize an individual's cognitions and, to a varying degree, place these cognitions within the context of the relationship and social norms. Sheeran et al. (1991) argued that these perspectives could be combined and that the best why to examine contraceptive use is as a product of (1) background; (2) intrapersonal; (3) interpersonal; and (4) situational factors. They defined these factors as follows.

BACKGROUND FACTORS

Research indicates that contraception use varies according to a number of background variables such as age, sex, ethnicity, social class and education (see Figures 7.2–7.4; Wellings et al. 1994; Bentley et al. 2009). Whether this effect is direct or through the effect of other factors such as knowledge and attitudes is unclear.

INTRAPERSONAL FACTORS

1 *Knowledge:* Whitley and Schofield (1986) analysed the results of 25 studies of contraceptive use and reported a correlation of 0.17 between objective knowledge and contraceptive use in both men and women, suggesting that knowledge is poorly linked to behaviour. However,

ignorance about contraception has also been shown by several studies. For example, Cvetkovich and Grote (1981) reported that, of their sample, 10 per cent did not believe that they could become pregnant the first time they had sex, and 52 per cent of men and 37 per cent of women could not identify the periods of highest risk in the menstrual cycle. In addition, Lowe and Radius (1982) reported that 40 per cent of their sample did not know how long sperm remained viable. Further, a leaflet-based intervention showed that a leaflet and questions could improve knowledge about the contraceptive pill (Little et al. 1998).

2 *Attitudes:* Fisher (1984) reported that positive attitudes towards contraception parallel actual use. Negative attitudes included beliefs that 'it kills spontaneity', 'it's too much trouble to use' and that there are possible side-effects. In addition, carrying contraceptives around is often believed to be associated with being promiscuous (e.g. Lowe and Radius 1982). Free and Ogden (2005) also reported a role for attitudes with users of emergency contraception reporting more positive attitudes than non-users. Further, Bryant (2009) concluded from her survey of diverse female college students that more positive attitudes to contraception were associated not only with contraception use but also consistent and effective use. This is particularly important as research indicates that many people show only partial adherence to contraception recommendations (see Chapter 10 for discussion of adherence).

3 *Personality:* many different personality types have been related to contraceptive use. This research assumes that certain aspects of individuals are consistent over time and research has reported associations between the following types of personality:

   • *Conservatism and sex role* have been shown to be negatively related to contraceptive use (e.g. McCormick et al. 1985).

   • *An internal locus of control* appears to correlate with contraceptive use but not with choice of type of contraception (Morrison 1985).

   • *Sex guilt and sex anxiety* positively relate to use and consistency of use of contraception (Herold and McNamee 1982).

   • *Personality* is often measured using the big-five factors (Goldberg 1999). These are *agreeableness, conscientiousness, emotional stability, extraversion* and *intellect*. Ingledew and Ferguson (2006) explored the role of personality in predicting riskier sexual behaviour. The results showed that agreeableness and conscientiousness reduced riskier behaviour. The results also showed that this effect was related to different forms of motivation.

INTERPERSONAL FACTORS

Research highlights a role for characteristics of the following significant others:

1 *Partner:* facets of the relationship may influence contraception use including duration of relationship, intimacy, type of relationship (e.g. casual versus steady), exclusivity, and ability to have overt discussions about contraception. For example, increased partner support was related to the use of emergency contraception (Free and Ogden 2005) and contraception in general (Coleman and Ingham 1998).

2 *Parents:* there is some evidence to suggest that increased parental permissiveness and explicit communication between mothers and daughters about contraception is related to contraception use (e.g. Herold and McNamee 1982). Research also indicates, however, that parents tend to underestimate their child's sexual activity which may place that child at risk of pregnancy (or STDs) if parents don't encourage them to use contraception (Jones et al. 2005; O'Donnell et al. 2008).

3 *Peers:* increased contraceptive use relates to peer permissiveness and peers' own contraceptive behaviour (e.g. Herold 1981). Peer norms have also been assessed within the framework of using social cognition models to predict contraception use (e.g. Albarracin et al. 2001).

SITUATIONAL FACTORS

Situational factors also contribute to contraceptive use, including the following:

1 *The spontaneity of sex:* spontaneity is often given as a reason for not using contraception (e.g. Holland et al. 1990b).

2 *Substance use prior to sex:* taking substances such as drugs or alcohol prior to sex may relate to risky sex (Cooper 2002).

3 *The accessibility of contraception:* research has examined whether easy access to contraception both in general (i.e. the provision of condom machines in pubs) and at the time of contemplating sex predicts contraception use (e.g. Sable et al. 2000).

Contraception use can therefore be seen as a result of demographics (background) (e.g. age, experience), intrapersonal variables (e.g. knowledge and attitudes), interpersonal variables (e.g. partner support) and the situation (e.g. accessibility, substance use). These different variables interact in order to predict contraception use. This approach reflects a combination of individual and social

Easy access to condoms can improve condom use

SOURCE: © Joshua Sherurcij/Wikimedia Commons

variables and highlights how sexual behaviour is an interaction between two people and how any explanation needs to include a role for the individual's social context. The broader role of the social context is considered later in this chapter in terms of negotiation, power dynamics and cultural norms.

SEX AS A RISK IN THE CONTEXT OF STDs/HIV AND AIDS

The HIV virus was identified in 1986 (see Chapter 14 for a discussion of HIV and AIDS). Since the beginning of the HIV/AIDS epidemic, sex as a risk has taken on a new dimension – the dimension of chronic illness and death. Research has therefore focused on the role of condoms in preventing STDs, HIV and AIDS. Early campaigns emphasized monogamy or at least cutting down on the number of sexual partners. Campaigns also promoted non-penetrative sex and suggested alternative ways to enjoy a sexual relationship. However, more recent campaigns emphasize safe sex and using a condom. In fact, Reiss and Leik (1989) argued that increased condom use (as opposed to abstinence, non-penetrative sex or a reduction in the number of partners) is likely to be the best approach to preventing HIV infection. As a result, research has examined the prerequisites to safer sex and condom use in an attempt to develop successful health promotion campaigns. This is particularly pertinent given that rates of other STDs have increased over the past 20 years in the UK (ONS 2005). This section will explore condom use in different populations and the predictors of condom use with a focus on social cognition models.

DO PEOPLE USE CONDOMS?

Young People

Since the late 1980s governments have funded several mass media campaigns to promote condom use in young people, yet during this time there has been an STDs increase. For example, in the UK, data indicate that there has been an increase in chlamydia and that the dramatic reduction in gonor-rhoea seen in the older population is not evident among younger people. Furthermore, new cases of STDs in the UK increased from 669,291 in 1991 to 1,332,910 in 2001 and by 2001 1,025 out of every 100,000 people suffered an STD compared to 350 per 100,000 in 1991. Richard and van der Pligt (1991) examined condom use among a group of Dutch teenagers and reported that only 50 per cent of those with multiple partners were consistent condom users. In an American study, 30 per cent of adolescent women were judged to be at risk from STDs, of whom 16 per cent used condoms consistently (Weisman et al. 1991). The Women, Risk and AIDS Project (WRAP) (e.g. Holland et al. 1990b) interviewed and collected questionnaires from heterosexual women aged 16–19 years and reported that 16 per cent of these used condoms on their own, 13 per cent had used condoms while on the pill, 2 per cent had used condoms in combination with spermicide and 3 per cent had used condoms together with a diaphragm. Overall only 30 per cent of their sample had ever used condoms, while 70 per cent had not. Fife-Schaw and Breakwell (1992) undertook an overview of the literature on condom use among young people and found that between 24 and 58 per cent of 16- to 24-year-olds had used a condom during their most recent sexual encounter. Hatherall et al. (2006) also explored condom use in young people and reported that 62 per cent said that they had used a condom in their most recent sexual experience. However, of these 31 per cent described putting on the condom after penetration at least once in the previous six months and 9 per cent reported having penetration after the condom had been removed. This suggests that even when condoms are used, they are not always used in the most effective way. Furthermore, Stone et al. (2006) explored the use of condoms during oral sex (which is recommended for the prevention of STD transmission) and the results showed that of those who had had oral sex only 17 per cent reported ever using a condom and only 2 per cent reported consistent condom use. Reasons for non-use included reduced pleasure and lack of motivation and reasons for use included hygiene and avoidance of the 'spit/swallow dilemma'. Condom use was assessed in a recent survey in the UK (ONS 2010). Condom use in the previous year by age and sex is shown in Figure 7.5. This indicates that men use condoms more often than women and that they are most commonly used by the younger age groups.

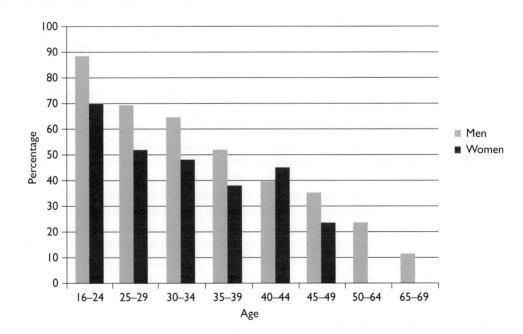

FIGURE 7.5

Condom use in the previous year by age and sex, from 2010 Report

SOURCE: ONS (2010)

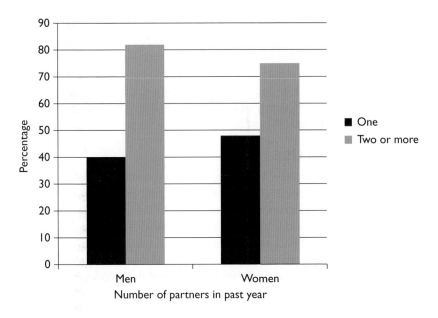

FIGURE 7.6

Condom use in the past year by number of partners, from 2010 Report

SOURCE: ONS (2010)

The survey also asked about condom use and number of partners. These data are shown in Figure 7.6. The results from this analysis indicate that condom use is more common in both men and women who have had more than one partner in the past year.

Gay Men

Research has examined condom use among homosexually active men. Weatherburn et al. (1991) interviewed 930 homosexually active men in England and Wales and reported that 270 of them had had insertive anal intercourse in the preceding month, with 38.9 per cent reporting always using a condom, 49.6 per cent never using a condom and 11.5 per cent sometimes using a condom. Of the 254 who reported having receptive anal sex in the preceding month, 42.5 per cent had always used a condom, 45.7 per cent had never used a condom and 11.8 per cent had sometimes used a condom. Weatherburn et al. reported that condom use was associated with casual, not regular, sexual partners and was more common in open and non-monogamous relationships. Research also shows that there was a consistent increase in condom use among gay men from the mid 1980s to the late 1990s following the identification of HIV and the subsequent recognition that condom use was the most effective form of prevention. Recent data, however, suggest that this trend is reversing with an increasing number of gay men practising unprotected anal sex (known as 'bare backing', see Ridge 2004) in both the US and the UK (Chen et al. 2002; Dodds and Mercey 2002). Therefore, within this high-risk group, condom use is low. In addition, research indicates that gay men who have unsafe sex talk about their behaviour in terms of a number of factors which justify or perpetuate the non-use of condoms. These include condom fatigue, unsafe sex as a sign of intimacy and optimistic beliefs about the effectiveness of treatments for HIV (Adam et al. 2005; Martin 2006).

Bisexuals

Boulton et al. (1991) asked 60 bisexual men about their sexual behaviour and their condom use. Over the previous 12 months, 80 per cent had had male partners, 73 per cent had had female partners and 60 per cent had had at least one male and one female partner. In terms of their condom use with their current partner, 25 per cent reported always using a condom with their current male partner, 12 per cent reported always using a condom with their current female partner, 27 per cent reported sometimes/never using a condom with their male partner and 38 per cent reported sometimes/never using a condom with their female partner. In terms of their non-current partner, 30 per cent had had unprotected sex with a man and 34 per cent had had unprotected sex with a woman. Bisexuals are believed to present a bridge between the homosexual and heterosexual populations and these data suggest that their frequency of condom use is low. This highlights a need to identify possible reasons for this behaviour.

PREDICTING CONDOM USE

Simple models using 'knowledge only' have been used to examine condom use. However, these models ignore the individual's beliefs and assume that simply increasing knowledge about HIV will promote safe sex. In order to incorporate an individual's cognitive state, social cognition models have been applied to condom use in the context of HIV and AIDS (see Chapter 3 for a discussion of these models). These models are similar to those used to predict other health-related behaviours, including contraceptive use for pregnancy avoidance, and illustrate varying attempts to understand cognitions in the context of the relationship and the broader social context.

Using Social Cognition Models

A number of social cognition models have been used to predict condom use in heterosexual and homosexual populations. For example, research has used the HBM for gay men (McCusker et al. 1989) and for heterosexual men and women (Winfield and Whaley 2002), and studies have used the TRA and the theory of planned behaviour (TPB) in similar populations (e.g. Fisher 1984; Boldero et al. 1992; Albarracin et al. 2001). Research has also explored the relative usefulness of the TRA compared with the TPB at predicting intentions to use condoms (Sutton et al. 1999). In general, results from these studies indicate the following:

- *The role of habit:* the most reliable predictor of future condom use behaviour is past condom use.
- *The role of norms:* peer, partner and social norms are good predictors of condom use. It remains more normal for men than women to carry condoms.
- *Support is important:* partner support is a good predictor of condom use.
- *Self-efficacy:* Self-efficacy predicts condom use. Abraham and Sheeran (1993) have emphasized the need for skills training as a means to promote self-efficacy.
- *A ceiling effect:* there is a consensus of perceptions of severity for HIV which presents the problem of a ceiling effect with only small differences in ratings of this variable.
- *A floor effect:* although people appear to know about HIV, its causes and how it is transmitted, feelings of immunity and low susceptibility ('it won't happen to me') are extremely common. This presents the problem of a floor effect with little individual variability (see later for discussions of risk perceptions).
- *Safer sex requires long-term maintenance of behaviour:* the HBM, TRA and TPB may be good predictors of short-term changes in behaviour (e.g. taking up an exercise class, stopping smoking in the short term), but safer sex is an ongoing behaviour which requires an ongoing determination to adopt condom use as a habit.

Problems with a Social Cognition Model Approach

Research using a social cognition models provides some insights into the predictors of this behavior but it also has its problems and neglects a number of key factors that might explain why people do or do not use condoms:

1 *Inconsistent findings:* the research examining condom use has not produced consistent results. Different studies have used very different populations (homosexual, heterosexual, adolescents, adults). Perhaps models of condom use should be constructed to fit the cognitive sets of

different populations. Certainly, attempts to develop one model for everyone may ignore the multitude of different cognitions held by different individuals within different groups.

2 *Sex as a result of individual cognitions:* models that emphasize cognitions and information processing intrinsically regard behaviour as the result of information processing – an individualistic approach to behaviour. In particular, early models tended to focus on representations of an individual's risks without taking into account their interactions with the outside world. Furthermore, models such as the HBM emphasize this process as rational. However, recent social cognition models have attempted to remedy this situation by emphasizing cognitions about the individual's social world (the normative beliefs) and by including elements of emotion (the behaviour becomes less rational).

3 *Perception of susceptibility:* in addition, these models predict that, because people appear to know that HIV is an extremely serious disease, and they know how it is transmitted, they will feel vulnerable (e.g. 'HIV is transmitted by unprotected sex, I have unprotected sex, therefore I am at risk from HIV'). This does not appear to be the case and many people underestimate their risk of HIV. Furthermore, the models predict that high levels of susceptibility will relate to less risk-taking behaviour (e.g. 'I am at risk, therefore I will use condoms'). Again this association is problematic.

Social norms predict condom use. But it's still more normal for men to carry condoms than women (is this a man or a woman?)

SOURCE: © Feferoni/Dreamstime

4 *Sex as an interaction between individuals – the relationship context:* models of condom use focus on cognitions. In attempts to include an analysis of the place of this behaviour (the relationship), variables such as peer norms, partner norms and partner support have been added. However, these variables are still accessed by asking one individual about their beliefs about the relationship. Perhaps this is still only accessing a cognition, not the interaction. But sex is an interaction between people and condom use requires some degree of communication and negotiation.

5 *Sex in a social context:* sex also takes place within a broader social context, involving norms about sexual practices, gender roles and stereotypes, the role of illness and theories of sexual behaviour. Cognitive models cannot address this broader context.

6 *Sex is emotional and involves a level of high arousal:* these factors are omitted in the social cognition models.

The rest of this chapter will address some of these issues.

SEX AS AN INTERACTION AND THE ROLE OF NEGOTIATION

Studying sexual behaviour is not straightforward from a psychological perspective as it presents a problem for psychologists – a problem of interaction. Social psychologists have spent decades emphasizing the context within which behaviour occurs. This is reflected in the extensive literature on areas such as conformity to majority and minority influence, group behaviour and decision-making, and obedience to authority. Such a perspective emphasizes that an individual's behaviour occurs as an interaction both with other individuals and with the broader social context. Sex highlights this interaction as it is inherently an interactive behaviour. However, health psychology draws on many other areas of psychology (e.g. physiological, cognitive, behavioural), which have tended to examine individuals *on their own*. In addition, psychological methodologies such as questionnaires and interviews involve an individual's experience (e.g. I felt, I believe, I think, I did). Even if individuals discuss their interactions with other individuals (e.g. we felt, we believe, we think, we did), or place their experiences in the context of others (e.g. I felt happy because she made me feel relaxed), only their own individual experiences are accessed using the psychological tools available. Furthermore, the recent emphasis on sex as a risk to health and resulting attempts to examine individuals' competence at protecting themselves from danger may have resulted in a more individualistic model of behaviour. This problem of interaction is exacerbated by the psychological methodologies available (unless the researcher simply observes two people having sex!). The problem of the interaction has been addressed in terms of the process of negotiation and partner support.

THE PROCESS OF NEGOTIATION

The WRAP interviewed 150 women from London and Manchester about their sexual histories and sexual behaviour and described the factors that related to the negotiation of condom use. Holland et al. (1990b: 4) stated that during sex 'words are likely to be the most difficult things to exchange' and suggested that the negotiation of condom use is far more complex than 'a simple, practical question about dealing rationally with risk, it is the outcome of negotiation between potentially unequal partners'. They suggested that although the process of negotiation may be hindered by embarrassment as suggested by some of the health promotion campaigns, this 'embarrassment over using condoms is not simply a question of bad timing but indicates a very complex process of negotiation'. Therefore they place condom use within the context of the relationship and, rather than see the interaction between individuals as only one component of the process of condom use, they place this interaction centrally.

The results from the WRAP study provide some insights into the process of negotiation and the interaction between individuals. Some of the interviewees reported no difficulties in demanding safe sex, with one woman saying, 'if they don't want to wear a condom, then tough, you know, go and find someone else'. Another woman said, 'He really hates using them, so I used to say to him, look, right, look, I have no intention of getting pregnant again and you have no intention to become a father so you put one of these on.' However, other women described how difficult it was to suggest safe sex to their partner with reasons for this relating to not wanting to hurt their boyfriend's feelings, not wanting to 'ruin the whole thing', and not being able to approach the subject. One woman said, 'when I got pregnant I thought to myself, "I'm not using a condom here, I'm not using anything" but I just couldn't say, just couldn't force myself to say, "look you know"'. Holland et al. (1990b) argued that safe sex campaigns present condoms as neutral objects, which can be easily negotiated prior to sex and that this did not appear to be the case with the women they interviewed. The qualitative data from the WRAP study provide some insights into the process of negotiation; they also emphasize sex as an interaction. In addition, these data provide a relationship context for individual beliefs and cognitions. In line with the WRAP study, Debro et al. (1994) examined the strategies use by 393 heterosexual college students to negotiate condom use and concluded that they used reward, emotional coercion, risk information, deception, seduction and withholding sex.

Noar et al. (2002) built upon Debro et al.'s work and developed and validated a measure to quantify negotiation strategies called the Condom Influence Strategy Questionnaire (CISQ). They conceptualized negotiation in terms of six strategies: withholding sex, direct request, education, relationship conceptualizing, risk information, and deception, and indicated that these factors account for variance in a range of safer sex variables such as behavioural intentions and actual condom use. Stone and Ingham (2002) also explored partner communication in the context of predicting the use of contraception at first intercourse. The study involved a survey of 963 students aged between 16 and 18 and explored the role of a range of individual, contextual and background factors. The results showed that communication with a partner was a significant predictor of contraception use for both men and women. In particular, young men's contraception use was predicted by discussing contraception beforehand, giving an intimate reason for having sex the first

BOX 7.1 Some Problems with . . . Sex Research

Below are some problems with research in this area that you may wish to consider.

1   Sexual behaviour involves two people and therefore results out of an interaction between two sets of beliefs, emotions and behaviours. Although ultimately all behaviour is located in its social context, sexual behaviour explicitly illustrates this and therefore results in specific problems in terms of understanding and measuring what factors relate to whether someone has sex or not and whether they engage in risky behaviours.

2   Sexual behaviour can generate embarrassment and is considered a sensitive and personal area of research. This can lead to problems gaining ethical approval and in encouraging people to speak openly and honestly.

3   Most sexual behaviour research focuses on the problems associated with sex such as STDs and HIV. To date, little research in health psychology has highlighted sex as a healthy and pleasurable activity. In part this is due to issues of embarrassment and in part to funders' emphasis on health problems.

4   Sexual behaviour research can be loaded with ideological perspectives in terms of whether people believe abstinence is the way forward, whether they are judgemental of homosexual behaviour, whether they believe in monogamy and whether they are critical of 'promiscuity'. Research may therefore be biased in terms of the areas of research selected, the data collected and funded and ways in which the research is interpreted and presented.

time (e.g. they loved their partner as opposed to losing their virginity) and having parents who portrayed sexuality positively. For young women, contraception use was predicted by discussing contraception beforehand, being older, expecting to have sex, comfort and ease of interacting with boys and not having visited a sexual health service provider prior to having sex (this last result was in contrast to much previous work). Wilkinson et al. (2002) also highlighted a role for partner cooperation. They asked 398 unmarried students to rate both their sexual behaviour and their perception of how cooperative their partner had been to practise safer sex. The results showed that partner cooperation was linked to safer sexual behaviour.

Qualitative and quantitative research has emphasized the importance of negotiation which seems to have been taken on board by health education campaigns with advertisements highlighting the problem of raising the issue of safer sex (e.g. when would you mention condoms?). However, do interviews really access the interaction? Can the interaction be accessed using the available (and ethical) methodologies? (It would obviously be problematic to observe the interaction!) Are qualitative methods actually accessing something different from quantitative methods? Are interviews simply another method of finding out about people's cognitions and beliefs? Debates about methodology (quantitative versus qualitative) and the problem of behaviour as an interaction are relevant to all forms of behaviour but are particularly apparent when discussing sex.

PERCEPTIONS OF RISK AND SUSCEPTIBILITY

Having a sexual career today involves a relationship to risk that is different to that seen previously. However, one of the most consistent findings to emerge from the research is the perception of personal invulnerability to HIV in heterosexual and homosexual populations. These feelings of invulnerability are shown by quantitative studies that have examined ratings of perceived susceptibility and unrealistic optimism (see Chapters 3 and 14). For example, Abrams et al. (1990: 49) concluded from their survey in 1988 that young people 'have a strong sense of AIDS invulnerability which seems to involve a perception that they have control over the risk at which they place themselves'. In a study of beliefs in a population of young people in Scotland from 1988 to 1989, the authors reported an increased sense of complacency and invulnerability over this time period.

In addition, qualitative methods have been used to further examine whether individuals feel that they are at risk from HIV. For example, Flowers et al. (1998) explored how gay men feel about sex in the context of HIV and argued that although they are aware of their risk in the abstract, this 'somewhat distant threat of HIV' can lose its meaning in the immediate context of sex and other more pertinent desires or concerns. Similarly, it has been argued that gay men have 'actual' rather than 'hypothetical' sexual encounters and that the rational decision to minimize the threat of HIV can get lost in the moment of having sex (Westhaver 2005; Martin 2006). Woodcock et al. (1992) interviewed 125 young people aged 16–25 about their sexual behaviour and examined how these individuals evaluated their own risk factors. The authors reported that many of the interviewees endorsed risky behaviour and gave reasons both acknowledging their own risk or denying that they had put themselves at risk. Their ways of coping with risk were as follows:

1 *Acknowledging risk:* one subject acknowledged that their behaviour had been risky, saying, 'I'm a chancer and I know I'm a chancer . . . with this AIDS thing, I know that I should use a condom.' However, most subjects, even though they acknowledged some degree of risk, managed to dismiss it in terms of 'it would show by now', 'it was in the past' or 'AIDS wasn't around in those days' (from a 21-year-old interviewee).

2 *Denying risk:* most commonly, people denied that they had ever put themselves at risk and the complex ways in which their sexual behaviour was rationalized illustrates how complicated the concept of susceptibility and 'being at risk' is. Woodcock et al. (1992) presented many ways of rationalizing risky behaviour. These included believing 'it's been blown out of proportion', that 'AIDS is a risk you take in living' and the authors reported that 'the theme of being run over, particularly by buses' was common and believing that 'it doesn't affect me' was also apparent. In addition, the interviewees evaluated their own risk in the context of the kinds of people with whom they had sex. For example, 'I don't go with people who go around a lot', 'He said, I've only slept with you in the last six months', and 'I do not have sex in risky geographical areas' – one interviewee said, 'London is the capital: has to be more AIDS.'

Most cognitive models emphasizing rational information processing suggest that condom use is related to feelings of susceptibility and being at risk from HIV. However, many people do not appear to believe that they themselves are at risk, which is perhaps why they do not engage in self-protective behaviour, and even when some acknowledgement of risk is made, this is often dismissed and does not appear to relate to behaviour change.

SEX EDUCATION

The decision to use contraception or condoms is informed by sex education that comes from a variety of different sources, including government health education campaigns, school sex education programmes and an individual's social world. These three sources of information will now be examined further.

SEXUAL HEALTH SERVICES

Specialist family planning clinics, genito-urinary clinics, general practitioners (GPs), the chemist and nurse practitioners all provide sexual health services offering access to contraception and sexual health information and advice. Even condom machines in public toilets and free condoms in youth clubs act as a form of sexual health service. Research shows that, to be effective, sexual health services must be user friendly, non-judgemental, accessible, approachable and confidential (Allen 1991; Stone and Ingham 2000). For example, Allen (1991) evaluated three new family planning and pregnancy counselling projects for young people set up in 1987 and subsequently monitored their use over an 18-month period. This evaluation identified a range of factors that made contraception services more or less acceptable to young people, including inconvenient opening times, embarrassment at being seen by other people while seeking sexual health advice, not feeling comfortable with the staff, judgemental or unhelpful staff, fear of the services not being confidential and having to give personal details. In a similar vein, Harden and Ogden (1999b) asked 967 16–19-year-olds about their beliefs and use of contraception services and reported that the chemist and the condom machine had been used by the largest number of respondents, with men favouring the condom machine and women favouring the GP or family planning clinic. In terms of beliefs, the condom machine was regarded as the easiest and most comfortable to use but the least confidential, with men reporting higher ratings for ease of use than women. Much research shows that young people in particular do not use sexual health services and often report finding contraceptives difficult (Stone and Ingham 2000). Stone and Ingham (2003) gave a questionnaire to 747 attendees at a youth-targeted sexual health service to investigate why they used the service. The results showed that 29 per cent had used a service before having ever had sex, 'to be prepared', but that the remainder had only used a service after having sex. The most common reasons for non-use of services were being embarrassed or scared, concern about confidentiality or not knowing how to access services.

GOVERNMENT HEALTH EDUCATION CAMPAIGNS

Ingham et al. (1991) examined UK campaigns that promoted safe sex and suggested that slogans such as 'Unless you're completely sure about your partner, always use a condom', 'Nowadays is it really wise to have sex with a stranger?' and 'Sex with a lot of partners, especially with people you don't know, can be dangerous' emphasize knowing your partner. They interviewed a group of young people in the south of England to examine how they interpreted 'knowing their partners'. The results suggest that 27 per cent of the interviewees had had sex within 24 hours of becoming a couple, that 10 per cent of the sample reported having sex on the first ever occasion on which they met their partner, and that over 50 per cent reported having sex within two weeks of beginning a relationship. In terms of 'knowing their partner', 31 per cent of males and 35 per cent of females reported knowing nothing of their partner's sexual history, and knowing was often explained in terms of 'she came from a nice family and stuff', and having 'seen them around'. The results from this study indicate that promoting 'knowing your partner' may not be the best way to promote safe sex as knowledge can be interpreted in a multitude of different ways. In addition, safer sex campaigns emphasize personal responsibility and choice in the use of condoms, and condoms are presented as a simple way to prevent contraction of the HIV virus. This presentation is epitomized by government health advertisement slogans such as 'You know the risks: the decision is yours'. This view of sex and condom use is in contradiction with the research suggesting that people believe that they are not at risk from HIV and that condom use involves a complex process of negotiation.

SCHOOL SEX EDUCATION PROGRAMMES

Information about sex also comes from sex education programmes at school. Holland et al. (1990a) interviewed young women about their experiences of sex education and concluded that such education in schools is impersonal, mechanistic and concerned with biology. The women in their study made comments such as 'it was all from the book, it wasn't really personal' and 'nobody ever talks to you about the problems and the entanglements, and what it means to a relationship when you start having sex'. It has been argued that this impersonal and objective approach to sex education is counterproductive (Aggleton 1989) and several alternatives have been suggested. Aggleton and Homans (1988) argued for a 'socially transformatory model' for AIDS education, which would involve discussions of: (1) ideas about sex; (2) social relations; (3) political processes involved; and (4) the problem of resource allocation. This approach would attempt to shift the emphasis from didactic teachings of facts and knowledge to a discussion of sex within a context of relationships and the broader social context. An additional solution to the problem of sex education is a skills training approach recommended by Abraham and Sheeran (1993). They argued that individuals could be taught a variety of skills, including buying condoms, negotiation of condom use and using condoms. These skills could be transmitted using tuition, role-play, feedback, modelling and practice. They are aimed at changing cognitions, preparing individuals for action and encouraging people to practise different aspects of the sequences involved in translating beliefs into behaviour. Ingham (2005) provides a detailed analysis of sex and relationship education. He explores how sex education is currently evaluated and highlights what is missing from current ideas about the nature of 'good education'. Further, he provides an analysis of how sex education could be improved. Central to Ingham's argument is the importance of teaching young people about desire and pleasure and how these are important both to physical and mental health. In particular, Ingham suggests that by learning about their bodies and how to achieve sexual pleasure, young people may feel more empowered to have healthier and happier sexual relationships. He argues that 'if young people are enabled to feel more relaxed about their own bodies, and about bodily pleasures then they may be less affected by the pressures to engage in sexual activity against their wishes or in ways that they do not feel comfortable about' (p. 385). Ingham then suggests that the use of small group teaching, organized around friendship groups with people at similar stages of sexual development and experience, could enable a deeper and more focused discussion of both the 'factual' and pleasure aspects of sex. These problems with school sex education reflect the debates about using psychological models to examine sexual behaviour and emphasize a need to place an individual's beliefs within the context of an interaction between individuals. In addition, the discussions about sex education in schools highlight the social context in which sex occurs.

AN INDIVIDUAL'S SOCIAL WORLD

Information about sex also comes from an individual's social world in terms of one's peers, parents and siblings. Holland et al. (1990a) argued that sex education and the process of learning about sex occur in the context of a multitude of different sources of information. They redefined the 'problem of sex education' as something that is broader than acquiring facts. They also argued that the resulting knowledge not only influences an individual's own knowledge and beliefs but also creates their sexuality. They identified the following five sources: school, peers, parents, magazines, and partners and relationships. Holland et al. argued that through these different sources, individuals learn about sex and their sexuality and suggested that 'the constructions which are presented are of women as passive, as potential victims of male sexuality or at best reproductive' (p. 43). However, they also argued that women do not simply passively accept this version of sexuality but are in a 'constant process of negotiating and re-negotiating the meaning which others give to their behaviour' (p. 43). Therefore, perhaps any understanding of sexual behaviour should take place within an understanding of the social context of sex education in the broadest sense.

POWER RELATIONS BETWEEN SEXUAL PARTNERS

Sex is an interaction between people and using contraception, particularly condoms, emerges out of this interaction, with or without explicit negotiation. But relationships between people are often unequal and research has explored the impact of power relations between sexual partners, both between men and women and between men and men.

MEN AND WOMEN

Holland et al. (1990b) argued that condom use 'must be understood in the context of the contradictions and tensions of heterosexual relationships' and the 'gendered power relations which construct and constrain choices and decisions'. They presented examples of power inequalities between men and women and the range of ways in which inequality can express itself, from coercion to rape. For example, one woman in their study said, 'I wasn't forced to do it but I didn't want to do it' and another explained her ambivalence to sex as 'like, do you want a coffee? Okay, fine, you drink the coffee, because you don't really like drinking coffee but you drink it anyway.' In fact, empirical research suggests that men's intentions to use condoms may be more likely to correlate with actual behaviour than women's, perhaps because women's intentions may be inhibited by the sexual context (Abraham et al. 1996). Sex should also be understood within the context of gender and power.

MEN AND MEN

Studies indicate that between one-fifth to one-third of men report having experienced some form of sexual coercion in their relationships with men (see Flowers et al. 1998; Ratner et al. 2003; Ridge 2004). Gavey et al. (2009) carried out focus groups with 40 gay and bisexual men in New Zealand to explore how coercion was experienced and its impact on safer sex practices and highlighted issues relating to drugs and alcohol, power and experience (see **Focus on Research 7.1** for details). Gavey et al. concluded that safe sex practices require choice and control and a process of negotiation, but that power relations between men can result in coercion which undermines these behaviours.

FOCUS ON RESEARCH 7.1: CONDOM USE IN GAY MEN

Understanding condom use and non-use in gay men and the impact of coercion (Gavey et al. 2009).

Power dynamics in relationships, coercion and rape are most commonly considered within the framework of relationships between men and women. However, there is much evidence emerging that men who have sex with men also experience coercion and power inequalities in their relationships and that this can result in unwanted and unsafe sex. This study used a qualitative design to explore gay men's experiences of coercion and the reasons for this.

METHODOLOGY

The data used in this paper were collected as part of a larger study that involved 18 interviews and six focus groups with gay and bisexual men and interviews with 23 key informants involved in gay men's welfare and issues of sexual violence. The interviews and focus groups focused on issues relating to sexual coercion.

Data Analysis

The data were analysed within a critical realist perspective which accepts the socially constructed nature of people's accounts but also accepts them as reasonable descriptions of real events.

RESULTS

The results from this study primarily showed how men can often find the ideals of choice and control much more precarious in practice than they would like. In addition, although the men described many accounts of being able to resist pressure to have unprotected sex, they also reported three key interrelated dynamics that made resisting this pressure impossible. These were as follows.

Drugs, Alcohol, Power and Sex

The results indicated how intoxication led men to change their 'usual sexual boundaries' leaving them more open to sexual coercion. Therefore, although it is already acknowledged that drugs and alcohol may change the boundaries of an individual's own desires, this paper argued that it also makes men unable to resist the unwanted desires of others. In fact many of the men described being plied with drink and drugs, often by older and more experienced men, and feeling out of control of their own behaviour.

Vulnerabilities of Youth and Inexperience

A related factor highlighted how one man's experience and age could change the power dynamics, thereby coercing the other man into having unsafe sex. For example, a participant described how his request to use a condom was deemed as 'a childlike' choice. He therefore went along with the pressure to have unsafe sex as 'he might've looked down on me'.

Coercive Dynamics within Relationships

The third factor illustrated coercion in the absence of an age or experience gap whereby men experienced an inability to say 'no' or to negotiate condom use and therefore had unsafe sex, but felt that they were doing so without actually giving consent. The authors discuss this in terms of 'the power of the norm' which is similar to that reported in heterosexual relationships (see Gavey 2005).

CONCLUSION

The results indicate that safe sex practices require choice and control but that these can be undermined by problems relating to power, inequality, experience and coercion. These results are interesting for health psychology in general as they illustrate how sexual behaviour (and other behaviours) occur as an interaction between people and that any attempt to understand, predict or change behaviour needs to address this dynamic.

SOCIAL NORMS OF THE GAY COMMUNITY

Sex between men also occurs within the context of gay communities, which have their own sets of norms and values. Studies by Flowers et al. (1997, 1998) explored 'the transformation of men who come to find themselves within a specific gay culture, one in which there are clear values which structure their new social world, shaping their relationships and their sexual behaviour'. Flowers et al. asked the question 'How do the social norms and values of the gay community influence gay men's sexual practices?' They interviewed 20 gay men from a small town in northern England about their experiences of becoming gay within a gay community. The results provided some interesting insights into the norms of gay culture and the impact of this social context on an individual's behaviour. First, the study describes how men gain access to the gay community: 'through sex and socialising they come to recognise the presence of other gay men where once . . . they only felt isolation'; second, the study illustrates how simply having a gay identity is not enough to prepare them for their new community and that they have 'to learn a gay specific knowledge and a gay language'; and third, the study describes how this new culture influences their sexual behaviour. For example, the interviewees described how feelings of romance, trust, love, commitment, inequality within the relationship, lack of experience and desperation resulted in having anal sex without a condom even though they had the knowledge that their behaviour was risky. Therefore sexual behaviour also occurs within the context of specific communities with their own sets of norms and values.

TO CONCLUDE

Early writings about sex emphasized it as a biological function whose outcome was reproduction. From the beginning of the twentieth century the emphasis shifted, first towards sex as an activity with an increasing focus on pleasure and then to sex as a risk to health. More recently these different perspectives have been combined to create a more holistic model of sexual health which encompasses physical, mental and social well-being. Psychologists have contributed to this literature in terms of an examination of sexual behaviour both in the context of pregnancy avoidance and HIV/AIDS. These behaviours have been predominantly understood using social cognition models, which emphasize individual differences and individual cognitions. However, sex presents a problem for psychologists as it is intrinsically an interactive behaviour involving more than one person. It also exists within a broader social context. This chapter has therefore explored this context in terms of the process of negotiation, perceptions of risk, sex education, power relations between sexual partners and the social norms of the gay community.

QUESTIONS

1 Outline changes in the ways in which sex has been described over the past 200 years.
2 Why do people not use contraception?
3 To what extent can social cognition models predict condom use?
4 How can qualitative research contribute to an understanding of condom use?
5 To what extent can psychology incorporate the context of a behaviour?
6 In what ways does the social context impact upon contraception and condom use?
7 To what extent do the problems highlighted by the sex literature relate to other health behaviours?
8 Describe a possible research study aimed at predicting condom use in adolescents.

FOR DISCUSSION

Health education campaigns frequently use billboards and magazines to promote safe sex. Consider a recent advertisement and discuss whether or not this would encourage you to use condoms.

ASSUMPTIONS IN HEALTH PSYCHOLOGY

The research into sex and contraceptive use highlights some of the assumptions that are central to psychology as follows:

1 *Methodology accesses information, it does not create it.* It is believed that questionnaires/interviews provide us with insights into what people think and believe. However, does the method of asking questions

influence the results? For example, do people have beliefs about risk until they are asked about risk? Do people have behavioural intentions prior to being asked whether they intend to behave in a particular way?

2　***Individuals can be studied separately from their social context.*** Social psychologists have studied processes such as conformity, group dynamics, obedience to authority and diffusion of responsibility, all of which suggest that individuals behave differently when on their own than when in the presence of others and also indicate the extent to which an individual's behaviour is determined by their context. However, much psychological research continues to examine behaviour and beliefs out of context. To what extent can psychological research incorporate the context? To what extent should it attempt to incorporate the environment?

3　***Theories are derived from data.*** Theories are not data themselves. It is assumed that eventually we will develop the best way to study sex, which will enable us to understand and predict sexual behaviour. However, perhaps the different approaches to sex can tell us something about the way we see individuals. For example, attempting to incorporate interactions between individuals into an understanding of sex may be a better way of understanding sex, and it may also suggest that we now see individuals as being interactive. In addition, examining the social context may also suggest that our model of individuals is changing and we see individuals as being social products.

FURTHER READING

Holland, J., Ramazanoglu, C. and Scott, S. (1990) Managing risk and experiencing danger: tensions between government AIDS health education policy and young women's sexuality, *Gender and Education*, 2: 125–46.
The WRAP study was an impressive piece of qualitative work that changed the ways in which people thought about sexual behaviour. This paper presents some of the results from the WRAP and examines how young women feel about their sexuality in the context of HIV.

Ingham, R. and Aggleton, P. (eds) (2005) *Promoting Young People's Sexual Health.* London: Routledge.
This book provides an excellent analysis of the practical and ideological barriers to enhancing sexual health in young people and offers a detailed account of cross-cultural differences and the problems faced in developing countries.

Lee, E., Clements, S., Ingham, R. and Stone, N. (2004) *A Matter of Choice? Explaining National Variations in Teenage Abortion and Motherhood.* York: Joseph Rowntree Foundation.
This book provides a detailed analysis of young people's sexual behaviour and their decisions about becoming a parent.

Robinson, B.B., Bockting, W.O., Rossner, BR. et al. (2002) The sexual health model: application of a sexological approach to HIV prevention, *Health Education Research*, 17: 43–57.
This paper presents the sexual health model described at the start of this chapter and illustrates a broader way of thinking about sex, condom use and sex as a core part of people's lives.

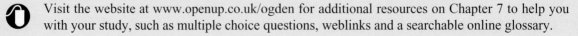 Visit the website at www.openup.co.uk/ogden for additional resources on Chapter 7 to help you with your study, such as multiple choice questions, weblinks and a searchable online glossary.

8 Health Promotion: Changing Health Behaviours

© Jeff Farmer, iStock

CHAPTER OVERVIEW

Chapter 3 explored factors that help understand and predict health-related behaviours. Chapters 4–7 then focused on individual health behaviours. This chapter explores a number of different approaches that have been developed to change health-related behaviour and describes those that target the individual and whole populations. Although there are a multitude of strategies that can be used to change individual behaviour, this chapter describes those that have been informed by four main theoretical perspectives: (1) learning theory and the use of behavioural strategies, modelling, cognitive behavioural therapy and relapse prevention; (2) social cognition theory and the use of social cognition models to frame interventions, information and planning; (3) stages of change theory (SOC) and the development of motivational interviewing; (4) theories of affect and the use of visualization, changes in affective cognitions, fear appeals and self-affirmation. The chapter then explores the impact of new technologies on behaviour change interventions such as texts, the identification of biological risk factors, the use of web-based intervention and the role of the mass media. Next, it describes commonalities across these different perspectives and the research which attempts to identify active ingredients, regardless of theoretical framework. Finally, it examines the characteristics of long-term successful changes in behaviour.

HOW TO CHANGE BEHAVIOUR

Behaviour and behaviour change can be seen as being either conscious and effortful, whereby the individual makes choices about how and whether to change their behaviour *or* effortless, whereby behaviour change occurs with no conscious processing. Effortful changes include decisions to eat more healthily, to stop smoking or to do more exercise. In contrast, effortless change is mostly a reaction to external changes in the environment as people alter their behaviour in response to a world that has also changed. Stopping smoking because it has been banned in public places or drinking less fizzy drinks because the machines have been removed from schools are examples of effortless changes.

Most psychological approaches encourage effortful changes in behaviour through interventions targeted at the individual. In contrast, public health interventions focus more on structural and environmental changes that bring about shifts in behaviour without the individual necessarily knowing they are involved in an intervention or even that they have changed their behaviour. This chapter will explore both effortful and effortless behaviour change strategies in the context of both individual and public health approaches to behaviour change. It will also explore how a range of strategies have evolved from a number of key psychological theories (see Chapter 4 for details on smoking- and alcohol-specific interventions). But first it explores the recent call for interventions that are based on theory.

THE NEED FOR THEORY-BASED INTERVENTIONS

Over recent years there has been a movement towards using psychological theories to inform and develop health behaviour interventions. This has been based upon two observations. First, it was observed that many interventions designed to change behaviour were only minimally effective. For example, reviews of early interventions to change sexual behaviour concluded that these interventions had only small effects (e.g. Oakley et al. 1995) and dietary interventions for weight loss may result in weight loss in the short term but the majority show a return to baseline by follow-up (e.g. NHS Centre for Reviews and Dissemination 1997). Second, it was observed that many interventions were not based upon any theoretical framework, nor were they drawing upon research that had identified which factors were correlated with the particular behaviour (e.g. Fisher and Fisher 1992). One interesting illustration of this involved the content analysis of health promotion leaflets to assess their theoretical basis. Abraham et al. (2002) collected sexual health leaflets from general practitioners' (GPs) surgeries and clinics for the treatment of sexually transmitted diseases (STDs) across Germany (37 leaflets) and the UK (74 leaflets). They included those that promoted the use of condoms and/or prevention of STDs including HIV and AIDS and were available widely. They excluded those that were aimed at lesbians due to their focus on protective measures other than condoms and those that targeted a limited audience such as HIV-positive men. The authors then identified the best cognitive and behavioural correlates of condom use based upon a meta-analysis by Sheeran et al. (1999), defined 20 correlate representative categories to reflect these correlates and then rated the leaflets according to the inclusion and frequency of these factors. The results showed very little association between theory and this form of behavioural intervention. Specifically, only 25 per cent of the leaflets referred to 10 or more of the correlates and two-thirds of the leaflets failed to frequently target more than two of the correlates. Although research is aimed at informing practice, it would seem that this is not often the case. However, many different approaches to behaviour change have been developed and tested. These can be classified as individual-based and population-based interventions.

Most psychology-based interventions target the individual and fall within the framework of four main theoretical perspectives. These will now be explored.

LEARNING AND COGNITIVE THEORIES

Learning theory forms the basis of much psychological work with its emphasis on associative learning, reinforcement and modelling. For example, from this perspective we eat chocolate when we are feeling fed up because we associate chocolate with feeling special from when we were children (associative learning), because our parents commented how lucky we were when they gave it to us (reinforcement) and because we saw them eat it (modelling). Cognitive theory added to this approach by encouraging psychologists to also explore how people think as well as how they behave. These theoretical perspectives have informed a number of therapeutic approaches which have been used to facilitate behaviour change. This chapter describes reinforcement, incentives, modelling, associative learning, exposure, cognitive behavioural therapy (CBT) and relapse prevention (see Figure 8.1).

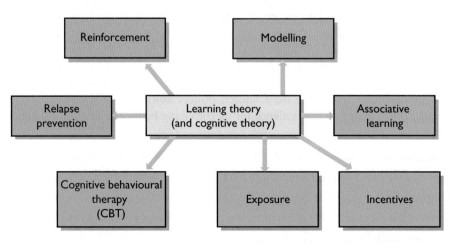

FIGURE 8.1

Behaviour change interventions derived from learning and cognitive theory

REINFORCEMENT

One way to change behaviour is to positively reinforce the desired behaviour and ignore or punish the less desired behaviour. For example, a child is more likely to eat fruit and vegetables if their parent smiles while they are eating them and an adult is less likely to return for a screening test if they found the last one embarrassing and painful. This process has been assessed by a number of different experimental studies and interventions. For example, Barthomeuf et al. (2007) explored whether the emotion expressed on people's faces could influence food preferences. Men and women were exposed to a series of pictures of liked and disliked food that were either on their own or accompanied by people eating them and expressing one of three emotions: disgust, pleasure or neutrality. The results showed that the expression of the eater influenced ratings of preference. Therefore, pairing a food with emotion changes the preference for that food. One intervention introduced a 'Kid's choice' school lunch programme whereby children were given tokens for eating fruit or vegetables which could be later traded for prizes. The results showed that preference and consumption increased at two weeks after the programme (Hendy et al. 1995). However by seven months, when the programme had finished, levels had returned to baseline: rewarding behaviour may change behaviour but this may not persist when the rewards are removed. The role of reinforcement is also implicit with several medical approaches to managing behaviour. For example, the drug Antabuse induces sickness if the individual also consumes alcohol and the drug orlistat causes anal leakage if taken with fatty foods. Both these consequences act as a deterrent for future behaviours (Finer 2002). Furthermore, research indicates that people often change their behaviour in the longer term when the old unhealthy behaviour is no longer functional. For example, people stop smoking when it no longer offers them a way to spend time with friends or change their diet when they find different foods more enjoyable (Ogden and Hills 2008).

INCENTIVES

Research has also explored the impact of financial incentives as a means to change behaviour. Incentivizing behaviour is rooted in a notion of reinforcement and has long been the standard tool of the retail industry which aims to encourage consumers to purchase a particular brand rather than a competitor's brand. In the context of health-related behaviours, incentivizing can take the form of centralized changes to the cost of products such as cigarettes, fatty foods and fizzy drinks or directly paying people to lose weight, stop smoking or be more physically active. Over the past few years research has addressed the effectiveness of these simple (and fairly crude) approaches and indicates that, in general, changes in cost and direct financial rewards can effectively change behaviour. For example, increased taxes on both alcohol and cigarettes over the past few decades have been linked with a reduction in drinking and alcohol (Sutherland et al. 2008) and current ongoing direct payment schemes include giving pregnant women in the UK £20 food vouchers for one-week smoking cessation, £40 after four weeks and £40 after one year (North East Essex NHS Trust 2009); paying men and women $45 in Tanzania to have regular tests for sexually transmitted diseases (World Bank 2008) and giving points to children in Scotland for eating healthy school meals which can be exchanged for donations to a Save the Children project abroad (East Ayrshire Council 2011). Marteau et al. (2009) reviewed the evidence for incentivizing behaviour change and concluded the following:

- The greater the incentive, the greater the likelihood of behaviour change.
- Incentives are better at producing short-term rather than longer-term changes.
- The impact of the incentive depends upon the financial state of the individual.
- Incentives are more effective if the money is paid as close as possible to that target behaviour.
- Incentives work better for discrete and infrequent behaviours such as having vaccinations rather than repeated habitual behaviours such as diet or smoking.

Marteau et al. also concluded that there may be three unintended consequences of incentivizing behaviour. These are:

- Incentives may undermine an individual's intrinsic motivation for carrying out a behaviour (e.g. 'I ate healthily but now I don't really like healthy foods').
- Incentives are a form of bribery which undermine an individual's informed consent and autonomy.
- Incentives may change the doctor–patient relationship if the patient is paid by the doctor to behave in certain ways.

Incentives therefore seem to change behaviour through a crude version of reinforcement. However, they may also have unintended consequences which may undermine changes in behaviour in the longer term.

MODELLING

Modelling healthy behaviour can also change behaviour: a child is more likely to smoke if their parents smoke and less likely to take up exercise if they see their parents sitting on the sofa watching TV. Research shows that adolescents are more likely to eat breakfast if their parents do (Pearson et al. 2009) and that adolescents are more likely to eat for emotional reasons such as boredom or comfort if their parents do this as well (Snoek et al. 2007). An intervention study explicitly used modelling to change children's eating behaviour (Lowe et al. 1998). This series of studies used video material of 'food dudes' – older children enthusiastically consuming refused food – which was shown to children with a history of food refusal. The results showed that exposure to the 'food dudes' significantly changed the children's food preferences and specifically increased their consumption of fruit and vegetables as the participants modelled their behaviour on that of the 'food dudes' in the video. Similarly, Sanderson and Yopyk (2007) showed young people a video consisting of other young people with positive attitudes towards condoms who modelled strategies for using them appropriately. The results showed increased intentions to have safe sex, higher self-efficacy to refuse unsafe sex and higher condom use four months later.

ASSOCIATIVE LEARNING

Associative learning involves pairing two variables together so that one variable acquires the value or meaning of the other. For example, in the classic early studies Pavlov's dogs heard a bell ring whenever they were given food and after a while they started to salivate when they heard the bell (even without the food). *Evaluative conditioning* is a form of associative learning whereby an attitude object is paired repeatedly with an object which is either viewed positively or negatively as a means to make the attitude object either more positive or negative. This method is frequently used in marketing as a means to make relatively neutral objects (e.g. perfume, cigarettes, pet food, air freshener) seem more positive by pairing them with something that is inherently attractive (e.g. attractive people, green fields, romantic music, etc.). Gibson (2008) tested this process experimentally and reported that evaluative conditioning could make participants predictably choose between Coca-Cola or Pepsi depending on which one had been paired with positive meaning. In terms of health, Hollands et al. (2011) used an evaluative conditioning procedure to increase the negative value attached to unhealthy snacks such as crisps and chocolate. Participants were shown images of unhealthy snacks interspersed with aversive unhealthy images of the body for the experimental condition (e.g. artery disease, obesity, heart surgery), or a blank screen for the control condition. The results showed that the intervention resulted in more positive implicit attitudes compared to the control condition. In addition, those in the experimental condition also chose fruit rather than high calorie snacks in a behavioural task.

Skills training for condom use can promote health behaviours through exposure to those behaviours in a safe context (this is a banana!)

SOURCE: © Atman/Dreamstime

EXPOSURE

One of the best predictors of future behaviour is past behaviour (see Chapter 3), as having already performed a behaviour makes that behaviour seem familiar and can increase an individual's confidence that they can carry out the behaviour again. Therefore, one of the simplest ways to change behaviour is through exposure to the behaviour, practice or skills training. In terms of eating habits, research shows that we eat what we are familiar with and have been exposed to. For example, Wardle et al. (2003) carried out a study whereby children aged 2–6 identified a vegetable they least liked and then were exposed to this vegetable for 14 days (compared to children who were either given information or were in the control group). The results showed that daily exposure resulted in the children eating more of the vegetable in a taste test and reporting greater preference for the vegetable than those in the other two groups. Similarly research indicates that children can identify and are willing to taste vegetables if their parents purchase them (Busick et al. 2008). Simple exposure can therefore change intake and preference. In a similar vein, actually performing a behaviour once can increase the chances that this behaviour will occur again in the future. For example, as part of sexual education interventions, research shows that basic skills training in negotiating how to ask for a condom, putting a condom on or buying a condom, which involves rehearsing these behaviours in a safe environment, improves the likelihood of these behaviours in the future (e.g. Weisse et al. 1995; see Chapter 7). Furthermore, not only does past behaviour predict future behaviour but it also predicts and changes cognitions that then predict behaviour (Gerrard et al. 1996). For example, if I think 'condoms are difficult to put on' and my behaviour is 'I don't use condoms' and then I put one on a banana during a skills training session, my cognition will shift to 'actually I can use condoms' and my behaviour will change as well to 'I now use condoms'.

COGNITIVE BEHAVIOURAL THERAPY

Behavioural strategies emphasize changing behaviour through reinforcement, modelling, exposure or associative learning and highlight a stimulus-response model of the individual. Much research, however, also includes a role for cognitions and interventions to change behaviour tend to combine cognitive and behaviour strategies into cognitive behavioural therapy (CBT). Freeman (1995) describes how CBT emphasizes the following:

- The link between thoughts and feelings.
- Therapy as a collaboration between patient and therapist.
- The patient as scientist and the role of experimentation.
- The importance of self-monitoring.
- The importance of regular measurement.
- The idea of an agenda for each session set by both patient and therapist.
- The idea that treatment is about learning a set of skills.
- The idea that the therapist is not the expert who will teach the patient how to get better.
- The importance of regular feedback by both patient and therapist.

CBT can vary according to client group and the problem being addressed, but involves a more structured form of intervention than most therapies and often includes the following cognitive and behavioural strategies:

1   *Keeping a diary:* many behaviours and thoughts occur without people being fully aware of them. For CBT, clients are asked to keep a diary of significant events and associated feelings,

thoughts and behaviours. This process of self-monitoring enables clients to understand the patterns in their lives and the ways in which they are responding to whatever is happening to them. For someone trying to change their diet, a diary could reveal that they eat while watching the TV or turn to food at work when feeling under stress.

2 *Gradually trying out new behaviours:* many behaviours are habitual and over time we learn to practise those behaviours which make us feel good and avoid those that make us feel uncomfortable. For CBT, clients are asked either on their own or with the therapist to try out new behaviours or face activities that have been avoided. This enables people to build confidence and familiarity with new behaviours and try to unlearn old behaviours.

3 *Cue exposure:* many people find that unhealthy behaviours can be triggered by certain situations (e.g. the desire to smoke when drinking alcohol). For CBT, clients are sometimes exposed to such situations when with the therapist in order to help them learn new coping responses and extinguish the old unhealthy reactions to these situations. For example, people addicted to drugs may be gradually exposed to the paraphernalia of drugs (e.g. silver foil, needles, cigarette papers, etc.) as a means to change their response to them.

4 *Relaxation techniques:* clients may use music, repeated clenching and relaxing of muscles, recordings of soothing voices or recordings of subliminal messages as a means to aid relaxation. This can help them to reduce their anxiety and negative thoughts about aspects of their lives.

5 *Distraction techniques:* distraction can be a powerful method for managing anxiety or preventing unhealthy responses to certain situations. In CBT, clients can be helped to find distraction strategies that work for them. For example, if a person feels the need to smoke when with certain friends, they can be taught how to focus on other aspects of their lives at these times or encouraged to use a telephone help line.

6 *Cognitive restructuring:* central to CBT is the notion that behaviour is maintained through a series of distorted cognitions and a vicious cycle between thoughts and behaviours which is perpetuated by irrational self-talk. Such distorted cognitions are:

- *Selective abstraction*, which involves focusing on selected evidence (e.g. 'drinking alcohol is the only way I can unwind after work').

- *Dichotomous reasoning*, which involves thinking in terms of extremes (e.g. 'If I am not in complete control, I will lose all control').

- *Overgeneralization*, which involves making conclusions from single events and then generalizing to all others (e.g. 'I failed last night so I will fail today as well').

- *Magnification*, which involves exaggeration (e.g. 'Stopping smoking will push me over the brink').

- *Superstitious thinking*, which involves making connections between unconnected things (e.g. 'If I do exercise, I will have another heart attack').

- *Personalization*, which involves making sense of events in a self-centred fashion (e.g. 'They were laughing, they must be laughing at me').

CBT then uses a number of cognitive strategies to challenge and change these distorted cognitions and replace them with more helpful ones. The main approach involves Socratic questions with the therapist challenging the client's cognitions by asking for evidence and attempting to help the client to develop a different perspective. Questions could include: 'What evidence do you have to support your thoughts?'; 'How would someone else view this situation?'; 'When you say "everyone", who do you mean?'; 'When you say "all the time", can you think of times when this is not the case?' To aid this process the therapist can use role play and role reversal so that the client can watch and hear someone else using their cognitions and learn to see how unhelpful and irrational they are.

CBT and Chronic Illness

Antoni and colleagues (Antoni et al. 2001, 2002) have developed structured guidelines for using CBT with a range of chronic illness patients including those with HIV and cancer as a means to change cognitions and promote behaviour change. They outline a detailed system for changing irrational thoughts using rational thought replacement which they call the ABCDE system. This is as follows:

Awareness: because much of our self-talk is automatic, the first step is to become aware of the cognitions we hold and the ways in which these impact upon emotional and physical responses. This awareness process can involve diary-keeping, reflection and talking to a therapist.

Beliefs: clients are then asked to rate their beliefs about each of the self-talk processes they hold to identify how strong their cognitions are. They should ask themselves 'How much do I believe that each of these cognitions is true?'.

Challenge: clients challenge their thoughts through questions which ask for evidence or encourage the client to think through what other people would think or do in the same situation.

Delete: Antoni and colleagues then argue that clients need to delete these self-statements and replace them with constructive cognitions. This can involve thinking through alternative explanations and different ways of making sense of what happens to them.

Evaluate: the final stage is for the client to evaluate how they feel after the cognitions have been deleted and whether they feel the process has been successful.

CBT has been most commonly used within the mental health domain to treat problems such as panic disorders, obsessive compulsive disorder (OCD) and eating disorders. It is also used in health psychology, particularly for a number of chronic conditions to change behaviours such as physical activity, diet, safe sex practices, smoking and alcohol intake (Antoni et al. 2001, 2002, 2006).

RELAPSE PREVENTION

CBT describes a number of cognitive and behavioural strategies to help people change their behaviour. Marlatt and Gordon (1985) developed a relapse prevention model to explore the processes that occur when a change in behaviour fails to last and people relapse. This model was developed in the context of addictions to substances such as nicotine, alcohol and drugs but has implications for understanding all other forms of behaviour change that may or may not be sustained. The relapse prevention model was based on the following concept of addictive behaviours:

- Addictive behaviours are learned and therefore can be unlearned; they are reversible.
- Addictions are not 'all or nothing' but exist on a continuum.
- Lapses from abstinence are likely and acceptable.
- Believing that 'one drink – a drunk' is a self-fulfilling prophecy.

Marlatt and Gordon distinguished between a lapse, which entails a minor slip (e.g. a cigarette, a couple of drinks), and a relapse, which entails a return to former behaviour (e.g. smoking 20 cigarettes, getting drunk). They examined the processes involved in the progression from abstinence to relapse and in particular assessed the mechanisms that may explain the transition from lapse to relapse (see Figure 8.2). These processes are described below.

Baseline State

Abstinence. If an individual sets total abstinence as the goal, then this stage represents the target behaviour and indicates a state of behavioural control.

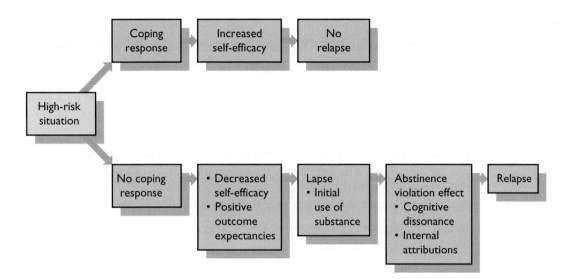

FIGURE 8.2

The relapse process

SOURCE: Adapted from Marlatt and Gordon (1985)

Pre-Lapse State

High-risk situation. A high-risk situation is any situation that may motivate the individual to carry out the behaviour. Such situations may be either external cues, such as someone else smoking or the availability of alcohol, or internal cues, such as anxiety. Research indicates that the most commonly reported high-risk situations are negative emotions, interpersonal conflict and social pressure. This is in line with social learning theories, which predict that internal cues are more problematic than external cues.

Coping behaviour. Once exposed to a high-risk situation the individual engages the coping strategies. Such strategies may be behavioural, such as avoiding the situation or using a substitute behaviour (e.g. eating), or cognitive, such as remembering why they are attempting to abstain.

Positive outcome expectancies. According to previous experience the individual will either have positive outcome expectancies if the behaviour is carried out (e.g. 'smoking will make me feel less anxious') or negative outcome expectancies (e.g. 'getting drunk will make me feel sick').

No Lapse or Lapse?

Marlatt and Gordon (1985) argue that when exposed to a high-risk situation, if an individual can engage good coping mechanisms and also develop negative outcome expectancies, the chances of a lapse will be reduced and the individual's self-efficacy will be increased. However, if the individual engages poor coping strategies and has positive outcome expectancies, the chances of a lapse will be high and the individual's self-efficacy will be reduced.

- *No lapse:* good coping strategies and negative outcome expectancies will raise self-efficacy, causing the period of abstinence to be maintained.
- *Lapse:* poor or no coping strategies and positive outcome expectancies will lower self-efficacy, causing an initial use of the substance (the cigarette, a drink). This lapse will either remain an isolated event and the individual will return to abstinence, or will become a full-blown relapse. Marlatt and Gordon describe this transition as the abstinence violation effect (AVE).

The AVE

The transition from initial lapse to full-blown relapse is determined by dissonance conflict and self-attribution. Dissonance is created by a conflict between a self-image as someone who no longer smokes or drinks and the current behaviour (e.g. smoking/drinking). This conflict is exacerbated by a disease model of addictions, which emphasizes 'all or nothing', and minimized by a social learning model, which acknowledges the likelihood of lapses.

Having lapsed, the individual is motivated to understand the cause of the lapse. If this lapse is attributed to the self (e.g. 'I am useless, it's my fault'), this may create guilt and self-blame. This internal attribution may lower self-efficacy, thereby increasing the chances of a full-blown relapse. However, if the lapse is attributed to the external world (e.g. the situation, the presence of others), guilt and self-blame will be reduced and the chances of the lapse remaining a lapse will be increased.

Marlatt and Gordon developed a relapse prevention programme based on cognitive behavioural techniques to help prevent lapses turning into full-blown relapses. This programme involved the following procedures:

- Self-monitoring (what do I do in high-risk situations?).
- Relapse fantasies (what would it be like to relapse?).
- Relaxation training/stress management.
- Skills training.
- Contingency contracts.
- Cognitive restructuring (learning not to make internal attributions for lapses).

How these procedures relate to the different stages of relapse is illustrated in Figure 8.3.

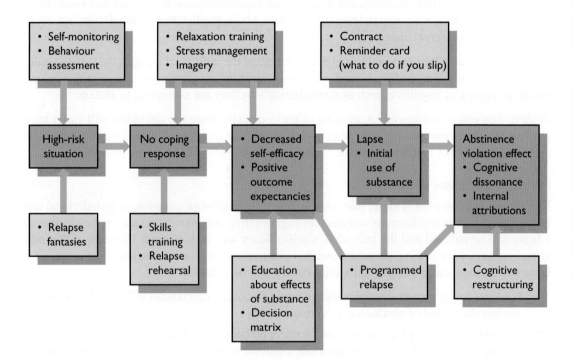

FIGURE 8.3

Relapse prevention intervention strategies

SOURCE: Adapted from Marlatt and Gordon (1985)

Relapse prevention has been used in a multitude of different contexts as a means to change behaviour either on its own or as part of a complex intervention. For example, Roske et al. (2008) explored the impact of a smoking cessation intervention using relapse prevention techniques in women post-pregnancy. The results showed that the intervention predicted both non-smoking and improved self-efficacy by six months. But by one year the intervention group showed smoking levels similar to the control group.

Learning theory (along with cognitive theory) therefore form the basis of many interventions to change behaviour. Some of these take the form of behavioural strategies with their emphasis on reinforcement, modelling and associative learning. Many incorporate both cognitive and behavioural strategies such as CBT (with its emphasis on behaviour change) and relapse prevention (with its emphasis on sustaining change and preventing relapse).

SOCIAL COGNITION THEORY

Social cognition theory was described in Chapter 3 and emphasizes expectancies, incentives and social cognitions (e.g. Bandura 1986). Expectancies include beliefs such as 'a poor diet can cause heart disease', 'if I changed my diet I could improve my health' and 'I could change my diet if I wanted to'. Incentives relate to the impact of the consequences of any behaviour and are closely aligned to reinforcements. For example, a healthy diet would be continued if an individual lost weight or had more energy but stopped if they became bored. Finally, social cognitions reflect an individual's representations of their social world in terms of what other people around think about any given behaviour. These constructs form the basis of social cognition models such as the theory of planned behaviour (TPB) and were described in Chapter 3 in the context of predicting how people behave. Recently this approach has been used to develop interventions to change behaviour with a focus on ways to change individual cognitions which in turn will result in changed behaviour. Further, as a development of this approach, research within the framework of social cognition theory has also explored the intention–behaviour gap and interventions that can be used to increase the likelihood that intentions will be translated into behaviour. These interventions consist of the use of planning, particularly implementation intentions. Finally, researchers have used knowledge- and information-based interventions as a means to change cognitions and therefore behaviour. These different types of intervention are shown in Figure 8.4 and will now be considered.

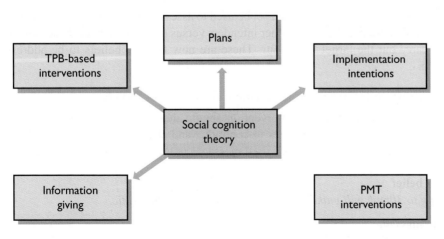

FIGURE 8.4

Behaviour change interventions derived from social cognition theory

SOCIAL COGNITION: PUTTING THEORY INTO PRACTICE

Given the call for more theory-based interventions, some researchers have outlined how this can be done with social cognition models. In particular, Sutton (2002b; 2010) draws upon the work of Fishbein and Middlestadt (1989) and describes a series of steps that can be followed to develop an intervention based upon the TPB, although he argued that the steps could also be applied to other models.

Step 1: Identify Target Behaviour and Target Population

Sutton argued that it is crucial that the target population and behaviour are clearly defined so that all measures used can be specific to that behaviour and population. This is in line with Ajzen's (1988) notion of correspondence or compatibility. For example, the behaviour should not just be 'healthy eating' but 'eating lettuce with my sandwich at lunchtime in the work canteen'. Accordingly the target behaviour should be defined in terms of action (eat healthily), target (lettuce), time (lunchtime) and context (at work).

Step 2: Identify the Most Salient Beliefs about the Target Behaviour in the Target Population Using Open-Ended Questions

Sutton then suggests that those developing the intervention carry out an elicitation study to identify the most salient beliefs about the target behaviour in the target population being studied. Elliot et al. (2005) designed an intervention to encourage drivers' compliance with speed limits and asked questions such as 'What do you think are the advantages of keeping within the speed limit whilst driving in a built-up area?'. The most common beliefs are known as *modal beliefs* and form the basis for the analysis.

Step 3: Conduct a Study Involving Closed Questions to Determine Which Beliefs are the Best Predictors of Behavioural Intention. Choose the Best Belief as the Target Belief

To further help to decide which beliefs to target in the intervention Sutton (2002, 2010) suggests carrying out a quantitative study including the salient beliefs identified in Step 2 involving the target population. These data can then be analysed to explore the best predictors of behavioural intentions as a means to decide whether all or only some of the TPB variables need to be included in the intervention.

Step 4: Analyse the Data to Determine the Beliefs that Best Discriminate Between Intenders and Non-Intenders. These Are Further Target Beliefs

Next, Sutton suggests that the same data set be used to assess which beliefs (including those identified in Step 2) differentiate between either intenders versus non-intenders or those who either do or do no not carry out the target behaviour. These are now the key beliefs to be addressed in the intervention.

Step 5: Develop an Intervention to Change These Target Beliefs

Finally, Sutton describes how the intervention should then aim to change these beliefs which mostly involves giving strong messages to contradict and change the target population's beliefs. Using this approach, Elliot et al. (2005) used messages to target individuals' beliefs as follows:

> **Target belief**
> *Keeping to 30mph will make it difficult to keep up with the traffic.*
>
> **Strong message**
> *Many drivers think that if they keep to the speed limit they will have difficulty keeping up with the traffic. However, this is a perception rather than a reality for the most part.*

Consider what driving in a 30mph area is typically like. Even on larger 30mph roads, there are roundabouts, traffic lights, pedestrian crossings and other things that make it necessary for traffic to slow down or stop. If a vehicle in front starts to pull away from you, you will often find that by maintaining a speed of 30mph you will catch up with that vehicle further up the road, because they have had to stop or slow down. They will have saved no significant amount of time and they will have gained little or no advantage.

From this perspective the TPB can be used as a framework for developing a behaviour change intervention. However, as Sutton (2002b; 2010) points out, although this process provides clear details about the preliminary work before the intervention, the intervention itself remains unclear. Hardeman et al. (2002) carried out a systematic review of 30 papers which used the TPB as part of an intervention and described a range of frameworks that had been used. These included persuasion, information, increasing skills, goal-setting and rehearsal of skills. These have recently been developed and integrated into a causal modelling approach for the development of behaviour change programmes (Hardeman et al. 2005). Sutton (2002b) indicates that two additional frameworks could also be useful. These are guided mastery experiences which involve getting people to focus on specific beliefs and the 'elaboration likelihood' model (Petty and Cacioppo 1986), which involves the presentation of 'strong arguments' and time for the recipient to think about and elaborate upon these arguments. Studies have also used a range of methods for their interventions including leaflets, videos, lectures and discussions.

USING SOCIAL COGNITION-BASED INTERVENTIONS

Over recent years an increasing number of behavioural interventions have been based upon social cognition models to change a range of behaviours. For example, Quine et al. (2001) followed the steps outlined earlier to identify salient beliefs about safety helmet wearing for children. They then developed an intervention based upon persuasion to change these salient beliefs. The results showed that after the intervention the participants showed more positive beliefs about safety helmet wearing than the control group and were more likely to wear a helmet at five months' follow-up. Similarly, McClendon and Prentice-Dunn (2001) targeted sun-tanning and developed an intervention based upon protection motivation theory (PMT). PMT variables were measured at baseline and one month follow-up and those in the intervention group were subjected to lectures, videos, an essay and discussions. The results showed that the intervention was associated with an increase in PMT variables and lighter skin as judged by independent raters. Other theory-based interventions have targeted behaviours such as the use of sports facilities (Sniehotta 2009), sun cream use (Castle et al. 1999), cervical cancer screening (Sheeran and Orbell 2000), children's fruit and vegetable intake (Gratton et al. 2007), and safer driving (Elliot et al. 2005).

There are some problems with using social cognition models for interventions, as follows.

- *How to change beliefs?* As Hardeman et al. (2002) found from their systematic review, although many interventions are based upon theory, this is often used for the design of process and outcome measures and to predict intention and behaviour rather than to design the intervention itself. Using the TPB for behaviour change interventions describes which beliefs should be changed but not how to change them.

- *Does behaviour change?* A TPB-based intervention assumes that changing salient beliefs will lead to changes in behaviour. However, studies indicate that there is an attenuation effect whereby any changes in beliefs are attenuated by the other variables in the model which reduce their impact upon behaviour (Armitage and Conner 2001; Sniehotta 2009). Further, although there is some evidence that theory-based interventions are successful, whether the use of theory relates to the success of the intervention remains unclear. For example,

Hardeman et al. (2002) reported that the use of the TPB to develop the intervention was not predictive of the success of the intervention.

- *Do they miss other important factors?* Sniehotta (2009) described the 'bottleneck' whereby interventions using the TPB assume that all changes in behaviour will be mediated through intentions. This, he argues, misses the opportunity to change other relevant factors which may influence behaviour directly such as changes in the environment and which do not need to pass through behavioural intentions.

Social cognition models have therefore been used to develop behaviour change interventions. To date, however, although they provide a clear structure for evaluating an intervention, the actual intervention and the means to be used to change beliefs require further attention.

MAKING PLANS AND IMPLEMENTATION INTENTIONS

Much research indicates that although an individual may make an intention to carry out a behaviour this intention is not always translated into practice. This is known as the intention–behaviour gap and appears to result from intenders who do not act rather than non-intenders who do act (Sheeran 2002). Research has highlighted a number of ways that this gap can be closed and in 1993 Gollwitzer defined the notion of implementation intentions which involve the development of simple but specific plans, after intentions, as to what an individual will do given a specific set of environmental factors. Therefore implementation intentions describe the 'what' and the 'when' of a particular behaviour. For example, the intention 'I intend to stop smoking' will be more likely to be translated into 'I have stopped smoking' if the individual makes the implementation intention 'I intend to stop smoking tomorrow at midday when I have finished my last packet'. Further, 'I intend to eat healthily' is more likely to be translated into 'I am eating healthily' if the implementation intention 'I will start to eat healthily by having a salad tomorrow at lunchtime' is made.

IMPLEMENTATION INTENTION INTERVENTIONS

Some experimental research has shown that encouraging individuals to make implementation intentions can actually increase the correlation between intentions and behaviour for a range of behaviours such as adolescent smoking (Conner and Higgins 2010), adult smoking (Armitage 2007b), fruit consumption (Armitage 2007a), fruit and vegetable consumption (Gratton et al. 2007), taking a vitamin C pill (Sheeran and Orbell 1998), reducing alcohol intake (Armitage 2009) and reducing dietary fat (Armitage 2004). Gollwitzer and Sheeran (2006) carried out a meta-analysis of 94 independent tests of the impact of implementation intentions on a range of behavioural goals and concluded that implementation intentions had a medium to large effect on goal attainment. Implementation intentions therefore provide a simple and easy way to promote and change health-related behaviours. There have, however, been some criticisms of this approach, as follows:

- *Do people make plans when asked to?* Research indicates that between 20 and 40 per cent of people do not make implementation intentions when they are asked to (Skar et al. 2008). This must influence the effectiveness of any intervention.
- *The impact of existing plans.* Implementation intention interventions ask people to make plans and then explore the impact of this on their behaviour. This assumes that people have not already made plans. Sniehotta et al. (2005) suggest that we need to differentiate between spontaneous plans and those made in response to the interventions.
- *Do people own their plans?* If people have made their own spontaneous plans they may well feel more ownership of these plans, making them more motivated to carry them out. This is not usually assessed in intervention studies.
- *Is all behaviour change volitional?* Central to a social cognition model approach to behaviour and the use of implementation intentions is the assumption that behaviour is volitional and

under the control of the individual. Much behaviour, however, may be either habitual or in response to environmental changes. These aspects are not addressed within this framework.

- *Not all plans are the same.* Sniehotta (2009) argues that research often treats all types of plans as the same but that it is important to differentiate between *action plans* and *coping plans*. Action plans involve choosing the behaviour that will achieve the goal (the where, when and how of the behaviour) and are what have been called implementation intentions. In contrast, coping plans prepare an individual for successfully managing high-risk situations in which strong cues might encourage them to engage in unwanted habits (without intention) or new unhealthy behaviours (with intention). Sniehotta et al. (2006) explored the relative impact of action and coping plans in promoting physical activity post-heart attack and concluded that those in the combined planning group did more activity that those in either the action planning group or the usual care group.

INFORMATION-GIVING

If a person believes 'I smoke but I am not at risk of getting lung cancer' or 'I eat a high fat diet but my heart is healthy', then the obvious first starting point to change their behaviour would be to improve their knowledge about their health. This has been the perspective of health education and health promotion campaigns for decades and has resulted in information provision through leaflets, billboards, TV advertisements and group-based seminars and lectures. Some research has evaluated the impact of information-giving using a range of mediums. For example, O'Brien and Lee (1990) manipulated knowledge about pap tests for cervical cancer by showing subjects an informative video and reported that not only did the video improve knowledge but that the resulting increased knowledge was related to future healthy behaviour. Further, Hammond et al. (2003) examined the effectiveness of the warning labels on cigarette packets and showed that the intention to stop smoking in the next six months and the number of quit attempts was higher in those who reported reading, thinking about and discussing the labels with other people. Similar results were also found in adolescents who were either established or occasional smokers (White et al. 2008; Germain et al. 2010). The provision of information is often incorporated into more complex interventions such as CBT, relapse prevention and psychoeducational interventions with people in rehabilitation (e.g. Dusseldorp et al. 1999; Sebregts et al. 2000; Rees et al. 2004). Generally it is accepted that giving information is not sufficient to change behaviour but that it is a useful and necessary adjunct to any other form of behaviour change strategy.

Social cognition theory has therefore informed much research on predicting and explaining health-related behaviours (see Chapter 3). It has also been the basis for behaviour change interventions, particularly through the use of the TPB and planning in the form of implementation intentions. In addition, interventions often use information and education as a means to improve knowledge and change cognitions. Such approaches are not without their problems however, particularly in terms of their narrow focus on intentions and behaviour and the focus on behaviour as a response to intentions and other related cognitions.

STAGE MODELS

Strategies to change behaviour based upon both learning theory and social cognition theory conceptualize behaviour as a continuum and change behaviour by encouraging people to move along the continuum from unhealthy to healthy ways of acting. In contrast, stage models of behaviour such as the SOC and the health action process approach (HAPA) emphasize differences between people who are at different stages (see Chapter 3). Stage models have influenced behaviour change interventions in two ways: the use of stage-matched interventions and the development of motivational interviewing.

STAGE-MATCHED INTERVENTIONS

A stage model approach to behaviour highlights how people show different levels of motivation to change their behaviour at different stages. Therefore someone at the pre-contemplation stage is less likely to attend a smoking cessation clinic or wear a nicotine replacement patch than someone at the contemplation or action stages. A stage approach has often been combined with the many strategies described above so that interventions can be targeted to people according to where they are in the process of change. This has taken the form of either tailored or stage-matched interventions. Participants are initially asked to rate their motivation as a means to assess their stage and then the intervention is delivered accordingly. At times this results in people being refused entry into the study as they are at the pre-contemplation stage and deemed not ready to change. Overall, it means that interventions tend to be more effective as the intervention makes more sense to the individual and those who would not have responded to the intervention are removed from the study. Stage-matched interventions have been used across a number of behaviours such as smoking cessation (Di Clemente et al. 1991; Aveyard et al. 2006), cervical cancer screening (Luszczynska et al. 2010) and in conjunction with a range of intervention approaches such as CBT, counselling, implementation intentions and planning.

MOTIVATIONAL INTERVIEWING

If people are at a stage when they are unmotivated to change their behaviour, then there seems little point in offering them an intervention or including them in a study, particularly as motivation is a consistently good predictor of behavioural intentions and behaviour (e.g. Jacobs et al. 2011). Motivational interviewing (MI) was developed by Miller and Rollnick (2002) as a way to help people consider changing their behaviour and to increase their motivation to change. From a stages of change perspective it takes people from a pre-contemplation to a contemplation stage in the behaviour change process. MI therefore doesn't show people *how* to change but encourages them to think about their behaviour in ways that may make them realize that they *should* change. MI was originally used with people with addictions but is now used across all health care settings and has become a core part of the toolkit of any health professional. The process of MI is based upon the idea that cognitive dissonance is uncomfortable and that people are motivated to get out of a state of dissonance by changing their cognitions (Festinger, 1957). For health-related behaviours conflicting beliefs such as 'My drug addiction lost me my job' and 'I like taking drugs' or 'My weight makes it difficult for me to move' and 'I like eating a lot' cause cognitive dissonance and are uncomfortable. The aim of MI is to encourage people to focus on these conflicting beliefs and therefore feel the discomfort more strongly. Questions asked would include:

'What are some of the good things about smoking/eating a lot/taking drugs?'

'What are the not so good things about smoking/eating a lot/taking drugs?'

The client is then encouraged to elaborate on the costs and benefits of their behaviour which are then fed back to them by the health professional to highlight the conflict between these two sets of cognitions:

'So your smoking makes you feel relaxed but you are finding it hard to climb stairs?'

'So taking drugs helps you cope but you have lost your job because of them?'

Next, the client is asked to describe how this conflict makes them feel and to consider how things could be different if they changed their behaviour. It is hoped that by focusing on their cognitive dissonance they will be motivated to change both their cognitions and behaviour as a means to resolve this dissonance. Obviously it is hoped that they will change towards being healthier, although this may not always be the case as the process could encourage people to see the benefits of their behaviour and decide to continue as they are.

Miller and Rollnick (2002) are very clear that their approach should be non-confrontational and should encourage people to think about the possibility of change rather than persuading them to change. This is particularly important for clients who may have already met much frustration and anger at their behaviour from other professionals or family members and may be very reluctant to speak openly. Miller and Rollnick also emphasize that professionals using MI should be empathic and non-judgemental and should assume that the client is responsible for the decision to change when and if they want to make that decision. A systematic review shows that MI is an effective tool for use by non-specialists for drug abuse treatment (Dunn et al. 2001). Research also shows that MI is effective across a number of problems including promoting attendance at a drug treatment programme (Carroll et al. 2001), enhancing medication compliance in people with schizophrenia (Bellack and DiClemente 1999), treating eating disorders (Killick and Allen, 1997), reducing problem drinking in inpatients with psychiatric problems (Hulse and Tait 2002), promoting healthy eating (Resnicow et al. 2001) and promoting a short-term increase in physical activity in a primary care setting (Harland et al. 1999). A systematic review of the use of MI in physical health care settings for problems such as diabetes, asthma and heart disease concluded that it was effective in the majority of studies for psychological, physiological and lifestyle change outcomes but that many of the studies had methodological weaknesses making broader conclusions problematic (Knight et al. 2006).

Stage models have therefore influenced behaviour change interventions through the use of tailored or stage-matched interventions and the development of motivational interviewing as a means to move people to a stage where they might consider entering an intervention to change their behaviour.

CHANGING AFFECT

One of the main criticisms of many psychological theories of behaviour and the strategies used to change behaviour is that they do not address an individual's emotions and consider people to be rational processors of information (van der Pligt et al. 1998; van den Berg et al. 2005). Some studies, however, have included a role for affect and this has taken various forms including visualization, affective attitudes, fear appeals and self-affirmation interventions. These are illustrated in Figure 8.5.

VISUALIZATION

The saying 'a picture paints a thousand words' reflects the belief that visual images may be more effective at conveying information or changing beliefs compared to language-based messages.

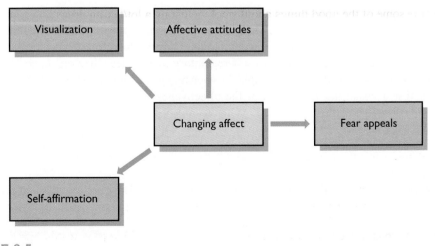

FIGURE 8.5

Behaviour change interventions based on a changing affect

This forms the basis of most advertising, marketing and health education campaigns and is central to the use of diagrams and illustrations throughout education. Some research has explored the impact of visual images in health research (see Chapter 9 for a discussion of imagery and changes in illness cognitions). For example, Hammond et al. (2003) examined the effectiveness of the cigarette warning labels and reported an association between reading and discussing the labels with a higher intention to stop smoking, more quit attempts and a reduction in smoking. Shahab et al. (2007) also reported that showing smokers images of their carotid arteries with a plaque compared to an artery without a plaque increased intentions to stop smoking in those with higher self-efficacy. Further, Karamanidou et al. (2008) reported that showing patients with renal disease a plastic container in which they could see how their phosphate binding mediation would work in their stomachs changed their beliefs about treatment (see **Focus on Research 8.1** for details). In a similar vein, Lee et al. (2011) used a web-based intervention to show participants images of heart disease (with or without text) and concluded that imagery caused more changes than text alone but that a combination of the two forms of information was the most effective. Images therefore seem to change cognitions and behaviour but to date little is known about the mechanisms behind this process. However, researchers have begun to theorize about this process and have suggested that images may be processed more rapidly than text and may be more memorable over time. In addition, images may also have a greater impact upon affect than text which in turn influences behaviour (Cameron 2008, 2009; Cameron and Chan 2008).

FOCUS ON RESEARCH 8.1: VISUAL IMAGES AND BEHAVIOUR CHANGE

Using visual images to change beliefs about treatment (Karamanidouet al. 2008).

It is well known in the advertising world that images are an effective method for changing beliefs and behaviour with images. Within health psychology, the use of images has become more common in recent years as a way to encourage behaviours such as smoking cessation, a healthy diet and exercise. This study used visual images to change patient beliefs about their medication and illustrates a simple way in which theory can be translated into practice.

BACKGROUND

Patients with renal disease have to take phosphate binding medication to avoid cardiovascular events which are the leading cause of death in this patient group. Adherence, however, is problematic as the treatment regimen is complex and there are no noticeable effects on symptoms. They are therefore expected to do something difficult with no immediate reward. Leventhal's self-regulatory model (see Chapters 9 and 10) argues that illness beliefs and beliefs about medication are linked to behaviour, including adherence. Accordingly, this study assessed whether a visual demonstration of the effectiveness of phosphate binding medication could change beliefs and subsequent adherence.

METHODOLOGY

Sample

Thirty-nine patients with end-stage renal disease, on haomodialysis for at least six months and receiving phosphate binding medication were recruited into the study.

Design

The study used a randomized control design and patients were alternatively allocated to the intervention group or the control group.

Follow-up

Assessments were made immediately before the intervention and one and four months post-intervention.

Measures

Patients completed measures of the following:

*   *Phosphate knowledge* (McGee et al. 1998).
*   *Treatment beliefs and understanding* (adapted from the Beliefs About Medicines questionnaire, BMQ, Horne et al. 1999).
*   *Coherence* ('My phosphate binding medication is a mystery to me').
*   *Understanding problems of high phosphate levels* ('How much do you feel you understand about how high phosphate levels can increase your risk of developing heart or bone disease?').
*   *Medication outcome efficacy belief* ('How much do you understand about how using phosphate binding medication incorrectly can increase risk of heart or bone disease?').
*   *General understanding* ('How easy would it be to explain to another patient how phosphate binding medication works?').
*   *Risk perception* ('How likely do you think you are to develop heart or bone disease?').
*   *Medication adherence* (MARS, Horne and Weinman 2002).

THE INTERVENTION

The intervention involved a visual demonstration of how the patient's medication binds with phosphates in their stomach. They were presented with a transparent container shaped like a stomach and asked to imagine that it was their stomach. Phosphate solution was then poured into the container and patients were asked to imagine that it was their favourite phosphate-containing food. Phosphate binding solution was then poured in and the patients were asked to describe what they saw as the medication bound with the phosphates. They were also given a leaflet further explaining the impact of their medication. Those in the control group received care as usual.

RESULTS

The results showed immediate effects in terms of knowledge, medication necessity, treatment coherence, risk perception, understanding problems and general understanding, and medication outcome efficacy with those in the intervention showing improvements for all these measures. However, by one month only general understanding remained significant but by four months general understanding, knowledge, understanding problems and medication outcome efficacy were significant. No effects were found for adherence.

CONCLUSION

The results indicate that a simple, theoretically informed visual intervention can change knowledge and treatment beliefs. They also show that although there was no additional interventions between one and four months, this effect increased. Showing people a visual representation of how their medication works seems to be an effective way to change their beliefs. This is particularly important when a condition is symptom-free or when the medication is experienced as if it has no effect upon a patient's health.

AFFECTIVE COGNITIONS

Affect is a difficult construct to measure as at its most pure it is probably a state that exists prior to language and description. It is therefore the feeling we have before that feeling is turned into words. This creates problems for researchers as most of our studies use language-based measures. One approach therefore has been to define affective cognitions which are measured using emotional words such as 'pleasant', 'enjoyable', 'exciting' and 'boring'. Affective attitudes have been shown to be good predictors of behaviour (e.g. Lawton et al. 2009; see Chapter 3) and some studies have therefore developed interventions to change behaviour through the modification of affective attitudes. For example, in 2011 Conner and colleagues explored the relative impact of affective versus cognitive messages on changes in self-reported exercise. They also assessed the role of individual differences in need for cognition (NFC) and need for affect (NFA) which reflect trait-like differences in the desirability for emotional or cognitive information. In study 1, participants were randomized to one of four conditions: (1) affective images (e.g. individuals smiling while exercising); (2) cognitive images (e.g. pictures of the heart); (3) both types of image; (4) no images, and rated their exercise levels at baseline and after three weeks. In study 2 participants also completed measures of NFC and NFA. The results showed that affective images produced a greater increase in exercise than the other conditions. In addition, this change was greater for those high in NFA and low in NFC. In parallel with this, Sirriyeh et al. (2010) explored the impact of affective cognitions of physical activity and whether these variables could be changed by a brief text-based intervention. Adolescents were therefore randomized to one of four groups: (1) affective texts (focusing on affective beliefs such as 'physical activity can make you feel cheerful' and 'physical activity can make you feel more enthusiastic'); (2) instrumental texts (e.g. 'physical activity can help maintain a healthy weight' and 'physical activity can keep your heart healthy'); (3) both types of text; (4) neutral texts. The results showed that affective texts significantly increased physical activity but only for those who had been inactive at baseline.

FEAR APPEALS

Protection motivation theory (PMT, see Chapter 3) was the first social cognition model to include a measure for emotion in the form of fear and it was argued that fear can motivate behaviour change (Rogers, 1983). As a result of this, many health promotion campaigns include fear appeals such as the tombstone images for AIDs in the 1980s in the UK, pictures of emaciated and wasted people to discourage drug use in the 2000s and cigarette warnings on packets describing problems of impotency and damage to unborn children. Fear appeals typically provide two types of message relating to fear arousal and safety conditions as follows:

1 Fear arousal which involves:
   • There is a threat: *'HIV infection', 'lung cancer'*.
   • You are at risk: *'Unsafe sex or sharing needles puts you at risk of HIV'*.
   • The threat is serious: *'HIV kills', 'Lung cancer kills'*.
2 Safety conditions which involve:
   • A recommended protective action: *'Use condoms', 'Don't share needles', 'Stop smoking'*.
   • The action is effective: *'Condoms prevent HIV', 'Stopping smoking prevents lung cancer'*.
   • The action is easy: *'Condoms are easy to buy and easy to use'*.

Together, fear arousals and safety conditions are designed to generate an emotional response (i.e. fear) and offer a simple way to manage the threat (i.e. behaviour change). However, research indicates that it is not clear whether, when or how fear appeals work. For example, originally it was believed that fear had a U-shaped impact on behaviour with maximum change resulting from moderate fear, while low fear caused no effect and high levels of fear resulted in denial, defensiveness and inaction (Janis 1967)). Subsequent research, however, indicates that a more linear relationship may exist with greater levels of fear being the most effective at changing behaviour, although this might be due to the kinds of fear that can be generated in the laboratory setting (see Ruiter et al. 2001 for a review). In the light of contradictory evidence researchers have highlighted two new avenues for study. One involves the need for the development of new constructs and models to distinguish between different types of responses to fear and an analysis of different types of fear-related information (e.g. Ruiter et al. 2001; Jessop and Wade 2008). The second involves the need to make fear appeals more effective. Self-affirmation theory is a promising approach to this.

Fear appeals: this gravestone advertisement was one of the first health promotion attempts after the identification of the HIV virus

SOURCE: © Department of Health

SELF-AFFIRMATION

When presented with messages trying to get them to change their behaviour, many people resist, using a number of strategies such as avoidance, ignoring and finding fault in the arguments used, or criticizing the mode of presentation (Jacks and Cameron 2003; Harris and Epton 2009). This is particularly the case if the message evokes a strong emotional response such as fear. Self-affirmation theory (Steele 1988) provides a framework not only for understanding the process of resistance but also as a means to encourage people to overcome this resistance and respond to the message in the desired way (see Chapter 3). It is grounded in the idea of 'self-integrity' and argues that people are inherently motivated to maintain their self-integrity and their sense of self as being 'adaptively and morally adequate' (Steele 1988). If their integrity is challenged by information indicating that their behaviour is damaging, then they resist this information as a means to preserve their sense of self. However, from this perspective such resistance can be reduced if the individual is encouraged to enhance their self-integrity by affirming their self-worth by focusing on other factors that are core to how they see themselves but unrelated to the threat (Harris and Epton 2009). A self-affirmation intervention can take many forms and studies have used methods such as providing positive feedback on a test, asking participants to rate themselves on a series of key values, writing an essay on their most important value or asking a series of questions about a universally valued construct such as kindness (e.g. 'Have you ever forgiven another person when they have hurt you?'). This process proceeds as follows using the example of someone who is obese:

- *Fear appeal:* 'being overweight can cause heart disease'.
- *Emotional response:* 'anxiety'.
- *Resistance:* Ignoring the message/thinking 'research is always wrong' or 'that leaflet isn't very well designed'.
- *Self-affirmation intervention:* 'Think of times when you have been kind to others'.
- *Emotional response:* 'I am reassured', 'I am a good person'.
- *Reaction to fear appeal:* 'Maybe I should lose some weight'.

Self-affirmation interventions are designed to do the following (Napper et al. 2009):

- Make a central and positive aspect of a person's sense of self more salient.
- Provide a reminder of 'who you are'.
- Offer reassurance that there are others aspects to the individual's sense of self other than that which is challenged by the fear appeal.

Harris and Epton (2009) provide a comprehensive review of 24 studies using self-affirmation interventions in the context of a range of different health problems and behaviours. In particular, they show that self-affirmation can increase message acceptance for information relating to caffeine consumption, smoking, sun safety, alcohol intake and safe sex (e.g. Sherman, et al. 2000; Harris and Napper 2005; Harris et al. 2007). It can change affect (Harris and Napper 2005; Harris et al. 2007) and attitudes (Jessop et al. 2009) and in general cause increases in behavioural intentions (Harris et al. 2007). Finally, the review also indicates that self-affirmation interventions can change behaviour in the short term (e.g. immediately taking a leaflet or buying condoms) but to date there is little evidence on longer-term changes in behaviour. Further, those most at risk (e.g. heavy drinkers, heavy smokers) seem to be more responsive to self-affirmation interventions than those less at risk.

Although many models within psychology have been criticized for ignoring the role of affect, some work with the behaviour change literature has addressed affect and methods have been developed to change how people feel. This has involved studies using visual imagery as a means to change cognition and behaviour via a change in affect, the direct manipulation of affective cognitions, delivering messages using fear appeals and the use of self-affirmation in order to minimize resistance and improve message acceptance and subsequent changes in behaviour.

MODERN TECHNOLOGIES

So far this chapter has described a number of key theories and strategies that have been used to change health-related behaviour. Recent developments in modern technologies have provided the opportunity for new ways to deliver such strategies and new sources of information that may help individuals change what they do. These include the use of 'ecological momentary interventions' (via palmtop computers or mobile phones), web-based interventions, the presentation of individualized biological risk data and the use of the mass media (see Figure 8.6). Some of these target individuals while others target populations as a means to change behaviour in a broader sense. Behaviour change interventions such as smoking bans, taxation and restricting or banning advertising are described in Chapter 4 in the context of addictive behaviours.

EMIs

Traditionally interventions occurred in the clinical setting with patients attending individual or group-based therapy sessions. It has long been recognized that interventions are more effective if

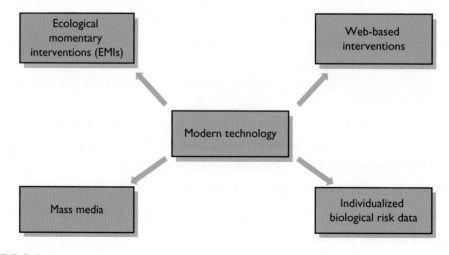

FIGURE 8.6

Modern technology-based behaviour change interventions

contact between therapist and patient can be extended beyond these interactions and until recently this has taken the form of homework to ensure that the patient takes the ideas discussed back into their day-to-day lives, or telephone helplines so that people can ring up whenever they need extra support when their resilience is weakened and addiction motivation is needed. The development of new technologies such as mobile phones and palmtop computers provides a simple and cost-effective way to extend therapy beyond the consultation and patients become accessible at all times. The term EMI refers to treatments provided to people during their everyday lives (i.e. in real time) and in natural settings (i.e. in the real world). Such treatments/interventions have been used for a wide range of behaviours such as smoking cessation, weight loss, anxiety, alcohol use, dietary change and exercise promotion. They have also been used across a number of different chronic illnesses including diabetes, coronary heart disease (CHD), eating disorders and obesity (see Heron and Smyth 2010 for a comprehensive review). They are particularly useful for hard-to-reach groups such as adolescents who would usually avoid contact with health professionals. For example, Sirriyeh et al. (2010) explored the impact of affective text messages and instrumental texts for promoting physical activity in adolescents, with those in the intervention groups receiving one text per day over a two-week period. The results showed that all participants increased their activity levels over the course of the study. In addition, affective texts such as 'exercise is enjoyable' were particularly effective at changing behaviour in those who were most inactive at baseline. For their review of the evidence, Heron and Smyth (2010) identified 27 interventions using EMIs to change behaviour and drew three conclusions. First, at the most practical level EMIs can be easily and successfully delivered to the target group. Second, this new approach is acceptable to patients, even those who are hard to reach such as adolescents, and third, EMIs are effective at changing a wide range of behaviours including smoking (Rodgers et al. 2005), physical activity (King et al. 2008), a reduction in calorie intake (Joo and Kim 2007), and diabetes self-management (Kwon et al. 2004), although most changes seem to be in the shorter rather than longer term. EMIs are a relatively new approach but offer a simple and cost-effective means to change behaviour for a wide section of the population.

WEB-BASED INTERVENTIONS
New developments in technologies have also led to the use of web-based interventions so that patients who may be unable or unwilling to attend to face-to-face consultations can now engage in a range of therapeutic strategies from their own home to fit in with their own time frame. For example, packages of web-based interventions have been developed for patients with a range of chronic illnesses such as diabetes, asthma, CHD and AIDS/HIV to deliver treatments such as CBT, relapse prevention, education and goal-setting. Many also address psychological problems such as depression and anxiety, OCD and body image disturbance. Rosser et al. (2009). carried out a systematic review of novel technologies for the management of chronic illnesses (both psychological and physical) and identified that most utilized web-based interventions (53 per cent) with other technologies being interactive CD-ROM programmes, online message boards, video presentations, email contact or virtual reality delivery. From this review they highlighted a number of packaged interventions such as 'MoodGYM', 'Diabetes Priority Programe', 'Beating the Blues' and 'CHESS'. Rosser et al. made three key observations about the studies they included in their review. First, they noted that sample sizes for the studies were extremely high (mean size at start of study n = 780) reflecting the ease with which patients can be targeted with this approach. Second, they highlighted the extremely high level of dropouts over the course of the studies as patients stopped engaging with the interventions (ranging, 0–84 per cent, mean sample size after dropouts n = 258). Finally, they noted that although the interventions were delivered remotely (i.e. by computer or email), 73 per cent still included some involvement with a therapist and that greater involvement with a therapist was associated with lower dropout rates. Overall, therefore, web-based interventions can reach large numbers of people who may not want to, or be able to, come into a consultation. They may be effective but they have high attrition rates and still seem to require therapist involvement to be more successful.

USING BIOLOGICAL RISK DATA

Most psychological theories of behaviour and behaviour change indicate that risk perception is a central variable for understanding why people either do or do not carry out health-related behaviours. For example, from a social cognition model perspective (see Chapter 3) if a person believes that they are at risk from lung cancer we would predict that they would be less likely to smoke. Many interventions therefore aim to increase an individual's perception of risk as a means to change their behaviour. Recent developments in DNA testing have offered a more refined way to present this risk as it means that risk information can be tailored specifically to the individual's own risk of any specific illness based upon their genetic predisposition for that illness. Therefore, rather than telling a smoker 'Your smoking might well cause lung cancer because it has done in many other people', following DNA testing a smoker could be told, 'You, personally, have a 75 per cent risk of developing lung cancer if you smoke.' This is in line with theories of attitude change which argue that personally salient information is more effective than general information. It also offers the chance to explore whether such information has a negative impact upon the individual by inducing fatalism and a sense that their pending illness in the future is inevitable. Marteau and colleagues have carried out much research in this area and recently have completed two systematic reviews of the literature (Marteau et al. 2010; Collins et al. 2011). The first review focused on the impact of DNA-based disease risk estimates in the context of heart disease, lung, breast and bowel cancer, inflammatory bowel disease and Alzheimer's disease. All these diseases include a role for health-related behaviors. Further, the risk of developing each of these diseases could be reduced by a change in behaviour. The review identified 14 papers using either clinical trials (n = 8) or analogue studies using vignettes (n = 6). The results from the clinical studies showed no significant effects of personalized risk estimates on smoking cessation, physical activity or medication and vitamin use. An effect, however, was found for improvements in diet. The analogue studies also showed significant effects for intentions to change behaviour. In their second review, Collins et al. (2011) identified five studies addressing obesity, depression, heart disease and diabetes and focused on the potentially negative impact of receiving personalized risk estimates. They concluded from this review that such risk estimates do not generate either fatalism or changes in perceived control. Overall, the authors concluded that DNA-based risk estimations may not be as effective as hoped for changing behaviour. However, it would also seem that such risk estimations do no harm in terms of negative changes in beliefs about any given condition.

THE MASS MEDIA

Television, the internet, magazines and outdoor advertising all constantly bombard us with information about what to buy, what to see and what to do. This has a major impact upon our health behaviours in both negative and positive ways. For example, after Eyton's *The F Plan Diet* (1982), which recommended a high fibre diet, was featured in a number of magazine articles and on numerous television programmes, sales of bran-based cereals rose by 30 per cent, whole-wheat bread sales rose by 10 per cent, wholewheat pasta by 70 per cent, and baked beans by 8 per cent. Similarly, when Edwina Curry, then junior health minister in the UK, said on television in December 1988 that 'most of the egg production in this country, sadly, is now infected with salmonella' egg sales fell by 50 per cent and by 1989 were still only at 75 percent of their previous levels (Mintel, 1990). Similarly, massive publicity about the health risks of beef in the UK between May and August 1990 resulted in a 20 per cent reduction in beef sales. The mass media can be used either as a means to make us more unhealthy or as a resource to help improve the health of the population.

THE MEDIA AS A NEGATIVE INFLUENCE

Although cigarette and alcohol adverts have now been banned across the USA and most of Europe, food adverts are still considered acceptable. For example, Radnitz et al. (2009) analysed the nutritional content of food on TV aimed at children under 5 and showed that unhealthy foods were given almost twice as much air time and were shown to be valued significantly more compared to healthy foods. Some research has explored the potential impact of TV adverts on eating behaviour. For example, Halford et al (2004) used an experimental design to evaluate the impact of exposure to food-related adverts. Lean, overweight and obese children were shown a series of food and non-food-related adverts and their snack food intake was then measured in a controlled environment. The results showed that overall the obese children recognized more of the food adverts than the other children and that the degree of recognition correlated with the amount of food consumed. Furthermore, all children ate more after exposure to the food adverts than the non-food adverts. Similarly, King and Hill (2008) showed children adverts for healthy or less healthy foods and measured their hunger, food choice and product recall. No effects were found for hunger or food choice but children could remember more of the less healthy than the healthy foods.

THE MEDIA AS A RESOURCE FOR POSITIVE CHANGE

Just Eat More
(fruit & veg)

Five a day: just eat more. A simple and memorable message

SOURCE: © Department of Health

The media has also been used by government and health promotion campaigns as a means to reach a wide audience and promote health behaviour. To date there is very little evidence as to whether these campaigns have been effective and it has been argued that perhaps such initiatives should be about raising awareness rather than changing behaviour (Stead et al. 2002). It is also possible that whereas individual campaigns may only raise awareness, repeated ongoing campaigns over many years may cause change through a 'drip drip effect' as successive generations gradually become accustomed to a new way of thinking or behaving. This is particularly apparent in the reduction in drink driving over the past decade. No one campaign may have made this happen but negative attitudes towards drink driving in the new generation of drivers may be a response to always having been aware that this was not an acceptable thing to do (Shinar et al. 1999).

One way to understand the impact of mass media campaigns is to identify those which are memorable and explore why this might be. Memorable campaigns over recent years include:

If you had another chance, what would you do differently?

THINK

Always wear a seat belt.

Promoting seat belts in the back seats of a car

SOURCE: © Department of Transport

- *'Five a day: just eat more':* this is a simple message using simple words and imagery and aims to promote healthy eating. Interestingly it encourages doing more rather than less of something which minimizes the chance of a rebound effect which is a common response to many other forms of dietary advice (see Chapter 5). It also offers clear rules of what to eat which are set slightly higher than the average intake but are also realistic.

- *'Most people are killed by someone they know':* this was the basis of an advert to promote seat-belt wearing in the back of cars to prevent those in the back seat from being thrown into the front during an accident. One advert involved a group of young men buying pizzas and setting off in the car without doing up their seat belts. They crashed and the ones in the back were flung forward and killed the ones in the front. The message was very simple.

A powerful image to discourage needle sharing

SOURCE: © Christine Osborne/Photographers Direct

The imagery was powerful and the solution it offered required very little effort. Also the target audience was clearly represented in the advert.

- *'Sharing your mate's works means sharing with everyone he's ever shared with':* this campaign showed a picture of a needle going through a series of arms and was designed to discourage needle-sharing in drug users for HIV prevention. It was effective as it illustrated rather than described the notion of needle-sharing. However, it also had implications for safe sex as it illustrated the idea that even though you might have sex with one person, this one person could connect you with a long line of other 'one persons'.

UNDERSTANDING MEDIA CAMPAIGNS

Media campaigns use a number of the psychological strategies described above to encourage us to change our behaviour. These include modeling (i.e. using people who are like us), fear appeals (i.e. being shocking), visual imagery (i.e. to change affect and maybe reduce denial or resistance), targeting a specific audience (i.e. those at the right stage of change and with a good level of motivation) and encouraging people to focus on the negative aspects of what they do (i.e. in line with motivational interviewing to create cognitive dissonance). The elaboration likelihood model (ELM, Petty and Cacioppo 1986) was developed as a model of persuasion and provides a framework for understanding why some media campaigns might be more successful than others and how they could be improved. The ELM is shown in Figure 8.7.

The ELM is a popular model in the area of persuasion across a range of fields including political persuasion, media influence and health behaviour change. It argues that in order for people to change their beliefs and behaviour, they need to do the following:

- Be motivated to receive the argument.
- Centrally process the argument.

This will occur if:

- The message is congruent with their existing beliefs.
- The message is personally relevant to them.
- The individual can understand the argument.

This central processing involves an assessment of arguments being presented which are then incorporated into the person's existing belief systems. This can result in a strong change in beliefs and longer-term changes in behaviour if this central processing determines that the case being made is strong and relevant. Only weak changes will occur that will not persist, however, if the case is deemed to be weak and not personally relevant. For example, if an overweight person has started to find it hard to climb the stairs and has realized that her clothes no longer fit, then she will be motivated to change and a message could be centrally processed. Such a message could be 'Eating less fat and more fruit and vegetables can help you lose weight, fit into your clothes and have more energy'.

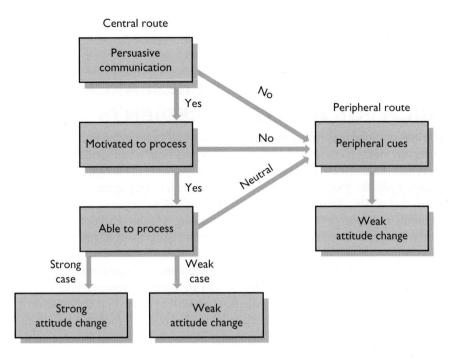

Central route

Peripheral route

FIGURE 8.7

The elaboration likelihood model (ELM)

But what if a person is not motivated in the first place? Given that most media campaigns are aimed at changing behaviour in those who are not already performing this behaviour, then many of these people will not fulfil the criteria for central processing as they will not be motivated. If this is the case, the ELM offers another route called 'peripheral processing'. This involves the following:

- Using direct cues and information.
- Maximizing the credibility of the source of the message.
- Maximizing the attractiveness of the source of the message.

For an overweight person who suffers no symptoms of breathlessness and has a wardrobe of larger clothes, the message above will not work. The campaign will therefore need to work harder to make a difference. For example, it could use indirect cues and information such as 'Weight loss clubs can be fun and are a good way to meet people'. It could increase the credibility of the message by using a more scientific approach (e.g. men in white coats, charts, data) and could make the message more attractive (e.g. a good-looking man in a white coat, images of friendly-looking people at a club, a smiling person selling fruit and vegetables). According to the ELM, messages using this peripheral processing route can change beliefs and behaviour but are likely to be less effective or long-lasting.

Over recent years there has been a rapid change in the development of new technologies in the form of mobile phones, palm- and laptop computers and the internet as well as more traditional methods of information-giving such as billboards and TV. In addition, advances in DNA testing mean that we can now offer personalized risk estimates to people based upon their own genetic data. Researchers have explored the possibility of using such technologies for changing health-related behaviours and although evidence is often still in its infancy, these approaches offer a new and often more cost-effective way of contacting people who may be averse to or unable to attend more traditional face-to-face consultations with health professionals.

IMPROVING INTERVENTION RESEARCH AND A SEARCH FOR ACTIVE INGREDIENTS

This chapter has outlined the wide range and number of different behaviour change strategies and complex interventions. Over the past few years there has been a call to identify which aspects of which interventions are effective and to promote improvements in the reporting and design of new interventions to make the process more transparent and easier to replicate (eg. Abraham and Michie 2008; Michie et al. 2009; 2010; West et al. 2010). This call to improve intervention research has involved a number of approaches including the following: (1) the development of a taxonomy of behaviour strategies to code and label which strategies are being used; (2) matching these strategies to their target behaviour and target populations; (3) calculating which strategies are most effective at producing change in which behaviours and which populations. Once completed, this could result in an exhaustive taxonomy of strategies that could be used to improve how interventions are designed and reported. In a recent review Michie et al. (2011) carried out a synthesis of all the different types of taxonomy as a means to identify essential conditions for behaviour change and how these could be turned into actual behaviour change. From this process, the researchers created a

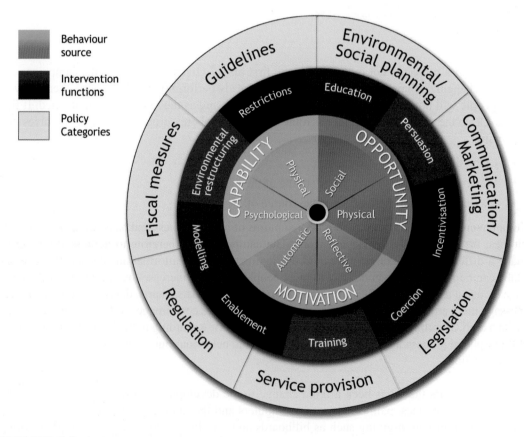

FIGURE 8.8

The behaviour change wheel

SOURCE: Michie et al. (2011)

behaviour change wheel with three levels illustrating the translational process from essential conditions, through intervention functions, to policy (see Figure 8.8).

- *Essential conditions:* the researchers identified three conditions which are deemed essential for behaviour and behaviour change: capability, motivation and opportunity. These constructs find parallels in many models of behaviour (see Chapter 3) but are deemed to capture the essence of how and why we act as we do.
- *Intervention functions:* it is argued that changing behaviour requires a change in these essential conditions and that a series of intervention functions can bring this change about. The nine functions identified in the behaviour change wheel reflect a synthesized version of the many strategies that are used to change behaviour and were derived from a detailed coding process.
- *Categories of policy:* finally, the researchers argue that policy changes are needed to enable the interventions to occur.

The end result of the behaviour change wheel would be that the policy enables interventions to occur, which in turn change the essential *conditions* of behaviour which bring about *changes* in behaviour. The model can be used to describe and understand why interventions do or do not work. It could also be used to design more effective interventions which could be linked to policy or even used to promote new policy.

UNDERSTANDING SUSTAINED BEHAVIOUR CHANGE

Even though there has been much research and a multitude of interventions, many people continue to behave in unhealthy ways. For example, although smoking in the UK has declined from 45 per cent in 1970 to 26 per cent in 2004, a substantial minority of the population still continue to smoke. Similarly, the prevalence of diet- and exercise-related problems, particularly obesity and overweight, is rising. Further, even though many people show initial changes in their health-related behaviours, rates of sustained behaviour change are poor, with many people reverting to their old habits. For example, although obesity treatments in the last 20 years have improved rates of initial weight loss, there has been very little success in weight loss maintenance in the longer term with up to 95 per cent of people returning to baseline weights by five years (NHS Centre for Reviews and Dissemination 1997; Jeffery et al. 2000; see Chapter 15). Similarly, nearly half of those smokers who make a quit attempt return to smoking within the year (see Chapter 4). If real changes are to be made to people's health status, then research needs to address the issue of behaviour change in the longer term. To date, however, most research has focused on the onset of new behaviours or changes in behaviour in the short term due to the use of quantitative methods, with prospective designs that have follow-ups varying from a few weeks only to a year, as longer-term follow-ups require greater investment of time and cost. Some research, however, has addressed the issue of longer-term behaviour change maintenance, particularly for weight loss, smoking cessation and exercise.

- *Weight loss maintenance:* research indicates that although the majority of the obese regain the weight they lose, a small minority show weight loss maintenance. The factors that predict this are described in detail in Chapter 15 and illustrate a role for profile characteristics such as baseline body mass index (BMI), gender and employment status, historical factors such as previous attempts at weight loss, the type and amount of help received and psychological factors including motivations and individuals' beliefs about the causes of their weight problem. In particular, research suggests that longer-term weight loss maintenance is associated with a behavioural model of obesity whereby behaviour is seen as central to both its cause and solution

(Ogden 2000). This is in line with much research on adherence and illness representations and is discussed in detail in Chapters 9 and 10.

- *Smoking cessation:* in terms of smoking cessation, much research has drawn upon a stage model approach and suggests that smoking cessation relates to factors such as action plans, goal-setting and the transition through stages (e.g. Prochaska and Velicer 1997, see Chapter 4). In contrast, however, West and Sohal (2006) asked almost 2,000 smokers and ex-smokers about their quit attempts and reported that nearly half had made quit attempts that were unplanned and that unplanned attempts were more likely to succeed than planned ones. They argue that longer-term smoking cessation may not always be the result of plans and the transition through stages and is often the result of 'catastrophes' which suddenly motivate change.

- *Exercise:* as with changes in diet and smoking, much research exploring exercise uptake has focused on short-term changes. From this perspective most research shows that exercise is related to social factors and enjoyment rather than any longer-term consideration of health goals (see Chapter 6). Armitage (2005) aimed to explore the problem of exercise maintenance and examined the predictors of stable exercise habits over a 12-week period. This study used the standard TPB measures and indicated that perceived behavioural control predicted behaviour in terms of both initiation and maintenance.

In general it would seem that there is a role for a range of demographic, psychological and structural factors in understanding longer-term changes in behaviour and that, while some changes in behaviour may result from the 'drip drip' effect illustrated by stages and plans, other forms of change are the result of more sudden shifts in an individual's motivation. To date, however, there remains very little research on longer-term changes in behaviour. Further, the existing research tends to focus on behaviour-specific changes rather than factors that may generalize across behaviours.

TO CONCLUDE

Changes in causes of illness and mortality over the past few decades highlight a central role for health behaviours such as diet, smoking, exercise, alcohol and drug use. Chapter 3 explored the predictors of these behaviours using a number of theoretical perspectives. This chapter has examined how these theories can inform the ways in which behaviours can be changed. First, it described learning theory and how together with cognitive theory this illustrates a role for reinforcement, modelling, associative learning, CBT and relapse prevention. Second, it described interventions derived from social cognition theory such as the use of the TPB to develop interventions, the role of planning and implementation intention and the impact of information-giving in changing cognitions. Next it explored interventions influenced by stage models including the use of stage-matched interventions and motivational interviewing. The chapter explored the role of emotions in behaviour change which have been incorporated into interventions in the form of the use of visual images, studies to change affective cognitions, fear appeals and the use of self-affirmation as a means to make messages more effective. The chapter described the development of new technologies which have been used as the basis for behaviour change interventions, such as palmtop computers and mobile phones, web-based interventions, the use of biological risk estimates and the role of mass media campaigns. These different approaches illustrate how a range of psychological theories have informed and can inform the development of interventions to change behaviour. The chapter then explored recent calls to identify the 'active ingredients' of behaviour change through the development of a taxonomy of change and the behaviour change wheel. Finally, the chapter explored a different sort of evidence; the characteristics of those who have shown sustained changes in their behaviour with or without structured interventions.

QUESTIONS

1 What is the evidence for behavioural strategies for changing health behaviour?
2 How can cognitive theories add to learning theory approaches to behaviour change?
3 In what ways can social cognitive theory inform behaviour change interventions?
4 Are implementation intentions effective?
5 Should interventions be stage matched?
6 Can affect be changed and would this aid behaviour change?
7 What is the evidence for self-affirmation-based interventions?
8 What new technologies can be used in behaviour change research?
9 How might mass media campaigns work?
10 How does knowing how people have already changed their behaviour add to the development of behaviour change interventions?

FOR DISCUSSION

People make small changes in their behaviour often without realizing it. Think of the last time you changed your behaviour (e.g. tried out a new clothes shop, had something different for breakfast, started to do more exercise) and think of all the reasons for this and explore how much these reasons related to the psychological theories and strategies described in this chapter.

FURTHER READING

Gollwitzer, P.M. and Sheeran, P. (2006) Implementation intentions and goal achievement: a meta-analysis of effects and processes, *Advances in Experimental Social Psychology*, 38: 69–119.
This paper provides a detailed account of the research using implementation intentions. It is also an excellent example of a meta-analysis and how this approach can be used effectively.

Leventhal, H., Weinman, J., Leventhal, E.A. and Phillips, A. (2008) Health psychology: the search for pathways between behaviour and health, *Annual Review of Psychology*, 59.
This paper explores problems with current theories of behaviour interventions and suggests new ways forward.

Ogden, J., and Hills, L. (2008) Understanding sustained changes in behaviour: the role of life events and the process of reinvention, *Health: An International Journal*, 12: 419–37.
This is one of my papers. I have included it here because it uses qualitative methods to explore how people make sense of their own successful changes in behaviour in terms of weight loss and smoking cessation. Work on success stories provides a different angle on what works for individuals. This paper focuses on the notion of identity shifts and reinventions which can be triggered by life events which make people see their futures differently.

Psychology and Health (2011) 26(2) Special edition: health promotion interventions.
This special edition of the journal was dedicated to research exploring the effectiveness of a number of different behaviour change interventions and explores behaviours such as exercise, diet, condom use and risk in pregnancy.

Rutter, D. and Quine, L. (eds) (2003) *Changing Health Behaviour: Intervention and Research with Social Cognition Models.* Maidenhead: Open University Press.
This edited book provides an excellent review of the intervention literature including an analysis of the problems with designing interventions and with their evaluation.

Thaler, R.H. and Sunstein, C.A. (2008) *Nudge: Improving Decisions About Health, Wealth, and Happiness.* New Haven, CT: Yale University Press.
This is a fairly accessible book which has generated much interest over the past couple of years. It describes the notion of 'nudge' and the ways in which small changes can 'nudge' people into changing aspects of their lives including their behaviour. The UK government has set up a 'nudge unit' to consider ways to nudge people to improve their behaviour. Roger Ingham recently suggested in the *Guardian* that if they turn their attention to sexual health, this should be called 'the nudge nudge unit' (see www.guardian.co.uk/theguardian/2010/nov/15/say-no-more-nudge-wink).

Visit the website at www.openup.co.uk/ogden for additional resources on Chapter 8 to help you with your study, such as multiple choice questions, weblinks and a searchable online glossary.

PART THREE
Becoming Ill

© JoseGirarte/iStock

9 Illness Cognitions

© Stephan Zabel/iStock

CHAPTER OVERVIEW

Chapter 3 described health beliefs, the models that have been developed to evaluate these beliefs and their relationship to health behaviours. Individuals, however, also have beliefs about illness. This chapter examines what it means to be 'healthy' and what it means to be 'sick', and reviews these meanings in the context of how individuals cognitively represent illness (their illness cognitions/illness beliefs). The chapter then assesses how illness beliefs can be measured and places these beliefs within Leventhal's self-regulatory model, with its focus on symptom perception, illness cognitions and coping. The relationship between these factors is then discussed and the association between illness cognitions and health outcomes explored with a focus on the central role of coherence. Finally, the chapter describes interventions to change illness cognitions and their impact on patient health.

WHAT DOES IT MEAN TO BE HEALTHY?

For the majority of people living in the western world, being healthy is the norm – most people are healthy for most of the time. Therefore, beliefs about being ill exist in the context of beliefs about being healthy (e.g. illness means not being healthy, illness means feeling different to usual, etc.). The World Health Organization (WHO) (1947) defined good health as 'a state of complete physical, mental and social well being'. This definition presents a broad multidimensional view of health that departs from the traditional medical emphasis on physical health only.

Over recent years this multidimensional model has emerged throughout the results of several qualitative studies from medical sociology that have asked lay people the question 'What does it mean to be healthy?' For example, Blaxter (1990) asked 9,000 individuals to describe someone whom they thought was healthy and to consider, 'What makes you call them healthy?' and 'What is it like when you are healthy?' A qualitative analysis was then carried out on a sub-sample of these individuals. For some, health simply meant not being ill. However, for many, health was seen in terms of a reserve, a healthy life filled with health behaviours, physical fitness, having energy and vitality, social relationships with others, being able to function effectively and an expression of psychosocial well-being. Blaxter also examined how a concept of health varied over the life course and investigated any sex differences. Calnan (1987) also explored the health beliefs of women in England and argued that their models of health could be conceptualized in two sets of definitions: positive definitions including feeling energetic, plenty of exercise, feeling fit, eating the right things, being the correct weight, having a positive outlook and having a good life/marriage; and negative definitions including not getting coughs and colds, only in bed once, rarely go to the doctor and have check-ups – nothing wrong.

The issue of 'What is health?' has also been explored from a psychological perspective with a particular focus on health and illness cognitions. For example, Lau (1995) found that when young healthy adults were asked to describe in their own words 'what being healthy means to you', their beliefs about health could be understood within the following dimensions:

- *Physiological/physical,* for example, good condition, have energy.
- *Psychological,* for example, happy, energetic, feel good psychologically.
- *Behavioural,* for example, eat, sleep properly.
- *Future consequences,* for example, live longer.
- *The absence of illness,* for example, not sick, no disease, no symptoms.

Lau argued that most people show a positive definition of health (not just the absence of illness), which also includes more than just physical and psychological factors. He suggested that healthiness is most people's normal state and represents the backdrop to their beliefs about being ill. Psychological studies of the beliefs of the elderly (Hall et al. 1989), those suffering from a chronic illness (Hays and Stewart 1990) and children (Schmidt and Frohling 2000) have reported that these individuals also conceptualize health as being multidimensional. This indicates some overlap between professional (WHO) and lay views of health (i.e. a multidimensional perspective involving physical and psychological factors).

WHAT DOES IT MEAN TO BE ILL?

In his study of the beliefs of young healthy adults, Lau (1995) also asked participants 'What does it mean to be sick?' Their answers indicated the dimensions they use to conceptualize illness:

- *Not feeling normal,* for example, 'I don't feel right'.
- *Specific symptoms,* for example, physiological/psychological.
- *Specific illnesses,* for example, cancer, cold, depression.
- *Consequences of illness,* for example, 'I can't do what I usually do'.
- *Time line,* for example, how long the symptoms last.
- *The absence of health,* for example, not being healthy.

These dimensions of 'what it means to be ill' have been described within the context of illness cognitions (also called illness beliefs or illness representations).

WHAT ARE ILLNESS COGNITIONS?

Leventhal and his colleagues (Leventhal et al. 1980, 2007a, 2007b; Leventhal and Nerenz 1985) defined illness cognitions as 'a patient's own implicit common sense beliefs about their illness'. They proposed that these cognitions provide patients with a framework or a schema for *coping with* and *understanding their illness,* and *telling them what to look out for if they are becoming ill.* Using interviews with patients suffering from a variety of different illnesses, Leventhal and his colleagues identified five cognitive dimensions of these beliefs (see Figure 9.1).

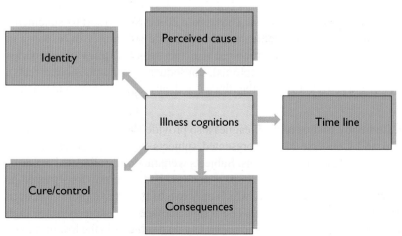

FIGURE 9.1

Illness cognitions: the five core dimensions

SOURCE: Adapted from Leventhal et al. (1980)

Some of these dimensions are similar to those described by attribution theory in Chapter 3:

1 *Identity:* this refers to the label given to the illness (the medical diagnosis) and the symptoms experienced (e.g. I have a cold – 'the diagnosis', with a runny nose – 'the symptoms').

2 *The perceived cause of the illness:* these causes may be biological, such as a virus or a lesion, or psychosocial, such as stress- or health-related behaviour. In addition, patients may hold representations of illness that reflect a variety of different causal models (e.g. 'My cold was caused by a virus', 'My cold was caused by being run down').

3 *Time line:* this refers to the patient's beliefs about how long the illness will last, whether it is acute (short term) or chronic (long term) (e.g. 'My cold will be over in a few days').

4 *Consequences:* this refers to the patient's perceptions of the possible effects of the illness on their life. Such consequences may be physical (e.g. pain, lack of mobility), emotional (e.g. loss of social contact, loneliness) or a combination of factors (e.g. 'My cold will prevent me from playing football, which will prevent me from seeing my friends').

5 *Curability and controllability:* patients also represent illnesses in terms of whether they believe that the illness can be treated and cured and the extent to which the outcome of their illness is controllable either by themselves or by powerful others (e.g. 'If I rest, my cold will go away', 'If I get medicine from my doctor, my cold will go away').

EVIDENCE FOR THE DIMENSIONS OF ILLNESS COGNITIONS

The extent to which beliefs about illness are constituted by these different dimensions has been studied using two main methodologies – qualitative and quantitative research.

Qualitative Research

Leventhal and his colleagues carried out interviews with individuals who were chronically ill, had been recently diagnosed as having cancer, and with healthy adults. The resulting descriptions of illness suggest underlying beliefs that are made up of the aforementioned dimensions. Leventhal argued that interviews are the best way to access illness cognitions as this methodology avoids the possibility of priming the subjects. For example, asking a subject 'To what extent do you think about your illness in terms of its possible consequences?' will obviously encourage them to regard consequences as an important dimension. However, according to Leventhal, interviews encourage subjects to express their own beliefs, not those expected by the interviewer.

Quantitative Research

Other studies have used more artificial and controlled methodologies, and these too have provided support for the dimensions of illness cognitions. Lau et al. (1989) used a card-sorting technique to evaluate how subjects conceptualized illness. They asked 20 subjects to sort 65 statements into piles that 'made sense to them'. These statements had been made previously in response to descriptions of 'your most recent illness'. They reported that the subjects' piles of categories reflected the dimensions of identity (diagnosis/symptoms), consequences (the possible effects), time line (how long it will last), cause (what caused the illness) and cure/control (how and whether it can be treated).

A series of experimental studies by Bishop and colleagues also provided support for these dimensions. For example, Bishop and Converse (1986) presented subjects with brief descriptions of patients who were experiencing six different symptoms. Subjects were randomly allocated to one of two sets of descriptions: high prototype in which all six symptoms had been previously rated as associated with the same disease, or low prototype in which only two of the six symptoms had been previously rated as associated with the same disease. The results showed that subjects in the high prototype condition labelled the disease more easily and accurately than subjects in the low prototype condition. The authors argued that this provides support for the role of the identity dimension (diagnosis and symptoms) of illness representations and also suggested that there is some consistency in people's concept of the identity of illnesses. In addition, subjects were asked to describe in their own words 'What else do you think may be associated with this person's situation?' They reported that 91 per cent of the given associations fell into the dimensions of illness representations as described by Leventhal. However, they also reported that the dimensions of consequences (the possible effects) and time line (how long it will last) were the least frequently mentioned.

There is also some evidence for a similar structure of illness representations in other cultures. Weller (1984) examined models of illness in English-speaking Americans and Spanish-speaking Guatemalans. The results indicated that illness was predominantly conceptualized in terms of contagion and severity. Lau (1995) argued that contagion is a version of the cause dimension (i.e. the illness is caused by a virus) and severity is a combination of the magnitude of the perceived consequences and beliefs about time line (i.e. how will the illness affect my life and how long will it last?) – dimensions that support those described by Leventhal. Hagger and Orbell (2003) carried out a meta-analysis of 45 empirical studies which used Leventhal's model of illness cognitions. They concluded from their analysis that there was consistent support for the different illness cognition dimensions and that the different cognitions showed a logical pattern across different illness types.

MEASURING ILLNESS COGNITIONS

Leventhal and colleagues originally used qualitative methods to assess people's illness cognitions. Since this time other forms of measurement have been used. These will be described in terms of questionnaires that have been developed and methodological issues surrounding measurement.

The Use of Questionnaires

Measuring Illness Beliefs

Although it has been argued that the preferred method to access illness cognitions is through interview, interviews are time-consuming and can only involve a limited number of subjects. In order to research further into individuals' beliefs about illness, researchers in New Zealand and the UK have developed the Illness Perception Questionnaire (IPQ) (Weinman et al. 1996). This questionnaire asks subjects to rate a series of statements about their illness. These statements reflect the dimensions of identity (e.g. a set of symptoms such as pain, tiredness), consequences (e.g. 'My illness has had major consequences on my life'), time line (e.g. 'My illness will last a short time'), cause (e.g. 'Stress was a major factor in causing my illness') and cure/control (e.g. 'There is a lot I can do to control my symptoms'). This questionnaire has been used to examine beliefs about illnesses such as chronic fatigue syndrome, diabetes and arthritis and has been translated in a number of different languages. A revised version of the IPQ has now been published (the IPQR; Moss-Morris et al. 2002) which has better psychometric properties than the original IPQ and includes three additional subscales: cyclical time line perceptions, illness coherence and emotional representations. A brief IPQ has also been developed which uses single items and is useful when participants don't have much time or when they are completing a large battery of different measures (the B-IPQ; Broadbent et al. 2006). In addition, researchers have created a version of the IPQ-R for use with healthy people (Figueiras and Alves 2007).

Measuring Treatment Beliefs

People also have beliefs about their treatment, whether it is medication, surgery or behaviour change. In line with this, Horne (1997; Horne et al. 1999) developed a Beliefs about Medicine Questionnaire (BMQ) which conceptualized such beliefs along four dimensions. Two of these are specific to the medication being taken: 'specific necessity' (to reflect whether their medicine is seen as important) and 'specific concerns' (to reflect whether the individual is concerned about side-effects); and two of these are general beliefs about all medicines: 'general overuse' (to reflect doctors' overuse of medicines) and 'general harm' (to reflect the damage that medicines can do). These two core dimensions of necessity and concerns have been shown to describe people's beliefs about anti-retroviral therapy for HIV/AIDS (V. Cooper et al. 2002; Horne et al. 2004) and to be relevant to a range of beliefs about medicines for illnesses such as asthma, renal disease, cancer, HIV and cardiac failure (e.g. Horne and Weinman 1999). Research also shows that although individuals may report a consistent pattern of beliefs, this pattern varies according to cultural background (Horne et al. 2004).

Measurement Issues

Although quantitative measures of illness and treatment beliefs are now commonly used, they are not without their limitations. Beliefs about illness can be assessed using a range of measures. Some research has used interviews (e.g. Leventhal et al. 1980, 2007a; Schmidt and Frohling 2000), some has used formal questionnaires (e.g. Horne and Weinman 2002; Llewellyn et al. 2003), some has used vignette studies (e.g. French et al. 2002) and other research has used a repertory grid method (e.g. Walton and Eves 2001). French and colleagues asked whether the form of method used to elicit beliefs about illness influenced the types of beliefs reported. In one study French et al. (2002) compared the impact of eliciting beliefs using either a questionnaire or a vignette. Participants were asked either simply to rate a series of causes for heart attack (the questionnaire) or to read a vignette about a man and to estimate his chances of having a heart attack. The results showed that the two different methods resulted in different beliefs about the causes of heart attack and different importance placed upon these causes. Specifically, when using the questionnaire, smoking and stress came out as more important causes than family history, whereas when using the vignette, smoking and family history came out as more important causes than stress. In a similar vein French et al. (2001) carried out a systematic review of studies involving attributions for causes of heart attack and compared these causes according to method used. The results showed that stressors, fate or luck were more common beliefs about causes when using interval rating scales (i.e. 1–5) than when studies used dichotomous answers (i.e. yes/no). French et al. (2005) also asked whether causal beliefs should be subjected to a factor analysis as a means to combine different sets of beliefs into individual

BOX 9.1 Some Problems with . . . Illness Cognitions Research

Below are some problems with research in this area that you may wish to consider.

1 Research often explores how people feel about their symptoms or illness by using existing questionnaires. It is possible that such measures change beliefs rather than simply access them (i.e. do I really have a belief about what has caused my headache until I am asked about it?). This is the same as the mere measurement effect described in Chapter 3.

2 Models of illness behaviour describe how the different constructs relate to each other (i.e. illness representations are associated with coping). It is not always clear, however, whether these two constructs are really discrete (e.g. 'I believe my illness is not going to last a long time' could either be an illness cognition or a coping mechanism).

3 Many of the constructs measured as part of research on illness behaviour are then used to predict health outcomes such as illness beliefs and coping. It is not clear how stable these constructs are and whether they should be considered states or traits. As a self-regulatory model, the changing nature of these constructs is central. However, it presents a real methodological problem in terms of when to measure what and whether variables are causes or consequences of each other.

constructs (e.g. external causes, lifestyle causes, etc.) and concluded that although many researchers use this approach to combine their data, it is unlikely to result in very valid groups of causal beliefs. In addition, the IPQ measures have been criticized for having ambiguous subscales, for been too general and not specific to the beliefs of each individual, and for not being sufficiently relevant for the characteristics of each individual condition (French and Weinman, 2008).

In summary, it appears that individuals may show consistent beliefs about illness that can be used to make sense of their illness and help their understanding of any developing symptoms. These illness cognitions have been incorporated into a model of illness behaviour to examine the relationship between an individual's cognitive representation of their illness and their subsequent coping behaviour. This model is known as the 'self-regulatory model of illness behaviour'.

LEVENTHAL'S SELF-REGULATORY MODEL OF ILLNESS BEHAVIOUR

Leventhal incorporated his description of illness cognitions into his self-regulatory model (SRM) of illness behaviour. This model is based on approaches to problem-solving and suggests that illness/symptoms are dealt with by individuals in the same way as other problems (see Chapter 10 for details of other models of problem solving). It is assumed that, given a problem or a change in the status quo, the individual will be motivated to solve the problem and re-establish their state of normality. Traditional models describe problem-solving in three stages: (1) interpretation (making sense of the problem); (2) coping (dealing with the problem in order to regain a state of equilibrium); and (3) appraisal (assessing how successful the coping stage has been). According to models of problem solving, these three stages will continue until the coping strategies are deemed to be successful and a state of equilibrium has been attained. In terms of health and illness, if healthiness is an individual's normal state, then any onset of illness will be interpreted as a problem and the individual will be motivated to re-establish their state of health (i.e. illness is not the normal state).

These stages have been applied to health using the SRM (see Figure 9.2) and are described briefly here and in more detail later on pp. 225–36.

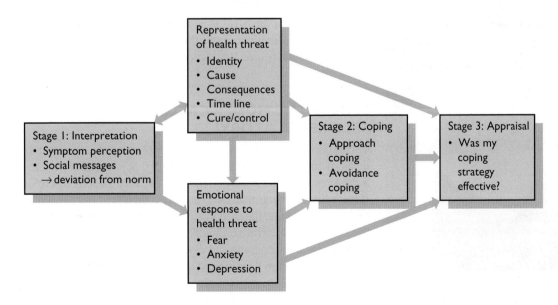

FIGURE 9.2

Leventhal's Self-Regulatory Model (SRM)

STAGE 1: INTERPRETATION

An individual may be confronted with the problem of a potential illness through two channels: *symptom perception* ('I have a pain in my chest') or *social messages* ('the doctor has diagnosed this pain as angina').

Once the individual has received information about the possibility of illness through these channels, according to theories of problem-solving, the individual is then motivated to return to a state of 'problem-free' normality. This involves assigning meaning to the problem. According to Leventhal, the problem can be given meaning by accessing the individual's illness cognitions. Therefore the symptoms and social messages will contribute towards the development of illness cognitions, which will be constructed according to the following dimensions: identity, cause, consequences, time line, cure/control. These cognitive representations of the 'problem' will give the problem meaning and will enable the individual to develop and consider suitable coping strategies.

However, a cognitive representation is not the only consequence of symptom perception and social messages. The identification of the problem of illness will also result in changes in emotional state. For example, perceiving the symptom of pain and receiving the social message that this pain may be related to coronary heart disease (CHD) may result in anxiety. Therefore, any coping strategies have to relate to both the illness cognitions and the emotional state of the individual.

STAGE 2: COPING

The next stage in the SRM is the development and identification of suitable coping strategies. Coping can take many forms, which will be discussed in detail later in this chapter and in Chapter 12. However, two broad categories of coping have been defined that incorporate the multitude of other

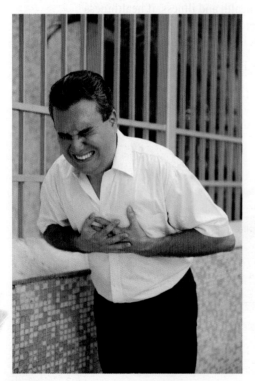

coping strategies: approach coping (e.g. taking pills, going to the doctor, resting, talking to friends about emotions) and avoidance coping (e.g. denial, wishful thinking). When faced with the problem of illness, the individual will therefore develop coping strategies in an attempt to return to a state of healthy normality.

STAGE 3: APPRAISAL

The third stage of the SRM is appraisal. This involves individuals evaluating the effectiveness of the coping strategy and determining whether to continue with this strategy or whether to opt for an alternative one.

WHY IS THE MODEL CALLED SELF-REGULATORY?

This process is regarded as self-regulatory because the three components of the model (interpretation, coping, appraisal) interrelate in order to maintain the status quo (i.e. they regulate the self). Therefore, if the individual's normal state (health) is disrupted (by illness), the model proposes that the individual is motivated to return the balance back to normality. This self-regulation involves the three processes interrelating in an ongoing and dynamic fashion. Therefore, interactions occur between the different stages. For example:

Experiencing symptoms can generate an emotional response and an illness representation

SOURCE: © Mangostock/Dreamstime

- Symptom perception may result in an emotional shift, which may exacerbate the perception of symptoms (e.g. 'I can feel a pain in my chest. Now I feel anxious. Now I can feel more pain as all my attention is focused on it.'

- If the individual opts to use denial as their coping strategy, this may result in a reduction in symptom perception, a decrease in any negative emotions and a shift in their illness cognition (e.g. 'This pain is not very bad' (denial); 'Now I feel less anxious' (emotions); 'This pain will not last for long' (time line); 'This illness will not have any serious consequences for my lifestyle' (consequences)).
- A positive appraisal of the effectiveness of the coping strategy may itself be a coping strategy (e.g. 'My symptoms appear to have been reduced by doing relaxation exercises' may be a form of denial).

PROBLEMS WITH ASSESSMENT

This dynamic, self-regulatory process suggests a model of cognitions that is complex and intuitively sensible, but poses problems for attempts at assessment and intervention. For example:

1 If the different components of the SRM interact, should they be measured separately? For example, is the belief that an illness has no serious consequences an illness cognition or a coping strategy?

2 If the different components of the SRM interact, can individual components be used to predict outcome or should the individual components be seen as co-occurring? For example, is the appraisal that symptoms have been reduced a successful outcome or is it a form of denial (a coping strategy)?

FOCUS ON RESEARCH 9.1: ILLNESS REPRESENTATIONS AND BEHAVIOURAL OUTCOMES

A study to explore the role of coherence in promoting the intentions to quit smoking (Hall et al. 2004).

This paper presents the results from two studies to examine the relationship between women's beliefs about cervical cancer and their intentions to quit smoking. In particular the study explored whether, by making beliefs about threat and behaviour more coherent with each other, people are more likely to be motivated to change their behaviour.

BACKGROUND

Research shows that women who smoke have twice the chance of developing cervical cancer than those who do not. Most women, however, are unaware of this association and, when told that smoking can increase the risk of cervical cancer, report finding this information confusing and nonsensical ('how [can] smoking a cigarette in your mouth cause you problems downstairs?'). Leventhal's SRM illustrates that people represent their illness in the form of illness representations. He also argues that if people are to act on threats to their health, they need to have a coherent model whereby their beliefs about the nature of the threat are coherent with their beliefs about any action that could be taken. The relationship between smoking and cervical cancer does not immediately make sense, suggesting that most people do not have a coherent model about the link between these factors. This study used an experimental design to present women with a coherent model of how smoking is linked to cervical cancer and to explore whether a more coherent model was associated with a greater intention to quit smoking.

STUDY I

Methodology

Design

The study used an experimental design with women receiving either a detailed leaflet about cervical cancer and smoking, a less detailed leaflet or no leaflet.

Sample

The sample consisted of female smokers aged between 20 and 64 who were recruited from two general practices in the UK.

Procedure

Women who received a leaflet in the post were then asked to complete a questionnaire a week later. Those who did not receive a leaflet were just sent the questionnaire.

Measures

Women completed measures of response efficacy (the extent to which stopping smoking would reduce vulnerability to cervical cancer), self-efficacy for smoking cessation, severity, coherence (the extent to which they believed they had a coherent explanation for the link between smoking and cervical cancer) and intentions to quit smoking in the next month. In addition, measures of smoking behaviour were taken.

Data Analysis

The results were analysed to assess the impact of the leaflets on women's level of coherence, beliefs and intentions. The results were then analysed to assess the relationship between level of coherence, beliefs and intentions.

Results

The results showed that the detailed and less detailed leaflet were equally as effective at producing a coherent model of the relationship between smoking and cervical cancer and were both more effective than receiving no leaflet. The results also showed that those who received a leaflet (regardless of level of detail) reported higher vulnerability to cervical cancer, greater response efficacy and higher intentions to quit smoking. Finally, in terms of the relationship between coherence, beliefs and intentions, the results showed that greater intentions to quit smoking were predicted by greater coherence, greater perceptions of severity, higher response efficacy and higher self-efficacy. Furthermore, greater perceptions of vulnerability to cervical cancer only predicted intentions to quit smoking in those women who showed a coherent model of the link between smoking and cervical cancer.

Conclusion

The results therefore show the importance of a coherent model in creating a link between beliefs and intentions. The results also show that coherence can be changed by a simple leaflet intervention.

STUDY 2

Because of the weakness of some of the measures in Study 1, the authors replicated their study with a further 178 women smokers and included an improved measure of vulnerability. The results directly replicated the findings of Study 1.

Conclusion

This study illustrates a role for coherence between beliefs about threat and subsequent action and supports Leventhal's model. Therefore people would seem more likely to intend to change their behaviour if they have a coherent model as to how this behaviour may impact upon their health status.

The individual processes involved in the SRM will now be examined in greater detail.

STAGE 1: INTERPRETATION IN GREATER DETAIL

The interpretation stage involves symptom perception and social messages. These result in the creation of illness cognitions and an emotional representation of the problem.

SYMPTOM PERCEPTION

It is often assumed that we experiences symptoms in response to some underlying physical problem. For example, we think that our headache reflects something going on in our head and that the worse it feels, the worse the damage in our head must be. Research exploring symptom perception indicates that this simple stimulus–response model of symptoms ignores the wealth of psychological factors that can make symptoms either better or worse. Research has addressed individual differences in symptom perception and the role of mood, cognition and the social context. These are illustrated in Figure 9.3.

Individual Differences in Symptom Perception

Symptoms such as a temperature, pain, a runny nose or the detection of a lump may indicate to the individual the possibility of illness. However, symptom perception is not a straightforward process and research indicates much variability between people (see Chapter 13 for details of pain perception and Chapter 16 for details of menopausal symptoms). For example, what might be a sore throat to one person could be another's tonsillitis, and whereas a retired person might consider a cough a serious problem, a working person might be too busy to think about it. Research has addressed this variability in terms of an internal/external focus, demographics and attachment styles.

Internal/External Focus

Pennebaker (1983) has argued that there are individual differences in the amount of attention people pay to their internal states and that whereas some individuals may sometimes be internally focused and more sensitive to symptoms, others may be more externally focused and less sensitive to any

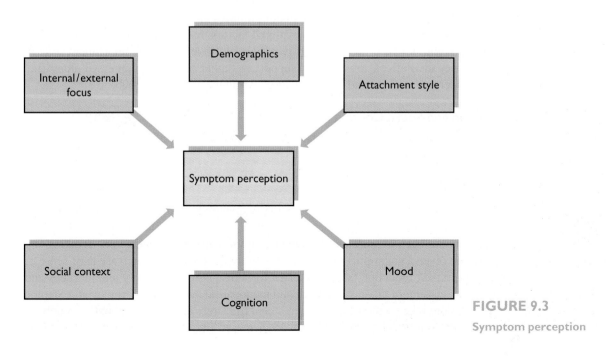

FIGURE 9.3

Symptom perception

internal changes. However, this difference is not always consistent with differences in how accurate people are at detecting their symptoms. For example, Pennebaker reported that individuals who were more focused on their internal states tended to overestimate changes in their heart rate compared with subjects who were externally focused. In contrast, Kohlmann et al. (2001) examined the relationship between cardiac vigilance and heart-beat detection in the laboratory and reported a negative correlation; those who stated they were more aware of their heart underestimated their heart rate. Being internally focused has also been shown to relate to a perception of slower recovery from illness (Miller et al. 1987) and to more health-protective behaviour (Kohlmann et al. 2001). Being internally focused may result in a different perception of symptom change, not a more accurate one.

Demographics

Research has also explored variability in symptom reporting by gender, time of day, day of week and family group (Michel 2006; 2007). For example, in one study parents and adolescents from 173 families completed measures of their somatic symptoms six times a day for seven consecutive days. The results showed that symptoms were more likely to be reported in the mornings and evenings than in the middle of the day and less likely to be reported on weekend evenings than week evenings. In addition, women reported more symptoms than men (during the day) and adolescents showed an increase in symptoms in the evenings compared to their parents (Michel 2007). In a parallel study, variation in symptom reporting was found at the individual level but not at the family level (Michel 2006).

Attachment Style

The notion of attachment style is derived from Bowlby's early work on how children internalize their interactions with their primary caregiver to form the basis for their beliefs and expectations of present and future interpersonal interactions (Bowlby 1973). Ainsworth et al. (1978) used this perspective to develop their three-factor model of attachment behaviour and classified attachment as secure ('my mother will respond to me'), anxious ambivalent ('my mother inconsistently responds to me') and avoidant ('my mother doesn't respond to me'). Attachment style has been used to inform much recent research across all areas of psychology including depression, stress, coping and anxiety. Within health psychology, research has identified a link between attachment style and symptom reporting and in general research indicates that those with secure attachment styles report fewer somatic symptoms than those with either anxious/ambivalent or avoidant styles (Taylor et al. 2000; Wearden et al. 2003). Research has also explored factors that may mediate this relationship and indicates that higher levels of symptoms may only relate to a less secure attachment style in those with either negative affect, lower social support or higher levels of suppressed anger (i.e. 'anger in', not 'anger out'), (Kidd and Sheffield 2005; Armitage and Harris 2006).

Mood, Cognition and Social Context

Skelton and Pennebaker (1982) suggested that symptom perception is also influenced by factors such as mood, cognitions and the social context.

Mood

The role of mood in symptom perception is particularly apparent in pain perception with anxiety increasing self-reports of the pain experience (see Chapter 13 for a discussion of anxiety and pain). In addition, anxiety has been proposed as an explanation for placebo pain reduction, as taking any form of medication (even a sugar pill) may reduce the individual's anxiety, increase their sense of control and result in pain reduction (see Chapter 13 for a discussion of anxiety and placebos and Chapter 16 for a discussion of anxiety and birth and menopausal symptoms). Cropley and Steptoe (2005) directly explored the relationship between recent life stress and general symptom reporting and found that higher stress was associated with an increased frequency of a range of symptoms.

In a similar vein, Charles and Almeida (2006) explored the relationship between state negative affect and a wide range of somatic symptoms and using a lagged design focused on the direction of the relationships between these factors in an attempt to determine what comes first – symptom or low mood. The results were complex with no simple story emerging but showed that whereas pain (e.g. headaches, backaches and muscle soreness) seemed to lead to lowered mood, lowered mood seemed to lead to gastrointestinal symptoms such as poor appetite, nausea/upset stomach or constipation. Stegen et al. (2000) likewise explored the impact of negative affectivity on the experience of symptoms but also focused on attributions for these symptoms. In an experimental study, participants were exposed to low-intensity somatic sensations induced by breathing air high in carbon dioxide. They were then told that the sensation would be either positive, negative or somewhere in between and were asked to rate both the pleasantness and intensity of their symptoms. The results showed that what the participants were told about the sensation influenced their ratings of its pleasantness. They also showed that although people who rated high on negative affectivity showed similar ratings of pleasantness to those low on negative affectivity, they also reported more negative meanings and worries about their symptoms. This indicates that expectations about the nature of a symptom can alter the experience of that symptom and that negative mood can influence the attributions made about a symptom. Similarly, Mora et al. (2007) explored the role of negative affect on symptom perception and the processes underlying this relationship. Their study involved both a cross-sectional and longitudinal design and assessed trait and state negative affect in adults with moderate and severe asthma. The results showed that higher trait negative affect was related to higher reports of all symptoms whether or not they were related to asthma. In addition, the results showed that only those who were worried about their asthma attributed their asthma symptoms to asthma. This suggests that negative affect increases symptom perception and further that worrying about asthma enables the individual to associate their symptoms with their illness.

In line with this relationship between mood and symptoms, a recent study explored the impact of manipulating psychological stress on symptom perception (Wright et al. 2005). Using an experimental design, 42 patients with heartburn and reflux were exposed either to a psychological stressor or a no-stress control condition. They then rated their state anxiety and symptom perception. In addition, objective ratings of reflux symptoms were taken. The results showed that the stressor resulted in increased subjective ratings of symptoms. The stressor, however, did not result in any increase in actual reflux. Therefore the stressor resulted in a greater dissociation between subjective and objective symptoms. This study is important as it not only illustrates the impact of stress on symptom perception but also illustrates that gap between objective and subjective accounts of symptoms. Further, a meta-analytic review of 244 observational studies of irritable bowel syndrome, non-ulcer dyspepsia, fibromyalgia and chronic fatigue syndrome reported a consistent impact of depression and anxiety on symptom perception (Henningsen et al. 2003) with parallel results also being reported for children and adolescents for stomach pain, headache and leg pain (Eminson 2007). Research therefore indicates a link between mood and symptom perception. Brosschot and Van der Doef (2006) explored whether a simple intervention could reduce this association. In their study, 171 teenagers were asked to record their 'worry' and any symptoms. In addition, half were asked to postpone their worry to a special 30-minute 'worry period' each day (the postponers) for six days and the results showed a reduction in their symptoms.

Cognition

An individual's cognitive state may also influence their symptom perception. This is illustrated by the placebo effect with the individual's expectations of recovery resulting in reduced symptom perception (see Chapter 13). It is also illustrated by Stegen et al.'s (2000) study of breathing symptoms with expectations changing symptom perception. Ruble (1977) carried out a study in which she manipulated women's expectations about when they were due to start menstruating. She gave subjects an 'accurate physiological test' and told women either that their period was due very shortly or that it was at least a week away. The women were then asked to report any premenstrual symptoms. The results showed that believing that they were about to start menstruating (even though they were not) increased the number of reported premenstrual symptoms. This indicates an association between cognitive state and symptom perception. Pennebaker also reported that symptom perception is related to an individual's attentional state and that boredom and the absence of environmental stimuli may result in over-reporting, whereas distraction and attention diversion may lead to under-reporting (Pennebaker 1983). One study provides support for Pennebaker's theory. Sixty-one women who had been hospitalized during pre-term labour were randomized to receive either information, distraction or nothing (van Zuuren 1998). The results showed that distraction had the most beneficial effect on measures of both physical and psychological symptoms, suggesting that symptom perception is sensitive to attention. Symptom perception can also be influenced by the ways in which symptoms are elicited. For example, Eiser (2000) carried out an experimental study whereby students were asked to indicate their symptoms, from a list of 30 alternatives, over the past month and the past year and also to rate their health status. However, whereas half were asked to endorse their symptoms (i.e. mark those they had had), half were asked to exclude their symptoms (i.e. mark those they had not had). The results showed that those in the 'exclude' condition reported 70 per cent more symptoms than those in the 'endorse' condition. In addition, those who had endorsed the symptoms rated their health more negatively than those who had excluded symptoms. This suggests that it is not only focus and attention that can influence symptom perception but also the ways in which this focus is directed.

Social Context

Symptom perception is therefore influenced by mood and cognitions. It is also influenced by an individual's social context. Cross-cultural research consistently shows variation in the presentation of psychiatric symptoms such as anxiety, psychosis and depression. For example, Minsky et al. (2003) explored diagnostic patterns in Latino, African American and European American psychiatric patients and reported that not only did the diagnoses of major depression and schizophrenic disorders vary by ethnic group, but so did symptom presentation, with Latinos reporting a higher frequency of psychotic symptoms than the other groups. Similarly, a consensus statement by the International Consensus Group of Depression and Anxiety (Ballenger et al. 2001) concluded that there was wide cultural variation not only in the diagnosis and responsiveness to treatment for depression and anxiety but also significant variation in symptom presentation. A similar pattern of variation can also be found for somatic symptoms such as headaches, fatigue, constipation and back pain although research in this area is less extensive. For example, epidemiological studies indicate that while headache is a common symptom in the USA and Western Europe, its prevalence remains much lower in China and in African and Asian populations (e.g. Ziegler 1990; Stewart et al. 1996; Wang et al. 1997). Similarly, large surveys of primary care attenders report that those from less developed countries and from Latin America tend to report more somatic symptoms in general (Gureje et al. 1997; Piccinelli and Simon 1997). One study explored cataract patients' reports of visual function and the extent to which they were bothered by their cataract, and also explored differences by culture (Alonso et al. 1998). The results showed that after controlling for clinical and sociodemographic characteristics, patients from Canada and Barcelona reported less trouble with their vision than patients from Denmark or the USA, suggesting cultural variation in the perception of visual symptoms. Symptom perception and diagnosis are therefore highly influenced by the individual's context and cultural background.

Mood, cognition and social context therefore influence symptom perception. These different factors may independently influence how symptoms are perceived, but often they interact together to make symptoms either worse or better. This is illustrated by three conditions: 'medical student disease', medically unexplained symptoms and post-traumatic stress symptoms.

A large component of the medical curriculum involves learning about the symptoms associated with a multitude of different illnesses. More than two-thirds of medical students incorrectly report that at some time they have had the symptoms they are being taught about. This was described by Mechanic (1962) as *'medical student disease'*. Perhaps this phenomenon can be understood in terms of the following:

- *Mood:* medical students become quite anxious due to their workload. This anxiety may heighten their awareness of any physiological changes, making them more internally focused.

- *Cognition:* medical students are thinking about symptoms as part of their course, which may result in a focus on their own internal states.

- *Social context:* once one student starts to perceive symptoms, others may model themselves on this behaviour.

People often experience symptoms which seem to have no obvious underlying pathology, and these are known as medically unexplained symptoms (MUS). For example, people may feel tired, have headaches, have stomach or bowel pain, or feel dizzy, yet medical tests can find nothing wrong with them. Such symptoms have been labeled 'functional' or 'psychosomatic' but are most often now referred to as MUS, which also includes clusters of symptoms (known as syndromes) such as chronic fatigue syndrome and irritable bowel syndrome. Such symptoms are even common in children, with the most common across age and sex being headache, abdominal pain and fatigue (Garber et al. 1991; Perquin et al. 2000). For example, one community survey of over 500 children found headache and fatigue to be present in around one quarter of participants; abdominal pain, muscle soreness and back pain were also common (Garber et al. 1991). Research exploring the reasons behind MUS focuses on a number of issues including predisposing factors (e.g. genetics, personality), perpetuating factors (e.g. attention to the problem, behaviour, mood) and precipitating factors (e.g. life events, stressors) (Deary et al. 2007). Central to this account of MUS is that symptoms can get worse or better according to how we react to them. This is supported by studies using cognitive behavioural therapy (CBT) to help reduce MUS which indicate that modifying a person's mood, cognitions and social context can help to reduce a range of symptoms such as pain, tiredness and stomach and bowel problems (Deary et al. 2007). This is also similar to research on pain and the placebo effect (see Chapter 13).

Post-traumatic stress disorder (PTSD) has mostly been the focus of clinical psychology rather than health psychology. Many people who have experienced a significant stressful life event also report somatic symptoms such as headaches, dizziness, nausea, upset stomach, breathlessness and muscle pain. For example, research has shown an increase in such symptoms after events such as a plane crash, a mass killing, a tornado or military action in a number of populations including military staff, bystanders, civilians, rescuers and relief workers (Bromet et al. 2002; Engel et al. 2002; Jones et al. 2002; North 2002; Slottje et al. 2008a, 2008b). Studies to date have tried to explain how these symptoms occur and have tended to focus the nature of the event itself (i.e. exposure to toxic substances, degree of physical damage inflicted on the individual, exposure to casualties of the disaster) or post-traumatic psychological symptoms (e.g. intrusive thoughts, anxiety). However, although it would seem that these factors may play a role, they only explain a small amount of the variance in actual somatic symptom experience (e.g. Schnurr and Green 2004; Slottje et al. 2008a, 2008b). Perhaps these somatic symptoms should be understood within the context of how all symptoms are perceived. From this perspective their onset and perpetuation may be influenced by the event itself and subsequent stress symptoms, but in line with other symptoms they may be made worse or better by the ways in which an individual reacts to them and the mood, cognitions and social context.

Research exploring symptom perception highlights how the severity and impact of symptoms can be changed by a number of factors such as mood, cognitions and the individual's social context. This assumes that there is the 'nugget' of a symptom there which is then made worse or better by the way we think about it. However, some research such as that addressing MUS indicates that symptoms might actually be created without this 'nugget'. From this perspective not only can the way we think change the severity of any symptom, it might also generate the symptom in the first place. Pennebaker (1982) explored this question and using an experimental design reported that people were more likely to start scratching if they sat next to a confederate who was also scratching. In a similar vein, research indicates that both smiling and yawning can be contagious (Wild et al. 2001; Platek et al. 2005; Schurman et al. 2005). This suggests that seeing a symptom may help to generate that symptom elsewhere. In 2009, Ogden and Zoukas carried out a similar experimental study to explore whether feeling itchy, cold or pain could be created by watching a film. Participants viewed a film showing either headlice in a head of hair (itchy), people swimming in icy water and running in snow (cold) or people sustaining broken limbs as part of football or boxing matches (pain). Participants then rated their symptoms and were observed for symptom-related behaviour (e.g. scratching, shivering, flinching). The results showed that the films did indeed generate their matched symptom (itchiness, cold, pain) on both subjective and objective measures but that cold symptoms were more easily generated than either itchiness or pain.

Symptom perception is therefore not a simple process and is influenced by a number of factors including mood, cognitions and social context. These factors can make symptoms worse or better. They may also be able to create symptoms in the first place.

SOCIAL MESSAGES

Information about illness also comes from other people in the form of a formal diagnosis from a health professional or a positive test result from a routine health check. Such messages may or may not be a consequence of symptom perception. For example, a formal diagnosis may occur after symptoms have been perceived, when the individual has subsequently been motivated to go to the doctor and has been given a diagnosis. However, screening and health checks may detect illness at an asymptomatic stage of development and therefore attendance for such a test may not have been motivated by symptom perception. Information about illness may also come from other lay individuals who are not health professionals. Before (and after) consulting a health professional, people often access their social network, which has been called their 'lay referral system' by Freidson (1970). This can take the form of colleagues, friends or family and involves seeking information and advice from multiple sources. For example, coughing in front of one friend may result in the advice to speak to another friend who had a similar cough, or a suggestion to take a favoured home remedy. Alternatively, it may result in a lay diagnosis or a suggestion to seek professional help from the doctor. In fact, Scambler et al. (1981) reported that three-quarters of those taking part in their study of primary care attenders had sought advice from family or friends before seeking professional help. In contrast, a study of men with symptoms of prostate disease such as dribbling, needing to urinate in the night and urgency showed that their delay in seeking help with their symptoms was related to the absence of any social messages from their friends or family as they were able to hide their symptoms due to a need to live up to traditional images of masculinity (Hale et al. 2007). Therefore, people may get or not get social messages which will influence how they interpret the 'problem' of illness and whether they decide to seek help.

The language used by the doctor is also an important source of information. Some research has explored how such language can influence how the patient feels about their problem. Ogden et al. (2003) explored the relative effect of calling a problem by its lay term (i.e. sore throat/stomach upset) or by its medical term (i.e. tonsillitis/gastroenteritis) and showed that whereas the medical terms made the patient feel that their symptoms were being taken seriously and reported greater confidence in the doctor, the lay terms made the patient feel more ownership of the problem which could be associated with unwanted responsibility and blame. Similarly, Tayler and Ogden (2005) explored the relative effect of describing a problem as either 'heart failure' or the doctors' preferred euphemism for the symptoms that are considered as heart failure – 'fluid on your lungs as your heart is not pumping hard enough'. The results showed that manipulating the name of the problem in this way resulted in significant shifts in people's beliefs about the problem. In particular, the term 'heart failure' resulted in people believing that the problem would have more serious consequences, would be more variable over time, would last for longer and made them feel more anxious and depressed about their problem compared to the euphemism. People therefore receive social messages about the nature of their problem which influence how they represent this problem and subsequently how they then behave.

People receive information about their health problem through symptom perception and social messages. This then leads to the formation of a cognitive representation of the problem in the form of illness cognitions and their different dimensions (identity, causes, control, consequences, time line) which have been described in detail above. It also leads to an emotional representation which might take the form of fear, denial, depression or anxiety. Compared to illness cognitions, the emotional response to symptom perception and social messages remains a much neglected part of the SRM.

STAGE 2: COPING IN GREATER DETAIL

There is a vast literature on how people cope with a range of problems including stress, pain and illness. Coping with stress and pain is covered in Chapters 12 and 13. This section will examine three approaches to coping with illness: (1) coping with the crisis of illness; (2) adjustment to physical illness and the theory of cognitive adaptation; (3) benefit-finding and post-traumatic growth. These different theoretical approaches have implications for understanding the differences between adaptive and maladaptive coping, and the role of reality and illusions in the coping process. They therefore have different implications for understanding the outcome of the coping process (see Figure 9.4).

COPING WITH THE CRISIS OF ILLNESS

Being diagnosed with a physical illness has been understood within the framework of crisis theory and the need to return to a state of equilibrium (Moos and Schaefer 1984).

What is Crisis Theory?

Crisis theory has been generally used to examine how people cope with major life crises and transitions and has traditionally provided a framework for understanding the impact of illness or injury. The theory was developed from work done on grief and mourning and a model of developmental crises at transition points in the life cycle. In general, crisis theory examines the impact of any form

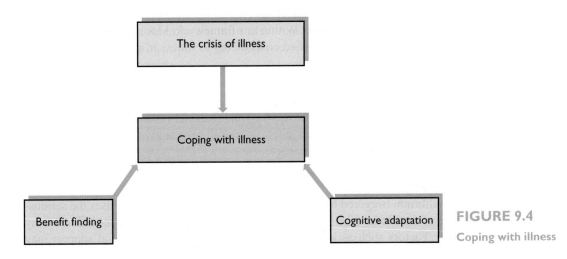

FIGURE 9.4

Coping with illness

of disruption on an individual's established personal and social identity. It suggests that psychological systems are driven towards maintaining homeostasis and equilibrium in the same way as physical systems. Within this framework any crisis is self-limiting as the individual will find a way of returning to a stable state; individuals are therefore regarded as self-regulators.

Physical Illness as a Crisis

Moos and Schaefer (1984) argued that physical illness can be considered a crisis as it represents a turning point in an individual's life. They suggest that physical illness causes the following changes, which can be conceptualized as a crisis:

- *Changes in identity:* illness can create a shift in identity, such as from carer to patient, or from breadwinner to person with an illness.
- *Changes in location:* illness may result in a move to a new environment such as becoming bed-ridden or hospitalized.
- *Changes in role:* a change from independent adult to passive dependant may occur following illness, resulting in a changed role.
- *Changes in social support:* illness may produce isolation from friends and family, effecting changes in social support.
- *Changes in the future:* a future involving children, career or travel can become uncertain.

In addition, the crisis nature of illness may be exacerbated by factors that are often specific to illness such as:

- *Illness is often unpredicted:* if an illness is not expected then the individual will not have had the opportunity to consider possible coping strategies.
- *Information about the illness is unclear:* much of the information about illness is ambiguous and unclear, particularly in terms of causality and outcome.
- *A decision is needed quickly:* illness frequently requires decisions about action to be made quickly (e.g. should we operate?, should we take medicines?, should we take time off from work?, should we tell our friends?).
- *Ambiguous meaning:* because of uncertainties about causality and outcome, the meaning of the illness for an individual will often be ambiguous (e.g. is it serious?, how long will it affect me?).
- *Limited prior experience:* most individuals are healthy most of the time. Therefore illness is infrequent and may occur to individuals with limited prior experience. This lack of experience has implications for the development of coping strategies and efficacy based on other similar situations (e.g. I've never had cancer before, what should I do next?).

Many other crises may be easier to predict, have clearer meanings and occur to individuals with a greater degree of relevant previous experience. Within this framework, Moos and Schaefer considered illness a particular kind of crisis, and applied crisis theory to illness in an attempt to examine how individuals cope with this crisis.

The Coping Process

Once confronted with the crisis of physical illness, Moos and Schaefer (1984) described three processes that constitute the coping process: (1) cognitive appraisal; (2) adaptive tasks; and (3) coping skills. These processes are illustrated in Figure 9.5.

Process 1: Cognitive Appraisal

At the stage of disequilibrium triggered by the illness, an individual initially appraises the seriousness and significance of the illness (e.g. Is my cancer serious? How will my cancer influence my life in the long run?). Factors such as knowledge, previous experience and social support may

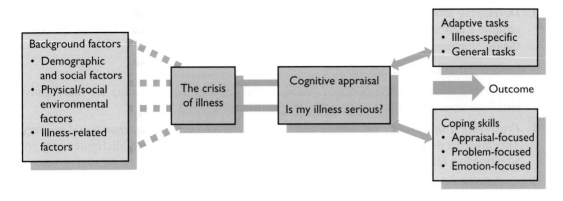

FIGURE 9.5

Coping with the crisis of illness

influence this appraisal process. In addition, it is possible to integrate Leventhal's illness cognitions at this stage in the coping process because such illness beliefs are related to how an illness will be appraised.

Process 2: Adaptive Tasks

Following cognitive appraisal, Moos and Schaefer describe seven adaptive tasks that are used as part of the coping process. These can be divided into three illness-specific tasks and four general tasks and are illustrated in Table 9.1.

The three illness-specific tasks can be described as:

1 *Dealing with pain, incapacitation and other symptoms.* This task involves dealing with symptoms such as pain, dizziness, loss of control and the recognition of changes in the severity of the symptoms.

2 *Dealing with the hospital environment and special treatment procedures.* This task involves dealing with medical interventions such as mastectomy, chemotherapy and any related side-effects.

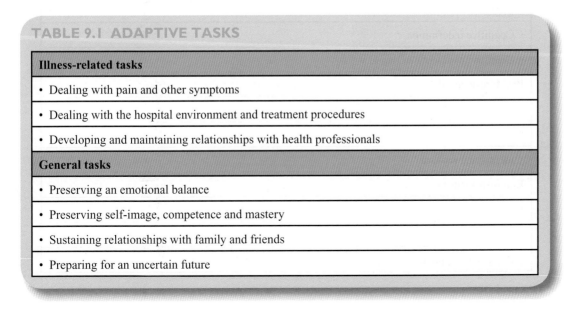

TABLE 9.1 ADAPTIVE TASKS

Illness-related tasks
• Dealing with pain and other symptoms
• Dealing with the hospital environment and treatment procedures
• Developing and maintaining relationships with health professionals
General tasks
• Preserving an emotional balance
• Preserving self-image, competence and mastery
• Sustaining relationships with family and friends
• Preparing for an uncertain future

3 *Developing and maintaining adequate relationships with health care staff.* Becoming ill requires a new set of relationships with a multitude of health professionals. This task describes the development of those relationships.

The four general tasks can be described as:

1 *Preserving a reasonable emotional balance.* This involves compensating for the negative emotions aroused by illness with sufficient positive ones.

2 *Preserving a satisfactory self-image and maintaining a sense of competence and mastery.* This involves dealing with changes in appearance following illness (e.g. disfigurement) and adapting to a reliance on technology (e.g. pacemaker).

3 *Sustaining relationships with family and friends.* This involves maintaining social support networks even when communication can become problematic due to changes in location and mobility.

4 *Preparing for an uncertain future.* Illness can often result in loss (e.g. of sight, lifestyle, mobility, life). This task involves coming to terms with such losses and redefining the future.

Process 3: Coping Skills

Following both appraisal and the use of adaptive tasks, Moos and Schaefer described a series of coping skills that are accessed to deal with the crisis of physical illness. These coping skills can be categorized into three forms: (1) appraisal-focused coping; (2) problem-focused coping; and (3) emotion-focused coping (see Table 9.2).

Appraisal-focused coping involves attempts to understand the illness and represents a search for meaning. Three sets of appraisal-focused coping skills have been defined:

1 Logical analysis and mental preparation, involving turning an apparently unmanageable event into a series of manageable ones.

TABLE 9.2 COPING TASKS

Appraisal-focused
• Logical analysis and mental preparation
• Cognitive redefinition
• Cognitive avoidance or denial
Problem-focused
• Seeking information and support
• Taking problem-solving action
• Identifying rewards
Emotion-focused
• Affective regulation
• Emotional discharge
• Resigned acceptance

2 Cognitive redefinition, involving accepting the reality of the situation and redefining it in a positive and acceptable way.

3 Cognitive avoidance and denial, involving minimizing the seriousness of the illness.

Problem-focused coping involves confronting the problem and reconstructing it as manageable. Three types of problem-focused coping skills have been defined:

1 Seeking information and support, involving building a knowledge base by accessing any available information.

2 Taking problem-solving action, involving learning specific procedures and behaviours (e.g. insulin injections).

3 Identifying alternative rewards, involving the development and planning of events and goals that can provide short-term satisfaction.

Emotion-focused coping involves managing emotions and maintaining emotional equilibrium. Three types of emotion-focused coping skills have been defined:

1 Affective, involving efforts to maintain hope when dealing with a stressful situation.

2 Emotional discharge, involving venting feelings of anger or despair.

3 Resigned acceptance, involving coming to terms with the inevitable outcome of an illness.

Therefore, according to this theory of coping with the crisis of a physical illness, individuals appraise the illness and then use a variety of adaptive tasks and coping skills which in turn determine the outcome.

However, not all individuals respond to illness in the same way and Moos and Schaefer (1984) argued that the use of these tasks and skills is determined by three factors:

1 Demographic and personal factors, such as age, sex, class, religion.

2 Physical and social/environmental factors, such as the accessibility of social support networks and the acceptability of the physical environment (e.g. hospitals can be dull and depressing).

3 Illness-related factors, such as any resulting pain, disfigurement or stigma.

The most commonly used tools to measure coping are the Ways of Coping checklist (Folkman and Lazarus 1988) and the COPE (Carver et al. 1989). These are described in detail in Chapter 12 in the context of stress and coping.

EVIDENCE FOR COPING WITH THE CRISIS OF ILLNESS

Much research has used the notion of crisis theory and coping with the crisis of illness to explore, predict and change how people respond to illness. In particular, research has explored the relative impact of different types of coping on a range of psychological outcomes following illness. For example, research exploring coping with rheumatoid arthritis suggests that active and problem-solving coping are associated with better outcomes whereas passive avoidant coping is associated with poorer outcomes (Manne and Zautra 1992; Newman et al. 1996). For patients with chronic obstructive pulmonary disease (COPD), wishful thinking and emotion-focused coping were least effective (Buchi et al. 1997). Similarly, research exploring stress and psoriasis shows that avoidant coping is least useful (e.g. Leary et al. 1998). Further, for women at risk of ovarian cancer, problem-focused coping predicted higher distress over time (in those with high levels of perceived control) and poorer attendance at screening appointments (Fang et al. 2006). Pollard and Kennedy (2007) explored changes in coping strategies, depression and anxiety following traumatic spinal cord injury and reported that all three variables were fairly stable over a 10-year period. In addition, the results indicated that although two-thirds of patients showed no signs or symptoms of depression, the level of depression at year 10 was predicted by more adaptive coping strategies at week

12 post-injury. A parallel link between adaptive coping and psychological morbidity was also found in a similar study but with a much larger sample across six European countries (n = 237) with a one-year follow up (Kennedy et al. 2010). Overall, reviews of the impact of coping indicate that poorer health outcomes tend to be predicted by avoidant coping strategies and ones which involve inhibiting emotional expression (de Ridder et al. 2008), although venting emotions per se does not always seem to be most effective either. In line with this, some research has also attempted to change the way people cope through coping skills training which aims to help them adjust to their illness, particularly through improving self-efficacy and encouraging individuals to prioritize coping resources towards those aspects of the illness which are most controllable and amenable to change. This approach has been used for a range of illnesses including HIV (Antoni et al. 2000, 2006), arthritis (Carson et al. 2006), diabetes (Grey et al. 2000) and sickle cell disease in children (Gil et al. 2001).

IMPLICATIONS FOR THE OUTCOME OF THE COPING PROCESS

Within this model, individuals attempt to deal with the crisis of physical illness via the stages of appraisal, the use of adaptive tasks and the employment of coping skills. The types of tasks and skills used may determine the outcome and such an outcome may be psychological adjustment or may be related to longevity or quality of life (see Chapter 12 for a discussion of coping and stress outcomes). According to crisis theory, individuals are motivated to re-establish a state of equilibrium and normality. This desire can be satisfied by either short-term or long-term solutions. Crisis theory differentiates between two types of new equilibrium: *healthy adaptation*, which can result in maturation, and a *maladaptive response* resulting in deterioration. In this perspective, healthy adaptation involves reality orientation, adaptive tasks and constructive coping skills. Therefore, according to this model of coping, the desired outcome of the coping process is reality orientation.

ADJUSTMENT TO PHYSICAL ILLNESS AND THE THEORY OF COGNITIVE ADAPTATION

In an alternative model of coping, Taylor and colleagues (e.g. Taylor 1983; Taylor et al. 1984) examined ways in which individuals adjust to threatening events. Based on a series of interviews with rape victims and cardiac and cancer patients, they suggested that coping with threatening events (including illness) consists of three processes: (1) a search for meaning; (2) a search for mastery; and (3) a process of self-enhancement. They argued that these three processes are central to developing and maintaining illusions and that these illusions constitute a process of cognitive adaptation. Again, this model describes the individual as self-regulatory and as motivated to maintain the status quo. In addition, many of the model's components parallel those described earlier in terms of illness cognitions (e.g. the dimensions of cause and consequence). This theoretical perspective will be described in the context of their results from women who had recently had breast cancer (Taylor et al. 1984) and is shown in Figure 9.6.

A SEARCH FOR MEANING

A search for meaning is reflected in questions such as 'Why did it happen?', 'What impact has it had?' and 'What does my life mean now?' A search for meaning can be understood in terms of a search for causality and a search to understand the implications.

A Search for Causality ('Why Did it Happen?')

Attribution theory suggests that individuals need to understand, predict and control their environment (e.g. Weiner 1986). Taylor et al. (1984) reported that 95 per cent of the women they interviewed offered an explanation of the cause of their breast cancer. For example, 41 per cent explained their cancer in terms of stress, 32 per cent held carcinogens such as the birth control pill, chemical

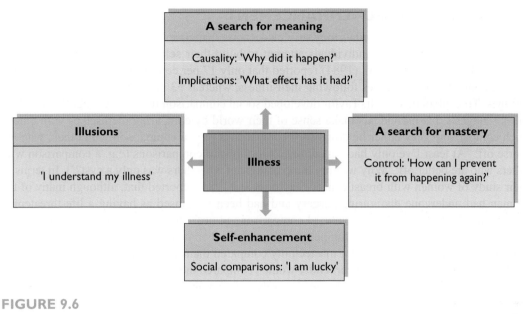

FIGURE 9.6

Cognitive adaptation theory

SOURCE: Adapted from Taylor et al. (1984)

dumps or nuclear waste as responsible, 26 per cent saw hereditary factors as the cause, 17 per cent blamed diet and 10 per cent considered a blow to the breast to blame. Several women reported multiple causes. Taylor (1983) suggested that no one perception of cause is better than any other, but that what is important for the process of cognitive adaptation is the search for any cause. People need to ask 'Why did it happen?'

Understanding the Implications ('What Effect Has it Had on My Life?')

Taylor (1983) also argued that it is important for the women to understand the implications of the cancer for their life now. Accordingly, over 50 per cent of the women stated that the cancer had resulted in them reappraising their life, and others mentioned improved self-knowledge, self-change and a process of reprioritization.

Understanding the cause of the illness and developing an insight into the implications of the illness gives the illness meaning. According to this model of coping, a sense of meaning contributes to the process of coping and cognitive adaptation.

A SEARCH FOR MASTERY

A search for mastery is reflected in questions such as 'How can I prevent a similar event reoccurring?' and 'What can I do to manage the event now?' Taylor et al. (1984) reported that a sense of mastery can be achieved by believing that the illness is controllable. In accordance with this, 66 per cent of the women in the study believed that they could influence the course or reoccurrence of the cancer. The remainder of the women believed that the cancer could be controlled by health professionals. Taylor reported that a sense of mastery is achieved either through psychological techniques such as developing a positive attitude, meditation, self-hypnosis or a type of causal attribution, or by behavioural techniques such as changing diet, changing medications, accessing information or controlling any side-effects. These processes contribute towards a state of mastery, which is central to the progression towards a state of cognitive adaptation.

THE PROCESS OF SELF-ENHANCEMENT

Following illness, some individuals may suffer a decrease in their self-esteem. The theory of cognitive adaptation suggests that individuals attempt to build their self-esteem through a process of self-enhancement. Taylor et al. (1984) reported that only 17 per cent of the women in their study reported only negative changes following their illness, whereas 53 per cent reported only positive changes. To explain this result, Taylor developed social comparison theory (Festinger 1957). This theory suggests that individuals make sense of their world by comparing themselves with others. Such comparisons may either be downward comparisons (e.g. a comparison with others who are worse off: 'At least I've only had cancer once'), or upward comparisons (e.g. a comparison with others who are better off: 'Why was my lump malignant when hers was only a cyst?'). In terms of their study of women with breast cancer, Taylor et al. (1984) reported that, although many of the women had undergone disfiguring surgery and had been diagnosed as having a life-threatening illness, most of them showed downward comparisons in order to improve their self-esteem. For example, women who had had a lumpectomy compared themselves with women who had had a mastectomy. Those who had had a mastectomy compared themselves with those who had a possibility of having generalized cancer. Older women compared themselves favourably with younger women, and younger women compared themselves favourably with older women. Taylor suggested that the women selected criteria for comparison that would enable them to improve their self-esteem as part of the process of self-enhancement. The role of social comparisons in coping is further discussed in terms of the response shift in Chapter 18.

THE ROLE OF ILLUSIONS

The search for meaning and mastery and the improvement of self-esteem involves developing illusions. Such illusions are not necessarily in contradiction to reality but are positive interpretations of that reality. For example, although there may be little evidence for the real causes of cancer, or for the ability of individuals to control the course of their illness, those who have suffered cancer wish to hold their own illusions about these factors (e.g. 'I understand what caused my cancer and believe that I can control whether it comes back'). Taylor and her colleagues argued that these illusions are a necessary and essential component of cognitive adaptation and that reality orientation (as suggested by other coping models) may actually be detrimental to adjustment.

The need for illusions raises the problem of disconfirmation of the illusions (what happens when the reoccurrence of cancer cannot be controlled?). Taylor argued that the need for illusions is sufficient to enable individuals to shift the goals and foci of their illusions so that those illusions can be maintained and adjustment can persist. The notion of illusions is similar to benefit-finding which is discussed later in this chapter.

EVIDENCE FOR COGNITIVE ADAPTATION THEORY

Research has used a cognitive adaptation theory approach to explore, predict and change the ways in which people cope with illness. For example, research indicates that forms of cognitive adjustment are linked to illness progression in people with HIV/AIDS (Reed et al. 1994, 1999; Bower et al. 1998), that cognitive adaptation influences how people manage cancer (Taylor 1983) and that it reflects the ways in which women respond to having a termination (Goodwin and Ogden 2007).

IMPLICATIONS FOR THE OUTCOME OF THE COPING PROCESS

According to this model of coping, the individual copes with illness by achieving cognitive adaptation. This involves searching for meaning ('I know what caused my illness'), mastery ('I can control my illness') and developing self-esteem ('I am better off than a lot of people'). These beliefs may not be accurate but they are essential to maintaining illusions that promote adjustment to the illness. Therefore, in this perspective the desired outcome of the coping process is the development of illusions, not reality orientation.

POST-TRAUMATIC GROWTH AND BENEFIT-FINDING

Most theories of coping emphasize a desire to re-establish equilibrium and a return to the status quo. Effective coping is therefore seen as that which enables adjustment to the illness and a return to normality. Some research, however, indicates that some people perceive benefits from being ill and see themselves as being better off because they have been ill. This approach is in line with positive psychology and its emphasis on positive rather than negative affect (see Chapters 11 and 12). For example, Laerum et al. (1988) interviewed 84 men who had had a heart attack and found that although the men reported some negative consequences for their lifestyle and quality of life, 33 per cent of them considered their life to be somewhat or considerably improved. Similarly, Collins et al. (1990) interviewed 55 cancer patients and also reported some positive shifts following illness. Sodergren and colleagues have explored positivity following illness and have developed a structured questionnaire called the Silver Lining Questionnaire (SLQ) (Sodergren et al. 2002). They concluded from their studies that the positive consequences of illness are varied and more common than often realized. They also suggest that positivity can be improved by rehabilitation. Such research has been framed within a number of different theoretical perspectives and has been given a range of names resulting from extensive debates about the nature of the construct. For example, research has focused on stress-related growth (Park 2004), benefit-finding (Tennen and Affleck 1999), meaning-making (Park and Folkman 1997), growth-orientated functioning and crisis growth (Holahan et al. 1996), and existential growth (Janoff-Bulham 2004). Tedeschi and Calhoun (2004) developed a self-regulatory model of post-traumatic growth in an attempt to draw together the existing literature on trauma and coping and described the role of factors including personality, optimism, social support and meaning-making.

EVIDENCE FOR POST-TRAUMATIC GROWTH AND BENEFIT-FINDING

The positive consequences of traumatic events have been explored in terms of the experience of positive growth, the role of positive growth in predicting patient outcomes and the predictors of positive growth. This will now be described.

The Experience of Positive Growth

Research has explored the ways in which individuals make sense of trauma and their experiences of growth or thriving. In particular, Tedeschi and Calhoun have carried out much work in this area and their synthesis of the literature concluded that post-traumatic growth was a more progressed form of positive adjustment than either just resilience or optimism, and involved a process of transformation. Further, they highlighted five main areas of growth which were: perceived changes in self; closer family relationships; changed philosophy in life; a better perspective in life; and a strengthened belief system (Tedeschi and Calhoun 2004, 2006). Recently, Hefferon et al. (2009) carried out a systematic review of the qualitative research and argued that traumas could be conceptualized as either external (e.g. natural disasters, bereavement, war) or internal (e.g. physical illness or injury), and that different types of trauma may result in different experiences. For their review they identified 57 qualitative papers which assessed the experience of physical illness and highlighted four key themes across the different studies. These were: reappraisal of life and priorities; trauma equals development of self; existential re-evaluation; and new awareness of the body. In addition, they concluded that the latter theme, in particular, was unique to internal rather than external trauma and that although there existed common elements to positive growth across traumas, there were also differences.

Predicting Post-Traumatic Growth

Research has also explored the role of different factors in predicting positive growth after trauma. For example, Tedeschi and Calhoun (2004) argued that the degree of post-traumatic growth relates to symptom severity, time elapsed since the event, age, gender, social support and a clear cause to the event. Similarly, McMillen (2004) emphasized the role of available support for recovery and Harvey et al. (2004) highlighted the positive and negative responses of others. Furthermore, when evaluating post-traumatic growth following cancer diagnosis, Cole et al. (2008) emphasized the role of spirituality and Cordova et al. (2001) reported that growth after breast cancer was related to talking about and assigning meaning to the experience as well as financial stability. Further, Dunn et al. (2011) reported that benefit-finding after cancer was associated with being a woman, greater optimism, high intrusive thinking and high social support. Research has also addressed growth following non-illness-related trauma. For example, McMillen et al. (1997) explored growth following a mass killing, surviving a tornado and a plane crash and reported that growth was predicted by being able to find benefit in the event and a stronger fear of death during the event.

The Role of Post-Traumatic Growth and Health Outcomes

Other studies have explored the role of post-traumatic growth in predicting patient outcomes. For example, Milam (2006) concluded that post-traumatic growth following a diagnosis of HIV was protective against certain physical illnesses and Reed et al. (1994) reported how 'realistic acceptance' of their HIV diagnosis illustrated by statements such as 'I tried to accept what has happened' and 'I prepare for the worst' was related to a higher chance of death at follow-up.

From the perspective of post-traumatic growth or benefit-finding at the end of the coping process, the individual ends up in a better place than they were before whatever traumatic event happened, whether it be an illness, a life event such as a divorce or a serious accident. The event is therefore coped with in such a way that the individual is able to find the positives in the event and incorporate these into a more fruitful future.

Coping research therefore explores the ways in which individuals manage and respond to any change in their lives. Health psychology draws upon coping with the crisis of illness and cognitive adaptation theories which emphasize how people are motivated to return to a state of normality. In contrast, research on post-traumatic growth and benefit-finding highlights how an illness may have positive consequences for the individual, and this is line with recent developments within the positive psychology movement. It is also similar to some work on sustained changes in behaviour following life events which is described in Chapters 3 and 8.

USING THE SRM TO PREDICT OUTCOMES

The self-regulatory model describes a transition from interpretation, through illness cognitions, emotional response and coping to appraisal. Early research used the model to ask the question: 'How do illness cognitions relate to coping?' More recent research, however, has also explored the impact of illness cognitions on psychological and physical health outcomes with a focus on adherence to treatment and recovery from illnesses including stroke, rheumatoid arthritis and myocardial infarction (MI – heart attack).

HOW DO ILLNESS COGNITIONS RELATE TO COPING?

Much correlational research has explored the links between the different components of the SRM with a focus on the associations between illness cognitions and coping across a number of different health problems. For example, Kemp et al. (1999) reported a link between perception of control over illness and problem-focused coping in patients with neuroepilepsy and Lawson et al. (2007)

concluded that more positive personal models (i.e. greater control, shorter time line, less consequences) were associated with more effective coping strategies in people with type 1 diabetes. Searle et al. (2007) argued that rather than just focusing on coping cognitions, research should also address coping behaviours in terms of what people actually *do* (e.g. taking medication, diet, physical activity). They then explored associations between illness cognitions, coping cognitions and coping behaviours in patients with type 2 diabetes. The results showed that illness cognitions predicted both aspects of coping. In addition the results showed that the link between illness cognitions and coping behaviours was direct and not mediated through coping cognitions. They argue that if we want to change people's behaviour (i.e. taking medication, diet, physical activity), it might be better to try and change their illness cognitions rather than their coping cognitions. Recent meta-analyses of the links between illness cognitions and coping indicate that in general a strong illness identity is associated with the use of avoidant coping strategies and those involving emotional expression, that perceived controllability of an illness is related to cognitive reappraisal, expressing emotions and problem-focused coping strategies and that avoidant and expressing emotion coping strategies are also correlated with perceptions of a chronic time line, serious consequences and ratings of a multitude of symptoms (Hagger and Orbell 2003; French et al. 2006a).

PREDICTING ADHERENCE TO TREATMENT

Beliefs about illness in terms of the dimensions described by Leventhal et al. (1980, 1997) have been shown to relate to coping. They have also been associated with whether or not a person takes their medication and/or adheres to suggested treatments. Some research shows that symptom perception is directly linked to adherence to medication. For example, Halm et al. (2006) explored asthmatics' beliefs about their problem, their perception of symptoms and their adherence to medication. The study involved 198 adults who had been hospitalized for their asthma over a 12-month period and identified a 'no symptoms, no asthma' belief, whereby people only believed they had asthma when they had symptoms, rather than seeing it as a chronic illness that is ongoing regardless of the level of symptomatology. Further, the results showed that those who held the 'acute asthma belief' were also less likely to take their medication. In a similar vein, Brewer et al. (2002) examined the relationship between illness cognitions and both adherence to medication and cholesterol control in patients with hypercholesterolaemia (involving very high cholesterol). The results showed that a belief that the illness has serious consequences was related to medication adherence. In addition, actual cholesterol control was related to the belief that the illness was stable, asymptomatic with serious consequences.

Some research has also included a role for treatment beliefs. For example, Horne and Weinman (2002) explored the links between beliefs about both illness and treatment and adherence to taking medication for asthma in 100 community-based patients. The results showed that non-adherers reported more doubts about the necessity of their medication, greater concerns about the consequences of the medication and more negative beliefs about the consequences of their illness. Overall, the analysis indicated that illness and treatment beliefs were better predictors of adherence than both clinical and demographic factors. In a similar study, Llewellyn et al. (2003) explored the interrelationships between illness beliefs, treatment beliefs and adherence to home treatment in patients with severe haemophilia. The results showed that poor adherence was related to beliefs about the necessity of the treatment, concerns about the consequences of treatment and beliefs about illness identity. Research also indicates that illness beliefs and treatment beliefs predict adherence to complementary therapies although the results from a study by Bishop et al. (2005) showed that much of the variance remained unexplained.

PREDICTING ILLNESS OUTCOMES

Research has also used the SRM to understand and predict illness outcomes for a range of conditions including rheumatoid arthritis (Carlisle et al. 2005), diabetes (Lawson et al. 2007), chronic fatigue syndrome (Deary 2008) and renal disease (Karamanidou et al. 2008). In particular, research has explored recovery from stroke and MI, and will now be described.

Recovery from Stroke

Partridge and Johnston (1989) used a prospective study and reported that individuals' beliefs about their perceived control over their problem predicted recovery from residual disability in stroke patients at follow-up. The results showed that this relationship persisted even when baseline levels of disability were taken into account. In line with this, Johnston (1999) also explored the relationship between perceived control and recovery from stroke and followed up 71 stroke patients one and six months after discharge from hospital. In addition, they examined the possible mediating effects of coping, exercise and mood. They asked the questions, 'Does recovery from stroke relate to illness cognitions?' and 'If so, is this relationship dependent upon other factors?' The results showed no support for the mediating effects of coping, exercise and mood but supported earlier work to indicate a predictive relationship between control beliefs and recovery. This was also supported by a further study which explored the role of a range of clinical, demographic and psychological factors to predict functional recovery three years following a stroke. The results showed that perceptions of control at baseline added to the variance accounted for by both clinical and demographic variables (Johnston et al. 2004). To further assess the factors that may relate to recovery from stroke, Johnston et al. (2006) developed a workbook-based intervention which was designed to change cognitions about control in patients who had just had a stroke. In particular the intervention focused on coping skills, encouraged self-management and offered encouragement. The results showed that at six months' follow-up, those receiving the intervention showed better disability recovery than those in the control group. However, it was unclear how the intervention had worked as the intervention group showed no significant changes in any psychological process variables apart from confidence in recovery, which did not itself relate to actual disability recovery. Research therefore indicates that control cognitions may relate to recovery from stroke. Further, an intervention to change such cognitions seems to improve recovery. It is not clear, however, which processes are involved in this change as the intervention did not actually change stroke patients' beliefs about control.

Recovery from MI

Research suggests that an individual's beliefs about their work capacity (Maeland and Havik 1987), helplessness towards future MIs (called 'cardiac invalidism') (Riegel 1993) and general psychological factors (Diederiks et al. 1991) relate to recovery from MI as measured by return to work and general social and occupational functioning. Using a self-regulatory approach, research has indicated that illness cognitions relate to recovery from MI. For example, the Heart Attack Recovery Project, which was carried out in New Zealand, followed 143 first-time heart attack patients aged 65 or under at 3, 6 and 12 months following admission to hospital. The results showed that those patients who believed that their illness had less serious consequences and would last a shorter time at baseline were more likely to have returned to work by six weeks. Furthermore, those with beliefs that the illness could be controlled or cured at baseline predicted attendance at rehabilitation classes (Petrie et al. 1996).

In a recent study authors not only explored the patients' beliefs about MI but also the beliefs of their spouse to discover whether congruence between spouse and patient beliefs was related to recovery from MI (Figueiras and Weinman 2003). Seventy couples in which the man had had an MI completed a baseline measure of the illness cognitions which were correlated with follow-up measures of recovery at 3, 6 and 12 months. The results showed that in couples who had similar positive beliefs about the identity and consequences of the illness, the patients showed improved recovery in terms of better psychological and physical functioning, better sexual functioning and lower impact of the MI on social and recreational activities. In addition, similar beliefs about time line were related to lower levels of disability and similar cure/control beliefs were associated with greater dietary changes. In a novel approach to assessing patients' beliefs about their MI, Broadbent et al. (2004) asked 69 patients who had just had an MI to draw their heart and how they felt it looked just after their heart attack. They also completed a series of questionnaires and repeated these drawings and measures at three and six months. The results showed that increases in the size of heart between baseline and three months were related to slower return to work, activity restriction and anxiety about having another MI as measured by a range of factors. The authors concluded that the increased size of the heart in the drawings may reflect the 'extent to which their heart condition plays on their mind'.

One study also explored the prevalence of PTSD in 44 patients who had either had an MI or a subarachnoid haemorrhage and examined the association with illness cognitions (Sheldrick et al. 2006). The results showed that the prevalence of PTSD was 16 per cent at two weeks, 35 per cent at six weeks and 16 per cent at three months after the medical event. The results also showed that beliefs relating to identity, time line, consequences and emotional representation were strongly correlated with PTSD symptoms at all time points. Further, the results indicated that baseline illness cognitions predicted PTSD at follow-up.

THE CENTRAL ROLE OF COHERENCE

Central to much research on illness beliefs and their relationship to outcome is the importance of a coherent model whereby beliefs about causes of the illness are consistent with beliefs about treatment (Leventhal et al. 1997). Leventhal and colleagues describe this association between causes and solutions in terms of the 'if . . . then rules'. For example, *if* I believe that breathlessness is caused by smoking, *then* I am more likely to decide to stop smoking. Similarly, *if* I believe that asthma symptoms are caused by bronchial constriction, *then* I am more likely to adhere to my medication that causes bronchial dilation. In contrast, an obese person who believes that their weight is caused by hormones rather than their diet is unlikely to eat less when advised to do so. Most research addressing the issue of coherence has focused on cross-sectional associations between the different sets of beliefs. For example, Horne and Weinman (2002) reported that adherence is more likely to occur when illness beliefs and treatment beliefs are coherent with each other. Similarly, Llewellyn et al. (2003) reported that adherence to medication for patients with haemophilia was also greater when beliefs about illness and treatment were matched. Some studies, however, have also explored whether or not beliefs can be changed to be more in line with each other. For example, although smoking increases the risk of cervical cancer, many women are not aware of this association. Therefore being told to stop smoking when having a cervical smear test makes no sense and women are therefore unlikely to take this advice on board – they do not have a coherent model of smoking as a cause of cervical cancer, and smoking cessation as a solution. As mentioned earlier, Hall et al. (2004, see **Focus on Research 9.1**) therefore examined whether giving people a leaflet containing information about the link between smoking and cervical cancer, which provided them with a coherent model of this association, could change intentions to quit smoking. The results showed that the leaflet did increase women's coherent model of the association. Further, the results showed that perceptions of vulnerability to cervical cancer were associated with intentions to quit smoking but only in those with a coherent model.

Ogden and Sidhu (2006) also explored the notion of coherence in the context of taking medication for obesity. Many people with obesity deem their hormones or genetics to be responsible for their condition. They do not blame their diet and therefore do not change their diet. An obesity drug called orlistat can result in weight loss but also produces highly visual side-effects if taken with fatty foods such as anal leakage and oily stools. Ogden and Sidhu explored the psychological mechanisms of the drug through interviews with patients and concluded that it can result in both adherence and behaviour change if the side-effects act as an education and bring people's beliefs about the causes of their obesity in line with a behavioural solution (see Chapter 15 for further details). People therefore see the side-effects after they have eaten fatty foods, realize the importance of their diet to their body weight and decide it is therefore worthwhile changing their diet.

Both these studies illustrate the importance of coherence and the benefits of changing beliefs. In contrast, Wright et al. (2003) explored the impact of informing smokers about their genetic predisposition towards nicotine dependence in terms of their choice of method for stopping smoking. In line with the studies described earlier, giving information did change beliefs. However, while those who believed that they were genetically prone to dependency were more likely to choose a medical form of cessation (a drug to reduce cravings), they were also likely to endorse relying upon their own willpower. Changing beliefs towards a more medical cause meant that smokers were less able to change their behaviour on their own and more in need of medical support. These results illustrate the importance of a coherent model, but they also illustrate that changing beliefs may not always be beneficial to subsequent changes in behaviour.

INTERVENTIONS TO CHANGE ILLNESS COGNITIONS

Research shows that people make sense of their illness and form illness cognitions which relate to their health outcomes. In line with this, interventions have been developed in an attempt to change illness cognitions and improve subsequent outcomes. Some interventions have used face-to-face consultations with a psychologist, while others, in line with the saying 'a picture paints a thousand words', have used visual information. (For a review of using the SRM for interventions see Wearden and Peters 2008 and related papers.)

FACE-TO-FACE CONSULTATIONS

Petrie et al. (2002) developed a three-session intervention for patients who had had an MI to change their beliefs about their condition and their health outcomes which was evaluated using a randomized control trial. Session 1 focused on the nature of an MI in terms of its symptoms and explored patients' beliefs about the causes of the MI. Session 2 explored beliefs about causes, helped the patient to develop a plan to minimize the future risk of a further MI and tried to increase patient control beliefs about their condition. In the final session, concerns about medication were explored and symptoms that were part of the recovery process, such as breathlessness upon exercise, were distinguished from those that were indicative of further pathology such as severe chest pain. The results showed that patients who received the intervention reported more positive views about their MI at follow-up in terms of beliefs about consequences, time line, control/cure and symptom distress. In addition, they reported that they were better prepared to leave hospital, returned to work at a faster rate and reported a lower rate of angina symptoms. No differences were found in rehabilitation attendance. The intervention therefore seemed to change cognitions and improve patients' functional outcome after MI. Broadbent et al. (2009) repeated this intervention and expanded it to include partners of those who had had an MI. The results showed changes in the partners' beliefs and reflect research indicating the importance of social support and concordance between the patient and their partner in health outcomes (e.g. Figueiras and Weinman 2003).

Moss-Morris et al. (2007) also carried out an intervention to change the illness beliefs of patients with chronic pain as part of a cognitive behavioural pain management programme. The results showed that patients reduced both their perceptions of consequences and their emotional representations of their pain and increased their sense of coherence of their condition. In addition, improved physical functioning was predicted by reduced beliefs about consequences and improved mental functioning was predicted by greater coherence and reduced emotional representations.

A complex intervention has also been developed to change the illness cognitions and health outcomes of those with diabetes (Skinner et al. 2006; Davies et al. 2009). The trial was known as DESMOND (diabetes education and self-management for ongoing and newly-diagnosed) and used a group-based intervention to elicit patients' beliefs about their condition and help them to develop feasible self-management plans. The results showed that after a year patients who had received the intervention endorsed more serious consequences, a longer time line and greater personal control beliefs for their condition. They also showed improved levels of smoking cessation and weight loss than those who received standard care. Such face-to-face interventions generally aim to elicit patient beliefs, change these beliefs and bring them in line with the desired changes in behaviour and patient health outcomes. Central to this is the notion of coherence and the bringing together or beliefs about causes and solutions.

IMAGERY-BASED INTERVENTIONS

Research shows that people often form mental images as a way of making sense of any given problem. In terms of health problems, studies have explored the images of breast cancer survivors (Harrow et al. 2008), how people think about skin cancer (Cameron 2008) and how patients make sense of their heart attack (Broadbent et al. 2004). In addition, research indicates that visual images may be an effective means to raise awareness about the risks of behaviours such as smoking and sun-bathing. For example, Hammond et al. (2003) examined the effectiveness of the warning labels that became a standard feature on cigarette packets in 2000 in Canada. The results showed that the graphic images had effectively drawn participants' attention to the health warnings although this decayed over time as people habituated to the messages. In addition, those who reported reading, thinking about and discussing the labels with other people were more likely to report an intention to stop smoking in the next six months and showed more successful and unsuccessful quit attempts and a reduction in smoking over a three-month period. Similar results were also found in adolescents who were either established or occasional smokers (White et al. 2008; Germain et al. 2010). Further, Shahab et al. (2007) reported that showing smokers images of their carotid arteries with a plaque compared to an artery without a plaque increased their perceptions of risk for smoking-related illnesses. Further, in those with higher self-efficacy, the images also increased their intention to stop smoking. In terms of sun-bathing, Mahler and colleagues (Mahler et al. 2003, 2007) designed a series of studies to increase awareness about the impact of UV radiation in terms of skin damage and the risk of cancer. In the two experiments (Mahler et al. 2003), students and beachgoers were shown UV photos of their own skin or a photo-ageing video. The results showed that the personalized photo of their own skin was related to stronger intentions to use sun-screen in the future. (For recent reviews of the impact of visual images on perceptions of risk, see Hollands et al. 2010, 2011 (see Figure 9.7)).

In line with this, some research has also used images to change illness cognitions. For example, Karamanidou et al. (2008) used an imagery-based intervention to change beliefs about the importance of phosphate levels in patients with end-stage renal disease (see Chapter 8). Patients were shown a stomach-shaped container which illustrated the digestion process and showed how their phosphate binding medication could effectively bind with phosphates from the foods being eaten. The results showed that patients in the intervention group reported a more coherent understanding of their medication and greater beliefs in the ability of their medication to control their disease. In a similar vein, Lee et al. (2011) explored the relative impact of image- versus text-based information

Image only

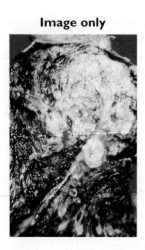

Text only

S M O K I N G
K I L L S

Image and text

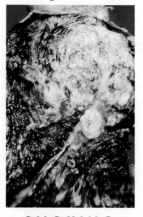

S M O K I N G
K I L L S

FIGURE 9.7

Using text and visual images to change beliefs and behaviour: Which is the most effective?

SOURCE: United States Government/Wikimedia Commons

for changing beliefs about the risk of heart disease and subsequent health-related behaviours using a web-based intervention. The results showed that imagery had an immediate impact on illness cognitions, worry, behavioural intentions and mental imagery relating to heart disease and that an increased sense of coherence and worry were sustained by one month follow-up. Imagery also resulted in increased healthy diet efforts after two weeks. The results showed that text resulted in immediate changes in beliefs about causes, mental imagery relating to clogged arteries and worry and that by two weeks follow-up participants also showed increased physical activity, and a greater sense of coherence by one month. Overall, the results indicate that imagery resulted in more changes than text alone but that a combination of both approaches is probably the most effective means to change cognitions and behaviour. Similarly, research indicates that viewing images of internal body parts can influence beliefs about susceptibility to a health problem (Green et al. 2006) as well as illness coherence (Brotherstone et al. 2006).

Visual information may not, however, always be beneficial. Recent changes in technology mean that patients can often view aspects of their body while undergoing invasive and non-invasive procedures. For example, screens are sometimes shown to patients for diagnostic procedures searching for explanations for symptoms such as vaginal or gastrointestinal bleeding, or unexplained pain. One such procedure is the hysteroscopy whereby a probe is placed inside a woman's uterus via the vagina and the results can be viewed by both health professional and patient on a screen. Although this is regarded as an advance in information-sharing, results from a randomized trial indicate that seeing the screen can lower patients, perceptions about the effectiveness of the treatment, raise anxiety and result in pain being described in more negative terms as well as in the health professional being perceived as less receptive to the patient (Ogden et al. 2009).

Research therefore shows that image-based information can be effective at changing beliefs about illness, its management and consequences. This has been called the 'image superiority theory'. To date, however, research exploring the mechanisms of *how* imagery influences cognitions and behaviour remains in its infancy. But it has been suggested that images not only imprint on memory better than verbal messages but may also generate changes in mood which make it more likely that they will be turned into cues to action and subsequent changes in behaviour (Cameron 2009). It has also been argued that visual imagery may change implicit rather than explicit attitudes which in turn may change behaviour. Therefore, although the use of visual images is central to many existing health education interventions at both the individual and population level, how they work, and why they may work better than words is yet to be fully understood.

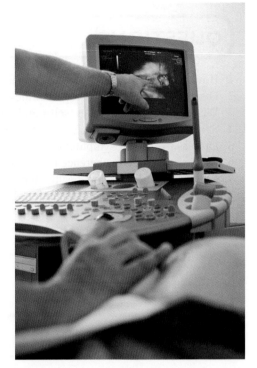

Seeing the screen during a procedure may change illness cognitions

SOURCE: © Pastoor/Dreamstime

TO CONCLUDE

In the same way that people have beliefs about health, they also have beliefs about illness. Such beliefs are often called 'illness cognitions' or 'illness representations'. Beliefs about illness appear to follow a pattern and are made up of: (1) identity (e.g. a diagnosis and symptoms); (2) consequences (e.g. beliefs about seriousness); (3) time line (e.g. how long it will last); (4) cause (e.g. caused by smoking, caused by a virus); and (5) cure/control (e.g. requires medical intervention). This chapter examined these dimensions of illness cognitions and assessed how they relate to the way in which an individual responds to illness via their coping and their appraisal of the illness. Further, it described the SRM and its implications for understanding and predicting health outcomes and the central role for coherence. Finally, it described interventions to change illness cognitions involving face-to-face consultations or the use of visual images.

QUESTIONS

1 How do people make sense of health and illness?
2 Discuss the relationship between illness cognitions and coping.
3 Why is Leventhal's model 'self-regulatory'?
4 Symptoms are more than just a sensation. Discuss.
5 Discuss the role of symptom perception in adjusting to illness.
6 Discuss the role of coherence in illness representations.
7 Illness cognitions predict health outcomes. Discuss.
8 To what extent can illness cognitions be changed?
9 Design a research project to assess the extent to which illness severity predicts patient adjustment and highlight the role that illness cognitions may have in explaining this relationship.

FOR DISCUSSION

Think about the last time you were ill (e.g. headache, flu, broken limb, etc.). Consider the ways in which you made sense of your illness, how they related to your coping strategies and how you recovered.

ASSUMPTIONS IN HEALTH PSYCHOLOGY

The literature examining illness cognitions highlights some of the assumptions in health psychology:

1 *Humans as information processors.* The literature describing the structure of illness cognitions assumes that individuals deal with their illness by processing the different forms of information. In addition, it assumes that the resulting cognitions are clearly defined and consistent across different people. However, perhaps the information is not always processed rationally and perhaps some cognitions are made up of only some of the components (e.g. just time line and cause), or made up of other components not included in the models.

2 *Methodology as separate to theory.* The literature also assumes that the structure of cognitions exists prior to questions about these cognitions. Therefore it is assumed that the data collected are separate from the methodology used (i.e. the different components of the illness cognitions pre-date questions about time line, causality, cure, etc.). However, it is possible that the structure of these cognitions is in part an artefact of the types of questions asked. In fact, Leventhal originally argued that interviews should be used to access illness cognitions as this methodology avoided 'contaminating' the data. However, even interviews involve the interviewer's own preconceived ideas which may be expressed through the structure of their questions, through their responses to the interviewee, or through their analysis of the transcripts.

FURTHER READING

Cameron, L. and Leventhal, H. (eds) (2003) *The Self-regulation of Health and Illness Behaviour.* London: Routledge.
This is a good book which presents a comprehensive coverage of a good selection of illness representations research and broader self-regulation approaches.

de Ridder, D. (1997) What is wrong with coping assessment? A review of conceptual and methodological issues, *Psychology and Health*, 12: 417–31.
This paper explores the complex and ever-growing area of coping and focuses on the issues surrounding the questions 'What is coping?' and 'How should it be measured?'

Ogden, J. and Sidhu, S. (2006) Adherence, behaviour change and visualisation: a qualitative study of patients' experiences of obesity medication, *The Journal of Psychosomatic Research*, 62: 545–52.
This paper provides an example of how beliefs about a problem can be changed through experience and how coherence is a essential part of illness representations. It also illustrates a qualitative approach to illness representations.

Petrie, K.J. and Weinman, J.A. (eds) (2006) *Perceptions of Health and Illness*. Amsterdam: Harwood.
This is an edited collection of projects using the SRM as their theoretical framework.

Taylor, S.E. (1983) Adjustment to threatening events: a theory of cognitive adaptation, *American Psychologist*, 38: 1161–73.
This is an excellent example of an interview-based study. It describes and analyses the cognitive adaptation theory of coping with illness and emphasizes the central role of illusions in making sense of the imbalance created by the absence of health.

Visit the website at www.openup.co.uk/ogden for additional resources on Chapter 9 to help you with your study, such as multiple choice questions, weblinks and a searchable online glossary.

10 Accessing Health Care

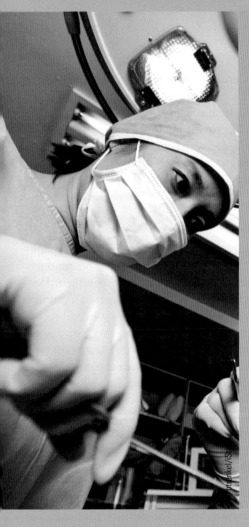

CHAPTER OVERVIEW

This chapter describes a number of factors relating to accessing health care and the use of the health care system. First it describes help-seeking behaviour, the problem of delay and why people do or do not go to the doctor. It then describes research on screening and how people are brought into contact with health care through screening interventions. It next describes consultations between patients and health professionals and the role of diagnosis, referral and the impact of health professionals' own health beliefs. Finally it describes the problem of adherence and factors which influence whether patients do or do not follow medical advice.

HEALTH CARE SYSTEMS

Many symptoms and illnesses are managed through self-care with no need for professional input. Most houses have cupboards with plasters and creams for cuts and bruises, pain relief pills for headaches, colds and flu and over-the-counter medicines to treat constipation, thread worms, allergies and thrush. In addition, the internet and self-help books provide photographs and descriptions of symptoms to aid self-diagnosis and self-medication, and alternative and complementary practitioners offer a range of herbal, nutritional and homeopathic cures. Many symptoms are therefore not taken to the doctor. When they are, however, in most countries across the world, they are met with a two-tiered system of primary and secondary care.

PRIMARY CARE

Primary care is the first contact with the health service and the patient is free to make an appointment whenever they feel they need one. In primary care they are met by generalist practitioners who have been trained to recognize and cope with whatever problems come through their door. Primary care is mainly offered by a doctor, the general practitioner (GP), who is part of a primary care team consisting of practice nurses, nurse practitioners, health visitors, midwives and receptionists. In most countries the primary care doctor would be different to the secondary care doctor, but in the USA some doctors are both generalists and specialists. The primary care team deal with a huge range of problems that vary vastly in their severity. For example, they see people with social problems such as housing issues, problems with benefits and those who are struggling with employment or relationships. They see people with chronic illnesses such as diabetes, cancer and heart disease who need weekly management through tests, repeat prescriptions and behaviour modification advice. They see common mild symptoms such as coughs, colds, stomach pain and tiredness and they see potentially serious symptoms (such as coughs, colds, stomach pain and tiredness!). They see people with coughs and colds who really want to talk about contraception or who really have piles but are too embarrassed to ask. The role of the primary care team is to diagnose and manage whatever problems fall within its range of expertise or to refer patients on to the hospital specialists in secondary care for a second opinion and further tests. The primary care team are therefore the gatekeepers into secondary care. This process prevents secondary care being inundated with less serious medical problems, but errors inevitably occur as minor problems are referred on and serious problems are missed.

SECONDARY CARE

If referred by their GP, a patient is then permitted to see a specialist in secondary care. In most countries access to secondary care can only occur via a referral letter from the GP although this is changing as patients are increasingly becoming consumers of health care and demanding their right to see whoever they want. Private practice also changes this division as patients can choose to pay to see secondary care specialists if they have the money or health insurance. Medicine in secondary care is further specialized as health professionals work in teams relating to body systems such as gastroenterology, respiratory medicine, obstetrics and gynaecology, cardiology and ear, nose and throat specialisms. Secondary care tends to be based in a hospital to provide access to beds and operates with an outpatient system (for check-ups, tests and follow-up consultations) and an inpatient system (having an operation, staying overnight).

The role of primary and secondary care health professionals raises some important questions about accessing health care and the care received:

- Why do patients attend their doctor's surgery for apparently trivial reasons?
- Why do patients delay seeking help for apparently serious reasons?
- How to doctors decide upon an appropriate diagnosis?
- Why do patients not always do as they are told?

These questions will be answered in terms of help-seeking and delay, screening procedures and their uptake, the medical consultation and adherence.

HELP-SEEKING AND DELAY

Help-seeking behaviour is also known as 'illness behaviour' and refers to the process of deciding to get professional help for a health-related problem. According to the medical model perspective, help-seeking relates to two factors:

- *Symptoms:* the patient has a headache, back problem or change in bowel habits that indicates that something is wrong.

- *Signs:* on examination the doctor identifies signs such as raised blood pressure, a lump in the bowel or hears rattling when listening to a patient's chest which indicates that there is a problem.

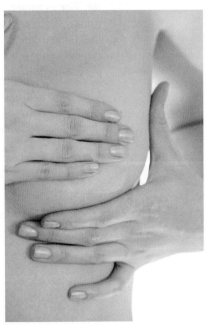

From this perspective the doctor is a detective and the patient is required to bring them the problem. Help-seeking, however, is not as simple as this as many people go to the doctor with very minor symptoms (e.g. 'I had a sore throat last week but it's gone now', 'I'm tired but keep going to bed late' or even 'I have a lump at the top of my back' (which is the top vertebrae!)). Furthermore, many patients don't go to their doctor when they have something serious (e.g. 'I have had this breast lump for about five years and it has now come through the skin', 'I have piles but the cream isn't working' (but actually it's anal cancer!)). This is known as the 'clinical iceberg' to reflect the vast number of problems that never reach the doctor. In addition, we all have symptoms all the time such as needing to go to the toilet, an itchy foot, feeling thirsty, feeling tired, coughing or a stiff neck that we do nothing about.

Help-seeking is therefore much more complex than the detection of symptoms and the identification of signs and can be understood in terms of a number of thresholds that need to be reached. Firstly, the patient needs to take a feeling − 'Ow' − and decide this is a symptom; then they need to decide if this symptom is normal or abnormal; next they need to decide whether it's serious enough to need help and finally they decide whether or not a doctor could help.

People have to decide whether a symptom is abnormal, or serious before they will seek help

SOURCE: © doram/iStock

In other words, these thresholds are as follows:

- *Is it a symptom?* 'I have a pain in my stomach.'
- *Is it normal or abnormal?* 'I have a pain in my stomach and it's not just wind.'
- *Do I need help?* 'I have a pain in my stomach, it's not just wind and it might be cancer.'
- *Could a doctor help?* 'I have a pain in my stomach, it's not just wind and it might be cancer and doctors know about cancer.'

These thresholds can be understood in terms of four processes which have been explored within both psychological and sociological research and are illustrated in Figure 10.1.

SYMPTOM PERCEPTION

The translation of a vague feeling into the concrete entity of a symptom involves the processes of symptom perception (see Chapter 9 for a detailed description). Research indicates that whether or not we perceive ourselves as having a symptom is influenced by four main sources of information:

- *Bodily data:* Gijsbers van Wijk and Kolk (1997) argued that one influence upon symptom perception is 'data driven' which comes from our bodies. It has also been argued that there is a competition between internal information (our bodies) and external information (our environment) which is why busy working people perceive fewer symptoms (Pennebaker 1982; Rief and Broadbent 2007). Research also indicates that some people show selective attention to their bodily symptoms and are therefore more aware of any changes (Gijsbers van Wijk and Kolk 1997). Symptom perception, however, is not as simple as receiving bodily data and symptom severity can be exacerbated or modified through mood, cognitions and the social context. Symptoms can be generated even in the absence of bodily data (e.g. watching a film of head lice can make people itch).

- *Mood:* stress and anxiety can make symptoms worse whereas relaxation can make them better. For example, a meta-analysis of 244 observational studies of a range of chronic conditions such as irritable bowel syndrome, fibromyalgia and chronic fatigue syndrome showed that higher depression and anxiety were consistently linked with greater symptom perception (Henningsen et al. 2003). Similar results have also being reported for children and adolescents for stomach pain, headache and leg pain (Eminson 2007).

- *Cognitions:* focusing on a symptom makes it worse while distraction makes it better. Therefore many strategies taught to those with chronic pain include encouraging distraction through being busy, talking to friends and staying employed if possible. Furthermore, during

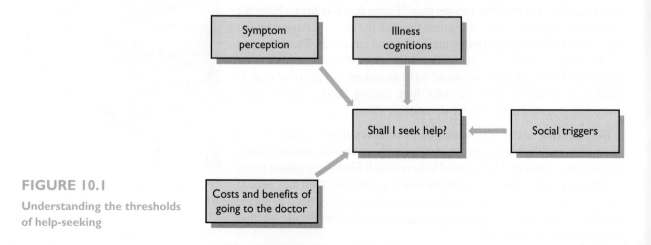

FIGURE 10.1

Understanding the thresholds of help-seeking

labour women are encouraged to stay distracted as long as possible by keeping active and staying out of hospital in the early stages. In an experimental study, 61 women who had been hospitalized during pre-term labour were randomized to receive either information, distraction or nothing (van Zuuren 1998). The results showed that physical and psychological symptoms were lower in the distraction group.

- *Social context:* symptoms also vary according to social context. For example, 'medical student's disease' describes how medical students often develop the symptoms of whatever condition they are studying (e.g. chest pain, backache, bowel problems) (Mechanic 1962) and research also indicates that smiling, yawning, shivering and itching can be contagious if people watch others experiencing these symptoms (Platek et al. 2005; Schurman et al. 2005).

The processes of symptom perception therefore helps to translate a vague experience into a concrete symptom. Before this leads to help-seeking, however, the individual also has to decide whether the symptom is abnormal and whether it requires formal help from a doctor. This is influenced by the development of illness cognitions.

ILLNESS COGNITIONS

Once a symptom has been perceived as such, a person then forms a mental representation of the problem. This has been called their 'illness cognitions' which are described in detail in Chapter 9. Research indicates that illness cognitions often consist of the same dimensions relating to identity ('What is it?'), time line ('How long will it last?'), causes ('What caused it?'), consequences ('Will it have a serious effect on my life?') and control/cure ('Can I manage it or do I need treatment?'). The formation of these cognitions will be helped by social messages from friends, family or the media to decide whether or not a symptom is serious, abnormal or manageable by self-care. It will also be influenced by the individual's own health history and expectations of their own level of health. For example, a patient who has recurring headaches may be less surprised by a new headache whereas someone who is always well may react more strongly to a less serious symptom. This process of *normalization* can pose problems for both the patient and the doctor (once in a consultation) as a heavy smoker may omit to tell the doctor that they are breathless as they always are and have become used to it. Further, if an individual lives in a family where indigestion is normal then chest pain may be more readily labelled 'indigestion' than 'possible heart attack'.

Therefore, illness cognitions take the symptom up to the next threshold as it is deemed to be abnormal (or not) and serious (or not).

SOCIAL TRIGGERS

The process of identifying a problem as abnormal (or not) is also influenced by what Zola (1973) called *social triggers* in his analysis of 'pathways to the doctor'. These triggers relate less to the individual's perception of the symptom itself and more the impact that the symptom will have on their daily lives. From this perspective our state of equilibrium can be disrupted by a symptom if it disturbs our normal life. Help-seeking is therefore a means to re-establish equilibrium. These social triggers are as follows:

- *Perceived interference with work or physical activity:* work and physical activity are core to most people's daily lives. A symptom that disrupts this will be identified as abnormal.

- *Perceived interference with social relations:* similarly, a symptom will also be perceived as abnormal if it interferes with our ability to interact with others.

- *An interpersonal crisis:* people have symptoms all the time that they normalize and habituate to. A sudden crisis such as an argument, divorce, change of job or retirement may trigger increased attention to a long-standing symptom leading to help-seeking for something that the patient appears to have had for a while.

- *Sanctioning:* the notion of sanctioning is similar to social messages as it involves other people encouraging a visit to the doctor so that patients often start a consultation saying, 'Sorry to bother you but my mother insisted I come to see you.'

Together, symptom perception, illness cognitions and social triggers take the individual up the thresholds towards help-seeking for a particular problem. The final set of factors that influence this process are the perceived costs and benefits of going to the doctor.

COSTS AND BENEFITS OF GOING TO THE DOCTOR

The final step before a patient seeks help involves weighing up the costs and benefits of seeing the doctor. These can be classified as follows:

- *Therapeutic:* first the patient needs to weigh up the therapeutic costs and benefits. Possible benefits include gaining access to effective treatments and being referred on to secondary care for more specialist advice and treatment. Help-seeking also comes with costs, however, such as being giving medicines to take for someone who doesn't like taking medicines, having to have a physical and potentially embarrassing examination or having to talk about a personal and embarrassing problem. Further, some patients may believe that medicine has nothing to offer them that they can't offer themselves.

- *Practical:* any visit to the doctor involves practical costs as it requires time off work, time away from the family, the cost of the fare and the effort of getting to the doctor's surgery.

- *Emotional:* many people enjoy visiting their doctor for more emotional reasons. For example, the trip can give a structure to their day, they might meet people to talk to at the surgery and the doctor can be reassuring, interesting, sympathetic and caring. There may, however, also be negative emotions generated by such a visit such as embarrassment or a feeling of being a nuisance to a doctor who is perceived as already too busy and overworked.

- *The sick role:* a doctor has the power to turn a person into a patient by legitimizing their symptoms. Therefore, although they may have been complaining of a sore throat, they will get more sympathy if they can say 'my doctor says I have tonsillitis'. Parsons (1951) described the notion of a *sick role* and argued that the doctor can legitimize a patient's experience and admit them into the sick role. According to Parsons, this comes with two benefits and two obligations:

  - *The benefits:* the main benefit of a sick role is that it excuses the patient from their normal roles and duties. This can be through a sick note which is used to miss work or simply being able to say 'my doctor says I mustn't lift things'. Therefore once in the sick role patients no longer have to work, do household chores or even have sex if they don't want to. The next benefit is that the sick role means they are no longer responsible for their illness as 'they are ill'. This means that the illness is no longer seen as self-inflicted or even as a punishment but the result of some biological process that has been identified by the doctor.

  - *The obligations:* Parsons also argues that once admitted into the sick role patients take on two obligations. The first is that they must want to get well and see the sick role as a temporary status. If the sick role goes on for too long, they will start to be seen as 'putting it on' or 'malingering'. The second obligation is that they will 'cooperate with technically competent help' – i.e. adhere to what the doctor says. Adherence is described in detail at the end of this chapter.

Patients therefore weigh up the costs and benefits of going to the doctor in terms of therapeutic, practical and emotional reasons and whether or not they want the benefits and obligations of the sick role.

Overall, help-seeking relates to a number of thresholds whereby an initial sensation ('Ow') is turned into a symptom which is deemed to be abnormal and serious enough to need professional help and whereby the benefits of seeing the doctor outweigh the costs. This process often means patients visit the doctor with appropriate symptoms at the appropriate time, but sometimes this goes wrong as patients attend with trivial symptoms *or* they delay help-seeking for more serious conditions.

DELAY

Some patients come to their doctor with symptoms that should have been treated months or even years before. Some don't phone an ambulance and end up having a heart attack at work after days of breathlessness and chest pain. Many treat serious symptoms with over-the-counter medicines or self-care when more effective treatments are needed. Delay in help-seeking presents a problem for health professionals as it undermines their chance to treat patients effectively. Delay can be understood in terms of all the factors described above that relate to help-seeking, but it is not an easy concept to define or measure, which in turn makes research on the predictors of delay problematic. This section will describe definitions of delay, the predictors of delay and interventions to reduce delay.

Definitions of Delay

Patient delay refers to the time between detecting a sign or symptom and the first contact with a health professional. Although this seems quite straightforward given all the factors described above, the notion of delay is more complex. For example, if detecting a symptom involves all the thresholds described above *and* the input of mood, cognitions, social context, illness cognitions and social triggers, than at what point can a symptom be declared 'detected'? It could be at the initial 'Ow' or it could be once the person has decided 'yes this is a symptom that is worth considering'. It is therefore very difficult to measure whether a patient has delayed their help-seeking and, if so, for how long.

Predictors of Delay

Research has identified a number of factors that predict delay which mostly incorporate aspects of symptom perception, illness cognitions, social triggers and the costs and benefits of going to the doctor as described above (see Scott et al. 2007; Scott et al. 2009 for some interesting research on delay for oral cancer). For example, a patient with chest pain would delay help-seeking if the following occurred:

Symptom perception
- 'I am too busy at work to think about my symptoms.'
- 'I am happy and not stressed.'

Illness cognitions
- 'It will go away soon.'
- 'It must be that curry I ate last night.'

Social triggers
- 'My friends have reassured me that this is normal.'
- 'My chest pain hasn't interfered with my work or relationships.'
- 'People in my family get a lot of indigestion.'

Costs and benefits of going to the doctor
- 'Doctors can't do much for indigestion.'
- 'I don't want to bother a busy doctor with my problems.'

Interventions for Delay

Interventions for adherence encourage patients to take their medicines and interventions for behaviour change encourage people to eat more healthily or stop smoking. For such interventions the outcome is clear – do more (or less) of whatever behaviour is being targeted. Interventions for delay, however, are more complicated. Symptoms of serious illnesses are more often than not the same as symptoms for minor illnesses. Up to 50 per cent of patients visiting the doctor seem to have 'nothing wrong with them' but have come in with their minor symptoms. If an intervention advised people to seek help whenever they experienced a symptom *and* as soon as this symptom started, then the system would collapse under the weight of demand. A good example of this is ovarian cancer. Ovarian cancer is most feared by women as it has a high mortality rate and presents late in its development. It is often too late to treat once it has been diagnosed. An intervention could therefore encourage women to come earlier to their doctor to give them a better chance of treatment. But ovarian cancer is a relatively silent cancer and the only symptom that women seem to perceive in retrospect is bloatedness. And if women came to the doctor when they felt bloated and doctors referred all women with bloatedness for scans, then the financial cost would be huge, the numbers of healthy people put through the inconvenience and potential danger of a scan would be vast and both primary and secondary services would lose resources from other potentially more cost-effective forms of treatment. Interventions to prevent delay therefore need to be extremely specific in terms of the advice they give and who they give it to, and should only intervene if early intervention has been *proven* to be both cost-effective and therapeutically effective.

SCREENING

Most people choose to come into contact with health care when they detect a symptom and seek help. This process relies upon two factors. First, patients need to identify that they have a symptom and conclude that health professionals will be able to help. This relates to help-seeking behaviours as described above. Second, this process relies upon an illness having symptoms that can be detected. Many health problems, however, such as cancer, hypertension and genetic disorders are asymptomatic in the early stages but are sometimes too far advanced for successful treatment once symptoms are severe enough to be noticeable. Health care has therefore introduced screening programmes as a means to pick up problems at a time when they cannot be detected by the patient on the premise that early detection leads to better treatment success.

WHAT IS SCREENING?

There are three forms of prevention aimed at improving a nation's health:

1 *Primary prevention* refers to the modification of risk factors (such as smoking, diet, alcohol intake) before illness onset. Health promotion campaigns are a form of primary prevention.

2 *Secondary prevention* refers to interventions aimed at detecting illness at an asymptomatic stage of development so that its progression can be halted or retarded. Screening is a form of secondary prevention.

3 *Tertiary prevention* refers to the rehabilitation of patients or treatment interventions once an illness has manifested itself.

Screening programmes (secondary prevention) take the form of health checks, such as measuring weight, blood pressure, height (particularly in children), urine, carrying out cervical smears and mammograms and offering genetic tests for illnesses such as Huntington's disease, some forms of breast cancer and cystic fibrosis. Until recently, two broad types of screening were defined: *opportunistic screening*, which involves using the time when a patient is involved with the medical services to measure aspects of their health (e.g. when seeing a patient for a sore throat the GP may decide to also check their blood pressure), and *population screening*, which involves setting up services specifically aimed at identifying problems. For example, current programmes involve cervical screening and breast screening. Recently a new form of screening has emerged in the form of *self-screening*. For example, people are encouraged to practise breast and testicular self-examination and it is now possible to buy over-the-counter kits to measure blood pressure, cholesterol and blood sugar levels.

The aim of all screening programmes is to detect a problem at the asymptomatic stage. This results in two outcomes. First, screening can discover a risk of the disease. This is called *primary screening*. For example, cervical screening may detect pre-cancerous cells which place the individual at risk of cervical cancer; genetic screening for cystic fibrosis would give the person an estimate of risk of producing children with cystic fibrosis; and cholesterol screening could place an individual at high risk of developing coronary heart disease (CHD). Second, screening can detect the illness itself. This is called *secondary screening*. For example, a mammogram may discover breast cancer, genetic testing may discover the gene for Huntington's disease and blood pressure assessment may discover hypertension. The recent enthusiasm for screening is reflected in an often repeated statement by Edward VII: 'If preventable, why not prevented?'

GUIDELINES FOR SCREENING

As a result of the enthusiasm for screening, sets of criteria have been established. Wilson (1965) outlined the following:

- *The disease*
  - an important problem
  - recognizable at the latent or early symptomatic stage
  - natural history must be understood (including development from latent to symptomatic stage)
- *The screen*
  - suitable test or examination (of reasonable sensitivity and specificity)
  - test should be acceptable by the population being screened
  - screening must be a continuous process
- *Follow-up*
  - facilities must exist for assessment and treatment
  - accepted form of effective treatment
  - agreed policy on whom to treat
- *Economy*
  - cost must be economically balanced in relation to possible expenditure on medical care as a whole

More recently, the criteria have been developed as follows:

- The disease must be sufficiently prevalent and/or sufficiently serious to make early detection appropriate.
- The disease must be sufficiently well defined to permit accurate diagnosis.
- There must be a possibility (or probability) that the disease exists undiagnosed in many cases (i.e. that the disease is not so manifest by symptoms as to make rapid diagnosis almost inevitable).
- There must be a beneficial outcome from early diagnosis in terms of disease treatment or prevention of complications.
- There must be a screening test that has good sensitivity and specificity and a reasonably positive predictive value in the population to be screened.

Research has explored screening in terms of: (1) the predictors of uptake; (2) the medical and social costs and benefits of screening; (3) the psychological impact of screening; and (4) whether screening is cost-effective.

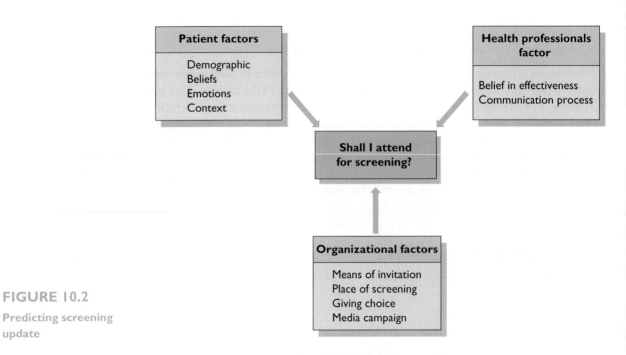

FIGURE 10.2

Predicting screening
update

THE PREDICTORS OF SCREENING UPTAKE

The numbers of individuals who attend different screening programmes vary enormously according to factors such as the country, the illness being screened and the time of the screening programme. For example, uptake for neonatal screening for phenylketonuria is almost 100 per cent. However, whereas up to 99 per cent of pregnant women in Sweden and France undertake HIV testing (Larsson et al. 1990; Moatti et al. 1990), in the UK and North America only a small minority elect to take the test. Marteau (1993) suggested that there are three main factors that influence uptake of screening: patient factors, health professional factors and organizational factors. These are illustrated in Figure 10.2.

BOX 10.1 Some Problems with ... Screening Research

Below are some problems with research in this area that you may wish to consider.

1 The ability of medicine to screen reflects new and ever-advancing medical technology. Because of this it is often seen by the health profession as a positive development. However, just because something can be done does not mean that it should be done. At times the research on screening can seem polarized between those who promote screening and the use of technology and those who seem wary of it. This can lead to contradictory findings or research that simply supports the ideological position of those involved.

2 Evaluating the impact of screening can involve measuring both psychological (e.g. fear, anxiety) and medical (e.g. health status, detection) outcomes. Sometimes these outcomes occur in opposite directions (it may make a person anxious but benefit their health status). Combining these contradictory outcomes and deciding upon the right way forward can be a complex and difficult process.

3 Screening may detect an illness at an early stage. Some people, however, may not wish to know that they have something wrong with them. This can present researchers and clinicians with a dilemma as medicine also emphasizes truth-telling, openness and patient autonomy. Balancing the different ethical positions and perspectives of medicine can prove difficult.

PATIENT FACTORS

Several studies have been carried out to examine which factors predict the uptake of screening. These have included demographic factors, health beliefs, emotional factors and contextual factors.

Demographic Factors

MacLean et al. (1984) reported that women who attended for breast screening were more likely to be of high socioeconomic status, and Owens et al. (1987) reported that older women were more likely to attend for breast screening than younger women. Similarly, Simpson et al. (1997) concluded that older women were more likely to attend a worksite screening programme for cardiovascular disease than either younger women or men. In addition, Waller et al. (1990) suggested that those individuals who are the most healthy are more likely to attend for an HIV test, and Sutton et al. (2000) reported that men, home-owners, non-smokers, those who have regular check-ups at the dentist and those with better subjective health were more likely to attend for flexible sigmoidoscopy which screens for colorectal cancer.

Health Beliefs

Health beliefs have also been linked to uptake and have been measured using a number of models (see Chapter 3). For example, Bish et al. (2000) used the health belief model (HBM) and the theory of planned behaviour (TPB) to predict uptake of a routine cervical smear test. The results showed that the TPB was a better predictor of behavioural intentions but that neither model successfully predicted actual uptake at follow-up. Pakenham et al. (2000) also used the HBM in conjunction with knowledge and sociodemographic variables to predict re-attendance for mammography screening. The results showed that although the re-attenders were older and more likely to be married, the HBM variable of perceived benefits of the mammography was a better predictor overall of re-attendance than sociodemographic variables. Similarly, Sutton et al. (2000) also included measures of beliefs and reported that a perception of fewer barriers and more benefits predicted attendance for sigmoidoscopy screening. Further, Dormandy et al. (2006) explored the predictors of screening for Down's syndrome in pregnant women and showed that although attitudes towards the test predicted both behavioural intentions and uptake of the test, this association was undermined by ambivalence measured by high scores on two items 'For me, having the screening test for Down's syndrome when I am 15 to 16 weeks pregnant will be a bad thing/not a bad thing' and 'For me, having the screening test for Down's syndrome when I am 15 to 16 weeks pregnant will be a good thing/not a good thing'. Some studies have also explored ways to increase uptake of screening through behavioural interventions. For example, Luszczynska et al. (2010) used a stage-matched intervention to encourage participants to focus on the pros of screening for cervical cancer and reported an increase in intentions to participate and Sandberg and Conner (2009) argued that simply completing measures of anticipated regret about not attending cervical screening increased actual attendance by follow-up.

Emotional Factors

Emotional factors such as anxiety, stress, fear, uncertainty and feeling indecent have also been shown to relate to uptake. Shiloh et al. (1997) examined the predictors of uptake for four screening programmes (a dental check-up, blood pressure measurement and cholesterol testing, a cervical smear, mammography) and suggested that both the cognitions derived from a range of models and emotional factors such as reassurance predicted uptake. However, they also argued that although beliefs and emotions predict screening uptake, the nature of these beliefs and emotions is very much dependent upon the screening programme being considered. In a similar vein researchers have also explored predictors of vaccination uptake. For example, Morison et al. (2010) explored parental uptake of a school-based vaccination programme for the HPV virus that can cause cervical cancer in 11–12-year-old girls. The results showed that intentions to vaccinate the child were predicted by a number of beliefs but also showed a significant role for anticipated regret if the child did not have the vaccine. Research, however, also shows that declining a test can result in elevated stress. For example, Almqvist et al. (2003) explored the longer-term consequences of either having or not having a genetic test for Huntington's disease and reported that those who declined the test were the most distressed over a period of 12 months. Some research has also focused on patients' need to reduce their uncertainty and to find 'cognitive closure'. For example, Eiser and Cole (2002) used a quantitative method based upon the stages of change (SOC) model and explored differences between individuals at different stages of attending for a cervical smear in terms of 'cognitive closure' and barriers to screening. The results showed that the pre-contemplators reported most barriers and the least need for closure and to reduce uncertainty. One qualitative study further highlighted the role of emotional factors in the form of feeling indecent. Borrayo and Jenkins (2001) interviewed 34 women of Mexican descent in five focus groups about their beliefs about breast cancer screening and their decision whether or not to take part. The analyses showed that the women reported a fundamental problem with breast screening as it violates a basic cultural standard. Breast screening requires women to touch their own breasts and to expose their breasts to health professionals. Within the cultural norms of respectable female behaviour for these women, this was seen as 'indecent'.

Contextual Factors

Finally, contextual factors have also been shown to predict uptake. For example, Smith et al. (2002) interviewed women who had been offered genetic testing for Huntington's disease. The results showed that the women often showed complex and sometimes contradictory beliefs about their risk status for the disease which related to factors such as prevalence in the family, family size, attempts to make the numbers 'add up' and beliefs about transmission. The results also showed that uptake of the test related not only to the individual's risk perception but also to contextual factors such as family discussion or a key triggering event. For example, one woman described how she had shouted at the cats for going on to the new stair carpet which had been paid for from her father's insurance money after he had died from Huntington's disease. This had made her resolve to have the test.

HEALTH PROFESSIONAL FACTORS

In a study of GPs' attitudes and screening behaviour, a belief in the effectiveness of screening was associated with an organized approach to screening and time spent on screening (Havelock et al. 1988). Such factors may influence patient uptake. In addition, the means of presenting a test may also influence uptake. For example, uptake rates for HIV testing at antenatal clinics are reported to vary from 3 to 82 per cent (Meadows et al. 1990). These rates may well be related to the way in which these tests were offered by the health professional, which in turn may reflect the health professional's own beliefs about the test. Some research has used qualitative methods to further analyse health professional factors. For example, Michie et al. (1999) used structured interviews to explore how clinical geneticists and genetic counsellors view the function of a genetic consultation in terms of its aims, the skills involved and patient expectations. The analyses showed that the interviewees described the consultations in terms of four main themes which were often contradictory. These were providing information that is both objective and full and tailored to the needs of the individual; dealing with emotion by both eliciting it and containing it; communicating both directively and non-directively; and performing sophisticated skills while having only minimal training. These themes and their contradictions suggest that consultations would vary enormously between patients and between clinicians. For example, while a clinician may offer full information for one patient, the same clinician might limit the information for another. Similarly, while one clinician might tend to be more directive, another might be less so. Such variation in health professional beliefs about the consultation and their subsequent behaviour could influence the patient's decision about whether or not to have a particular test.

ORGANIZATIONAL FACTORS

Many organizational factors may also influence the uptake of screening. Research has examined the effects of the means of invitation on the uptake rate and indicates that if the invitation is issued in person, and if the individual is expected to opt out, not in, the rates of uptake are higher (Mann et al. 1988; Smith et al. 1990). The place of the screening programme may also be influential, with more accessible settings promoting higher uptake. In addition, making attendance at a screening programme mandatory rather than voluntary will also obviously have an effect (Marteau 1993). Uptake may also be influenced by education and media campaigns. For example, Fernbach (2002) evaluated the impact of a large media campaign designed to influence women's self-efficacy and uptake of cervical screening. The media campaign was called the 'Papscreen Victoria' campaign and took place in Australia. It was evaluated by face-to-face interviews with 1,571 women at baseline and two follow-ups. The results showed that women reported an increase in awareness of cervical screening and rated this as a greater health priority than before the campaign. However, the results were not all positive. The women also stated after the campaign that they would find it more difficult to ring up for test results and reported lowered self-efficacy.

THE MEDICAL AND SOCIAL COSTS AND BENEFITS

Skrabanek (1988) suggested that screening should be subjected to the same rigours as any experimental procedure, that the possible risks should be evaluated and that the precept of 'first do no harm' should be remembered. Research has therefore explored the costs and benefits of screening in terms of both medical and social factors.

The Medical Costs

Electronic foetal monitoring was introduced as a way of improving obstetric outcomes. However, the results from two well-controlled trials indicated that such monitoring may increase the rate of caesarean section without any benefit to the babies both immediately after birth (MacDonald et al. 1985) and at 4 years of age (Grant and Elbourne 1989). In addition, electronic foetal monitoring appeared to increase the rate of cerebral palsy measured at 18 months of age (Shy et al. 1990). In a recent review of the effects of antenatal blood pressure screening on the incidence of pre-eclampsia (high blood pressure in pregnancy, which threatens the mother's life), the authors concluded that the introduction of antenatal screening has had no significant effect on pre-eclampsia, suggesting that this screening process does not benefit the individual. Papers have also questioned the efficacy of screening for congenital dislocation of the hip in neonates (Leck 1986), hypertension, breast cancer and cervical cancer in terms of the relative effectiveness of early (rather than later) medical interventions and the effects of simply increasing the lead time (the period of time between detection and symptoms).

Harm to the Individual

Some of the techniques used to monitor an individual's health may have a detrimental effect on their biological state. This is of particular concern in terms of the frequent use of mammography for the detection of breast cancer. Evidence for the harmful effects of the irradiation of breast tissue and the links to cancer can be found in reports of breast cancer in women who have been treated for benign conditions using radiation therapy (Metler et al. 1969; Simon 1977), in survivors of the bombings of Hiroshima and Nagasaki (Wanebo et al. 1968) and in women who have been given fluoroscopy for tuberculosis (MacKenzie 1965). It has been argued that there is a threshold below which radiation could be considered totally safe, and that the above examples of an association between irradiation and breast cancer are due to the unusually high levels of radiation (Perquin et al. 1976). However, there is some disagreement with this view. In particular, Upton et al. (1977) suggested that exposure to 1 rad would increase the risk of breast cancer by 1 per cent. Furthermore, Strax (1978) suggested that if 40 million women were screened for 20 years, 120 would die from radiation-induced breast cancer. However, since these concerns were raised, the dose of radiation used in mammography has been reduced, although some concerns still remain. All tests are fallible and none can promise 100 per cent accuracy. Therefore there is always the chance of false positives and false negatives. A false-positive result may lead to unnecessary treatment interventions and the associated anxiety and uncertainty. A false-negative result may lead to an illness remaining undetected, untreated and consequently progressing without medical intervention. In addition, a false-negative result may lead to subsequent signs of illness (e.g. a breast lump, vaginal discharge) being ignored by the patient. A recent review of the effectiveness of screening for breast cancer concluded that it reduced breast cancer mortality by 15 per cent but led to 30 per cent over-diagnosis and overtreatment. This means that for every 2,000 women invited for screening over 10 years, one will have her life expectancy increased but 10 will have unnecessary treatment. The report also concluded that 200 will experience psychological distress because of these false-positive findings (Gotzsche and Neilsen 2011).

Social Harm

Zola (1973) has argued that medicine is a means of social control and suggested that there is a danger if individuals become too reliant on experts. In terms of screening, monitoring and surveillance of populations could be seen as a forum for not only examining individuals but controlling them. This argument is also made by Illich in his book *Medical Nemesis* (1974), where he argued that medicine is taking over the responsibility for people's health and creating a society of medical addicts. Screening epitomizes this shift towards social control in that not only are the ill seen by the medical profession but also the healthy, as all individuals are now 'at risk' from illness (Armstrong 1995). Skrabanek (1988: 1155) argued that screening with the medicalization of health 'serves as a justification for State intrusion into people's private lives, and for stigmatising those who do not conform'.

The possibility that screening may exacerbate existing stigma of particular social groups is particularly relevant to screening for genetic disorders. At present, society is constituted of a variety of individuals, some of whom have genetic deficits such as Down's syndrome, cystic fibrosis and sickle-cell anaemia. Although these individuals may be subjected to stereotyping and stigma, society provides treatment and support and attempts to integrate them into the rest of the population. It is possible, however, that screening for such disorders would lead to terminations of pregnancy and a reduction in this stigmatized population. Although this would lead to fewer individuals with these disorders (this may be a positive consequence, as no one wants to suffer from sickle-cell anaemia), the individuals who are born with these problems may face increased stigma as they would be part of a greatly reduced minority existing in a world with reduced social provisions for support and treatment.

The Medical Benefits

Screening has also been found to benefit individuals. In terms of screening for hypertension, Hart (1987) has argued 'we are surely under a moral if not legal obligation to record blood pressure at least once in every five year span for every registered adult in our practice'. In terms of cervical screening it has been estimated that for every 40,000 smears, one life has been saved (*Lancet* 1985). Results concerning the benefits of breast screening have also been reported following a systematic review of seven trials which indicated that breast cancer screening leads to a 15 per cent reduction in cancer mortality (although 30 per cent of women had unnecessary treatment) (Gotzsche and Nielsen 2011). Jones (1992) argued that screening for colorectal cancer may also be beneficial. He suggested that the 'evidence and arguments ... are becoming compelling' and noted that the death rate due to colorectal cancer was 10 times that due to cervical cancer, for which there is an existing screening programme. In addition, the identification of the absence of illness through screening may also benefit the patient in that a negative result may 'give health back' (Grimes 1988).

THE PSYCHOLOGICAL IMPACT

Screening therefore has medical and social costs and benefits. The negative consequences of screening have been described as 'the intangible costs' (Kinlay 1988) but research suggests that they are indeed experienced by the individuals involved. These psychological consequences can be a result of the various different stages of the screening process:

1   *The receipt of a screening invitation.* Research indicates that sending out invitations to enter into a screening programme may not only influence an individual's behaviour, but also their psychological state. Fallowfield et al. (1990) carried out a retrospective study of women's responses to receiving a request to attend a breast screening session. Their results showed that 55 per cent reported feeling worried although 93 per cent were pleased. Dean et al. (1984) sent a measure of psychological morbidity to women awaiting breast screening and then followed them up six months later. The results showed no significant increases in psychological morbidity. However, when asked in retrospect 30 per cent said that they had become anxious after receiving the letter of invitation. Therefore receiving a screening invitation may increase anxiety. However, some research suggests that this is not always the case (Cockburn et al. 1994).

2   *The receipt of a negative result.* It may be assumed that receiving a negative result (i.e. not having the condition being tested for) would only decrease an individual's anxiety. Most research suggests that this is the case and that a negative result may create a sense of reassurance (Orton et al. 1991) or no change in anxiety (Sutton et al. 1995). Further, Sutton (1999), in his review of the literature on receiving a negative result following breast cancer screening, concluded that 'anxiety is not a significant problem among women who receive a negative screening result'. However, some research points towards residual levels of anxiety which do not return to baseline (Baillie et al. 2000) and that, even following negative results, some people attend for further tests even though these tests have not been clinically recommended (e.g. Lerman et al. 2000; Michie et al. 2002). Michie et al. (2003) used qualitative methods to explore why negative genetic results can fail to reassure. They interviewed nine people who had received a negative result for familial adenomatous polyposis (FAP) which is a genetic condition and results in polyps in the bowel which can become cancerous if not detected and removed by surgery. They argued that people may not be reassured by a negative result for two reasons. First, they may hold a belief about the cause of the illness that does not directly map onto the cause being tested for. In the case of FAP, people described how they believed that it was caused by genetics but that genetics could change. Therefore, although the test indicated that they did not have the relevant genes, this may not be the case in the future. Second, they may show a lack of faith in the test itself. For FAP, people were sceptical about the ability of a blood test to inform about a disease that occurred in the bowel. Some research has also explored the ways in which a negative result is presented. In the UK in 1997 the policy recommendation for cervical smear results stated that the term 'negative result' could be confusing as women would feel 'positive' to such a 'negative' result and that the term 'normal' smear result should be used instead. Marteau et al. (2006) explored the impact of receiving a result that was either presented as 'normal', or normal and a series of statements of risk, that is, 'you are at low risk of having or developing cervical cancer in the next five years' and a range of numerical presentations of risk. Participants were then asked to describe their levels of perceived risk. The results showed that, when only told that their smear result was 'normal' without any description of risk, women described feeling less at risk than when they received 'normal' and the description of risk. Marteau et al. (2006) argued that a negative smear result still implies a low risk of getting cervical cancer and that the term 'normal' makes people underestimate this risk.

3   *The receipt of a positive result.* As expected, the receipt of a positive result can be associated with a variety of negative emotions ranging from worry to anxiety and shock. For example, an abnormal cervical smear may generate anxiety, morbidity and even terror (Wilkinson et al.

1990). Psychological costs have also been reported after screening for CHD (Stoate 1989), breast cancer (Fallowfield et al. 1990) and genetic diseases (Marteau et al. 1992). However, some research suggests that these psychological changes may only be maintained in the short term and quickly return to baseline levels (Broadstock et al. 2000). This decay in the psychological consequences has been particularly shown with the termination of pregnancy following the detection of foetal abnormalities (Black 1989) and following the receipt of a positive genetic test result (Broadstock et al. 2000). Collins et al. (2011) carried out a systematic review of screening procedures for a number of health problems and concluded that receiving a positive test result results in a small increase in depression but that this is short-lasting. Some research has also explored the impact of receiving a positive genetic test result upon individuals' beliefs about their condition and subsequent behaviour. Such an approach is in line with a self-regulatory model (see Chapter 9). For example, Marteau et al. (2004) explored the impact of telling people that they had tested positive for familial hypercholesterolaemia on their beliefs about the nature of their condition and their behaviour. The results showed that those who were told that they had a genetic mutation reported a lower belief that their cholesterol could be managed by diet. Therefore, being given a medical model of their problem made them less likely to endorse a behavioural solution. No effect was found, however, for perceptions of control, adherence to medication or risk-reducing behaviours. Similarly two systematic reviews of the impact of communication of personalized genetic risk to patients concluded that such information had no impact upon beliefs about fatalism or perceptions of control and no impact on actual behaviours such as smoking and physical activity (Marteau et al. 2010; Collins et al. 2011).

4   *The receipt of an inadequate test result.* Although many tests produce either positive or negative results, some produce inadequate results which neither confirm nor disconfirm the presence of the condition. An example of this is cervical screening whereby the test can be 'ruined' due to the presence of pus or the absence of sufficient number of cervical cells. French et al. (2004, 2006b) explored the immediate and longer-term psychological consequences of receiving either an inadequate test result (n = 180) or a normal test result (n = 226). The results showed that women with an inadequate result reported more anxiety and more concern about their result, perceived themselves to be more at risk of cervical cancer and were less satisfied with the information they had received immediately following the result. By three months' follow-up, the women who had the inadequate results were no longer more anxious. They were, however, more concerned about their test results and less satisfied with the information they had received even after having normal results from subsequent tests.

5   *Being involved in a screening programme.* Most research has explored the relative impact of receiving a positive or negative result from a screening procedure. Collins et al. (2011) carried out a systematic review to explore the impact of taking part in a screening procedure regardless of the test results. They identified 12 randomized controlled trials for a range of problems including cancer, type 2 diabetes, CHD and a genetic risk for lung cancer and explored changes in psychological morbidity both before and after four weeks. The results showed no evidence for raised levels of either depression or anxiety or reduced quality of life in the longer term (more than four weeks). Insufficient data were available for an analysis of short-term effects. They argued that their results illustrate a process of self-regulation, with initial negative responses being minimized by one month as people draw upon a number of cognitive strategies to reduce their sense of threat.

6   *The existence of a screening programme.* Marteau (1993) suggested that the existence of screening programmes may influence social beliefs about what is healthy and may change society's attitude towards a screened condition. In a study by Marteau and Riordan (1992), health professionals were asked to rate their attitudes towards two hypothetical patients, one of whom had attended a screening programme and one who had not. Both patients were

described as having developed cervical cancer. The results showed that the health profession-als held more negative attitudes towards the patient who had not attended. In terms of the wider effects of screening programmes, it is possible that the existence of such programmes encourages society to see illnesses as preventable and the responsibility of the individual, which may lead to victim-blaming of those individuals who still develop these illnesses. This may be relevant to illnesses such as CHD, cervical cancer and breast cancer, which have established screening programmes. In the future, it may also be relevant to genetic disorders which could have been eradicated by terminations.

IS SCREENING COST-EFFECTIVE?

Screening has medical, social and psychological consequences which can be either positive or negative. It also has cost implications which can be evaluated using a cost-effective analysis. This involves assessing either how to achieve a set objectives at minimum cost or how to use a fixed resource to produce the best output. In terms of screening, this raises issues about the objectives of screening (to detect asymptomatic illness, which can be treated) and the degree of resources required to achieve these objectives (minimum interventions such as opportunistic weighing versus expensive interventions such as breast screening clinics). The economic considerations of screen-ing have been analysed for different policies for cervical screening (Smith and Chamberlain 1987). The different policies include: (1) opportunistic screening (offer a smear test when an individual presents at the surgery); (2) offer a smear test every five years; (3) offer a smear test every three years; and (4) offer a smear test annually. The results from this analysis are shown in Figure 10.3. These different policies have been offered as possible solutions to the problem of screening for cervical cancer. The results suggest that annual screening in England and Wales would cost £165 million and would potentially prevent 4,300 cancers, whereas smears every five years would cost £34 million and would potentially prevent 3,900 cancers.

The problem of cost-effectiveness is also highlighted by a discussion of the OXCHECK and Family Heart Study results (Muir et al. 1994; Wood et al. 1994). Both studies indicated that inten-sive screening, counselling and health checks have only a moderate effect on risk factors and the authors discuss these results in terms of the implications for government policies for health promo-tion through doctor-based interventions.

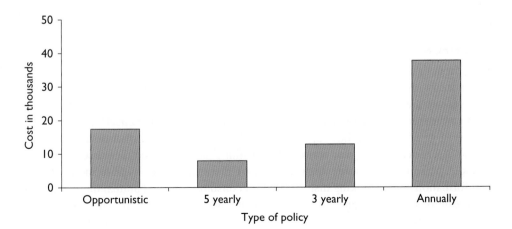

FIGURE 10.3

Costs per potential cancer prevented for different screening policies

SOURCE: Adapted from Smith and Chamberlain (1987)

The Family Heart Study

The Family Heart Study (Wood et al. 1994) examined the effects of screening and lifestyle interventions on cardiovascular risk factors in families over a one-year period. The study involved 26 general practices in 13 towns in Britain and recruited 12,472 individuals aged 40–59 years. The total sample consisted of 7,460 men and 5,012 women. The practices within each town were paired according to sociodemographic characteristics and were randomly designated as either the intervention or the comparison practice. Intervention practices were then randomly allocated either to a further comparison group or to an intervention group. This provided both an internal and external comparison with the subjects receiving the intervention. All intervention practices received screening, but only the intervention group of these practices received lifestyle counselling and follow-up within the one-year period. All subjects from all practices were followed up at one year. The screening process involved an appointment with a trained research nurse, who asked about demographic, lifestyle and medical factors and measured height, weight, carbon monoxide, blood pressure, blood glucose and blood cholesterol. The subjects in the intervention group also received lifestyle counselling and repeated follow-up. The counselling used a client-centred family approach and involved an assessment of the patients' risk status, educational input and a booklet for the subject to document their personally negotiated lifestyle changes. All subjects were then offered follow-up every 1, 2, 3, 4, 6 or 12 months, depending on their risk status. Outcome was measured at the follow-up in terms of changes in the main risk factors for CHD and the Dundee Risk Score, which is dependent on serum cholesterol concentration, systolic blood pressure, and previous and current smoking behaviour. Outcome was compared within the intervention practices, between the intervention practice and the internal comparison practice, and between the intervention practice and practices in the external comparison group. The results showed a 16 per cent reduction in overall risk score in the intervention practices at one year, a 4 per cent reduction in smoking, a small reduction in systolic (7mmHg) and diastolic (3mmHg) blood pressure and marginal reductions in weight (1kg) and cholesterol concentrations (0.1m). The results showed no changes in blood glucose levels. In addition, the greatest changes in risk status were reported in subjects with the highest risk levels. Although this intensive screening and intervention did result in changes in risk for CHD in the correct direction, Wood et al. (1994: 319) concluded that 'whether these small reductions can be sustained long term is not known, but even if they were, they would correspond only to a 12 per cent lower risk of coronary heart disease events'. The authors also concluded that the government-sponsored health promotion clinics 'would probably have achieved considerably less and possibly no change at all' (Wood et al. 1994: 319) and that 'the government's screening policy cannot be justified by these results' (1994: 313).

The OXCHECK Study

The results from the OXCHECK study also produced similarly pessimistic conclusions (Muir et al. 1994). This study involved 6,124 patients recruited from five urban practices in Bedfordshire and aimed to evaluate the effectiveness of health checks by nurses in general practice in reducing risk factors for cardiovascular disease. All subjects received an initial health check and the intervention group received an additional follow-up health check after one year (further results were also collected for subjects over a four-year period). The health checks involved the nurse recording information about personal and family history of heart disease, stroke, hypertension, diabetes and cancer. Information about smoking history, alcohol consumption and habitual diet, height, weight, serum cholesterol concentration and blood pressure was also recorded. The nurses were also instructed to counsel patients about risk factors and to negotiate priorities and targets for risk reduction. The re-examination was briefer than the original health check but it involved re-measurement of the same profile and lifestyle factors. The results showed a lower cholesterol level (by 2.3 per cent) in the intervention group than the control group, lower systolic (2.5 per cent) and diastolic (2.4 per cent) blood pressure, and no differences in body mass index (BMI), or smoking prevalence or quit rates. The authors concluded that using health checks to reduce smoking may be ineffective as the effectiveness of health information may be diluted if the health check attempts to change too many risk factors at once. They suggested that the reduction in blood pressure was probably due to an accommodation effect, suggesting that the health checks were ineffective. Muir et al. (1994: 312) also concluded that, although the health checks did appear to reduce serum cholesterol concentration, 'it is disappointing that the difference . . . was smaller in men than in women in view of the greater effect of cholesterol concentration on absolute risk in men' and they questioned whether such a shift in concentration could be sustained in the long term in the light of a previous trial in Oxfordshire. Therefore, although the results of the OXCHECK study suggested some reduction in risk factors for cardiovascular disease, the authors were fairly pessimistic in their presentation of these reductions.

Both of the above studies suggested that screening and minimal interventions are not cost-effective, as the possible benefits are not worthy of the amount of time and money needed to implement the programmes.

THE MEDICAL CONSULTATION

The core component of any interaction with a health care system is the consultation between patient and health professional as this is the context within which key decisions about diagnosis and management strategy are made.

Traditional models of the consultation regarded doctors as having an objective knowledge set that came from their extensive medical education and was communicated to a passive patient who absorbed any suggestions and responded accordingly. Therefore doctors were the experts and patients needed to be educated. Over time this model has evolved towards the notion of the 'expert patient' who has their own beliefs and expectations and doctors who have become more 'human', based upon both personal and professional experience. This shift in perspective is in part a response to an increase in consumerism, patient knowledge and rights, and the availability of medical information through the internet. It is also due to a recognition of the problem of doctor variability and the many factors involved in doctors' decision-making. This section will describe the problem of doctor variability, how doctors make decisions, the role of health professionals' beliefs and the nature of the modern consultation with its focus on patient-centredness, shared decision-making and informed consent.

THE PROBLEM OF DOCTOR VARIABILITY

If doctors were simply the experts who behaved according to their extensive knowledge and training then it could be predicted that doctors with similar levels of knowledge and training would behave in similar ways. Considerable variability has been found, however, among doctors in terms of different aspects of their practice (see Figure 10.4). For example, Anderson et al. (1983) reported that doctors differ in their diagnosis of asthma. Mapes (1980) suggested that they vary in terms of their prescribing behaviour, with a variation of 15–90 per cent of patients receiving drugs. Bucknall et al. (1986) reported variation in the methods used by doctors to measure blood

The medical consultation is core to most health care decisions

SOURCE: © Justmeyo/Dreamstime

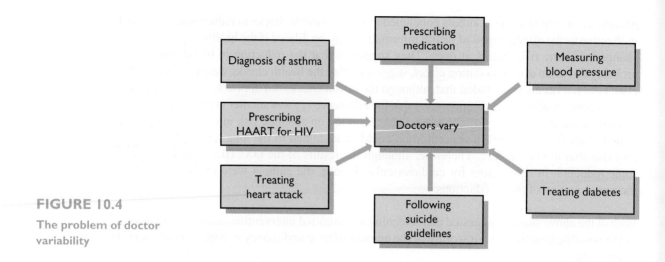

FIGURE 10.4

The problem of doctor variability

pressure, Marteau and Baum (1984) also reported that doctors vary in their treatment of diabetes and Hanbury et al. (2009) indicated that health professionals varied in their adherence to guidelines regarding suicide prevention. Similar variation was also shown in a study of doctor attitudes towards prescribing HAART for patients with HIV infection (Moatti et al. 2000). For example, although a large majority of doctors stated that they would prescribe HAART in line with official recommendations when all patient details were presented, there was much variability in prescribing for patients with less clear histories indicating that the same patient would receive a different management procedure if they visited more than one doctor. Similar variability can be seen for the treatment of acute myocardial infarction (AMI, heart attack) (Venturini et al. 1999). Although there is clear evidence that AMI should be treated immediately, a study of 1,976 patients from 10 countries showed wide variability with 63.7 per cent being given thrombolysis, 88 per cent being given aspirin and 65.9 per cent being given beta-adrenergic blocking agents. Guidelines indicate that all patients should be given all of these treatments. According to a traditional educational model of doctor–patient communication, this variability could be understood in terms of differing levels of knowledge and expertise. However, this variability can also be understood by examining the other factors involved in the clinical decision-making process.

HOW DOCTORS MAKE DECISIONS

Health professionals are not just confronted with patients with illnesses, diseases or syndromes such as cancer, heart disease or multiple sclerosis: they have patients sitting opposite them with a huge range of vague and often very common symptoms such as headaches, back pain, tiredness and bowel changes, and their role is to decide what these symptoms mean. This involves differentiating between the pain in the chest that means 'indigestion' and the one that means 'heart disease', and the raised temperature that means 'a cold' and the one that means 'meningitis'. Once a problem has been diagnosed, they then have to decide on an appropriate management strategy which could range from 'do nothing, it will go away', to 'prescribe medicine', to 'refer as a non-urgent patient for a second opinion', to 'refer urgently' or 'call the ambulance'. The doctor's role is therefore highly skilled and complex. It is further complicated by the high numbers of people coming through their doors with housing, relationship and benefit issues, symptoms that 'they had last week', patients who come every week with a different symptom and patients who are too embarrassed to describe the real reason for their visit but spend the consultation describing another symptom that is really irrelevant. Therefore, the process of clinical decision-making has been understood within the framework of problem-solving.

A Model of Problem-Solving

Clinical decision-making processes are a specialized form of problem-solving and have been studied within the context of problem-solving and theories of information processing. It is often assumed that clinical decisions are made by the process of *inductive reasoning*, which involves collecting evidence and data and using these data to develop a conclusion and a hypothesis. For example, within this framework, a GP would start a consultation with a patient without any prior model of their problem. The GP would then ask the appropriate questions regarding the patient's history and symptoms and develop a hypothesis about the presenting problem. However, doctors' decision-making processes are generally considered within the framework of the *hypothetico-deductive* model of decision-making. This perspective emphasizes the development of hypotheses early on in the consultation and is illustrated by Newell and Simon's (1972) model of problem-solving, which emphasizes hypothesis testing. Newell and Simon suggested that problem-solving involves a number of stages that result in a solution to any given problem. This model has been applied to many different forms of problem-solving and is a useful framework for examining clinical decisions (see Figure 10.5).

The stages involved are as follows:

1. *Understand the nature of the problem and develop an internal representation.* At this stage, the individual needs to formulate an internal representation of the problem. This process involves understanding the goal of the problem, evaluating any given conditions and assessing the nature of the available data.

2. *Develop a plan of action for solving the problem.* Newell and Simon differentiated between two types of plan: heuristics and algorithms. An algorithm is a set of rules that will provide a correct solution if applied correctly (e.g. addition, multiplication, etc. involve algorithms). However, most human problem-solving involves heuristics, which are 'rules of thumb'. Heuristics are less definite and specific but provide guidance and direction for the problem-solver. Heuristics may involve developing parallels between the present problem and previous similar ones.

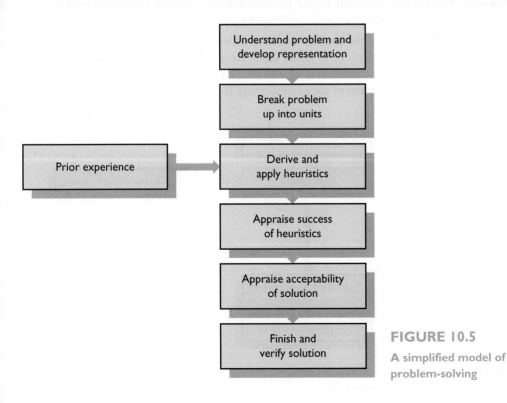

FIGURE 10.5

A simplified model of problem-solving

3   *Apply heuristics.* Once developed, the plans are then applied to the given situation.

4   *Determine whether heuristics have been fruitful.* The individual then decides whether the heuristics have been successful in the attempt to solve the given problem. If they are considered unsuccessful, the individual may need to develop a new approach to the problem.

5   *Determine whether an acceptable solution has been obtained.*

6   *Finish and verify the solution.* The end-point of the problem-solving process involves the individual deciding that an acceptable solution to the problem has been reached and that this solution provides a suitable outcome.

According to Newell and Simon's model of problem-solving, hypotheses about the causes and solutions to the problem are developed very early on in the process. They regarded this process as dynamic and ever-changing and suggested that at each stage the individual applies a 'means end analysis', whereby they assess the value of the hypothesis, which is either accepted or rejected according to the evidence. This type of model involves information processing whereby the individual develops hypotheses to convert an open problem, which may be unmanageable with no obvious end-point, to one that can be closed and tested by a series of hypotheses.

Clinical Decisions as Problem-Solving

Clinical decisions can be conceptualized as a form of problem-solving and involve the development of hypotheses early on in the consultation process. These hypotheses are subsequently tested by the doctor's selection of questions. Models of problem-solving have been applied to clinical decision-making by several authors (e.g. MacWhinney 1973), who have argued that the process of formulating a clinical decision involves the stages show in Figure 10.6.

1   *Accessing information about the patient's symptoms.* The initial questions in any consultation from the health professional to the patient will enable the health professional to understand the nature of the problem and to form an internal representation of the type of problem.

2   *Developing hypotheses.* Early on in the problem-solving process, the health professional develops hypotheses about the possible causes and solutions to the problem.

3   *Search for attributes.* The health professional then proceeds to test the hypotheses by searching for factors either to confirm or to refute them. Research into the hypothesis-testing process has indicated that although doctors aim to either confirm or refute their hypothesis by asking balanced questions, most of their questioning is biased towards confirmation of their

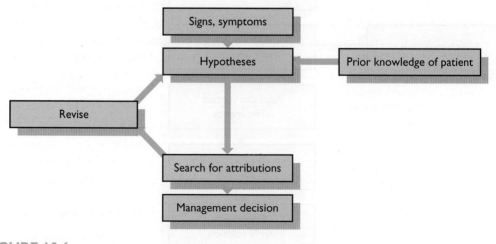

FIGURE 10.6

Diagnosis as a form of problem-solving

original hypothesis. Therefore an initial hypothesis that a patient has a psychological problem may cause the doctor to focus on the patient's psychological state and ignore the patient's attempt to talk about their physical symptoms. Studies have shown that doctors' clinical information collected subsequent to the development of a hypothesis may be systematically distorted to support the original hypothesis (Wallsten 1978). Furthermore, the type of hypothesis has been shown to bias the collection and interpretation of any information received during the consultation (Wason 1974).

4   *Making a management decision.* The outcome of the clinical decision-making process involves the health professional deciding on the way forward. The outcome of a consultation and a diagnosis, however, is not an absolute entity, but is itself a hypothesis and an informed guess that will be either confirmed or refuted by future events.

Explaining Variability

Variability in the behaviour of health professionals can therefore be understood in terms of the processes involved in clinical decisions. For example, health professionals may:

- Access different information about the patient's symptoms.
- Develop different hypotheses.
- Access different attributes either to confirm or to refute their hypotheses.
- Have differing degrees of a bias towards confirmation.
- Consequently reach different management decisions.

HEALTH PROFESSIONALS' HEALTH BELIEFS

The hypothesis-testing model of clinical decision-making provides some understanding of the possible causes of variability in health professionals' behaviour. Perhaps the most important stage in the model that may lead to variability is the development of the original hypothesis. Patients are described as having lay beliefs, which are individual and variable. Health professionals are usually described as having professional beliefs, which are often assumed to be consistent and predictable. However, the development of the original hypothesis involves the health professional's own health beliefs, which may vary as much as those of the patient (see Chapter 3). Components of models such as the HBM, protection motivation theory (PMT) and attribution theory have been developed to examine health professionals' beliefs. The beliefs involved in making the original hypothesis can be categorized as follows:

1   *The health professional's own beliefs about the nature of clinical problems.* Health professionals have their own beliefs about health and illness. This pre-existing factor will influence their choice of hypothesis. For example, if a health professional believes that health and illness are determined by biomedical factors (e.g. lesions, bacteria, viruses) then they will develop a hypothesis about the patient's problem that reflects this perspective (e.g. a patient who reports feeling tired all the time may be anaemic). However, a health professional who views health and illness as relating to psychosocial factors may develop hypotheses reflecting this perspective (e.g. a patient who reports feeling tired all the time may be under stress).

2   *The health professional's estimate of the probability of the hypothesis and disease.* Health professionals will have pre-existing beliefs about the prevalence and incidence of any given health problem that will influence the process of developing a hypothesis. For example, some doctors may regard childhood asthma as a common complaint and hypothesize that a child presenting with a cough has asthma, whereas others may believe that childhood asthma is rare and so will not consider this hypothesis.

3   *The seriousness and treatability of the disease.* Health professionals are motivated to consider the 'payoff' involved in reaching a correct diagnosis and that this will influence their choice

of hypothesis. This payoff is related to their beliefs about the seriousness and treatability of an illness. For example, a child presenting with abdominal pain may result in an original hypothesis of appendicitis as this is both a serious and treatable condition, and the benefits of arriving at the correct diagnosis for this condition far outweigh the costs involved (such as time-wasting) if this hypothesis is refuted.

4 *Personal knowledge of the patient.* The original hypothesis will also be related to the health professional's existing knowledge of the patient. This may include the patient's medical history, knowledge about their psychological state, an understanding of their psychosocial environment and a belief about why the patient uses medical services.

5 *The health professional's stereotypes.* Stereotypes are sometimes seen as problematic and as confounding the decision-making process. However, most meetings between health professionals and patients are time-limited and consequently stereotypes play a central role in developing and testing a hypothesis and reaching a management decision. Stereotypes reflect the process of 'cognitive economy' and may be developed according to a multitude of factors such as how the patient looks/talks/walks or whether they remind the health professional of previous patients. Without stereotypes, consultations between health professionals and patients would be extremely time-consuming.

Other factors that may influence the development of the original hypothesis include the following:

1 *The health professional's mood.* The health professional's mood may influence the choice of hypotheses and the subsequent process of testing this hypothesis. Isen et al. (1991) manipulated mood in a group of medical students and evaluated the effect of induced positive affect on their decision-making processes. Positive affect was induced by informing subjects in this group that they had performed in the top 3 per cent of all graduate students nationwide in an anagram task. All subjects were then given a set of hypothetical patients and asked to decide which one was most likely to have lung cancer. The results showed that those subjects in the positive affect group spent less time to reach the correct decision and showed greater interest in the case histories by going beyond the assigned task. The authors therefore concluded that mood influenced the subjects' decision-making processes.

2 *The profile characteristics of the health professional.* Factors such as age, sex, weight, geographical location, previous experience and the health professional's own behaviour may also affect the decision-making process. For example, smoking doctors have been shown to spend more time counselling about smoking than their non-smoking counterparts (Stokes and Rigotti 1988). Further, thinner practice nurses have been shown to have different beliefs about obesity and offer different advice to obese patients than overweight practice nurses (Hoppe and Ogden 1997).

In summary, variability in health professionals' behaviour can be understood in terms of the factors involved in the decision-making process. In particular, many factors pre-dating the development of the original hypothesis such as the health professional's own beliefs may contribute to this variability.

COMMUNICATING BELIEFS TO PATIENTS

If health professionals hold their own health-related beliefs, these may be communicated to their patients. This has particularly been studied in the domain of risk communication. A study by McNeil et al. (1982) examined the effects of health professionals' language on the patients' choice of hypothetical treatment. They assessed the effect of offering surgery either if it would 'increase the probability of survival' or would 'decrease the probability of death'. The results showed that patients are more likely to choose surgery if they believed it increased the probability of survival rather than if it decreased the probability of death. The phrasing of such a question would very much reflect the individual beliefs of the doctor, which in turn influence the choices of the patients. Similarly, Senior et al. (2000) explored the impact of framing risk for heart disease or arthritis as either genetic or unspecified using hypothetical scenarios. The results showed that how risk was presented influenced both the participants' ratings of how preventable the illness was and their beliefs about causes. In a similar vein, Misselbrook and Armstrong (2000) asked patients whether they would accept treatment to prevent stroke and presented the effectiveness of this treatment in four different ways. The results showed that although all the forms of presentation were actually the same, 92 per cent of the patients said they would accept the treatment if it reduced their chances of stroke by 45 per cent (relative risk); 75 per cent said they would accept the treatment if it reduced their risk from 1 in 400 to 1 in 700 (absolute risk); 71 per cent said they would accept it if the doctor had to treat 35 patients for 25 years to prevent one stroke (number needed to treat); and only 44 per cent said they would accept it if the treatment had a 3 per cent chance of doing them good and a 97 per cent chance of doing no good or not being needed (personal probability of benefit). Therefore, although the actual risk of the treatment was the same in all four conditions, the ways of presenting the risk varied and this resulted in a variation in patient uptake. Harris and Smith (2005) carried out a similar study but compared absolute risk (high versus low risk) with comparative risk (above average versus below average). They asked participants to read information about deep-vein thrombosis (DVT) and to rate a range of beliefs. Participants were then told to imagine their risk of DVT in either absolute or comparative terms. The results showed that the US sample were more disturbed by absolute risk. A detailed analysis of risk communication can be found in Berry (2004).

However, doctors not only have beliefs about risk but also about illness, which could be communicated to patients. Ogden et al. (2003) used an experimental design to explore the impact of type of diagnosis on patients' beliefs about common problems. Patients were asked to read a vignette in which a person was told either that they had a problem using a medical diagnostic term (tonsillitis/gastroenteritis) or using a lay term (sore throat/stomach upset). The results showed that, although doctors are often being told to use lay language when speaking to patients, patients

BOX 10.2 Some Problems with … Communication Research

Below are some problems with research in this area that you may wish to consider.

1 Research exploring the communication process highlights how health professionals' beliefs relate to their behaviour in terms of diagnosis, management or referral. It is possible, however, that their behaviour also influences their beliefs and that beliefs and behaviour exist in a dynamic relationship.

2 The current emphasis within clinical care is on patient-centredness, shared decision-making and informed decisions. This emphasizes respecting the patient's perspective and understanding the patient's beliefs. However, health professionals also have training and expertise which encourages them to feel they know what is the correct mode of management and the correct way forward. At times these two perspectives can clash. For example, an epileptic patient may believe that they can manage their problem through self-care and the use of alternative medicines. The doctor may disagree and feel that anti-epileptic drugs are the safest option. How these two perspectives can sit alongside each other while enabling the doctor to be both patient-centred and safe is unclear. Sometimes the literature appears to be trying to have it all ways.

3 Research exploring the interaction between health professional and patient uses a variety of methods. Some studies ask each party about the interaction, some record the interaction, some code the interaction and some observe the interaction. All these methods involve a level of interpretation (by the researcher, the health professional or the patient). Trying to access what 'really' goes on in a consulting room is not really possible.

actually preferred the medical labels as it made the symptoms seem more legitimate and gave the patient more confidence in the doctor. In contrast the lay terms made the patients feel more to blame for the problem. Therefore, if a doctor holds particular beliefs about risk or the nature of an illness, and chooses language that reflects these beliefs, then these beliefs may be communicated to the patient in a way that may then influence the patient's own beliefs and their subsequent behaviour.

THE MODERN CONSULTATION

The explanations of variability in health professionals' behaviour presented so far have focused on the health professional in isolation. The educational model emphasizes the knowledge of the health professional and ignores the factors involved in the clinical decision-making process and their health beliefs. This perspective accepts the traditional divide between lay beliefs and professional beliefs. Emphasizing the clinical decision-making processes and health beliefs represents a shift from this perspective and attempts to see the divide between these two types of belief as problematic; health professionals have their own individualized 'lay beliefs' similar to patients. However, this explanation of variability ignores another important factor, namely the patient. Any variability in health professionals' behaviour exists in the context of both the health professional and the patient. Therefore, in order to understand the processes involved in health professional–patient communication, the resulting management decisions and any variability in the outcome of the consultation, both the patient and health professional should be considered as a dyad. The modern consultation involves two individuals and a communication process that exists between them. This shift from an expert model towards an interaction is reflected in the emphasis on patient-centredness, agreement between the health professional and patient and recent concerns about informed choice.

Patient-Centredness

First developed by Byrne and Long in 1976, the concept of patient-centredness has become increasingly in vogue over recent years. The prescriptive literature has recommended patient-centredness as the preferred style of doctor–patient communication as a means to improve patient outcomes (Pendleton et al. 1984; Neighbour 1987; McWhinney 1995). Further, empirical research has explored both the extent to which consultations can be deemed to be patient-centred. For example, in one classic study Tuckett et al. (1985) analysed recorded consultations and described the interaction between doctor and patient as a 'meeting between experts'. Research has also addressed whether patient-centredness is predictive of outcomes such as patient satisfaction, compliance and health status (Savage and Armstrong 1990). Such research has raised questions concerning both the definition of patient-centredness and its assessment, which has resulted in a range of methodological approaches. For example, some studies have used coding frames such as the Stiles Verbal Response Mode System (Stiles 1978) or the Roter Index (Roter et al. 1997) as a means to code whether a particular doctor is behaving in a patient-centred fashion. In contrast, other studies have used interviews with patients and doctors (Tuckett at al. 1985) while some have used behavioural checklists (Byrne and Long 1976). Complicating the matter further, research studies exploring the doctor–patient interaction and the literature proposing a particular form of interaction have used a wide range of different but related terms such as 'shared decision-making' (Elwyn et al. 1999), 'patient participation' (Guadagnoli and Ward 1998) and 'patient partnership' (Coulter 1999).

In general, patient-centredness is considered to consist of three central components:

- A receptiveness by the doctor to the patient's opinions and expectations, and an effort to see the illness through the patient's eyes.
- Patient involvement in the decision-making and planning of treatment.
- An attention to the affective content of the consultation in terms of the emotions of both the patient and the doctor.

This framework is comparable to the six interactive components described by Levenstein et al. (1986) and is apparent in the five key dimensions described by Mead and Bower (2000) in their comprehensive review of the patient-centred literature. Finally, it is explicitly described by Winefield et al. (1996) in their work comparing the effectiveness of different measures. Patient-centredness is now the way in which consultations are supposed to be managed. It emphasizes negotiation between doctor and patient and places the interaction between the two as central. In line with this approach, research has explored the relationship between health professional and patient with an emphasis not on either the health professional or the patient but on the interaction between the two in terms of the level of agreement between health professional and patient and the impact of this agreement on patient outcome.

Agreement between Health Professional and Patient

If health professional–patient communication is seen as an interaction between two individuals, then it is important to understand the extent to which these two individuals speak the same language, share the same beliefs and agree as to the desired content and outcome of any consultation. This is of particular relevance to general practice consultations where patient and health professional perspectives are most likely to coincide. For example, as noted, Tuckett et al. (1985) argued that the consultation should be conceptualized as a 'meeting between experts' and emphasized the importance of the patient's and doctor's potentially different views of the problem. Recent research has examined levels of agreement between GPs' and patients' beliefs about different health problems. Ogden et al. (1999) explored GPs' and patients' models of depression in terms of symptoms (mood and somatic), causes (psychological, medical, external) and treatments (medical and non-medical). The results showed that GPs and patients agreed about the importance of mood-related symptoms, psychological causes and non-medical treatments. However, the GPs reported greater support for somatic symptoms, medical causes and medical treatments. Therefore the results indicated that GPs hold a more medical model of depression than patients. From a similar perspective, Ogden et al. (2001b) explored GPs' and patients' beliefs about obesity. The results showed that the GPs and patients reported similar beliefs for most psychological, behavioural and social causes of obesity. However, they differed consistently in their beliefs about medical causes. In particular, the patients rated a gland/hormone problem, slow metabolism and overall medical causes more highly than did the GPs. For the treatment of obesity, a similar pattern emerged with the two groups reporting similar beliefs for a range of methods, but showing different beliefs about who (GP or patient) was most helpful. Whereas the patients rated the GP as more helpful, the GPs rated the obese patients themselves more highly. Therefore, although GPs seem to have a more medical model of depression, they have a less medical model of obesity. Research has also shown that doctors and patients differ in their beliefs about the role of the doctor (Ogden et al. 1997), about the value of patient-centred consultations (Ogden et al. 2002), about the very nature of health (Ogden et al. 2001), about chronic disease and the role of stress (Heijmans et al. 2001) and in terms of what it is important to know about medicines (Berry et al. 1997). If health professional–patient communication is seen as an interaction, then these studies suggest that it may well be an interaction between two individuals with very different perspectives. Do these different perspectives influence patient outcomes?

The Role of Agreement in Patient Outcomes

If doctors and patients have different beliefs about illness, different beliefs about the role of the doctor and about medicines, does this lack of agreement relate to patient outcomes? It is possible that such disagreement may result in poor compliance to medication ('Why should I take anti-depressants if I am not depressed?'), poor compliance to any recommended changes in behaviour ('Why should I eat less if obesity is caused by hormones?') or low satisfaction with the consultation ('I wanted emotional support and the GP gave me a prescription'). To date little research has explored these possibilities. One study did, however, examine the extent to which a patient's expectations of a GP consultation were met by the GP and whether this predicted patient satisfaction. Williams et al. (1995) asked 504 general practice patients to complete a measure of their expectations of the consultation with their GP prior to it taking place and a measure of whether their expectations were actually met afterwards. The results showed that having more expectations met was related to a higher level of satisfaction with the consultation. However, this study did not explore compliance, nor did it examine whether the GP and patient had a shared belief about the nature of the consultation.

Informed Choice

Gaining informed consent has become a central requirement for any research study or clinical intervention and aims to ensure that the participants have understood what they are about to take part in and any side-effects that it might have. Informed consent can be either written or verbal depending on the nature of the study and is an essential requirement for gaining ethical approval. Medical councils across the world stipulate that patients must be given sufficient information to enable them to consent to any procedure in an informed way. Informed consent therefore relates to a formal process prior to research or clinical work. Within health psychology, researchers have also focused on informed choice and informed decision-making, although defining the differences between these is often difficult. It is generally agreed that an informed decision is one that is made effectively but whether effectiveness relates to evaluations of the final choice (i.e. the outcome) or the way in which the decision is made (i.e. the process) is unclear. Bekker (2003) provides a good analysis of these two different perspectives and highlights the theoretical positions that inform the emphasis on either outcome or process.

- *Outcome.* Bekker (2003) describes how the emphasis on outcome reflects classical decision or rational choice theory which suggests that a choice can be deemed effective if it conforms to expected utility theory. This means that a choice is effective if the individual has surveyed all the decision options, evaluated the consequences of each option in terms of likelihood (i.e. the expected probability of the consequences occurring), assessed the attractiveness of the outcome of each option (utility) and then created an 'expected utility' value for each option by combining the likelihood of consequence (expected probability) and attractiveness (utility) and then choosing the option that has the greatest expected utility. This approach therefore emphasizes the outcome of a decision. The problem is that most decisions are not made in this rational way and so would be judged to be ineffective decisions. Further, it is possible that even if the individual were to be so rational, they may be basing their decisions on inaccurate information. If this were to occur, the decision(s) would be deemed effective but the final decision would be incomplete.

- *Process.* In contrast to this approach is one that emphasizes process. Bekker (2003) argues that this approach is informed by reasoned choice models which suggest that an effective decision is one that has met three criteria in terms of the process used to make the decision. These criteria are: the decision is based on information about the alternatives and their consequences; the likelihood and desirability of the consequences are evaluated accurately; a trade-off between these factors is evident. Further, central to this approach is a role for the individual's own beliefs as the evaluation of the consequences and desirability of the options takes place in the context of any existing values or beliefs.

Adding Behaviour

O'Connor and O'Brien-Pallas (1989) take a process approach to informed choice but also add in the individual's behaviour. They describe an effective decision as one that is informed, consistent with the decision-maker's values and then behaviourally implemented.

Measuring Informed Choice

As a means to assess informed choice Marteau et al. (2001) developed a new measure of informed choice which was based upon O'Connor and O'Brien-Pallas's definition and included measures of knowledge, attitudes and behaviour. They argued that when these three components are consistent with each other, then the person can be deemed to have made an informed choice. There are therefore different ways of defining informed choice and informed decision-making. To date, however, there remains no consensus as to the nature of informed choice or decision-making although these terms are still widely used and regarded as essential to the research and clinical process.

The medical consultation is at the heart of most interactions between the patient and the health care system. Traditional models of the consultation regarded the doctor as the expert and the patient as a passive recipient of this expertise who simply responded to what the doctor said. Doctors, however, vary in their decisions and behaviours more than this model would allow for, suggesting a role for other factors in their decision-making processes. Research has therefore explored clinical decision-making as a form of problem-solving and has highlighted a role for health professionals' own beliefs, behaviours, past experiences and mood. Nowadays the modern consultation is seen much more as a meeting between experts and the emphasis is on patient-centred care, shared decision-making and a level of agreement between doctor and patient. It also highlights a role for patient autonomy which is reflected in the notion of informed choice. The consultation has therefore changed enormously in the past 100 years. But one issue that still remains a problem for the medical world is that of adherence. However much medical advances improve the effectiveness of medical care, it cannot work is patients don't behave in ways that doctors would like.

ADHERENCE

In 1987, HIV was a terrifying, acute and fatal illness and many people who were infected died within a couple of years. Nowadays, in the West, it is regarded as a chronic illness and people have survived for over 20 years. In the main, this is due to medical advances and the development of HAART (see p. 375). In Africa the picture is completely different as people do not have the same access to treatment that we do (see Figures 2.13 and 2.14, p. 25). They are desperate for medicines. Yet people in the West who are prescribed their treatment don't always take it. From the outside this non-adherence seems inexplicable. Why would people not take a drug that can stop them from dying? But this is the very essence of research on adherence. Medicine invents treatments that research shows can prevent illness, manage illness and cure illness, yet the people with the illnesses do not take the medicines as prescribed. This section explores definitions of adherence, measuring adherence, why adherence is important, models of adherence, predictors of adherence and how adherence can be changed.

DEFINING ADHERENCE

The concept of adherence used to be referred to as 'compliance', which was defined by Haynes et al. (1979) as 'the extent to which the patient's behaviour (in terms of taking medications, following diets or other lifestyle changes) coincides with medical or health advice'. Compliance excited an enormous amount of clinical and academic interest and it was calculated that 3,200 articles on compliance in English were listed between 1979 and 1985 (Trostle 1988). The term 'compliance', however, was deemed too paternalistic and was seen to relate to a more traditional model of the consultation with the doctor as expert and the patient as a passive recipient of this expertise who wasn't doing as they were told. The term 'adherence' was therefore introduced in the 1990s as a means to encapsulate a more active and empowered patient and most research nowadays uses this term. Adherence has been defined as the extent to which a patient's behaviour matches agreed recommendations from their health professional (Horne 2006; NICE 2009). Although this appears similar to the notion of compliance the terms 'agreed', and 'recommendations' illustrate a shift in perspective away from a paternalistic doctor towards one who negotiates and agrees management plans with their patient. This is in line with ideas of patient-centredness and shared decision-making. Adherence is mostly explored in the context of medication-taking and the extent to which patients take their drugs as recommended. It also, however, relates to other behaviours such as smoking, dietary change and exercise, if these are what the doctor has recommended. As a means to understand why people do not adhere, researchers have further defined non-adherence as being either 'unintentional non-adherence' which occurs when an individual simply forgets or has misunderstood the instructions and 'intentional non-adherence' which describes those times when a patient chooses not to take their medicine or engage in a risk-reducing behaviour. As mentioned in earlier chapters, an obesity drug called orlistat causes unpleasant side-effects (anal leakage and oily stools) if taken with fatty foods. People therefore often have 'drug holidays' to enable them to have a meal out every now and again. This is a form of intentional non-adherence.

MEASURING ADHERENCE

Before any construct can be measured it needs to be clearly operationalized and adherence is particularly difficult for two key reasons. First, self-reported adherence may be inaccurate due to issues such as memory, social desirability and the wish to be prescribed further medicines in the future ('I can't remember whether I took my pills last Wednesday', 'If I tell them I didn't take my medication as I wanted a break, then they might not give me any more'). Second, the behaviour itself can be highly complex. For example, recommended medication-taking may involve instructions about time of day, amount, whether with or with food, number of days or legitimate reasons for not taking the medication such as illness or side-effects. Deciding whether or not a patient has been adherent therefore requires a decision on whether they need to meet all, some or most of these recommended criteria. For example, a patient could be told to take two pills, four times a day for seven days. But if they miss a day and then take them all the next day is this adherence or not? Measures of adherence are broadly objective or subjective with each having their strengths and weaknesses. Horne and Clatworthy (2010) provide a detailed analysis of measurement which is summarized as follows:

Objective measures

- *Observation:* researchers/clinicians can directly observe how many pills a patient takes. This is accurate but time-consuming and not always feasible.

- *Blood or urine samples:* these can be taken to assess blood levels of the drug. This is objective but costly, time-consuming and varies according to how drugs are metabolized by different individuals.

- *Pill counting:* patients are asked to bring their remaining pills in to be counted. This requires face-to-face meetings which are time-consuming and inconvenient and patients may throw away pills in order to appear adherent.

- *Electronic monitors:* pill bottles can contain a computer chip to record each time the bottle is opened. This can provide detailed information about drug-taking. But it assumes that a pill is taken each time the bottle is opened and is expensive.

- *Assessing prescriptions:* records can be made of when patients ask for new prescriptions. This assumes that patients have taken the used pills and that they ask for a new prescription exactly when they have run out.

Subjective measures

- *Self-report:* patients can rate their own adherence either during an interview or using a questionnaire. This is inexpensive and simple but may be contaminated by recall problems and social desirability. It is possible to 'normalize' non-adherence as a means to reduce social desirability but this may in fact promote non-adherence. A commonly used self-report measure is the Medication Adherence Report Scale (MAARS, Horne and Weinman 2002).

WHY IS ADHERENCE IMPORTANT?

Adherence is considered to be important primarily because following the recommendations of health professionals is believed essential to patient recovery. For example, DiMatteo et al. (2002) reviewed 63 studies of adherence to a wide range of recommendations (e.g. medication, diet, physical activity) and concluded that the odds of having a good treatment were three times higher in those that showed good adherence. Similarly, Simpson et al. (2006) reported that the odds of dying were halved if people took their medication. Interestingly they also showed an adherence effect whereby adherence, regardless of whether it was to an active drug or a placebo, also halved the odds of dying. This is discussed further in the section on placebos in Chapter 13. Adherence is therefore related to health outcomes. Yet studies estimate that about half of the patients with chronic illnesses, such as diabetes and hypertension, are non-adherent with their medication regimens and that even adherence for a behaviour as apparently simple as using an inhaler for asthma is poor (e.g. Dekker et al. 1992). In addition, the WHO (2003) estimated that about a third of all prescribed drugs are not taken as directed. This also has cost implications as money is wasted when drugs are prescribed, prescriptions are cashed, but the drugs not taken. In the UK this has been estimated at about £4 billion per year (NICE 2009).

MODELS OF ADHERENCE

Researchers have developed models as a means to understand, predict and possibly change adherence.

Cognitive Hypothesis Model

An early model of adherence was developed by Ley (1989) who described a cognitive hypothesis model of compliance (as it was then). This model is illustrated in Figure 10.7.

From this model it was predicted that a patient would adhere to their doctor's recommendations if they understood these recommendations, could recall the instructions and were satisfied with the consultation.

The Perceptions and Practicalities Approach

From a different perspective Horne (2001) developed a model of adherence that emphasized perceptions and practicalities of adherence and focused on the predictors of unintentional non-adherence and intentional non-adherence. From this perspective adherence is seen as relating to motivation ('I want to get well') and resources ('I have access to my pills') and perceptual barriers ('My medicine isn't really necessary') and practical barriers ('I can't get to the pharmacist') are deemed to prevent adherence from happening. This model is shown in Figure 10.8.

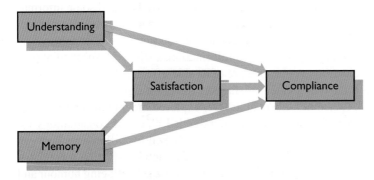

FIGURE 10.7

Ley's cognitive hypothesis model of compliance

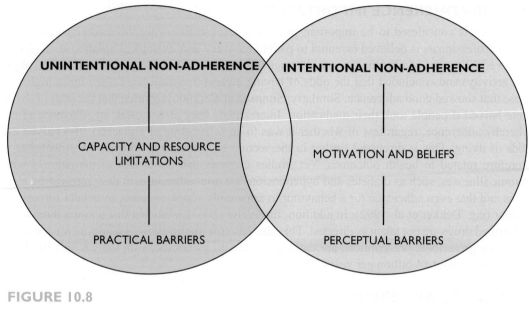

FIGURE 10.8

The perceptions and practicalities approach

SOURCE: Horne (2001)

These two models provide a different structure for understanding adherence. However, there are several similarities in terms of the constructs used. These will now be explored in terms of the predictors of adherence.

PREDICTORS OF ADHERENCE

The models described above highlight a number of factors that may predict adherence. Some of these remain to be tested explicitly whereas others are more evidence-based.

Patient Satisfaction

Ley (1988) examined the extent of patient satisfaction with the consultation. He reviewed 21 studies of hospital patients and found that 41 per cent of patients were dissatisfied with their treatment and that 28 per cent of general practice patients were also dissatisfied. Ley also reported that satisfaction is determined by the content of the consultation and that patients want to know as much information as possible, even if this is bad news. For example, in studies looking at cancer diagnosis, patients showed improved satisfaction if they were given a diagnosis of cancer rather than if they were protected from this information. Berry et al. (2003) explored the impact on satisfaction of making information more personal to the patient. Participants were asked to read some information about medication and then to rate their satisfaction. Some were given personalized information, such as 'If you take this medicine, there is a substantial chance of you getting one or more of its side-effects', whereas some were given non-personalized information, such as 'A substantial proportion of people who take this medication get one or more of its side-effects'. The results showed that a more personalized style was related to greater satisfaction, lower ratings of the risks of side-effects and lower ratings of the risk to health. Sala et al. (2002) explored the relationship between humour in consultations and patient satisfaction. The authors coded recorded consultations for their humour content and for the type of humour used. They then looked for differences between high and low satisfaction-rated consultations. The results showed that high satisfaction was related to the use of more light humour, more humour that relieved tension, more self-effacing humour and more positive-function humour. Patient satisfaction therefore relates to a range of professional and patient variables and is increasingly used in health care assessment as an indirect measure of health outcome based on the assumption that a satisfied patient will be a healthier patient. It is possible that in line with Ley's model increased satisfaction may predict increased adherence.

Patient Understanding

Several studies have also examined the extent to which patients understand the content of the consultation. Boyle (1970) examined patients' beliefs about the location of organs and found that only 44 per cent correctly located the heart, 20 per cent located the stomach. 42 per cent located the kidneys and 49 per cent located the liver. Forty years after this original study, Weinman et al. (2009) assessed whether understanding was still as poor in a large sample of 776 patients and members of the general public (see Figure 10.9).

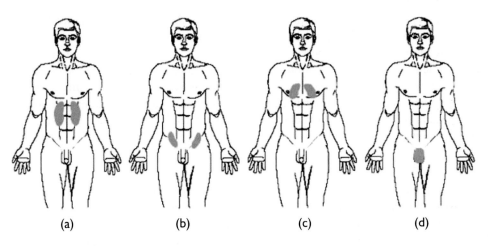

FIGURE 10.9

Assessing anatomical knowledge

SOURCE: Weinman et al. (2009)

The results showed no significant improvements since the earlier study and that knowledge got worse the older the participant. If the doctor gives advice to the patient or suggests that they follow a particular treatment programme and the patient does not understand the causes of their illness, the correct location of the relevant organ or the processes involved in the treatment, then this lack of understanding is likely to affect their compliance with the advice.

Patients' Recall

Researchers also examined the process of recall of the information given during the consultation. Bain (1977) examined the recall from a sample of patients who had attended a GP consultation and found that 37 per cent could not recall the name of the drug, 23 per cent could not recall the frequency of the dose and 25 per cent could not recall the duration of the treatment. A further study by Crichton et al. (1978) found that 22 per cent of patients had forgotten the treatment regime recommended by their doctors. In a meta-analysis of the research into recall of consultation information, Ley (1989) found that recall is influenced by a multitude of factors. For example, Ley argued that the greater the anxiety, medical knowledge, intellectual level, importance of the statement, primacy effect and number of statements all increase recall. However, he concluded that recall is not influenced by the age of the patient, which is contrary to some predictions of the effect of ageing on memory and some of the myths and counter-myths of the ageing process. Recalling information after the consultation may be related to compliance.

Beliefs About the Illness

Research shows that patients hold beliefs about their illness and that these consistently relate to key dimensions of cause, consequences, time line, control and identity (see Chapter 9 for a discussion of illness cognitions). In addition, research indicates that these beliefs predict adherence. For example, Halm et al. (2006) explored 198 asthmatics' beliefs about their problem, their perception of symptoms and their adherence to medication. The results showed that those who believed they only had asthma when they had symptoms (the 'acute asthma belief') showed lower levels of adherence. Similarly, Brewer et al. (2002) examined the relationship between illness cognitions and adherence to medication in patients with hypercholesterolaemia (involving very high cholesterol). The results showed that a belief that the illness has serious consequences was related to medication adherence.

Beliefs About the Behaviour

People also hold beliefs about their health-related behaviours and within the framework of social cognition models adherence can be predicted by beliefs about the costs and benefits of taking medication, perceptions of risk for illness, self-efficacy for taking drugs, the norms of those around the patient and their attitudes to medication. Norman et al. (2003) used PMT to predict children's adherence to wearing an eye patch. Parents of children diagnosed with eye problems completed a baseline questionnaire concerning their beliefs and described their child's adherence after two months. The results showed that higher adherence was predicted by greater perceived susceptibility and lower response costs.

Beliefs About Medication

One area of research that has received much attention over the past few years is the specific beliefs that people have about their medication. Horne (1997) identified two key sets of beliefs labelled 'necessity' beliefs '('How much do I need this medicine?') and 'concerns' beliefs ('I worry about side-effects'). This has been called the necessity/concerns framework (NCF) (Horne 1997; Horne and Weinman 2002) and research indicates that beliefs about necessity and concerns are good predictors of adherence in the context of illnesses such as asthma (Horne and Weinman 2002); diabetes, cancer and CHD (Horne and Weinman 1999); HIV/AIDS (Horne et al. 2007) and rheumatoid arthritis (Neame and Hammond 2005). Therefore the lower the beliefs about necessity and the higher the beliefs about concern, the lower the levels of adherence.

Adherence to medication may therefore be predicted by a number of variables. Some of these such as patient satisfaction, recall and understanding are central to Ley's cognitive hypothesis model and others find reflection in Horne's perceptions and practicalities approach and research on health and illness beliefs. Understanding the predictors of adherence is a step towards improving adherence.

HOW CAN ADHERENCE BE IMPROVED?

Adherence is considered essential to patient well-being. Studies have therefore explored how adherence can be improved with a focus on information-giving to improve recall and changing cognitions and emotions.

The Role of Information

Researchers have examined the role and the type of information used to improve patient adherence. Using a meta-analysis, Mullen et al. (1985) found that 64 per cent of patients were more adherent when using instructional and educational information. Haynes (1982) reported that information could improve adherence from 52 to 66 per cent. Information-giving could improve adherence in the following ways.

Oral Information

Ley (1989) suggested that oral information can improve adherence in the following ways by facilitating understanding and recall:

- Primacy effect – patients have a tendency to remember the first thing they are told.
- Stressing the importance of adherence.
- Simplifying the information.
- Using repetition.
- Being specific.
- Following up the consultation with additional interviews.

Written Information

Researchers also looked at the use of written information in improving adherence. Ley and Morris (1984) examined the effect of written information about medication and found that it increased knowledge in 90 per cent of the studies, increased compliance in 60 per cent of the studies and improved outcome in 57 per cent of the studies. Interventions have therefore explored the role of information-giving in improving adherence and suggestions have been to made to make information clearer and easier to remember. However, Haynes et al. (2002) concluded from their review of the literature that although information-based interventions can improve adherence for short-term regimens (less or equal to two weeks), more complex interventions are needed for longer-term medication taking. Similarly, Kripalini et al. (2007) carried out a systematic review of interventions to improve medication adherence in chronic conditions and concluded that although good information is important, it is not sufficient to improve adherence.

Changing Beliefs and Emotions

Because knowledge is not enough to improve adherence, research has turned its focus onto changing cognitions and emotions. This is in line with the interventions to change other health-related behaviours described in Chapter 8. It can involve behavioural strategies such as reinforcement, incentives or modelling, social cognition theory-based interventions such as implementation intentions or the use of stage models and motivational interviewing. Haynes et al. (2002) carried out a review of 33 randomized controlled trials design to improve medication adherence for a range of psychiatric (e.g. depression, psychosis) or chronic medical conditions (e.g. hypertension, asthma, HIV/AIDs). The interventions included counselling, education, family systems therapy, self-monitoring, face-to-face consultations, group sessions and behaviour therapy. Although their review included a diverse number of problems and interventions, they concluded that 49 per cent of the studies reported significant improvements in medication adherence and that the most effective used the most complex interventions involving a combination of all forms of behaviour modification strategy. However, even the most effective still showed modest results.

Adherence is important as appropriate medicine-taking is believed to be a core part of effective treatment and non-adherence has both health and cost implications. Over the past few decades the term 'compliance' has been replaced with 'adherence' as a means to reflect a more empowered model of the patient and a less paternalistic model of the doctor. In line with most behaviours, adherence is difficult to measure due to problems of social desirability and recall for subjective measures and cost and time for more objective measures. Research, however, has identified possible predictors of adherence with a focus on patient satisfaction, understanding, recall and beliefs relating to behaviour, illness and a patient's treatment regimen. Research has also explored ways in which adherence can be improved, drawing upon a range of intervention strategies, although, in line with all attempts at behaviour change, short-term changes seem easier to create compared to changes in the longer term.

TO CONCLUDE

Accessing health care involves a number of different pathways to the doctor. The patient then encounters a health professional, usually within primary care, who makes a diagnosis and decides how to manage their problem. The patient can then choose whether or not to follow this advice. This chapter has explored this process in terms of help-seeking and delay whereby the patient is responsible for their first point of contact with health care, or screening, which involves the patient being asked to attend. The chapter then described the medical consultation in terms of the changing nature of interaction with health professionals, how doctors make decisions and the role of their health beliefs. Finally the chapter described the issue of adherence and how this can be predicted or improved.

QUESTIONS

1 Why do some people seek help for seemingly minor problems?
2 Why do some people delay seeking help for serious problems?
3 What are the costs and benefits of a screening programme?
4 To what extent is a medical diagnosis based upon knowledge and expertise?
5 Discuss the role of health professionals' beliefs in the communication process.
6 Consider the problems inherent in determining whether someone has made an informed choice.
7 Health professionals should attempt to respect and share the beliefs of their patients. Discuss.
8 Patients should be made to adhere to their medication regimen. Discuss.
9 What factors influence whether or not a patient takes their medicine?

FOR DISCUSSION

Consider the last time you had contact with a health professional (e.g. doctor, dentist, nurse, etc.). Discuss why you went to the doctor and how the health professional's health beliefs may have influenced how they decided to manage you.

ASSUMPTIONS IN HEALTH PSYCHOLOGY

Some of the research cited in this chapter illustrates the kinds of assumptions that underlie the study of accessing and using health care and also provides insights into the assumptions of health psychology.

1 *The mind–body split.* Health psychology attempts to challenge the biomedical model of health and illness. This involves challenging biomedical assumptions such as the mind–body split. However, perhaps by emphasizing the mind (attitudes, cognitions, beliefs) as a separate entity, the mind–body split is not challenged but reinforced.

2 *Biomedical outcomes.* Challenging the biomedical model also involves questioning some of the outcomes used by medicine. For example, appropriate help-seeking, adherence with recommendations for drug-taking, accuracy of recall, and following advice are all established desired outcomes. Health psychology accepts these outcomes by examining ways in which doctor–patient communication can be improved, patient and doctor variability can be understood and reduced, and adherence can be promoted. However, again, accepting these outcomes as legitimate is also a way of supporting biomedicine. Perhaps variability is acceptable. Perhaps inaccuracy of recall sums up what happens in communication (psychologists who study memory would argue that memory is the only process that is defined by its failures – memory is about reconstruction). Even though psychology adds to a biomedical model, by accepting the same outcomes, it does not challenge it.

3 *Adding the social context.* Individuals exist within a social world and yet health psychology often misses out this world. An emphasis on the interaction between health professionals and patients represents an attempt to examine the cognitions of both these groups in the context of each other (the relationship context). However, this interaction is still accessed through an individual's beliefs. Is asking someone about the interaction actually examining the interaction or is it examining their cognitions about the interaction?

FURTHER READING

Berry, D. (2004) *Risk, Communication and Health Psychology.* Maidenhead: Open University Press. The communication of risk is a central part of many consultations. This book provides a comprehensive overview of research on risk communication.

Marteau, T.M. and Johnston, M. (1990) Health professionals: a source of variance in health outcomes, *Psychology and Health*, 5: 47–58.

This is quite an old paper now but it set the scene for much psychological research in the area of health professional behaviour. It examines the different models of health professionals' behaviour and emphasizes the role of health professionals' health beliefs.

Marteau, T.M. and Weinman, J. (2006) Self-regulation and the behavioural response to DNA risk information: a theoretical analysis and framework for future research, *Social Science and Medicine*, 62: 1360–8.

This is an interesting theoretical paper which describes existing research on reactions to DNA risk information and illustrates how these reactions can be understood within a self-regulatory model. In particular it highlights the importance of a 'fit' between existing cognitive representations of the problem and any new information.

Tuckett, D., Boulton, M., Olson, C. and Williams, A. (1985) *Meetings Between Experts*. London: Tavistock.

This is a classic book which describes a study involving consultation analysis. It set the scene for much subsequent research and shifted the emphasis from doctor as expert to seeing the consultation as an interaction.

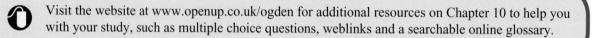

Visit the website at www.openup.co.uk/ogden for additional resources on Chapter 10 to help you with your study, such as multiple choice questions, weblinks and a searchable online glossary.

11 Stress

© Fitjoe/iStock

CHAPTER OVERVIEW

This chapter examines definitions of stress and looks at the early models of stress in terms of the fight/flight response, the general adaptation syndrome and life events theory. It then describes the concept of appraisal and Lazarus's transactional model of stress which emphasizes psychology as central to eliciting a stress response. The chapter then describes the physiological model of stress and explores the impact of stress on changes in physiological factors such as arousal and cortisol production. Finally, it describes how stress has been measured both in the laboratory and in a more naturalistic setting and compares physiological and self-report measurement approaches.

WHAT IS STRESS?

The term 'stress' means many things to many different people. A layperson may define stress in terms of pressure, tension, unpleasant external forces or an emotional response. Psychologists have defined stress in a variety of different ways. Contemporary definitions regard stress from the external environmental as a stressor (e.g. problems at work), the response to the stressor as stress or distress (e.g. the feeling of tension), and the concept of stress as something that involves biochemical, physiological, behavioural and psychological changes. Researchers have also differentiated between stress that is harmful and damaging (distress) and stress that is positive and beneficial (eustress). In addition, researchers differentiate between acute stress, such as an exam or having to give a public talk, and chronic stress, such as job stress and poverty. The most commonly used definition of stress was developed by Lazarus and Launier (1978), who regarded stress as a transaction between people and the environment and described stress in terms of 'person–environment fit'. If a person is faced with a potentially difficult stressor such as an exam or having to give a public talk, the degree of stress they experience is determined first by their appraisal of the event ('Is it stressful?') and second by their appraisal of their own personal resources ('Will I cope?'). A good person–environment fit results in no or low stress and a poor fit results in higher stress.

Stress involves a person–environment fit: What is stressful to one person may not be to another

THE DEVELOPMENT OF STRESS MODELS

Over the past few decades, models of stress have varied in terms of their definition of stress, their differing emphasis on physiological and psychological factors, and their description of the relationship between individuals and their environment.

CANNON'S FIGHT-OR-FLIGHT MODEL

One of the earliest models of stress was developed by Cannon (1932). This was called the fight-or-flight model of stress, which suggested that external threats elicited the fight-or-flight response involving an increased activity rate and increased arousal. He suggested that these physiological changes enabled the individual to either escape from the source of stress or fight. Within Cannon's model, stress was defined as a response to external stressors, which was predominantly seen as physiological. Cannon considered stress to be an adaptive response as it enabled the individual to manage a stressful event. However, he also recognized that prolonged stress could result in medical problems.

SELYE'S GENERAL ADAPTATION SYNDROME

Selye's general adaptation syndrome (GAS) was developed in 1956 and described three stages in the stress process (Selye 1956). The initial stage was called the 'alarm' stage, which described an increase in activity, and occurred as soon as the individual was exposed to a stressful situation. The second stage was called 'resistance', which involved coping and attempts to reverse the effects of the alarm stage. The third stage was called 'exhaustion', which was reached when the individual had been repeatedly exposed to the stressful situation and was incapable of showing further resistance. This model is shown in Figure 11.1.

PROBLEMS WITH THE CANNON AND SELYE MODELS

Cannon's early fight/flight model and Selye's GAS laid important foundations for stress research. However, there are problems with them:

1 Both regarded the individual as automatically responding to an external stressor and described stress within a straightforward stimulus–response framework. They therefore did not address the issue of individual variability and psychological factors were given only a minimal role. For example, while an exam could be seen as stressful for one person, it might be seen as an opportunity to shine to another.

2 Both also described the physiological response to stress as consistent. This response is seen as non-specific in that the changes in physiology are the same regardless of the nature of the stressor. This is reflected in the use of the term 'arousal' which has been criticized by more recent researchers. Therefore these two models described individuals as passive and as responding automatically to their external world.

LIFE EVENTS THEORY

In an attempt to depart from both the Selye and Cannon models of stress, which emphasized physiological changes, life events theory was developed to examine stress and stress-related changes

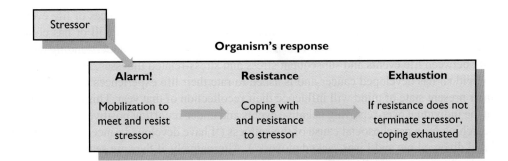

FIGURE 11.1

Selye's (1956) three-stage general adaptation syndrome (GAS)

as a response to life experiences. Holmes and Rahe (1967) developed the Schedule of Recent Experiences (SRE), which provided respondents with an extensive list of possible life changes or life events. These ranged in supposed objective severity from events such as 'death of a spouse', 'death of a close family member' and 'jail term', to more moderate events such as 'son or daughter leaving home' and 'pregnancy', to minor events such as 'vacation', 'change in eating habits', 'change in sleeping habits' and 'change in number of family get-togethers'. Originally the SRE was scored by simply counting the number of actual recent experiences. For example, someone who had experienced both the death of a spouse and the death of a close family member would receive the same score as someone who had recently had two holidays. It was assumed that this score reflected an indication of their level of stress. Early research using the SRE in this way showed some links between individuals' SRE score and their health status. However, this obviously crude method of measurement was later replaced by a variety of others, including a weighting system whereby each potential life event was weighted by a panel, creating a degree of differentiation between the different life experiences. A recent longitudinal study explored the impact of life events on mortality at 17 years follow-up (Phillips et al. 2008). Participants were 968 Scottish men and women aged 56 years old who completed measures of stressful life events for the preceding 2 years at baseline, then after 8 or 9 years and then at 11/13 years. By 17 years 266 participants had died. The results showed that when sex, occupational status, smoking, body mass index (BMI) and systolic blood pressure were controlled for the number of health-related life events, the stress load they imposed (not health *un*related life events) was strongly predictive of mortality.

PROBLEMS WITH LIFE EVENTS THEORY

The use of the SRE and similar measures of life experiences have been criticized for the following reasons:

1 *The individual's own rating of the event is important.* It has been argued by many researchers that life experiences should not be seen as either objectively stressful or benign, but that this interpretation of the event should be left to the individual. For example, a divorce for one individual may be regarded as extremely upsetting, whereas for another it may be a relief from an unpleasant situation. Pilkonis et al. (1985) gave checklists of life events to a group of subjects to complete and also interviewed them about these experiences. They reported that a useful means of assessing the potential impact of life events is to evaluate the individual's own ratings of the life experience in terms of: (1) the desirability of the event (was the event regarded as positive or negative?); (2) how much control they had over the event (was the outcome of the event determined by the individual or others?); and (3) the degree of required adjustment following the event. This methodology would enable the individual's own evaluation of the events to be taken into consideration.

2 *The problem of retrospective assessment.* Most ratings of life experiences or life events are completed retrospectively, at the time when the individual has become ill or has come into contact with the health profession. This has obvious implications for understanding the causal link between life events and subsequent stress and stress-related illnesses. For example, if an individual has developed cancer and is asked to rate their life experiences over the last year, their present state of mind will influence their recollection of that year. This effect may result in the individual over-reporting negative events and under-reporting positive events if they are searching for a psychosocial cause of their illness ('I have developed cancer because my husband divorced me and I was sacked at work'). Alternatively, if they are searching for a more medical cause of their illness they may under-report negative life events ('I developed cancer because it is a family weakness; my lifestyle and experiences are unrelated as I have had an uneventful year'). The relationship between self-reports of life events and causal models of

illness is an interesting area of research. Research projects could select to use this problem of selective recall as a focus for analysis. However, this influence of an individual's present state of health on their retrospective ratings undermines attempts at causally relating life events to illness onset.

3 *Life experiences may interact with each other.* When individuals are asked to complete a checklist of their recent life experiences, these experiences are regarded as independent of each other. For example, a divorce, a change of job and a marriage would be regarded as an accumulation of life events that together would contribute to a stressful period of time. However, one event may counter the effects of another and cancel out any negative stressful consequences. Evaluating the potential effects of life experiences should include an assessment of any interactions between events.

4 *What is the outcome of a series of life experiences?* Originally, the SRE was developed to assess the relationship between stressful life experiences and health status. Accordingly, it was assumed that if the life experiences were indeed stressful then the appropriate outcome measure was one of health status. The most straightforward measure of health status would be a diagnosis of illness such as cancer, heart attack or hypertension. Within this framework, a simple correlational analysis could be carried out to evaluate whether a greater number of life experiences correlated with a medical diagnosis. Apart from the problems with retrospective recall and so on, this would allow some measure of causality – subjects with higher numbers of life events would be more likely to get a medical diagnosis. However, such an outcome measure is restrictive, as it ignores lesser 'illnesses' and relies on an intervention by the medical profession to provide the diagnosis. In addition, it also ignores the role of the diagnosis as a life event in itself. An alternative outcome measure would be to evaluate symptoms. Therefore the individual could be asked to rate not only their life experiences but also their health-related symptoms (e.g. pain, tiredness, loss of appetite, etc.). Within this framework, correlational analysis could examine the relationship between life events and symptoms. However, this outcome measure has its own problems: is 'a change in eating habits' a life event or a symptom of a life event? Is 'a change in sleeping habits' a stressor or a consequence of stress? Choosing the appropriate outcome measure for assessing the effects of life events on health is therefore problematic.

5 *Stressors may be short term or ongoing.* Traditionally, assessments of life experiences have conceptualized such life events as short-term experiences. However, many events may be ongoing and chronic. Moos and Swindle (1990) identified domains of ongoing stressors, which they suggested reflect chronic forms of life experiences:

- physical health stressors (e.g. medical conditions)
- home and neighbourhood stressors (e.g. safety, cleanliness)
- financial stressors
- work stressors (e.g. interpersonal problems, high pressure)
- spouse/partner stressors (e.g. emotional problems with partner)
- child stressors
- extended family stressors
- friend stressors.

They incorporated these factors into their measure – the Life Stressors and Social Resources Inventory (LISRES) – which represented an attempt to emphasize the chronic nature of life experiences and to place them within the context of the individual's coping resources. Moos and Swindle argued that life events should not be evaluated in isolation but should be integrated into two facets of an individual's life: their ongoing social resources (e.g. social support networks, financial resources) and their ongoing stressors.

A ROLE FOR PSYCHOLOGICAL FACTORS IN STRESS

Both Cannon's and Selye's early models of stress conceptualized stress as an automatic response to an external stressor. This perspective is also reflected in versions of life events theory, which suggests that individuals respond to life experiences with a stress response that is therefore related to their health status. However, the above criticisms of life events theory suggest a different approach to stress, an approach that includes an individual who no longer simply passively *responds* to stressors but actively *interacts* with them. This approach to stress provides a role for an individual's psychological state and is epitomized by Lazarus's transactional model of stress and his theory of appraisal.

THE TRANSACTIONAL MODEL OF STRESS
THE ROLE OF APPRAISAL

In the 1970s, Lazarus's work on stress introduced psychology to understanding the stress response (Lazarus and Cohen 1973; Lazarus 1975; Lazarus and Folkman 1987). This role for psychology took the form of his concept of *appraisal*. Lazarus argued that stress involved a transaction between the individual and their external world, and that a stress response was elicited if the individual appraised a potentially stressful event as actually being stressful. Lazarus's model therefore described individuals as psychological beings who appraised the outside world, rather than simply passively responding to it. Lazarus defined two forms of appraisal: primary and secondary. According to Lazarus, the individual initially appraises the event itself – defined as *primary appraisal*. There are four possible ways that the event can be appraised: (1) irrelevant; (2) benign and positive; (3) harmful and a threat; (4) harmful and a challenge. Lazarus then described *secondary appraisal*, which involves the individual evaluating the pros and cons of their different coping strategies. Therefore primary appraisal involves an appraisal of the outside world and secondary appraisal involves an appraisal of the individual themselves. This model is shown in Figure 11.2.

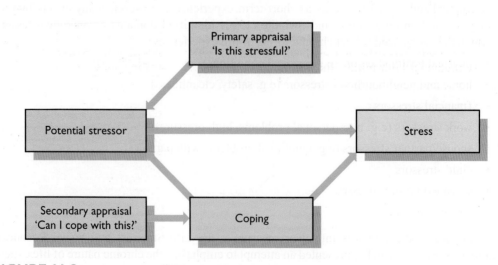

FIGURE 11.2

The role of appraisal in stress

The form of the primary and secondary appraisals determines whether the individual shows a stress response or not. According to Lazarus's model this stress response can take different forms: (1) direct action; (2) seeking information; (3) doing nothing; or (4) developing a means of coping with the stress in terms of relaxation or defence mechanisms.

Lazarus's model of appraisal and the transaction between the individual and the environment indicated a novel way of looking at the stress response – the individual no longer passively responded to their external world, but interacted with it.

DOES APPRAISAL INFLUENCE THE STRESS RESPONSE?

Several studies have examined the effect of appraisal on stress and have evaluated the role of the psychological state of the individual on their stress response. In an early study by Speisman et al. (1964), subjects were shown a film depicting an initiation ceremony involving unpleasant genital surgery. The film was shown with three different soundtracks. In condition 1, the trauma condition, the soundtrack emphasized the pain and the mutilation. In condition 2, the denial condition, the soundtrack showed the participants as being willing and happy. In condition 3, the intellectualization condition, the soundtrack gave an anthropological interpretation of the ceremony. The study therefore manipulated the subjects' appraisal of the situation and evaluated the effect of the type of appraisal on their stress response. The results showed that subjects reported that the trauma condition was most stressful. This suggests that it is not the events themselves that elicit stress, but the individuals' interpretation or appraisal of those events. Similarly, Mason (1975) argued that the stress response needed a degree of awareness of the stressful situation and reported that dying patients who were unconscious showed less signs of physiological stress than those who were conscious. He suggested that the conscious patients were able to appraise their situation whereas the unconscious ones were not. These studies therefore suggest that appraisal is related to the stress response. However, in contrast, some research indicates that appraisal may not always be necessary. For example, Repetti (1993) assessed the objective stressors (e.g. weather conditions, congestion) and subjective stressors (e.g. perceived stress) experienced by air traffic controllers and reported that both objective and subjective stressors independently predicted both minor illnesses and psychological distress.

This could indicate that either appraisal is not always necessary or that at times individuals do not acknowledge their level of subjective stress. In line with this possibility some researchers have identified 'repressors' as a group of individuals who use selective inattention and forgetting to avoid stressful information (Roth and Cohen 1986). Such people show incongruence between their physiological state and their level of reported anxiety. For example, when confronted with a stressor they say, 'I am fine' but their body is showing arousal. This suggests that although appraisal may be central to the stress response there may be some people in some situations who deny or repress their emotional response to a stressor.

An event needs to be appraised as stressful to elicit a stress response

SOURCE: © Wjphoto/Dreamstime

WHICH EVENTS ARE APPRAISED AS STRESSFUL?

Lazarus has argued that an event needs to be appraised as stressful before it can elicit a stress response. It could be concluded from this that the nature of the event itself is irrelevant – it is all down to the individual's own perception. However, research shows that some types of event are more likely to result in a stress response than others.

- *Salient events.* People often function in many different domains such as work, family and friends. For one person, work might be more salient, while for another their family life might be more important. Swindle and Moos (1992) argued that stressors in salient domains of life are more stressful than those in more peripheral domains.
- *Overload.* Multitasking seems to result in more stress than the chance to focus on fewer tasks at any one time. Therefore a single stressor which adds to a background of other stressors will be appraised as more stressful than when the same stressor occurs in isolation – commonly known as the 'straw that broke the camel's back'.
- *Ambiguous events.* If an event is clearly defined, then the person can efficiently develop a coping strategy. If, however, the event is ambiguous and unclear, then the person first has to spend time and energy considering which coping strategy is best. This is reflected in the work stress literature which illustrates that poor job control and role ambiguity in the workplace often result in a stress response.
- *Uncontrollable events.* If a stressor can be predicted and controlled, then it is usually appraised as less stressful than a more random uncontrollable event. For example, experimental studies show that unpredictable loud bursts of noise are more stressful than predictable ones (Glass and Singer 1972). The issue of control is dealt with in more depth later on.

SELF-CONTROL AND STRESS

Recently theories of stress have emphasized forms of self-control as important in understanding stress. This is illustrated in theories of self-efficacy, hardiness and feelings of mastery.

1 *Self-efficacy.* In 1987, Lazarus and Folkman suggested that self-efficacy was a powerful factor for mediating the stress response. Self-efficacy refers to an individual's feeling of confidence that they can perform a desired action. Research indicates that self-efficacy may have a role in mediating stress-induced immunosuppression and physiological changes such as blood pressure, heart rate and stress hormones (e.g. Bandura et al. 1988; Wiedenfeld et al. 1990). For example, the belief 'I am confident that I can succeed in this exam' may result in physiological changes that reduce the stress response. Therefore a belief in the ability to control one's behaviour may relate to whether or not a potentially stressful event results in a stress response.

2 *Hardiness.* This shift towards emphasizing self-control is also illustrated by Kobasa's concept of 'hardiness' (e.g. Maddi and Kobasa 1984). Hardiness was described as reflecting: (1) personal feelings of control; (2) a desire to accept challenges; and (3) commitment. It has been argued that the degree of hardiness influence an individual's appraisal of potential stressors and the resulting stress response. Accordingly, a feeling of being in control may contribute to the process of primary appraisal.

3 *Mastery.* Karasek and Theorell (1990) defined the term 'feelings of mastery', which reflected an individual's control over their stress response. They argued that the degree of mastery may be related to the stress response.

In summary, most current stress researchers consider stress as the result of a person–environment fit and emphasize the role of primary appraisal ('Is the event stressful?') and secondary appraisal ('Can I cope?'). Psychological factors are seen as a central component to the stress response. However, they are always regarded as co-occurring with physiological changes.

BOX 11.1 Some Problems with . . . Stress Research

Below are some problems with research in this area that you may wish to consider.

1 Defining stress can be difficult as it can be assessed using self-report or physiological changes which have their problems. Self-report can be open to bias and a desire to appear more or less stressed depending upon the person and the situation. Physiological measures may be intrusive and actually create stress and may change the way in which a person responds to their environment.

2 The appraisal model suggests that people appraise the stressor and then appraise their coping mechanisms. This conceptualizes these two processes as separate and discrete. However, it is likely that they are completely interdependent as a stressor is only really stressful in the context of whether the individual feels they can or cannot cope with it.

3 Stress is considered to be made up of both psychological and physiological changes. However, how these two sets of processes interact is unclear as it is possible to perceive stress without showing physiological changes or to show a physiological reaction without labelling it as stress.

STRESS AND CHANGES IN PHYSIOLOGY

The physiological consequences of stress have been studied extensively, mostly in the laboratory using the acute stress paradigm which involves bringing individuals into a controlled environment, putting them into a stressful situation such as counting backwards, completing an intelligence task or giving an unprepared speech, and then recording any changes. This research has highlighted two main groups of physiological changes (see Figure 11.3):

1 *Sympathetic activation:* when an event has been appraised as stressful it triggers responses in the sympathetic nervous system. This results in the production of catecholamines (adrenalin and noradrenalin, also known as epinephrine and norepinephrine) which cause changes in factors such as blood pressure, heart rate, sweating and pupil dilation and is experienced as a feeling of arousal. This process is similar to the fight-or-flight response described by Cannon (1932). Catecholamines also have an effect on a range of the body's tissues and can lead to changes in immune function.

2 *Hypothalamic-pituitary-adrenocortical (HPA) activation:* in addition to the aforementioned sympathetic activation, stress also triggers changes in the HPA system. This results in the production of increased levels of corticosteroids, the most important of which is cortisol, which results in more diffuse changes such as the management of carbohydrate stores and inflammation. These changes constitute the background effect of stress and cannot be detected by the individual. They are similar to the alarm, resistance and exhaustion stages of stress described by Selye (1956). In addition, raised levels of the brain opioids beta endorphin and enkephalin have been found following stress which are involved in immune-related problems.

The physiological aspects of the stress response are linked to stress reactivity, stress recovery, the allostatic load and stress resistance.

STRESS REACTIVITY

Changes in physiology are known as 'stress reactivity' and vary enormously between people. For example, some individuals respond to stressful events with high levels of sweating, raised blood pressure and heart rate while others show only a minimal response. This, in part, is due to whether the

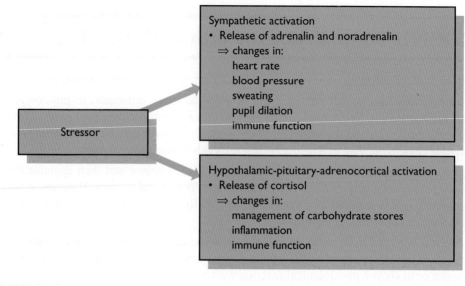

FIGURE 11.3
Stress and changes in physiology

stressor is appraised as stressful (primary appraisal) and how the individual appraises their own coping resources (secondary appraisal). However, research also shows that some people are simply more reactive to stress than others, regardless of appraisal. Two people may show similar psychological reactions to stress but different physiological reactions. In particular, there is some evidence for gender differences in stress reactivity, with men responding more strenuously to stressors than women and women showing smaller increases in blood pressure during stressful tasks than men (Stoney et al. 1990). This indicates that gender may determine the stress response to a stressful event and consequently the effect of this response on the illness or health status of the individual. Stress reactivity is thought to be dispositional and may either be genetic or a result of prenatal or childhood experiences.

STRESS RECOVERY

After reacting to stress, the body then recovers and levels of sympathetic and HPA activation return to baseline. However, there is great variability in the rate of recovery both between individuals, as some people recover more quickly than others, and within the same individual across the lifespan. Chafin et al. (2004) reported that classical music (not jazz or pop music) improved recovery in the laboratory after a three-minute stressful challenge involving a mental arithmetic task.

ALLOSTATIC LOAD

Stress recovery is linked with *allostatic load* which was described by McEwan and Stellar (1993). They argued that the body's physiological systems constantly fluctuate as the individual responds and recovers from stress – a state of allostasis – and that, as time progresses, recovery is less and less complete and the body is left increasingly depleted.

STRESS RESISTANCE

To reflect the observation that not all individuals react to stressors in the same way, researchers developed the concept of stress resistance to emphasize how some people remain healthy even when stressors occur (e.g. Holahan and Moos 1990). Stress resistance includes adaptive coping strategies, certain personality characteristics and social support.

Stress reactivity, stress recovery, allostatic load and stress resistance all influence an individual's reaction to a stressor. They also all affect the stress–illness link. This is described in Chapter 12.

MEASURING STRESS

Stress has been measured both in the laboratory and in a naturalistic setting, and using both physiological measures and those involving self-report.

LABORATORY SETTING

Many stress researchers use the acute stress paradigm to assess stress reactivity and the stress response. This involves taking people into the laboratory and asking them either to complete a stressful task such as an intelligence test, a mathematical task, giving a public talk or watching a horror film, or exposing them to an unpleasant event such as a loud noise, white light or a puff of air in the eye. The acute stress paradigm has enabled researchers to study gender differences in stress reactivity, the interrelationship between acute and chronic stress, the role of personality in the stress response and the impact of exercise on mediating stress-related changes (e.g. Pike et al. 1997; Stoney and Finney 2000).

NATURALISTIC SETTING

Some researchers study stress in a more naturalistic environment. This includes measuring stress responses to specific events such as a public performance, before and after an examination, during a job interview or while undergoing physical activity. Naturalistic research also examines the impact of ongoing stressors such as work-related stress, normal 'daily hassles', poverty or marriage conflicts. These types of study have provided important information on how people react to both acute and chronic stress in their everyday lives.

COSTS AND BENEFITS OF DIFFERENT SETTINGS

Both laboratory and naturalistic settings have their costs and benefits:

1 The degree of stressor delivered in the laboratory setting can be controlled so that differences in stress response can be attributed to aspects of the individual rather than to the stressor itself.
2 Researchers can artificially manipulate aspects of the stressor in the laboratory to examine corresponding changes in physiological and psychological measures.
3 Laboratory researchers can artificially manipulate mediating variables such as control and the presence or absence of social support to assess their impact on the stress response.
4 The laboratory is an artificial environment which may produce a stress response that does not reflect that triggered by a more natural environment. It may also produce associations between variables (i.e. control and stress) which might be an artefact of the laboratory.
5 Naturalistic settings allow researchers to study real stress and how people really cope with it.
6 However, there are many other uncontrolled variables which the researcher needs to measure in order to control for it in the analysis.

PHYSIOLOGICAL MEASURES

Physiological measures are mostly used in the laboratory as they involve participants being attached to monitors or having fluid samples taken. However, some ambulatory machines have been developed which can be attached to people as they carry on with their normal activities. To assess stress reactivity from a physiological perspective, researchers can use a polygraph to measure heart rate, respiration rate, blood pressure and the galvanic skin response (GSR), which is effected by sweating. They can also take blood, urine or saliva samples to test for changes in catecholamine and cortisol production.

SELF-REPORT MEASURES

Researchers use a range of self-report measures to assess both chronic and acute stress. Some of these focus on life events and include the original Social Readjustment Rating Scale (SRRS) (Holmes and Rahe 1967) which asks about events such as 'death of a spouse', 'changing to a different line of work' and 'change of residence'. Other measures focus more on an individual's own perception of stress. The Perceived Stress Scale (PSS) (Cohen et al. 1983) is the most commonly used scale to assess self-perceived stress and asks questions such as 'In the last month how often have you been upset because of something that happened unexpectedly?', and 'In the last month how often have you felt nervous or stressed?' Some researchers also assess minor stressors in the form of 'daily hassles'. Kanner et al. (1981) developed the Hassles Scale which asks participants to rate how severe a range of hassles have been over the past month including 'misplacing or losing things', 'health of a family member' and 'concerns about owing money'. Johnston et al. (2006) used a small hand-held computer called a personal digital assistant (PDA) which participants carry around with them and which prompts them at pre-set intervals to complete a diary entry describing their level of stress. Self-report measures have been used to describe the impact of environmental factors on stress whereby stress is seen as the outcome variable (i.e. 'a poor working environment causes high stress'). They have also been used to explore the impact of stress on the individual's health status whereby stress in seen as the input variable (i.e. 'high stress causes poor health').

COSTS AND BENEFITS OF DIFFERENT MEASURES

Physiological and self-report measures of stress are used in the main to complement each other. The former reflect a more physiological emphasis and the latter a more psychological perspective. A researcher who has a greater interest in physiology might argue that physiological measures are more central to stress research, while another researcher who believes that experience is more important might favour self-report. Most stress researchers measure both physiological and psychological aspects of stress and study how these two components interact. However, in general the different types of measures have the following costs and benefits:

1 Physiological measures are more objective and less affected by the participant's wish to give a desirable response or the researcher's wish to see a particular result.

2 Self-report measures reflect the individual's experience of stress rather than just what their body is doing.

3 Self-report measures can be influenced by problems with recall, social desirability, and different participants interpreting the questions in different ways.

4 Self-report measures are based upon the life events or hassles that have been chosen by the author of the questionnaire. One person's hassle, such as 'troublesome neighbours' which appears on the Hassles Scale, may not be a hassle for another, whereas worries about a child's school might be, which doesn't appear on this scale.

ASSOCIATIONS BETWEEN RESEARCH IN DIFFERENT SETTINGS USING DIFFERENT MEASURES

Given that stress research takes place in both the laboratory and in more naturalistic settings and uses both physiological and self-report measures it is important to know how these different studies relate to each other. This is illustrated in **Focus on Research 11.1**.

FOCUS ON RESEARCH 11.1: RELAXATION TRAINING IN CHILDREN

Psychophysiological effects of relaxation training in children (Lohaus et al. 2001).

BACKGROUND

Stress is conceptualized as involving both physiological and subjective changes that can be assessed using laboratory and self-report procedures. This study assessed the impact of two types of relaxation training on different aspects of the stress response. It is interesting as it allows an insight into how these different aspects of stress may interrelate. It also illustrates the impact of relaxation training on children who are a rarely studied subject group.

AIMS

The study aimed to explore the relative impact of two types of relaxation training on children's physiological and self-report responses. The training types were progressive muscle relaxation and imagery-based relaxation.

Participants

The study involved 64 children from a school in Germany who were aged between 10 and 12.

Design

The study used a randomized control trial design and participants were randomly allocated to one of three arms of the trial: progressive muscle relaxation, imagery-based relaxation or the control group.

The Interventions

Each intervention involved five training sessions. Each session lasted about 30 minutes. The children were asked to sit quietly for 5 minutes (baseline period), then they took part in the intervention, and the children were then asked to sit quietly again for 5 minutes (follow-up).

- *Progressive muscle relaxation.* Children were asked to tense and relax specific muscle groups for a period of 7 minutes. These were hand muscles, arms, forehead, cheeks, chest, shoulders, stomach and thighs.
- *Imagery-based relaxation.* Children in this group were asked to imagine that they were a butterfly going on a fantasy journey such as to a meadow, a tree or a boat.
- *Control group.* Children in this group listened to audiotapes of neutral stories which were designed not to elicit any feeling of either tension or relaxation.

Measures

The study involved physiological and self-report measures. Subjective measurements were taken before and after the baseline period, after the intervention and after the follow-up period. Physiological measurements were taken continuously throughout.

- *Physiological measures.* Measures were taken of heart rate, skin temperature and skin conductance level.
- *Self-report measures.* Measures were also taken of the children's mood (e.g. sensation of perceived calmness, subjective feeling of wellness, feeling of perceived attentiveness) and their physical well-being (e.g. calmness of their heart beats, subjective body warmth, perceived dampness of the hands).

RESULTS

The results were assessed to examine the impact of relaxation training regardless of type of relaxation and also to explore whether one form of relaxation training was more effective.

- *Physiological changes.* The results showed that imagery relaxation was related to a decrease in heart rate and skin conductance but did not result in changes in skin temperature. In contrast, progressive muscle relaxation resulted in an increase in heart rate during the training session.
- *Self-report changes.* The results showed increased ratings of mood and physical well-being during baseline and training sessions for all interventions.

CONCLUSIONS

The authors conclude that relaxation training can result in psychophysiological changes but that these vary according to the type of training. What is also interesting, however, is the degree of variability between the different measures of change. In particular, differences were found in the changes between different aspects of the children's physiology – a change in heart rate did not always correspond to a change in skin temperature. Further, changes in physiology did not always correspond to changes in self-reported mood or physical well-being. Therefore a measure indicating that heart rate had gone down did not always correspond with a self-report that the individual's heart was more calm.

LABORATORY VERSUS NATURALISTIC RESEARCH

Laboratory research is artificial whereas real-life research is uncontrolled. Some studies, however, illustrate high levels of congruence between physiological responses in the laboratory and those assessed using ambulatory machines in real life. For example, Matthews et al. (1986) reported similarity between reactivity following laboratory tasks and public speaking and Turner and Carroll (1985) reported a correlation between the response to video games and real-life stress identified from diaries. However, other studies have found no relationship or only some relationship with some measures (e.g. Johnston et al. 1990). Johnston and colleagues (Anastasiades et al. 1990; Johnston et al. 1990, 1994) designed a series of studies to try to explain this variability. Using a battery of tasks to elicit stress in the laboratory and ambulatory machines to assess stress reactivity in real life, they concluded that physiological measures taken in the laboratory concord if the following conditions are met: the field measure is taken continuously; the analysis takes into account physical activity levels (as this produces a similar response to the stressor); and when the laboratory task involves active coping such as a video game rather than a passive coping task such as the cold pressor task (i.e. placing the hand in icy water). In addition, they argued that appraisal is central to the congruence between laboratory and naturalistic measures and that higher congruence is particularly apparent when the stressors selected are appraised as stressful by the individual rather than identified as stressful by the researcher. This indicates that laboratory assessments may be artificial but do bear some resemblance to real-life stress.

PHYSIOLOGICAL VERSUS SELF-REPORT MEASURES

Stress is considered to reflect both the experience of 'I feel stress' and the underlying physiological changes in factors such as heart rate and cortisol levels. But do these two sets of measures relate to each other? This question is central not only to stress research but also to an understanding of mind–body interactions. Research has addressed this association and has consistently found no or only poor relationships between physiological and perceived measures of stress (see **Focus on Research 11.1**, p. 301). This is surprising given the central place that perception is given in the stress response. It is possible, however, that this lack of congruence between these two types of measure reflects a role for other mediating variables. For example, it might be that physiological measures only reflect self-report measures when the stressor is controllable by the individual, when it is considered a threat rather than a challenge or when the individual draws upon particular coping strategies.

THE INTERACTION BETWEEN PSYCHOLOGICAL AND PHYSIOLOGICAL ASPECTS OF STRESS

Stress is generally considered to illustrate the interaction between psychological and physiological factors. The psychological appraisal of a stressor is central to the stress response and without appraisal, physiological changes are absent or minimal. Further, the degree of appraisal also influences the extent of the physiological response. However, there is little research illustrating a link between how stressed people say they are feeling (perceived stress) and how their body is reacting (physiological stress). It is likely that the mind–body interactions illustrated by stress are dynamic and ongoing. Therefore, rather than appraisal causing a change in physiology which constitutes the response, appraisal probably triggers a change in physiology which is then detected and appraised causing a further response and so on. In addition, psychological factors such as control, personality, coping and social support will impact upon this ongoing process. This psychophysiological model of the stress response is described in Figure 11.4.

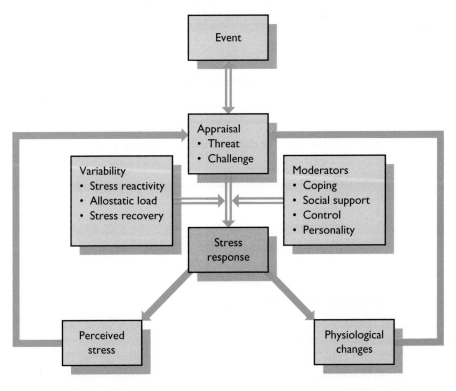

FIGURE 11.4

The interaction between psychological and physiological aspects of stress

TO CONCLUDE

This chapter has examined the different models of stress, the psychological and physiological responses to stress and the way in which stress has been measured. Early models of stress regarded it as an automatic response to an external stressor. However, the introduction of the concept of appraisal suggested that stress was best understood as an interaction between the individual and the outside world. Accordingly, a stress response would be elicited if an event were appraised as stressful. Once appraised as a stressor, the individual then shows a stress response involving both a sense of being stressed and physiological changes including both sympathetic activation and activation of the hypothalamus pituitary axis. The stress response can be measured either in the laboratory or in a more naturalistic setting and can be assessed using either physiological measures or those involving self-report.

QUESTIONS

1 Stress is an automatic response to external stressors. Discuss.
2 Discuss the role of appraisal in the stress response.
3 How does stress cause changes in physiology?
4 How and where can stress be measured and what are the costs and benefits of each measurement approach?
5 Design a study to show whether or not appraisal is necessary for the stress response to occur.

FOR DISCUSSION

Consider the last time you felt stressed. What were the characteristics of the stressful event that made it feel stressful?

ASSUMPTIONS IN HEALTH PSYCHOLOGY

Stress research highlights some of the assumptions in health psychology:

1 *Dividing up the soup.* Stress research defines appraisal as central to eliciting stress as a means to progress beyond the more simplistic stimulus response theories of Cannon and Selye. Therefore it states that appraisal ('Is it stressful?', 'Can I cope?') is necessary for a stressor to elicit stress. However, research then explores whether coping *reduces* the stress response. Coping and stress are sometimes one construct and sometimes two constructs which can be associated.

2 *The problem of mind–body split.* Although much stress research examines how the mind may influence the body (e.g. appraisal relates to the release of stress hormones, social support relates to resulting stress-related illnesses), how this process occurs is unclear. In addition, although these relationships suggest an interaction between the mind and the body, they still define them as separate entities which influence each other, not as the same entity.

3 *The problem of progress.* It is often assumed that the most recent theories are better than earlier theories. Therefore models including appraisal, social support and so on are better than those describing stress as a knee-jerk reaction to a stressor. Perhaps these different theories are not necessarily better than each other, but are simply different ways of describing the stress process.

FURTHER READING

Cohen, S., Kessler, R.C. and Gordon, L.U. (eds) (1995) *Measuring Stress: A Guide for Health and Social Scientists.* New York: Oxford University Press.
This is a comprehensive edited collection for anyone interested in the details of stress measurement using physiological and self-report approaches.

Jones, F. and Bright, J. (2001) *Stress: Myth, Theory and Research.* Harlow: Prentice Hall.
This is a highly accessible book that describes and analyses the research and theories of stress and particularly addresses the methodological problems with this area.

Lazarus, R.S. (2000) Towards better research on stress and coping, *American Psychologist*, 55: 665–73.
This paper is part of a special issue on stress and coping, and reflects Lazarus's own comments on recent developments and critiques of the stress literature.

 Visit the website at www.openup.co.uk/ogden for additional resources on Chapter 11 to help you with your study, such as multiple choice questions, weblinks and a searchable online glossary.

12 Stress and Illness

© craftvision/iStock

CHAPTER OVERVIEW

This chapter first assesses whether stress causes illness and then explores a chronic and acute model of the mechanisms behind this association. The chapter then explores the relationship between stress and illness in terms of behavioural and physiological pathways. It goes on to outline the approach of psychoneuroimmunology and explores the impact of psychological factors such as mood, beliefs, emotional expression and stress on immunity. Finally, it highlights the role of coping, social support, personality and control as moderators of the stress–illness link.

DOES STRESS CAUSE ILLNESS?

One of the reasons that stress has been studied so consistently is because of its potential effect on the health of the individual. Research shows that hypertension rates are more common in those with high-stress jobs such as air traffic controllers (Cobb and Rose 1973) than in less stressed occupations such as nuns (Timio et al. 1988) and that higher life stress is associated with greater reporting of physical symptoms (Cropley and Steptoe 2005). Both cross-sectional and longitudinal studies also show that stressful occupations are associated with an increased risk of coronary heart disease (CHD) (Karasek et al. 1981; Kivimaki et al. 2002). Further, Phillips et al. (2008) reported from their longitudinal study of 968 men and women aged 56 that the number of health-related life events at baseline and their stress load predicted mortality by 17 years (266 participants had died) (see **Focus on Research 12.1**). In addition, Appels and Mulder (1989) and Appels et al. (2002) indicated that 'vital exhaustion' is common in the year preceding a heart attack. In one study people were given nasal drops either containing viruses responsible for the common cold or placebo saline drops. Their level of stress was then assessed in terms of life events during the past year (Cohen et al. 1991). The results showed that not everyone who was given the virus contracted the virus and not everyone who did contract the virus actually exhibited cold symptoms and became ill. Stress was shown to predict, first, who contracted the virus, and second, who developed symptoms. However, these studies involved a cross-sectional, prospective or retrospective design which raises the problem of causality as it is unclear whether stress causes illness or illness causes stress (or stress ratings). To solve this problem some research has used an experimental design which involves inducing stress and assessing subsequent changes in health. Because of the ethical problems with such a design most experimental work has been done using animals. A classic series of animal studies by Manuck, Kaplan and colleagues (e.g. Kaplan et al. 1983; Manuck et al. 1986) experimentally manipulated the social groupings of Bowman Gray monkeys who have a strong social hierarchy. The results showed that the monkeys illustrated not only behavioural signs of stress but also a marked increase in the disease of their coronary arteries. In addition, stress management, which involves experimentally reducing stress, has had some success in reducing CHD (Johnston 1989, 1992) and in reducing recurrent cold and flu in children (Hewson-Bower and Drummond 2001).

FOCUS ON RESEARCH 12.1: LIFE EVENTS AND MORTALITY

Stressful life events and 17 years mortality (Phillips et al. 2008).

This is an impressive piece of work exploring the links between life events and mortality as it uses a prospective design with an exceptionally long follow-up (17 years) and predicts the ultimate outcome variable – death.

In addition, the sample is substantial and the study differentiates between health-related life events and health-unrelated events.

METHODOLOGY

Participants

Data was collected as part of the West of Scotland Twenty-07 study and the follow-up was the 07 which followed a cohort of participants from 1988 to 2000/1. Baseline life events data for this paper was collected in 1992/3 and the follow-up data 17 years later in 2000/1. The sample was from the Glasgow area in Scotland and was around 56 years old when the study started in 1988. The sample for this study was 968 men and women and by follow-up 266 had died.

Procedure

Trained nurses interviewed participants in their own homes at each time point and participants completed questionnaires. The following measures were taken:

- *Occupational status.* This was assessed in terms of the occupational status of the head of household and was classified as manual versus non-manual.
- *Smoking behaviour.* Participants were asked 'Do you ever smoke tobacco now? I am thinking of a pipe, cigars and your own roll-ups as well as cigarettes you might buy?' If they answered 'No' they were also asked 'Did you ever used to smoke any kind of tobacco?'. Participants were then classified as 'never smokers', 'ex-smokers' or 'current smokers'.
- *Height and weight.* This was assessed to compute body mass index (BMI).
- *Resting blood pressure.* This was taken after five minutes of relaxed sitting.
- *Major life events.* Life events over the past two years at each time point were assessed by presenting participants with eight cards which listed a number of major life events in the following domains: health, marriage, relationships, bereavement, work, housing, finance, general. The participants were asked to indicate up to six events which had happened to either them or someone they cared about. They were then asked to specify how much each event had disrupted or changed their life and how stressful it had been 'then' and 'now'.
- *Mortality.* This was assessed using the death certificates of those who had died which were sent to the study office.

Data Analysis

The results were analysed using Cox's regression models to predict all-cause mortality from life events while adjusting for sex, occupational status, smoking, BMI and systolic blood pressure.

RESULTS

By the 17-year follow-up 27 per cent (n = 266) had died. The mean age of death was 66 years and the major causes of death were cancers (34 per cent), cardiovascular (24 per cent), respiratory (12 per cent) and other causes (30 per cent). More men (33 per cent) than women (23 per cent) had died and more people classified as manual (32 per cent) compared to non-manual (21 per cent) had died.

Predicting All-Cause Mortality

Overall life events experience predicted 17-year mortality in terms of disruption at the time, disruption now and stressfulness now. These were significant even after all potential risk factors were controlled for.

The Type of Life Event

Health-related life events significantly predicted 17-year mortality in terms of disruption at the time, disruption now, stressfulness at the time and stressfulness now (again controlling for risk factors). Non-health-related events were not significantly predictive of mortality.

Number of Life Events

Overall, the number of life events predicted 17-year mortality, however when looked at separately, while health-related life events were predictive, non-health related events were not.

CONCLUSION

This study illustrates a strong link between life events and mortality over a long period of time in a large sample. Further, it indicates that it is not life events per se but those that are health-related that have significance. However, it is unclear whether this is due to the psychological impact of such events (e.g. having an operation or being diagnosed with a worrying illness) (i.e. these events are stressful) or whether it is just a marker for serious morbidity.

HOW DOES STRESS CAUSE ILLNESS?

Johnston (2002) argued that stress can cause illness through two interrelated mechanisms and developed his model of the stress–illness link which involves chronic and acute processes (see Figure 12.1).

THE CHRONIC PROCESS

The most commonly-held view of the link between stress and illness suggests that stress leads to disease due to a prolonged interaction of physiological, behavioural and psychological factors. For example, chronic work stress may cause changes in physiology and changes in behaviour which over time lead to damage to the cardiovascular system. In particular, chronic stress is associated with atherosclerosis, which is a slow process of arterial damage that limits the supply of blood to the heart. Further, this damage might be greater in those individuals with a particular genetic tendency. This chronic process is supported by research indicating links between job stress and cardiovascular disease (Karasek et al. 1981; Kivimaki et al. 2002). Such an approach is parallel to Levi's (1974) 'stress-diathesis' model of illness which is illustrated in Figure 12.2.

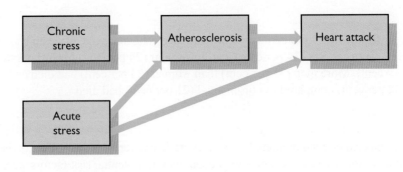

FIGURE 12.1

Chronic/acute model of stress–illness link

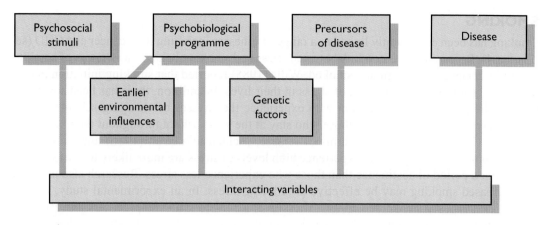

FIGURE 12.2

Stress-diathesis model

SOURCE: Adapted from Levi (1974)

However, there are several problems with a purely chronic model of the stress–illness link:

1 Exercise protects against the wear and tear of stress with more active individuals being less likely to die from cardiovascular disease than more sedentary individuals (Kivimaki et al. 2002). However, exercise can also immediately precede a heart attack.

2 The wear and tear caused by stress can explain the accumulative damage to the cardiovascular system, but this chronic model does not explain why coronary events occur when they do.

In the light of these problems, Johnston (2002) argues for an acute model.

THE ACUTE PROCESS

Heart attacks are more likely to occur following exercise, following anger, upon wakening, during changes in heart rate and during changes in blood pressure (e.g. Muller et al. 1994; Moller et al. 1999). They are acute events and involve a sudden rupture and thrombogenesis. Johnston (2002) argues that this reflects an acute model of the link between stress and illness with acute stress triggering a sudden cardiac problem. This explains how exercise can be protective in the longer term but a danger for an at-risk individual. It also explains why and when a heart attack occurs.

LINKS BETWEEN THE ACUTE AND CHRONIC PROCESSES

The acute and chronic processes are intrinsically interlinked. Chronic stress may simply be the frequent occurrence of acute stress; acute stress may be more likely to trigger a cardiac event in someone who has experienced chronic stress; and acute stress may also contribute to the wear and tear on the cardiovascular system. Furthermore, both the chronic and acute processes highlight the central role for stress-induced changes in behaviour and changes in physiology. These will now be considered.

STRESS AND CHANGES IN BEHAVIOUR

Stress has been mostly studied in the context of CHD. However, there are also studies exploring links between illnesses such as cancer, diabetes and recovery from surgery. Research exploring the links between stress and CHD highlights the impact of stress on the classic risk factors for CHD, namely raised blood cholesterol, raised blood pressure and smoking. These risk factors are strongly influenced by behaviour and reflect the behavioural pathway between stress and illness (Krantz et al. 1981). In line with this, some research has examined the effect of stress on specific health-related behaviours.

SMOKING

Smoking has been consistently linked to a range of illnesses including lung cancer and CHD (see Chapter 4). Research suggests a link between stress and smoking behaviour in terms of smoking initiation, relapse and the amount smoked. Wills (1985) reported that smoking initiation in adolescents was related to the amount of stress in their lives. In addition, there has been some support for the prediction that children who experience the stressor of changing schools may be more likely to start smoking than those who stay at the same school throughout their secondary education (Santi et al. 1991). In terms of relapse, Lichtenstein et al. (1986) and Carey et al. (1993) reported that people who experience high levels of stress are more likely to start smoking again after a period of abstinence than those who experience less stress. Research also indicates that increased smoking may be effective at reducing stress. In an experimental study, Perkins et al. (1992) exposed smokers to either a stressful or a non-stressful computer task and asked the subjects to smoke a cigarette or sham smoke an unlit cigarette. The results showed that, regardless of whether the smokers smoked or not, all subjects reported an increased desire to smoke in the stressful condition. However, this desire was less in those smokers who were actually allowed to smoke. This suggests that stress causes an increased urge for a cigarette, which can be modified by smoking. In a more naturalistic study, smokers were asked to attend a stressful social situation and were instructed either to smoke or not to smoke. Those who could not smoke reported the occasion as more socially stressful than those who could smoke (Gilbert and Spielberger 1987). Similarly, Metcalfe et al. (2003) used the Reeder Stress Inventory to relate stress to health behaviours and concluded that higher levels of stress were associated with smoking more cigarettes. This association was also found in one large-scale study of over 6,000 Scottish men and women which showed that higher levels of perceived stress were linked to smoking more (Heslop et al. 2001).

ALCOHOL

High alcohol intake has been linked to illnesses such as CHD, cancer and liver disease (see Chapter 4). Research has also examined the relationship between stress and alcohol consumption. Many authors have suggested that work stress, in particular, may promote alcohol use (e.g. Herold and Conlon 1981). The tension-reduction theory suggests that people drink alcohol for its tension-reducing properties (Cappell and Greeley 1987). Tension refers to states such as fear, anxiety, depression and distress. Therefore, according to this model, negative moods are the internal stressors, or the consequence of an external stressor, which cause alcohol consumption due to the expected outcome of the alcohol. For example, if an individual feels tense or anxious (their internal state) as a result of an exam (the external stressor) and believes that alcohol will reduce this tension (the expected outcome), they may drink alcohol to improve their mood. This theory has been supported by some evidence of the relationship between negative mood and drinking behaviour (Violanti et al. 1983), suggesting that people are more likely to drink when they are feeling depressed or anxious. Similarly, both Metcalfe et al. (2003) and Heslop et al. (2001) reported an association between perceived stress and drinking more alcohol (if a drinker). Furthermore, it has been suggested that medical students' lifestyle and the occurrence of problem drinking may be related to the stress they experience (Wolf and Kissling 1984). In one study, this theory was tested experimentally and the health-related behaviours of medical students were evaluated both before and during a stressful examination period. The results showed that the students reported a deterioration in mood in terms of anxiety and depression and changes in their behaviour in terms of decreases in exercise and food intake (Ogden and Mtandabari 1997). However, alcohol consumption also went down. The authors concluded that acute exposure to stress resulted in negative changes in those behaviours that had only a minimal influence on the students' ability to perform satisfactorily. Obviously chronic stress may have more damaging effects on longer-term changes in behaviour.

EATING

Diet can influence health either through changes in body weight or via the over- or underconsumption of specific dietary components (see Chapter 5). Greeno and Wing (1994) proposed two hypotheses concerning the link between stress and eating: (1) the *general effect model*, which predicts that stress changes food intake generally; and (2) the *individual difference model*, which predicts that stress only causes changes in eating in vulnerable groups of individuals. Most research has focused on the individual difference model and has examined whether either naturally-occurring stress or laboratory-induced stress causes changes in eating in specific individuals. For example, Michaud et al. (1990) reported that exam stress was related to an increase in eating in girls but not in boys; Baucom and Aiken (1981) reported that stress increased eating in both the overweight and dieters and Cools et al. (1992) reported that stress was related to eating in dieters only. Furthermore, O'Conner et al. (2008) concluded from their study that the snacking–stress relationship was stronger in those with higher levels of dietary restraint, more emotional eating, greater disinhibition, higher levels of external eating, women and obese participants. Research has also addressed whether the link between stress and eating behaviour can be explained by cortisol reactivity. Research indicates that there is much individual variability in the extent to which individuals react to stressors (see Chapter 11). Newman et al. (2007) carried out a laboratory-based study in which 50 women were subjected to a stressor in the laboratory and then completed ratings of daily hassles and snack intake over the next 14 days. The results showed that, overall, higher levels of daily hassles were associated with a higher intake of snacks. However, when this association was related to the responses to the stressor, daily hassles resulted in snacking only in those that showed greater cortisol reactivity. Therefore gender, cortisol reactivity, weight, levels of dieting and aspects of eating style (see Chapter 5) seem to be important predictors of a link between stress and eating. However, the research is not always consistent with this suggestion. For example, Conner et al. (1999) examined the link between daily hassles and snacking in 60 students who completed diaries of their snacking and hassles for seven consecutive days. Their results showed a direct association between increased daily hassles and increased snacking but showed no differences according to either gender or dieting. Such inconsistencies in the literature have been described by Stone and Brownell (1994) as the 'stress eating paradox' to explain how at times stress causes overeating and at others it causes undereating without any clear pattern emerging.

EXERCISE

Exercise has been linked to health in terms of its impact on body weight and through its beneficial effects on CHD (see Chapter 6). Research indicates that stress may reduce exercise (e.g. Heslop et al. 2001; Metcalfe et al. 2003) whereas stress management, which focuses on increasing exercise, has been shown to result in some improvements in coronary health. One recent study explored the impact of gardening on relief following experimentally induced stress (Van den Berg and Custers 2011). For this study 30 allotment gardeners performed a stressful Stroop task (see **Focus on Research 6.1**, p. 145) and were then randomly allocated to outdoor gardening or indoor reading on their allotment plot. The results showed that although both groups showed a decrease in salivary cortisol this was greater in the gardening group. It is not clear, however, whether this is due to gardening as a form of exercise, gardening as a form of creativity or whether simply being outdoors created this effect.

ACCIDENTS

Accidents are a very common and rarely studied cause of injury or mortality. Research has also examined the effects of stress on accidents and correlational research suggests that individuals who experience high levels of stress show a greater tendency to perform behaviours that increase their chances of becoming injured (Wiebe and McCallum 1986). Further, Johnson (1986) has also suggested that stress increases accidents at home, at work and in the car.

ILLNESS AS A STRESSOR

Being ill itself could be a stressful event. If this is the case then the stress following illness also has implications for the health of individuals. Such stress may influence individuals' behaviour in terms of their likelihood to seek help, their compliance with interventions and medical recommendations, and also their adopting healthy lifestyles. Therefore stress may cause behaviour changes, which are related to the health status of the individual.

STRESS AND CHANGES IN PHYSIOLOGY

The physiological consequences of stress and their effects on health have been studied extensively. Research indicates that stress causes physiological changes that have implications for promoting both the onset of illness and its progression. Stress has also been linked with wound healing.

STRESS, ILLNESS ONSET AND PROGRESSION

Stress causes changes in both sympathetic activation (e.g. heart rate, sweating, blood pressure) via the production of catecholamines and the hypothalamic-pituitary-adrenocortical (HPA) activation via the production of cortisol. These changes can directly impact upon health and illness onset.

Sympathetic Activation

The prolonged production of adrenalin and noradrenalin can result in the following:

- blood clot formation
- increased blood pressure
- increased heart rate
- irregular heart beats
- fat deposits
- plaque formation
- immunosuppression.

These changes may increase the chances of heart disease and kidney disease and leave the body open to infection.

HPA Activation

The prolonged production of cortisol can result in the following:

- decreased immune function
- damage to neurons in the hippocampus.

These changes may increase the chances of infection, psychiatric problems and losses in memory and concentration.

These physiological changes can be further understood in terms of Johnston's (2002) chronic and acute model of the stress–illness link. Chronic stress is more likely to involve HPA activation and the release of cortisol. This results in ongoing wear and tear and the slower process of atherosclerosis and damage to the cardiovascular system. Acute stress operates primarily through changes in sympathetic activation with changes in heart rate and blood pressure. This can contribute to atherosclerosis and kidney disease but is also related to sudden changes such as heart attacks.

INTERACTION BETWEEN THE BEHAVIOURAL AND PHYSIOLOGICAL PATHWAYS

Stress can therefore influence health and illness by changing behaviour or by directly impacting upon an individual's physiology. So far the behavioural and physiological pathways have been presented as separate and discrete. However, this is very much an oversimplification. Stress may cause changes in behaviours such as smoking and diet which impact upon health by changing the individual's physiology. Likewise, stress may cause physiological changes such as raised blood pressure but this is often most apparent in those who also exhibit particularly unhealthy behaviours (Johnston 1989). Therefore, in reality, stress is linked to illness via a complex interaction between behavioural and physiological factors. Further, Johnston (1989) argued that these factors are multiplicative, indicating that the more factors that are changed by stress, the greater the chance that stress will lead to illness.

INDIVIDUAL VARIABILITY IN THE STRESS–ILLNESS LINK

Not everyone who experiences stress becomes ill. To some extent this is due to the role of variables such as coping, control, personality and social support which are described in detail later on. However, research indicates that this variability is also due to individual differences in stress reactivity, stress recovery, the allostatic load and stress resistance.

STRESS REACTIVITY

Some individuals show a stronger physiological response to stress than others which is known as their level of 'cardiovascular reactivity' or 'stress reactivity'. This means that when given the same level of stressor and regardless of their self-perceived stress, some people show greater sympathetic activation than others (e.g. Vitaliano et al. 1993). Research suggests that greater stress reactivity may make people more susceptible to stress-related illnesses. For example, individuals with both hypertension and heart disease have higher levels of stress reactivity (e.g. Frederickson et al. 1991, 2000). However, these studies used a cross-sectional design which raises the problem of causality. Some research has therefore used a prospective design. For example, in an early study Keys et al. (1971) assessed baseline blood pressure reaction to a cold pressor test and found that higher reactivity predicted heart disease at follow-up 23 years later. Similarly, Boyce et al. (1995) measured baseline levels of stress reactivity in children following a stressful task and then rated the number of family stressors and illness rates over the subsequent 12 weeks. The results showed that stress and illness were not linked in the children with low reactivity but that those with higher reactivity showed more illness if they had experienced more stress. Everson and colleagues (1997) also assessed baseline stress reactivity and explored cardiac health using echo cardiography at follow-up. The results showed that higher stress reactivity at baseline was predictive of arterial deterioration after four years. In addition, stress reactivity has been suggested as the physiological mechanism behind the impact of coronary-prone behaviours on the heart (Suarez et al. 1991). This doesn't mean that individuals who show greater responses to stress are more likely to become ill. It means that they are more likely to become ill *if subjected to stress* (see Figure 12.3).

STRESS RECOVERY

After reacting to stress the body recovers and levels of sympathetic and HPA activation return to baseline. However, some people recover more quickly than others and some research indicates that this rate of recovery may relate to a susceptibility to stress-related illness. This is reflected in Selye's (1956) notion of 'exhaustion' and the general wear and tear caused by stress. Some research has focused particularly on changes in cortisol production, suggesting that slower recovery from raised cortisol levels could be related to immune function and a susceptibility to infection and illness (e.g. Perna and McDowell 1995).

ALLOSTATIC LOAD

McEwan and Stellar (1993) described the concept of 'allostatic load' to reflect the wear and tear on the body which accumulates over time after exposure to repeated or chronic stress. They argued

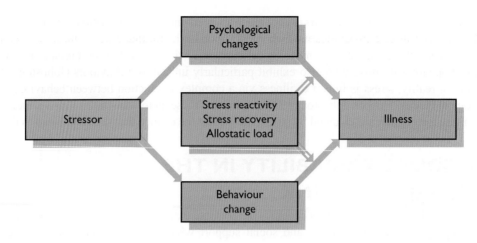

FIGURE 12.3

The stress–illness link: physiological moderators

that the body's physiological systems constantly fluctuate as the individual responds and recovers from stress – a state of allostasis – and that as time progresses, recovery is less and less complete and the body is left increasingly depleted. Therefore, if exposed to a new stressor the person is more likely to become ill if their allostatic load is quite high.

STRESS RESISTANCE

To reflect the observation that not all individuals react to stressors in the same way, researchers have developed the concept of stress resistance to emphasize how some people remain healthy even when stressors occur (e.g. Holahan and Moos 1990). Stress resistance includes adaptive coping strategies, certain personality characteristics and social support. These factors are dealt with in detail later on.

Stress has therefore been linked to a range of illnesses and research highlights the role of both a behavioural and physiological pathway. One area of research that emphasizes the physiological pathway and has received much interest over recent years is psychoneuroimmunology (PNI).

PSYCHONEUROIMMUNOLOGY

PNI is based on the prediction that an individual's psychological state can influence their immune system via the nervous system. This perspective provides a scientific basis for the 'mind over matter', 'think yourself well' and 'positive thinking, positive health' approaches to life. PNI can be understood in terms of: (1) what the immune system is; (2) conditioning the immune system; (3) measuring immune changes; and (4) psychological state and immunity.

THE IMMUNE SYSTEM

The role of the immune system is to distinguish between the body and its invaders and to attack and protect the body from anything that is considered foreign. These invaders are called 'antigens'. When the immune system works well, the body is protected and infections and illnesses are kept at bay. If the immune system overreacts, then this can lead to allergies. If the immune system mistakes the body itself for an invader, then this can form the basis of autoimmune disorders. The main organs of the immune system are the lymphoid organs which are distributed throughout the body and include the bone marrow, lymph nodes and vessels, the spleen and thymus. These organs produce a range of 'soldiers' which are involved in identifying foreign bodies and disabling them. There are three levels of immune system activity. The first two are called specific immune processes and are 'cell mediated immunity' and 'humoral mediated immunity'. Cell mediated immunity involves a set of lymphocytes called T cells (killer T cells, memory T cells, delayed hypersensitivity T cells, helper T cells and suppressor T cells). These operate within the cells of the body and are made within the thymus (hence 'T'). Humoral mediated immunity involves B cells and antibodies and takes place in the body's fluids before the antigens have entered any cells. Third, there is non-specific immunity which involves phagocytes which non-specifically attack any kind of antigen. Immunocompetence is when the immune system is working well. Immunocompromise is when the immune system is failing in some way.

CONDITIONING THE IMMUNE SYSTEM

Originally it was believed that the immune system was autonomous and did not interact with any other bodily systems. However, research indicates that this is not the case and that not only does the immune system interact with other systems, but it can be conditioned to respond in a particular way using the basic rules of classical and operant conditioning. The early work in this area was carried out by Ader and Cohen (1975, 1981) and showed that changes in the immune system brought about by an immunosuppressive drug could be paired with a sweet taste. This meant that after several pairings, the sweet taste itself began to bring about immunosuppression. These results were important for two reasons. First, they confirmed that the immune system could be manipulated. Second, the results opened up the area for PNI and the possibility that psychological factors could change an individual's immune response.

MEASURING IMMUNE CHANGES

Although it is accepted that the immune system can be changed, measuring such changes has proved to be problematic. The four main markers of immune function used to date have been as follows: (1) tumour growth, which is mainly used in animal research; (2) wound healing, which can be used in human research by way of the removal of a small section of the skin and can be monitored to follow the healing process; (3) secretory immunoglobulin A (sIgA), which is found in saliva and can be accessed easily and without pain or discomfort to the subject; and (4) natural killer cell cytoxicity (NKCC), T lymphocytes and T helper lymphocytes, which are found in the blood.

All these markers have been shown to be useful in the study of immune functioning (see Chapter 14 for a discussion of immunity and longevity in the context of HIV/AIDs). However, each approach to measurement has its problems. For example, both wound healing and tumour growth present problems of researcher accuracy. But both these measures are actual rather than only proxy measures of outcome (i.e. a healed wound is healthier than an open one). In contrast, whereas measures of sIgA, NKCC, T lymphocytes and T helper cells are more accurate, their link to actual health status is more problematic. In addition, the measurement of immune function raises questions such as 'How long after an event should the immune system marker be assessed?' (i.e. is the effect immediate or delayed?), 'How can baseline measures of the immune system be taken?' (i.e. does actually taking blood/saliva, etc. cause changes in immune functioning?) and 'Are changes in immune functioning predictive of changes in health?' (i.e. if we measure changes in a marker, do we really know that this will impact on health in the long term?).

PSYCHOLOGICAL STATE AND IMMUNITY

Research has focused on the capacity of psychological factors to change immune functioning. In particular, it has examined the role of mood, beliefs, emotional expression and stress.

Mood

Studies indicate that positive mood is associated with better immune functioning (as measured by sIgA), that negative mood is associated with poorer functioning (Stone et al. 1987) and that humour appears to be specifically beneficial (Newman and Stone 1996). Johnston et al. (1999) explored the impact of mood on the progression of the disease, disability and survival in patients with amyotrophic lateral sclerosis/motor neurone disease. The study used a prospective design with 38 consecutive patients completing measures of mood (anxiety and depression), self-esteem, well-being and disability at time of diagnosis and after six weeks. Survival and disability were also measured after six months. Ten patients had died by six months. Controlling for disease severity, the results showed that those who died reported lower mood at the six-week interview and that low mood at six weeks was also predictive of greater disability in the survivors.

Beliefs

It has also been suggested that beliefs may themselves have a direct effect on the immune system. Kamen and Seligman (1987) reported that an internal, stable, global attributional style (i.e. a pessimist approach to life whereby the individual blames themselves when things go wrong) predicted poor health in later life. This was supported by Seligman et al. (1988) who argued that pessimism may be related to health through a decrease in T-cells and immunosuppression. The authors argued that this was not mediated through behavioural change but was indicative of a direct effect of attributional style and beliefs on physiology. In a further study, Greer et al. (1979) suggested that denial and a fighting spirit, not hopelessness, predicted survival for breast cancer, suggesting again that beliefs might have a direct effect on illness and recovery. Similarly, Gidron et al. (2001) measured hopelessness (defined as pessimism and helplessness) at baseline and assessed change in a serological marker for breast cancer in women with breast cancer after four months. The results showed that helplessness but not pessimism was related to poorer outcome (see Chapter 14 for a discussion of cancer).

Emotional Expression

There is evidence that certain coping styles linked to emotional expression may relate to illness onset and progression. For example, some studies have looked at suppression and denial and have reported associations with poorer health outcomes (e.g. Kune et al. 1991; Gross and Levenson 1997). Other studies have focused on emotional (non-) expression and an emotionally inexpressive coping style known as 'type C', and have described a link with illness (e.g. Solano et al. 2001, 2002; Nykliček et al. 2002), while other researchers have highlighted the importance of a repressive coping style (e.g. Myers 2000). This research consistently indicates that non-expression of emotions, particularly negative emotions in stressful situations, can be harmful for health. There is also evidence that encouraging emotional expression through writing or disclosure groups may be beneficial. This work has been particularly pioneered by Pennebaker (e.g. 1993, 1997) using his basic writing paradigm. This has involved randomly allocating participants to either the experimental or control group with both groups being asked to write for three to five consecutive days for 15 to 30 minutes each day. The experimental group is asked to 'write about your very deepest thoughts and feelings about an extremely emotional issue that has affected you and your life. In your writing I'd really like you to let go and explore your very deepest emotions and thoughts . . .'. The control group is asked to write about more superficial topics such as how they spend their time. This intervention has been used with a range of people including adults, children, students, patients, maximum-security prisoners and survivors of the Holocaust who disclose a range of traumatic experiences including relationship break-ups, deaths and abuse. The writing paradigm has been shown to impact upon a range of outcome measures. Some research has shown a reduction in subsequent visits to the doctor (e.g. Pennebaker and Beall 1986; Greenberg and Stone 1992), re-employment following job loss (e.g. Spera et al. 1994), absenteeism from work (Francis and Pennebaker 1992), reduction in self-reported physical symptoms (Greenberg and Stone 1992;

Petrie et al. 1995), pain reduction in patients with rheumatoid arthritis (Danoff-Burg et al. 2006) and changes in negative mood (Petrie et al. 1995). In terms of PNI, emotional expression through writing has also been shown to affect the immune system. For example, it has resulted in changes in T helper cell responses (Pennebaker et al. 1988; Petrie et al. 1998), natural killer cell activity (Futterman et al. 1992; Christensen et al. 1996) and CD4 (T lymphocyte) levels (Booth et al. 1997). It has even been shown to improve wound healing after a small punch biopsy (Weinman et al. 2008). Therefore this simple intervention provides support for the PNI model, suggesting a link between an individual's psychological state and their immune system. However, as with all associations, research indicates that the impact of emotional expression might vary according to aspects of the task and aspects of the individual. Smyth and Pennebaker (2008) refer to this as the 'boundary conditions' that may or may not make the intervention work.

Aspects of the Task

Writing versus Talking

Some research has compared the effectiveness of writing versus talking either into a tape recorder or to a therapist (e.g. Donnelly and Murray 1991; Esterling et al. 1994). The results showed that both writing and talking about emotional topics were more effective than writing about superficial topics.

Type of Topic

Some research has shown that changes in outcome only occur after writing about particularly traumatic experiences (e.g. Greenberg and Stone 1992). Others have found that it is the relevance of the topic to the outcome variable that is important. For example, Pennebaker and Beall (1986) found that writing about the experience of coming to college had a greater impact upon college grades than writing about 'irrelevant' traumatic experiences.

Amount of Writing

Research using the writing paradigm has varied the stipulated time of writing both in terms of the length of sessions (from 15 to 30 minutes) and the spread of sessions (over a few days to over a month). Smyth (1998) carried out a meta-analysis and concluded that writing over a longer period might be the most effective approach.

Aspects of the Individual

Demographics

Pennebaker (1997) concludes that the effectiveness of emotional expression does not seem to vary according to age, level of education, language or culture. However, a meta-analysis of writing studies by Smyth (1998) indicated that men may benefit more from writing than women and those who do not naturally talk openly about their emotion may benefit more than those who do.

Personality and Mood

Pennebaker (1997) also concludes that anxiety, inhibition or constraint do not influence the effectiveness of writing. However, Christensen et al. (1996) concluded that individuals high on hostility scores benefited more from writing than those low on hostility.

Use of Language

To explain the effectiveness of writing Pennebaker et al. (2001) developed a computer programme to analyse the content of what people were writing during the task. They coded the transcripts in terms of the types of words used: negative emotion words (sad, angry), positive emotion words (happy, laugh), causal words (because, reason) and insight words (understand, realize). The results from this analysis showed that greater improvement in health was associated with a high number of positive emotion words and a moderate number of negative emotion words. More interestingly, they also found that those who showed a shift towards more causal and insight words also showed greater improvement (Pennebaker et al. 1997). They concluded from this that this shift in language use reflected a shift from poorly organized descriptions towards a coherent story and that a coherent story was associated with better health status. However, in contrast to this Graybeal et al. (2002) directly assessed story-making and found no relationship with health outcomes.

STRESS AND IMMUNITY

Stress can cause illness through physiological changes such as raised heart rate, blood pressure, heartbeat irregularities and an increase in fatty deposits (see earlier). It can also result in changes in immune function. Research on rats showed that stressors such as tail pinching, a loud noise and electric shocks could produce immunosuppression (Moynihan and Ader 1996). Research in humans shows a similar picture. One area of research which has received much attention relates to the impact of caregiver stress. In an early study, Kiecolt-Glaser et al. (1995) explored differences in wound healing between people who were caring for a person with Alzheimer's disease and a control group. Using a punch biopsy, which involves removing a small area of skin and tissue, they explored the relationship between caregiver stress and the wound healing process. The results showed that wound healing was slower in the caregivers than the control group. The wound healing paradigm has also been used to show links between stress and slower healing in students during an exam period (Marucha et al. 1998) and slower healing using high resolution ultrasound scanning which is more accurate than the more traditional measurement strategies involving photography (Ebrecht et al. 2004). Herbert and Cohen (1993) carried out a meta-analysis of 38 studies which had explored the stress–immune system link. They concluded that stress consistently resulted in changes in immune function in terms of proliferative response to mitogens and NK cell activity, and was related to greater numbers of circulating white blood cells, immunoglobulin levels and antibody titers to herpes viruses. They also concluded that greater changes in immune response were found following objectively rather than subjectively rated stressful events and that immune response varied according to the duration of the stressor and whether the stressor involved interpersonal or non-social events.

Given that stress can change health behaviours (see earlier), it is possible that stress causes changes in the immune system by changing behaviour. Ebrecht et al. (2004) examined this possibility by assessing the link between perceived stress and wound healing and controlling for alcohol consumption, smoking, sleeping, exercise and diet. The results showed that stress was related to wound healing regardless of changes in behaviour, indicating that the stress–immunity link may not be explained by an unhealthy lifestyle. In contrast, however, a review of 12 studies exploring the impact of smoking and smoking cessation on recovery following surgery concluded that a longer period of smoking cessation prior to surgery was related to fewer post-operative complications. Health behaviours may not have an association with wound healing when measured following a punch biopsy and when smoking is measured at the same time, but in real life and when smoking changes are assessed, there may well be a link.

Research also indicates that stress may relate to illness progression. Kiecolt-Glaser and Glaser (1986) argued that stress causes a decrease in the hormones produced to fight carcinogens and repair DNA. In particular, cortisol decreases the number of active T cells, which could increase the rate of tumour development. This suggests that stress while ill could exacerbate the illness through physiological changes. Such stress may occur independently of the illness. However, stress may also be a result of the illness itself, such as relationship breakdown, changes in occupation or simply the distress from a diagnosis. Therefore, if the illness is appraised as being stressful, this itself may be damaging to the chances of recovery. The relationship between stress and illness progression has particularly been explored in the context of HIV. For example, Pereira et al. (2003) explored the progression of cervical problems in women with HIV. Women who are HIV positive are more at risk from cervical intraepithelial neoplasia (CIN) and cervical cancer. Pereira et al. explored the relationship between the likelihood of developing the lesions associated with CIN and life stress. The results showed that higher life stress increased the odds of developing lesions by sevenfold over a one-year period. Life stress therefore seemed to link with illness progression. Some research has also addressed the stress–illness link with a focus on stress management interventions. For example, Antoni et al. (2006) randomized 130 gay men who were HIV positive to receive either a cognitive behavioural stress management intervention (CBSM) and anti-retroviral medication adherence training (MAT), or to receive MAT alone. The men were then followed up after 9 and 15 months in terms of viral load. The results showed no differences overall between the two groups. When only those men who already showed detectable viral loads at baseline were included (i.e. those with a lot of virus in the blood already), differences were found. In particular, for these men, those who received the stress management showed a reduction in their viral load over the 15-month period even when medication adherence was controlled for. The authors conclude that for HIV-positive men who already show a detectable viral load, stress management may enhance the beneficial effects of their anti-retroviral treatment. In a similar study, the mechanisms behind the impact of stress management were explored (Antoni et al. 2005). For this study 25 HIV-positive men were randomized to receive stress management or a waiting list control. Urine samples were taken before and after the intervention period. The results again showed that stress management was effective and that this effect was related to reduction in cortisol and depressed mood. The authors conclude that stress management works by reducing the stress induced by being ill with a disease such as HIV. Therefore, whereas stress can exacerbate illness, stress management can aid the effectiveness of treatment and reduce the consequences of the stress resulting from being ill.

STRESS AND WOUND HEALING

One marker of how well the immune system is working is the speed of wound healing and research indicates that stress is linked to this, which has implications for how patients are supported after surgery and the impact of any stressors on their health outcomes. Research in this area has either used acute and chronic clinical wounds, including patients post-surgery for hernia, oral surgery, burn injuries and coronary artery bypass grafting, or experimentally-induced wounds using either tape stripping, a blister chamber model or punch biopsies. Wound healing and stress have then

---

BOX 12.1 Some Problems with . . . Stress and Illness Research

Below are some problems with research in this area that you may wish to consider.

1 Research indicates that stress is linked to illness. However, without some degree of stress we probably wouldn't get many of the pleasures from life (e.g. rewards from hard work, satisfaction of small children, etc.). What differentiates stress that produces illness and that which produces a sense of worth is unclear.

2 Stress is seen to cause illness through either a direct route via physiological shifts or an indirect route via behaviour. Much research considers these two pathways as separate. However, it is likely that they constantly interact and that behaviour and physiology exist in a dynamic relationship. This has implications for both measuring and predicting the stress–illness link.

3 Factors such as coping, social support and control are considered to mediate the stress–illness link. From this perspective the stress–illness link is seen as occurring first, which in turn can then be influenced by these factors. It is likely, however, that the very identification of a stressor in the first place, which may or may not then lead to illness, is determined by the degree of coping, social support or control.

been measured. A recent review explored the evidence in this field and identified 21 papers for a systematic review and 11 papers for a meta-analysis (Walburn et al. 2009). The results indicated that in 17 of the 21 studies stress was associated with impaired wound healing. The effect size was estimated at r = −0.42. This indicates a fairly strong impact of stress on wound healing. The authors conclude that although this link seems fairly well established, more needs to be discovered about what factors mediate this link, including variables such as health-related behaviours, social support and coping (see p. 324).

THE IMPACT OF CHRONIC STRESS

Most research described to date has explored the impact of acute stress induced in the laboratory or individual stressors such as life events. However, many people exist in a life of ongoing chronic stressors including poverty, unemployment, job stress and marital conflict. There is much research linking these social factors to health inequalities, with results consistently showing that psychological distress, CHD and most cancers are more prevalent among lower-class individuals who have more chronic stress in their lives (e.g. Adler et al. 1993; Marmot 1998). However, untangling this relationship is difficult: although chronic stressors such as poverty may cause heart disease, they are also linked to a range of other factors such as nutrition, hygiene, smoking and social support which are also linked to health status. Furthermore, whereas lower socioeconomic position is linked to chronic stressors such as poverty, higher socioeconomic position is linked to higher perceived stress (Heslop et al. 2001). As a result of these methodological problems many researchers have focused on specific areas of chronic stress including job stress and relationship stress.

JOB STRESS

Occupational stress has been studied primarily as a means to minimize work-related illness but also because it provides a forum to clarify the relationship between stress and illness. Early work on occupational stress highlighted the importance of a range of job-related factors including work overload, poor work relationships, poor control over work and role ambiguity. Karasek and colleagues integrated many of these factors into their job demand–job control model of stress, central to which is the notion of job strain (Karasek et al. 1981; Karasek and Theorell 1990). According to the model, there are two aspects of job strain: *job demands*, which reflect conditions that affect performance, and *job autonomy*, which reflects the control over the speed or the nature of decisions made within the job. Karasek's job demand–job control model suggests that high job demands and low job autonomy (control) predict CHD. Karasek and co-workers have since developed the job demand–control hypothesis to include social support. Within this context, social support is defined as either *emotional support*, involving trust between colleagues and social cohesion, or *instrumental social support*, involving the provision of extra resources and assistance. It is argued that high social support mediates and moderates the effects of low control and high job demand. Karasek and Theorell (1990) reported a study in which subjects were divided into low social support and high social support groups, and their decisional control and the demands of their job were measured. The results indicated that subjects in the high social support group showed fewer symptoms of CHD than those subjects in the low social support group. In addition, within those groups high job control and low job demands predicted fewer CHD symptoms.

A series of studies have tested and applied Karasek's model of job strain and associations have been reported between job strain and risk factors for heart disease and heart disease itself (Marmot 1998; Tsutsumi et al. 1998) as well as psychiatric morbidity (Cropley et al. 1999). For example, Kivimaki et al. (2002) used a prospective design to explore the links between job strain and subsequent death from cardiovascular disease. A total of 812 employees from a metal factory in Finland that manufactures paper machines, tractors and firearms along with other equipment completed a baseline assessment in 1973 including measures of their behavioural and biological risks and their work stress. Those with cardiovascular disease at baseline were excluded. Cardiovascular mortality was then recorded between 1973 and 2001 using the national mortality register. The results showed that 73 people had died from cardiovascular disease since the study onset, who were more likely to be older, male, have low worker status, to smoke, have a sedentary lifestyle, high blood pressure, high cholesterol and higher BMI. Further, when age and sex were controlled for, death was predicted by high job strain and low job control. However, after occupational group was also controlled for (i.e. a measure of class), high job strain remained the best predictor.

In line with the emphasis on job strain some research has also explored the impact of changing work and domestic patterns on women's health. Whereas 50 years ago women may have worked until they had children, and then given up work to be at home with their offspring, nowadays an increasing number of women take on multiple roles and balance working with being a parent and a partner. There are two contrasting models of the impact of such multiple roles. The first is the *enhancement model* which suggests that multiple roles have a positive effect on health as they bring benefits such as economic independence, social contact and self-esteem (Collijn et al. 1996; Moen 1998). In contrast the *role strain model* suggests that multiple roles can be detrimental to health as people only have limited resources and can experience role overload and role conflict (Weatherall et al. 1994). Steptoe et al. (2000) explored the effect of multiple roles on cardiovascular activity throughout the day. They monitored the blood pressure and heart rate throughout the working day and evening in 162 full-time teachers and explored the impact of whether the teacher was also married and/or a parent with a child at home. The results showed that marital status or parenthood had no effect on cardiovascular changes throughout the working day. However, these factors did affect the day–evening drop in blood pressure. In particular, parents who reported good social support showed the greatest drop in blood pressure between the end of the working day and evening. The authors conclude that this supports the enhancement model of job strain as those who worked and were parents with support (i.e. had multiple roles) showed a lower allostatic load. This may have been because they found it easier to switch off from their work stress at the end of the day.

To explain the possible effects of multiple roles recent research has focused on the impact of *rumination*. Rumination is defined as 'unintentional preservative thoughts in the absence of obvious external cues' (Cropley and Millward Purvis 2003) and has been linked with anxiety, physical symptoms and depression. Rumination about work is essentially thinking about work out of work hours when the individual no longer wants to think about work. In terms of its relationship with job strain, research shows that higher job strain is associated with more rumination. Further, research indicates that people report more ruminative thoughts about work when alone than with family or friends (Cropley and Millward Purvis 2003). Job strain would seem to be damaging to health and may also result in rumination. If people go home at the end of a busy day to partners or children they are less likely to ruminate and thus continue feeling the stress of work than if they go home to be on their own.

RELATIONSHIP STRESS

There is much evidence indicating an association between relationship status, psychological distress and health status. For example, separated and divorced people have the highest rates of both acute and chronic medical problems even when many demographic factors are controlled for (Verbrugge 1979). In addition, these people also have higher rates of mortality from infectious diseases such as pneumonia and are also over-represented in both inpatient and outpatient psychiatric populations (Crago 1972; Bachrach 1975). However, it is not just the presence or absence or a relationship that is important. The quality is also linked to health. For example, whereas marital happiness is one of the best predictors of global happiness, those in troubled marriages show more distress than those who are unmarried (Glenn and Weaver 1981). These links between relationship status and quality have been understood using a range of literatures including attachment theory, life events theory and self-identity theory. Kiecolt-Glaser et al. (1987, 2003) have explored these links within the context of stress and the role of immune function. In one study they assessed the associations between marital status and marital quality and markers of immune function. Their results showed that poor marital quality was associated with both depression and a poorer immune response. In addition, they reported that women who had been recently separated showed poorer immune response than matched married women and that time since separation and attachment to the ex-husband predicted variability in this response (Kiecolt-Glaser et al. 1987). In another study they explored the relationship between measures of stress hormones during the first year of marriage and marital status and satisfaction 10 years later. The results showed that those who were divorced at follow-up had shown higher levels of stress hormones during conflict, throughout the day and during the night than those who were still married. Further, those whose marriages were troubled at follow-up also showed higher levels of stress hormones at baseline than those whose marriages were untroubled. This suggests that stress responses during the first year of marriage are predictive of marital dissatisfaction and divorce 10 years later (Kiecolt-Glaser et al. 2003).

Research therefore shows a link between stress and illness. For many, this stress takes the form of discrete events. However, many people also experience chronic stress caused by factors such as poverty, unemployment or work load. Much research has focused on two aspects of chronic stress, namely job stress and relationship stress. This research indicates an association between chronic stress and illness, with a role for changes in immune function. However, there exists much variability in the stress–illness link. In part this can be explained by factors such as stress reactivity and stress recovery which have already been described. However, research also highlights a role for other moderating variables which will now be considered.

WHICH FACTORS MODERATE THE STRESS–ILLNESS LINK?

The relationship between stress and illness is not straightforward, and there is much evidence to suggest that several factors may moderate the stress–illness link. These factors are as follows:

Exercise can help to alleviate stress

- *Exercise.* This can cause a reduction in stress (see Chapter 6).
- *Coping styles.* The individual's type of coping style may well mediate the stress–illness link and determine the extent of the effect of the stressful event on their health status (see Chapter 9 for a discussion of coping with illness).
- *Social support.* Increased social support has been related to a decreased stress response and a subsequent reduction in illness.
- *Personality.* It has been suggested that personality may influence the individual's response to a stressful situation and the effect of this response on health. This has been studied with a focus on type A behaviour and personality and the role of hostility (see Chapter 15 for details in the context of CHD).
- *Actual or perceived control.* Control over the stressor may decrease the effects of stress on the individual's health status.

Coping with stress, social support, personality and control will now be examined in greater detail (see Figure 12.4).

COPING

Over the past few years the literature on coping has grown enormously and has explored different types of coping styles, the links

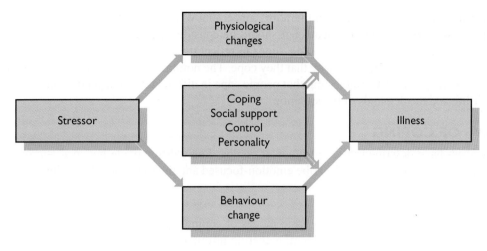

FIGURE 12.4
The stress–illness link: psychological moderators

between coping and a range of health outcomes and the nature of coping itself. How individuals cope with illness was described in Chapter 9 with a focus on crisis theory, cognitive adaptation theory and benefit-finding. This section will describe how coping relates to stress and the stress–illness link.

WHAT IS COPING?

Coping has been defined by Lazarus and colleagues as the process of managing stressors that have been appraised as taxing or exceeding a person's resources and as the 'efforts to manage . . . environmental and internal demands' (Lazarus and Launier 1978). In the context of stress, coping therefore reflects the ways in which individuals interact with stressors in an attempt to return to some sort of normal functioning. This might involve correcting or removing the problem, or it might involve changing the way a person thinks about the problem or learning to tolerate and accept it. For example, coping with relationship conflict could involve leaving the relationship or developing strategies to make the relationship better. In contrast, it could involve lowering one's expectations of what a relationship should be like. Lazarus and Folkman (1987) emphasized the dynamic nature of coping which involves appraisal and reappraisal, evaluation and re-evaluation. Lazarus's model of stress emphasized the interaction between the person and their environment. Likewise, coping is also seen as a similar interaction between the person and the stressor. Further, in the same way that Lazarus and colleagues described responses to stress as involving primary appraisal of the external stressor and secondary appraisal of the person's internal resources, coping is seen to involve regulation of the external stressor and regulation of the internal emotional response. Cohen and Lazarus (1979) defined the goals of coping as:

1 To reduce stressful environmental conditions and maximize the chance of recovery.
2 To adjust or tolerate negative events.
3 To maintain a positive self-image.
4 To maintain emotional equilibrium.
5 To continue satisfying relationships with others.

Styles, Processes and Strategies

When discussing coping, some research focuses on 'styles', some on 'processes' and some on 'strategies'. At times this may just reflect a different use of terminology. However, it also reflects an ongoing debate within the coping literature concerning whether coping should be considered a 'trait' similar to personality, or whether it should be considered a 'state' which is responsive to time and situation. The notion of a 'style' tends to reflect the 'trait' perspective and suggests that people are quite consistent in the way that they cope. The notions of 'process' or 'strategy' tend to reflect a 'state' perspective suggesting that people cope in different ways depending upon the time of their life and the demands of the situation.

WAYS OF COPING

Researchers have described different types of coping. Some differentiate between approach and avoidance coping, while others describe emotion-focused and problem-focused coping.

Approach versus Avoidance

Roth and Cohen (1986) defined two basic modes of coping: approach and avoidance. *Approach coping* involves confronting the problem, gathering information and taking direct action. In contrast, *avoidant coping* involves minimizing the importance of the event. People tend to show one form of coping or the other, although it is possible for someone to manage one type of problem by denying it and another by making specific plans. Some researchers have argued that approach coping is consistently more adaptive than avoidant coping. However, research indicates that the effectiveness of the coping style depends upon the nature of the stressor. For example, avoidant coping might be more effective for short-term stressors (Wong and Kaloupek 1986), but less effective for longer-term stressors (Holahan and Moos 1986). Therefore it might be best to avoid thinking about a one-off stressor such as going to the dentist but make plans and attend to a longer-term stressor such as marital conflict. Some researchers have also explored repressive coping (Myers 2000) and emotional (non-) expression (Solano et al. 2001) which are similar to avoidance coping.

Problem-Focused versus Emotion-Focused Coping (Instrumentality–Emotionality)

In contrast to the dichotomy between approach and avoidant coping, the problem- and emotion-focused dimensions reflect types of coping strategies rather than opposing styles. People can show both problem-focused coping and emotion-focused coping when facing a stressful event. For example, Tennen et al. (2000) examined daily coping in people with rheumatoid arthritis and showed that problem-focused and emotion-focused coping usually occurred together and that emotion-focused coping was 4.4 times more likely to occur on a day when problem-focused coping had occurred than when it had not.

Problem-Focused Coping

This involves attempts to take action to either reduce the demands of the stressor or to increase the resources available to manage it. Examples include devising a revision plan and sticking to it, setting an agenda for a busy day, studying for extra qualifications to enable a career change and organizing counselling for a failing relationship.

Emotion-Focused Coping

This involves attempts to manage the emotions evoked by the stressful event. People use both behavioural and cognitive strategies to regulate their emotions. Examples include talking to friends about a problem, turning to drink or smoking more, or getting distracted by shopping or watching a film. Examples of cognitive strategies include denying the importance of the problem and trying to think about the problem in a positive way.

Several factors have been shown to influence which coping strategy is used:

- *Type of problem.* Work problems seem to evoke more problem-focused coping whereas health and relationship problems tend to evoke emotion-focused coping (Vitaliano et al. 1990).
- *Age.* Children tend to use more problem-focused coping strategies whereas emotion-focused strategies seem to develop in adolescence (Compas et al. 1991, 1996). Folkman et al. (1987)

reported that middle-aged men and women tended to use problem-focused coping whereas the elderly used emotion-focused coping.

- *Gender.* It is generally believed that women use more emotion-focused coping and that men are more problem-focused. Some research supports this belief. For example, Stone and Neale (1984) considered coping with daily events and reported that men were more likely to use direct action than women. However, Folkman and Lazarus (1980) found no gender differences.
- *Controllability.* People tend to use problem-focused coping if they believe that the problem itself can be changed. In contrast they use more emotion-focused coping if the problem is perceived as being out of their control (Lazarus and Folkman 1987).
- *Available resources.* Coping is influenced by external resources such as time, money, children, family and education (Terry 1994). Poor resources may make people feel that the stressor is less controllable by them, resulting in a tendency not to use problem-focused coping.
- *Coping training.* Kaluza (2000) evaluated an intervention designed to change the coping profiles of 82 healthy working men and women. The intervention lasted for 12 weeks and focused on assertiveness, cognitive restructuring, time management, relaxation, physical activities and the scheduling of pleasant activities. Changes were compared to a control group who received no intervention. The results showed significant improvements in emotion-focused coping and problem-focused coping which were related to the individual's original coping profiles. In particular, those who were originally more problem-focused became more emotion-focused and those who were more avoidant copers became more problem-focused. The authors suggest that the intervention changed unbalanced coping profiles. In addition, these changes were related to improvements in aspects of well-being.

MEASURING COPING

The different styles of coping have been operationalized in several measures which have described a range of specific coping strategies. The most commonly used measures are the Ways of Coping Checklist (Folkman and Lazarus 1988) and COPE (Carver et al. 1989). The coping strategies described by these measures include the following:

- *Active coping* (e.g. 'I've been taking action to try to make the situation better').
- *Planning* (e.g. 'I've been trying to come up with a strategy about what to do').
- *Positive reframing* (e.g. 'I've been looking for something good in what is happening').
- *Self-distraction* (e.g. 'I've been turning to work or other activities to take my mind off things').
- *Using emotional support* (e.g. 'I've been getting emotional support from others').
- *Substance use* (e.g. 'I've been using alcohol or other drugs to help me get through it').
- *Behavioural disengagement* (e.g. 'I've given up trying to deal with it').
- *Denial* (e.g. 'I've been saying to myself, "this isn't real"').
- *Self-control* (e.g. 'I've tried to keep my feelings to myself').
- *Distancing* (e.g. 'I didn't let it get to me. I refused to think about it too much').
- *Escape/avoidance* (e.g. 'I wished that the situation would go away').

Some of these strategies are clearly problem-focused coping such as active coping and planning. Others are more emotion-focused such as self-control and distancing. Some strategies, however, are a mix of both problem- and emotion-focused coping. For example, positive reframing involves thinking about the problem in a different way as a means to alter the emotional response to it. Some strategies can also be considered approach coping such as using emotional support and planning, whereas others reflect a more avoidance coping style such as denial and substance use.

According to models of stress and illness, coping should have two effects. First, it should reduce the intensity and duration of the stressor itself. Second, it should reduce the likelihood that stress will lead to illness. Therefore effective coping can be classified as that which reduces the stressor and minimizes the negative outcomes. Some research has addressed these associations. In addition, recent research has shifted the emphasis away from just the absence of illness towards positive outcomes.

Coping and the Stressor

According to Lazarus and colleagues, one of the goals of coping is to minimize the stressor. Much research has addressed the impact of coping on the physiological and self-report dimensions of the stress response. For example, Harnish et al. (2000) argued that effective coping terminates, minimizes or shortens the stressor.

Coping and the Stress–Illness Link

Some research indicates that coping styles may moderate the association between stress and illness. For some studies the outcome variable has been more psychological in its emphasis and has taken the form of well-being, psychological distress or adjustment. For example, Kneebone and Martin (2003) critically reviewed the research exploring coping in carers of persons with dementia. They examined both cross-sectional and longitudinal studies and concluded that problem-solving and acceptance styles of coping seemed to be more effective at reducing stress and distress. In a similar vein, research exploring coping with rheumatoid arthritis suggests that active and problem-solving coping are associated with better outcomes whereas passive avoidant coping is associated with poorer outcomes (e.g. Newman et al. 1996). For patients with chronic obstructive pulmonary disease (COPD), wishful thinking and emotion-focused coping were least effective (Buchi et al. 1997). Similarly, research exploring stress and psoriasis shows that avoidant coping is the least useful (e.g. Leary et al. 1998). Other studies have focused on more illness-associated variables. For example, Holahan and Moos (1986) examined the relationship between the use of avoidance coping, stress and symptoms such as stomach-ache and headaches. The results after one year showed that, of those who had experienced stress, those who used avoidance coping had more symptoms than those who used more approach coping strategies.

Coping and Positive Outcomes

Over recent years there has been an increasing recognition that stressful events such as life events and illness may not only result in negative outcomes but may also lead to some positive changes in people's lives. This phenomenon has been given a range of names including *stress-related growth* (Park et al. 1996), *benefit-finding* (Tennen and Affleck 1999), *meaning-making* (Park and Folkman 1997), *growth-orientated functioning* and *crisis growth* (Holahan et al. 1996). This finds reflection in Taylor's (1983) cognitive adaptation theory and is in line with a new movement called 'positive psychology' (Seligman and Csikszentmihalyi 2000). Though a new field of study, research indicates that coping processes that involve finding meaning in the stressful event, positive reappraisal and problem-focused coping are associated with positive outcomes (Folkman and Moskowitz 2000). (See Chapter 9 for further discussion of benefit-finding following illness.)

Coping is considered to moderate the stress–illness link and to impact upon the extent of the stressor. Much research has involved the description of the kinds of coping styles and strategies used by people and a few studies suggest that some styles might be more effective than others.

SOCIAL SUPPORT

WHAT IS SOCIAL SUPPORT?

Social support has been defined in a number of ways. Initially, it was defined according to the number of friends that were available to the individual. However, this has been developed to include not only the number of friends supplying social support, but the satisfaction with this support (Sarason et al. 1983). Wills (1985) has defined several types of social support:

- *Esteem support:* whereby other people increase one's own self-esteem.
- *Support:* whereby other people are available to offer advice.
- *Companionship:* which involves support through activities.
- *Instrumental support:* which involves physical help.

Lett et al. (2005) also put forward a definition of social support that differentiates between two types:

- *Structural support (or network support):* which refers to the type, size, density and frequency of contact with the network of people available to any individual.
- *Functional support:* which refers to the perceived benefit provided by this structure. This has also be classified into *available functional support* (i.e. potential access to support) and *enacted functional support* (i.e. actual support received) (Tardy 1985).

The term 'social support' is generally used to refer to the perceived comfort, caring, esteem or help one individual receives from others (e.g. Wallston et al. 1983).

Since the 1990s researchers have also explored the notion of 'social capital' which has been shown to have an impact on health (e.g. Putnam 1993; Veenstra 2000; Almedon 2005). Social capital is a broad construct that incorporates trust, social networks, social participation, successful cooperation and reciprocity. Therefore rather than a person having social capital, it could be argued that a town or village is high on social capital if there is a strong sense of community and mutual support. Social capital is hard to measure as it contains components at both the individual (i.e. trust) and group (i.e.

Some communities are high on social capital which can reduce stress

social networks) levels. Within psychology, therefore, the focus has tended to be upon social support from a more individualistic perspective, although Abbott and Freeth (2008) argued that social capital, particularly the elements of trust and reciprocity, could be useful in understanding ways to reduce stress.

MEASURING SOCIAL SUPPORT

Given the definitions of social support above, the focus of measuring social support tends to be on the numbers of people available to provide support and the benefit of this to the individual. The most commonly used measure is the Social Support Questionnaire (SSQ; Sarason et al. 1987) which comes as a long and short version and asks people to list the number of those people they could turn to when in need (i.e. network support) and to rate how helpful they would find this support (i.e. functional support). Some researchers use the SSQ-N just to measure the number of people available to their participants. There are problems with this approach as it is possible that one person could have 20 available people whom they didn't really like, while someone else could have only 2 that they felt really close to. Therefore if the researcher wants to network support and functional support they need to use the complete measure.

DOES SOCIAL SUPPORT AFFECT HEALTH?

A number of studies have examined whether social support influences the health status of the individual. For example, Lynch (1977) reported that widowed, divorced or single individuals have higher mortality rates from heart disease than married people and suggested that heart disease and mortality are related to lower levels of social support. However, problems with this study include the absence of a direct measure of social support and the implicit assumption that marriage is an effective source of social support.

Berkman and Syme (1979) reported the results of a prospective study whereby they measured social support in 4,700 men and women aged 30–69, whom they followed up for nine years. They found that increased social support predicted a decrease in mortality rate. This indicates a role for social support in health. Research has also indicated that birth complications are lower in women who have high levels of social support, again suggesting a link between social support and health status (Oakley 1992). Research has also examined the effects of social support on immune functioning and consequently health. For example, Arnetz et al. (1987) examined the immune function of 25 women who were either employed (n = 8) or unemployed (n = 17). The unemployed group received either standard economic benefits only or received benefits as well as a psychosocial support programme. The results showed that those who received the psychosocial support showed better immune functioning than those who received benefits only. It would seem that social support reduced immunosuppression, thus promoting health.

HOW DOES SOCIAL SUPPORT INFLUENCE HEALTH?

If social support does influence or mediate the stress–illness link, then what are the possible mechanisms? Two theories have been developed to explain the role of social support in health status:

1   The *main effect hypothesis* suggests that social support itself is beneficial and that the absence of social support is itself stressful. This suggests that social support mediates the stress–illness link, with its very presence reducing the effect of the stressor and its absence acting as a stressor.

2   The *stress buffering hypothesis* suggests that social support helps individuals to cope with stress, therefore mediating the stress–illness link by buffering the individual from the stressor; social support influences the individual's appraisal of the potential stressor. This process, which has been described using *social comparison theory*, suggests that the existence of other people enables individuals exposed to a stressor to select an appropriate coping strategy by comparing themselves with others. For example, if an individual was going through a stressful life event, such as divorce, and existed in a social group where other people had dealt with divorces, the experiences of others would help them to choose a suitable coping strategy. The stress buffering hypothesis has also been described using role theory. This suggests that social support enables individuals to change their role or identity according to the demands of the stressor. Role theory emphasizes an individual's role and suggests that the existence of other people offers choices as to which role or identity to adopt as a result of the stressful event.

The Physiological Effects of Social Support

Research has also explored the impact of social support on illness via changes in physiology. The main theory used to explore this mechanism is the *social support reactivity hypothesis* (Lepore 1998) which argues that social support reduces physiological responses to stress, particularly cardiovascular reactivity. This is important as prolonged cardiovascular reactivity has been linked with hypertension and CHD (Treiber et al. 2003; see p. 315 for a discussion of reactivity). Using this approach research has explored the impact of different types of social support on reactivity in the laboratory. For example, separate studies indicate that enacted support (i.e. getting actual support, e.g. Lepore et al. 1993) and the availability of functional support (i.e. potential access to support, e.g. Uchino and Garvey 1997) are associated with reduced reactivity to stressors in the laboratory setting. In a detailed analysis of the relative impact of different types of social support, O'Donovan and Hughes (2008) explored the role of both perceived network support and the availability of functional support on reactivity (measured as heart rate and blood pressure) in response to an acute stressor (a video-recorded and assessed reading out loud). Female participants rated their network support and those scoring in the top or bottom tertiles (n = 152) were included in the study (i.e. those with the most and least people who could help them). They were then randomly allocated to one of three conditions: (1) *functional support, available* (i.e. they were told by the researcher 'My job is to be available to you with help if you need it during your task'); (2) *functional support, not available* (i.e. they were told by the researcher 'My job is to supervise the experiment. If there are any words in any of the passages that are unfamiliar . . . I will not help you in any way'); (3) *control* (i.e. support not mentioned). The results showed a complex relationship between network support and the availability (or not) of functional support for heart rate (not blood pressure). In particular, when functional support was available (i.e. from the researcher), those with low network support (i.e. not many friends and family) showed lower heart rate reactivity than those with high network support. However, when functional support was not available (i.e. not from the researcher), those with low network support had higher heart rate reactivity. This indicates that network support moderates the effect of functional support and that available functional support can compensate for lower network support.

IS SOCIAL SUPPORT ALWAYS A GOOD THING?

Although most research points to the beneficial effects of social support, some studies suggest that at times social support may be detrimental to how an individual responds to stress. For example, laboratory results indicate that high perceived network support (i.e. a large number of people) sometimes relates to increased responses to stressors (Hughes and Curtis 2000; Hughes 2007). There have been several explanations for the negative impact of social support including the following:

- A high number of social ties could increase the chances of vicarious distress if someone in one's social group is upset (Rook et al. 1991).
- People with large social networks may prefer social forms of coping and therefore respond less well to stressors in isolated laboratory settings (Hughes 2007).
- Large social networks provide the opportunity for upward social comparisons which may be detrimental to health (Hughes 2007).
- The impact of social support may be mediated through other variables (O'Donovan and Hughes 2008).
- Different types of social support may have either positive or negative effects. For example, de Ridder et al. (2005) identified 'overprotection' as a potentially harmful form of support.

Research therefore indicates that stress can cause illness. Research also indicates that social support may mediate this relationship.

PERSONALITY

Early research exploring the role of personality as a moderator of the stress–illness link focused on type A behaviour. For example, Friedman and Rosenman (1959) initially defined type A behaviour in terms of excessive competitiveness, impatience, hostility and vigorous speech. Using a semi-structured interview, three types of type A behaviour were identified. Type A1 reflected vigour, energy, alertness, confidence, loud speaking, rapid speaking, tense clipped speech, impatience, hostility, interrupting, frequent use of the word 'never' and frequent use of the word 'absolutely'. Type A2 was defined as being similar to type A1, but not as extreme, and type B was regarded as relaxed, showing no interruptions and quieter (e.g. Rosenman 1978). The Jenkins Activity Survey was developed in 1971 to further define type A behaviour. Support for a relationship between type A behaviour and CHD using the Jenkins Activity Survey has been reported by a number of studies (Rosenman et al. 1975; Haynes et al. 1980). However, research has also reported no relationship between type A behaviour and CHD. For example, Johnston et al. (1987) used Bortner's (1969) questionnaire to predict heart attacks in 5,936 men aged 40–59 years, who were randomly selected from British general practice lists. All subjects were examined at the start of the study for the presence of heart disease and completed the Bortner questionnaire. They were then followed up for morbidity and mortality from heart attack and for sudden cardiac death for an average of 6.2 years. The results showed that non-manual workers had higher type A scores than manual workers and that type A score decreased with age. However, at follow-up the results showed no relationship between type A behaviour and heart disease.

More recently, however, research has focused on other aspects of personality. For example, O'Connor et al. (2009) explored the role of conscientiousness on moderating the link between daily hassles and changes in health behaviours. Using a prospective design, 422 employees completed ratings of daily hassles and health behaviours over a four-week period. The results showed that greater daily hassles were linked to a higher intake of high fat snacks, a greater consumption of caffeinated drinks, higher levels of smoking but lower intakes of alcohol, vegetables and less exercise. Furthermore, the results indicated that these associations were influenced by conscientiousness. Much research has also focused on hostility and aspects of anger expression as being linked to stress and illness. Hostility has most frequently been measured using the Cook Medley Hostility Scale (Cook and Medley 1954) which asks people to rate statements such as 'I have often met people who were supposed to be experts who were no better than I', 'It is safer to trust nobody', and 'My way of doing things is apt to be misunderstood by others'. Agreement with such statements is an indication of high hostility. Hostility has also been classified according to cynical hostility and neurotic hostility. Research has asked 'Who is hostile?', 'How does hostility link to stress?' and 'How does hostility link to illness?'

WHO IS HOSTILE?

Hostility is higher in men than women (Matthews et al. 1992), higher in those of lower socioeconomic status (e.g. Siegman et al. 2000) and seems to run in families (Weidner et al. 2000). It seems to be more common in people whose parents were punitive, abusive or interfering and where there was a lot of conflict (Matthews et al. 1996), and Houston and Vavak (1991) have argued that it relates to feelings of insecurity and negative feelings about others.

HOW DOES HOSTILITY LINK TO STRESS?

As described earlier, individuals vary in their physiological reactions to stress, with some showing greater stress reactivity than others. Researchers have argued that hostility may be the social manifestation of this heightened reactivity. To assess this, Guyll and Contrada (1998) explored the relationship between hostility and stress reactivity and reported that chronically hostile people showed greater reactivity to stressors involving interpersonal interactions than non-hostile people. In addition, Fredrickson et al. (2000) indicated that hostile people show larger and longer-lasting changes in blood pressure when made to feel angry. Therefore hostility and stress reactivity seem to be closely linked. What are the implications of this for the stress–illness link?

HOW DOES HOSTILITY LINK TO ILLNESS?

Much research has shown an association between hostility and CHD. In particular, researchers have argued that hostility is not only an important risk factor for the development of heart disease (e.g. Miller et al. 1996) but is also a trigger for heart attack (Moller et al. 1999). However, it may not be hostility per se that predicts heart disease but how this hostility is expressed. Ramsay et al.

(2001) and McDermott et al. (2001) explored associations between a range of components of hostility and symptoms of coronary artery disease (CAD) in men with CAD versus a control group of men attending a fracture clinic. Results at baseline and at two-year follow-up showed that the best predictor of CAD symptoms was not hostility but anger *expression*. Similarly, Siegman and Snow (1997) argued that the expression of anger and hostility might be a better predictor of stress reactivity and subsequent health outcomes than the state of either anger or hostility on their own. So how might hostility and the expression of hostility cause illness? The link between hostility and heart disease illustrates a role for a physiological pathway with the associated heightened stress reactivity leading to cardiac damage. However, research also suggests that hostility may impact upon health through two other pathways. First, hostility is linked to unhealthy behaviours such as smoking, alcohol intake, caffeine consumption and poorer diet (e.g. Lipkus et al. 1994). Second, hostility may be associated with other moderating factors. For example, hostile individuals may avoid social support and refuse to draw upon any help when under stress. In fact, this is implicit within some of the measures of hostility with responses to statements such as 'No one cares much what happens to me'. Hostility may also relate to coping as believing that 'It is safer to trust nobody' could be seen to reflect an avoidant coping style.

CONTROL

The final potential mediator of the stress–illness link is control. The effect of control on the stress–illness link has also been extensively studied.

WHAT IS CONTROL?

Control has been studied within a variety of different psychological theories.

1 *Attributions and control.* Kelley's (1967) attributional theory examines control in terms of attributions for causality (see Chapter 3 for a discussion of attribution theory). If applied to a stressor, the cause of a stressful event would be understood in terms of whether the cause was controllable by the individual or not. For example, failure to get a job could be understood in terms of a controllable cause (e.g. 'I didn't perform as well as I could in the interview', 'I should have prepared better') or an uncontrollable cause (e.g. 'I am stupid', 'The interviewer was biased').

2 *Self-efficacy and control.* Control has also been discussed by Bandura (1977) in his self-efficacy theory. Self-efficacy refers to an individual's confidence to carry out a particular behaviour. Control is implicit in this concept.

3 *Categories of control.* Five different types of control have been defined by Thompson (1986): behavioural control (e.g. avoidance); cognitive control (e.g. reappraisal of coping strategies); decisional control (e.g. choice over possible outcome); informational control (e.g. the ability to access information about the stressor); and retrospective control (e.g. 'Could I have prevented that event from happening?').

4 *The reality of control.* Control has also been subdivided into perceived control (e.g. 'I *believe* that I can control the outcome of a job interview') and actual control (e.g. 'I *can* control the outcome of a job interview'). The discrepancy between these two factors has been referred to as *illusory control* (e.g. 'I control whether the plane crashes by counting throughout the journey'). However, within psychological theory, most control relates to perceived control.

DOES CONTROL AFFECT THE STRESS RESPONSE?

Research has examined the extent to which the controllability of the stressor influences the stress response to this stressor, both in terms of the subjective experience of stress and the accompanying physiological changes.

1   *Subjective experience.* Corah and Boffa (1970) examined the relationship between the controllability of the stressor and the subjective experience of stress. Subjects were exposed to a loud noise (the experimental stressor) and were either told about the noise (the stressor was predictable) or not (an unpredictable stressor). The results indicated that if the noise was predictable, there was a decrease in subjective experiences of stress. The authors argued that predictability enables the subject to feel that they have control over the stressor, and that this perceived control reduces the stress response. Baum et al. (1981) further suggested that if a stressor is predicted, there is a decrease in the stress response, and reported that predictability or an expectation of the stress enables the individual to prepare their coping strategies.

2   *Physiological changes.* Research has also examined the effect of control on the physiological response to stress. For example, Meyer et al. (1985) reported that if a stressor is regarded as uncontrollable, the release of corticosteroids is increased.

DOES CONTROL AFFECT HEALTH?

If control influences the stress response, does control also influence the effect of stress on health and illness? This question has been examined by looking at both animal and human models.

Animal Research

Seligman and Visintainer (1985) reported the results of a study whereby rats were injected with live tumour cells and exposed to either controllable or uncontrollable shocks. The results indicated that the uncontrollable shocks resulted in promotion of the tumour growth. This suggests that controllability may influence the stress response, which may then promote illness. In a further study, the relationship between control and CHD was studied in monkeys (Manuck et al. 1986). Some breeds of monkey exist in social hierarchies with clearly delineated roles. The monkeys are categorized as either dominant or submissive and this hierarchy is usually stable. However, the authors introduced new members to the groups to create an unstable environment. They argued that the dominant monkeys showed higher rates of CHD in the unstable condition than the dominant monkeys in the stable condition, or the submissive monkeys in the stable condition. It was suggested that the dominant monkeys had high expectations of control, and were used to experiencing high levels of control. However, in the unstable condition, there was a conflict between their expectations of control and the reality which, the authors argued, resulted in an increase in CHD. These animal models are obviously problematic in that many assumptions are made about the similarities between the animals' experience of control and that of humans. However, the results indicate an association between control and health in the predicted direction.

Human Research

Human models have also been used to examine the effect of control on the stress–illness link. For example, the job strain model was developed to examine the effects of control on CHD (e.g. Karasek and Theorell 1990). The three factors involved in the model are (1) psychological demands of the job in terms of workload; (2) the autonomy of the job, reflecting control; and (3) the satisfaction with the job. This model has been used to predict CHD in the USA (Karasek et al. 1988), and in Sweden (Karasek et al. 1981). The results of these studies suggest that a combination of high workload (i.e. high demand), low satisfaction and low control are the best predictors of CHD.

HOW DOES CONTROL MEDIATE THE STRESS–ILLNESS LINK?

A number of theories have been developed to explain how control influences health and mediates the stress–illness link:

- *Control and preventive behaviour.* It has been suggested that high control enables the individual to maintain a healthy lifestyle by believing that 'I can do something to prevent illness'.

- *Control and behaviour following illness.* It has also been suggested that high control enables the individual to change behaviour after illness. For example, even though the individual may have low health status following an illness, if they believe there is something they can do about their health, they will change their behaviour.

- *Control and physiology.* It has been suggested that control directly influences health via physiological changes.

- *Control and personal responsibility.* It is possible that high control can lead to a feeling of personal responsibility and consequently personal blame and learned helplessness. These feelings could lead either to no behaviour change or to unhealthy behaviours resulting in illness.

THE POSSIBLE BENEFITS OF LOW CONTROL

Most theories of the relationship between control and stress suggest that high control (such as predictability, responsibility, etc.) relates to a reduction in stress and is therefore beneficial to health. However, in certain situations a perception of low control may result in lowered stress. For example, flying in a plane can be made less stressful by acknowledging that there is nothing one can do about the possibility of crashing. To an extent this perception of helplessness may be less stressful than attempting to control an uncontrollable situation.

TO CONCLUDE

Cross-sectional and prospective research suggests an association between stress and illness and some experimental studies indicate that stress can cause illness. Theories of the stress–illness link suggest that stress may cause illness through chronic and acute processes involving chronic and acute stress. Both these pathways include changes in behaviour and changes in physiology. The behavioural pathway involves changes in health behaviours such as smoking, alcohol consumption, eating and exercise, whereas the physiological pathway involves changes in sympathetic activation or HPA activation. This chapter has also explored research in the area of PNI which provides some insights into how psychological factors such as emotional expression, mood, belief and stress might directly influence health. However, there is much variability in the link between stress and illness and this chapter has also examined coping, social support, personality and control as possible moderators of this association.

QUESTIONS

1 Stress causes illness. Critically analyse the evidence to support this statement.
2 To what extent might the acute and chronic pathways of stress interact?
3 Describe the mechanisms behind the stress–illness association.
4 How might the behavioural and physiological pathways interact?
5 Discuss the role of PNI in explaining the stress–illness link.
6 How might expressive writing influence health?
7 Is social support always a good thing?
6 Discuss the possible factors that moderate the stress–illness link.
7 Describe a study designed to assess the potential effect of perceived control on the development of illness.

FOR DISCUSSION

Think of the last time you were placed under stress. Consider what factors made this experience either better or worse and discuss the extent stress may have impacted upon your health.

ASSUMPTIONS IN HEALTH PSYCHOLOGY

The stress research highlights some of the assumptions in health psychology.

1 *The problem of mind–body split.* Although much of the stress research examines how the mind may influence the body (e.g. appraisal relates to the release of stress hormones, social support relates to resulting stress-related illnesses), how this process occurs is unclear. In addition, although these relationships suggest an interaction between the mind and the body, they still define them as separate entities which influence each other, not as the same entity.

2 *The problem of progress.* It is often assumed that the most recent theories are better than earlier theories. Therefore models including appraisal, social support and so on, are better than those describing stress as a knee-jerk reaction to a stressor. Perhaps these different theories are not necessarily better than each other, but are simply different ways of describing the stress process.

3 *The problem of methodology.* It is assumed that methodology is neutral and separate to the data collected. For example, factors such as hardiness, self-efficacy and control exist before they are measured. Perhaps, however, methodology is not so neutral, and asking subjects questions relating to these factors actually encourages them to see themselves/the world in terms of hardiness, self-efficacy and control.

FURTHER READING

Evans, P., Hucklebridge, F. and Clow, A. (2000) *Mind, Immunity and Health: The Science of Psychoimmunology.* London: Free Association Books.
This book provides a good introduction to the area of PNI and explains how factors such as stress, depression and conditioning can affect the immune system.

Johnston, D. (1992) The management of stress in the prevention of coronary heart disease, in S. Maes, H. Leventhal and M. Johnston (eds) *International Review of Health Psychology.* London: Wiley.
This chapter reviews the literature relating to the role of stress on CHD and evaluates the effectiveness of interventions aimed at reducing stress in individuals.

Jones, F., Burke, R.J. and Westmen, M. (eds) (2006) *Work–Life Balance: A Psychological Perspective.* Hove: Psychology Press.
This book is an edited collection of chapters which describe and explore different aspects of the work–life balance including the changing nature of work, the legal and policy context of work, managing home and work, managing family and work and recovery after work.

Vedhara, K. and Irwin, M. (eds) (2005) *Human Psychoneuroimmunology.* Oxford: Oxford University Press.
This book provides an excellent overview of the research on PNI and covers key concepts, research and methods.

 Visit the website at www.openup.co.uk/ogden for additional resources on Chapter 12 to help you with your study, such as multiple choice questions, weblinks and a searchable online glossary.

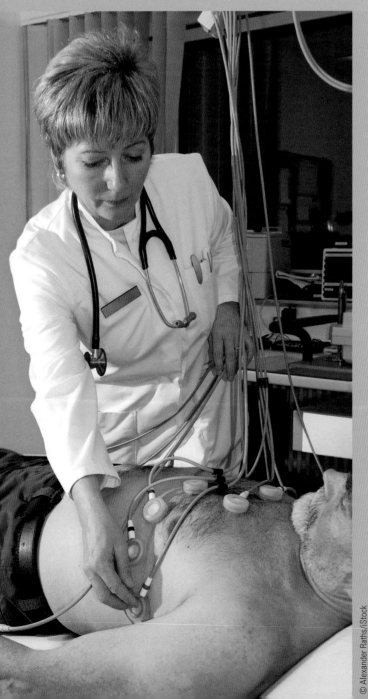

PART FOUR
Being Ill

© Alexander Raths/iStock

13 Pain and the Placebo Effect

© FotografiaBasica/iStock

> ## CHAPTER OVERVIEW
>
> This chapter examines early models of pain and their description of pain as a sensation. It then examines the increasing emphasis on a role for psychology in pain, the shift towards the notion of pain perception and the development of gate control theory. The chapter then describes the three-process model of pain with a focus on how cognitive, affective and behavioural factors can either exacerbate or reduce pain perception. Next, the role of psychology in treating and managing pain is discussed. The chapter examines the problems with pain measurement and the ways in which pain can be assessed. Finally, the chapter explores the placebo effect which is central to pain perception but also to all other areas of health psychology.

WHAT IS PAIN?

Pain seems to have an obvious function. It provides constant feedback about the body, enabling us to make adjustments to how we sit or sleep. Pain is often a warning sign that something is wrong and results in protective behaviour such as avoiding moving in a particular way or lifting heavy objects. Pain also triggers help-seeking behaviour and is a common reason for patients visiting their doctor. Pain also has psychological consequences and can generate fear and anxiety. From an evolutionary perspective therefore, pain is a sign that action is needed. It functions to generate change either in the form of seeking help or avoiding activity. However, pain is not that simple. Some pain seems to have no underlying cause and functions to hinder rather than to help a person carry on with their lives. Such pain has a strong psychological component. Researchers differentiate between acute pain and chronic pain. Acute pain is defined as pain that lasts for six months or less. It usually has a definable cause and is mostly treated with painkillers. A broken leg or a surgical wound is an example of acute pain. In contrast, chronic pain lasts for longer than six months and can be either benign, in that it varies in severity, or progressive, in that it gets gradually worse. Chronic low back pain is often described as chronic benign pain whereas illnesses such as rheumatoid arthritis result in chronic progressive pain. Most of the research described in this chapter is concerned with chronic pain which shows an important role for psychological factors.

Giving a child's pain meaning illustrates the role of psychological factors in pain perception

Imagine a small child falling over. They look up at you and you have a split second to turn their experience into 'nothing' or 'pain'. So if you say, 'Never mind, up you get' and smile enthusiastically, chances are they will get up and carry on playing. But if you look frightened and say, 'Oh, that must have hurt, give me a cuddle', then they will cry. In that split second all the psychological factors that influence the pain experience come into play and translate the signals being sent to the brain into something that hurts or something that is OK. Without these factors pain would be considered a *sensation*. But this example illustrates why pain is considered a *perception* and not a sensation (if their arm is hanging off, they will cry regardless of what you do!).

EARLY PAIN THEORIES: PAIN AS A SENSATION

Early models of pain described it within a biomedical framework as an automatic response to an external factor. Descartes, perhaps the earliest writer on pain, regarded it as a response to a painful stimulus. He described a direct pathway from the source of pain (e.g. a burnt finger) to an area of the brain that detected the painful sensation. Von Frey (1895) developed the *specificity theory of pain*, which again reflected this very simple stimulus–response model. He suggested that there were specific sensory receptors which transmit touch, warmth and pain, and that each receptor was sensitive to specific stimulation. This model was similar to that described by Descartes in that the link between the cause of pain and the brain was seen as direct and automatic. In a similar vein, Goldschneider (1920) developed a further model of pain called the *pattern theory*. He suggested that nerve impulse patterns determined the degree of pain and that messages from the damaged area were sent directly to the brain via these nerve impulses. Therefore these three models of pain describe the sensation in the following ways:

- Tissue damage causes the sensation of pain.
- Psychology is involved in these models of pain only as a consequence of pain (e.g. anxiety, fear, depression). Psychology has no causal influence.
- Pain is an automatic response to an external stimulus. There is no place for interpretation or moderation.
- The pain sensation has a single cause.
- Pain was categorized into being either *psychogenic pain* or *organic pain*. Psychogenic pain was considered to be 'all in the patient's mind' and was a label given to pain when no organic basis could be found. Organic pain was regarded as being 'real pain' and was the label given to pain when some clear injury could be seen.

INCLUDING PSYCHOLOGY IN THEORIES OF PAIN

The early simple models of pain had no role for psychology. However, psychology came to play an important part in understanding pain during the twentieth century. This was based on several observations.

First, it was observed that medical treatments for pain (e.g. drugs, surgery) were, in the main, only useful for treating *acute* pain (i.e. pain with a short duration). Such treatments were fairly ineffective for treating *chronic* pain (i.e. pain that lasts for a long time). This suggested that there must be something else involved in the pain sensation which was not included in the simple stimulus–response models.

It was also observed that individuals with the same degree of tissue damage differed in their reports of the painful sensation and/or painful responses. Beecher (1956) observed soldiers' and civilians' requests for pain relief in a hospital during the Second World War. He reported that although soldiers and civilians often showed the same degree of injury, 80 per cent of the civilians requested medication, whereas only 25 per cent of the soldiers did. He suggested that this reflected a role for the meaning of the injury in the experience of pain; for the soldiers, the injury had a positive meaning as it indicated that their war was over. This meaning mediated the pain experience.

The third observation was *phantom limb pain*. The majority of amputees tend to feel pain in an absent limb. This pain can actually get worse after the amputation, and continues even after complete healing. Sometimes the pain can feel as if it is spreading and is often described as a hand being clenched with the nails digging into the palm (when the hand is missing) or the bottom of the foot being forced into the ankle (when the foot is missing). Phantom limb pain has no peripheral physical basis because the limb is obviously missing. In addition, not everybody feels phantom limb pain and for those who do, they do not experience it to the same extent. Further, even individuals who are born with missing limbs sometimes report phantom limb pain.

These observations, therefore, suggest variation between individuals. Perhaps this variation indicates a role for psychology.

THE GATE CONTROL THEORY OF PAIN

Melzack and Wall (1965), developed the gate control theory of pain (GCT), which represented an attempt to introduce psychology into the understanding of pain. This model is illustrated in Figure 13.1. It suggested that, although pain could still be understood in terms of a stimulus–response pathway, this pathway was complex and mediated by a network of interacting processes. Therefore the GCT integrated psychology into the traditional biomedical model of pain and not only described a role for physiological causes and interventions, but also allowed for psychological causes and interventions.

INPUT TO THE GATE

Melzack and Wall suggested that a gate existed at the spinal cord level, which received input from the following sources:

- *Peripheral nerve fibres.* The site of injury (e.g. the hand) sends information about pain, pressure or heat to the gate.
- *Descending central influences from the brain.* The brain sends information related to the psychological state of the individual to the gate. This may reflect the individual's behavioural state (e.g. attention, focus on the source of the pain); emotional state (e.g. anxiety, fear, depression); and previous experiences or self-efficacy (e.g. 'I have experienced this pain before and know that it will go away') in terms of dealing with the pain.
- *Large and small fibres.* These fibres constitute part of the physiological input to pain perception.

OUTPUT FROM THE GATE

The gate integrates all of the information from these different sources and produces an output. This output from the gate sends information to an action system, which results in the perception of pain.

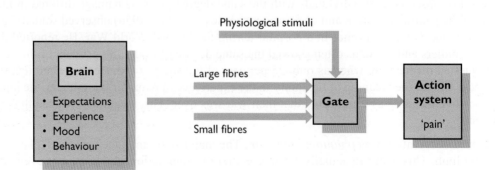

FIGURE 13.1

The gate control theory (GTC) of pain

HOW DOES THE GCT DIFFER FROM EARLIER MODELS OF PAIN?

The GCT differs from earlier models in a number of fundamental ways:

- *Pain as a perception.* According to the GCT, pain is a perception and an experience rather than a sensation. This change in terminology reflects the role of the individual in the degree of pain experienced. In the same way that psychologists regard vision as a perception, rather than a direct mirror image, pain is described as involving an active interpretation of the painful stimuli.

- *The individual as active, not passive.* According to the GCT, pain is determined by central and peripheral fibres. Pain is seen as an active process as opposed to a passive one. The individual no longer just responds passively to painful stimuli, but actively interprets and appraises painful stimuli.

- *The role of individual variability.* Individual variability is no longer a problem in understanding pain but central to the GCT. Variation in pain perception is understood in terms of the degree of opening or closing of the gate.

- *The role for multiple causes.* The GCT suggests that many factors are involved in pain perception, not just a singular physical cause.

- *Is pain ever organic?* The GCT describes most pain as a combination of physical and psychological. It could, therefore, be argued that within this model pain is never totally either organic or psychogenic.

- *Pain and dualism.* The GCT attempts to depart from traditional dualistic models of the body and suggests an interaction between the mind and the body.

PROBLEMS WITH THE GCT

The GCT represented an important advancement on previous simple stimulus–response theories of pain. It introduced a role for psychology and described a multidimensional process rather than a simple linear one. However, there are several problems with the theory:

- Although there is plenty of evidence illustrating the mechanisms to increase and decrease pain perception, no one has yet actually located the 'gate' itself.

- Although the input from the site of physical injury is mediated and moderated by experience and other psychological factors, the model still assumes an organic basis for pain. This integration of physiological and psychological factors can explain individual variability and phantom limb pain to an extent, but because the model still assumes some organic basis it is still based on a simple stimulus–response process.

- The GCT attempted to depart from traditional dualistic models of health by its integration of the mind and the body. However, although the GCT suggests some integration or interaction between mind and body, it still sees them as separate processes. The model suggests that physical processes are influenced by the psychological processes, but that these two sets of processes are distinct.

BOX 13.1 Some Problems with . . . Pain Research

Below are some problems with research in this area that you may wish to consider.

1 Pain cannot be observed and is a subjective experience. Therefore measuring pain is problematic. Self-report measures are reliant upon the individual attempting to give an accurate description of how they feel which may well be influenced by how they want other people to believe that they feel and the ability of

the existing measures to describe their experience. More objective measures such as the observation of pain behaviour or medication use may miss the subjective nature of the pain experience.

2   Pain research highlights the interaction between biological and psychological processes. This is particularly apparent in the GCT and the role of affect and cognitions in mediating the pain experience. However, how these different processes actually interact remains unclear. Why is it that focusing on pain actually makes it hurt more?

3   Pain research emphasizes the role of psychological factors in promoting chronic pain and exacerbating acute pain. Little, however, is known about pain onset. Why do some people get headaches while others do not? Why is there such cultural variation in where and when people experience pain? (see Chapter 9 for a discussion of symptom onset).

4   Pain is difficult to measure, difficult to define and treatment studies often use different protocols, different outcomes and different time points. This makes synthesizing evidence across studies difficult. This is discussed in detail in Eccleston et al. (2010) and Moore et al. (2010).

THE ROLE OF PSYCHOSOCIAL FACTORS IN PAIN PERCEPTION

The GCT was a development from previous theories in that it allowed for the existence of mediating variables, and emphasized active perception rather than passive sensation. That theory, and the subsequent attempts at evaluating the different components of pain perception, reflect a *three-process model* of pain. The components of this model are: physiological processes; subjective–affective–cognitive processes; and behavioural processes. Physiological processes involve factors such as tissue damage, the release of endorphins and changes in heart rate. The subjective–affective–cognitive and behavioural processes are illustrated in Figure 13.2 and are described in more detail below.

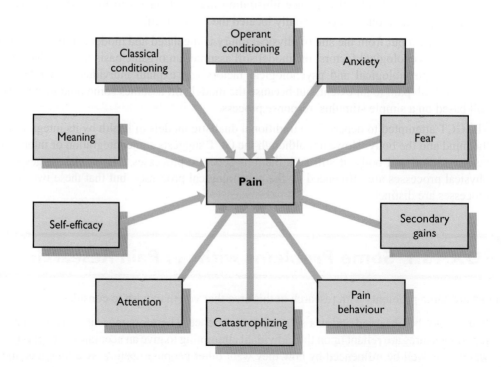

FIGURE 13.2

Psychosocial aspects of pain

SUBJECTIVE–AFFECTIVE–COGNITIVE PROCESSES
THE ROLE OF LEARNING
Classical Conditioning

Research suggests that *classical conditioning* may have an effect on the perception of pain. As described by theories of associative learning, an individual may associate a particular environment with the experience of pain. For example, if an individual associates the dentist with pain due to past experience, the pain perception may be enhanced when attending the dentist due to this expectation. In addition, because of the association between these two factors, the individual may experience increased anxiety when attending the dentist, which may also increase pain. Jamner and Tursky (1987) examined the effect of presenting migraine sufferers with words associated with pain. They found that this presentation increased both anxiety and pain perception and concluded that the words caused a change in mood, which caused a change in the subject's perception of pain. This is further discussed in terms of the impact of anxiety.

Operant Conditioning

Research suggests that there is also a role for *operant conditioning* in pain perception. Individuals may respond to pain by showing pain behaviour (e.g. resting, grimacing, limping, staying off work). Such pain behaviour may be positively reinforced (e.g. sympathy, attention, time off work), which may itself increase pain perception (see below).

THE ROLE OF AFFECT
Anxiety

Some research has explored how patients worry about their pain. For example, Eccleston et al. (2001) asked 34 male and female chronic pain patients to describe their experience of pain over a seven-day period. The results showed that the patients reported both pain-related and non-pain-related worry and that these two forms of worry were qualitatively different. In particular, worry about chronic pain was seen as more difficult to dismiss, more distracting, more attention grabbing, more intrusive, more distressing and less pleasant than non-pain-related worry. Other research has explored how worry and anxiety relate to pain perception. Fordyce and Steger (1979) examined the relationship between anxiety and acute and chronic pain. They reported that anxiety has a different relationship to these two types of pain. In terms of acute pain, pain increases anxiety; the successful treatment for the pain then decreases the pain which subsequently decreases the anxiety. This can then cause a further decrease in the pain. Therefore, because of the relative ease with which acute pain can be treated, anxiety relates to this pain perception in terms of a cycle of pain *reduction*. However, the pattern is different for chronic pain. Because treatment has very little effect on chronic pain, this increases anxiety, which can further increase pain. Therefore, in terms of the relationship between anxiety and chronic pain, there is a cycle of pain *increase*. Research has also shown a direct correlation between high anxiety levels and increased pain perception in children with migraines and sufferers of back pain and pelvic pain (Feuerstein et al. 1987; McGowan et al. 1998). In an experimental study, participants took part in the cold pressor test which involves placing the hand and arm in icy water as a means to induce pain. Their trait anxiety was assessed and some were actively distracted from thinking about their pain (James and Hardardottir 2002). The results showed that both distraction and low anxiety reduced the pain experience.

Fear

Many patients with an experience of pain can have extensive fear of increased pain or of the pain reoccurring which can result in them avoiding a whole range of activities that they perceive to be high risk. For example, patients can avoid moving in particular ways and exerting themselves to any extent. However, these patients often do not describe their experiences in terms of fear but rather in terms of what they can and cannot do. Therefore they do not report being frightened of making the pain worse by lifting a heavy object, but they state that they can no longer lift heavy objects. Fear of pain and fear avoidance beliefs have been shown to be linked with the pain experience in terms of triggering pain in the first place. For example, Linton et al. (2000) measured fear avoidance beliefs in a large community sample of people who reported no spinal pain in the preceding year. The participants were then followed up after one year and the occurrence of a pain episode and their physical functioning were assessed. The results showed that 19 per cent of the sample reported an episode of back pain at follow-up and that those with higher baseline scores of fear avoidance were twice as likely to report back pain and had a 1.7 times higher risk of lowered physical functioning. The authors argued that fear avoidance may relate to the early onset of pain. Some research also suggests that fear may be involved in exacerbating existing pain and turning acute pain into chronic pain. For example, Crombez et al. (1999) explored the interrelationship between attention to pain and fear. They argued that pain functions by demanding attention which results in a lowered ability to focus on other activities. Their results indicated that pain-related fear increased this attentional interference, suggesting that fear about pain increased the amount of attention demanded by the pain. They concluded that pain-related fear can create a hyper-vigilance towards pain which could contribute to the progression from acute to chronic pain. These conclusions were further supported by a comprehensive review of the research. This indicates that treatment that exposes patients to the very situations they are afraid of, such as going out and being in crowds, can reduce fear avoidance beliefs and modify their pain experience (Vlaeyen and Linton 2000).

THE ROLE OF COGNITION

Catastrophizing

Patients with pain, particularly chronic pain, often show *catastrophizing*. Keefe et al. (2000) described catastrophizing as involving three components: (1) rumination – a focus on threatening information, both internal and external ('I can feel my neck click whenever I move'); (2) magnification – overestimating the extent of the threat ('The bones are crumbling and I will become paralysed'); and (3) helplessness – underestimating personal and broader resources that might mitigate the danger and disastrous consequences ('Nobody understands how to fix the problem and I just can't bear any more pain'). Catastrophizing has been linked to both the onset of pain and the development of longer-term pain problems (Sullivan et al. 2001). For example, in the prospective study described earlier by Linton et al. (2000), the authors measured baseline levels of pain catastrophizing. The results showed some small associations between this and the onset of back pain by follow-up. Crombez et al. (2003) developed a new measure of catastrophizing to assess this aspect of pain in children which consisted of three subscales reflecting the dimensions of catastrophizing – namely rumination, magnification and helplessness. They then used this measure to explore the relationship between catastrophizing and pain intensity in a clinical sample of 43 boys and girls aged between 8 and 16. The results indicated that catastrophizing independently predicted both pain intensity and disability regardless of age and gender. The authors argued that catastrophizing functions by facilitating the escape from pain and by communicating distress to others.

Meaning

Although at first glance any pain would seem to be only negative in its meaning, research indicates that pain can have a range of meanings to different people. For example, the pain experienced during childbirth, although intense, has a very clear cause and consequence. If the same kind of pain were to happen outside childbirth then it would have a totally different meaning and would probably be experienced in a very different way. Beecher (1956), in his study of soldiers' and civilians' requests for medication, was one of the first people to examine this and asked the question, 'What does pain mean to the individual?' Beecher argued that differences in pain perception were related to the meaning of pain for the individual. In this study, the soldiers benefited from their pain. This has also been described in terms of *secondary gains* whereby the pain may have a positive reward for the individual.

Self-Efficacy

Some research has emphasized the role of self-efficacy in pain perception and reduction. Turk et al. (1983) suggested that increased pain self-efficacy may be an important factor in determining the degree of pain perception. In addition, the concept of pain *locus of control* has been developed to emphasize the role of individual cognitions in pain perception (Manning and Wright 1983).

Attention

There has also been research exploring the impact of attention on pain and much work shows that attention to the pain can exacerbate it whereas distraction can reduce the pain experience. For example, Chapman and Martin (2010) reported that patients with irritable bowel syndrome paid more attention to pain words compared to controls when exposed to an exogenous cuing task. The results also showed that those who paid more attention to the pain words also reported more symptoms and took more time off work. However, this study was cross-sectional in design and only shows associations rather than causal relationships. Further, it addresses attention to pain words rather than pain itself. In the experimental study described earlier, however, James and Hardardottir (2002) illustrated that increasing attention to pain increased the pain experience using the cold pressor task. Eccleston and Crombez have carried out much work in this area which they reviewed in the *Psychological Bulletin* in 1999. They illustrated how patients who attend to their pain experience more pain than those who are distracted. This association explains why patients suffering from back pain who take to their beds and therefore focus on their pain take longer to recover than those who carry on working and engaging with their lives. This association is also reflected in relatively recent changes in the general management approach to back pain problems – bed rest is no longer the main treatment option. In addition, Eccleston and Crombez provide a model of how pain and attention are related (Eccleston 1994; Eccleston and Crombez 1999). They argue that pain interrupts and demands attention and that this interruption depends upon pain-related characteristics such as the threat value of the pain and environmental demands such as emotional arousal. They argue that pain causes a shift in attention towards the pain as a way to encourage escape and action. The result of this shift in attention is a reduced ability to focus on other tasks, resulting in attentional interference and disruption. This disruption has been shown in a series of experimental studies indicating that patients with high pain perform less well on difficult tasks that involve the greatest demand of their limited resources (e.g. Eccleston 1994; Crombez et al. 1998a, 1999).

BEHAVIOURAL PROCESSES

Pain Behaviour and Secondary Gains

The way in which an individual responds to pain can itself increase or decrease the pain perception. In particular, research has looked at pain behaviours which have been defined by Turk et al. (1985) as facial or audible expression (e.g. clenched teeth and moaning), distorted posture or movement (e.g. limping, protecting the pain area), negative affect (e.g. irritability, depression) or avoidance of activity (e.g. not going to work, lying down). It has been suggested that pain behaviours are reinforced through attention, the acknowledgement they receive, and through secondary gains, such as not having to go to work. Positively reinforcing pain behaviour may increase pain perception. Pain behaviour can also cause a lack of activity and muscle wastage, no social contact and no distraction leading to a sick role, which can also increase pain perception. Williams (2002) provides an evolutionary analysis of facial expressions of pain and argues that if the function of pain is to prioritize escape, recovery and healing, facial expressions are a means to communicate pain and to elicit help from others to achieve these goals. Further, she argues that people often assume that individuals have more control over the extent of their pain-induced facial expressions than they actually do and are more likely to offer help or sympathy when expressions are mild. Stronger forms of expression are interpreted as amplified and as indications of malingering.

THE INTERACTION BETWEEN THESE DIFFERENT PROCESSES

The three-process model describes the separate components that influence pain perception. However, these three processes are not discrete but interact and are at times interchangeable. For example, emotional factors may influence an individual's physiology and cognitive factors may influence an individual's behaviour. Further, the different components within each process also interact. For example, association may increase pain in terms of learning. However, it is likely that this process can be explained by changes in anxiety and focus, with places and experiences that have previously been associated with pain resulting in increased anxiety and increased attention to pain, therefore increasing the pain experience. Likewise, pain behaviours may exacerbate pain by limiting physical movement. But it is also likely that they operate by increasing focus and anxiety – staying in bed leaves the individual with nothing to do other than think and worry about their pain. Research also indicates that fear influences attention, that fear interacts with catastrophizing and that catastrophizing influences attentional interference (Crombez et al. 1998a, 1998b, 1999; Van Damme et al. 2002). The three-process model offers a framework for mapping out the different factors that influence pain. However, this categorization is probably best seen as a framework only, with the different components being interrelated rather than discrete categories of discrete factors.

THE EXPERIENCE OF PAIN

So far this chapter has explored the kinds of factors that contribute to why people feel pain and theories that can explain pain onset, maintenance and the translation of acute pain into chronic pain. What is missing in this research, however, is how pain is *experienced*. Some of the measures of pain capture these experiences by asking people whether their pain can be described by words such as 'flickering', 'punishing', 'cruel', 'killing' or 'annoying' (see p. 355 for a discussion of pain measures). Qualitative research has further explored the pain experience. For example, Osborn and Smith (1998) interviewed nine women who experienced chronic back pain and analysed the transcripts using interpretative phenomenological analysis (IPA) (Smith and Osborn 2003). The results showed that the patients experienced their pain in a range of ways which were conceptualized into four main themes. First, they showed a strong motivation to understand and explain their situation and to know why they had developed chronic pain. They also described how they could not believe that nothing else could be done for their condition, how they felt poorly informed about their pain and often described their pain as acting of its own volition. Their need to make sense of their pain was therefore frustrated, leaving them with feelings of uncertainty and ambiguity about their experience. Second, they showed a process of social comparison and compared themselves with others and with themselves in the past and future. In general they saw their pain as denying them the chance to be who they once were and who they wanted to be in the future and attempts to boost their self-esteem by making comparisons with those more unfortunate seemed to fail as they only acted as reminders of their gloomy prognosis. Third, they described how they were often not believed by others as they had no visible signs to support their suffering or disability. Finally, they described how their pain had resulted in them withdrawing from public view as they felt a burden to others and felt that when in public they had to hide their pain and appear healthy and mobile. For these sufferers, chronic back pain seemed to have a profound effect on their lives, impacting on how they felt about themselves and how they interacted with others.

In a further qualitative study, McGowan et al. (2007) asked 32 women with chronic pelvic pain to write stories about their illness trajectories. The data were analysed using a narrative approach to explore why women disengaged from their treatment and often become dissatisfied with the care they received. The results showed that the women wanted validation and recognition of their experiences and therefore engaged with the process of finding a diagnosis. But they often felt that they weren't listened to and opted out of this process, leaving them with a sense of disempowerment and being in limbo. Much of this failure was attributed to the medical consultation and its dualistic model of the mind and body being separate. The experience of pain is further discussed in **Focus on Research 13.1**.

FOCUS ON RESEARCH 13.1: THE EXPERIENCE OF PAIN

A study to examine how people experience chronic benign back pain (Smith 2007).

BACKGROUND

Chronic benign pain is any pain that lasts longer than six months and is unrelated to any ongoing disease. It does not seem to have any biological function and is generally experienced as acute pain that simply does not go away. Chronic benign low back pain is most often a midlife condition and is the single largest cause of disability and time lost at work in the western world. This study aimed to explore participants' experiences of their chronic benign back pain in the context of their sense of self, with a focus on their subjective experience. It is an interesting study as it presents a clear picture of what it is like to suffer chronic pain and illustrates how this ongoing problem challenges people's sense of who they are.

METHODOLOGY

The study used a qualitative method using semi-structured interviews which included questions such as 'How did your pain start?', 'Has your pain changed things for you at all?', 'How would you describe yourself as a person?' and 'Has having pain changed the way you think or feel about yourself?'.

Sample

Six people were interviewed who had all been recently referred to a pain clinic in the UK. They were a reasonably homogenous sample, being European, Caucasian, from a working-class background and in middle adulthood and had been in pain for between 5 and 15 years. None was taking major opiates or waiting for any medical interventions and none had any prior experience of a pain clinic.

Data Analysis

The data were analysed using IPA (Smith and Osborn 2003).

RESULTS

The results showed that pain had a powerful negative impact upon the sufferers' self and identity. In particular, the interviewees described how their pain resulted in them often experiencing themselves as two separate identities; the 'nice person' and the 'mean me' and that these two selves created a struggle for the individual as they attempted to retain the good self. In addition, they described how they moved between these two selves and employed coping strategies in an attempt to prevent the pain eroding the good self. Further, they described how this struggle over self was exacerbated by the public arena as they were concerned about how others would see them. This often led to the pain sufferers becoming socially isolated or consciously acting when with others. They also described how they sometimes directed the 'mean me' at others by stopping caring and taking pleasure in the suffering of others. Finally, some also described how they felt they may be punished in some way for being so negative towards others.

CONCLUSION

Smith concludes from his analysis that the pain experience generates a cycle of negative thoughts, with the sufferer having negative thoughts which get internalized, which are then discharged onto others which in turn leads to further negative thoughts. Further, he suggests that this has a serious debilitating impact on the person's sense of self which is further exacerbated by the public arena. This study therefore offers an insight into chronic benign back pain and illustrates how an ongoing problem can change how an individual feels about themselves and in addition influence how they react to the world around them.

THE ROLE OF PSYCHOLOGY IN PAIN TREATMENT

Acute pain is mostly treated with pharmacological interventions. Chronic pain has proved to be more resistant to such approaches and recently pain clinics have been set up that adopt a multidisciplinary approach to pain treatment. The goals set by such clinics include the following:

- *Improving physical and lifestyle functioning.* This involves improving muscle tone, self-esteem, self-efficacy and distraction, and decreasing boredom, pain behaviour and secondary gains.
- *Decreasing reliance on drugs and medical services.* This involves improving personal control, decreasing the sick role and increasing self-efficacy.
- *Increasing social support and family life.* This aims to increase optimism and distraction and decrease boredom, anxiety, sick role behaviour and secondary gains.

Current treatment philosophy also emphasizes early intervention to prevent the transition of acute pain to chronic pain.

Research shows that psychology is involved in the perception of pain in terms of factors such as learning, anxiety, worry, fear, catastrophizing, meaning and attention. Multidisciplinary pain clinics increasingly place psychological interventions at their core. There are several methods of pain treatment, which reflect an interaction between psychology and physiological factors. These methods can be categorized as respondent, cognitive and behavioural methods and are illustrated in Figure 13.3.

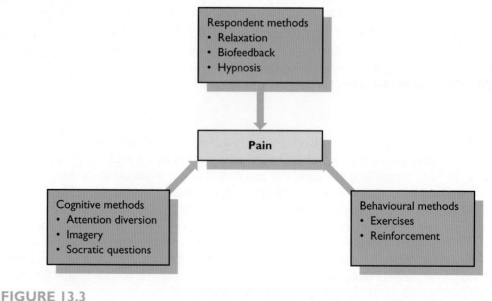

FIGURE 13.3

Psychology and pain treatment

- *Respondent methods.* Respondent methods are designed to modify the physiological system directly by reducing muscular tension. Examples are relaxation methods which aim to decrease anxiety and stress and consequently to decrease pain and biofeedback which is used to enable the individual to exert voluntary control over their bodily functions. Biofeedback aims to decrease anxiety and tension and therefore to decrease pain. However, some research indicates that it adds nothing to relaxation methods. Hypnosis is also used as a means to relax the individual. It seems to be of most use for acute pain and for repeated painful procedures such as burn dressing.

- *Cognitive methods.* A cognitive approach to pain treatment focuses on the individual's thoughts about pain and aims to modify cognitions that may be exacerbating their pain experience. Techniques used include attention diversion (i.e. encouraging the individual not to focus on the pain), imagery (i.e. encouraging the individual to have positive, pleasant thoughts) and the modification of maladaptive thoughts by the use of Socratic questions. Socratic questions challenge the individual to try to understand their automatic thoughts and involve questions such as 'What evidence do you have to support your thoughts?' and 'How would someone else view this situation?' The therapist can use role play and role reversal (see Chapter 8 for a discussion of cognitive behavioural therapy – CBT – and Socratic questions).

- *Behavioural methods.* Some treatment approaches draw upon the basic principles of operant conditioning and use reinforcement to encourage the individual to change their behaviour. For example, if a chronic pain patient has stopped activities that they believe may exacerbate their pain, the therapist will incrementally encourage them to become increasingly more active. Each change in behaviour will be rewarded by the therapist and new exercises will be developed and agreed to encourage the patient to move towards their pre-set goal.

The three components of psychological therapy are often integrated into a cognitive behavioural treatment package (see Chapter 8 for a discussion of CBT in the context of behaviour change).

COGNITIVE BEHAVIOURAL THERAPY

CBT is increasingly used with chronic pain patients and is based upon the premise that pain is influenced by four sources of information: cognitive sources such as the meaning of the pain ('it will prevent me from working'); emotional sources such as the emotions associated with the pain ('I am anxious that it will never go away'); physiological sources such as the impulses sent from the site of physical damage; and behavioural sources such as pain behaviour that may either increase the pain (such as not doing any exercise) or decrease the pain (such as doing sufficient exercise). CBT focuses on these aspects of pain perception and uses a range of psychological strategies to enable people to unlearn unhelpful practices and learn new ways of thinking and behaviours. CBT draws upon the three treatment approaches described earlier, namely respondent methods such as relaxation and biofeedback, cognitive methods such as attention diversion and Socratic questioning, and behavioural methods involving graded exercises and reinforcement. Several individual studies have been carried out to explore the relative effectiveness of CBT compared to other forms of intervention and/or waiting list controls. Recently systematic reviews have been published which have synthesized these studies in terms of CBT for adults and for children and adolescents.

CBT and Adults

Van Tulder et al. (2000) carried out a systematic review of randomized controlled trials which had used behavioural therapy for chronic non-specific low back pain in adults. Their extensive search of the databases produced six studies of sufficient quality for inclusion and involved methodological practices such as blinding of outcome assessment, adequate length of follow-up and a high-quality randomization procedure. The analysis showed that behavioural treatments effectively reduced pain intensity, increased functional status (e.g. return to work) and improved behavioural outcomes (e.g. activity level). In a similar vein, Eccleston et al. (2009b) carried out a systematic review of trials of CBT and behaviour therapy for chronic pain in 4,781 adults excluding headache. Their database search produced 40 trials for inclusion and the control conditions were treatment as usual and active control. The analysis showed that behaviour therapy was effective at reducing pain but only immediately following treatment when compared to treatment as usual. The results for CBT were more positive but the effects were small, showing improvements in pain, disability, depression and anxiety. In addition, some of these improvements were maintained at six-month follow-up. The authors concluded that psychological therapies that include CBT seem to be an effective way to reduce aspects of chronic pain but that the effects are often small. Further they argued that although the quality of trials to evaluate the effectiveness of CBT and behaviour therapy has improved over time, the quality of the treatments has not.

CBT and Children and Adolescents

Children with chronic and/or recurrent pain are also increasingly offered some form of psychological intervention. At times this takes the form of CBT. However, it also takes the form of individual components such as relaxation, coping skills training, biofeedback and hypnosis. Eccleston et al. (2009a) carried out a systematic review of interventions using psychological therapies for the management of chronic and recurrent pain in children and adolescents and 29 trials that included some form of psychological therapy and sufficient information were entered into the analysis. These trials were for chronic or recurrent headache, abdominal pain, musculoskeletal pain, sickle-cell pain and fibromyalgia and involved 1,432 patients with about half receiving the psychological treatment which was mostly relaxation or CBT. The control groups received standard medical care, placebo or were waiting list controls. The results of their analysis showed that psychological therapies were very effective at reducing headache pain, musculoskeletal pain and recurrent abdominal pain in children and adolescents. The results also showed that these effects persisted by six-month follow-up. There were no significant effects for mood or disability.

Psychological factors can therefore exacerbate pain perception. Research indicates that they are also important in the treatment and management of pain, although they seem to be more effective in children than adults.

THE OUTCOME OF PAIN TREATMENT AND MANAGEMENT: A ROLE FOR PAIN ACCEPTANCE?

The psychological treatment of pain includes respondent, cognitive and behavioural methods. These are mostly used in conjunction with pharmacological treatments involving analgesics or anaesthetics. The outcome of such interventions has traditionally been assessed in terms of a reduction in pain intensity and pain perception. Recently, however, some researchers have been calling for a shift in focus towards pain acceptance. Risdon et al. (2003) asked 30 participants to describe their pain using a Q factor analysis. This methodology encourages the participant to describe their experiences in a way that enables the researcher to derive a factor structure. From their analysis the authors argued that the acceptance of pain involves eight factors. These were: taking control, living day-by-day, acknowledging limitations, empowerment, accepting loss of self, a belief that there's more to life than pain, a philosophy of not fighting battles that can't be won and spiritual strength. In addition, the authors suggest that these factors reflect three underlying beliefs: (1) the acknowledgement that a cure for pain is unlikely; (2) a shift of focus away from pain to non-pain aspects of life; and (3) a resistance to any suggestion that pain is a sign of personal weakness. In a further study McCracken and Eccleston (2003) explored the relationship between pain acceptance, coping with pain and a range of pain-related outcomes in 230 chronic pain patients. The results showed that pain acceptance was a better predictor than coping with pain adjustment variables such as pain intensity, disability, depression and anxiety and better work status. The authors of these studies suggest that the extent of pain acceptance may relate to changes in an individual's sense of self and how their pain has been incorporated into their self-identity. In addition, they argue that the concept of pain acceptance may be an important way forward for pain research, particularly given the nature of chronic pain. Similarly, Samwel et al. (2009) concluded from their study of 220 participants, half of whom attended a chronic pain multidisciplinary clinic, that pain acceptance at baseline predicted greater reduction in pain intensity in the intervention but not the control group. This indicates not only that pain acceptance relates to pain intensity, but also that those who show pain acceptance may benefit most from pain treatment.

MEASURING PAIN

Whether it is to examine the causes or consequences of pain or to evaluate the effectiveness of a treatment for pain, pain needs to be measured. This has raised several questions and problems. For example, 'Are we interested in the individual's own experience of the pain?' (i.e. what someone says is all important), 'What about denial or self-image?' (i.e. someone might be in agony but deny it to themselves and to others), 'Are we interested in a more objective assessment?' (i.e. can we get over the problem of denial by asking someone else to rate their pain?) and 'Do we need to assess a physiological basis to pain?' These questions have resulted in three different perspectives on pain measurement: self-reports, observational assessments and physiological assessments, which are very similar to the different ways of measuring health status (see Chapter 18). In addition, these different perspectives reflect the different theories of pain.

SELF-REPORTS

Self-report scales of pain rely on the individual's own subjective view of their pain level. They take the form of visual analogue scales (e.g. 'How severe is your pain?' Rated from 'not at all' (0) to 'extremely' (100)), verbal scales (e.g. 'Describe your pain: no pain, mild pain, moderate pain, severe pain, worst pain') and descriptive questionnaires (e.g. the McGill Pain Questionnaire (MPQ); Melzack 1975). The MPQ attempts to access the more complex nature of pain and asks individuals to rate their pain in terms of three dimensions: sensory (e.g. flickering, pulsing, beating), affective (e.g. punishing, cruel, killing) and evaluative (e.g. annoying, miserable, intense). Some self-report measures also attempt to access the impact that the pain is having upon the individual's level of functioning and ask whether the pain influences their ability to do daily tasks such as walking, sitting and climbing stairs. Similarly, pain is often assessed within the context of quality of life scales which include a pain component (e.g. see Chapter 18 for a discussion of quality of life scales).

OBSERVATIONAL ASSESSMENT

Observational assessments attempt to make a more objective assessment of pain and are used when the patient's own self-reports are considered unreliable or when they are unable to provide them. For example, observational measures would be used for children, some stroke sufferers and some terminally ill patients. In addition, they can provide an objective validation of self-report measures. Observational measures include an assessment of the pain relief requested and used, pain behaviours (such as limping, grimacing and muscle tension) and time spent sleeping and/or resting.

PHYSIOLOGICAL MEASURES

Both self-report measures and observational measures are sometimes regarded as unreliable if a supposedly 'objective' measure of pain is required. In particular, self-report measures are open to the bias of the individual in pain and observational measures are open to errors made by the observer. Therefore physiological measures are sometimes used as an index of pain intensity. Such measures include an assessment of inflammation and measures of sweating, heart rate and skin temperature. However, the relationship between physiological measures and both observational and self-report measures is often contradictory, raising the question, 'Are the individual and the rater mistaken or are the physiological measurements not measuring pain?'

THE PLACEBO EFFECT

PLACEBOS AND PAIN REDUCTION

Traditionally, placebos were used in randomized control trials to compare an active drug with the effects of simply taking 'something'. However, placebos have been shown to have an effect on pain relief. Beecher (1955) suggested that 30 per cent of chronic pain sufferers experience pain relief after taking placebos. In the 1960s Diamond et al. (1960) carried out several sham operations to examine the effect of placebos on pain relief. A sham heart bypass operation involved the individual believing that they were going to have a proper operation, being prepared for surgery, being given a general anaesthetic, cut open and then sewed up again without any actual bypass being carried out. The individual therefore believed that they had had an operation and had the scars to prove it. This procedure obviously has serious ethical problems. However, the results suggested that angina pain can actually be reduced by a sham operation by comparable levels to an actual operation for angina. This suggests that the expectations of the individual change their perception of pain, again providing evidence for the role of psychology in pain perception. Placebos will now be explored in more details in terms of definitions of a placebo, a brief history of inert treatments, how placebos work and their implications for health psychology in terms of pain and other key areas.

WHAT IS A PLACEBO?

Placebos have been defined as follows:

- Inert substances that cause symptom relief (e.g. 'My headache went away after having a sugar pill').
- Substances that cause changes in a symptom not directly attributable to specific or real pharmacological actions of a drug or operation (e.g. 'After I had my hip operation I stopped getting headaches').
- Any therapy that is deliberately used for its non-specific psychological or physiological effects (e.g. 'I had a bath and my headache went away').

These definitions illustrate some of the problems with understanding placebos. For example:

- What are specific/real versus non-specific/unreal effects? For example, 'My headaches went after the operation': is this an unreal effect (it was not predicted) or a real effect (it definitely happened)?
- Why are psychological effects non-specific? (e.g. 'I feel more relaxed after my operation': is this a non-specific effect?).
- Are there placebo effects in psychological treatments? For example, 'I specifically went for cognitive restructuring therapy and ended up simply feeling less tired': is this a placebo effect or a real effect?

The problems inherent in the distinctions between specific versus non-specific effects and physiological versus psychological effects are illustrated by examining the history of apparently medically inert treatments.

A HISTORY OF INERT TREATMENTS

For centuries, individuals (including doctors and psychologists) from many different cultural backgrounds have used (and still use) apparently inert treatments for various different conditions. For example, medicines such as wild animal faeces and the blood of a gladiator were supposed to increase strength, and part of a dolphin's penis was supposed to increase virility. These so-called 'medicines' have been used at different times in different cultures but have no apparent medical (active) properties. In addition, treatments such as bleeding by leeches to decrease fever or travelling to religious sites such as Lourdes in order to alleviate symptoms have also continued across the years without any obvious understanding of the processes involved. Faith healers are another example of inert treatments, including Jesus Christ, Buddha and Krishna. The tradition of faith healers has persisted, although our understanding of the processes involved is very poor.

Such apparently inert interventions, and the traditions involved with these practices, have lasted over thousands of years. In addition, the people involved in these practices have become famous and have gained a degree of credibility. Furthermore, many of the treatments are still believed in. Perhaps the maintenance of faith, both in these interventions and in the people carrying out the treatments, suggests that they were actually successful, giving the treatments themselves some validity. Why were they successful? It is possible that there are medically active substances in some of these traditional treatments that were not understood in the past and are still not understood now (e.g. gladiators' blood may actually contain some still unknown active chemical). It is also possible that the effectiveness of some of these treatments can be understood in terms of modern-day placebo effects.

MODERN-DAY PLACEBOS

More recently, placebos have been studied specifically and have been found to have a multitude of effects. For example, Haas et al. (1959) listed a whole series of areas where placebos have been shown to have some effect, such as allergies, asthma, cancer, diabetes, enuresis, epilepsy, multiple sclerosis, insomnia, ulcers, obesity, acne, smoking and dementia.

Perhaps one of the most studied areas in relation to placebo effects is pain. Beecher (1955), in an early study of the specific effects of placebos in pain reduction, suggested that 30 per cent of chronic pain sufferers show relief from a placebo when using both subjective (e.g. 'I feel less pain') and objective (e.g. 'You are more mobile') measures of pain. In addition, as noted above, Diamond et al. (1960) reported a sham operation for patients suffering from angina pain and reported that half the subjects with angina pain were given a sham operation, and half of the subjects were given a real heart bypass operation. The results indicated that pain reduction in both groups was equal, and the authors concluded that the belief that the individual had had an operation was sufficient to cause pain reduction and alleviation of the angina.

PLACEBOS: TO BE TAKEN OUT OF AN UNDERSTANDING OF HEALTH?

Since the 1940s, research into the effectiveness of drugs has used randomized controlled trials and placebos to assess the real effects of a drug versus the unreal effects. Placebos have been seen as something to take out of the health equation. However, if placebos have a multitude of effects as already discussed, perhaps, rather than being taken out, they should be seen as central to health status. For this reason it is interesting to examine how placebos work.

HOW DO PLACEBOS WORK?

If placebos have a multiple number of possible effects, what factors actually mediate these changes? Several theories have been developed to try to understand the process of placebo effects. These can be described as *non-interactive* theories in that they examine individual characteristics,

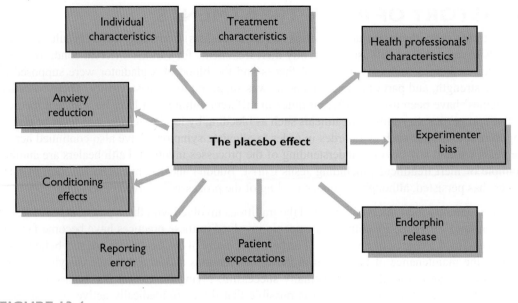

FIGURE 13.4

The placebo effect

characteristics of the treatment and characteristics of the health professional, or *interactive* theories in that they involve an examination of the processes involved in the interactions between patients, the treatment and the health professional. These mechanisms are illustrated in Figure 13.4.

NON-INTERACTIVE THEORIES

Characteristics of the Individual

Individual trait theories suggest that certain individuals have characteristics that make them susceptible to placebo effects. Such characteristics have been described as emotional dependency, extroversion, neurosis and being highly suggestible. Research has also suggested that individuals who respond to placebos are introverted. However, many of the characteristics described are conflicting and there is little evidence to support consistent traits as predictive of placebo responsiveness.

Characteristics of the Treatment

Other researchers have focused on treatment characteristics and have suggested that the characteristics of the actual process involved in the placebo treatment relate to the effectiveness or degree of the placebo effect. For example, if a treatment is perceived by the individual as being serious, the placebo effect will be greater. Accordingly, surgery, which is likely to be perceived as very serious, has the greatest placebo effect, followed by an injection, followed by having two pills versus one pill. Research has also looked at the size of the pill and suggests that larger pills are more effective than small pills in eliciting a change.

The placebo effect: which pill do you think would be more effective?

SOURCE: © Natalia7/Dreamstime

Characteristics of the Health Professional

Research has also looked at the characteristics of the health professional, suggesting that the kind of professional administering the placebo treatment may determine the degree of the placebo effect. For example, higher professional status and higher concern have been shown to increase the placebo effect.

Problems with the Non-Interactive Theories

Theories that examine only the patient, only the treatment or only the professional ignore the interaction between patient and health professional that occurs when a placebo effect has taken place. They assume that these factors exist in isolation and can be examined independently of each other. However, if we are to understand placebo effects then perhaps theories of the interaction between health professionals and patients described within the literature (see Chapter 10) can be applied to understanding placebos.

INTERACTIVE THEORIES

It is therefore necessary to understand the process of placebo effects as an active process, which involves patient, treatment and health professional variables. Placebo effects should be conceptualized as multidimensional processes that depend on an interaction between a multitude of different factors. To understand such processes, research has looked at possible mechanisms of the placebo effect. Many of these mechanisms are similar to the factors highlighted in the three-process model of pain perception described above.

Experimenter Bias

Experimenter bias refers to the impact that the experimenter's expectations can have on the outcome of a study. For example, if an experimenter were carrying out a study to examine the effect of seeing an aggressive film on a child's aggressive behaviour (a classic social psychology study), then the experimenter's expectations may themselves be responsible for changing the child's behaviour (by their own interaction with the child), not the film. This phenomenon has been used to explain placebo effects. For example, Gracely et al. (1985) examined the impact of doctors' beliefs about the treatment on the patients' experience of placebo-induced pain reduction. Subjects were allocated to one of three conditions and were given either an analgesic (a painkiller), a placebo or naloxone (an opiate antagonist, which increases the pain experience). The patients were therefore told that this treatment would either reduce, have no effect or increase their pain. The doctors giving the drugs were themselves allocated to one of two conditions. They believed that either the patients would receive one of three of these substances (a chance of receiving a pain killer), or that the patient would receive either a placebo or naloxone (no chance of receiving a pain killer). Therefore one group of doctors believed that there was a chance that the patient would be given an analgesic and would show pain reduction, and the other group of doctors believed that there was no chance that the patient would receive some form of analgesia. In fact, all subjects were given a placebo. This study, therefore, manipulated both the patients' beliefs about the kind of treatment they had received and the doctors' beliefs about the kind of treatment they were administering. The results showed that the subjects who were given the drug treatment by the doctor who believed they had a chance to receive the analgesic showed a decrease in pain whereas the patients whose doctor believed that they had no chance of receiving the painkiller showed no effect. This suggests that if the doctors believed that the subjects may show pain reduction, this belief was communicated to the subjects who actually reported pain reduction. However, if the doctors believed that the subjects would not show pain reduction, this belief was also communicated to the subjects who accordingly reported no change in their pain experience. This study highlights a role for an interaction between the doctor and the patient and is similar to the effect described as 'experimenter bias' described within social psychology. Experimenter bias suggests that the experimenter is capable of communicating their expectations to the subjects who respond in accordance with these expectations. Therefore, if applied to placebo effects, subjects show improvement because the health professionals expect them to improve.

Patient Expectations

Research has also looked at the expectations of the patient. Ross and Olson (1981) examined the effects of patients' expectations on recovery following a placebo. They suggested that most patients experience spontaneous recovery following illness as most illnesses go through periods of spontaneous change and patients attribute these changes to the treatment. Therefore, even if the treatment is a placebo, any change will be understood in terms of the effectiveness of this treatment. This suggests that because patients want to get better and expect to get better, any changes that they experience are attributed to the drugs they have taken. However, Park and Covi (1965) gave sugar pills to a group of neurotic patients and actually told the patients that the pills were sugar pills and would therefore have no effect. The results showed that the patients still showed some reduction in their neuroticism. It could be argued that in this case, even though the patients did not expect the treatment to work, they still responded to the placebo. However, it could also be argued that these patients would still have some expectations that they would get better otherwise they would not have bothered to take the pills.

Conditioning Effects

Traditional conditioning theories have also been used to explain placebo effects (Wickramasekera 1980). It is suggested that patients associate certain factors with recovery and an improvement in their symptoms. For example, the presence of doctors, white coats, pills, injections and surgery are associated with improvement, recovery and effective treatment. According to conditioning theory, the unconditioned stimulus (treatment) would usually be associated with an unconditioned response (recovery). However, if this unconditioned stimulus (treatment) is paired with a conditioned stimulus (e.g. hospital, a white coat), the conditioned stimulus can itself elicit a conditioned response (recovery, the placebo effect). The conditioned stimulus might be comprised of a number of factors, including the appearance of the doctor, the environment, the actual site of the treatment or simply taking a pill. This stimulus may then elicit placebo recovery. For example, people often comment that they feel better as soon as they get into a doctor's waiting room, that their headache gets better before they have had time to digest a pill and that symptoms disappear when a doctor appears. According to conditioning theory, these changes would be examples of placebo recovery. Several reports provide support for conditioning theory. For example, research suggests that taking a placebo drug is more effective in a hospital setting when given by a doctor than if taken at home and given by someone who is not associated with the medical profession. This suggests that placebo effects require an interaction between the patient and their environment. In addition, placebo pain reduction is more effective with clinical and real pain than with experimentally created pain. This suggests that experimentally created pain does not elicit the association with the treatment environment, whereas the real pain has the effect of eliciting memories of previous experiences of treatment, making it more responsive to placebo intervention.

Anxiety Reduction

Placebos have also been explained in terms of anxiety reduction. Downing and Rickels (1983) argued that placebos decrease anxiety, thus helping the patient to recover. For example, according to gate control theory, anxiety reduction may close the gate and reduce pain, whereas increased anxiety may open the gate and increase pain (see p. 344). Placebos may decrease anxiety by empowering the individual and encouraging them to feel that they are in control of their pain. This improved sense of control may lead to decreased anxiety, which itself reduces the pain experience. Placebos may be particularly effective in chronic pain by breaking the anxiety–pain cycle (see p. 347). The role of anxiety reduction is supported by reports that placebos are more effective in reducing real pain than reducing experimental pain, perhaps because real pain elicits a greater degree of anxiety, which can be alleviated by the placebo, whereas experimentally induced pain does not make the individual anxious. However, there are problems with the anxiety-reducing theory of placebos. Primarily, there are many other effects of placebos besides pain reduction. In addition, Butler and Steptoe (1986) reported that although placebos increased lung function in asthmatics, this increase was not related to anxiety.

PHYSIOLOGICAL THEORIES

Physiologists have also developed theories to explain placebo effects, with a specific focus on pain reduction. Levine et al. (1978) argued that placebos increase endorphin (opiate) release – the brain's natural painkiller – which therefore decreases pain. Evidence for this comes in several forms. Placebos have been shown to create dependence, withdrawal and tolerance, all factors that are similar to those found in abstinent heroin addicts, suggesting that placebos may well increase opiate release. In addition, results suggest that placebo effects can be blocked by giving naloxone, which is an opiate antagonist. This indicates that placebos may increase the opiate release, but that this opiate release is blocked by naloxone, supporting the physiological theory of placebos. However, the physiological theories are limited as pain reduction is not the only consequence of placebos.

BOX 13.2 Some Problems with . . . Placebo Research

Below are some problems with research in this area that you may wish to pause to consider.

1 Central to understanding the placebo effect is the role of expectations, with people seeming to feel pain or get better if they expect to do so. But how can the role of expectations be tested, as taking part in any study or being offered any medication will ultimately change an individual's expectations? It is not really possible therefore to 'placebo' the placebo effect.

2 Placebo research suggests that expecting to get better, even just in the form of adhering to medication, seems to make people better. However, it is not clear how this process actually works. How does a placebo effect make a wound heal faster, a pain go away or lungs function better?

3 Placebos illustrate a direct relationship between a person's mind and their body. This is central to health psychology. We still, however, do not know how this works – it seems to have a magical feel to it which remains unexplained.

THE CENTRAL ROLE OF PATIENT EXPECTATIONS

Galen is reported to have said about the physician, 'He cures most in whom most are confident'. In accordance with this, all the theories of placebo effects described so far involve the patient *expecting* to get better. Experimenter bias theory describes the expectation of the doctor, which is communicated to the patient, changing the patient's expectation. *Expectancy effects theory* describes directly the patients' expectations derived from previous experience of successful treatment. *Reporting error theory* suggests that patients expect to show recovery and therefore inaccurately report recovery, and *theories of misattribution* argue that patients' expectations of improvement are translated into understanding spontaneous changes in terms of the expected changes. In addition, *conditioning theory* requires the individual to expect the conditioned stimuli to be associated with successful intervention, and *anxiety-reduction theory* describes the individual as feeling less anxious after a placebo treatment because of the belief that the treatment will be effective. Finally,

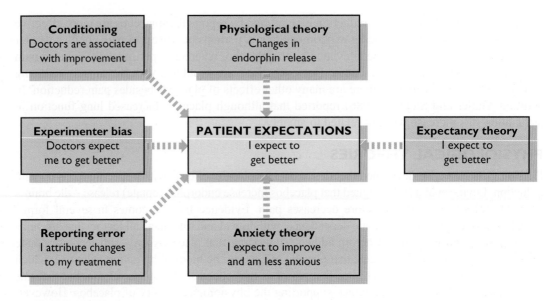

FIGURE 13.5

The central role of patient expectations in placebo effects

even *physiological theory* assumes that the individual will expect to get better. The central role of patient expectations is illustrated in Figure 13.5.

Ross and Olson (1981) summarize the placebo effects as follows:

- The direction of placebo effects parallels the effects of the drug under study.
- The strength of the placebo effect is proportional to that of the active drug.
- The reported side-effects of the placebo drug and the active drug are often similar.
- The time needed for both the placebo and the active drug to become active are often similar.

As a result, they conclude that 'most studies find that an administered placebo will alter the recipient's condition (or in some instances self-report of the condition) in accordance with the placebo's expected effects' (1981: 419). Therefore, according to the above theories, placebos work because the patient and the health professionals expect them to work. This emphasizes the role of expectations and regards placebo effects as an interaction between individuals and between individuals and their environment.

COGNITIVE DISSONANCE THEORY

The theories of placebos described so far emphasize patient expectations. The *cognitive dissonance theory* of placebos developed by Totman (1987) attempted to remove patient expectations from the placebo equation and emphasized justification and dissonance. Totman placed his cognitive dissonance theory of placebos in the following context: 'Why did faith healing last for such a long time?' and 'Why are many of the homeopathic medicines, which have no medically active content, still used?' He argued that faith healing has lasted and homeopathic medicines are still used because they work. In answer to his question why this might be, Totman suggested that the one factor that all of these medically inert treatments have in common is that they require an investment by the individual in terms of money, dedication, pain, time or inconvenience. He argued that if medically inactive drugs were freely available, they would not be effective and that if an individual lived around the corner to Lourdes then a trip to Lourdes would have no effect on their health status.

FOCUS ON RESEARCH 13.2: 'DOING AS YOU'RE TOLD' AS A PLACEBO

A study to examine the role of adhering to medical treatment in predicting recovery from a heart attack – taking pills (whether active or not) as a placebo (Horwitz et al. 1990).

For a long time, medicine has regarded adherence (compliance) with medical recommendations as important for recovery: 'take these drugs and you will get better'. However, this study suggests that simply adhering to medical recommendations to take pills may be beneficial to recovery following a heart attack, regardless of whether the pills taken are active pills or placebo pills. This has implications for understanding the relationship between the mind and the body ('I believe that I have taken my medication' is related to actually getting better) and for understanding the central role of beliefs and expectations in health and illness. It also provides an insight into the role of adherence which was described in Chapter 10.

BACKGROUND

Randomized controlled trials have been used since the 1940s to assess the effectiveness of drugs compared with placebos. For these trials, subjects are randomly allocated to either the experimental condition (and receive the real drug) or the control condition (and receive the placebo drug). Placebo drugs are used as a comparison point in order to distinguish the 'real' effects of the chemically active drug from both the 'placebo effects' and changes that may spontaneously happen over time. This methodology acknowledges that changes in symptoms may occur following a placebo drug, but regards these as less important than the real changes that occur following the real drug. However, in 1982, data from the Coronary Drug Project were published which suggested that the best predictor of mortality in men who had survived a heart attack was not taking the lipid-lowering drug compared with taking the placebo drug, but adherence to taking *any drug at all* (whether an active drug or a placebo drug). The results indicated that adherers had lower mortality at five years than the non-adherers in both the experimental and placebo groups. Horwitz et al. set out to examine whether adherence was a good predictor of risk of death in a large beta-blocker heart attack trial (Beta-blocker Heart Attack Trial Research Group 1982) and to evaluate whether any effects of adherence could be explained by social and behavioural characteristics (e.g. were the non-adherers also the smokers with stressful lives?).

METHODOLOGY

The researchers reported a reanalysis of the data collected as part of the beta-blocker heart attack trial, which was a multicentre, randomized, double-blind trial comparing proprandol (a beta-blocker) with a placebo drug in patients who had survived an acute heart attack (this is known as secondary data analysis).

Subjects

The original study included 3,837 men and women aged 30–69 who were reassessed every three months for an average of 25 months. The data from 1,082 men in the experimental condition (who had received the beta-blocker) and 1,094 men in the placebo condition were analysed (all women and those men who had not completed the psychosocial measures were excluded from the analysis). Follow-up data were analysed for 12 months.

Design

The study was prospective, with subjects completing initial measures six weeks after hospital discharge and subsequent follow-up measures every three months.

Measures

Measures were taken of psychosocial factors, adherence and clinical characteristics:

- *Psychosocial factors.* The subjects completed a structured interview six weeks after discharge. The answers to this were grouped to form four psychosocial variables: levels of life stress, social isolation, depression and type A behaviour pattern. In addition, data were collected concerning their health practices both at baseline and at follow-up (e.g. smoking, alcohol use, diet, physical activity other than work).
- *Adherence.* For each follow-up interval (three months), adherence was calculated as the amount of medication divided by the amount prescribed. The subjects were divided into poor adherers (taking less than or equal to 75 per cent of prescribed medication) and good adherers (taking more than 75 per cent of prescribed medication).
- *Clinical characteristics.* Measures were also taken of the clinical severity of the heart attack (congestive heart failure, severity of heart attack, age) and sociodemographic features (ethnicity, marital status, education).
- *Mortality.* Mortality was measured after 12 months.

RESULTS

Adherence and Mortality

The results were analysed to examine the relationship between adherence and mortality, and showed that, compared with patients with good adherence, those with poor adherence were twice as likely to have died at one-year follow-up. This association was also present when the data were analysed according to treatment category (i.e. for both the experimental group and the control group). Therefore, regardless of what the drug was (whether a beta-blocker or a placebo), taking it as recommended halved the subjects' chances of dying.

The Role of Psychosocial and Clinical Factors

The results showed that death after one year was higher for those subjects who had a history of congestive heart failure, were not married, and had high social isolation and high life stress. In addition, those who had died after one year were more likely to have been smokers at baseline and less likely to have given up smoking during the follow-up. However, even when the data were analysed to take into account these psychosocial and clinical factors, adherence was still strongly associated with mortality at one year.

CONCLUSION

These results therefore indicate a strong link between adherence to medical recommendations and mortality, regardless of the type of drug taken. This effect does not appear to be due to psychosocial or clinical factors (the non-adherers did not simply smoke more than the adherers). Therefore 'doing as the doctor suggests' appears to be beneficial to health, but not for the traditional reasons ('the drugs are good for you') but perhaps because by taking medication the patient *expects* to get better. The authors concluded in a review article that 'perhaps the most provocative explanation for the good effect of good adherence on health is the one most perplexing to clinicians: the role of patient expectancies or self-efficacy'. They suggested that 'patients who expect treatment to be effective engage in other health practices that lead to improved clinical outcomes' (Horwitz and Horwitz 1993). In addition, they suggested that the power of adherence may not be limited to taking drugs but may also occur with adherence to recommendations of behaviour change. Adherence may be a measure of patient expectation, with these expectations influencing the individual's health status – adherence is an illustration of the placebo effect and a reflection of the complex interrelationship between beliefs, behaviour and health.

THE EFFECT OF INVESTMENT

Totman (1987) suggested that investment results in the individual having to go through two processes: (1) the individual needs to justify their behaviour; and (2) the individual needs to see themselves as rational and in control. If these two factors are in line with each other (e.g. 'I spent money on a treatment and it worked'), then the individual experiences low dissonance. If, however, there is a conflict between these two factors (e.g. 'I spent money on a treatment and I do not feel any better'), the individual experiences a state of high dissonance. Totman argued that high justification (it worked) results in low guilt and low dissonance (e.g. 'I can justify my behaviour, I am rational and in control'). However, low justification (e.g. 'it didn't work') results in high guilt and high dissonance (e.g. 'I cannot justify my behaviour, I am not rational or in control'). The best way to resolve this dissonance, according to Totman, is for there to be an outcome that enables the individual to be able to justify their behaviour and to see themselves as rational and in control. Accordingly, Totman argued that when in a state of high dissonance, unconscious regulating mechanisms are activated which may cause physical changes that improve the health of the individual, which in turn enables the individual to justify their behaviour, and this resolves the dissonance. Totman therefore suggested that for a placebo effect to occur, the individual does not require an expectation that they will get better, but a need to find justification for their behaviour and a state of cognitive dissonance to set this up.

THE ROLE OF PLACEBO EFFECTS IN HEALTH PSYCHOLOGY

Placebos have implications for understanding pain perception and the factors that may exacerbate or ease an individual's pain experience. Placebos, however, are also relevant to many other areas of health psychology described in this book.

HEALTH BELIEFS

For a placebo to have an effect, the individual needs to have a belief that the intervention will be effective. For example, a placebo in the form of a pill will work if the individual subscribes to a medical model of health and illness and believes that traditional medical interventions are effective. A placebo in the form of herbal tea may only be effective if the individual believes in alternative medicines and is open to non-traditional forms of intervention. Furthermore, the conditioning effects, reporting error and misattribution process may only occur if the individual believes that health professionals in white coats can treat illness, that hospitals are where people get better and that medical interventions should produce positive results.

ILLNESS COGNITIONS

For a placebo to have an effect, the individual needs to hold particular beliefs about their illness. For example, if an illness is seen as long-lasting without episodes of remission, times of spontaneous recovery may not happen, which therefore cannot be explained in terms of the effectiveness of the treatment. Likewise, if an individual believes that their illness has a medical cause, then a placebo in the form of a pill would be effective. However, if the individual believes that their illness is caused by their lifestyle, a pill placebo may not be effective.

HEALTH PROFESSIONALS' HEALTH BELIEFS

Placebos may also be related to the beliefs of the health professional. For example, a doctor may need to believe in the intervention for it to have an effect. If the doctor believes that an illness is the result of lifestyle, and can be cured by changes in that lifestyle, then a placebo in the form of a medical intervention may not work, as the doctor's expectation of failure may be communicated to the patient.

HEALTH-RELATED BEHAVIOURS

A placebo may function via changes in health-related behaviour. If an individual believes that they have taken something or behaved in a way that may promote good health, they may also change other health-related behaviours (e.g. smoking, drinking, exercise), which may also improve their health.

STRESS

Placebos also have implications for understanding responses to stress. If placebos have an effect either directly (physiological change) or indirectly (behaviour change), then this is in parallel with theories of stress. In addition, placebos may function by reducing any stress caused by illness. The belief that an individual has taken control of their illness (perceived control) may reduce the stress response, reducing any effects this stress may have on the illness.

TO CONCLUDE

Early biomedical models of pain suggested that it was a simple response to external stimuli and categorized the individual as a passive responder to external factors. Such models had no causal role for psychology. However, gate control theory, developed in the 1960s and 1970s by Melzack and Wall, included psychological factors. As a result, pain was no longer understood as a sensation but as an active *perception*. Due to this inclusion of psychological factors into pain perception, research has examined the role of factors such as learning, anxiety, fear, catastrophizing, meaning, attention and pain behaviour in either decreasing or exacerbating pain. As psychological factors appear to have a role to play in eliciting pain perception, multidisciplinary pain clinics have been set up to use psychological factors in treatment. These often use psychological therapies, particularly CBT, which have been shown to be effective for adults, children and adolescents. Recently researchers suggested a role for pain acceptance as a useful outcome measure and some research indicates that acceptance rather than coping might be a better predictor of adjustment to pain and changes following treatment. This chapter also explored the role of placebo effects which are central not only to understanding pain and its management but also have implications for all other areas of health psychology.

QUESTIONS

1 Pain is a response to painful stimuli. Discuss.
2 To what extent does gate control theory depart from biomedical models of pain?
3 What are the implications of gate control theory for the mind–body debate?
4 Pain is a perception. Discuss.
5 How might psychological factors exacerbate pain perception?
6 To what extent can psychological factors be used to reduce pain perception?
7 Self-report is the only true way of measuring pain. Discuss.
8 Develop a research protocol to examine the role of secondary gains in pain perception.
9 Placebos are all in the mind. Discuss.
10 Placebos are a useful treatment for pain. Discuss.
11 Discuss the role of patient expectations in improvements in health.

FOR DISCUSSION

Consider the last time you experienced pain (e.g. period pain, headache, sports injury) and discuss the potential cognitive, emotional and behavioural factors that may have exacerbated that pain.

ASSUMPTIONS IN HEALTH PSYCHOLOGY

The research into pain highlights some of the assumptions underlying health psychology.

1 *The mind–body split.* Early models of pain regarded the physical aspects of pain as 'real' and categorized pain as either 'organic' or 'psychogenic'. Such models conceptualized the mind and body as separate and conform to a dualistic model of individuals. Recent models of pain have attempted to integrate the mind and the body by examining pain as a perception that is influenced by a multitude of different factors. However, even within these models the mind and the body are still regarded as separate.

2 *The problem of progression.* Over the last 100 years, different theories have been developed to explain pain. It is often assumed that changes in theoretical perspective over time represent improvement, with the recent theories reflecting a better approximation to the truth of 'what pain really is'. However, perhaps these different theories can also be used themselves as data to show how psychologists have thought in the past and how they now think about individuals. For example, in the past pain was seen as a passive response to external stimuli; therefore individuals were seen as passive responders. However, today pain is increasingly seen as a response to the individual's self-control – pain is a sign of either successful or failed self-control. Therefore contemporary individuals are seen as having self-control, self-management and self-mastery. Perhaps the different theories over time reflect different (not necessarily better) versions of individuality.

FURTHER READING

Dekker, J., Lundberg, U. and Williams, A. (eds) (2001) *Behavioural Factors and Interventions in Pain and Musculoskeletal Disorders: A Special Issue of the International Journal of Behavioural Medicine.* Mahawah, NJ: Lawrence Erlbaum Associates.
This provides a detailed analysis of the psychosocial factors involved in the development of chronic pain.

Main, C.J. and Spanswick, C.C. (eds) (2000) *Pain Management: An Interdisciplinary Approach.* Edinburgh: Churchill Livingstone.
This edited collection provides a detailed account of contemporary approaches to treating pain.

Simpson, S.H., Eurich, D.T., Majumdar, S.R. et al. (2006) A meta-analysis of the association between adherence to drug therapy and mortality, *British Medical Journal*, 333: 15.
This is an excellent review of the literature exploring how simply adhering to medication has a powerful placebo effect which is linked with improved mortality.

Totman, R.G. (1987) *The Social Causes of Illness*. London: Souvenir Press.

This book provides an interesting perspective on placebos and the interrelationship between beliefs, behaviours and health.

Turk, D.C. and Melzack, R. (eds) (2001) *Handbook of Pain Assessment*, 2nd edn. New York: Guilford Press.

This edited collection provides an excellent overview of how pain can be measured and the problems inherent within pain assessment.

Visit the website at www.openup.co.uk/ogden for additional resources on Chapter 13 to help you with your study, such as multiple choice questions, weblinks and a searchable online glossary.

14 HIV and Cancer: Psychology Throughout the Course of Illness

© dra_schwartz/iStock

CHAPTER OVERVIEW

This chapter and the next examine the role that psychology plays at each stage of a chronic illness, from illness onset, through the adaptation to illness, its progression, the psychological consequences and longevity. They do not aim to be comprehensive overviews of the immense literature on illness, but to illustrate the possible varied role of psychology in illness. This chapter uses the examples of HIV and cancer and Chapter 15 focuses on obesity and coronary heart disease (CHD). However, these psychological factors are relevant to a multitude of other chronic and acute illnesses including multiple sclerosis, rheumatoid arthritis, asthma, chronic fatigue syndrome and chronic pain. Rather than being seen as a passive response to biomedical factors, such chronic illnesses are better understood in terms of a complex interplay of physiological and psychological processes.

CHRONIC ILLNESS AND PSYCHOLOGY

From a biomedical perspective (see Chapter 1) psychology is purely a consequence of chronic illness – having cancer makes people depressed. From a health psychology perspective, however, the role of psychology is far more complex and psychological factors such as beliefs, behaviours, coping, symptom perception, stress, adaptation and quality of life are seen as having a part in illness from onset through coping with illness to illness progression and the final outcome.

HIV AND AIDS

The first part of this chapter examines the history of HIV, what HIV is and how it is transmitted. It then evaluates the role of psychology in understanding HIV in terms of susceptibility to HIV and AIDS, progression from HIV to AIDS and longevity. A detailed discussion of condom use in the context of HIV and AIDS can be found in Chapter 7 and a detailed description of psychoneuroimmunology (PNI) can be found in Chapter 12. Chapter 8 also provides a description of behaviour change interventions, Chapter 3 describes the role of beliefs in predicting behaviour and Chapter 10 describes adherence to medication.

THE HISTORY OF HIV

AIDS (acquired immune deficiency syndrome) was identified as a new syndrome in 1981. At that time, it was regarded as specific to homosexuality and was known as GRIDS (gay-related immune deficiency syndrome). As a result of this belief a number of theories were developed to try to explain the occurrence of this new illness among homosexuals. These ranged from the suggestion that AIDS may be a response to the over-use of recreational drugs such as 'poppers' or to over-exposure to semen, and focused on the perceived lifestyles of the homosexual population. In 1982, however, AIDS occurred in haemophiliacs. As haemophiliacs were seen not to have lifestyles comparable with the homosexual population, scientists started to reform their theories about AIDS and suggested, for the first time, that perhaps it was caused by a virus. Such a virus could reach haemophiliacs through their use of Factor VIII, a donated blood-clotting agent.

The HIV virus was first isolated in 1983. However, there is debate as to whether this was achieved by Gallo in the USA or/and Montagnier in France. Both these researchers were looking for a retrovirus, having examined a cat retrovirus that caused leukaemia and appeared to be very similar to what they thought was causing this new illness. In 1984, the human immunodeficiency virus type 1 (HIV 1) was identified, and in 1985 HIV 2 was identified in Africa.

WHAT IS HIV?

The Structure of HIV

The HIV virus is a *retrovirus*, a type of virus containing RNA. There are three types of retrovirus: oncogenic retroviruses which cause cancer, foamy retroviruses which have no effect at all on the health status of the individual, and lentiviruses, or slow viruses, which have slow long-term effects. HIV is a lentivirus.

The HIV virus is structured with an outer coat and an inner core. The RNA is situated in the core and contains eight viral genes, which encode the proteins of the envelope and the core, and also contains enzymes, which are essential for replication.

The Transmission of HIV

In order to be transmitted from one individual to the next, the HIV virus generally needs to come into contact with cells that have CD4 molecules on their surface. Such cells are found within the immune system and are called T-helper cells. The process of transmission of the HIV virus involves the following stages:

1 HIV binds to the CD4 molecule of the T-helper cell.
2 HIV virus is internalized into the cytoplasm of the cell.
3 The cell itself generates a pro-viral DNA, which is a copy of the host cell.
4 This pro-virus enters the nucleus of the host cell.
5 The host cell produces new viral particles, which it reads off from the viral code of the viral DNA.
6 These viral particles bud off and infect new cells.
7 Eventually, after much replication, the host T-helper cell dies.

THE PROGRESSION FROM HIV TO AIDS

The progression from HIV to HIV disease and AIDS varies in time. AIDS reflects a reduction in T-helper cells and specifically those that are CD4-positive T-cells. This causes immune deficiency and the appearance of opportunistic infections. The progression from initial HIV seroconversion through to AIDS tends to go through the following stages:

1 The initial viral seroconversion illness.
2 An asymptomatic stage.
3 Enlargement of the lymph nodes, onset of opportunistic infections.
4 AIDS-related complex (ARC).
5 AIDS.

THE PREVALENCE OF HIV AND AIDS

At the end of 2005 there were 38.6 million people living with HIV and in 2005 4.1 million became newly-infected and 2.8 million died from the virus. Generally, the incidence of HIV peaked in the late 1990s and has now mostly stabilized. However, the numbers of people living with HIV has increased due to population growth as have the numbers of people now taking antiretroviral therapy which has significantly improved the life expectancy of those infected with the HIV virus (see Figures 2.3, 2.13 and 2.14 in Chapter 2 for worldwide prevalence rates of HIV and the impact of medication on life expectancy). Although much western interest has been on the incidence of HIV within the gay populations of the western world, the epicentre of the global epidemic is in Sub-Saharan Africa. Rates are also very high in parts of Asia, particularly India and China. At the end of 2005 there were 5.5 million people in Sub-Saharan Africa who were living with HIV. This includes about 18.8 per cent of adults, and about one in three pregnant women attending antenatal care in 2004 were found to be HIV positive. In Asia about 8.3 million people were living with HIV at the end of 2005 and most of these were in India. In China, about 650,000 were living with HIV in 2005 and of these 44 per cent were injecting drug users. In Europe the highest incident rate is in the Russian Federation. Overall, the prevalence of HIV is very low in the Middle East and North Africa (except the Sudan). In terms of changing rates of HIV, there was a decline in new cases across the USA and Europe in the 1990s although there is some evidence of a resurgent epidemic in men who have sex with men in the USA and some European countries. There has also been a recent increase in the UK, mostly due to heterosexual transmission with an increasing number of women accounting for the rise in numbers. It is estimated that about 80 per cent of these cases are due to the virus being contracted in countries where there are much higher rates. There have been declines in rates in some parts of Sub-Saharan Africa (Kenya and Zimbabwe), declines in some parts of India (Tamil Nadu) but no signs of decline in most of southern Africa, and increases in China, Indonesia, Papua New Guinea, Bangladesh and Pakistan. Across Europe the highest rates of people living with HIV per million people are Portugal (79.6), Spain (43.0), Switzerland (42.8) and Italy (29.2). By the end of 2004 about 300,000 people across Europe were living with HIV and about 170,000 had died. In the UK, by the end of 2004, 58,000 people were living with HIV. In 2005 there were 7,205 new diagnoses and of the 22,281 diagnoses ever, 17,014 people had died. Worldwide incidence rates of newly-diagnosed people with HIV in 2008 are shown in Figure 14.1 which shows that the highest prevalence rates are in Africa, North, Central and South America. Figure 14.2 shows the estimated number of adults living with HIV (both diagnosed and undiagnosed) in the UK in 2009. The data from this graph indicate that the highest rates of HIV in the UK are in men who have sex with men (MSM) followed by heterosexual women born in Africa.

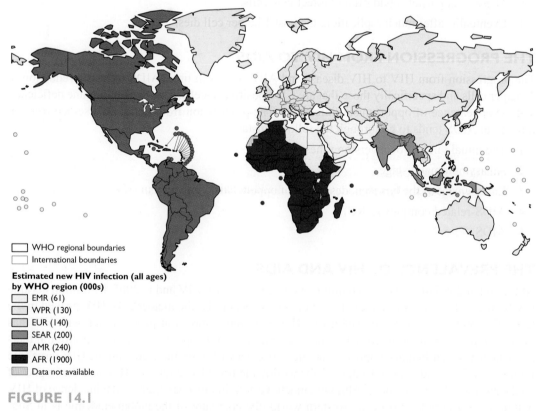

WHO regional boundaries
International boundaries

Estimated new HIV infection (all ages)
by WHO region (000s)
EMR (61)
WPR (130)
EUR (140)
SEAR (200)
AMR (240)
AFR (1900)
Data not available

FIGURE 14.1

Worldwide newly-infected HIV adults and children in 2008

SOURCE: WHO (2010)

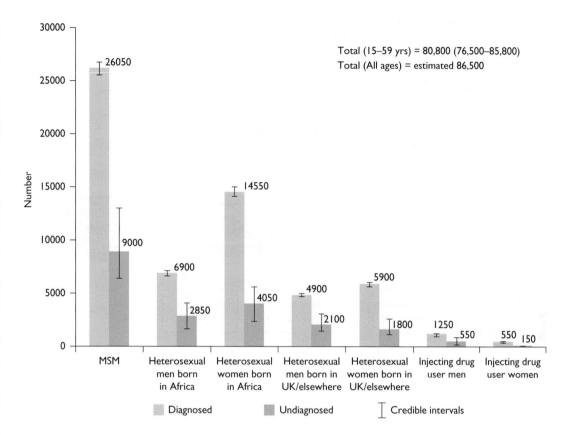

FIGURE 14.2

Number of adults living with HIV (both diagnosed and undiagnosed) in the UK, 2009

SOURCE: Health Protection Agency (2010)

THE ROLE OF PSYCHOLOGY IN THE STUDY OF HIV

HIV is transmitted mostly because of people's behaviour (e.g. sexual intercourse, needle use). Health psychology has studied HIV in terms of attitudes to HIV, changing these attitudes, examining predictors of behaviour and the development of interventions to change behaviour. The following observations suggest that psychology has an additional role to play in HIV:

- *Not everyone exposed to the HIV virus becomes HIV positive.* This suggests that psychological factors may influence an individual's susceptibility to the HIV virus.
- *The time for progression from HIV to AIDS is variable.* Psychological factors may have a role in promoting the replication of the HIV virus and the progression from being HIV positive to having AIDS.
- *Perhaps not everyone with HIV dies from AIDS.* Psychological factors may have a role to play in determining the longevity of the individual.

The potential role of psychological factors in understanding HIV and AIDS is shown in Figure 14.3.

The role of psychology in AIDS in terms of susceptibility to AIDS, progression from HIV to AIDS and longevity will now be examined. Chapters 3–12 provide further insights into aspects of beliefs, behaviours, medication adherence, behaviour change interventions and the immune function which are all relevant to understanding the role of psychology in HIV and AIDS.

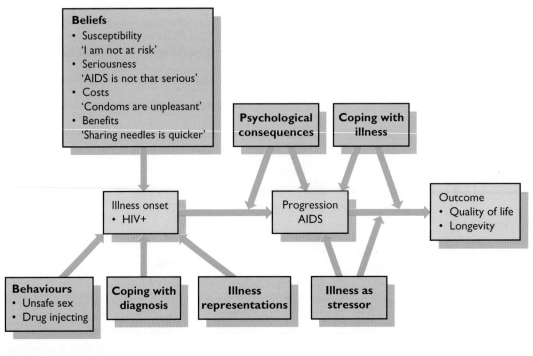

FIGURE 14.3

The potential role of psychology in HIV

PSYCHOLOGY AND SUSCEPTIBILITY TO THE HIV VIRUS

Psychology may have a role to play in an individual's susceptibility to the HIV virus once exposed to it. Several studies have examined the possibility that not all those individuals who come into contact with HIV become HIV positive, and have suggested several reasons for this. One train of thought argues that the lifestyle of an individual may increase their chances of contracting HIV once exposed to the virus. Van Griensven et al. (1986) suggested that the use of other drugs, such as nitrates and cannabis, increases the chance of contracting HIV once exposed to the virus. Lifson et al. (1989) also argued that the existence of other viruses, such as herpes simplex and cytomegalovirus (CMV), in the bloodstream may increase the chances of contracting HIV. These viruses are also thought to be associated with unsafe sex and injecting drugs. Therefore unhealthy behaviours may not only be related to exposure to the HIV virus but also to the likelihood that an individual will become HIV positive. However, much of the lifestyle literature surrounding susceptibility to HIV was based on the beliefs about HIV that existed during the 1980s, when HIV was still regarded as a homosexual illness. It therefore focused on the lifestyles of homosexuals and made generalizations about this lifestyle in order to explain susceptibility to the virus.

PSYCHOLOGY AND THE PROGRESSION FROM HIV TO AIDS

Research has also examined the role of psychology in the progression from HIV to AIDS. It has been argued that HIV provides a useful basis for such research for the following reasons: (1) there are large numbers of individuals who can be identified at the asymptomatic stage of their illness, allowing an analysis of disease progression from a symptom-free stage; (2) as people with HIV tend to be young, the problem of other coexisting diseases can be avoided; and (3) the measurement of disease progression using numbers of CD4 T-helper cells is accurate (S. Taylor et al. 1998).

This research points to roles for lifestyle, adherence to medication, stress, cognitive adjustment and type C coping style in the progression of the illness.

Lifestyle

It has been suggested that injecting drugs further stimulates the immune system, which may well influence replication, and thereby points to a role for drug use not only in contracting the virus but also for its replication. In addition, research has indicated that replication of the HIV virus may be influenced by further exposure to the virus, suggesting a role for unsafe sex and drug use in its progression. Furthermore, it has been suggested that contact with drugs, which may have an immuno-suppressive effect, or other viruses, such as herpes complex and CMV, may also be related to an increase in replication.

Adherence to Medication

Over recent years the life expectancy and quality of life of those with HIV have improved dramatically (e.g. Mocroft et al. 1998). Much of this has been attributed to the success of highly active anti-retroviral therapy (HAART) and HIV is often now described as a chronic illness rather than a terminal one. Many people who are offered HAART, however, do not take the treatment. For example, Steinberg (2001) reported that only 75 per cent of those eligible for treatment received treatment. Of those who did not receive treatment, 58 per cent had declined the offer. Research has therefore explored the reasons behind adherence and non-adherence to medication (see p. 279–286 for a discussion of adherence). Before HAART the most common medication was AZT mono-therapy. Siegel et al. (1992) reported that reasons for non-adherence included lack of trust in doctors, feelings of well-being, negative beliefs about medical treatments, the belief that AZT would make the person worse and the belief that taking AZT would reduce treatment options in future. In a similar vein, V. Cooper et al. (2002) explored people's beliefs about HAART. They interviewed 26 gay men about their views about HAART shortly after it had been recommended by their doctor. The results showed that the men held beliefs about the necessity of their medication in terms of whether they felt it could control their HIV or whether they were inclined to let their condition take its natural course; they described their concerns about taking the drugs in terms of side-effects, the difficulties of the drug regimen and its effectiveness; and they described feelings about their control over the decision to take the medication. In an associated study, Gellaitry et al. (2005) further examined beliefs about HAART and linked them with adherence. These results showed that concerns about the adverse effects of HAART were related to declining treatment.

Stress

Sodroski et al. (1984) suggested that stress or distress may well increase the replication of the HIV virus, causing a quicker progression to AIDS. Women who are HIV positive are more at risk from cervical intraepithelial neoplasia (CIN) and cervical cancer. Pereira et al. (2003) explored the relationship between the likelihood of developing the lesions associated with CIN and life stress. The results showed that higher life stress increased the odds of developing lesions by sevenfold over a one-year period. Life stress therefore seemed to link with illness progression. Some research has also addressed the effectiveness of stress management in slowing down the progression of HIV. Antoni et al. (2006) randomized 130 gay men who were HIV positive to receive either a cognitive behavioural stress management

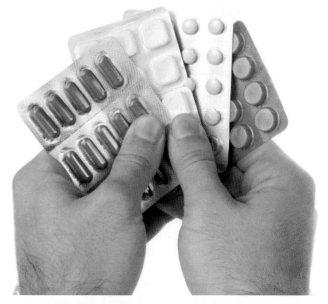

The treatment regimen for AIDs can be complex and can lead to non-adherence

SOURCE: © Nomadsoul1/Dreamstime

intervention (CBSM) and anti-retroviral medication adherence training (MAT), or to receive MAT alone. The men were then followed up after 9 and 15 months in terms of viral load. The results showed that men who already showed a detectable viral load at baseline (i.e. those with a lot of virus in the blood already) who received the stress management showed a reduction in their viral load over the 15-month period even when medication adherence was controlled for. The authors concluded that for HIV-positive men who already show a detectable viral load, stress management may enhance the beneficial effects of their anti-retroviral treatment. In a similar study, the mechanisms behind the impact of stress management were explored (Antoni et al. 2005). For this study 25 HIV-positive men were randomized to receive stress management or a waiting list control. Urine samples were taken before and after the intervention period. The results again showed that stress management was effective and that this effect was related to reduction in cortisol and depressed mood. The authors concluded that stress management works by reducing the stress induced by being ill with a disease such as HIV. This supports the early work of Solomon and Temoshok (1987), who argued that social homophobia may well cause stress in individuals who have contracted HIV, which could exacerbate their illness.

Cognitive Adjustment

Research from the Multi Center AIDS Cohort Study (MACS) in the USA has suggested a role for forms of cognitive adjustment to bereavement and illness progression (Bower et al. 1998; Reed et al. 1999). In the first part of this study, 72 men who were HIV positive, asymptomatic and half of whom had recently experienced the death of a close friend or primary partner, completed measures of their psychosocial state (HIV-specific expectancies, mood state and hopelessness) and had the number of their CD4 T-helper cells recorded. They were then followed up over a six-year period. The results showed that about half the sample showed symptoms over the follow-up period. However, the rate and extent of the disease progression were not consistent for everyone. In particular, the results showed that symptom development was predicted by baseline HIV-specific expectancies, particularly in those who had been bereaved. Therefore it would seem that having more negative expectancies of HIV progression is predictive of actual progression. In the second part of this study, 40 HIV-positive men who had recently lost a close friend or partner to AIDS were interviewed about how they made sense of this death. These interviews were then classified according to whether the individual had managed to find meaning in the death in line with Taylor's cognitive adaptation theory of coping (Taylor 1983) (see Chapter 9). An example of meaning would be: 'What his death did was snap a certain value into my behaviour, which is "Listen, you don't know how long you've got. You've just lost another one. Spend more time with the people that mean something to you".' The results showed that those who had managed to find meaning maintained their levels of CD4 T-helper cells at follow-up, whereas those who did not find meaning showed a decline.

Type C Coping Style

Research has also explored the link between how people cope with HIV and the progression of their disease with a focus on type C coping style which reflects emotional inexpression and a decreased recognition of needs and feelings. For example, Solano et al. (2001, 2002) used CD4 cells as a measure of disease status, assessed baseline coping and followed 200 patients up after 6 and 12 months. The results showed that type C coping style predicted progression at follow-up, suggesting that a form of coping that relies upon a lack of emotional expression may exacerbate the course of HIV disease. However, the results also showed that very high levels of emotional expression were also detrimental. The authors conclude that working through emotions rather than just releasing them may be the most protective coping strategy for people diagnosed as HIV positive (see **Focus on Research 14.1**).

FOCUS ON RESEARCH 14.1: EMOTIONAL EXPRESSION AND IMMUNE FUNCTION

The relationship between emotional expression and immune function on individuals with HIV (Solano et al. 2001).

This study uses a cross-sectional design to explore the relationship between emotional expression and the capacity to express in general, and biological markers of immune status in people who are HIV positive and having treatment. The results are interesting because they illustrate a link between emotional expression and health but also provide insights into the kind of emotional expression that might be most effective.

BACKGROUND

Emotions and health have been linked across a number of different literatures including stress and coping (see Chapter 12), adaptation to illness (see Chapter 9) and the expressive writing paradigm which has been used in wide range of settings (see Chapter 12). It is also central to much therapeutic work with the assumption being that talking about emotions rather than bottling them up has to be beneficial. Prior to this study research had shown a link between emotional expression in cancer (e.g. Temoshok et al. 1987) and HIV (Solano et al. 2002). This study aimed to explore the ways in which emotional expression may relate to immune status.

METHODOLOGY

Design

The study used a cross-sectional design.

Participants

A total of 42 asymptomatic patients with HIV who were outpatients of a clinic in Rome were recruited into the study. Twenty-four were men and 18 were women. They ranged in age from 22 to 47. Fifteen were heterosexual (non-drug dependent), 13 were heterosexual (drug dependent), 13 were homosexual and 1 was bisexual.

The interview

All participants were interviewed by a trained psychologist and asked the question, 'How are things going for you in this period?'. For all interviews only the first 10 minutes was transcribed and analysed in order to equalize interview length.

MEASURES

- *Physiological measures:* blood was taken immediately after the interview and immunological assessments were made in terms of CD4+ levels.
- *Interview coding:* the interviews were coded for emotional content and style of language.
- *Emotional content:* the interviews were coded using a Gottschalk and Gleser method for content analysis (1969) for five affect scales: anxiety, hostility directed outwards, overt and covert hostility, hostility directed inwards, ambivalent hostility.
- *Style of language:* an observer-rated scale was also used called the Referential Activity Scale (Bucci 1995) which codes the interview in terms of the types of language used. The provides a measure of the capacity to express. Using this, the interviews were rated in terms of:
  i *concreteness* (i.e. the extent to which expressions rate to actual things, e.g. 'my heart was pounding like a hammer');
  ii *specificity* (i.e. the quantity of detail, e.g. 'There were old broken dirty shoes, a greasy old recipe book');

iii *clarity* (i.e. the speaker's ability to be understandable to the listener); and

iv *imagery* (i.e. the vividness in the speaker's language, e.g. 'The red ripeness of round leaves').

Data Analysis

The results were analysed to explore relationships between emotional content and immune function and style of language and immune function.

RESULTS

Emotional Content

The results showed a significant curvilinear and cubic relationship between 'hostility directed inwards' and CD4+ cells with those with either the highest or the lowest 'hostility directed inwards' having the poorest immune function. Those with the best immune function showed intermediate levels of 'hostility directed inwards'.

Style of Language

In terms of style of language used, the results showed a linear relationship between most of the measures of the referential activity scale and immune function (apart from imagery). This indicates that a greater capacity for expression is related to improved immune function.

CONCLUSION

The authors concluded from their study that there is an association between form of emotional expression and immune function but that this is not linear, as sometimes expected. Therefore it is not just that more emotional expression is always better, and the authors argued that working through emotions rather than just expressing them may have the best impact upon an individual's health status. However, there was a linear relationship with the capacity to be expressive, indicating that learning to become more emotionally articulate may help an individual's immune status.

PSYCHOLOGY AND LONGEVITY

Research has also examined the role of psychological factors in longevity following infection with HIV. In particular, this has looked at the direct effects of beliefs and behaviour on the state of immunosuppression of the individual (see Chapter 12 for a discussion of PNI). In 1987, Solomon et al. studied 21 AIDS patients and examined their health status and the relationship of this health status to predictive baseline psychological variables. At follow-up, they found that survival was predicted by their general health status at baseline, their health behaviours, hardiness, social support, type C behaviour (self-sacrificing, self-blaming, not emotionally expressive) and coping strategies. In a further study, Solomon and Temoshok (1987) reported an additional follow-up of AIDS patients. They argued that a positive outcome was predicted by perceived control over illness at baseline, social support, problem-solving, help-seeking behaviour, low social desirability and the expression of anger and hostility. This study indicated that type C behaviour was not related to longevity.

Reed et al. (1994) also examined the psychological state of 78 gay men who had been diagnosed with AIDS in terms of their self-reported health status, psychological adjustment and psychological responses to HIV, well-being, self-esteem and levels of hopelessness. In addition, they completed measures of 'realistic acceptance', which reflected statements such as 'I tried to accept what might happen', 'I prepare for the worst' and 'I go over in my mind what I say or do about this problem'. At follow-up, the results showed that two-thirds of the men had died. However, survival was predicted by 'realistic acceptance' at baseline, with those who showed greater acceptance of their own death dying earlier. Therefore psychological state may also relate to longevity.

SUMMING UP

The study of HIV and AIDS illustrates the role of psychology at different stages of an illness. Psychological factors are important not only for attitudes and beliefs about HIV and the resulting behaviour (see Chapters 3, 7 and 8), but may also be involved in an individual's susceptibility to contracting the virus, the replication of the virus once it has been contracted and their subsequent longevity.

CANCER

The second part of this chapter examines what cancer is, looks at its prevalence and then assesses the role of psychology in understanding cancer in terms of its initiation and promotion, its psychological consequences, dealing with the symptoms of cancer, longevity and the promotion of a disease-free interval. Chapters 3–10 provide detailed descriptions of health and illness beliefs, coping, health behaviour, screening and adherence to medication which are all relevant to understanding cancer in terms of its onset and impact upon the individual.

WHAT IS CANCER?

Cancer is defined as an uncontrolled growth of abnormal cells, which produces tumours called neoplasms. There are two types of tumour: *benign* tumours, which do not spread throughout the body, and *malignant* tumours, which show metastasis (the process of cells breaking off from the tumour and moving elsewhere). There are three types of cancer cell: *carcinomas*, which constitute 90 per cent of all cancer cells and which originate in tissue cells; *sarcomas*, which originate in connective tissue; and *leukaemias*, which originate in the blood.

THE PREVALENCE OF CANCER

In 2008, cancer accounted for 7.6 million deaths worldwide (around 13 per cent of all deaths) and is now the leading cause of death. The main types of cancer are lung (1.4 million deaths); stomach

BOX 14.1 Some Problems with ... HIV and Cancer Research

Below are some problems with research in this area that you may wish to consider.

1 Much psychological research explores the predictors of becoming HIV positive in terms of safer sex behaviour and needle-sharing. HIV, however, is a worldwide problem which affects people from all religions and cultural backgrounds. The reasons that people do or do not engage in risky behaviours are highly linked to their specific cultures. It is therefore very difficult to generalize from one study to populations outside the study group.

2 The management of HIV and AIDS has changed enormously over the past 20 years, resulting in an increase in longevity due to combination therapies. HIV is now seen as a chronic illness rather than a terminal one. This means that combining research on longevity across the years is difficult as people at different times have been managed in very different ways.

3 Research on cancer shows some commonalities across different types of cancers. However, there are also vast differences in ways in which different cancers impact upon people's lives and are and should be managed. Generalizations across cancers should therefore be limited to those areas where there is consistent cross-cancer variation. For example, while screening and early detection for breast cancer can result in improved management and health outcomes, screening for prostate cancer may result in anxiety, a painful procedure and a recommendation of watchful waiting which can make people regret knowing about their condition in the first place.

(740,000 deaths); liver (700,000 deaths); colorectal (610,000 deaths) and breast (460,000 deaths). Deaths from cancer worldwide are projected to continue to rise to over 11 million in 2030. In the UK, in 2008, cancer was the second most common cause of death (after cardiovascular disease) and was responsible for 29 per cent of deaths in men and 26 per cent of deaths in women. In Europe these figures were 21 and 17 per cent respectively. The main causes of cancer mortality in the UK were lung cancer (men: 7 per cent; women: 5 per cent), colorectal cancer (men and women: 3 per cent) and breast cancer in women (4 per cent). (Rates of lung cancer across Europe and by deprivation level can be seen in Chapter 2, Figures 2.4 and 2.8.) The incidence of newly-diagnosed cancer in the UK in 2007 is shown in Figure 14.4, which shows that the most commonly diagnosed

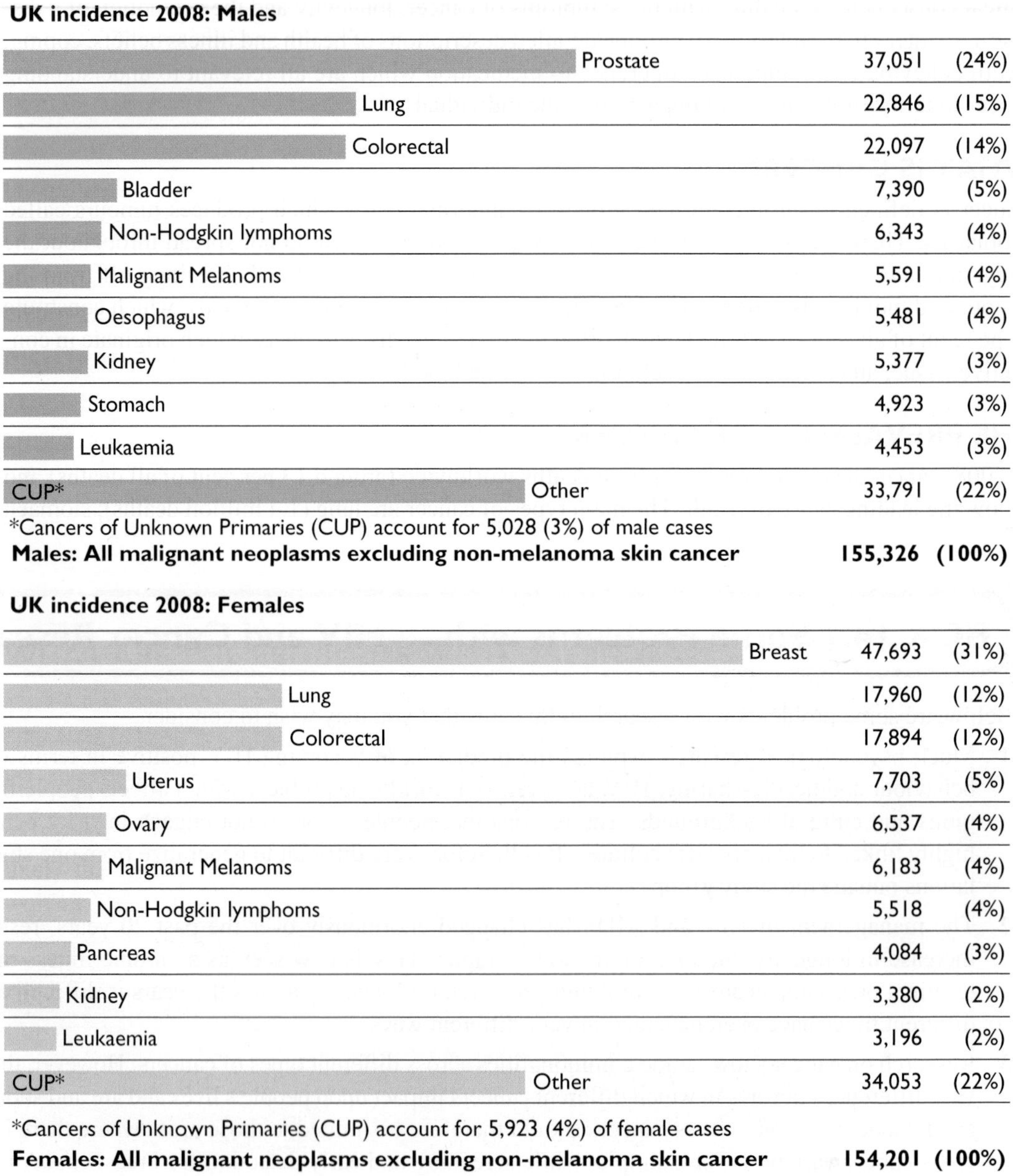

UK incidence 2008: Males

Cancer	Cases	%
Prostate	37,051	(24%)
Lung	22,846	(15%)
Colorectal	22,097	(14%)
Bladder	7,390	(5%)
Non-Hodgkin lymphoms	6,343	(4%)
Malignant Melanoms	5,591	(4%)
Oesophagus	5,481	(4%)
Kidney	5,377	(3%)
Stomach	4,923	(3%)
Leukaemia	4,453	(3%)
CUP* Other	33,791	(22%)

*Cancers of Unknown Primaries (CUP) account for 5,028 (3%) of male cases

Males: All malignant neoplasms excluding non-melanoma skin cancer   155,326 (100%)

UK incidence 2008: Females

Cancer	Cases	%
Breast	47,693	(31%)
Lung	17,960	(12%)
Colorectal	17,894	(12%)
Uterus	7,703	(5%)
Ovary	6,537	(4%)
Malignant Melanoms	6,183	(4%)
Non-Hodgkin lymphoms	5,518	(4%)
Pancreas	4,084	(3%)
Kidney	3,380	(2%)
Leukaemia	3,196	(2%)
CUP* Other	34,053	(22%)

*Cancers of Unknown Primaries (CUP) account for 5,923 (4%) of female cases

Females: All malignant neoplasms excluding non-melanoma skin cancer   154,201 (100%)

FIGURE 14.4

UK incidence of newly-diagnosed cancers for men and women

SOURCE: Cancer Research UK (2009)

cancers in men are prostate cancer (24 per cent) and lung cancer (22 per cent) and in women are breast cancer (31 per cent) and colorectal cancer (12 per cent).

THE ROLE OF PSYCHOLOGY IN CANCER

A role for psychology in cancer was first suggested by Galen in AD 200–300, who argued for an association between melancholia and cancer, and also by Gedman in 1701, who suggested that cancer might be related to life disasters. In addition, more than 30 per cent of cancer deaths are thought to be preventable. Psychology therefore plays a role in cancer in a number of ways. First, psychological factors are important in terms of cancer onset and a discussion of health and illness beliefs, health behaviours and behaviour change interventions can be found in Chapters 3–8. Second, psychology is involved in factors such as screening, help-seeking, delay and adherence which are described in Chapters 9 and 10. Further, sufferers of cancer report psychological consequences, which have implications for coping, adjustment and a person's quality of life (see Chapters 9 and 18). The role of psychology in cancer is also illustrated by the following observations:

- *Cancer cells are present in most people but not everybody gets cancer.* In addition, although research suggests a link between smoking and lung cancer, not all heavy smokers get lung cancer. Perhaps psychology is involved in the susceptibility to cancer.

- *All those who have cancer do not always show progression towards death at the same rate.* Perhaps psychology has a role to play in the progression of cancer.

- *Not all cancer sufferers die of cancer.* Perhaps psychology has a role to play in longevity.

The potential role of psychology in understanding cancer is shown in Figure 14.5.

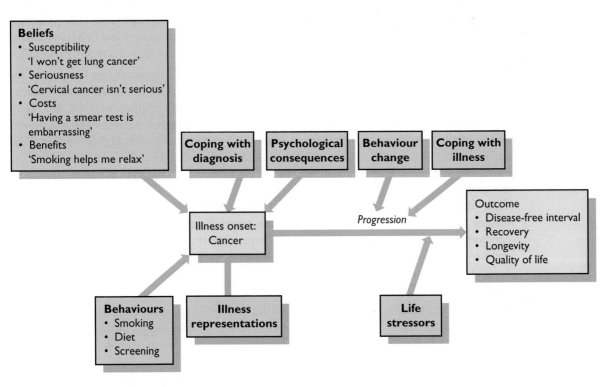

FIGURE 14.5

The potential role of psychology in cancer

The role of psychology in cancer will now be examined in terms of: (1) the initiation and promotion of cancer; (2) the psychological consequences of cancer; (3) dealing with the symptoms of cancer; and (4) longevity and promoting a disease-free interval.

THE PSYCHOSOCIAL FACTORS IN THE INITIATION AND PROMOTION OF CANCER

1 *Behavioural factors.* Behavioural factors have been shown to play a role in the initiation and promotion of cancer with research indicating that up to 75 per cent of all cancers are linked to behaviours such as smoking, poor diet, alcohol and sexual behavior (e.g. Doll and Peto 1981; Mokdad et al. 2004; Khaw et al. 2008). These behaviours can be predicted by examining individual health beliefs (see Chapters 3–7). They can also be modified using behaviour change interventions (see Chapter 8). In addition, screening, help-seeking behaviour and symptom perception all influence early detection which may influence health outcomes (see Chapters 9 and 10). For example, Mason and White (2008) concluded that the components of the theory of planned behaviour (TPB) could predict breast self-examination in young women, Hale et al. (2007) identified a number of barriers to seeking help in men with prostate disease and Fang et al. (2006) highlighted the role of perceptions of control and coping in predicting screening uptake for ovarian cancer.

2 *Stress.* Stress has also been shown to have a role to play in cancer. Laudenslager et al. (1983) reported a study that involved exposing cancer-prone mice to stress (shaking the cage). They found that if this stressor could be controlled, there was a decrease in the rate of tumour development. However, if the stressor was perceived as uncontrollable, this resulted in an increase in the development. This suggests a role for stress in the initiation of cancer. However, Sklar and Anisman (1981) argued that an increase in stress increased the *promotion* of cancer, not its *initiation* (see Chapter 12 for a discussion of the relationship between stress and illness). Furthermore, stress following diagnosis may also influence whether or not an individual makes positive changes to their health-related behaviours (e.g. Park et al. 2008).

3 *Life events.* It has also been suggested that life events play a role in cancer (see Chapter 11 for a discussion of life events). A study by Jacobs and Charles (1980) examined the differences in life events between families who had a cancer victim and families who did not. They reported that in families who had a cancer victim, there were higher numbers who had moved house, higher numbers who had changed some form of their behaviour, higher numbers who had had a change in health status other than the cancer person, and higher numbers of divorces, indicating that life events may well be a factor contributing to the onset of cancer. However, the results from a meta-analysis by Petticrew et al. (1999) do not support this suggestion. They identified 29 studies, from 1966 to 1997, which met their inclusion criteria (adult women with breast cancer, group of cancer-free controls, measure of stressful life events) and concluded that although several individual studies report a relationship between life events and breast cancer, when methodological problems are taken into account and when the data across the different studies are merged, 'the research shows no good evidence of a relationship between stressful life events and breast cancer'.

4 *Control.* Control also seems to play a role in the initiation and promotion of cancer and it has been argued that control over stressors and control over environmental factors may be related to an increase in the onset of cancer (see Chapter 12 for a discussion of control and the stress–illness link).

5 *Coping styles.* Coping styles are also important. If an individual is subjected to stress, then the methods they use to cope with this stress may well be related to the onset of cancer. For example, maladaptive, disengagement coping strategies, such as smoking and alcohol, may

have a relationship with an increase in cancer (see Chapters 9 and 12 for a discussion of coping).

6 *Depression.* Bieliauskas (1980) highlighted a relationship between depression and cancer and suggested that chronic mild depression, but not clinical depression, may be related to cancer.

7 *Personality.* Some research has also explored the relationship between personality and cancer. Temoshok and Fox (1984) argued that individuals who develop cancer have a 'type C personality', which is described as passive, appeasing, helpless, 'other focused' and unexpressive of emotion. Eysenck (1990) described 'a cancer-prone personality', and suggested that this is characteristic of individuals who react to stress with helplessness and hopelessness, and individuals who repress emotional reactions to life events. An early study by Kissen (1966) supported this relationship between personality and cancer and reported that heavy smokers who develop lung cancer have a poorly developed outlet for their emotions, perhaps suggesting type C personality. In 1987, Shaffer et al. carried out a prospective study to examine the predictive capacity of personality and its relationship to developing cancer in medical students over 30 years. At follow-up they described the type of individual who was more likely to develop cancer as having impaired self-awareness, being self-sacrificing and self-blaming, and not being emotionally expressive. The results from this study suggest that those individuals who had this type of personality were 16 times more likely to develop cancer than those individuals who did not. However, the relationship between cancer and personality is not a straightforward one. It has been argued that the different personality types predicted to relate to illness are not distinct from each other and also that people with cancer do not consistently differ from either healthy people or people with heart disease in the predicted direction (Amelang and Schmidt-Rathjens 1996).

8 *Hardiness.* Kobasa et al. (1982) described a coping style called 'hardiness', which has three components: control, commitment and challenge. Low control suggests a tendency to show feelings of helplessness in the face of stress. Commitment is defined as the opposite of alienation: individuals high in commitment find meaning in their work, values and personal relationships. Individuals high in challenge regard potentially stressful events as a challenge to be met with expected success. Hardiness may be protective against developing cancer.

PSYCHOLOGICAL CONSEQUENCES OF CANCER

Psychology also has a role to play in cancer in terms of how people respond to their diagnosis.

Lowered Mood

Up to 20 per cent of cancer patients may show severe depression, grief, lack of control, personality change, anger and anxiety. Depression seems to be particularly high in those with head and neck cancer (Humphris and Ozakinci, 2006). Some patients also report a sense of hopelessness (Abbey et al. 2006) and Nanton et al. (2009) highlighted feelings of uncertainty in men with prostate cancer. Pinder et al. (1993) examined the emotional responses of women with operable breast cancer and reported that these can differ widely from little disruption of mood to clinical states of depression and anxiety. The emotional state of breast cancer sufferers appears to be unrelated to the type of surgery they have (Kiebert et al. 1991), whether or not they have radiotherapy (Hughson et al. 1987) and is only affected by chemotherapy in the medium term (Hughson et al. 1986). However, persistent deterioration in mood does seem to be related to previous psychiatric history (Dean 1987), lack of social support (Bloom 1983), age and lack of an intimate relationship (Pinder et al. 1993). Pinder et al. also reported that in sufferers with advanced cancer, psychological morbidity was related to functional status (how well the patient functioned physically) and suggested that lowered functional status was associated with higher levels of depression, which was also related to lower social class.

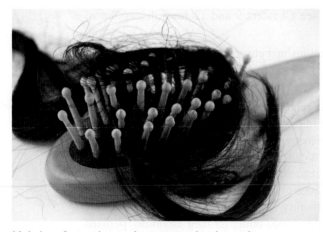

Hair loss from chemotherapy can be damaging to a
patient's body image and self-esteem

SOURCE: © Szefei/Dreamstime

Body Image

Lowered mood is not the only emotional consequence of cancer. Women with breast cancer often
report changes in their sense of femininity, attractiveness and body image. This has been shown to be
greater in women who have radical mastectomies
rather than lumpectomies (e.g. Moyer 1997) and to
occur across a range of ethnic groups (e.g. Petronis
et al. 2003). Harcourt and Frith (2008) carried out a
qualitative interview study with 19 women having
chemotherapy for breast cancer, focusing on how
the treatment could alter their physical appearance.
The results indicated that the women were anxious
that the treatment would make them identifiable as
a 'person with cancer' which would change their
interactions with others. In a similar vein, Frith
et al. (2007) particularly focused on the impact of
hair loss and identified a number of ways in which
women actively anticipate and manage their hair loss and use both affective and behavioural
rehearsal strategies even before they have lost their hair as a means to feel more in control.

Cognitive Adaptation

Research has also examined cognitive responses to cancer and suggests that a 'fighting spirit' is
negatively correlated with anxiety and depression while 'fatalism', 'helplessness' and 'anxious
preoccupation' are related to lowered mood (Watson et al. 1991). Taylor (1983) examined the
cognitive adaptation of 78 women with breast cancer. She reported that these women responded to
their cancer in three ways. First, they made a search for meaning, whereby the cancer patients
attempted to understand why they had developed cancer. Meanings that were reported included
stress, hereditary factors, ingested carcinogens such as birth control pills, environmental carcinogens such as chemical waste, diet, and a blow to the breast. Second, they also attempted to gain a
sense of mastery by believing that they could control their cancer and any relapses. Such attempts
at control included meditation, positive thinking and a belief that the original cause was no longer
in effect. Third, the women began a process of self-enhancement. This involved social comparison,
whereby they tended to analyse their condition in terms of others they knew. Taylor argued that
they showed 'downward comparison', which involved comparing themselves to others worse off,
thus improving their beliefs about their own situation. According to Taylor's theory of cognitive
adaptation, the combination of meaning, mastery and self-enhancement creates illusions which are
a central component of attempts to cope. This theory is discussed in more detail in Chapter 9. In a
similar vein, Jim and Andersen (2007) also explored meaning-making in cancer survivors but
focused on a patient's meaning of life rather than the meaning of cancer. In this study, cancer survivors completed measures of social and physical functioning, distress and the meaning of their
lives. The authors concluded that the negative social and physical consequences of cancer cause
distress but that this association is mediated through the ways in which cancer disrupts a person's
meaning of life.

Benefit-Finding

Not all consequences of cancer are negative and many patients report finding benefit in their illness.
This has been explored within the frameworks of stress-related growth, post-traumatic growth,
benefit-finding, meaning-making and existential growth (see Chapter 9 for details). In terms of
cancer, research indicates that positive shifts are common following diagnosis and treatment and

that greater benefit-finding is predicted by factors such as spirituality, talking and assigning meaning to the illness, financial stability, being a woman, greater optimism, high intrusive thinking and high social support (Cordova et al. 2001; Cole et al. 2008; Dunn et al. 2011).

PSYCHOLOGY AND THE ALLEVIATION OF SYMPTOMS

Psychology has a role to play in the alleviation of symptoms of cancer, and in promoting quality of life (see Chapter 18 for a discussion of quality of life theory and measurement). Cartwright et al. (1973) described the experiences of cancer sufferers, which included very distressing pain, breathing difficulties, vomiting, sleeplessness, loss of bowel and bladder control, loss of appetite and mental confusion. Psychosocial interventions have therefore been used to attempt to alleviate some of the symptoms of the cancer sufferer and to improve their quality of life:

1 *Pain management.* One of the main roles of psychology is in terms of pain management, and this has taken place through a variety of different pain management techniques (see Chapter 13). For example, biofeedback and hypnosis have been shown to decrease pain. Turk and Rennert (1981) encouraged patients with cancer to describe and monitor their pain, encouraged them to develop coping skills, taught them relaxation skills, encouraged them to do positive imagery and to focus on other things. They reported that these techniques were successful in reducing the pain experience.

2 *Social support interventions.* Social support interventions have also been used through the provision of support groups, which emphasize control and meaningful activities and aim to reduce denial and promote hope. It has been suggested that although this intervention may not have any effect on longevity, it may improve the meaningfulness of the cancer patient's life. In line with this, Holland and Holahan (2003) explored the relationship between social support, coping and positive adaptation to breast cancer in 56 women. The results showed that higher levels of perceived social support and approach-coping strategies were related to positive adjustment.

3 *Treating nausea and vomiting.* Psychology has also been involved in treating the nausea and vomiting experienced by cancer patients. Patients are often offered chemotherapy as a treatment for their cancer, which can cause anticipatory nausea, vomiting and anxiety. Respondent conditioning and visual imagery, relaxation, hypnosis and desensitization have been shown to decrease nausea and anxiety in cancer patients. Redd (1982) and Burish et al. (1987) suggested that 25–33 per cent of cancer patients show conditioned vomiting and 60 per cent show anticipatory anxiety. It is reported that relaxation and guided imagery may decrease these problems.

4 *Body image counselling.* The quality of life of cancer patients may also be improved through altered body image counselling, particularly following the loss of a breast and, more generally, in dealing with the grief at loss of various parts of the body.

5 *Cognitive adaptation strategies.* Research also suggests that quality of life may be improved using cognitive adaptation strategies. Taylor (1983) used such strategies to improve patients' self-worth, their ability to be close to others, and the meaningfulness of their lives. Such methods have been suggested to involve self-transcendence and this has again been related to improvement in well-being and decrease in illness-related distresses.

6 *Fear reduction.* Many patients experience enduring fear that their cancer will return which can impact upon their adjustment and ability to plan for the future. Humphris and Ozakinci (2008) developed a programme called AFTER (Adjustment for the Fear, Threat or Expectation of Recurrence) to help patients with head and neck cancer manage their fear of recurrence. The intervention targets fears, inappropriate checking behaviour and beliefs about cancer and is based upon Leventhal's self-regulatory model (see Chapter 9). Preliminary evidence indicates that it is acceptable and may be of use to patients with a number of different cancers.

Adjuvant Psychological Therapy

Greer et al. (1992) suggested that, in addition to physical interventions, patients with breast cancer should be offered adjuvant psychological therapy. This involves encouraging patients to examine the personal meaning of their cancer and what they can do to cope with it (see **Focus on Research 14.2**).

FOCUS ON RESEARCH 14.2: TREATING CANCER SYMPTOMS

A randomized controlled trial to examine the effects of adjuvant psychological therapy on the psychological sequelae of cancer (Greer et al. 1992).

Research has examined the psychological consequences of having cancer. This study examined changes in cancer patients' psychological state as a result of adjuvant psychological therapy (APT). The study used a randomized controlled trial design in order to compare changes in measures of quality of life in patients receiving APT with those receiving no therapy.

BACKGROUND

Evidence suggests that a substantial minority of cancer patients show psychological ill health, particularly in terms of depression and anxiety. As a result, a number of psychotherapeutic procedures have been developed to improve cancer patients' emotional well-being. However, evaluating the effectiveness of such procedures raises several ethical and methodological problems, and these are addressed by Greer et al. These are: (1) the ethical considerations of having a control group (can patients suffering from psychological distress not be given therapy?); (2) the specificity of any psychological intervention (terms such as 'counselling' and 'psychotherapy' are vague and any procedure being evaluated should be clarified); and (3) the outcome measures chosen (many measures of psychological state include items that are not appropriate for cancer patients, such as weight loss and fatigue, which may change as a result of the cancer, not the individual's psychological state). The authors of this study aimed to examine the effects of APT on the psychological state of cancer patients in the light of these problems.

METHODOLOGY

Subjects

A total of 174 patients attending the Royal Marsden Hospital in the UK were recruited for the study using the following criteria: (1) any form of cancer except cerebral tumours and benign skin cancers; (2) a life expectancy of at least 12 months; (3) aged 18–74; (4) no obvious intellectual impairments, psychotic illness or suicide risk; (5) residence within 65km of the hospital; and (6) psychological morbidity defined above a set of cut-off points for anxiety, depression and helplessness, and below a cut-off point for fighting spirit. Altogether, 153 subjects completed the baseline and eight-week measures and 137 completed all measures.

Design

All subjects completed measures of their psychological state at baseline. They were then allocated to either the experimental group (and received eight weeks of APT) or the control group. The subjects then completed follow-up measures at eight weeks and four months.

Measures

Subjects completed the following measures at baseline (before randomization), at eight weeks' and four months' follow-up:

- *The Hospital Anxiety and Depression Scale.*
- *The Mental Adjustment to Cancer Scale:* this measures four dimensions of adjustment: fighting spirit, helplessness, anxious preoccupation and fatalism.
- *The Psychosocial Adjustment to Illness Scale:* this measures health care orientation, work adjustment, domestic environment, sexual relationships, extended family relationships, the social environment and psychological distress.
- *The Rotterdam Symptom Checklist:* this measures quality of life in terms of both physical and psychological symptoms.

The Intervention

The subjects were randomly allocated to either the experimental (APT) or the control group. ATP is a cognitive behavioural treatment developed specifically for cancer patients. Therapy involved approximately eight one-hour weekly sessions with individual patients and their spouses (if appropriate). However, many patients in the present study did not attend all these sessions and several received additional sessions throughout the four months. The therapy focused on the personal meaning of the cancer for the patient, examined their coping strategies, and emphasized the current problems defined jointly by the therapist and the patient. APT uses the following cognitive behavioural techniques:

- Identifying the patient's strengths and using these to develop self-esteem, overcome feelings of helplessness and promote fighting spirit.
- Teaching patients to identify any automatic thoughts underlying their anxiety and depression and developing means to challenge these thoughts.
- Teaching patients how to use imagination and role play as a means of coping with stressors.
- Encouraging patients to carry out activities that give them a sense of pleasure and achievement in order to promote a sense of control.
- Encouraging expression of emotions and open communication.
- Teaching relaxation to control anxiety.

RESULTS

The results showed that at eight weeks the patients receiving the APT had significantly higher scores on fighting spirit and significantly lower scores on helplessness, anxious preoccupation, fatalism, anxiety, psychological symptoms and orientation towards health care than the control patients. At four months, patients receiving the APT had significantly lower scores than the controls on anxiety, psychological symptoms and psychological distress.

CONCLUSION

The authors concluded that APT improves the psychological well-being of cancer patients who show increased psychological problems and that some of these improvements persist for up to four months. They suggested that APT relates to 'improvement in the psychological dimension of the quality of life of cancer patients'.

PSYCHOLOGICAL FACTORS IN LONGEVITY

The final question about the role of psychology in cancer is its relationship to longevity: do psychosocial factors influence longevity?

Cognitive Responses and Longevity

Greer et al. (1979) carried out a prospective study in which they examined the relationship between cognitive responses to a breast cancer diagnosis and disease-free intervals. Using semi-structured interviews, they defined three types of responder: those with 'fighting spirit', those who showed denial of the implications of their disease and those who showed a hopeless/helpless response. The authors reported that the groups who showed either 'fighting spirit' or 'denial' had a longer disease-free interval than the other group. In addition, at a further 15-year follow-up, both a fighting spirit and denial approach also predicted longevity. However, there were problems with this study. At baseline the authors did not measure several important physiological prognostic indicators, such as lymph node involvement, as these measures were not available at the time. These physiological factors may have contributed to both the disease-free interval and the survival of the patients. More recently, Gidron et al. (2001) examined the role of hopelessness defined as 'helplessness' and 'pessimism' in predicting changes in breast cancer. Clinical data, measures of hopelessness, life changes and measures of affect were collected at baseline from 49 Israeli women diagnosed with breast cancer. Follow-up data were collected over a four-month period. The results showed that hopelessness was related to aspects of mood. In addition, helplessness (not pessimism) predicted changes in CA15–3, which was used as the marker for breast cancer development.

Life Stress and Disease-Free Interval

In a case control study, Ramirez et al. (1989) examined the relationship between life stress and relapse in operable breast cancer. The life events and difficulties occurring during the disease-free interval were recorded in 50 women who had developed their first recurrence of breast cancer and 50 women who were in remission. The two subject groups were matched for the main physical and pathological factors believed to be associated with prognosis and for the sociodemographic variables believed to be related to life events and difficulties. The results showed that life events rated as severe were related to first recurrence of breast cancer. However, the study was cross-sectional in nature, which has implications for determining causality.

Personality/Coping Style and Longevity

In 1991, Eysenck and Grossarth-Maticek reported a study whereby they selected 'at risk' individuals who were healthy (the controls) and another group of individuals (the experimental group) who showed conflict-avoiding and emotion-suppression type personality (a type C/cancer-prone personality). The experimental group received CBT in an attempt to change how they dealt with stress. At follow-up, the authors reported that this group showed a decrease in mortality rate compared with the controls who did not receive the CBT. In a further study by Temoshok and Fox (1984), the results from a 15-year follow-up of women with breast cancer indicated that poor outcome was associated with a passive, helpless coping style. However, it has been questioned as to whether the personality styles predicted to be associated with different illnesses are distinct (Amelang and Schmidt-Rathjens 1996).

There Is No Relationship between Psychological Factors and Longevity

Not all research has pointed to an association between psychological factors and longevity. Barraclough et al. (1992) measured severe life events, social difficulties and depression at baseline in a group of breast cancer patients, and followed them up after 42 months. Of a total of 204 subjects, 26 died and 23 per cent relapsed. However, the results showed no relationship between these outcomes and the psychosocial factors measured at baseline. These results caused debate in the light of earlier studies and it has been suggested that the absence of a relationship between life events and outcome may be due to the older age of the women in Barraclough's study, the short follow-up period used, and the unreported use of chemotherapy (Ramirez et al. 1992).

SUMMING UP

Psychology has many roles to play in cancer in terms of illness onset through behaviours such as smoking and diet, the ways in which people adjust and cope with their illness, illness progression and ultimate health outcomes. This part of the chapter has particularly focused on beliefs and behaviours, which may be related to the onset of cancer, psychological consequences such as lowered mood, altered body image, cognitive adaptation and benefit-finding, the treatment of symptoms through pain relief, relaxation or fear management and improving quality of life, disease-free intervals and longevity.

TO CONCLUDE

Psychology has a role to play in understanding chronic illness in terms of illness onset, adaptation, coping, illness progression and health outcomes. This chapter has focused on two examples, namely HIV/AIDS and cancer, although the theories and evidence presented are also relevant to any number of chronic illnesses.

QUESTIONS

1 Discuss the role of psychological factors in the progression to full-blown AIDS.
2 To what extent is the transmission of the HIV virus due to a lack of knowledge?
3 AIDS kills. Discuss.
4 Discuss the factors that may explain why patients do not take their medication for AIDS.
5 Describe the role of psychology in cancer onset.
6 Discuss the impact that cancer may have upon the individual.
7 Discuss the role of psychological factors in a disease-free interval following a diagnosis of breast cancer.
8 To what extent do psychological factors relate to the recovery from cancer?

FOR DISCUSSION

Do you know anyone who has had either HIV or cancer? Think about how psychological factors such as behaviour, beliefs and coping have influenced their state of health.

ASSUMPTIONS IN HEALTH PSYCHOLOGY

An examination of the role of psychological factors in illness highlights some of the assumptions in health psychology:

1 ***The mind–body split.*** By examining the role of psychology in illness, it is implicitly assumed that psychology and illness (the body) are separate. This promotes a model of an individual who has a physical and a mental world which interact but are separate. Although this interaction is an attempt at a holistic approach to health and illness, it is still intrinsically dualistic.

2 ***Correlational studies.*** Many of the research studies carried out in health psychology are cross-sectional (i.e. they examine the relationship between variables measured at the same time). For example, 'What is the relationship between coping style and immune status?', and 'What is the relationship between life stressors and illness?' Studies using cross-sectional designs often make statements about causality (e.g. 'coping style causes changes in immune status', 'stressors cause illness'). However, it is quite possible that the relationship between these variables is either causal in the opposite direction (e.g. illness causes high reports of stressors, 'I am now ill and remember the last six months differently'), or non-existent (e.g. 'I am ill and I have had lots of stressful events in my life recently but they are unrelated' (the third variable problem)). Prospective studies are used as an attempt to solve this problem, but even they only examine the correlation between variables – it is still difficult to talk about causality.

FURTHER READING

Barraclough, J. (2000) *Cancer and Emotion: A Practical Guide to Psycho-oncology.* Chichester: Wiley. A thorough and accessible review of the research and theories exploring links between psychological factors and cancer in terms of onset, progression and recovery.

Mulder, C.L. and Antoni, M.H. (1992) Psychosocial correlates of immune status and disease progression in HIV-1 infected homosexual men: review of preliminary findings and commentary, *Psychology and Health*, 6: 175–92.
This paper reviews the literature on the role of behavioural and psychological factors in the course of HIV infection. It is also a good introduction to PNI.

Vedhara, K. and Irwin, M. (eds) (2005) *Human Psychoneuroimmunology.* Oxford: Oxford University Press.
This book provides an excellent up-to-date overview of the research on PNI and covers key concepts, research and methods.

 Visit the website at www.openup.co.uk/ogden for additional resources on Chapter 14 to help you with your study, such as multiple choice questions, weblinks and a searchable online glossary.

15 Obesity and Coronary Heart Disease: Psychology Throughout the Course of Illness

© mark wragg/iStock

CHAPTER OVERVIEW

This chapter focuses on obesity and coronary heart disease (CHD). First it examines definitions of obesity, its prevalence and potential consequences. It then examines the role of physiological factors, the obesogenic environment and behaviour in causing obesity. The chapter moves on to look at obesity treatment with a focus on dietary management, medication and surgery and the first part concludes by exploring the factors associated with successful weight loss maintenance. In the second half, the chapter looks at CHD, describing what it is, how it is defined and the role of psychology in its aetiology. The psychological consequences of CHD are then explored, along with the role of psychology in patient rehabilitation. The chapter concludes with descriptions of the predictors of patient health outcomes, with a focus on quality of life and mortality.

OBESITY

THE ROLE OF PSYCHOLOGICAL FACTORS

Psychology has a role to play in obesity in terms of its onset and the role of beliefs and behaviours, how people cope with and adjust to this condition, how obesity is managed and the consequences on an individual's physical and psychological well-being. Most of the chapters in this book so far are relevant to understanding obesity, particularly those relating to beliefs, behaviour, diet and exercise (see Chapters 3, 5, 6 and 8 in particular). The first half of this chapter explores what obesity is and then examines the role of psychology in understanding obesity in terms of its consequences, causes and treatment. The potential role of psychological factors in obesity is illustrated in Figure 15.1.

WHAT IS OBESITY?

Obesity can be defined in a number of ways:

- *Population means.* Population means involves exploring mean weights, given a specific population, and deciding whether someone is below average weight, average or above average in terms of percentage overweight. Stunkard (1984) suggested that obesity should be categorized as either mild (20–40 per cent overweight), moderate (41–100 per cent overweight) or severe (100 per cent overweight). This approach is problematic as it depends on which population is being considered – someone could be obese in India but not in the USA.

- *BMI.* Body mass index (BMI) is calculated using the equation weight (kg)/height (m2). This produces a figure that has been categorized as normal weight (20–24.9); overweight (grade 1, 25–29.9); clinical obesity (grade 2, 30–39.9); and severe obesity (grade 3, 40) (see Figure 15.2). This is the most frequently used definition of obesity. However, it does not allow for differences in weight between muscle and fat – a bodybuilder would be considered obese.

- *Waist circumference.* BMI is the most frequently used measure of obesity but it does not allow for an analysis of the *location* of fat. This is important as some problems such as diabetes are predicted by abdominal fat rather than lower body fat. Researchers originally used waist:hip ratios to assess obesity but recently waist circumference on its own has become the preferred approach. For men, low waist circumference is < 94cm; high is 94–102cm and very high is > 102cm. For women, low waist circumference is < 80cm; high is 80–88cm and very high is > 88cm. Weight reduction is recommended when waist circumference is greater than

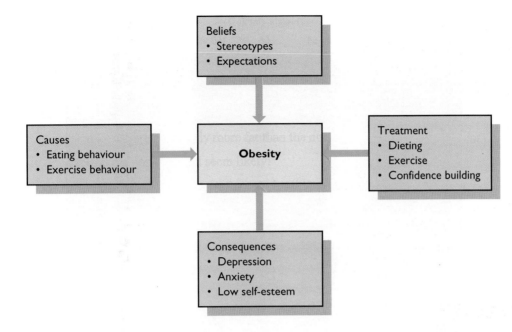

FIGURE 15.1

Potential role of psychology in obesity

102cm in men and 88cm in women (Lean et al. 1995). A reduction in waist circumference is associated with a reduction in cardiovascular risk factors and abdominal obesity is associated with insulin resistance and the development of type 2 diabetes (Chan et al. 1994; Han et al. 1997). Waist circumference has been suggested as the basis for routine screening in primary care (Despres et al. 2001) although Little and Byrne (2001) have argued that more evidence is needed before such a programme should be implemented.

- *Percentage body fat.* As health is mostly associated with fat rather than weight per se, researchers and clinicians have also developed methods of measuring percentage body fat directly. At its most basic this involves assessing skinfold thickness using callipers, normally around the upper arm and upper and lower back. This is not suitable for those individuals who are severely obese and misses abdominal fat. At a more advanced level, body fat can be measured using bioelectrical impedence which involves passing an electrical current between a person's hand and foot. As water conducts electricity and fat is an insulator, the impedence of the current can be used to calculate the ratio between water and fat and therefore an overall estimate of percentage body fat can be made.

HOW COMMON IS OBESITY?

In the UK the rates of obesity increased dramatically from 1993 to about 2007 but have been relatively stable for the past five or six years. If obesity is defined as a BMI greater than 30, reports show that in 1980, 6 per cent of men and 8 per cent of women were obese and that this had increased to 13 per cent and 16 per cent in 1994, to 18 per cent and 24 per cent respectively by 2005 and to 22 and 24 per cent respectively in 2009. In 2009 the mean BMI was 27 for both men and women. Rates of obesity in the UK from 1994 to 2008 are shown in Figure 15.3.

For children in England, Chinn and Rona (2001) reported that in 1994, 9 per cent of boys and 13.5 per cent of girls were overweight, that 1.7 per cent of boys and 2.6 per cent of girls were obese and that these figures were more than 50 per cent higher than 10 years earlier. Estimates for the

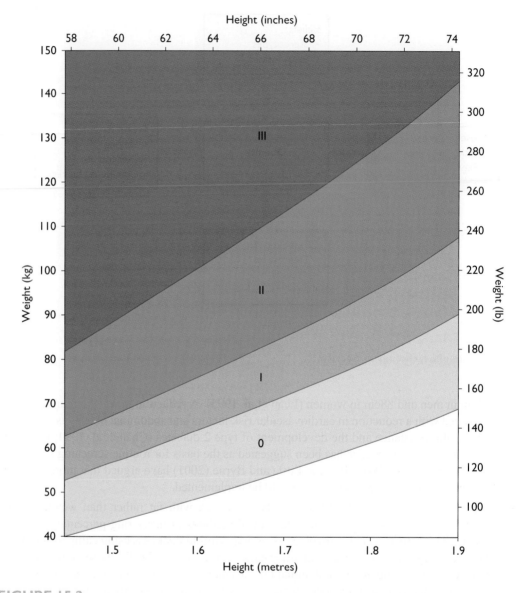

FIGURE 15.2

Grades of obesity by height and weight

SOURCE: Adapted from Garrow (1984)

USA suggest that roughly half of American adults are overweight, that a third are obese, that women have grown particularly heavier in recent years and that the prevalence of overweight children has doubled in the past 20 years (National Institutes of Health 1998; Ogden et al. 2007). Across the world, the World Health Organization (WHO 2006) estimates that 1.5 billion adults worldwide are overweight and 400 million are obese. Figure 15.4 shows obesity rates across the world for men and Figure 15.5 shows rates for women.

The highest rates of obesity are found in Tunisia, the USA, Saudi Arabia and Canada, and the lowest are found in China, Mali, Japan, Sweden and Brazil; the UK, Australia and New Zealand are all placed in the middle of the range (WHO 2007). Even though the rates are low in China and Japan they are steadily increasing and reports indicate that the prevalence of childhood obesity has tripled in Japan and that 1 in 10 children in China is now obese (Ogden et al. 2007). Across Europe,

FIGURE 15.3

Obesity and overweight prevalence in the UK, 1993–2008

SOURCE: Copyright © 2011, re-used with the permission of The Health and Social Care Information Centre, all rights reserved

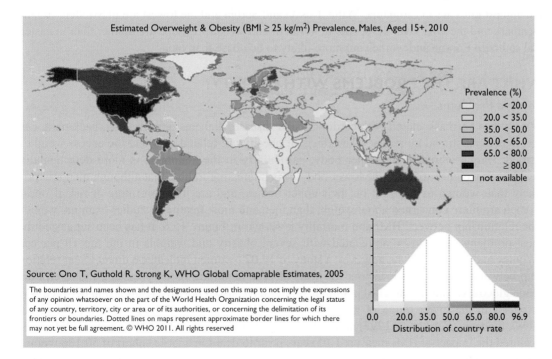

FIGURE 15.4

Worldwide obesity prevalence rates for men

SOURCE: WHO Global Infobase (online)

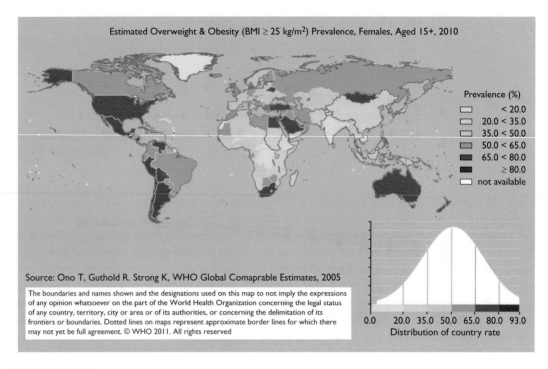

Estimated Overweight & Obesity (BMI ≥ 25 kg/m^2) Prevalence, Females, Aged 15+, 2010

Prevalence (%)
- < 20.0
- 20.0 < 35.0
- 35.0 < 50.0
- 50.0 < 65.0
- 65.0 < 80.0
- ≥ 80.0
- not available

Source: Ono T, Guthold R. Strong K, WHO Global Comaprable Estimates, 2005

The boundaries and names shown and the designations used on this map to not imply the expressions of any opinion whatsoever on the part of the World Health Organization concerning the legal status of any country, territory, city or area or of its authorities, or concerning the delimitation of its frontiers or boundaries. Dotted lines on maps represent approximate border lines for which there may not yet be full agreement. © WHO 2011. All rights reserved

0.0   20.0 35.0 50.0 65.0 80.0 93.0
Distribution of country rate

FIGURE 15.5

Worldwide obesity prevalence rates for women

SOURCE: WHO Global Infobase (online)

the highest rates are in Lithuania, Malta, Russia and Serbia and the lowest are in Sweden, Ireland, Denmark and the UK. Overall, people in northern and western Europe are thinner than in eastern and southern Europe and women are more likely to be obese than men.

WHAT ARE THE PROBLEMS WITH OBESITY?

Physical Problems

Obesity has been associated with cardiovascular disease, diabetes, joint trauma, back pain, cancer, hypertension and mortality. The effects of obesity are related to where the excess weight is carried; weight stored in the upper body, particularly in the abdomen, is more detrimental to health than weight carried in the lower body. It is interesting to note that although men are more likely than women to store fat on their upper bodies, and are therefore more at risk if obese, women are more concerned about weight than men and most treatment studies examine women. The relationship between BMI and mortality is shown in Figure 15.6. It has been suggested that most problems seem to be associated with severe obesity and weights in the top 10 per cent (Wooley and Wooley 1984); however, a study of 14,077 women indicated a direct linear relationship between BMI and risk factors for heart disease including blood pressure, cholesterol and blood glucose (Ashton et al. 2001). Similar studies have also reported a relationship between BMI increases in the lower range of the spectrum and hypertension (National Institutes of Health 1998), diabetes (Ford et al. 1997) and heart attack (Willett et al. 1995). Moore et al. (2008) also explored the impact of BMI measured 10 years prior to death in a large cohort of 50,186 women. The results showed a direct relationship between BMI and mortality (see Romero-Corral et al. 2006 for a systematic review of the literature). Further, in 2002, research by the House of Commons Special Select Committee in the UK estimated that 6.8 per cent of all deaths in England were attributable to obesity.

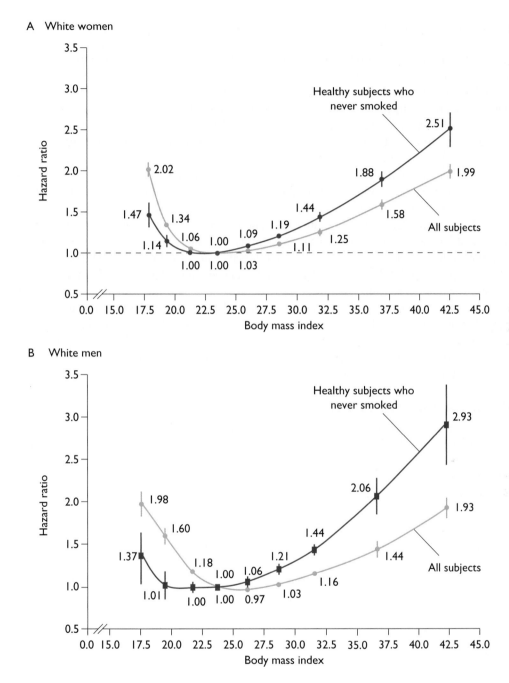

FIGURE 15.6

Relationship between BMI and mortality

SOURCE: de Gonzalez et al. (2010)

Psychological Problems

Research has examined the relationship between psychological problems and obesity. The contemporary cultural obsession with thinness, the aversion to fat found in both adults and children and the attribution of blame to the obese may promote low self-esteem and poor self-image in those individuals who do not conform to the stereotypically attractive thin image. Some studies have explored levels of depression in those waiting for surgical treatment for their obesity and consistently show that such patients report more depressive symptoms than average-weight individuals (e.g. Wadden et al. 1986). In addition, Rand and MacGregor (1991) concluded that individuals who had lost weight following gastric bypass surgery stated that they would rather be deaf, dyslexic, diabetic or have heart disease or acne than return to their former weight. More recently, Simon et al. (2006) carried out a large survey on over 9,000 adults in the USA and concluded that obesity was associated with increased lifetime diagnosis of major depression, bipolar disorder, panic disorder or agoraphobia. In line with this, Ogden and Clementi (2011) carried out a qualitative study of the experience of being obese and reported that the obese describe a multitude of negative ways in which their weight impacts upon their self-identity and that this is exacerbated by living in a society that stigmatizes their condition. However, it is possible that depressed obese individuals are more likely to seek treatment for their obesity than those who are not depressed and that there may be many obese individuals who are quite happy and therefore do not come into contact with health professionals. Ross (1994) addressed this possibility and interviewed a random sample of more than 2,000 adults by telephone. These were individuals who varied in weight and were not necessarily in the process of seeking help for any weight-related issues. The results from this large-scale study showed that overweight was *unrelated* to depression. There was a small subgroup in Ross's study who were both overweight and depressed, and these tended to be the most educated. Ross argued that these individuals were also dieting to lose weight and that it was the *attempt* to lose weight rather than the weight per se that was distressing. Therefore, although many obese people may experience their obesity in negative ways, there is no consistent support for a simple relationship between body size and psychological problems.

WHAT CAUSES OBESITY?

The theories relating to the causes of obesity include physiological theories, the role of the obesogenic environment and behavioural theories.

Physiological Theories

Several physiological theories describe the possible causes of obesity.

Genetic Theories

Size appears to run in families and the probability that a child will be overweight is related to the parents' weight. For example, having one obese parent results in a 40 per cent chance of producing an obese child, and having two obese parents results in an 80 per cent chance. In contrast, the probability that thin parents will produce overweight children is very small, about 7 per cent (Garn et al. 1981). This observation has been repeated in studies exploring populations from different parts of the world living in different environments (Maes et al. 1997). However, parents and children share both environment and genetic constitution, so this likeness could be due to either factor. To address this problem, research has examined twins and adoptees.

- *Twin studies.* Twin studies have examined the weight of identical twins reared apart, who have identical genes but different environments. Studies have also examined the weights of non-identical twins reared together, who have different genes but similar environments. The results show that the identical twins reared apart are more similar in weight than non-identical twins reared together. For example, Stunkard et al. (1990) examined the BMI in 93 pairs of identical twins reared apart and reported that genetic factors accounted for 66–70 per cent in the variance in their body weight, suggesting a strong genetic component in determining obesity. However, the role of genetics appears to be greater in lighter twin pairs than in heavier pairs.
- *Adoptee studies.* Research has also examined the role of genetics in obesity using adoptees. Such studies compare the adoptees' weight with both their adoptive parents and their biological

parents. Stunkard et al. (1986) gathered information about 540 adult adoptees in Denmark, their adopted parents and their biological parents. The results showed a strong relationship between the weight class of the adoptee (thin, median weight, overweight, obese) and their biological parents' weight class but no relationship with their adoptee parents' weight class. This suggests a major role for genetics and was also found across the whole range of body weight. Interestingly, the relationship to the biological mother's weight was greater than the relationship with the biological father's weight.

Research therefore suggests a strong role for genetics in predicting obesity. It also suggests that the primary distribution of this weight (upper versus lower body) is also inherited (Bouchard et al. 1990). However, how this genetic predisposition expresses itself is unclear. *Metabolic rate* and *appetite regulation* may be two factors influenced by genetics.

Metabolic Rate Theory

The body uses energy to carry out the chemical and biological processes which are essential to being alive (e.g. respiration, heart rate, blood pressure). The rate of this energy use is called the *resting metabolic rate*, which has been found to be highly heritable (Bouchard et al. 1990). One theory of obesity has argued that the obese may have lower metabolic rates and that they burn up fewer calories when they are resting, and therefore require less food intake to carry on living. There is some tentative support for this suggestion. For example, research in the USA evaluated the relationship between metabolic rate and weight gain. A group in Phoenix assessed the metabolic rates of 126 Pima Indians by monitoring their breathing for a 40-minute period. The study was carried out using Pima Indians because they have an abnormally high rate of obesity – about 80 to 85 per cent – and are considered an interesting population. The subjects remained stationary and the levels of oxygen consumed and carbon dioxide produced were measured. The researchers then followed any changes in weight and metabolic rate for a four-year period and found that the people who gained a substantial amount of weight were the ones with the lowest metabolic rates at the beginning of the study. In a further study, 95 subjects spent 24 hours in a respiratory chamber and the amount of energy used was measured. The subjects were followed up two years later and the researchers found that those who had originally shown a low level of energy use were four times more likely to also show a substantial weight increase (Ravussin et al. 1988). Tataranni *et al.* (2003) used state-of-the art methods to assess energy intake and energy expenditure in 92 free-living, adult Pima Indians in Arizona. These methods allowed the researchers to measure energy intake and total energy expenditure accurately outside the laboratory in order to test their role in the aetiology of obesity prospectively. The results demonstrate for the first time that baseline total energy intake is a key determinant of long-term changes in body weight in Pima Indians, and also confirm that a low resting metabolic rate is a risk factor for weight gain in this population. In addition, baseline energy expenditure, due to physical activity, was not found to be associated with changes in body weight.

These results indicate a possible relationship between metabolic rate and the tendency for weight gain. If this is the case, then some individuals are predisposed to become obese because they require fewer calories to survive than thinner individuals. A genetic tendency to be obese may therefore express itself in lowered metabolic rates. However, most research does not support this theory. In particular, there is no evidence to suggest that obese people generally have lower metabolic rates than thin people. In fact, research suggests that overweight people tend to have slightly higher metabolic rates than thin people of similar height (Garrow 1987). The obese also expend more energy than thin people for a given activity (Prentice et al. 1989). To explain these apparently contradictory findings it has been suggested that obese people may have lower metabolic rates to start with, which results in weight gain, and this weight gain itself results in an increase in metabolic rate (Ravussin and Bogardus 1989). This view has not gone unchallenged, however, and Garrow and Webster (1985) have argued that this is an unlikely explanation which is unsupported by the evidence. In sum, the 'slow metabolism' theory of obesity may be held by many lay people, but it is no longer considered to be backed by research.

Appetite Regulation

A genetic predisposition may also be related to appetite control. Over recent years researchers have attempted to identify the gene, or collection of genes, responsible for obesity. Although some work using small animals has identified a single gene that is associated with profound obesity, for humans the work is still unclear. Two children have, however, been identified with a defect in the 'ob gene', which produces leptin, which is responsible for telling the brain to stop eating (Montague et al. 1997). It has been argued that the obese may not produce leptin and therefore overeat. To support this, researchers have given these two children daily injections of leptin, which has resulted in a decrease in food intake and weight loss at a rate of 1–2kg per month (Farooqi et al. 1999). Despite this, the research exploring the role of genetics on appetite control is still in the very early stages.

In summary, there is strong evidence for a genetic basis to obesity, but how this genetic basis expresses itself remains unclear, as the research on lowered metabolic rate has mostly been refuted and the genetics of appetite control remains in its infancy. There are also some problems with genetic studies which need to be considered. For example, the sample size of studies is often small, zygosity needs to be confirmed, and there remains the problem of the environment. Twin studies assume that the environment for twins is constant and that only the genetic makeup of non-identical twins is different. It is possible, however, that identical twins are brought up more similarly because they are identical whereas parents of non-identical twins emphasize their children's differences. In addition, adopted children often go to the homes of parents who are similar to their biological parents. There also remains a substantial amount of variance in body fat which is unexplained by genetics, and the recent increased prevalence of obesity in the West within populations whose gene pool has remained relatively constant points to a role for additional factors. This has led to researchers examining the impact of our changing environment.

The Obesogenic Environment

Physiological models emphasize a number of different mechanisms to explain obesity onset. They cannot, however, explain why the prevalence of obesity has increased so rapidly over the past few decades. Our genetics, neural mechanisms and metabolic rates take far longer to change than just years, and yet obesity is now considered an epidemic. To address this change, researchers have turned their attention to the role of the external world which has been labelled an *obesogenic environment* (Hill and Peters 1998). For example, they have highlighted the impact of the food industry with its food advertising, food labelling and the easy availability of energy-dense foods such as fast foods and takeaways. They have identified environmental factors which encourage us to live an increasingly sedentary lifestyle such as a reduction in manual labour, the use of cars, computers and television and the design of towns whereby walking is prohibited through the absence of streetlights, pavements and large distances between residential areas and places of entertainment or shops, and they have focused on factors which make it more and more difficult to eat well and be active such as the presence of lifts and escalators which detract from stair use and the cheapness of prepared foods which discourages food shopping and cooking. Accordingly, this obesogenic environment creates a world in which it is easy to gain weight. Furthermore, the changes in our environment coincide with the increased prevalence of obesity. From a public health perspective, therefore, environmental factors are key to understanding obesity and any attempts to prevent obesity onset should focus on changing the environment. In line with this, governments provide subsidies for leisure centres, trying to make them more accessible for everyone. There are local campaigns to encourage stair climbing by putting prompts near lifts and stairwells and there is legislation limiting food advertising. Furthermore, some companies encourage their staff to be active in their lunch breaks by organizing walking groups and offering gym facilities, and school and work canteens are supported in their attempts to offer healthier meals. In the same way that many governments have now finally responded to the knowledge that smoking kills by banning it in public places, steps are being made to intervene at an environmental and policy level to control the obesity epidemic.

From a psychological perspective, however, understanding the environmental factors which promote obesity does not seem to be a sufficient explanatory model. Psychology focuses on beliefs and behaviour and as Prentice (1999: 38) argued, 'Obesity can only occur when energy

The obesogenic environment changes our behaviour

SOURCE: © Jfeinstein/Dreamstime

intake remains higher than energy expenditure, for an extended period of time. This is an incontrovertible cornerstone on which all explanations must be based.' Research has therefore examined the role of behaviour in explaining obesity, and behavioural theories of obesity focus on physical activity and eating behaviour.

Behavioural Theories

Behavioural theories of obesity have examined both physical activity and eating behaviour. Further details about exercise and diet can be found in Chapters 5 and 6.

Physical Activity

Increases in the prevalence of obesity coincide with decreases in daily energy expenditure due to improvements in transport systems, and a shift from an agricultural society to an industrial and increasingly information-based one. As a simple example, a telephone company in the USA has suggested that in the course of one year an extension phone upstairs – which means the person no longer needs to run downstairs – saves an individual approximately one mile of walking, which could be the equivalent of 2–3lb of fat or up to 10,500 kcals (Stern 1984). Imagine how much energy a mobile phone saves! Further, at present only 20 per cent of men and 10 per cent of women are employed in active occupations and for many people leisure times are dominated by inactivity (see Chapter 6 for a discussion of physical activity). Although data on changes in activity levels are problematic, there exists a useful database on TV viewing which shows that, whereas the average viewer in the 1960s watched 13 hours of TV per week, in England this had doubled to 26 hours per week (OPCS 1994). Overall, data seem to indicate that the majority of people do not meet the recommended targets for activity, that generally people get more sedentary and less active as they get older and that men are more active than women particularly when young, but watch more TV than women as they get older. This is further exacerbated by the increased use of videos and computer games by both children and adults. It has therefore been suggested that obesity may be caused by inactivity. In a survey of adolescent boys in Glasgow in 1964 and 1971, whereas daily food diaries indicated a decrease in daily energy intake from 2,795kcals to 2,610kcals, the boys in 1971 showed an increase in body fat from 16.3 per cent to 18.4 per cent. This suggests that decreased physical activity was related to increased body fat (Durnin et al. 1974). To examine the role of physical activity in obesity, research has asked, 'Are changes in obesity related to changes in activity?', 'Do the obese exercise less?' and 'What effect does exercise have on energy expenditure?' These questions will now be examined.

ARE CHANGES IN OBESITY RELATED TO CHANGES IN ACTIVITY?

This question can be answered in two ways, first using epidemiological data on a population and second using prospective data on individuals.

In 1995, Prentice and Jebb presented epidemiological data on changes in physical activity from 1950 to 1990, as measured by car ownership and TV viewing, and compared these with changes in the prevalence of obesity. The results from this study suggested a strong association between an increase in both car ownership and TV viewing and an increase in obesity (see Figure 15.7). They commented that 'it seems reasonable to conclude that the low levels of physical activity now prevalent in Britain must play an important, perhaps dominant role in the development of obesity by greatly reducing energy needs'. However, their data were only correlational. Therefore it remains unclear whether obesity and physical activity are related (the *third factor problem* – some other variable may be determining both obesity and activity), and whether decreases in activity cause increases in obesity or whether, in fact, increases in obesity actually cause decreases in activity. In addition, the data are at the population level and therefore could miss important individual differences (i.e. some people who become obese could be active and those who are thin could be inactive).

In an alternative approach to assessing the relationship between activity and obesity a large Finnish study of 12,000 adults examined the association between levels of physical activity and excess weight gain over a five-year follow-up period (Rissanen et al. 1991). The results showed that lower levels of activity were a greater risk factor for weight gain than any other baseline measures. In a recent study the authors analysed data from 146 twin pairs as a means to assess the relative contribution of genetics and physical activity over a 30-year period (Waller et al. 2008). The results showed that persistent physical activity across the 30 years of the study was related to smaller waist circumference and a decreased weight gain as the active twin showed less weight gain than the inactive twin even though they shared the same genetic make-up and childhood environment. However, although these data were prospective, it is still possible that a third factor may explain the relationship (i.e. those with lower levels of activity at baseline were women, the women had children and therefore put on more weight). Unless experimental data are collected, conclusions about causality remain problematic.

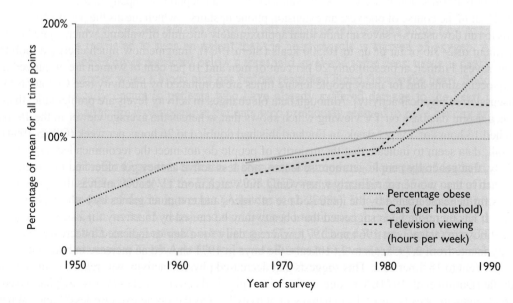

FIGURE 15.7

Changes in physical activity and obesity

DO THE OBESE EXERCISE LESS?

Research has also examined the relationship between activity and obesity using a cross-sectional design to examine differences between the obese and non-obese. In particular, several studies in the 1960s and 1970s examined whether the obese exercised less than the non-obese. Using time-lapse photography, Bullen et al. (1964) observed girls considered obese and those of normal weight on a summer camp. They reported that during swimming the obese girls spent less time swimming and more time floating, and while playing tennis the obese girls were inactive for 77 per cent of the time compared with the girls of normal weight, who were inactive for only 56 per cent of the time. In addition, research indicates that the obese walk less on a daily basis than the non-obese and are less likely to use stairs or walk up escalators. For example, to assess the impact of stair climbing Shenassa et al. (2008) explored the relationship between BMI and floor of residence in nearly 3,000 normal weight adults across eight European cities. The results showed that for men, higher floor was associated with lower BMI. This association was not, however, found for women. The authors concluded that daily stair climbing may reduce weight and therefore should be encouraged. Why the association was not there for women is unclear.

Further cross-sectional data in 2008 from the UK explored the relationship between body weight and being sedentary in the week and at the weekend. The results are shown in Figure 15.8 for men and women. The results from this data indicate that the obese are more sedentary at both the weekend and in the week than either those who are overweight or those of normal weight. These studies are cross-sectional and whether reduced exercise is a cause or a consequence of obesity is unclear. It is possible that the obese take less exercise due to factors such as embarrassment and stigma and that exercise plays a part in the maintenance of obesity but not in its cause.

WHAT EFFECT DOES EXERCISE HAVE ON ENERGY EXPENDITURE?

Exercise burns up calories. For example, 10 minutes of sleeping uses up to 16kcals, standing uses 19kcals, running uses 142kcals, walking downstairs uses 88kcals and walking upstairs uses 229kcals (Brownell 1989). In addition, the amount of calories used increases with the individual's body weight. Therefore, exercise has long been recommended as a weight loss method. However, the number of calories that exercise burns up is relatively few compared with those in an average meal. In addition, exercise is recommended as a means to increase metabolic rate, however, only intense and prolonged exercise appears to have an effect on that rate.

The role of exercise in obesity is still unclear. There appears to be an association between population decreases in activity and increases in obesity. In addition, prospective data support this association and highlight lower levels of activity as an important risk factor. Further, cross-sectional data indicate that the obese appear to exercise less than the non-obese. However, whether inactivity is a cause or consequence of obesity is questionable. It is possible that an unidentified third factor may be creating this association, and it is also debatable whether exercise has a role in reducing food intake and promoting energy expenditure. However, exercise may have psychological and general health effects, which could benefit the obese either in terms of promoting weight loss or simply by making them feel better about themselves (see Chapter 6 for the effects of exercise on mood and health).

EATING BEHAVIOUR

In an alternative approach to understanding the causes of obesity, research has examined eating behaviour. Chapter 5 described a number of different approaches to understanding eating behaviour. These perspectives emphasize mechanisms such as exposure, modelling and associative learning, beliefs and emotions, body dissatisfaction and dieting, all of which can help explain obesity. For example, it is possible that the obese have childhoods in which food is used to reward good behaviour, or have parents who overeat, or hold cognitions about food which drive eating behaviour. It is also possible that dieting when moderately overweight (or just feeling fat) triggers episodes of overeating which themselves cause increases in body fat. It is therefore important to ask the following

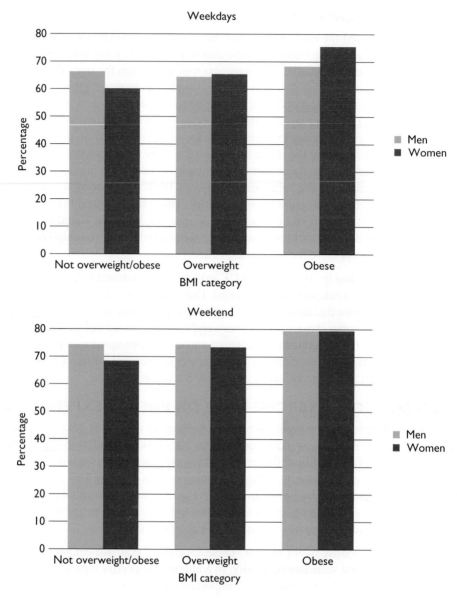

FIGURE 15.8

Body weight and being sedentary on a weekday and at the weekend

SOURCE: Copyright © 2011, re-used with the permission of The Health and Social Care Information Centre, all rights reserved

questions to link diet and obesity: 'Are changes in food intake associated with changes in obesity?', 'Do the obese eat for different reasons than the non-obese?' and 'Do the obese eat more than the non-obese?'

Are Changes in Food Intake Associated with Changes in Obesity?

The UK National Food Survey collects data on food intake in the home, which can be analysed to assess changes in food intake over the past 50 years. The results from this database illustrate that, although overall calorie consumption increased between 1950 and 1970, since 1970 there has been a distinct decrease in the amount we eat (see Figure 15.9). However, this data relates *only* to food intake in the home and does not take into account meals and snacking in cafés and restaurants or on the move.

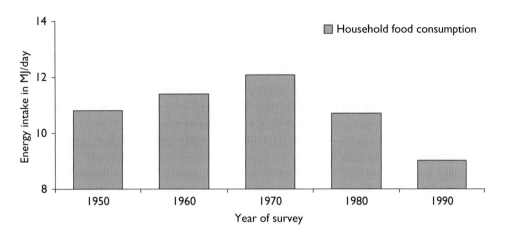

FIGURE 15.9

Changes in food intake from the 1950s to the 1990s

Prentice and Jebb (1995) examined the association between changes in food intake in terms of energy intake and fat intake and changes in obesity. Their results indicated no obvious association between the increase in obesity and the changes in food intake (see Figure 15.10). Therefore, using population data, there appears to be no relationship between changes in food intake and changes in obesity.

Do the Obese Eat for Different Reasons than the Non-Obese?

Throughout the 1960s and 1970s theories of eating behaviour emphasized the role of food intake in predicting weight. Original studies of obesity were based on the assumption that the obese ate for different reasons than people of normal weight (Ferster et al. 1962). Schachter's *externality theory* suggested that, although all people were responsive to environmental stimuli such as the

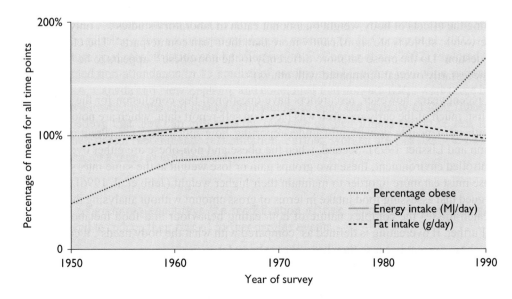

FIGURE 15.10

Changes in calorie consumption and obesity

sight, taste and smell of food, and that such stimuli might cause overeating, the obese were highly and sometimes uncontrollably responsive to external cues. It was argued that normal-weight individuals mainly ate as a response to internal cues (e.g. hunger, satiety) and obese individuals tended to be under-responsive to their internal cues and over-responsive to external cues. Within this perspective, research examined the eating behaviour and eating style of the obese and non-obese in response to external cues such as the time of day, the sight of food, the taste of food and the number and salience of food cues (e.g. Schachter and Gross 1968; Schachter and Rodin 1974). The results from these studies were fairly inconsistent. Research has also addressed the *emotionality theory* of eating behaviour. For example, Bruch (e.g. 1974) developed a psychosomatic theory of eating behaviour and eating disorders which argued that some people interpret the sensations of such emotions as emptiness as similar to hunger and that food is used as a substitute for other forms of emotional comfort. Van Strien et al. (2009) explored the relationship between dietary restraint, emotional and external eating, overeating and BMI to assess how people resist (or not) the opportunity to become overweight offered by the obesogenic environment. The results showed that although overeating was associated with being overweight, this association was moderated by both restraint and emotional eating (not external eating). They drew two conclusions from their data. First, they argued that the impact of overeating is limited by dietary restraint; second, they argued that emotional eating is a better predictor of body weight than external eating.

Do the Obese Eat More than the Non-Obese?

Research has also examined whether the obese eat more than the non-obese, focusing on the amount consumed per se, how they eat and the type of food consumed.

The Amount Eaten

Because it was believed that the obese ate for different reasons than the non-obese, it was also believed that they ate more. Research explored the food intake of the obese in restaurants and at home, and examined what food they bought. For example, Coates et al. (1978) suggested that perhaps the obese were overeating at home and went into the homes of 60 middle-class families to examine what was stored in their cupboards. They weighed all members of the families and found no relationship between body size and the mass and type of food they consumed at home. In an attempt to clarify the problem of whether the obese eat more than the non-obese, Spitzer and Rodin (1981) examined the research into eating behaviour and suggested that 'of twenty-nine studies examining the effects of body weight on amount eaten in laboratory studies . . . only nine reported that overweight subjects ate significantly more than their lean counterparts'. Therefore the answer to the question 'Do the obese eat more/differently to the non-obese?' appears to be 'no'; the obese do not necessarily overeat (compared with others).

Over recent years, however, researchers have questioned this conclusion for the following reasons. First, much of the early research was based on self-report data, which are notoriously unreliable, with most people consistently under-reporting how much they eat (Prentice et al. 1986; Heitmann and Lissner 1995). Second, when the obese and non-obese are either over- or underfed in a controlled environment, these two groups gain or lose weight at the same rate, suggesting that the obese must eat more in order to maintain their higher weight (Jebb et al. 1996). Finally, it has been argued that assessing food intake in terms of gross amount without analysing the *types* of food being eaten misses the complex nature of both eating behaviour and food metabolism (Prentice 1995). Further, if overeating is defined as 'compared with what the body needs', it could be argued that the obese overeat because they have excess body fat.

Eating Differently

One recent study asked whether the obese eat at different times of day to the non-obese. Berg et al. (2009) used a sample of 3,610 women and men from Sweden and explored their BMI and meal patterns. The results showed that those who were obese were more likely to skip breakfast, skip lunch and eat at night and reported larger portion sizes at meal times. Similarly, Laessle et al. (2007) explored whether the obese ate differently in a laboratory study in Germany. The results showed that compared to normal weight participants the obese showed a faster initial rate of eating, took larger spoonfuls and had an overall greater intake of food.

Type of Food

Over recent years, research has focused on the eating behaviour of the obese not in terms of calories consumed, or in terms of amount eaten, but more specifically in terms of the type of food eaten. Population data indicate that calorie consumption has decreased since the 1970s and that this decrease is unrelated to the increase in obesity (see Figures 15.9, 15.10). However, these data also show that the ratio between carbohydrate consumption and fat consumption has changed; whereas we now eat less carbohydrate, we eat proportionally more fat (Prentice and Jebb 1995, see Figure 15.11).

One theory that has been developed is that, although the obese may not eat more than the non-obese overall, they may eat proportionally more fat. Further, it has been argued that not all calories are equal (Prentice 1995) and that calories from fat may lead to greater weight gain than calories from carbohydrates. To support this theory, one study of 11,500 people in Scotland showed that men consuming the lowest proportion of carbohydrate in their diets were four times more likely to be obese than those consuming the highest proportion of carbohydrate. A similar relationship was also found for women, although the difference was only two- to threefold. Therefore it was concluded that relatively lower carbohydrate consumption is related to lower levels of obesity (Bolton-Smith and Woodward 1994). A similar study in Leeds also provided support for the fat proportion theory of obesity (Blundell and Macdiarmid 1997). This study reported that high fat eaters who derived more than 45 per cent of their energy from fat were 19 times more likely to be obese than those who derived less than 35 per cent of their energy from fat. Therefore these studies suggest that the obese do not eat more overall than the non-obese, nor do they eat more calories, carbohydrate or fat per se than the non-obese. But they do eat more fat

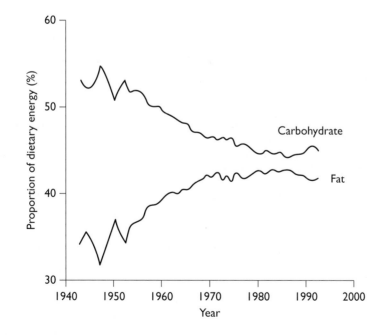

FIGURE 15.11

Changes in fat and carbohydrate consumption in the UK

SOURCE: Prentice and Jebb (1995)

compared with the amount of carbohydrate; the proportion of fat in their diet is higher. So how might a relative increase in fat consumption relate to obesity?

As a possible explanation of these results, research has examined the role of fat and carbohydrates in appetite regulation. Three possible mechanisms have been proposed (Blundell et al. 1996; Blundell and Macdiarmid 1997):

1 *The benefits of complex carbohydrates to energy use.* It has been suggested that it takes more energy to burn carbohydrates than fat. Further, as the body prefers to burn carbohydrates than fat, carbohydrate intake is accompanied by an increase in carbohydrate oxidation. In contrast, increased fat intake is not accompanied by an increase in fat oxidation. Therefore carbohydrates are burned, fat is stored.

2 *The benefits of complex carbohydrates to hunger.* It has been suggested that complex carbohydrates (such as bread, potatoes, pasta, rice) reduce hunger and cause reduced food intake due to their bulk and the amount of fibre they contain. In addition, they switch off the desire to eat. Therefore carbohydrates make you feel fuller faster.

3 *The costs of fat to hunger.* It has been suggested that fat does not switch off the desire to eat, making it easier to eat more and more fat without feeling full.

WHAT DOES ALL THIS RESEARCH MEAN?

The evidence for the causes of obesity is therefore complex and can be summarized as follows:

- There is good evidence for a genetic basis to obesity. The evidence for how this is expressed is weak.
- The prevalence of obesity has increased at a similar rate to decreases in physical activity.
- There is some evidence that the obese exercise less than the non-obese.

BOX 15.1 Some Problems with ... Obesity and CHD Research

Below are some problems with research in this area that you may wish to consider.

1 Measuring and defining obesity are problematic as they rely upon assessments of body weight and body size, whereas the factor that is most linked to health status is probably body fat. Therefore research can show contradictory evidence for the consequences of obesity which probably illustrates the drawbacks of using proxy measures (i.e. BMI and waist circumference) for what the real measurement should be (i.e. body fat).

2 Obesity is a product of biological factors (e.g. genetics), social factors (e.g. the food industry, town planning) and psychological factors (e.g. diet, exercise, beliefs). Research tends to focus on the contribution of one set of these factors. How they all interact remains unclear. This means that most research misses the complexity of the obesity problem. However, if research were to try to address all these factors, the studies would become unwieldy and the conclusions would be too complex to put into practice.

3 CHD illustrates the impact of stress and behaviour on illness. Research focuses on how these factors can predict CHD and how they can be changed to prevent the development of CHD or prevent the reoccurrence of a myocardial infarction in the future. Central to this is the measurement of stress and behaviour which is problematic due to the reliance upon self-report. This may be particularly biased if a person has been identified as having CHD and wishes to seem to be compliant with any recommendations they have been given by their health professional.

- The prevalence of obesity has increased at a rate unrelated to the overall decrease in calorie consumption (but measured in the home).
- There is inconsistent evidence as to whether the obese eat more calories than the non-obese.
- The obese may eat differently and for different reasons than the non-obese.
- The relative increase in fat is parallel to the increase in obesity.
- The obese may eat proportionally more fat than the non-obese.

Therefore the following points would seem likely:

- Some individuals have a genetic tendency to be obese.
- Obesity is related to lack of exercise.
- Obesity is related to consuming relatively more fat and relatively less carbohydrates.

The causes of obesity remain complex and unclear. Perhaps an integration of all theories is needed before proper conclusions can be drawn.

OBESITY TREATMENT

TRADITIONAL TREATMENT APPROACHES

The traditional treatment approach to obesity was a corrective one, the assumption being that obesity was a product of overeating and underactivity. Treatment approaches therefore focused on encouraging the obese to eat 'normally' and this consistently involved putting them on a diet. Stuart and Davis (1972) developed a behavioural programme for obesity involving monitoring food intake, modifying cues for inappropriate eating and encouraging self-reward for appropriate behaviour, which was widely adopted by hospitals and clinics. The programme aimed to encourage eating in response to physiological hunger and not in response to mood cues such as boredom or depression, or in response to external cues such as the sight and smell of food or the sight of other people eating. In 1958, Stunkard concluded his review of the past 30 years' attempts to promote weight loss in the obese with the statement, 'Most obese persons will not stay in treatment for obesity. Of those who stay in treatment, most will not lose weight, and of those who do lose weight, most will regain it.' More recent evaluations of their effectiveness indicate that although traditional behavioural therapies may lead to initial weight losses of, on average, 0.5kg per week (Brownell and Wadden 1992), 'weight losses achieved by behavioural treatments for obesity are not well maintained'.

However, it is now generally accepted that obesity is not simply a behavioural problem and, as Brownell and Steen said somewhat optimistically in 1987, 'psychological problems are no longer inferred simply because an individual is overweight'. Therefore traditional behavioural programmes make some unsubstantiated assumptions about the causes of obesity by encouraging the obese to eat 'normally' like individuals of normal weight.

MULTIDIMENSIONAL BEHAVIOURAL PROGRAMMES

The failure of traditional treatment packages for obesity resulted in longer periods of treatment, an emphasis on follow-up and the introduction of a multidimensional perspective to obesity treatment. Recent comprehensive, multidimensional cognitive behavioural packages aim to broaden the perspective for obesity treatment and combine traditional self-monitoring methods with information, exercise, cognitive restructuring, attitude change and relapse prevention (e.g. see Chapter 8 for a discussion of behaviour change strategies). Brownell and Wadden (1991) emphasized the need for a multidimensional approach, the importance of screening patients for entry onto a treatment programme and the need to match the individual with the most appropriate package. State-of-the-art behavioural treatment programmes aim to encourage the obese to eat less than they do *usually* rather than encouraging them to eat less than the non-obese. Analysis of the effectiveness of this treatment approach suggests that average weight loss during the treatment programme is 0.5kg per week, that approximately 60–70 per cent of the weight loss is maintained during the first year but that follow-up at three and five years tends to show weight gains back to baseline weight (Brownell and Wadden 1992). In a comprehensive review of the treatment interventions for obesity, Wilson (1994) suggested that although there has been an improvement in the effectiveness of obesity treatment since the 1970s, success rates are still poor.

Wadden (1993) examined both the short- and long-term effectiveness of both moderate and severe caloric restriction on weight loss. He reviewed all the studies involving randomized controlled trials in four behavioural journals and compared his findings with those of Stunkard (1958). Wadden concluded that 'Investigators have made significant progress in inducing weight loss in the 35 years since Stunkard's review.' Wadden stated that 80 per cent of patients stayed in treatment for 20 weeks and that 50 per cent achieved a weight loss of 20lb or more. Therefore modern methods of weight loss produced improved results in the short term. However, Wadden also concluded that 'most obese patients treated in research trials still regain their lost weight'. This conclusion has been further supported by a systematic review of interventions for the treatment and prevention of obesity, which identified 92 studies that fitted the authors' inclusion criteria (NHS Centre for Reviews and Dissemination 1997). The review examined the effectiveness of dietary, exercise, behavioural, pharmacological and surgical interventions for obesity and concluded that 'the majority of the studies included in the present review demonstrate weight regain either during treatment or post intervention'. Further, Fabricatore and Wadden in 2006 argued that the weight losses achieved with non-surgical approaches 'have remained virtually unchanged over the past 20 years'. Accordingly, the picture for long-term weight loss is still fairly pessimistic.

THE ROLE OF DIETING

With the exception of the surgical interventions now available (see p. 412), all obesity treatment programmes involve recommending dieting in one form or another. Traditional treatment programmes aimed to correct the obese individual's abnormal behaviour, and recent packages suggest that the obese need to readjust their energy balance by eating less than they usually do. But both styles of treatment suggest that to lose weight the individual must impose cognitive restraint upon their eating behaviour. They recommend that the obese deny food and set cognitive limits to override physiological limits of satiety. And this brings with it all the problematic consequences of restrained eating (see Chapter 5).

Psychological Problems and Obesity Treatment

Wadden et al. (1986) reported that dieting resulted in increased depression in a group of obese patients and Loro and Orleans (1981) indicated that obese dieters report episodes of bingeing precipitated by 'anxiety, frustration, depression and other unpleasant emotions'. This suggests that the obese respond to dieting in the same way as the non-obese, with lowered mood and episodes of overeating, both of which are detrimental to attempts at weight loss. The obese are encouraged to impose a cognitive limit on their food intake, which introduces a sense of denial, guilt and the inevitable response of overeating. Consequently any weight loss is precluded by episodes of overeating, which are a response to the many cognitive and emotional changes that occur during dieting (see Chapter 5 for a discussion of the consequences of dieting).

Physiological Problems and Obesity Treatment

In addition to the psychological consequences of imposing a dieting structure on the obese, there are physiological changes which accompany attempts at food restriction. Heatherton et al. (1991) reported that restraint in the non-obese predicts weight fluctuation, which parallels the process of *weight cycling* or *'yo-yo' dieting* in the obese. Research on rats suggests that repeated attempts at weight loss followed by weight regain result in further weight loss becoming increasingly difficult due to a decreased metabolic rate and an increase in the percentage of body fat (Brownell et al. 1986a). Human research has found similar results in dieters and athletes who show yo-yo dieting (Brownell et al. 1989). Research has also found that weight fluctuation may have negative effects on health, with reports suggesting an association between weight fluctuation and mortality and morbidity from CHD (Hamm et al. 1989) and all-cause mortality (Lissner et al. 1991). Repeated failed attempts at dieting, therefore, may be more detrimental to physical health than remaining statically obese.

Dieting, Obesity and Health

Restraint theory (see Chapter 5) suggests that dieting has negative consequences, and yet the treatment of obesity recommends dieting as a solution. This paradox can be summarized as follows:

- Obesity is a physical health risk, but restrained eating may promote weight cycling, which is also detrimental to health.
- Obesity treatment aims to reduce food intake, but restrained eating can promote overeating.
- The obese may suffer psychologically from the social pressures to be thin (although evidence of psychological problems in the non-dieting obese is scarce), but failed attempts to diet may leave them depressed, feeling a failure and out of control. For those few who do succeed in their attempts at weight loss, Wooley and Wooley (1984: 187) suggest that they 'are in fact condemned to a life of weight obsession, semi-starvation and all the symptoms produced by chronic hunger . . . and seem precariously close to developing a frank eating disorder'.

If restraint theory is applied to obesity, the obese should not be encouraged to restrain their food intake. Obesity may not be caused by overeating but overeating may be a consequence of obesity if restrained eating is recommended as a cure.

SHOULD OBESITY BE TREATED AT ALL?

The problems with treating obesity raise the question of whether it should be treated at all. In order to answer this it is necessary to examine the benefits of treatment, the treatment alternatives and the role of individual responsibility.

THE BENEFITS

Although failed obesity treatment may be related to negative mood, actual weight loss has been found to be associated with positive changes such as elation, self-confidence and increased feelings of well-being (Stunkard 1984). This suggests that, whereas failed dieting attempts are detrimental, successful treatment may bring with it psychological rewards. The physical effects of obesity treatment also show a similar pattern of results. Yo-yo dieting and weight fluctuation may increase the chances of CHD and death, but actual weight loss of only 10 per cent may result in improved blood pressure and benefits for type 2 diabetes (Wing et al. 1987; Aucott 2008). These results again suggest that actual weight loss can be beneficial. Halmi et al. (1980) reported significant psychological and physical benefits of weight loss in the severely obese. They compared a group of severely obese subjects who received surgery with a comparison group who received a behavioural diet programme. The results indicated that the surgery group showed higher rates of both weight loss and weight maintenance. In addition, the diet group reported significantly higher changes in psychological characteristics, such as preoccupation with food and depression, than the surgery group. Thus permanent weight loss through surgery brought both physical and psychological benefits. Weight loss can therefore be beneficial in the obese, but *only* if treatment is successful and the results are permanent. Therefore dieting may be rejected as a treatment but weight loss may still be seen as beneficial.

An argument for treating severe obesity can be made, but only if a positive outcome can be guaranteed, as failed treatment may be more detrimental than no treatment attempts at all.

THE TREATMENT ALTERNATIVES

The implications of restraint theory suggest that the obese should avoid restrained eating. Dieting offers a small chance of weight loss and a high chance of both negative physical and psychological consequences. Taking dieting out of the treatment equation leaves us primarily with drug treatments and surgery.

Drug Treatments

Drug therapy is only legally available to patients in the UK with a BMI of 30 or more and government bodies have become increasingly restrictive on the use of anti-obesity drugs. For example, both fenfluramine and dexfenfluramine were recently withdrawn from the market because of their association with heart disease even though they were both quite effective at bringing about weight loss. Current recommendations state that drugs should be used only when other approaches have failed, that they should not be prescribed for longer than three months in the first instance and should be stopped if a 10 per cent reduction in weight has not been achieved. Continued drug use beyond this time should be accompanied by review and close monitoring (Kopelman 1999). There are currently two groups of anti-obesity drugs available which are offered in conjunction with dietary and exercise programmes. The first group work on the central nervous system and suppress appetite. The most commonly used of these are phentermine, which acts on the catecholamine pathway, and sibutramine, which acts on the noradronergic and serotonergic pathways. There is some evidence for the effectiveness of these drugs although they can be accompanied by side-effects such as nausea, dry mouth and constipation (Lean 1997). The second group of drugs act on the gastrointestinal system and the more successful of these reduce fat absorption. Orlistat is one of these and has been shown to cause substantial weight loss in obese subjects (Sjostrom et al. 1998; Rossner et al. 2000). It can be, however, accompanied by a range of unpleasant side-effects including liquid stools, an urgency to go to the toilet and anal leakage which are particularly apparent following a high-fat meal. Although Orlistat is designed to work by reducing fat absorption, it probably also has a deterrent effect as eating fat causes unpleasant consequences. Ogden and Sidhu (2006) carried out a qualitative study exploring patients' experiences of taking Orlistat and concluded that, although it constitutes a medical approach to obesity, it provides a window into the processes of adherence to medication and behaviour change and also has some interesting effects on the individual's psychological state. The results from this study suggest that adherence to the drug was related to being motivated to lose weight by a life event rather than just the daily hassles of being obese. Further, if the unpleasant, highly visual side-effects were regarded as an education into the relationship between fat eaten and body fat, then they helped to change the patient's model of their problem by encouraging a model that emphasized behaviour. Such a behavioural model of obesity was then related to behaviour change. This is similar to the importance of coherent models described in Chapter 9.

Surgical Treatments

Although there are 21 different surgical procedures for obesity (Kral 1995), the two most popular are the gastric bypass and gastric banding. Researchers in Sweden have carried out the large-scale Swedish Obese Subjects (SOS) study which explored nearly 1,000 matched pairs of patients who received either surgery or conventional treatment for their obesity (Torgerson and Sjostrom 2001). The results showed an average weight loss of 28kg in the surgical group after two years compared to only 0.5kg in the conventional group. After eight years the weight loss in the surgical group remained high (average of 20kg) while the control group had gained an average of 0.7kg. The weight loss in the surgical group was associated with a reduction in diabetes and hypertension at two years and diabetes at eight years. This study indicated that surgery can be effective for both weight loss and maintenance and brings with it a reduction in the risk factors for cardiovascular disease. The surgical management of obesity has been endorsed by expert committees in the USA (Institute of Medicine 1995) and the UK (Garrow 1997) and is recommended for those with a BMI over 40 (or > 35 with complications of obesity), who have not lost weight with dietary or pharmacological interventions, as long as they are made aware of the possible side-effects. Obesity surgery, however, does not only affect weight. Some research has also explored post-operative changes in aspects of the individual's psychological state such as health status and psychological morbidity and a series of studies have shown significant improvements, particularly in those patients who show sustained weight loss. For example, cross-sectional research has illustrated improved quality of life in surgical patients compared to control subjects (De Zwann et al. 2002; Ogden et al. 2005) which has been supported by studies using either retrospective or longitudinal designs. In particular, in a large-scale follow-up of the SOS patients, Karlsson et al. (1998) reported an improvement in health-related quality of life operationalized in terms of mood disorders, mental well-being, health perceptions and social interaction. Bocchieri et al. (2002) carried out a comprehensive review of much of the literature examining the impact of obesity surgery on psychosocial outcomes and concluded that in general 'the empirical evidence . . . seems to be pointing in a positive direction'. Ogden et al. (2006a) carried out a qualitative study to explore patients' experiences of obesity surgery and concluded that by imposing control and limited choice upon how much and what they could eat, surgery and the process of making their stomach much smaller paradoxically made them feel more in control of their weight and eating behaviour (see **Focus on Research 15.1** for details). This is in contrast to much of the literature on communication and choice discussed in Chapter 10.

FOCUS ON RESEARCH 15.1: THE EXPERIENCE OF OBESITY SURGERY

The psychological impact of obesity surgery and the paradox of control (Ogden et al. 2006a).

Given the failure rates of many dietary and medical forms of management for obesity, bariatric surgery is currently the preferred treatment for those with a BMI > 40 (>35 with co-morbidity). The two most common operations are the gastric bypass and the gastric band which reduce the amount of food that can be consumed. The bypass also reduces food absorption. This qualitative study explored patients' experiences of having obesity surgery and the results were surprising. In particular, although it may have been predicted that having a much smaller stomach and not being able to eat would make people feel hungry and preoccupied with food, for most patients the reverse happened. Overall, the results indicated that taking control and choice *away* from patients by imposing a physical limitation on their capacity to eat can feel liberating and paradoxically make them feel more in control.

METHODOLOGY

Fifteen patients who had undergone surgery in the past four years were interviewed about their reasons for having surgery and their subsequent experiences. Fourteen had shown significant weight loss but two had regained weight recently due to problems with the banding.

Data Analysis

The interviews were transcribed and analysed using interpretative phenomenological analysis (IPA, Smith 1996).

RESULTS

Personal Histories

Patients described their histories of weight gain, failed attempts at weight loss and weight cycling. The majority attributed their weight problem to factors such as illness, pregnancy or their genetics and illustrated a preference for a biological model of the aetiology of obesity and one which shifted responsibility away from their own behaviour. The patients also provided detailed accounts of the vast array of interventions which had been tried and had failed. Throughout these personal histories emerged a central sense of a lack of control, with patients feeling out of control both of their weight gain and also of any subsequent weight loss.

Decision-Making

Overall, the decision-making processes involved in seeking surgery included a role for background motivations and immediate triggers. This pathway towards surgery reflected a shift from seeing obesity as an unpleasant consequence of biology to seeing it as a serious threat to health and life itself precipitated by the onset of symptoms. It also illustrated a concurrent change in patients' understanding of responsibility from a patient reliant upon self-help to one with a desire to hand over control to the 'experts'. This was in line with the patients' analysis of their personal histories, as it reflected a central role for control as they described feeling out of control of their weight, out of control of any attempts at weight loss and expressed a desire to shift the control of their problem over to something outside themselves.

The Impact of Surgery

The third area to emerge from the interviews was the patients' experiences of surgery that can be understood in terms of two distinct phases: the initial impact of the surgery (involving feelings of shock and a range of negative side-effects) and the subsequent phase of adjustment involving changes in eating behaviour and a shift in their relationship with food. Given the unpleasant consequences experienced after eating and the reduction in food intake, it could be predicted that food would acquire an even greater importance in the patients' lives. However, paradoxically, the majority of patients described how surgery had resulted in a fundamental shift in their relationship with food in terms of the role of food, control and hunger, with food and eating becoming increasingly related to a biological necessity rather than a psychological support. Furthermore, the results suggested that although, for some, this increase in control was experienced as relating directly to their new stomach size, others believed that they had 'relearned' to control their eating behaviour in addition to any physically imposed limitations.

The Impact of Weight Loss

Finally, the fourth area described related to the impact of weight loss. This included changes in their confidence, body image, energy and general quality of life with many patients describing a sense of rebirth and as having been given a new chance in life.

The Paradox of Control

Patients conceptualized weight gain as a result of uncontrollable factors and chose to have surgery through a belief that they were out of control of their weight and eating and through a desire to hand over control to an external force. Further, although the initial stage post-surgery was characterized by a sense of shock, the majority of patients described how they adjusted to the physical limitations imposed by the operation and developed a new sense of control over both their weight and eating. This new sense of control appeared to take two forms. For some, it took the form of an externally imposed control that was welcomed as a release from their previous sense of responsibility and ongoing battle with themselves. Many, however, experienced an internalization of control resulting in a new psychological state. Further, this new state of mind appeared to generalize to other areas of life with many reporting not only feeling more in control over what they ate but also over their lives in the broadest sense. The authors labelled this process the *paradox of control* to describe how by imposing a reduction in food intake and taking choice away from the individual, surgery paradoxically resulted in an improved sense of control not only over what the patients ate and how they felt around food but also over all other areas of their lives.

CONCLUSION

Much psychology research and therapy emphasize encouraging individuals to take control and terms such as 'self-efficacy', 'empowerment' and 'confidence' are central to psychological literature. This study indicates that at times too much choice and control may be overwhelming for people and that limiting choice and control may actually be liberating. This finds reflection in the notion of government and public health interventions which encourage behaviour change through the imposition of laws such as the seat belt law and smoking bans: effectively taking away rather than encouraging choice.

THE SUCCESS STORIES

Randomized controlled trials examining the effectiveness of interventions indicate that, although the majority of individuals may lose weight initially, the large majority eventually return to their baseline weight. Within each trial, however, a small minority not only lose weight initially, but successfully maintain this loss. Klem et al. (1997) examined the psychological states of 784 men and women who had both lost weight and maintained their weight loss and concluded that weight suppression was not associated with psychological distress. In contrast, as noted above, Wooley and Wooley (1984: 187) suggested that the minority of 'success stories' are 'in fact condemned to a life of weight obsession'.

What factors distinguish between the majority of failures and the minority of long-term successes? To date, some studies have specifically examined this minority group. This research, together with data from the trials of obesity treatment, provides some preliminary insights into the factors that predict and/or correlate with successful weight loss and maintenance. In particular, the literature highlights a role for a range of variables which can be conceptualized as profile characteristics, historical factors, help-seeking behaviours, psychological factors and life events.

Profile Characteristics

Research suggests that baseline BMI predicts weight loss and maintenance; however, while some studies indicate that lower baseline weight is predictive of greater success (Ogden 2000), others show the reverse effect (Wadden et al. 1992). Research also suggests that employment outside the home, higher income and being older are predictive of weight loss and maintenance (Wong et al. 1997; Ogden 2000). Some research has also looked at gender although the data remain contradictory (e.g. Colvin and Olson 1983).

Historical Factors

Some research points to an individual's previous dieting attempts and their weight history as important for successful weight loss and maintenance. In particular, studies indicate that a history of dieting for longer and a higher number of dieting attempts predict success (Hoiberg et al. 1994; Ogden 2000). In contrast, Kiernan et al. (1998) concluded that success was greater in those who did *not* have a history of repeated weight loss. Whether the 'try, try and try again' ethos holds for dieting therefore remains unclear. It is also possible that changes in smoking behaviour (e.g. Klesges and Klesges 1988) and an individual's reproductive history may be contributory factors to success as weight gain and maintenance often follow smoking cessation and childbirth (e.g. Ohlin and Rossner 1990).

Help-Seeking Behaviours

There appear to be several help-seeking factors which are predictive of success. Primarily research highlights a role for the types and intensity of weight loss methods used. For example, many studies have emphasized the importance of dietary changes (e.g. McGuire et al. 1999) although Ogden (2000) reported that calorie-controlled diets were associated with weight loss and regain rather than maintenance. Many studies have also highlighted the role of exercise and general increases in physical activity (Hoiberg et al. 1994; French and Jeffrey 1997; Klem et al. 1997; Wong et al. 1997). Furthermore, research has highlighted the relative effectiveness of different interventions involving contact with a range of health professionals. These include psychological interventions such as CBT, counselling, self-help groups and medical interventions involving drug therapy and surgery (see NHS Centre for Reviews and Dissemination 1997 for review). The general conclusion from this research is that the more intense the intervention, the longer the follow-up period and the greater the professional contact, the higher the probability of successful weight loss and maintenance.

Psychological Factors

Rodin et al. (1977) reported the results from a study designed to assess the baseline psychological predictors of successful weight loss. The results indicated a role for the individual's beliefs about the causes of obesity and their motivations for weight loss. Kiernan et al. (1998) indicated that individuals who were more dissatisfied with their body shape at baseline were more successful, suggesting that motivations for weight loss guided by a high value placed on attractiveness may also be important. Ogden (2000) examined differences in psychological factors between weight loss regainers, stable obese and weight loss maintainers who were classified as those individuals who had been obese (BMI > 29.9), lost sufficient weight to be considered non-obese (BMI < 29.9) and maintained this weight loss for a minimum of three years. The results showed that the weight loss maintainers were more likely to endorse a psychological model of obesity in terms of its consequences such as depression and low self-esteem and to have been motivated to lose weight for psychological reasons such as wanting to increase their self-esteem and feel better about themselves. Further, they showed less endorsement of a medical model of causality including genetics and hormone imbalance. These results suggest that it is not only what an individual *does* that is predictive of success, but also what they *believe*. Accordingly, for an obese person to lose weight and keep this weight off it would seem that they need both to change their behaviour and believe that their own behaviour is important. Further, they need to perceive the consequences of their behaviour change as valuable. This supports the research exploring the psychological effects of taking obesity medication (Ogden and Sidhu 2006) and reflects the role of coherent models described in Chapter 9.

The Role of Life Events and Reinvention

Most research exploring successful weight loss maintenance emphasizes the impact of structured interventions or focuses on gradual changes in the individual's psychological state. Both approaches see change as the result of a 'drip drip' effect that occurs slowly over time. However, some changes in behaviour, and subsequent body weight, may occur in a more dichotomous fashion following a specific event and this has been explored using a number of different terms including 'teachable moments', 'life events', 'life crises', 'epiphanies' and 'medical triggers'. This is in line with life events theory, which was a central part of psychological theory and research towards the end of the twentieth century (eg. Brown and Harris 1978). In a recent qualitative study Ogden and Hills (2008) carried out a series of interviews with those who had shown sustained behaviour change in terms of either smoking cessation (n = 10) or weight loss maintenance (n = 24) and highlighted the role for a number of different life events. In particular, many participants described how their behaviour change had been triggered by events relating to their health (e.g. heart attack, symptoms of diabetes), relationships (e.g. divorce) or salient milestones (e.g. important birthday). The results also illustrated that the impact of these life events was mediated through three key sustaining conditions – namely, reduced choice over the previous unhealthy behaviour, reduced function of their past behaviour and a model of their health which emphasized behavioural causes and solutions. Using the example of weight loss maintenance, it was argued that the initial change in diet triggered by the life event is translated into sustained behaviour change if the event reduces the individual's choice about when and how much to eat, if it reduces the function and benefits attached to eating and if the individual believes that their weight problem is caused by their behaviour. Further, it was concluded that sustained behaviour change is facilitated through a process of reinvention as individuals respond to the life event by reinventing themselves as a healthier and thinner person.

In summary, a small minority of individuals show successful weight loss and maintenance which relates to their profile characteristics, dieting history, help-seeking behaviours, their beliefs about obesity and the impact of life events. To answer the question 'Should obesity be treated at all?' it is necessary to consider the following points:

- Obesity is a health risk.
- Obesity is caused by a combination of physiological and behavioural factors – it is not simply a product of overeating.
- Treating obesity with dieting emphasizes personal responsibility ('you can make yourself well'), but may result in overeating, which could exacerbate the weight problem.
- Treating obesity with drugs and/or surgery emphasizes the physiological causes and places the obese in the hands of the medical profession ('we can make you well'). This can result in weight loss but has side-effects and can result in medical complications and weight regain. These medical approaches to obesity also have an impact upon the individual's psychological state.
- Any treatment intervention should therefore weigh up the potential benefits of any weight loss (e.g. improved self-esteem, reduced risk of CHD, etc.) against the potential costs of intervention (e.g. overeating, weight fluctuations).

SUMMING UP

Obesity is related to several health problems and a number of theories have been developed in an attempt to understand its aetiology. In particular, research has suggested that there may be a strong genetic predisposition to obesity, which is reflected in underactivity and the relative overconsumption of fat. However, the research examining the causes of obesity is often contradictory, suggesting that the story is not yet complete. In terms of interventions, research indicates that all forms of intervention are effective at promoting weight loss but weight maintenance is particularly poor for dieting-based treatments. The fact that all treatments have side-effects raises the question 'Should obesity be treated at all?' The answer seems to be that it should be treated as long as the costs and benefits of any intervention are assessed and both physical and psychological consequences are taken into account.

CORONARY HEART DISEASE

CHD is another example of chronic illness which shows a strong role for a range of psychological factors. The remainder of this chapter examines what CHD is, its prevalence, risk factors, beliefs about CHD, the psychological impact, rehabilitation and the modification of risk factors, and the predictors of patient health outcomes. The potential role of psychology in CHD is shown in Figure 15.12.

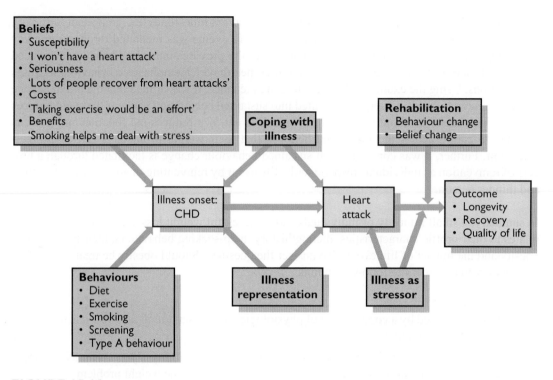

FIGURE 15.12

The potential role of psychology in CHD

WHAT IS CHD?

CHD refers to a disease of the heart involving coronary arteries which are not functioning properly. The most important diseases are angina, acute myocardial infarction (AMI – heart attack) and sudden cardiac death. All these forms of CHD are caused by atherosclerosis which involves a narrowing of the arteries due to fatty deposits which obstruct the flow of blood. Angina is a powerful pain in the chest, which sometimes radiates down the left arm. It develops when blood flow to the coronary arteries is restricted to such an extent that the heart muscle is starved of oxygen. An AMI occurs when blood flow is restricted below a threshold level and some heart tissue is destroyed. It also seems to happen when a blood clot has further restricted blood flow to the heart. Sudden cardiac death typically occurs in patients who have already suffered damage to the heart through previous AMIs although it can occur in patients who previously seemed to have healthy arteries.

THE PREVALENCE OF CHD

CHD is responsible for 43 per cent of deaths in men across Europe and 54 per cent of deaths in women (Allender et al. 2008a, 2008b). In the UK, in 2008 CHD was responsible for 35 per cent of deaths in men and 34 per cent of deaths in women (Allender et al. 2008a). It is the main cause of premature death in the UK (i.e. under 75 years) and worldwide it is estimated that 17 million people die from CHD each year with the highest death rates being in China, India and Russia. Deaths from CHD have declined in recent years in North America and across Europe mainly due to the decline in smoking and other lifestyle factors. The highest death rates from CHD are found in men and women in the manual classes, and men and women of Asian origin. In middle age, the death rate is up to five times higher for men than for women; this evens out, however, in old age when CHD is the leading cause of death for both men and women. In the UK about 150,000 people each year survive the acute stage of MI with women showing poorer recovery than men in terms of both mood and activity limitations.

RISK FACTORS FOR CHD

Many risk factors for CHD have been identified such as educational status, social mobility, social class, age, gender, stress reactivity, family history, ethnicity, smoking, diet, obesity, sedentary lifestyle, perceived work stress and personality. Details of many of these factors can be found in Chapters 3, 4, 5, 6, 8, 11 and 12. Key modifiable risk factors are as follows:

1 *Smoking.* One in four deaths from CHD is thought to be caused by smoking. Smoking more than 20 cigarettes a day increases the risk of CHD in middle age threefold. In addition, stopping smoking can halve the risk of another heart attack in those who have already had one. Smoking cessation is discussed in Chapter 4.

2 *Diet.* Diet, in particular cholesterol levels, has also been implicated in CHD. It has been suggested that the 20 per cent of a population with the highest cholesterol levels are three times more likely to die of heart disease than the 20 per cent with the lowest levels. Cholesterol levels may be determined by the amount of saturated fat consumed (derived mainly from animal fats). Cholesterol reduction can be achieved through a reduction in total fats and saturated fats, an increase in polyunsaturated fats and an increase in dietary fibre. Dietary change is discussed in Chapters 5 and 8.

3 *High blood pressure.* High blood pressure is also a risk factor for CHD – the higher the blood pressure, the greater the risk. It has been suggested that a 10mmHg decrease in a population's average blood pressure could reduce the mortality attributable to heart disease by 30 per cent. Blood pressure appears to be related to a multitude of factors such as genetics, obesity, alcohol intake and salt consumption. Some research also points to a role for caffeine intake (see Chapter 4).

4 *Type A behaviour and hostility.* Type A behaviour and its associated characteristic, hostility, are probably the most extensively studied risk factor for CHD (see Chapters 11 and 12 for details). Support for a relationship between type A behaviour and CHD has been reported by a number of studies (Rosenman et al. 1975; Haynes et al. 1980). However, research has also reported no relationship between type A behaviour and CHD (e.g. Johnston et al. 1987). More recent research has focused on hostility which has been shown to predict stress reactivity and to be linked to the development of CHD (e.g. Miller et al. 1996).

5 *Stress.* Stress has also been studied extensively as a predictor of CHD and research has shown links between stress reactivity and CHD, life events and CHD, and job stress and CHD (see Chapters 11 and 12). Stress management is used to reduce stress in people already diagnosed with CHD.

BELIEFS ABOUT CHD

Chapter 9 described the kinds of beliefs that people have about their illness and explored how these beliefs may influence the development and progression of the disease. Some research has specifically examined the beliefs that people have about CHD with a particular focus on beliefs about causes. For example, French et al. (2002a) explored how members of the general public understand MI and differentiated between beliefs about proximal causes that directly cause MI and distal causes that are mediated by other causal factors. The results showed that even though the respondents did not have CHD, they still had quite complex beliefs about its causes. In particular, type of work was seen as a distal cause of MI which operated through stress and high blood pressure: stress was seen to operate via raised blood pressure rather than behaviour and genes were seen to have a direct effect on CHD which was not mediated by any behavioural or physiological processes. French et al. (2005a) further explored people's beliefs about MI in 12 patients who had had an MI. The results showed that, while people were aware of many possible causes of MI, they tended to focus on a single cause for their MI which was often related to their symptoms. This was driven by a need to understand why they had had their MI 'now' which was further motivated by a desire not to blame themselves or others while at the same time trying to assert control over having another MI in the future.

Gudmundsdottir et al. (2001) also explored people's beliefs about CHD but examined the beliefs of people who had had an MI in the past year. Using a longitudinal design they assessed the patients' beliefs within 72 hours of admission into hospital and interviewed the patients about the causes of their MI. Patients were then followed up three times over the next year. In addition, the study used four different types of method to explore causal attributions. These were spontaneous attributions (i.e. responses to an open question about the illness), elicited attributions (i.e. responses to an open question about the cause of the MI), cued attributions (i.e. responses to a list of possible causes) and most important attribution (i.e. selected cause from the given list). The results showed that the most common causes derived from all methods were 'smoking', 'stress', 'it's in the family', 'working' and 'eating fatty foods'. The results also showed some changes over time, with patients being less likely to blame their behaviour and/or personality as time went on. Therefore both sufferers and non-sufferers of CHD seem to hold beliefs about the cause of MI which might influence their subsequent risky behaviour and reflect a process of adjustment once they have become ill.

THE PSYCHOLOGICAL IMPACT OF CHD

Research has addressed the psychological impact of having an MI in terms of anxiety and depression, post-traumatic stress disorder (PTSD) and finding meaning.

Anxiety and Depression

Lane et al. (2002) used a longitudinal design to assess changes in depression and anxiety immediately post-MI, 2–15 days post-MI and after 4 and 12 months. The results showed that during hospitalization 30.9 per cent of patients reported elevated depression scores and 26.1 per cent reported elevated anxiety scores. The results also indicated that this increase in psychological morbidity persisted over the year of study. Holahan et al. (2006) explored gender and ethnic group differences in depressive symptoms in cardiac patients from the USA and reported that depressive symptoms were higher in women than men and in Hispanic patients compared to non-Hispanic white patients. The results also showed that higher levels of depression were predicted by greater physical and role limitations and less social support. Similarly, Gum et al. (2006) concluded that depressive symptoms three months after having a stroke were predicted by baseline levels of hopeful thinking about one's ability fulfil one's own goals in the future. Further, Boersma et al. (2005) concluded from their study of patients post-MI that goal disturbance predicted both depression and health-related quality of life. Some research has also explored whether such changes in psychological morbidity can be modified. For example, Johnston et al. (1999b) evaluated the impact of nurse counsellor-led cardiac counselling compared to normal care. The study used an randomized design with a one-year follow-up and patients and their partners were recruited within 72 hours of the patients' first MI. The results showed that although patients did not show particularly raised levels of anxiety and depression while still in hospital, those who did not receive counselling showed an increase in these factors following discharge. Counselling seemed to minimize this increase. In contrast to the patients, the partners did show very high levels of anxiety and depression while the patients were still in hospital. This dropped to normal levels in those that received counselling.

PTSD

Research has also explored the prevalence and predictors of PTSD following either stroke or MI and indicates rates of about 16 per cent, with people experiencing intrusive thoughts, elevated levels of arousal, psychological numbing and avoidance of reminders of the trauma (e.g. Sheldrick et al. 2006). Research also indicates that symptoms of PTSD vary over time and are strongly predicted and correlated with illness cognitions, particularly identity, time line, consequences and emotional representations (Sheldrick et al. 2006). In addition, such symptoms are associated with a history of psychological problems and dysfunctional coping strategies.

Finding Meaning

Bury (1982) argued that illness can be seen as a form of biographical disruption which requires people to question 'what is going on here?' and results in a sense of uncertainty. Radley (1984, 1989) has drawn upon this perspective to explore how people adjust and respond to CHD. In particular, Radley argues that patients diagnosed with CHD try to resolve the dual demands of symptoms and society. He suggests that people with a chronic illness such as CHD need to establish a new identity as someone who has been ill but can be well again. This need occurs against a backdrop of family and friends who are worried about their health and often results in the ill person persistently acting in a 'healthy way' as a means to communicate that things are 'back to normal'. This approach finds reflection in theories of coping and the re-establishment of equilibrium described in Chapter 9.

REHABILITATION OF PATIENTS WITH CHD

Psychology also plays a role in the rehabilitation of individuals who have been diagnosed with CHD in terms of angina, stroke, atherosclerosis or heart attack. Rehabilitation programmes use a range of techniques including health education, relaxation training and counselling, and have been developed to encourage CHD sufferers to modify their risk factors (see Chapter 8 for a description of these techniques). Research has explored predictors of uptake of rehabilitation programmes and whether they can modify factors such as exercise, type A behaviour, general lifestyle factors, illness cognitions and stress.

PREDICTING UPTAKE OF REHABILITATION

Although MI is the primary cause of premature mortality in many western countries, over 60 per cent of patients will survive their MI. Furthermore, if risk factors can be modified then the likelihood of a further MI is greatly reduced. Rehabilitation programmes are therefore designed to reduce these risk factors. Despite the benefits of rehabilitation, however, many patients fail to attend either some or all of the classes. For example, in a systematic review of the literature, attendance rates across 15 studies varied from 13 to 74 per cent, although what constituted 'attendance' also varied from missing a few sessions to missing all sessions (A.F. Cooper et al. 2002). So why do people not turn up if rehabilitation can be effective? A.F. Cooper et al. (2002) explored the factors that predicted non-attendance in 15 studies of cardiac rehabilitation involving patients from Europe, the USA, Canada and New Zealand, and concluded that non-attenders were more likely to be older, to have lower income and greater deprivation, to deny the severity of their illness, to be less likely to believe that they can influence the outcome of their illness and to be less likely to perceive that their doctor recommends rehabilitation. Further, women are less likely to be referred for rehabilitation than men, as are the elderly.

MODIFYING RISK FACTORS

Rehabilitation programmes encourage the modification of risk factors to improve the patient's quality of life and to reduce their risk of further cardiac events.

Exercise

Most rehabilitation programmes emphasize the restoration of physical functioning through exercise, with the assumption that physical recovery will in turn promote psychological and social recovery. Meta-analyses of these exercise-based programmes have suggested that they may have favourable effects on cardiovascular mortality (e.g. Oldridge et al. 1988). Whether

Exercise is a standard part of rehabilitation after a heart attack

these exercise-based programmes influence risk factors other than exercise, such as smoking, diet and type A behaviour, is questionable.

Type A Behaviour

The Recurrent Coronary Prevention project was developed by Friedman et al. (1986) in an attempt to modify type A behaviour. This programme was based on the following questions: can type A behaviour be modified? If so, can such modification reduce the chances of a recurrence of a heart attack? The study involved 1,000 subjects and a five-year intervention. Subjects had all suffered a heart attack and were allocated to one of three groups: cardiology counselling, type A behaviour modification or no treatment. Type A behaviour modification involved discussions of the beliefs and values of type A, discussing methods of reducing work demands, relaxation and education about changing the cognitive framework of the individuals. At five years, the results showed that the type A modification group had a reduced recurrence of heart attacks, suggesting that not only can type A behaviour be modified but that, when modified, there may be a reduction of reinfarction. However, the relationship between type A behaviour and CHD is still controversial, with recent discussions suggesting that type A may at times be protective against CHD.

General Lifestyle Factors

Rehabilitation programmes have been developed which focus on modifying other risk factors such as smoking and diet. For example, van Elderen et al. (1994) developed a health education and counselling programme for patients with cardiovascular disease after hospitalization, with weekly follow-ups by telephone. Thirty CHD sufferers and their partners were offered the intervention and were compared with a group of 30 control patients who received standard medical care only. The results showed that after two months the patients who had received health education and counselling reported a greater increase in physical activity and a greater decrease in unhealthy eating habits. In addition, within those subjects in the experimental condition (receiving health education and counselling), those whose partners had also participated in the programme showed greater improvements in their activity and diet and, in addition, showed a decrease in their smoking behaviour. At 12 months, subjects who had participated in the health education and counselling programme maintained their improvement in their eating behaviour. The authors concluded that, although this study involved only a small number of patients, the results provide some support for including health education and counselling in rehabilitation programmes.

More recently, however, van Elderen and Dusseldorp (2001) reported results from a similar study which produced more contradictory results. They explored the relative impact of providing health education, psychological input, standard medical care and physical training to patients with CHD and their partners after discharge from hospital. Overall, all patients improved their lifestyle during the first three months and showed extra improvement in their eating habits over the next nine months. However, by one-year follow-up many patients had increased their smoking again and returned to their sedentary lifestyles. In terms of the relative effects of the different forms of intervention the results were more complex than the authors' earlier work. Although health education and the psychological intervention had an improved impact on eating habits over standard medical care and physical training, some changes in lifestyle were more pronounced in the patients who had only received the latter. For example, receiving health education and psychological intervention seemed to make it more difficult to quit a sedentary lifestyle, and receiving health education seemed to make it more difficult to stop smoking. Therefore, although some work supports the addition of health education and counselling to rehabilitation programmes, at times this may have a cost. In 2010, Huttunen-Lenz et al. carried out a meta-analysis of psychoeducational interventions focusing on smoking cessation for CHD patients. Their analysis identified 14 studies and the results showed that although the interventions had no significant impact on mortality, they did significantly increase smoking cessation rates.

Illness Cognitions

Research illustrates that patients' beliefs about their MI may relate to health outcomes in terms of attendance at rehabilitation, return to work and adjustment (see Chapter 9 for illness cognitions and outcomes). In line with this, Petrie et al. (2002) developed an intervention designed to change illness cognitions and explored the subsequent impact upon a range of patient outcomes. In particular the intervention consisted of three sessions of about 40 minutes with a psychologist and was designed to address and change patients' beliefs about their MI. For session 1 the psychologist gave an explanation about the nature of an MI in terms of its symptoms and explored patients' beliefs about the causes of the MI. In session 2 the psychologist further explored beliefs about causes, helped the patient to develop a plan to minimize the future risk of a further MI and tried to increase patient control beliefs about their condition. In the final session, this action plan was reviewed, concerns about medication were explored and symptoms that were part of the recovery process such as breathlessness upon exercise were distinguished from those that were indicative of further pathology such as severe chest pain. Throughout the intervention the information and discussion were targeted to the specific beliefs and concerns of the patient. The results showed that patients who had received the intervention reported more positive views about their MI at follow-up in terms of beliefs about consequences, time line, control/cure and symptom distress (see Chapter 9 for a description of these dimensions). In addition, they reported that they were better prepared to leave hospital, returned to work at a faster rate and reported a lower rate of angina symptoms. No differences were found in rehabilitation attendance. The intervention therefore seemed to change cognitions and improve patients' functional outcome after MI.

Stress

Stress management involves teaching individuals about the theories of stress, encouraging them to be aware of the factors that can trigger stress, and teaching them a range of strategies to reduce stress, such as 'self-talk', relaxation techniques and general life management approaches, such as time management and problem-solving. Stress management has been used successfully to reduce some of the risk factors for CHD, including raised blood pressure (Johnston et al. 1993), blood cholesterol (Gill et al. 1985) and type A behaviour (Roskies et al. 1986). Further, some studies also indicate that it can reduce angina, which is highly predictive of heart attack and/or death. For example, Gallacher et al. (1997) randomly allocated 452 male angina patients to receive either stress management or no intervention at all. The results showed that at six months' follow-up, those who had received stress management reported a reduced frequency of chest pain when resting. In a similar trial, Bundy et al. (1998) examined both the independent and the combined effect of stress management and exercise on angina compared with a control group taken from a waiting list. The results indicated that those who undertook both stress management and exercise reported fewer angina attacks and reduced reliance on medication. Therefore stress management appears to reduce angina, which in turn could reduce the occurrence of MIs.

PREDICTING PATIENT HEALTH OUTCOMES

Research has explored the role of psychological factors in predicting patient health outcomes with a focus on quality of life, level of functioning, and mortality.

QUALITY OF LIFE AND LEVEL OF FUNCTIONING

Research exploring the predictors of quality of life and level of functioning in patients with CHD has focused on perceptions of control, goal disturbance, depression, social support and illness cognitions.

Perceptions of Control

Research shows a consistent link between baseline levels of perceived control and recovery from stroke in terms of level of functioning (e.g. Johnston et al. 2004; Bonetti and Johnson 2008). Johnston et al. (2006) developed a workbook-based intervention to change perceptions of control in patients who had just had a stroke and showed that at six months' follow-up those receiving the intervention showed better disability recovery than those in the control group. In a similar vein, Chan et al. (2006) explored the role of resilience in predicting outcome in CHD patients in Hong Kong. Resilience was defined as closely aligned to perceived control and was a composite measure including optimism, perceived control and self-esteem. The results showed that those high in resilience showed better outcomes after an eight-week rehabilitation programme in terms of lower cholesterol, higher physical and mental health status and a better performance on a six-minute walk test. In addition, personal resilience was also predictive of greater post-traumatic growth (see Chapter 9).

Goal Disturbance

MI and stroke often result in a reduction in physical functioning through impaired speech or movement. They can also trigger a sense of goal disturbance. According to goal theory (Carver and Scheier 1999) behaviour is driven by a hierarchy of goals that make life feel meaningful. Lower-order goals could involve eating, getting to work or getting enough sleep, while higher-order goals include 'supporting others' or 'ensuring my safety'. It has been argued that a major health event such as a stroke or MI can disturb an individual's usual means of attaining their goals, which in turn can challenge how an individual sees themselves or their future (eg. Kuijer and De Ridder 2003). In terms of CHD, research indicates that goal disturbance at baseline predicts both depression and lowered health-related quality of life at follow-up (Boersma et al. 2005; Joekes et al. 2007).

Depression

Depression post-MI is quite common (see p. 420). Although for many patients levels of depressive symptoms reduce over time, research indicates a link between depression at baseline and health-related quality of life by four months follow-up (e.g. Lane et al. 2000).

Social Support

Research also shows a role for social support in predicting patient quality of life post-MI, although perceived rather than actual support is more important (e.g. Bosworth et al. 2001). Not all social support is positive, however, and although 'active engagement' by partners of those who have had an MI may predict better outcomes, 'over-protection' can result in decreased levels of physical functioning over time (Joekes et al. 2007).

Illness Cognitions

Research shows a role for beliefs in predicting recovery from MI and quality of life as measured by return to work and general social and occupational functioning. In particular, studies indicate that those with more negative beliefs about their work capacity (Maeland and Havik 1987), a greater perception of helplessness towards future MIs (called 'cardiac invalidism'; Riegel 1993) and beliefs that their MI has more serious consequences and will last a longer time at baseline

(Petrie et al. 1996) show poorer outcomes. Further, beliefs that the illness can be controlled or cured at baseline predict attendance at rehabilitation classes which itself predicts better outcomes (Petrie et al. 1996) (see Chapter 9 for further details).

MORTALITY

Research has explored the predictors of survival or mortality in patients with CHD. There are many biological predictors including cholesterol levels, blood pressure, previous MIs, long-term health history and a number of biological markers. The results also, however, show a role for more psychological factors such as health-related behaviours and depression.

Health Behaviours

Research indicates that the behaviours which predict CHD onset also predict mortality. In addition, other health conditions, which are also related to health-related behaviours, also predict CHD mortality. For example, large-scale cohort studies and systematic reviews indicate that mortality post-MI or stroke is predicted by smoking, obesity and diabetes (Panagiotakos et al. 2003; Pearte et al. 2006; Prugger et al. 2008). Research also shows a similar pattern for predicting mortality after coronary artery bypass surgery (e.g. Ketonen et al. 2008). A recent meta-analysis showed a role for sleep duration with both low and long sleep duration being predictive of cardiovascular mortality (Cappuccio et al. 2011), although the mechanism of this association is less clear.

Depression

Research indicates that depression post-MI and stroke is common and can relate to an individual's subsequent quality of life (see p. 420). Research, however, also indicates that depression predicts mortality. Barth et al. (2004) carried out a meta-analysis of 20 studies and reported that although depression had no impact on mortality by six months, by two years those with clinical depression were twice as likely to have died. Similar results have been found when follow-up times were extended to 12 years, with depression being predictive of mortality in both men and women (Ahto et al. 2007).

SUMMING UP

CHD is a common cause of death across the developing and western world. It illustrates the role of psychology in illness in terms of the risk factors for its onset, beliefs people have about CHD, the psychological consequences of a diagnosis, rehabilitation, the modification of risk factors and the predictors of quality of life and mortality.

TO CONCLUDE

Illnesses such as obesity and CHD illustrate the role of psychology throughout the course of an illness. For example, psychological factors play a role in illness onset (e.g. health beliefs, health behaviours, personality, coping mechanisms), illness progression (e.g. psychological consequences, adaptation, health behaviours) and longevity (e.g. health behaviours, coping mechanisms, quality of life). These psychological factors are also relevant to a multitude of other chronic and acute illnesses, such as diabetes, asthma, chronic fatigue syndrome and multiple sclerosis. This suggests that illness is best conceptualized not as a biomedical problem but as a complex interplay of physiological and psychological factors.

QUESTIONS

1 To what extent can obesity be explained by physiological factors?
2 Discuss the role of psychological factors in explaining the recent increase in the prevalence of obesity.
3 To what extent is obesity a social problem?
4 Treating obesity causes more problems than it solves. Discuss.
5 How can obesity be treated effectively?
6 CHD is a product of lifestyle. Discuss.
7 How might beliefs about CHD influence its onset and progression?
8 What are the psychological consequences of CHD?
9 To what extent can a reinfarction be prevented?
10 Is death from a heart attack inevitable?

FOR DISCUSSION

In the light of the literature on obesity and CHD, discuss the possible role of psychological factors throughout the course of an alternative chronic illness (e.g. diabetes, rheumatoid arthritis, multiple sclerosis).

ASSUMPTIONS IN HEALTH PSYCHOLOGY

The research into obesity and CHD highlights some of the assumptions in health psychology:

1 *The role of behaviour in illness.* Throughout the twentieth century there was an increasing emphasis on behavioural factors in health and illness. Research examined the problem of obesity from the same perspective and evaluated the role of overeating as a causal factor. However, perhaps not all problems are products of behaviour.

2 *Treatment as beneficial.* Drug and surgical interventions are stopped if they are found to be either ineffective or to have negative consequences. However, behavioural interventions to promote behaviour change, such as smoking cessation, exercise and weight loss programmes, are developed and promoted even when the evidence for their success is poor. Within health psychology, behavioural programmes are considered neutral enough to be better than nothing. However, obesity treatment using dieting is an example of the potential negative side-effects of encouraging individual responsibility for health and attempting to change behaviour. Perhaps behavioural interventions can have as many negative consequences as other medical treatments.

3 *The mind–body problem.* Research into obesity and CHD raises the problem of the relationship between the mind and the body. Theories are considered either physiological or psychological and treatment perspectives are divided in a similar fashion, thereby maintaining a dualistic model of individuals.

FURTHER READING

Brownell, K.D. (1991) Personal responsibility and control over our health: when expectation exceeds reality, *Health Psychology*, 10: 303–10.
This paper discusses the emphasis on patient responsibility for health and suggests that encouraging the obese to diet may be an example of attempting to control the uncontrollable. It is an interesting paper as it challenges the core of much health psychology thinking by suggesting that some illnesses are beyond the control of the individual. It is a good paper to generate debate.

Ogden, J. (2010) *The Psychology of Eating: From Health to Disordered Behaviour*, 2nd edn. Oxford: Blackwell.
This book provides an account of the continuum of eating behaviour from healthy eating, through dieting and body dissatisfaction, to obesity and eating disorders. In particular, it provides a detailed analysis of obesity and its treatment.

Romero-Corral, A., Montori, V.M., Somers, V.K. et al. (2006) Association of body weight with total mortality and with cardiovascular events in coronary artery disease: a systematic review of cohort studies, *Lancet*, 368: 666–78.
This paper provides an up-to-date analysis of research exploring the links between body weight and CHD.

 Visit the website at www.openup.co.uk/ogden for additional resources on Chapter 15 to help you with your study, such as multiple choice questions, weblinks and a searchable online glossary.

16 Women's Health Issues

© Anton Hlushchenko/iStock

> ## CHAPTER OVERVIEW
>
> Chapter 2 highlighted how health and illness vary by a number of demographic factors, including gender. This chapter focuses on three key health issues specific to women. First, it examines the psychological impact of having a miscarriage. Next, it describes issues relating to having a termination of pregnancy in terms of contact with the health care system and the short- and longer-term psychological consequences. Finally, it describes women's experiences of the menopause. These health issues are managed in different ways and central to this chapter is a description of how the mode of treatment or intervention used can impact upon women's experiences.

GENDER AND HEALTH

Chapter 2 highlighted how health and illness vary according to social class, geographical location, time and gender. In terms of gender, much research shows that although women live longer than men, they are more likely to be diagnosed and treated for a wide range of health problems, from headaches and constipation through to depression, obesity and diabetes. Such gender differences can be understood in terms of all the factors described throughout this book such as health beliefs and behaviour, symptom perception, help-seeking, coping, adherence to medication and behaviour change. There are, however, a few health problems which are gender-specific. For example, while men suffer from baldness, impotence and prostate cancer, women get breast cancer, endometriosis and uterine cancer. They also suffer miscarriages, receive terminations of pregnancy and experience the menopause.

MISCARRIAGE

Miscarriage is a relatively common phenomenon occurring in 15–20 per cent of known pregnancies, with 80 per cent of these occurring within the first trimester (Broquet 1999). Miscarriage or 'spontaneous abortion' has been defined as the unintended end of a pregnancy before a foetus can survive outside the mother, which is recognized as being before the twentieth week of gestation (Borg and Lasker 1982). Despite the frequency with which miscarriage occurs, it has only been in the last 10 to 15 years that research has begun to identify and explore the consequences of early pregnancy loss. This section explores the psychological consequences of miscarriage in terms of the quantitative and qualitative research and then examines the impact of how miscarriage is managed in terms of women's experiences of this event.

QUANTITATIVE RESEARCH

Quantitative research has tended to conceptualize women's reactions to miscarriage in terms of grief, depression and anxiety, or coping.

- *Grief.* One main area of research has conceptualized miscarriage as a loss event, assuming that after miscarriage women experience stages of grief parallel to that of the death of a loved one (Herz 1984). The main symptoms identified are sadness, yearning for the lost child, a desire to talk to others about the loss and a search for meaningful explanations (Herz 1984; Athey and Spielvogel 2000). In addition, research has highlighted grief reactions that are unique to the miscarriage experience. For example, women often perceive themselves as failures for not being able to have a healthy pregnancy and this loss is often not acknowledged by the community because there are no rituals that can be performed (Herz 1984).

- *Depression and anxiety.* Other research has focused on depression and anxiety following miscarriage. Friedman and Gath (1989) used the Present State Examination (PSE) to assess psychiatric 'caseness' in women four weeks post-miscarriage. They found that 48 per cent of the sample had sufficiently high scores on the scale to qualify as 'case' patients, which is over four times higher than that in women in the general population. When analysed, these women were all classified as having depressive disorders. Klier et al. (2000) similarly found that women who had miscarried had a significantly increased risk of developing a minor depressive disorder in the six months following their loss, compared to a cohort drawn from the community. Thapar and Thapar (1992) also found that women who had miscarried experienced a significant degree of anxiety and depression at both the initial interview and at the six-week follow-up compared to the control group. In contrast, Prettyman et al. (1993) used the Hospital Anxiety and Depression Scale (HADS) and found that anxiety rather than depression was the predominant response at 1, 6 and 12 weeks after miscarriage. Further, Beutel et al. (1995) reported that immediately after the miscarriage the majority of the sample experienced elevated levels of psychological morbidity compared to a community cohort and a pregnant control group, much of which persisted up until the 12-month follow-up. The authors concluded that depression and grief should be considered as two distinct reactions to pregnancy loss, with grief being the normal reaction and depression only developing when certain circumstances are met. This study also showed that a large minority reported no negative emotional reaction post-miscarriage, suggesting that a focus on anxiety, depression and grief may only tap into a part of the miscarriage experience.

- *Coping.* A small number of studies have considered the experience of miscarriage from a coping viewpoint. For example, Madden (1988) completed 65 structured interviews with women two weeks post-miscarriage and concluded that, rather than self-blame, external blame for the miscarriage and the ability to be able to control the outcome of future pregnancies were predictive of depressive symptoms post-miscarriage. Tunaley et al. (1993) drew upon the theory of cognitive adaptation (Taylor 1983) which focuses on meaning, self-enhancement and mastery, to explore the miscarriage experience (see Chapter 9). They found that 86 per cent of the sample had established their own set of reasons as to why the miscarriage had occurred, ranging from medical explanations to feelings of punishment and judgement, which finds reflection in work on attributions for heart disease (e.g. French et al. 2001) and breast cancer (Taylor 1983). In terms of self-enhancement, 50 per cent of the sample made downward social comparisons with women who had reproductive problems. By comparing themselves with women who were worse off than themselves, they were able to increase their own self-esteem. The search for mastery was less visible. There was little evidence that the women in the sample tried to gain control over their lives in general. Although 81 per cent of the sample believed that they could make changes to prevent future miscarriage, they had little or no confidence in the difference these changes would make to future outcomes (Tunaley et al. 1993).

The quantitative research has therefore explored the reaction to miscarriage in terms of grief, anxiety and depression and coping. Other research has used a qualitative method to assess women's broader experience of having a miscarriage.

QUALITATIVE RESEARCH

In an early study, Hutti (1986) conducted in-depth interviews at two time points with two women. The results showed that although both women referred to a similar inventory of events, the significance that they attached to these events was different and dependent upon their previous experience. For example, one woman had had a previous miscarriage and was described as taking more control over her medical treatment; she found her grief to be less severe than with her first miscarriage. In contrast, the woman who had experienced her first miscarriage represented the miscarriage as a 'severe threat to her perception of herself as a childbearing woman' (p. 383). On a larger scale, Bansen and Stevens (1992) focused on 10 women who had experienced their first pregnancy loss of a wanted pregnancy. The authors concluded that miscarriage was a 'silent event' which was not discussed within the wider community. The women were described as being unable to share their experiences and felt isolated as a result. When they did get the opportunity to talk about their loss, they realized how common miscarriage is and that was a source of comfort to them. The authors concluded that miscarriage constituted a major life event that changed the way in which women viewed their lives in the present and affected the way in which they planned for the future.

Maker and Ogden (2003) carried out in-depth interviews with a heterogenous sample of 13 women who had experienced a miscarriage up to five weeks previously. The women described their experiences using a range of themes which were conceptualized into three stages: turmoil, adjustment and resolution. For the majority, the turmoil stage was characterized by feelings of being unprepared and negative emotions. Some women who had had an unwanted pregnancy described their shock at the physical trauma of miscarriage but described the experience as a relief. The women then described a period of adjustment involving social comparisons, sharing and a search for meaning. The latter included a focus on causality which left a minority, particularly those who had had previous miscarriages, feeling frustrated with the absence of a satisfactory medical explanation. The final resolution stage was characterized by a decline in negative emotions, a belief by some that the miscarriage was a learning experience and the integration of the experience into their lives. This resolution seemed more positive for those with children and more negative if the miscarriage was not their first. The authors argued that, rather than being a trigger to psychological morbidity, a miscarriage should be conceptualized as a *process* involving the stages of turmoil, adjustment and resolution.

IMPACT OF MODE OF TREATMENT

Miscarriages can occur throughout a pregnancy but most occur during the first trimester (Steer et al. 1989). Until recently, the standard management of first trimester miscarriages involved the evacuation of the retained products of conception (ERPC), also sometimes known as a D&C (dilatation and curettage). This uses either a general or local anaesthetic and surgically removes the lining of the womb and the foetus if it is still there. This occasionally causes infection, uterine perforation and bowel damage and brings with it all the associated risks of an anaesthetic. Expectant management is a possible alternative and has been adopted by several clinics across the UK. This involves letting the miscarriage take its natural course and enables the woman to be at home as the miscarriage occurs. Trials suggest that expectant management might produce less infection (Neilson and Hahlin 1995) and observational studies show that it usually results in complete evacuation of the products of conception (Sairam et al. 2001; Luise et al. 2002). It would seem to be feasible, effective and safe and may be the preferred treatment by many women (Luise et al. 2002). Rates of surgical management of miscarriage vary by age and are shown in Figure 16.1.

Little is known about what women expect, or about their subsequent experiences of each management approach. Ogden and Maker (2004) assessed women's reasons for deciding upon a given treatment and the impact of treatment type upon their subsequent experiences. The choice of expectant management was motivated by a desire for a natural solution and a fear of surgery. Women described how pain and bleeding had made them anxious that something was wrong and how they felt unprepared for how gruelling the experience would be. Some also described how their support had dwindled as the miscarriage progressed. In contrast, women who chose surgery valued a quick resolution and focused on the support from hospital staff, although some commented that their emotional needs had not always been met. The mode of treatment therefore seemed to influence how the miscarriage was experienced. Furthermore, even though expectant management is becoming increasingly common, women feel unprepared for how this will make them feel.

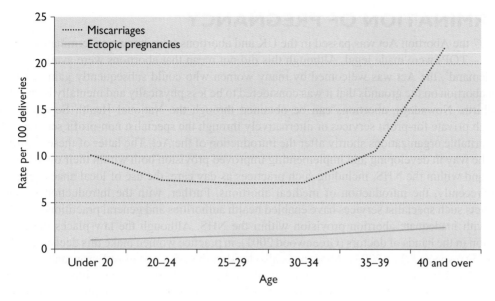

FIGURE 16.1

Rates of miscarriage that require a hospital stay vary by age of mother

SOURCE: Adapted from NHS Maternity Statistics, Department of Health, 2003–4

PROBLEMS WITH MISCARRIAGE RESEARCH

Research into miscarriage is problematic in the following ways:

1 Miscarriage is very common. Many women come into contact with health professionals as they visit their GP or are referred to a hospital clinic. Some, however, have early miscarriages that are considered to be late periods or miscarriages that will resolve themselves without medical intervention. To date, most research focuses on those who seek help. This offers an unrepresentative sample and means that very little is known about those women who experience miscarriage but never seek help.

2 Research exploring miscarriage tends to use either quantitative or qualitative methods. To date, there has been no use of mixed methods or any real integration of the two literatures. Future research needs to take the findings from the qualitative approaches and test them quantitatively.

3 The use of expectant management is relatively new. Women's experiences of this approach are coloured by the lack of familiarity in recommending it by the professionals. Research is needed to explore how women experience expectant management as it becomes the more 'normal' approach used.

4 Research to date has focused on women's experiences of miscarriage. Future research could explore how men feel about this form of pregnancy loss.

SUMMING UP

Research exploring the psychological impact of having a miscarriage has used both quantitative and qualitative research methods. The results indicate that miscarriage can result in feelings of grief, anxiety and depression. In addition, women experience their miscarriage as a *process*, involving a series of stages which can result in women reassessing both their past and future experiences. Furthermore, research indicates that a woman's experience is clearly influenced by how it is managed, and that, although the medical management of miscarriage brings with it the risks associated with surgery, a more 'natural' approach can leave women feeling misinformed and unprepared.

TERMINATION OF PREGNANCY

In 1967 the Abortion Act was passed in the UK and abortions (also known as termination of pregnancy – TOP) were made legal. Although this did not mean that abortions were available simply 'on demand', the Act was welcomed by many women who could subsequently gain access to a legal abortion on the grounds that it was considered to be less physically and mentally harmful than childbirth. Nowadays, abortions can be obtained through the National Health Service (NHS), through private for-profit services or alternatively through the specialist non-profit services set up by charitable organizations shortly after the introduction of the Act. The latter of these continue to lead the way in developing and implementing improved provision both within their own organizations and within the NHS, including such practices as day care, the use of local anaesthetics and, more recently, the introduction of medical abortions. Further, with the introduction of agency contracts such specialist services have enabled health authorities and general practitioners (GPs) to deal with inadequate abortion provision within the NHS. Although the law places the abortion decision in the hands of doctors (Greenwood 2001), in practice women make this decision and their choice is respected (Lee 2003). Abortion is also legal in the USA and most European countries. In England and Wales one in three women is likely to have an abortion in their lifetime (calculated from The Abortion Statistics England and Wales 2001); however, debate continues over the moral status of a human foetus and consequently also over that of abortions (Gillon 2001). The abortion rate by age is shown in Figure 16.2.

Up until recently all abortions involved the surgical removal of the foetus using a D&C and a general anaesthetic. Nowadays, however, women can choose to have their abortion using either the D&C with a general or local anaesthetic, a suction technique which can involve general or local anaesthetic or no anaesthetic, or the abortion pill which induces a miscarriage (later miscarriages may be managed through inducing labour). The type of abortion procedure depends upon the gestation of the pregnancy, the preference of the woman and the methods preferred by the clinic involved. In the UK an abortion is legal up until the 24th week of gestation although abortions occur within the first trimester. Abortion is illegal in a number of countries in all circumstances except to save a woman's life. These include Brazil, Chile, Mexico, Venezuela, Angola, Congo,

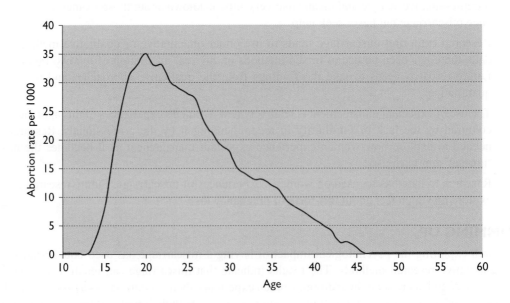

FIGURE 16.2

Abortion rate in England and Wales by age, 2005

SOURCE: Adapted from the Department of Health (2005)

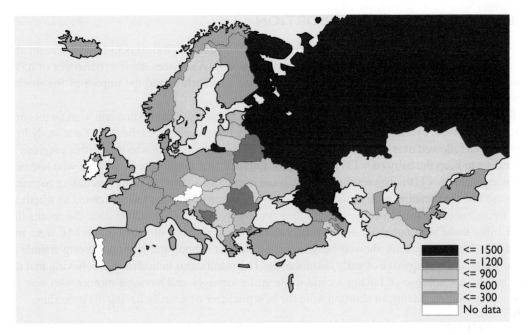

FIGURE 16.3

Abortion rates across Europe and Asia

SOURCE: Adapted from WHO European Health for All Database, Del (2004 accessed)

Mali, Niger, Nigeria, Uganda, Afghanistan, Iran, Egypt, Libya, Syria, Bangladesh, Ireland and Malta. In addition, many countries only allow abortion to protect a woman's health. These include Argentina, Peru, Cameroon, Ethiopia, Malawi, Zimbabwe, Kuwait, Saudi Arabia, Pakistan, Thailand, Poland and Portugal. Rates of abortions across the world are shown in Figure 16.3 and the rates of unsafe abortions are shown in Figure 16.4.

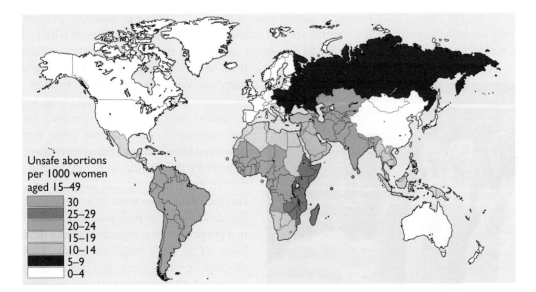

FIGURE 16.4

Worldwide rates of unsafe abortions

SOURCE: Adapted from Gunta Lazone (2005)

DECIDING TO HAVE AN ABORTION

Research focusing on abortions has addressed a range of issues including deciding to have an abortion, the provision of services, women's experiences of such services, their experiences of having an abortion, the longer-term consequences of having an abortion and the impact of the mode of intervention used.

Research has explored how women decide whether or not to have an abortion and what factors influence this decision. Freeman and Rickels (1993) reported the results from the Penn State study in the USA which followed over 300 black teenagers aged 13–17 for two years who were either pregnant and intending to keep the baby (n = 137), had terminated their first pregnancy (n = 94) or who had never been pregnant (n = 110). The results were analysed to explore a range of factors including contraception use and the meaning of pregnancy. The study also examined what factors related to whether or not the teenager decided to continue with their pregnancy. Using quantitative data, the results illustrated that those who opted for an abortion had more employment in their households, were more likely to still be in school, showed better course grades at school and reported having friends and family who did not approve of early childbearing. The results also indicated that believing that their mother did not approve of having a child while still a teenager and having a mother who was very supportive of them having an abortion were the best predictor of actually having the procedure.

In a similar vein, Lee et al. (2004) carried out a qualitative study involving in-depth interviews with 103 women aged between 15 and 17 in the UK who had been pregnant and either continued with the pregnancy or had an abortion, and with older people in communities with high abortion rates. The interviews explored the influences upon their decision-making. The results showed that their decisions were mostly related to the social and economic context of their lives rather than any abstract moral views. Further, the results indicated that similar factors influenced the decision-making processes for women regardless of their age. For example, the decision to have an abortion was related to social deprivation. In particular, the results indicated that although there are higher numbers of conceptions in young women in deprived areas, these women are less likely to terminate their pregnancy than those in less deprived areas. In addition, those who believed that their future life would include higher education and a career, who had higher expectations of their life in the present, who had a lack of financial independence and who felt that they lacked the stable relationships to support them if they became a mother were more likely to have an abortion. In contrast, keeping the baby was related to a positive view of motherhood that was not associated with lack or loss, and those who viewed motherhood as rewarding, associating it with responsibility and seeing it as an achievement, were more likely to carry on with the pregnancy. Further, the decision-making process seemed to be highly related to the views of the women's family and community. For example, some women described how having children early was considered by their world to be acceptable and normal and these tended to have the baby. In contrast, those who went on to have an abortion described how their parents saw abortion in a pragmatic way, regarding young motherhood as a more negative event. Finally, although most women had made up their minds whether or not to have an abortion before they had any contact with a health professional, the results showed an association between the abortion rate and provision of

Social support can be important for new mothers

local family planning provision, higher pro-
portions of female GPs and a greater independent sector providing abortion services.
This suggests that, although much of the decision-making process is influenced by social
and economic factors prior to professional
contact, structural factors such as service provision also have a role to play. Deciding to
have an abortion seems to relate to the context
of the woman's life and the beliefs and support
offered by those important to her.

THE PROVISION OF SERVICES

In line with the role of structural factors
already described, some research has examined the changes in both the provision and
accessibility of services. For example, research
has highlighted that, despite increasing provi-

Deciding whether or not to have an abortion is influenced by
the views of others

SOURCE: © Monkeybusinessimages/Dreamstime

sion for abortion in the UK within the NHS, there remains wide variation in the level of NHS provision in different health authorities (Abortion Law Reform Association 1997). In particular, figures
revealed that, while on average 70.5 per cent of abortions are funded by the NHS in England and
Wales, this figure ranges from 28 to 96 per cent across regional and district health authorities (Office
for National Statistics Population and Health Monitors 1995). A report by the Abortion Law Reform
Association examined the reasons for this variation and found that informal means testing is applied
by many health authorities and GPs, resulting in targets for abortion services being set below the local
known need (Abortion Law Reform Association 1997).

Other studies from this perspective have mapped the stages involved in accessing and using the
abortion services. For example, Clarke et al. (1983) examined why half the women in their study
had their abortion in a private or charitable clinic despite generous provision of NHS abortion services. The study showed that an important reason for women bypassing the NHS was that they
either thought or had been actually told by their GP or another doctor that it was difficult to get an
abortion on the NHS. Other reasons for not having an abortion on the NHS included not wanting
to delay the abortion, expectation of better personal treatment in a private clinic and wanting to
ensure anonymity. The results also indicated that women feared insensitive treatment from local
NHS hospitals, and this resonates with a survey of abortion patients carried out in the UK (Pro-
choice Alliance 1993). This is supported by studies of women's experiences of having an abortion
which suggest that women may have a more positive experience if they are managed through specialist independent clinics (Lee et al. 2004).

WOMEN'S EXPERIENCES OF SERVICES

Sociological research has emphasized the importance of women's experiences of having an
abortion. For some, this has involved a study of the factors that are likely to impinge upon a
woman's experience. For example, reports indicate that decisions about the provision of services
are often based upon moral judgements (MacIntyre 1977). In addition, it has been shown that
referrals to services and therefore service access are also influenced by judgements and assumptions concerning a woman's circumstances (e.g. marital status) rather than health need (MacIntyre
1977). Accordingly, several authors have noted that such a judgemental context is likely to
impact negatively upon women's experiences of such services (Doyal 1985; Hadley 1996).

In contrast, some psychological research has examined women's experiences directly. In terms of
surgical abortion, an analysis of women's experiences of seeking an abortion in Australia (Ryan et al.

1994) found that limitations in current service provision and the legal and health contexts in which women sought abortion had an impact on women's experience and treatment. In particular, it was reported that confusion in the laws surrounding abortion could lead to women facing long drawn-out referral procedures as a result of the idiosyncratic eligibility criteria that a particular GP or gynaecologist applied in a given case. Furthermore it was found that the women had many ideas about how abortion services could be improved. These ranged from specific issues such as the importance of accessibility of information and recommendations that abortion be treated as an urgent rather than elective procedure, to the wider social context of abortion regarding women's ownership and respect for their decisions and the removal of the stigma that surrounds the procedure.

Harden and Ogden (1999a) interviewed 54 women aged between 16 and 24 up to three hours after their abortion about their experiences. They reported that, overall, having an unwanted pregnancy was experienced as a rare event which was accompanied by feelings of lack of control and loss of status. Further, the process of arranging and having an abortion led to a reinstatement of status, control and normality. However, this process was sometimes hindered by inaccessible information, judgemental health professionals and the wider social context of abortion in which it is seen as a generally negative experience. In the main, however, most of these negative experiences were associated with accessing the abortion service and the professionals who act as gatekeepers to the service rather than those who work within the service itself. Therefore, although young women's experiences were wide-ranging and varied, most were positive and at times even negative expectations were compensated by supportive staff, indicating that abortion services may not be as judgemental in the late twentieth century as suggested in previous decades.

PSYCHOLOGICAL IMPACT

Much research has addressed the psychological consequences of abortion (see Coleman et al. 2005 for a comprehensive review). Some of this has explored the extent of emotional reactions post-abortion. For example, Zolese and Blacker (1992) argued that approximately 10 per cent of women experience depression or anxiety that is severe or persistent after an abortion. Other authors have used case studies of women who are distressed to suggest that this may be more widespread (Butler and Llanedeyrn 1996). In contrast, although Major et al. (2000) found that 20 per cent of their sample experienced clinical depression within two years of an abortion, they argued that this is equivalent to population rates. Adler et al. (1990) reviewed the most methodologically sound US studies and concluded that incidence of severe negative responses was low, that distress was greatest before an abortion and reactions were often positive. They argued that abortion can be considered within a stress and coping framework and that the small numbers of women who experience distress are insignificant from a public health perspective.

Some research has also considered what type of psychological reactions occur after an abortion. Söderberg et al. (1998) conducted interviews with a large sample of Swedish women (n = 845) a year after their abortion and found that 55 per cent experienced some form of emotional distress. In contrast, however, Kero et al. (2004) interviewed 58 women in Sweden a year after their abortion and concluded that most reported no distress and that more than half reported only positive experiences. Other researchers have found that relief is commonly expressed after an abortion (Rosenfeld 1992) and Major et al. (2000) found that 72 per cent of their sample were satisfied with their decision two years after. Similarly, Alex and Hammarström (2004) conducted a study in Sweden of five women's experiences and concluded that the women reported gaining a sense of maturity and experience.

LONGER-TERM IMPACT

It would therefore seem that, although some women experience emotional distress post-abortion, others experience more positive reactions such as relief, a return to normality and satisfaction. But do these emotional states persist over time? Russo and Zierk (1992) followed up women eight years after their abortion and compared them to those who had kept the child. They found that having an abortion was related to higher global self-esteem than having an unwanted birth, suggesting that any initial negative reactions decay over time. In a similar vein, Major et al. (2000) explored the variation in emotional reactions over time and reported that negative emotions increased between the time of the abortion and two years, and satisfaction with the decision decreased. These results also suggest a linear pattern of change but one towards worse rather than better adaptation. In contrast, however, some researchers have argued that emotional responses do not always alter in a linear way. For example, Kumar and Robson (1987) found that neurotic disturbances during pregnancy were significantly higher in those who had had a previous termination than those who had not, and suggested that this is due to unresolved feelings about the abortion that had been reawakened by the pregnancy. In contrast, however, Adler et al. (1990) argued that research from other life stressors has found that if no severe negative responses are present from a few months to a year after the event, it is unlikely that they will develop later.

The research therefore illustrates variability both in terms of the initial emotional reactions to an abortion and how these reactions change over time. Some research has addressed which factors may explain variability in the initial response. For example, immediate distress has been reported as being higher in those women who belong to a society that is antagonistic towards abortion (Major and Gramzow 1999), in those who experienced difficulty making the decision (Lyndon et al. 1996), and in those who are younger, unmarried, have the abortion later in pregnancy (which may be due to the features of women who delay), show low self-esteem or an external locus of control, have had multiple abortions, and self-blame for the pregnancy or abortion (Harris 2004). Further, believing in the human qualities of the foetus has also been associated with higher levels of distress (Conklin and O'Connor 1995). Goodwin and Ogden (2006) explored women's reactions to their abortion up to nine years later and examined how they believed their feelings about the abortion had changed over time. The results showed that, although a few women reported a linear pattern of change in their emotions, some also described different patterns including persistent upset that remained ongoing many years after the event, negative reappraisal some time after the event and a positive appraisal at the time of the event with no subsequent negative emotions. The results also provide some insights into this variability. Those who described how they had never been upset or experienced a linear recovery also tended to conceptualize the foetus as less human, reported having had more social support and described either a belief that abortions are supported by society or an ability to defend against a belief that society is judgemental. In contrast, patterns of emotional change involving persistent upset or negative appraisal were entwined with a more human view of the foetus, a lack of social support and a belief that society is either overly judgemental or negates the impact that an abortion can have on a woman.

IMPACT OF MODE OF INTERVENTION

An abortion can be carried out using a D&C (surgical), vacuum aspiration (suction) or the abortion pill (medical) and may or may not involve a general or local anaesthetic. Some research has explored the relative impact of type of procedure on women's experiences. For example, Slade et al. (1998) examined the impact of having either a medical or surgical abortion. The results showed that those opting for surgical procedure had to wait longer and were more advanced by the time of the abortion but that the two groups showed similar emotional responses prior to having the abortion. After the abortion, however, the medical procedure was seen as more stressful and was associated with more post-termination problems. It was also seen as more disruptive to life. Further, seeing the foetus was associated with more intrusive events such as nightmares, flashbacks and unwanted thoughts. Fifty-three per cent of the medical group said they would have the same procedure again whereas 77 per cent of the surgical group felt this. Similarly, Goodwin and Ogden (2006) suggest from their study that the abortion pill technique may result in a more negative experience for several women than other methods, as some women described seeing the foetus as it was expelled from their bodies. In contrast, Lowenstein et al. (2006) compared surgical and medical management of abortion and reported no differences in anxiety by two weeks following the abortion. In line with this, Howie et al. (1997) reported no differences in emotional change two years after having either a medical abortion or vacuum aspiration. Perhaps the mode of intervention does result in short-term differences in the women's experiences but after a while the differences begin to disappear. Given the increasing use of these newer modes of intervention, research is required to assess their relative impact on women's short- and longer-term adjustment.

PROBLEMS WITH TERMINATION RESEARCH

People have extremely strong views about terminations which are reflected in alliances such as 'pro-choice' and 'pro-life'. However hard they try, researchers are not immune to their own political or moral positions. Research exploring the impact of termination is therefore problematic because the researcher's own views and experiences are highly likely to influence the research process. For example, an ideological position either for or against termination could affect the choice of research design, the selection of participants, the ways the data are analysed or the ways the data are interpreted and the results presented. Furthermore, the existence of such views may also promote a more black and white view of women's experiences. For example, a researcher who is pro-life may encounter women's experiences which illustrate the times when termination is acceptable (against the researcher's own beliefs) but she may be reluctant to report this. Similarly, a researcher who is pro-choice may encounter data that suggest that abortion is not always a 'good thing' but may be similarly reluctant to add such accounts to the literature. Therefore the highly moral nature of terminations makes the research open to bias. Furthermore, even the existence of an understanding of the moral nature of the subject matter may encourage researchers to be more polarized in their positions.

SUMMING UP

Research exploring abortions has focused on women's experiences of access to services, the short- and longer-term impact of having a termination of pregnancy and the impact of the mode of treatment on women's experiences. In general, the research indicates that access to services varies according to locality but that private specialized services are experienced in a more positive way than state-run services. Further, the results indicate that, although some women report negative mood changes following an abortion, many describe a return to normality and relief, although this varies according to a range of individual and social factors as well as the type of intervention used.

BOX 16.1 Some Problems with . . . Women's Health Research

Below are some problems with research in this area that you may wish to consider.

1   Much women's health research generates political and ideological perspectives. For example, termination and menopause management can create a strong sense of what is right or wrong. Research in these areas may therefore be biased in terms of what questions are asked, how data are collected and how the results are interpreted and presented.

2   Many areas of women's health are constantly changing. For example, the use of hormone replacement therapy (HRT) for the menopause, the management of miscarriages and that of terminations change from year to year. Summarizing results within these areas across time is therefore difficult.

3   Research in women's health is often addressed from many different theoretical perspectives, of which psychology is only one. Integrating research and theories from sociology, gender studies, medicine and anthropology can either produce conflicting conclusions or ones that are so complex and multifactorial that they become difficult to summarize or put into any useful practice.

THE MENOPAUSE

The word 'menopause' means the end of monthly menstruation and for the average woman this occurs at the age of 51 years, with 80 per cent of women reaching the menopause by age 54. In general, the menopause is considered to be a transition which has been classified according to three stages (WHO 1996). The *pre-menopause* refers to the whole of the woman's reproductive life up until the end of the last menstrual period. The *peri-menopause* is the time prior to the final menstrual period when hormonal changes are taking place and continues until a year after the last menstrual period. The *post-menopause* stage refers to any time after the last menstrual period but has to be defined retrospectively after 12 months of no menstruation. Therefore the menopause reflects the end point of a gradual change in biological function which is finally lost as the woman stops producing eggs and the level of oestrogen produced is reduced as it is no longer required to stimulate the lining of the womb in preparation for fertilization. The cessation of menstruation for 12 consecutive months is the required period of time for a doctor to define a woman as menopausal, with research showing that around 75 per cent of women present to their doctor about the menopause (Hope et al. 1998). Although there is a strong genetic determinant of the time of the menopause, with mothers and daughters tending to become menopausal at a similar age, smoking can result in an earlier menopause and being heavier can result in a later menopause. In addition to the cessation of periods, the menopause brings with it other symptoms while it is happening and results in longer-term physical changes due to the reduction in female hormones.

SYMPTOMS

During the menopause women report a range of symptoms, some of which are clearly linked to a reduction in oestrogen while others have unclear origins. These illustrate the complex nature of symptoms and the role of social and psychological factors in influencing symptom perception. The most common symptoms are the following:

- Change in pattern and heaviness of periods.
- Hot flushes.
- Night sweats.
- Tiredness.
- Poor concentration.
- Aches and pains in joints.
- Vaginal dryness.
- Changes in the frequency of passing urine.

As part of a large-scale survey, 413 women completed a questionnaire about their experiences of menopausal symptoms and their perceptions of severity, and the results showed that the most common symptoms were hot flushes, night sweats and tiredness, and of these, night sweats seemed to cause the most distress with over a third describing their night sweats as severe (Ballard 2003). The results from this study are illustrated in Figure 16.5.

PHYSICAL CHANGES

Women also experience a range of physical changes which persist after the menopause has passed. In particular they show changes in their breasts and it is suggested that older women should have regular mammograms to check for breast cancer. There is a post-menopausal increase in cholesterol in the blood which places women more at risk of heart disease; bone loss becomes more rapid, increasing the chance of osteoporosis; the urinary organs can become less elastic and pliable, resulting in many women suffering from incontinence; and finally women experience vaginal dryness, making sexual intercourse uncomfortable.

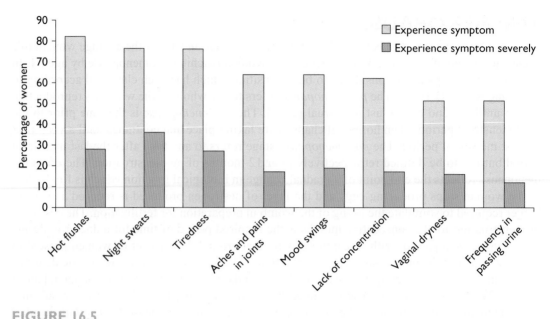

FIGURE 16.5

The frequency and severity of menopausal symptoms

SOURCE: Adapted from Ballard (2003)

The menopause therefore signifies the end of a woman's reproductive capacity and brings with it a wide range of symptoms and physical changes. Ballard (2003) describes how the menopause experience is influenced by a range of social, cultural and biological factors which in turn have a psychological impact upon the individual. This reflects why the menopause is also referred to as 'the change of life'. This is illustrated in Figure 16.6.

Research exploring the impact of the menopause has highlighted the experience as a life transition and the social and psychological factors that affect this transition.

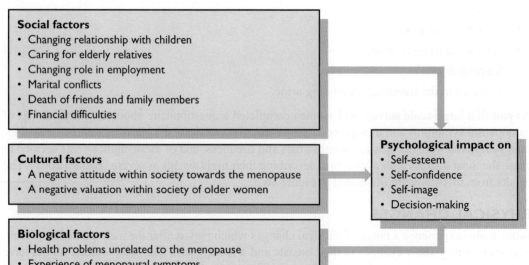

FIGURE 16.6

The menopause as a biopsychosocial event

THE MENOPAUSE AS A TRANSITION

As part of a larger-scale cohort study which has collected data regularly from people born during the first week of March 1946 (see Wadsworth 1991; Wadsworth and Kuh 1997; Ballard et al. 2001), 1,572 women described their menopausal years. The women completed questions about their symptoms and health in general and then 65 per cent also completed a 'free comments' section. These data were then analysed using both quantitative and qualitative methods. From this study the authors conclude that women experience the menopause as a 'status passage' which involves five stages. These are as follows:

1 *Expectations of symptoms.* The results illustrate that, prior to the menopause onset, women are searching for symptoms and looking for signs of any biological changes. At this point some women seek help from the doctor and start to find further information.

2 *Experience of symptoms and loss of control.* Women then start to experience symptoms such as night sweats, hot flushes and mood swings, which for some interfere with their sense of well-being and can make them feel out of control.

3 *Confirmation of the menopause.* Once women sense a loss of control, they then try to confirm the onset of the menopause by visiting their doctor as a means to regain control. The doctor can use blood tests to measure hormone levels to confirm the onset of the menopause and at this stage many women are offered hormone replacement therapy (HRT).

4 *Regaining control.* Women try to regain control in several ways. Some try to minimize the impact of their symptoms by taking HRT while others try a range of methods such as wearing different clothes to cope with hot flushes or taking alternative medicines.

5 *Freedom from menstruation.* The end of menstruation is often welcomed by women as, for the majority, decisions about family size have been made long ago. Women therefore feel relieved that they do not have to experience the pain and bleeding from periods any more and the inconvenience that this can cause.

The menopause is therefore seen as a process through which women go, which starts with a sense of expectation and loss of control and finishes with a sense of freedom and regained control. For many women and doctors this transition is managed through the use of HRT as the symptoms and changes associated with the menopause are attributed to changes in hormone levels. For some researchers, however, this perspective has been seen as over-medicalizing the menopause which provides a platform for medicine to take control of women's bodies (Oakley 1984; Doyal 1994). The results from the large-scale women's health study (Ballard et al. 2001) suggest that, although many women conceptualize the menopause as a medical event, they also locate it within the complex social and psychological changes that also occur at this time.

SOCIAL FACTORS

The menopause happens at a time in a woman's life when she is probably also experiencing a range of other changes. Whether or not such changes have a direct or indirect effect upon the menopausal experience, research indicates that the menopause needs to be understood in the context of these changes and describes them and their effect upon the menopause as follows (Ballard et al. 2001; Ballard 2003):

1 *Elderly relatives.* At the time of the menopause women often find that they are also increasingly responsible for caring for elderly relatives. Further, this may come at a time when women are just starting to enjoy a newfound freedom from the children leaving home. The added pressure of elderly relatives can make women feel under stress and guilty and can affect their physical health, all of which may exacerbate their menopausal symptoms.

2 *Changes in employment and finance.* In middle life many women increase their hours of work as the children leave home. This may bring with it new opportunities and a sense of rebirth.

However, it can also be an extra stressor, particularly if women still have the primary responsibility for the home. In contrast, some women retire in middle life which brings with it its own sets of stresses in terms of readjustment and a need to develop a new self-image. Both these types of changes in employment can influence the menopause and its associated symptoms.

3 *Changing relationships.* At the time of the menopause women often experience changes in their role as a mother as this is the time when children leave home, and a change in their relationship with their partner as they renegotiate a new life without children. Such changes can make the menopause seem more pertinent as it reflects the end of an era.

4 *Death of family or friends.* As women reach their fifties they may experience the death of similar-age family or friends. The menopause may represent a sense of mortality which can be exacerbated by a sense of loss.

According to Ballard et al. (2001) these social factors coexist alongside the time of the menopause and can influence the ways in which the menopause is experienced. In turn they result in subsequent changes in the individual's psychological state.

PSYCHOLOGICAL EFFECTS

Psychological factors influence the menopause in terms of symptom perception because symptoms such as hot flushes, night sweats, lack of concentration and tiredness are all influenced by processes such as distraction, focus, mood, meaning and the environment (see Chapter 9). In addition, the menopause has more direct effects upon the individual's psychological state. Ballard (2003) describes these as the following:

1 *Changes in body image.* The menopause brings with it physical changes such as dryer skin, changing fat distribution and softer breasts, which can all impact upon a woman's body image. In addition, becoming 50 is also seen as a milestone, particularly within a society that associates getting older with being less attractive. Ballard provides interesting descriptions of how women can suddenly catch themselves in a mirror and think 'it's my mum' or 'you are getting old'. Such changes in body image and body dissatisfaction are in line with those described in Chapter 5.

2 *Mood changes.* Some women report experiencing moods such as anxiety and depression and some report having panic attacks. Given the many life changes that co-occur with the menopause, it is not surprising that women experience changes in their mood. However, many women view their emotional shifts as directly linked to their changing hormone levels. This therefore raises the problem of attribution as there is a danger of all menopausal women's emotional shifts being attributed to their biological state, which makes them seem 'unstable'. However, there is also the converse problem that 'real' biological mechanisms are ignored and that emotions are inappropriately attributed to more social reasons.

3 *Self-esteem and self-confidence.* Some women also report decreases in their self-esteem and self-confidence. They describe not feeling confident in everyday tasks such as cooking or work, and feeling less able to manage relationships.

4 *Lack of concentration.* Several surveys report that women describe how the menopause disrupts their cognitive function in terms of concentration and memory (Rubin and Quine 1995; Ballard et al. 2001). Experimental studies in controlled conditions, however, show no evidence for any cognitive decline that could be attributed to the menopause above and beyond standard age effects (Herlitz et al. 1997).

The research exploring women's experiences of the menopause therefore shows that it is experienced as a transition which is accompanied by symptoms and longer-term physical changes. Although many of these factors may be related to underlying shifts in a woman's biology, the research also indicates that the experience of the menopause needs to be understood in the context of other social changes which in turn influence a woman's psychological state. The menopause can therefore be conceptualized as one part of a series of changes that happen to a woman during her midlife.

MODE OF MANAGEMENT

The menopause can be managed in a range of ways. Some women simply carry on with their lives and wait for the symptoms to pass. They may manage these symptoms using 'tricks of the trade' – such as wearing layered clothes rather than thick jumpers to make removing clothes easier should they have a hot flush, sleeping with the window open to cope with night sweats and buying lubricants to manage vaginal dryness – but they do not necessarily present their symptoms to the doctor. Others may try alternative medicines for symptom relief including herbal remedies, homeopathy and acupuncture, preferring a more natural approach. Many, however, do visit their doctor and are prescribed HRT. Further, the numbers of women taking HRT increased threefold between 1981 and 1990, up to 19 per cent, and increased to a rate of 60 per cent by 2000 (Moorhead et al. 1997; Kuh et al. 2000; Ballard 2002). HRT was originally developed to reduce menopausal symptoms but has subsequently been shown to treat and prevent osteoporosis, Alzheimer's disease, cardiovascular disease and depression. It also has its own risks, however, and has been associated with breast and endometrial cancer, heart attack, cerebrovascular disease and thromboembolic disease (see Writing Group for the Women's Health Initiative Investigators 2002; Beral et al. 2005 for a comprehensive review). Research has explored how women decide whether or not to take HRT and the impact of taking HRT upon symptoms.

DECIDING HOW TO MANAGE

HRT may help to alleviate menopausal symptoms and can protect against menopause-related diseases, but at the same time evidence indicates that it can increase the risk of longer-term health problems. Women therefore have to weigh up the pros and cons of HRT if they are to decide how to manage their menopause. Ballard (2002) analysed questionnaire data from 413 women of menopausal age to explore why women take HRT. The results showed that the main reason was for the relief of symptoms, particularly hot flushes, tiredness and irritability. Similarly, Welton et al. (2004) carried out eight focus groups with 82 women aged between 50 and 69. The results showed that, for those taking HRT, the main reason was perceived improvement in quality of life regardless of either the costs or benefits in the longer term. In addition, however, Ballard (2002) also reported that 58 per cent also took HRT to prevent osteoporosis. Symptom relief would therefore be the main factor influencing the decision-making process. Protection from illness, however, also seems to have a role to play. As a means to further understand the decision-making process, Buick et al. (2005) carried out a systematic review of the literature between 1980 and 2002 to explore women's beliefs about HRT. The results support those described earlier and indicate that use and discontinuation of HRT are more related to symptom relief than considerations of long-term benefits. Further, the results indicate that those women who refuse HRT often believe that the menopause is a natural event that does not require chemical intervention and that women's beliefs about the benefits of HRT are often countered by their concerns about potential adverse events (see Chapters 9 and 10 for a discussion of beliefs about medicines and adherence). Research has also used the theory of planned behaviour (TPB) to predict the use of HRT, showing a role for attitudes to HRT and self-efficacy (Huston et al. 2010). Not all women, however, take HRT and Wathen (2006) explored women's use of complementary and alternative medicines. This study used a mixed method approach and reported that 57 per cent of the Canadian sample had either considered or used alternative medicines as an alternative to HRT and that these women tended to be younger and had experienced worse symptoms than those who had not tried such remedies.

IMPACT OF HRT ON SYMPTOMS

Women report a wide range of menopausal symptoms which vary in their severity and the impact they have on their quality of life. HRT was invented as a means to relieve these symptoms and, as described earlier, those who take HRT do so mostly for symptom relief. Much research has explored the extent to which HRT does actually relieve menopausal symptoms. From the perspective of the patient, research indicates that women feel better when taking HRT and report improvements in their symptoms and quality of life. For example, Abraham et al. (1995) explored 60 women's beliefs about HRT when they were pre-menopausal and then 10 years later when they were post-menopausal. Thirty-eight of these had taken HRT. The results showed that the majority of the women believed that HRT helped hot flushes, non-specific emotional changes, vaginal dryness, insomnia and loss of muscle tone. In contrast, however, a large randomized trial, which explored the effectiveness of HRT compared to a placebo, suggested that HRT may not be as effective as believed (Utian et al. 1999). In particular this double-blind placebo-controlled study showed that HRT was only effective at relieving vasomotor symptoms such as hot flushes and night sweats. Similarly, another placebo-controlled trial showed that HRT only improved vaginal dryness, increased frequency of passing urine and the tendency to get urinary infections (Eriksen and Rasmussen 1992). These data suggest no effect for insomnia and mood. Further, they were placebo controlled, suggesting that such changes cannot simply be attributed to women wanting to feel better. Rymer et al. (2003) explored the effectiveness of HRT and suggested that this discrepancy between perceived effectiveness and actual effectiveness may illustrate a domino effect. In particular, while HRT may only relieve hot flushes and vaginal dryness, which can be directly explained by oestrogen deficiency, such changes may in turn improve mood, sleep and general quality of life.

PROBLEMS WITH MENOPAUSE RESEARCH

Problems with research on the menopause include the following:

1 The menopause happens to all women regardless of class, culture or time. Most research to date, however, has explored the experiences of western women for whom the menopause is often seen as an event that needs to be managed medically. It is likely that other cultures have very different beliefs and experiences of the menopause and that this influences their management strategies. More cross-cultural research is needed to explore how cultural factors impact upon the menopause experience.

2 New research is constantly being published about the risks and benefits of HRT. Studies exploring women's beliefs and use of HRT must therefore be located within the time that the data were collected and the current state of evidence at this time. This means that aggregating studies is problematic and drawing conclusions across time is difficult.

3 The menopause and HRT generate strong beliefs in researchers, clinicians and patients according to the need for any medical intervention, the dangers of HRT and the dangers of menopause-related disease. Interpreting research is therefore problematic as results and the ways in which results are presented may well reflect the beliefs of the people involved.

4 Research on the menopause and HRT illustrates the complex problem of risk analysis and risk communication because symptoms, side-effects and longer-term costs and benefits will have different meanings to all the parties involved. There is a tendency within the literature to attempt to find the state of 'truth' within all these risks and probabilities. Future psychological research could focus on how different risks are managed and communicated without attempting to synthesize them.

SUMMING UP

The menopause reflects the end of a woman's reproductive life and brings with it a range of symptoms and longer-term physical changes. Research has explored how women experience the menopause and suggests that it is considered a life transition which results in a range of psychological shifts and changes. However, the research also suggests that, although some of these changes may be directly related to the biological nature of the menopause, they are also created or exacerbated by the multitude of social changes that occur in a woman's life at the same time. The menopause is therefore best understood as a time where biological, social and psychological factors come together. Research has also explored how women choose to manage their menopause and the impact of HRT on menopausal symptoms. The results indicate that many women choose HRT primarily for symptom relief but that its effect on symptoms may not be as straightforward as once believed.

TO CONCLUDE

There are many areas of health that are specific to women. This chapter has explored three of these which were chosen because they seemed to have generated the most research and most closely reflect the interests of the health psychology community. Miscarriage, termination and the menopause are generally regarded as negative events that women often have to endure. The results from the studies described in this chapter indicate that, although these are difficult and often unpleasant times for women, many women report how they can also see the benefit in these experiences. In particular, miscarriage is sometimes seen as a pivotal point in a woman's life, enabling her to re-evaluate her past and future self; termination is often accompanied by feelings of relief and a return to normality; and the menopause introduces a new period of life and a sense of liberation. Furthermore, the research illustrates how women's experiences of these events are influenced by the mode of management as all can be managed either medically or in a more natural way.

QUESTIONS

1 To what extent are women's responses to miscarriage similar to those following bereavement?
2 Discuss the problems inherent in carrying out research into the experience of having an abortion.
3 To what extent is the experience of having an abortion influenced by the social context?
4 To what extent are women's experiences of the menopause a response to the biological changes that occur at this time?
5 How are women's experiences of their health problems influenced by the mode of management chosen?

FOR DISCUSSION

Consider how someone you know (your mother, friend, etc.) experienced the menopause. Reflect upon how this experience may have been affected by other factors that were changing at the same time.

ASSUMPTIONS IN HEALTH PSYCHOLOGY

1 *The mind–body split.* Research often assumes that the mind and the body are separate. Women's health issues illustrate how the physical changes caused by factors such as miscarriage, termination and the menopause have a direct influence upon the individual's psychological state. From this perspective the body influences the mind. It is also likely, however, that the actual physical changes themselves are also affected by the individual's psychology.

2 *Progression.* It is often assumed that research and technology result in improvements. In terms of women's health issues there have been many developments that have resulted in changes in how these issues are managed, such as the invention of HRT and the development of new procedures for the management of termination and miscarriage. Whether such developments are of benefit, however, is unclear as they often illustrate the issue of iatrogenesis: although they are new solutions, they can end up causing harm.

3 *Research as theory-generating.* Research aims to be objective and explore and generate ideas. Much research in the area of women's health is very contentious and touches upon highly politicized and ideological areas. The research is therefore likely to be open to researcher bias and the desired objectivity will be undermined by the researcher's own perspective.

FURTHER READING

Freeman, E.W. and Rickels, K. (1993) *Early Childbearing: Perspectives of Black Adolescents on Pregnancy, Abortion and Childbearing.* Thousand Oaks, CA: Sage.
This book is based upon the Penn study of black teenagers' experiences and provides detailed descriptions of their beliefs about pregnancy, abortion and childbearing. It also explores the longer-term impact of their decisions and behaviour and locates them within the literature. Although focusing on a very specific sample, the results resonate with the wider literature.

Lee, C. (1998) *Women's Health: Psychological and Social Perspectives.* London: Sage.
This book covers a wide range of issues relating to women's health not covered by the present chapter, including pre-menstrual syndrome, post-partum depression and fertility control. It therefore offers a useful background into the areas not addressed by this book.

Moulder, C. (1998) *Understanding Pregnancy Loss: Perspectives and Issues in Care.* London: Macmillan.
This is an excellent book that draws upon the experiences of women who have had either a miscarriage, termination or stillbirth and locates their experiences within the existing literature. It explores a range of factors including health care prior to admission, experiences of being in hospital, health professionals' views and care after discharge.

 Visit the website at www.openup.co.uk/ogden for additional resources on Chapter 16 to help you with your study, such as multiple choice questions, weblinks and a searchable online glossary.

17 Men's Health Issues

© Hakan Caglav/iStock

CHAPTER OVERVIEW

Research in the past has been criticized for ignoring women and treating men as the norm or the standard against which health and illness can be judged. In response to the protestations of feminism, research has become increasingly 'gendered' and primarily this has led to a proliferation of research on women's health (see Chapter 16). For some, however, the pendulum has swung too far and there has recently been a call for more work on men's health issues. This chapter addresses some of the key issues relating to men's health, beginning with some basic statistics which suggest that health and illness differ between men and women. Next the chapter explores possible explanations for this and describes men's health behaviour, their risk-taking behaviours and their help-seeking behaviours. The chapter then addresses recent theories which have analysed why men behave in different ways to women with a focus on health beliefs, social norms of masculinity and emotional expression. Finally, the chapter addresses three case examples which highlight many of the key issues for men's health: prostate cancer, suicide and coronary heart disease (CHD).

GENDER DIFFERENCES IN HEALTH AND ILLNESS

Chapter 2 described health inequalities and highlighted the ways in which health and illness vary across a number of domains, including gender. For example Figures 2.4 and 2.7–12 illustrated gender differences in lung cancer, obesity, diabetes, a wide range of illnesses and a wide range of physical symptoms. In general, we know the following about the ways in which men and women differ (see Lee and Glynn Owens 2002 for a comprehensive review):

- Worldwide, men live three years less than women.
- This varies across regions.
- In Eastern Europe men live on average 11 years less than women.
- In the UK men live on average 4 years less than women; 6 years less in the USA.
- In Australia indigenous men live on average 23 years less than non-indigenous women and 19 years less than non-indigenous men.
- In Afghanistan men live on average 1 year longer than women.
- Men are twice as likely to develop and die from the 10 most common cancers which affect both men and women.
- Although CHD is a leading cause of death for both men and women, men die younger from this illness than women.
- Of those who die from a heart attack in the USA under the age of 65, nearly 75 per cent are men.

There are therefore consistent differences between men and women, with men dying younger than women worldwide and being more likely to develop and die from the leading causes of death. Such gender differences have been understood in terms of the role of biological factors such as oestrogen, which improves lipid profiles and can protect against cardiovascular disease, and the general robustness of females illustrated by the higher neonatal death rate of male babies compared to females. Furthermore, in evolutionary terms women may need to be stronger than men in order to survive childbirth and whereas maternal mortality reduced women's life expectancy in the past, women have now overtaken men because the risk of dying during labour is much reduced. However, these biological differences cannot be the complete picture as the gap between men and

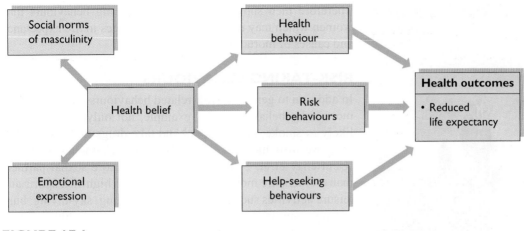

FIGURE 17.1

Understanding men's health

women's life expectancy is not only changing over time but also shows great variation across geographical location, suggesting a strong role for psychological and social factors. Over the past few years there have been several extremely thorough and well-researched reviews of the research on men's health which have identified a number of key areas as explanations for gender differences (see Courtenay et al. 2002; Lee and Glynn Owens 2002). This chapter draws upon these reviews to explore behaviour in men's health, health beliefs, social norms and emotional expression in explaining gender differences in health and behaviour. The role of these variables is shown in Figure 17.1.

THE ROLE OF BEHAVIOUR IN MEN'S HEALTH

So why do men die earlier than women? And why are they more likely to die once they become ill? Research points to a key role for behaviour in terms of health behaviours, risky behaviours and help-seeking behaviours.

HEALTH BEHAVIOURS

This book has extensively described the role of health behaviours in health and illness. For example, Chapters 3–8 described behaviours such as smoking, alcohol use, diet, exercise and safe sex and how these can be predicted by beliefs and changed using a number of different interventions. Furthermore, Chapter 12 illustrated how stress may trigger unhealthy behaviours which in turn cause disease and Chapters 14 and 15 illustrated the role of behaviour in chronic illness. Much research indicates that men are often more likely to carry out unhealthy behaviours than women. For example, Courtenay et al. (2002) carried out a survey of 1,816 students from the USA and concluded that men showed more risky unhealthy behaviours than women in terms of their diet and substance use. In particular, men eat more meat, fat and salt and less fibre and fruit and vegetables than women and are more likely to smoke and show higher levels of alcohol and drug use. Similar results have also been found from surveys in Germany, Austria and Scotland across a range of age groups (Uitenbroek et al. 1996; Stronegger et al. 1997; Reime et al. 2000). Men also show less motivation to engage in lifestyle changes than women and whereas older men believe it is 'too late' to change, younger men believe that they don't need to change 'yet' (Gabhainn et al. 1999). In addition, following divorce or widowhood, men show a greater deterioration in their diet, use of alcohol and drugs than women (Byrne et al. 1999). In fact, the only health-related behaviour that men consistently perform more than women is physical activity (e.g. Dubbert and Martin 1988).

Physical exercise – a positive part of men's health behaviour

Therefore men show fewer health-promoting behaviours than women which may explain gender differences in life expectancy and causes of mortality.

RISK-TAKING BEHAVIOURS

In addition to general health-related behaviours, men also show more risky behaviours. For example, not only are they more likely to smoke, drink alcohol and take drugs than women but they are also more likely to do these behaviours to excess (Courtenay et al. 2002). Men also have more sexual partners than women, are more likely to take part in high-risk sports and leisure activities such as rugby, snowboarding, sky-diving, bungee-jumping and rally driving (Courtenay et al. 2002). These risky behaviours are reflected in higher rates of accidental injury and death among men. For example, research shows the following:

- An Australian study showed that boys are twice as likely to die in play-related accidents (Lam et al. 1999).
- A US study showed boys are twice as likely to die or be injured from falling out of a window (Stone et al. 2000).
- In Argentina boys are more likely to suffer from head injuries (Murgio et al. 1999).
- The death rate for men is higher than women for motor vehicle accidents and drowning (Courtenay 2002).
- The large majority of all fatal and non-fatal injuries recorded in hospitals are for men (Watson and Ozanne-Smith 2000).
- Men are four times more likely than women to fracture their clavicle (e.g. from sporting accidents) and sustain spinal cord injuries (e.g. from diving) than women (Van Asbeck et al. 2000).
- Many of these injuries are sustained after heavy drinking (Kolakowsky-Hayner et al. 1999).

Men therefore engage in more risky behaviours than women and are also more likely to be injured or die as a result. Interestingly, the data also indicate that in the main accidental injury or death is directly related to the level of exposure to the high-risk activity. This means that more men die from injuries because they engage in more activities that expose them to risk. There are two good examples of this. First, research shows that men are more likely to die from accidental injury while employed in the armed forces. However, although the armed forces are overwhelmingly men, when this is accounted for, women in the army are more likely to be injured than men (Snedecor et al. 2000). Likewise, although overall men have more motor vehicle accidents, accidents are best predicted by being younger, heavy drinking and not wearing a seatbelt than by gender per se (Bell et al. 2000). Accordingly, men are more likely to be injured or die from their injuries than women because they are more likely to behave in risky ways.

Men engage in more high-risk activities than women

SOURCE: © carlofranco/iStock

TABLE 17.1 WHY MEN MIGHT NOT SEEK HELP: THE ROLE OF PSYCHOLOGICAL PROCESSES

	Help-seeking	**Delay**
Symptom perception	I have a pain in my stomach	I am too busy to think about myself
Illness cognitions	This pain could be serious	I will try to ignore it until it goes away
Social triggers	My friends tell me that this pain isn't normal	My colleagues tell me to stop making a fuss
Costs and benefits of seeing the doctor	My doctor is lovely. She will be really understanding. It will be nice to have a chat	I feel embarrassed about seeing a doctor/I should be able to manage this on my own/I don't want someone I don't know interfering
Help-seeking	I will see the doctor after I have dropped the kids at school	I don't have a doctor/I am too busy at work/I work a long way from my doctor

HELP-SEEKING BEHAVIOURS

One core component of being healthy and staying well is the appropriate use of health care services. Chapter 10 described a number of factors involved in the use of health care including help-seeking behaviour and screening which bring individuals into contact with health care professionals. Research indicates that in general men use health care services less than women and show greater delay in seeking help and identifying symptoms (e.g. Gijsbers van Wijk et al. 1999; Schappert 1999). Further, they are less likely to have seen their general practitioner (GP) in the past 12 months, have fewer hospital admissions and are less likely to have a screening test or a general health check (DH 2001; Bayram et al. 2003; National Statistics Online 2006; Eurostat 2007). Importantly, these differences persist even when reproductive and sex-specific conditions are accounted for but start to diminish when a health problem is serious (Courtenay 2000a, 2000b). A similar pattern can also be seen for mental health problems with only third of all clients seeking psychological support being men and with men delaying help-seeking until their problems are more serious and entrenched (Good et al. 1989). Chapter 10 described a series of psychological processes that help to explain help-seeking behaviour and why at times people either go to their doctor when they have nothing wrong with them or delay seeking help when they have a serious problem. These processes are *symptom perception, illness cognitions, social triggers* and the *perceived costs and benefits of going to the doctor* and can be used to explain why men use health care less than women (see Table 17.1).

EXPLAINING MEN'S HEALTH-RELATED BEHAVIOURS AND ILLNESS PROFILES

So why do men behave in ways that are damaging to their health? Research highlights the role of the following factors.

HEALTH BELIEFS

Chapter 3 described the ways in which health beliefs predict health behaviours such as smoking, diet, exercise and alcohol use. Similarly, Chapter 10 explored the factors involved in help-seeking, screening and adherence to medication. Research indicates that men may have different beliefs about their health which in turn influence their behaviours.

Risk Perception

In general, men appear to underestimate their risk for illness or injury compared to women. For example, research indicates the following:

- Men of all ages perceive that they are less at risk from smoking, drug or alcohol use (e.g. Kauffman et al. 1997; Gustafson 1998).
- Men perceive that they are less at risk of skin cancer and rate the risks of sun exposure as less than women (e.g. Flynn et al. 1994).
- Even though men are more likely to have HIV/AIDs than women, they perceive that they are less at risk of contracting the HIV virus than women rate their own risk (Flynn et al. 1994).
- Men also rate the risks of dangerous driving as less than women (Savage 1993).

Perceived Control

The research into perceptions of control is less clear-cut although some studies indicate that men believe that they have less control over their health than women (Furnham and Kirkclady 1997). Given the consistent link between perceived control and health behaviours (see Chapter 3), this may account for why men behave in less healthy ways than women.

Perceived Health Status

Ironically, although men die younger than women and tend to seek help at a later stage of disease, research indicates that men rate their subjective health status as higher than women rate theirs (Ross and Bird 1994). In addition, men also rate their behaviours as healthier than their peers whereas women tend to see their own behaviour as worse or comparable to those around them (Rakowski 1986). This suggests a mismatch between 'objective' and 'subjective' assessments of health which may relate to symptom perception and illness cognitions, as discussed above. Interestingly, one study compared self-reported seatbelt-wearing with observed seatbelt-wearing and concluded that more men were likely to say they always wore a seatbelt (when they didn't) compared to women – perceptions of health and behaviour may not always map onto 'real' health and behaviour.

Readiness to Change Behaviour

Chapter 3 described the stages of change (SOC) model which emphasizes behaviour change as progressing through a series of discrete stages. At times research using this approach has explored gender differences and illustrates that men are less likely to be contemplating changing their behaviour, less likely to be maintaining any healthy behaviour changes and more likely to deny that their behaviours are problematic (e.g. Leforge et al. 1999; Weinstock et al. 2000). Men therefore show a profile of health beliefs which may contribute to behaving in less healthy ways and in turn having shorter life expectancy than women.

Social Norms of Masculinity

Within men's health research there has been an increasing interest in the impact of social norms of masculinity on the ways in which men behave and how this might impact upon their health (see Courtenay 2000; Lee and Glynn Owens 2002; Robertson 2007; Gough and Robertson 2010 for comprehensive debates).

Central to this literature is the notion of 'hegemonic masculinity' which reflects dominant ideals of masculinity within any given context (Carrigan et al. 1985). From this perspective hegemonic masculinity represents that version of masculinity which has become a 'male script', illustrating and describing the most acceptable way for men to think, feel and behave (Lohan 2010). In contemporary society concern for health is considered a feminine characteristic while 'men are positioned as naturally "strong", resistant to disease, unresponsive to pain and physical distress and unconcerned with minor symptoms' (Lee and Glynn Owens 2002). Furthermore, society encourages men to engage in stereotypically male behaviour to define themselves as 'not female' and

What is your idea of masculinity?
SOURCE: Studio/Dreamstime

the ways in which they do this often involve unhealthy behaviours. From this perspective hegemonic masculinity promotes a version of being male which encourages beliefs and behaviours which are ultimately damaging to health and longevity. Research indicates that more traditional beliefs about masculinity in men have been shown to be associated with:

- Health behaviours including smoking, diet, alcohol and drug use, and sexual behaviour (e.g. Eisler et al. 1988).
- Higher stress reactivity following stressors (see Chapter 11 for discussion).
- Slower help-seeking when ill (O'Neil et al. 1995).
- Poorer adherence to medication and recommended lifestyle changes following a diagnosis of heart disease (Helgeson 1994).

Thus, hegemonic masculinity encourages men to engage in unhealthy behaviours and they are also slower to seek help when ill. In line with this, some behaviour change interventions have been based upon the assumed relationship between hegemonic masculinity and health behaviours. For example, interventions have targeted men at their place of work, have been offered during work-friendly hours and have been made available at places occupied by men (e.g. Watson 2000; McKinlay 2005). In addition, health-related messages have been framed in 'male friendly' language with unhealthy bodies being described as cars which need tuning (Doyal 2001b). To date such initiatives have not been overly effective which has raised three questions about the link between hegemonic masculinity and men's health. First, it has been argued that it is not only men themselves that limit their help-seeking behaviour; health professionals' gendered beliefs may also be a barrier to men who want to seek help (Robertson and Williamson 2005; Hale et al. 2010; see **Focus on Research 17.1**). Second, it has been argued that although social norms of masculinity may well impact upon men's health, men are not a homogenous group and not all men adhere to the same male script of how they should be (Robertson 2007). This has led to a call for understanding the plurality of masculinity and a recognition that the stereotype of maleness is not a case of 'one size fits all'. Finally, it has been argued that masculinity is not all bad and that there are some benefits to being male. In particular, the masculine traits of being independent, decisive and assertive may help men cope with cancer and chronic illness (Charmaz 1995; Gordon 1995).

FOCUS ON RESEARCH 17.1: MEN'S HELP-SEEKING BEHAVIOUR

Why do men not seek help when they are ill? The impact of the GP (Hale, et al. 2010).

BACKGROUND

Research indicates that men are slower to seek help for their symptoms which can result in problems remaining undiagnosed and presentation being delayed to a point whereby illnesses have become untreatable. Some research has explored the reasons for this phenomenon and has highlighted the role of men's health beliefs and their notion that seeking help is a sign of weakness. It is possible that men also don't seek help due to the beliefs of health care providers which may act as a deterrent for men with symptoms. This qualitative study explored the beliefs of male GPs about men who seek help.

METHODOLOGY

Sample

Ten male GPs ranging in age from 35 to 53 took part in the study. A snowball sampling method was used with the earlier GPs providing details of other GPs to contact. The GPs were from the North of England from both urban and suburban practices.

Interview Schedule

The interview consisted of open-ended questions concerned with men's health, men's pattern of self-referral and men's use of health care services. Interviews lasted between 30 and 40 minutes and were audio-recorded and transcribed verbatim.

Data Analysis

The data were analysed using Interpretative Phenomenological Analysis (IPA – Smith 1996).

RESULTS

Analysis revealed three superordinate themes relating to 'managing demand', 'men in consultation' and 'men first, doctors second'. The authors argued that all the themes illustrated the impact of social norms of masculinity.

1 *Managing demand.* The GPs spoke extensively about their workload and how many younger patients were very demanding, consulting over what were seen as 'trivial things' and making 'irresponsible demands'. This was explained in terms of a change in people's perception of the role of the GP which was managed by distancing themselves from patients and delegating to nurses. Within this context men who didn't attend were seen as a relief and as one GP said, 'I think they all come, they all come all the time! I wish I did have a group that didn't come' (p. 705).

2 *Men in consultation.* The GPs described men's help-seeking patterns and how their lack of contact with health care services was seen as the need to be 'brave and manly' and 'reluctant to admit weakness'. Within this context those who did attend their GP were seen as being at the extremes: as having a 'real health problem' or 'hypochondriacal'. Some were described as being brought in by their wives, 'very similar to a child consultation sometimes', while some avoided coming in until their illness had progressed with 'infections heading off towards pneumonia'. The authors concluded that male GPs are ambivalent about men who seek help unless they consult with what is considered a 'legitimate' problem.

3 ***Men first, doctors second.*** The authors drew strong comparisons between the male patients and the ways in which the male doctors described their own health and self-management. In particular, despite recommending health checks for their patients, the GPs described avoiding their own GPs and delaying help-seeking in the same way as some of their more stoical male patients.

CONCLUSION

Overall, the authors concluded from their study that due to their heavy workload GPs are sometimes relieved that men don't seek help as often as women. Further, they argue that GPs can be quite critical of the male patients who do attend and see them as childlike or hypochondriacal unless they have a 'real' problem that is legitimate. The authors argue that such negative attitudes from GPs may act as a barrier for men to seek help if they feel they will be judged by their doctor. The results from this study therefore provide a broader context for men's help-seeking behaviour and illustrate that the decision whether or not to visit the doctor is not only influenced the patient's beliefs but also by those of the health professional.

Emotional Expression

One central component to current social norms of masculinity is the focus on men not sharing their emotions or asking for help when upset (Petersen 1998). Lupton (1998) has also argued that men who express their emotions are considered weak, effeminate and possibly gay, and that they are expected to show mastery and control over their feelings. To reflect this, research indicates that men are less likely to cry than women and overall report less fear and emotional distress (Courtenay et al. 2002). Furthermore, men express fewer negative internally focused emotions such as grief and fewer positive externally focused emotions such as tenderness, than do women (Brody 1999; Lee and Glynn Owens 2002). Such lowered levels of emotional expression have implications for health and behaviour. For example, Chapter 12 described how emotional expression through writing or talk relates to a wide range of health outcomes including mood, immune functioning and return to work (see Chapter 12 for discussion). Similarly, research also describes how repressive coping and denial may be detrimental to one's health status (Myers 2000; Solano et al. 2001). The one exception in terms of emotional expression is anger, and research indicates that men express more anger and hostility than women (Brody 1999). In line with research on type behaviour described in Chapter 12 the expression of negative emotions may be linked to cardiovascular disease which is the leading cause of death in men (Rosenman 1978). Men also report higher thresholds for and greater tolerance of pain (Unruh et al.1999). This may reflect biological factors such as hormones which may influence pain perception. It may, however, also reflect a determination not to acknowledge pain in order to present a more masculine image to the world. In line with this, men have been shown to express less pain in front of female compared to male health professionals (Puntillo and Weiss 1994). Accordingly the perception of pain may be influenced by issues relating to identity ('I am not the kind of person to feel pain'). It may also relate to the processes of symptom perception ('I am too busy to think about my pain') and illness cognitions ('This pain is nothing and will go away'), which were discussed earlier (see Chapter 13 for a discussion of pain perception).

Men in general are therefore less emotionally expressive than women which may relate to their health behaviours, help-seeking and experience of illness.The data in this area, however, are not always consistent and research indicates that not all men conform to this stereotypical presentation of their ways of coping with their lives. For example, Lucas and Gohm (2000) collated data from several large-scale surveys from different countries and concluded that although there was a tendency for men to be less expressive of some negative emotions, this certainly wasn't consistent for all men and for all emotions. Accordingly, in line with the call to consider the plurality of

```
┌─────────────────────────────────────────────────────────────┐
```
BOX 17.1 Some Problems with ... Men's Health Research

Below are some problems with research in this area that you may wish to consider:

1 Research into men's health often makes very clear distinctions between men and women, emphasizing how different they are. This can result in a highly stereotypical version of gender differences and emphasizes differences rather than similarities. It is important to remember that not all men behave like 'men' and not all women behave like 'women', and that there is much variability in the ways in which both men and women think and act.

2 Over the past few years there has been a debate about the notion of *cisgenderism* – the prejudicial belief that there are only two genders (i.e. men and women). In line with this, some researchers have called for an understanding of a multitude of different genders and have highlighted many different cultures in which a binary version of gender doesn't exist. The focus on men's and women's health as presented in this book falls into the camp of cisgenderism as it reinforces the belief that the world can be broken down into only two genders.

3 At the beginning of the twentieth century men in general lived longer than women. Then this turned around. Nowadays, however, the gap between men's and women's life expectancy is getting smaller year on year. Soon we may all be equal or men may start living longer than women again. Any analysis of men's (and women's) health needs to take this historical perspective into account.

masculinity, it would seem that patterns of emotional inexpression are more varied than they are sometimes presented as being.

In sum, research indicates consistent gender differences for life expectancy and causes of morbidity and mortality and that much of this difference can be attributed to men's behaviour, with men being more likely to engage in unhealthy and risky behaviours and less likely to perform health-protective or help-seeking behaviours. From this perspective differences in life expectancy, mortality and health-related behaviours can be seen as 'gendered' as they reflect the ways in which men behave within the confines of what is expected. This will now be explored in the context of three case examples: prostate cancer, suicide and CHD.

CASE EXAMPLES: HOW BEING MALE CAN IMPACT UPON HEALTH

CASE 1: PROSTATE CANCER

Prostate cancer is now the most common form of male cancer and accounts for 23 per cent of all new male cancer diagnoses (Cancer Research UK 2006). There has been a significant increase in the prevalence of prostate cancer since the 1980s and whereas it used to be said that 'men die with it not of it' as many elderly men have prostate cancer but die from another cause, this is now changing, with more younger men both being diagnosed with and dying from this disease (Broom 2004). Prostate cancer illustrates many of the issues relating to men's health in the following ways.

Help-Seeking

The most common symptoms of prostate cancer are dribbling after urination, a frequent need to urinate, urination during the night and a feeling that the bladder is never empty. Although these symptoms are intrusive and upsetting, they are not always qualitatively different from normal urination behaviour which means that they can be normalized or ignored. Research indicates that many men choose to manage their symptoms on their own and delay seeking help. Hale et al. (2007) carried out a qualitative study of men's help-seeking behaviour for prostate symptoms and concluded that the men tended to ignore their symptoms or put them down to age or general 'wear and tear'. They also described how the men didn't want to inconvenience the doctor and as one participant said: 'I'm not the sort of person who would necessarily bother a GP or run to a GP, you know, sort of straight away.' This lack of help-seeking resulted from embarrassment and a desire not to trouble anyone else with their problems due to a need to live up to traditional images of masculinity. This in turn led to an absence of any social messages from others about their condition.

Broom (2010) similarly carried out a study on men in Australia and illustrated how men wanted to manage their health. Partcicipants' responses included, 'I think it's part of the male image thing' and 'I'm not going to let anyone else know I've got the problem and I'm going to figure it out myself.' Eventual help-seeking was often triggered by the appearance of blood in the urine or pain which was seen as a more legitimate symptom that required formal help. This explains why many men present late with their symptoms when the disease has already progressed.

Uptake of Tests

Once deciding to seek help a man with prostate symptoms will need to undergo tests to determine whether the problem is cancer, prostate disease or simply a normal variation of urination. These tests are painful, intrusive and embarrassing and involve inserting a probe either up the man's anus and/or into the end of the penis. Broom (2010) concluded from his qualitative study of men at varying stages of prostate diagnosis and treatment that these intrusive procedures impacted 'upon the participants' perceptions of being men' (p. 189) and were associated with feelings of 'shame', 'humiliation' and 'embarrassment'. The anticipation of such tests therefore be a barrier to seeking help, exacerbating problems of delayed help-seeking. As one man said, 'My brother said he is not going to let anyone stick anything up his backside. That's an issue for a lot of people' (Broom 2010: 186–7).

Treatment

The most common treatments for prostate cancer are radical prostatectomy and radiation treatments which are painful and can result in serious and unpleasant side-effects such as incontinence and impotence. Although studies indicate that most men are prepared to trade potency for survival (Kunkel et al. 2000), Broom (2010) argued that concerns about masculinity were central both to a patient's decision about choice of treatment and their adaptation after treatment. For some men in Broom's study these concerns resulted in their choosing to have alternative treatments as a means to maintain their sense of masculinity. As one man said: 'My sexual performance is very important even to an older bloke like me . . . if you take that away from the male, you change the male . . . you change him entirely' (2010: 194). Others had the treatment but found it hard to adjust to their diminished sex lives. One man said: 'Masculinity is an incredibly important thing . . . my wife and I had reached a stage in our lives where sex had become really important . . . I was 55, my boys were off at uni and we had some time to ourselves . . . we've never got that back' (2010: 193).

Prostate cancer is increasingly common and illustrates many of the issues relating to men's health. In particular, many men delay seeking help by normalizing their symptoms and not talking to others about their problem. Furthermore, the tests and treatments are embarrassing, impacting directly on aspects of masculinity which may further exacerbate problems with delay and also influence men's choice of intervention.

CASE 2: SUICIDE

There are two common sayings about gender and health. The first is 'women get ill but men die younger' and the second is 'women get depressed but men commit suicide'. Research shows that the rates of suicide are higher in men than women across all age groups with child, adolescent and adult males being four times more likely to commit suicide than females of comparable age in most western societies (Taylor et al. 1998; Lee et al. 1999). In contrast, rates of suicide are equal in Hong Kong for men and women and in China the rates are slightly lower for men (Yip et al. 2000). Suicide in men illustrates some of the factors described earlier in this chapter in terms of health, risky and help-seeking behaviours, emotional expression and social norms of masculinity. For example, the evidence shows the following:

- Men who are marginalized from mainstream society are more at risk of suicide (e.g. gay, migrant, or indigenous populations) (Lee et al. 1999). Such marginalization seems to affect men more than women, perhaps because they have fewer social resources to draw upon.

- Suicide attempts and actual suicide are strongly associated with other unhealthy and risky behaviours such as alcohol and drug use, smoking and fighting (Woods et al. 1997). Men show more of all these behaviours.

- Men tend to use more immediate and successful forms of suicide such as shooting (rather than poisoning) which are less likely to be discovered and prevented. It has been argued that failed suicide is seen as weak and effeminate (Canetto 1997).

- Men respond more negatively to divorce or bereavement than women and are more likely to commit suicide (Kposowa 2000). This may reflect their lower levels of emotional expression and help-seeking.

- Although more women are diagnosed with depression, many men are depressed but delay seeking help. This may result in suicide as their emotional needs are not acknowledged or met (Lee and Glynn Owens 2002).

Men are therefore more likely to commit suicide than women. This seems to reflect the factors discussed in this chapter in terms of their health and risky behaviours, levels of emotional expression and social norms of masculinity.

CASE 3: CHD

About half of all male deaths are caused by CHD across Europe and in 2008 in the UK CHD was responsible for 35 per cent of deaths in men and 34 per cent of deaths in women (Allender et al. 2008a). Worldwide it is estimated that 17 million people die from CHD each year with the highest death rates being in China, India and Russia. In middle age, the death rate is up to five times higher for men than for women but this evens out in old age (see Chapter 15 for a detailed discussion of CHD in terms of prevalence, causes and consequences). CHD takes the form of angina, heart attack or sudden death and highlights many of the issues central to understanding men's health as follows:

- Unhealthy behaviours such as poor diet and smoking are key causes of CHD. Men are more likely to show these behaviours than women (see Chapters 4 and 5).

- Heart attack can be treated more effectively the earlier it is diagnosed. Men are more likely to delay help-seeking for symptoms of heart attack such as chest pain (see Chapters 9, 10 and 15).

- Following a heart attack, patients will be offered cardiac rehabilitation which encourages behaviour changes and often offers cognitive behavioural therapy (CBT) to change health-related cognitions. Men are less likely to attend rehabilitation than women (see Chapter 15).

- CHD is linked to stress, including chronic stressors such as work. Men are more likely to work full time, have a poorer work–life balance and are more likely to ruminate after work than women. This may be linked to the onset of their CHD (see Chapters 11 and 12).

- Men, however, are more physically active than women which is protective of CHD (see Chapter 6).

CHD is therefore a common cause of death in men and is linked to an unhealthy lifestyle, particularly poor diet and smoking. Men often have poorer lifestyles. Furthermore, recovery can be facilitated through early help-seeking, attending a rehabilitation programme and subsequent behaviour change. Men, however, may be less likely to seek help either before or after they have had a heart attack. All these aspects of CHD can be seen to be gendered which may help to explain gender differences in life expectancy and causes of mortality.

TO CONCLUDE

Research indicates that men have a shorter life expectancy than women and when they become ill, they are more likely to die sooner. This chapter has explored possible causes for these gender differences with a focus on health, risk and help-seeking behaviours, health beliefs, social norms of masculinity and emotional expression. From the literature described it can be argued that men's well-being is undermined by their behaviour which is influenced by a male script encouraging them to neglect their health in order to conform to a dominant sense of what it is to be male. The chapter has illustrated these processes with a focus on three case examples which highlight the interrelationship between behaviour, individual beliefs and those held by society as a whole.

QUESTIONS

1 In what ways is men's health worse than women's?
2 How might behaviour influence men's health status?
3 Discuss the role of health beliefs in men's health behaviours.
4 Where might men's beliefs about their health come from?
5 Consider the evidence that men are less emotionally expressive than women.
6 To what extent do men conform to hegemonic masculinity?

FOR DISCUSSION

Talk to a male friend about their health beliefs and behaviour. Consider to what extent they are (or are not) conforming to social norms of masculinity.

ASSUMPTIONS IN HEALTH PSYCHOLOGY

The research into men's health highlights some of the assumptions in health psychology:

1 *The role of behaviour in illness.* Throughout the twentieth century there was an increasing emphasis on behavioural factors in health and illness. Research has examined men's health from the same perspective

and evaluated the role of behaviours such as diet and smoking. However, perhaps not all problems are products of behaviour.

2 ***Treatment as beneficial.*** In research on men's health it is assumed that early help-seeking and treatment are beneficial and that men should be encouraged to identify their symptoms and seek help at an early stage. Although this may be the case for some illnesses, it is not the case for all. Focusing on symptoms can cause health anxiety, frequent and unnecessary visits to the GP, unnecessary and potentially dangerous diagnostic tests and over-medicalization, resulting in the inappropriate prescribing and use of drugs. Furthermore, if everyone went to the doctor every time they noticed a change in their bodies, the health service would be flooded and unable to function effectively.

3 ***Dividing up the soup.*** Psychological research divides the world up into chunks so that it can then understand the relationship between these chunks but in doing so it perpetuates the belief that these chunks really are separate. The focus on men's health (and women's health) helps to create the 'chunk' called gender and highlights the ways in which men and women are different. But this is not a benign process because simply by describing men and women as different, it encourages the belief that gender differences are true and worthy of study.

FURTHER READING

Courtenay, W.H. (2000) Constructions of masculinity and their influence on men's well being: a theory of gender and health, *Social Science and Medicine*, 50(10): 1385–401.
Will Courtenay has written extensively on male health issues. This is one of his more theoretical papers which provides an interesting discussion on masculinity and health. Other papers by him are also useful and can be found in the reference list at the end of this book.

Gough, B. and Robertson, S. (eds) (2010) *Men, Masculinities and Health: Critical Perspectives.* Basingstoke: Palgrave Macmillan.
This is an edited collection of an interesting series of studies which explore men's health issues such as fatherhood, body image and chest pain. The study on prostate cancer by Broom that I cite in this chapter is from this book. The book takes a critical perspective and has an excellent introductory chapter outlining the theoretical stance being used.

Lee, C. and Glynn Owens, R. (2002) *The Psychology of Men's Health.* Maidenhead: Open University Press.
This is an excellent text which clearly describes a range of aspects of men's health and locates them within a sense of gender and notions of masculinity.

Robertson, S. (2007) *Understanding Men and Health: Masculinities, Identity and Well-being.* Maidenhead: Open University Press.
This is a very thorough book that describes in depth many of the theoretical issues outlined in this chapter such as identity and hegemonic masculinity. It draws upon qualitative data and emphasizes the diversity of the male experience.

 Visit the website at www.openup.co.uk/ogden for additional resources on Chapter 17 to help you with your study, such as multiple choice questions, weblinks and a searchable online glossary.

18 Measuring Health Status: From Mortality Rates to Quality of Life

© Oleg Kozlov/iStock

CHAPTER OVERVIEW

This chapter examines the different ways in which health status has been measured from mortality rates to quality of life. In addition, it describes the ways in which quality of life has been used in research both in terms of the factors that predict quality of life (quality of life as an outcome variable) and the association between quality of life and longevity (quality of life as a predictor). Finally, it describes the notion of a response shift and the ways in which a person's evaluation of their quality of life changes over the course of an illness.

MORTALITY RATES

At its most basic, a measure of health status takes the form of a very crude mortality rate, which is calculated by simply counting the number of deaths in one year compared with either previous or subsequent years. The question asked is, 'Has the number of people who have died this year gone up, gone down or stayed the same?' An increase in mortality rate can be seen as a decrease in health status and a decrease as an increase in health status. This approach, however, requires a denominator: a measure of who is at risk. The next most basic form of mortality rate therefore includes a denominator reflecting the size of the population being studied. Such a measure allows for comparisons to be made between different populations: more people may die in a given year in London when compared with Bournemouth, but London is simply bigger. In order to provide any meaningful measure of health status, mortality rates are corrected for age (Bournemouth has an older population and therefore we would predict that more people would die each year) and sex (men generally die younger than women and this needs to be taken into account). Furthermore, mortality rates can be produced to be either age specific, such as infant mortality rates, or illness specific, such as sudden death rates. As long as the population being studied is accurately specified, corrected and specific, mortality rates provide an easily available and simple measure: death is a good reliable outcome.

MORBIDITY RATES

Laboratory and clinical researchers and epidemiologists may accept mortality rates as the perfect measure of health status. However, the juxtaposition of social scientists to the medical world has challenged this position to raise the now seemingly obvious question, 'Is health really only the absence of death?' In response to this, there has been an increasing focus upon morbidity. However, in line with the emphasis upon simplicity inherent within the focus on mortality rates, many morbidity measures still use methods of counting and recording. For example, the expensive and time-consuming production of morbidity prevalence rates involves large surveys of 'caseness' to simply count how many people within a given population suffer from a particular problem. Likewise, sickness absence rates simply count days lost due to illness and caseload assessments count the number of people who visit their general practitioner (GP) or hospital within a given time frame. Such morbidity rates provide details at the level of the population in general. However, morbidity is also measured for each individual using measures of functioning.

MEASURES OF FUNCTIONING

Measures of functioning ask the question, 'To what extent can you do the following tasks?' and are generally called activity of daily living scales (ADLs). For example, Katz et al. (1970) designed the

Index of Activities of Daily Living to assess levels of functioning in the elderly. This was developed for the therapist and/or carer to complete and asked the rater to evaluate the individual on a range of dimensions including bathing, dressing, continence and feeding. ADLs have also been developed for individuals themselves to complete and include questions such as, 'Do you or would you have any difficulty: washing down/cutting toenails/running to catch a bus/going up/down stairs?' Measures of functioning can either be administered on their own or as part of a more complex assessment involving measures of subjective health status.

SUBJECTIVE HEALTH STATUS

Over recent years, measures of health status have increasingly opted for measures of subjective health status, which all have one thing in common: they ask the individuals themselves to rate their health. Some of these are referred to as subjective health measures, while others are referred to as either quality of life scales or health-related quality of life scales. Research has also addressed other related outcome variables such as benefit-finding, post-traumatic growth, adjustment and meaning-making which all reflect the ways in which an illness impacts upon an individual's life (see Chapter 9). However, the literature in the area of subjective health status and quality of life is plagued by two main questions: 'What is quality of life?' and 'How should it be measured?'

WHAT IS QUALITY OF LIFE?

Reports of a Medline search on the term 'quality of life' indicate a surge in its use from 40 citations (1966–74), to 1,907 citations (1981–85), to 5,078 citations (1986–90) (Albrecht 1994). Quality of life is obviously in vogue. However, to date there exists no consensus as to what it actually *is*. For example, it has been defined as 'the value assigned to duration of life as modified by the impairments, functional states, perceptions and social opportunities that are influenced by disease, injury, treatment or policy' (Patrick and Ericson 1993), 'a personal statement of the positivity or negativity of attributes that characterise one's life' (Grant et al. 1990) and by the World Health Organization (WHO) as 'a broad ranging concept affected in a complex way by the person's physical health, psychological state, level of independence, social relationships and their relationship to the salient features in their environment' (WHOQoL Group 1993). Further, while some researchers treat the concepts of quality of life as interchangeable, others argue that they are separate (Bradley 2001).

Such problems with definition have resulted in a range of ways of operationalizing quality of life. For example, following the discussions about an acceptable definition of quality of life, the European Organization for Research on Treatment of Cancer operationalized quality of life in terms of 'functional status, cancer and treatment specific symptoms, psychological distress, social interaction, financial/economic impact, perceived health status and overall quality of life' (Aaronson et al. 1993). In line with this, their measure consisted of items that reflected these different dimensions. Likewise, the researchers who worked on the Rand Corporation health batteries operationalized quality of life in terms of 'physical functioning, social functioning, role limitations due to physical problems, role limitations due to emotional problems, mental health, energy/vitality, pain and general health perception', which formed the basic dimensions of their scale (e.g. Stewart and Ware 1992). Furthermore, Fallowfield (1990) defined the four main dimensions of quality of life as psychological (mood, emotional distress, adjustment to illness), social (relationships, social and leisure activities), occupational (paid and unpaid work) and physical (mobility, pain, sleep and appetite).

CREATING A CONCEPTUAL FRAMEWORK

In response to the problems of defining quality of life, researchers have recently attempted to create a clearer conceptual framework for this construct. In particular, they have divided quality of life measures either according to who devises the measure or in terms of whether the measure is considered objective or subjective.

Who Devises the Measure?

Browne et al. (1997) differentiated between the standard needs approach and the psychological processes perspective. The first of these is described as being based on the assumption that 'a consensus about what constitutes a good or poor quality of life exists or at least can be discovered through investigation' (Browne et al. 1997: 738). In addition, the standard needs approach assumes that needs rather than wants are central to quality of life and that these needs are common to all, including the researchers. In contrast, the psychological processes approach considers quality of life to be 'constructed from individual evaluations of personally salient aspects of life' (Browne et al. 1997: 737). Therefore Browne et al. conceptualized measures of quality of life as being devised either by researchers or by the individuals themselves.

Is the Measure Objective or Subjective?

Muldoon et al. (1998) provided an alternative conceptual framework for quality of life based on the degree to which the domains being rated can be objectively validated. They argued that quality of life measures should be divided into those that assess objective functioning and those that assess subjective well-being. The first of these reflects those measures that describe an individual's level of functioning, which they argue must be validated against directly observed behavioural performance, and the second describes the individual's own appraisal of their well-being.

Therefore some progress has been made to clarify the problems surrounding measures of quality of life. However, until a consensus among researchers and clinicians exists, it remains unclear what quality of life is, and whether quality of life is different to subjective health status and health-related quality of life. In fact, Annas (1990) argued that we should stop using the term altogether. However, 'quality of life', 'subjective health status' and 'health-related quality of life' continue to be used and their measurement continues to be taken. The range of measures developed will now be considered in terms of (1) unidimensional measures and (2) multidimensional measures.

HOW SHOULD IT BE MEASURED?

Unidimensional Measures

Many measures focus on one particular aspect of health. For example, Goldberg (1978) developed the General Health Questionnaire (GHQ), which assesses mood by asking questions such as 'Have you recently: been able to concentrate on whatever you're doing/spent much time chatting to people/been feeling happy or depressed?' The GHQ is available as long forms, consisting of 30, 28 or 20 items, and as a short form, which consists of 12 items. While the short form is mainly used to explore mood in general and provides results as to an individual's relative mood (i.e. is the person better or worse than usual?), the longer forms have been used to detect 'caseness' (i.e. is the person depressed or not?). Other unidimensional measures include the following: the Hospital Anxiety and Depression Scale (HADS) (Zigmond and Snaith 1983) and the Beck Depression Inventory (BDI) (Beck et al. 1961), both of which focus on mood; the McGill Pain Questionnaire, which assesses pain levels (Melzack 1975); measures of self-esteem, such as the Self-esteem Scale (Rosenberg 1965) and the Self-esteem Inventory (Coopersmith 1967); measures of social support (e.g. Sarason et al. 1983, 1987); measures of satisfaction with life (e.g. Diner et al. 1985); and measures of symptoms (e.g. deHaes et al. 1990). These unidimensional measures assess health in terms of one specific aspect of health and can be used on their own or in conjunction with other measures.

Multidimensional Measures

Multidimensional measures assess health in the broadest sense. However, this does not mean that such measures are always long and complicated. For example, researchers often use a single item such as, 'Would you say your health is: excellent/good/fair/poor?' or 'Rate your current state of health on a scale ranging from "poor" to "perfect"'. Further, some researchers simply ask respondents to make a relative judgement about their health on a scale from 'best possible' to 'worst possible'. In addition to these measures of self-reported health, researchers have also assessed self-reported fitness (Phillips et al. 2010). Although these simple measures do not provide as much detail as longer measures, they have been shown to correlate highly with other more complex measures and to be useful as outcome measures (Idler and Kasl 1995). Furthermore, they have also been shown to be good predictors of mortality at follow-ups ranging from 2 to 28 years even when a wide range of factors including demographics, smoking and medical diagnoses are taken into account (Idler and Benyamini 1997; Phillips et al. 2010). This indicates that how healthy people think they are predicts when they die!

Composite Scales

In the main, researchers have tended to use *composite scales*. Because of the many ways of defining quality of life, many different measures have been developed. Some focus on particular populations, such as the elderly (McKee et al. 2002), children (Jirojanakul and Skevington 2000), or those in the last year of life (Lawton et al. 1990). Others focus on specific illnesses, such as diabetes (Bradley et al. 1999), arthritis (Meenan et al. 1980), heart disease (Rector et al. 1993), HIV (Skevington and O'Connell 2003) and renal disease (Bradley 1997). In addition, generic measures of quality of life have also been developed, which can be applied to all individuals. These include the Nottingham Health Profile (NHP) (Hunt et al. 1986), the Short Form 36 (SF36) (Ware and Sherbourne 1992), the Sickness Impact Profile (SIP) (Bergner et al. 1981) and the WHOQoL-100 (Skevington et al. 2004a, 2004b). Research using these generic measures has explored quality of life in people from different cultures, with different levels of health and different levels of economic security (e.g. Skevington et al. 2004a, 2004b). All of these measures have been criticized for being too broad and therefore resulting in a definition of quality of life that is all-encompassing, vague and unfocused. In contrast, they have also been criticized for being too focused and for potentially missing out aspects of quality of life that may be of specific importance to the individual concerned. In particular, it has been suggested that by asking individuals to answer a predefined set of questions and to rate statements that have been developed by researchers, the individuals' own concerns may be missed. This has led to the development of individual quality of life measures.

Individual Quality of Life Measures

Measures of subjective health status ask the individual to rate their own health. This is in contrast to measures of mortality, morbidity and most measures of functioning, which are completed by carers, researchers or an observer. However, although such measures enable individuals to rate their own health, they do not allow them to select the dimensions along which to rate it. For example, a measure that asks about an individual's work life assumes that work is important to this person, but they might not want to work. A measure that asks about family life might be addressing the question to someone who is glad not to see their family. How can one set of individuals who happen to be researchers know what is important to the quality of life of another set of individuals? In line with this perspective, researchers have developed individual quality of life measures, which not only ask the subjects to rate their own health status but also to define the dimensions along which it should be rated. One such measure, the Schedule for Evaluating Individual Quality of Life (SEIQoL) (McGee et al. 1991; O'Boyle et al. 1992), asks subjects to select five areas of their lives that are important to them, to weight them in terms of their importance and then to rate how satisfied they currently are with each dimension (see **Focus on Research 18.1**).

FOCUS ON RESEARCH 18.1: EVALUATING HIP REPLACEMENT SURGERY

Individual quality of life in patients undergoing hip replacement (O'Boyle et al. 1992).

This is an interesting paper as it illustrates how a measurement tool, developed within a psychological framework, can be used to evaluate the impact of a surgical intervention. In addition, it compared the use of composite scales with an individual quality of life scale.

BACKGROUND

There are a multitude of measures of quality of life available, most of which ask patients to rate a set of statements that a group of researchers consider to reflect quality of life. However, whether this approach actually accesses what the patient thinks is unclear. Therefore O'Boyle et al. devised their own measure of quality of life (the SEIQoL) which asks the patients themselves to decide what is important to them. In addition, the authors wanted to compare the results using SEIQoL with those of more traditional assessment tools: 'We wanted to know whether SEIQoL could answer the question, "What does the patient think?"'.

METHODOLOGY

Subjects

Consecutive patients attending a hospital in Dublin for osteoarthritis of the hip were asked to participate. These were matched to control subjects from local general practices in terms of age, sex and class. The study consisted of 20 subjects, who underwent hip replacement operations, and 20 controls.

Design

The study used a repeated-measures design with measures completed before (baseline) and after (six-month follow-up) unilateral total hip replacement surgery.

Measures

The subjects completed the following measures at baseline and follow-up:

- *Individual quality of life.* This involved the following stages. First, the subjects were asked to list the five areas of life that they considered to be most important to their quality of life. Second, the subjects were asked to rate each area for their status at the present time, ranging from 'as good as could possibly be' to 'as bad as could possibly be'. Finally, in order to weight each area of life, the subjects were presented with 30 randomly generated profiles of hypothetical people labelled with the five chosen areas and were asked to rate the quality of life of each of these people. These three ratings were then used to compute total quality of life score (i.e. adding up each current rating, multiplied by weighting per area).

- *Global health status.* The subjects completed the McMaster Health Index Questionnaire, which assesses physical, social and emotional functioning (Chambers et al. 1982).

- *Disease-specific health status.* Subjects completed the Arthritis Impact Scale which assesses nine aspects of functioning: mobility, physical activity, dexterity, household activities, social activity, activities of daily living, pain, anxiety and depression (Meenan et al. 1980).

RESULTS

The results were analysed in terms of the areas of life selected as part of the individual quality of life scale and to assess the impact of the hip replacement operation in terms of changes in all measures from baseline to follow-up and differences in these changes between the patients and the controls.

- *Areas of life selected.* Social/leisure activities and family were nominated most frequently by both groups. Happiness, intellectual function and living conditions were nominated least frequently. Health was nominated more frequently by the control than the patients who rated independence and finance more frequently.
- *The impact of the hip replacement operation.* The results showed that all measures of quality of life improved following the hip replacement operation.

CONCLUSION

The authors concluded that their individual quality of life measure can be used to elicit the views of patients and in addition can detect changes in quality of life over time. Further, they argued that 'a major advantage of a patient-centred measure such as SEIQoL especially with elicited cues is that it is applicable across all patients, illnesses and diseases and is not specific to any one culture'. Therefore this study illustrates the usefulness of an individual quality of life measure in evaluating the effectiveness of a surgical procedure.

A SHIFT IN PERSPECTIVE

Health status can be assessed in terms of mortality rates, morbidity, levels of functioning and subjective health measures. Subjective health measures overlap significantly with measures of quality of life and health-related quality of life. These different measures illustrate a shift among a number of perspectives (see Figure 18.1).

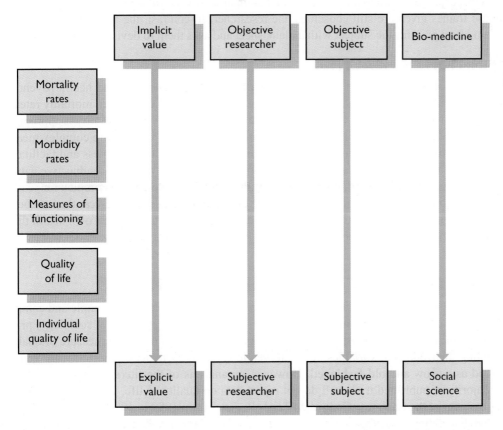

FIGURE 18.1

A shift in perspective in measuring health

VALUE

The shift from mortality rates to subjective health measures represents a move from implicit value to attempts to make this value explicit. For example, mortality and morbidity measures assume that what they are measuring is an absolute index of health. The subjects being studied are not asked, 'Is it a bad thing that you cannot walk upstairs?' or the relatives asked, 'Did they want to die?' Subjective health measures attempt to make the value within the constructs being studied explicit by asking, 'To what extent are you prevented from doing the things you would like to do?'

SUBJECTIVITY OF THE SUBJECT

Mortality and morbidity measures are assumed to be objective scientific measures that access a reality that is uncontaminated by bias. In contrast, subjective measures make this bias the essence of what they are interested in. For example, mortality data are taken from hospital records or death certificates, and morbidity ratings are often made by the health professionals rather than the individuals being studied. However, subjective health measures ask the individual for their own experiences and beliefs in terms of 'How do you rate your health?' or 'How do you feel?' They make no pretence to be objective and, rather than attempting to exclude the individuals' beliefs, they make them their focus.

SUBJECTIVITY OF THE RESEARCHER

In addition, there is also a shift in the ways in which measures of health status conceptualize the researcher. For example, mortality and morbidity rates are assumed to be consistent regardless of who collected them; the researcher is assumed to be an objective person. Subjective measures, however, attempt to address the issue of researcher subjectivity. For example, self-report questionnaires and the use of closed questions aim to minimize researcher input. However, the questions being asked and the response frames given are still chosen by the researcher. In contrast, the SEIQoL (O'Boyle et al. 1992) in effect presents the subject with a blank sheet and asks them to devise their own scale.

DEFINITION OF HEALTH

Finally, such shifts epitomize the different perspectives of biomedicine and health psychology. Therefore, if health status is regarded as the presence or absence of death, then mortality rates provide a suitable assessment tool. Death is a reliable outcome variable and mortality is appropriately simple. If, however, health status is regarded as more complex than this, more complex measures are needed. Morbidity rates account for a continuum model of health and illness and facilitate the assessment of the greyer areas, and even some morbidity measures accept the subjective nature of health. However, if health psychology regards health status as made up of a complex range of factors that can only be both chosen and evaluated by the individuals themselves, then it could be argued that it is only measures that ask the individuals themselves to rate their own health that are fully in line with a health psychology model of what health means.

USING QUALITY OF LIFE IN RESEARCH

Quality of life measures, in the form of subjective health measures and both simple and composite scales, play a central role in many debates within health psychology, medical sociology, primary care and clinical medicine. Most funded trials are now required to include a measure of quality of life among their outcome variables, and interventions that only focus on mortality are generally regarded as narrow and old-fashioned. However, an analysis of the literature suggested that the vast majority of published trials still do not report data on quality of life. For example, following an assessment of the Cochrane Controlled Trials Register from 1980 to 1997, Sanders et al. (1998) reported that, although the frequency of reporting quality of life data had increased from 0.63 to 4.2 per cent for trials from all disciplines, from 1.5 to 8.2 per cent for cancer trials and from 0.34 to 3.6 per cent for cardiovascular trials, less than 5 per cent of all trials reported data on quality of life.

Furthermore, they showed that this proportion was below 10 per cent even for cancer trials. In addition, they indicated that, while 72 per cent of the trials used established measures of quality of life, 22 per cent used measures developed by the authors themselves. Therefore it would seem that, although quality of life is in vogue and is a required part of outcome research, it still remains underused. For those trials that do include a measure of quality of life, it is used mainly as an outcome variable and the data are analysed to assess whether the intervention had an impact on the individual's health status, including their quality of life. The use of quality of life as an outcome variable and a predictor of mortality will now be discussed. In addition, research has also explored the notion of the *response shift* which reflects the ways in which an individual's evaluation of their quality of life changes and adjusts over the course of an illness.

QUALITY OF LIFE AS AN OUTCOME MEASURE

At its simplest, research using cross-sectional and longitudinal designs has explored the impact of an illness on an individual's quality of life. For example, Wiczinski et al. (2009) explored the association between obesity and quality of life in 2,732 participants from Germany. The results indicated that obesity was associated with reduced physical but not mental quality of life as measured by the SF-12 in men and women and that this link was only mediated by strong social support in men. Research has examined how a range of interventions influence an individual's quality of life using a repeated-measures design. For example, a trial of breast reduction surgery compared women's quality of life before and after the operation (Klassen et al. 1996). The study involved 166 women who were referred for plastic surgery, mainly for physical reasons, and their health status was assessed using the SF36 to assess general quality of life, the 28-item GHQ to assess mood and Rosenberg's self-esteem scale. The results showed that the women reported significantly better quality of life both before and after the operation than a control group of women in the general population and, further, that the operation resulted in an improvement in the women's physical, social and psychological functioning, including their levels of 'caseness' for psychiatric morbidity. Accordingly, the authors concluded that breast reduction surgery is beneficial for quality of life and should be included in NHS purchasing contracts.

Quality of life has also been included as an outcome variable for disease-specific randomized controlled trials. For example, Grunfeld et al. (1996) examined the relative impact of providing either hospital (routine care) or primary care follow-ups for women with breast cancer. The study included 296 women with breast cancer who were in remission and randomly allocated them to

BOX 18.1 Some Problems with . . . Health Status Research

Below are some problems with research in this area that you may wish to consider.

1 Health status can be measured using either tools that include predefined domains or those that rely on the individual themselves to generate the domains. Both are problematic.

2 Quality of life measures are sometimes criticized for missing important domains and for being too simple. Sometimes they are criticized for being over-inclusive, unwieldy and difficult to use. The choice of measure therefore has to be pragmatic and based upon what a particular person is deemed able to complete at any particular time rather than perfect theoretical principles.

3 Research measuring health outcomes often includes a range of health status, quality of life and physiological measures. Often these measures contradict each other. For example, while an intervention may improve longevity, it may be detrimental to quality of life. How these different outcomes are combined is unclear and can cause conflict or confusion for health professionals.

receive follow-up care either in hospital or by their GP. Quality of life was assessed using some of the dimensions from the SF36 and the HADS. The results showed that general practice care was not associated with any deterioration in quality of life. In addition, it was not related to an increased time to diagnose any recurrence of the cancer. Therefore the authors concluded that general practice care of women in remission from breast cancer is as good as hospital care.

Other studies have explored the impact of an intervention for a range of illnesses. For example, the DAFNE study group (2002) explored the impact of teaching diabetic patients flexible intensive treatment which combines dietary freedom and insulin adjustment (dose adjustment for normal eating – DAFNE). The results showed that this approach to self-management improved both the patients' glycaemic control and their quality of life at follow-up. Shepperd et al. (1998) also used quality of life as an outcome measure. They examined the relative effectiveness of home versus hospital care for patients with a range of problems, including hip replacement, knee replacement and hysterectomy. Quality of life was assessed using tools such as the SF36 and disease-specific measures, and the results showed no differences between the two groups at a three-month follow-up. Therefore the authors concluded that if there are no significant differences between home and hospital care in terms of quality of life, then the cost of these different forms of care becomes an important factor.

PROBLEMS WITH USING QUALITY OF LIFE AS AN OUTCOME MEASURE

Research uses quality of life as an outcome measure for trials that have different designs and are either focused on specific illnesses or involve a range of problems. However, there are the following difficulties with such studies:

- Different studies use different ways of measuring quality of life: generalizing across studies is difficult.
- Some studies use the term 'quality of life' while others use the term 'subjective health status': generalizing across studies is difficult.
- Some studies report results from the different measures of quality of life, which are in the opposite direction to each other: drawing conclusions is difficult.
- Some studies report the results from quality of life measures, which are in the opposite direction to mortality or morbidity data: deciding whether an intervention is good or bad is difficult.

QUALITY OF LIFE AS A PREDICTOR OF LONGEVITY

Most research using quality of life explores its predictors and therefore places this variable as the end-point. However, it is possible that quality of life may also be a predictor of future events, particularly longevity. This is suggested indirectly by several studies that indicate that mortality is higher in the first six months after the death of a spouse, particularly from heart disease or suicide (e.g. Schaefer et al. 1995; Martikainen and Valkonen 1996). Further, some studies suggest a link between life events and longevity (see Chapters 11 and 14). Perhaps these links could be explained by quality of life. Furthermore, research indicates that simple self-report measures of health status that ask an individual to rate their own health using single item scales are predictive of mortality at follow-ups ranging from 2 to 28 years (Idler and Benyamini 1997; Phillips et al. 2010; see **Focus on Research 18.2**).

Subjective health status can predict mortality: Spike Milligan's joke about his tombstone

The comedian Spike Milligan was reported to have joked that he wanted the words 'I told you I was ill' on his tombstone. Milligan recognized that subjective health status was a good predictor of mortality! Therefore quality of life may not only be an outcome variable in itself but a predictor of further outcomes in the future.

FOCUS ON RESEARCH 18.2: 'I KNEW I WAS ILL' AS A PREDICTOR OF MORTALITY

The role of subjective health status in predicting mortality (Phillips et al. 2010).

BACKGROUND

There are many measures of health status ranging from subjective measures and the use of questionnaires to more objective markers of health such as blood pressure and a wide range of biological factors that can be determined from blood tests or scans using the most up-to-date medical technology. This study explored the simplest measure of health status, namely self-reported health, and assessed the role of this variable along with self-reported fitness in predicting the most objective measure we have – mortality.

METHODOLOGY

Sample

Data for this study was drawn from a large cohort study called the West of Scotland Twenty-07 study which involved participants from the Glasgow region. For this study, wave 2 data were selected as the baseline (data collected in 1991/92) as this database included measures of both self-reported health and self-reported fitness. At baseline the sample (n = 858) were almost all white, 46 per cent were male, 38 per cent were current smokers, 71 per cent had a long-standing illness and participants had a mean age of 59. Mortality data was collected after 16.5 years when 247 of the original sample had died. The mean age of death was 69 and the most common causes were cardiovascular disease (39 per cent), cancer (34 per cent), respiratory disease (13 per cent) and other (14 per cent).

Procedure

Data was collected using face-to-face interviews in the participants' homes by a trained nurse.

Measures

As well as standard measures of demographics participants rated the following aspects of their health status:

- *Self-reported health:* participants were asked 'would you say that for someone your own age your own health is . . .' with the response options being excellent/good/fair/poor.
- *Self-reported fitness:* participants were also asked 'would you say that for someone your own age your fitness is . . .' with the response options being very good/good/moderate/poor/very poor.

Mortality data was acquired from the UK's NHS central registry which provided notification of death and cause of death.

RESULTS

The results were analysed using Cox's regression models. First separate models were run for self-reported health and self-reported fitness. Then a final model was run including both these variables. All models controlled for potential confounding variables (sex, occupational group, smoking status, body mass index (BMI), blood pressure, long-standing illness). Overall, the results showed that those with either poor ratings of health or poor ratings of fitness at baseline were twice as likely to die by 16.5 years follow-up. Further, in the individual models both self-reported health and self-reported fitness were significant predictors of mortality after controlling for potential confounding variables. In addition, when both measures of health status were entered into the equation, both remained significant with those with both poor health and poor fitness at baseline being 2.7 times more likely to die by follow-up.

CONCLUSION

The results showed that self-reported health and self-reported fitness predicted mortality independently of each even when other possible risk factors had been controlled for. Furthermore, the existence of both poor self-reported health and poor self-reported fitness appeared to be a particularly lethal combination. There are several possible explanations for these findings. First, these subjective measures may simply be good proxy measures for more objective levels of health and fitness. From this perspective, 'I think I am unhealthy' predicts dying because 'I am really unhealthy'. However, in this and other related studies the self-report scales seem to predict death even when other more objective risk factors are controlled for. Second, believing that one is healthy may then influence health behaviours, making someone behave in a more healthy way and thus making them live longer. Finally, perhaps believing that you are well creates a state of mind which actually makes you live longer regardless of behaviour. To date, however, the mechanisms behind the predictive capacity of subjective health and fitness remain only poorly understood. This study therefore highlights the predictive capacity of simple measures. It also raises some fundamental questions about the relationship between the mind, body and the mediating role of behavior.

THE RESPONSE SHIFT

Quality of life research is often inconsistent, presenting challenges to those involved in its measurement. For example, people often rate their quality of life differently at different time points even though there are no observable changes to their lives and often there seems to be no relationship between any objective assessment of quality of life and the person's own ratings of their health status. Some of this variation has been attributed to measurement error. Increasingly, however, it is seen as an illustration of the appraisal processes involved in making quality of life assessments and has been addressed within the context of the *response shift* (Rapkin and Schwartz 2004). Rapkin and Schwartz argued that each time a person judges their quality of life they must establish a 'frame of reference' which determines how they comprehend the questions being asked (what do the words 'health', 'mood', 'family', 'work' mean to them?). Next they decide upon 'standards of comparison', which include both between- and within-subject comparisons, to decide whether to judge their quality of life in terms of their own past history, their expectations of themselves or other people they know ('Am I better off or worse off than I have been or than other people?'). Then they decide upon a 'sampling strategy' to determine which parts of their life they should assess ('Should I think of right now or how far back should I go?'). People then combine these three sets of appraisals to formulate a response. From this perspective, inconsistencies in the quality of life literature are no longer seen as a product of measurement error but as illustrations of the complex ways in which people make judgements about their health. Accordingly, studies show that although immediately after diagnosis of an illness or the

People can show an improvement in their quality of life even after a serious illness or injury – the response shift

SOURCE: © MichaelSvoboda/iStock

occurrence of a serious injury people's rated quality of life might be poor, several months later it may well be high again even though their physical condition has remained constant. Dempster, Carney and McClements (2010) concluded from their study of cardiac patients that the response shift occurred over the course of a cardiac rehabilitation programme and that it was related to changes in an individual's internal standards and correlated with active coping strategies.

TO CONCLUDE

This chapter has explored the different ways of measuring health status. In particular, it has examined the use of mortality rates, morbidity rates, measures of functioning, measures of subjective health status and quality of life. It then described how the change from mortality rates to quality of life reflects a shift from implicit to explicit value, an increasing subjectivity on behalf of both the subject being studied and the researcher, and a change in the definition of health from a biomedical dichotomous model to a more complex psychological one. Further, it explored definitions of quality of life and the vast range of scales that have been developed to assess this complex construct, and their use in research. Finally it described the use of quality of life in research as an outcome variable, as a predictor of longevity and within the context of the response shift.

QUESTIONS

1 Mortality rates are the most accurate measure of health status. Discuss.
2 The views of the subject get in the way of measuring health. Discuss.
3 The views of the researcher get in the way of measuring health. Discuss.
4 To what extent is quality of life a useful construct?
5 Should all outcome research include an assessment of quality of life?
6 To what extent can quality of life predict mortality?
7 Describe the mechanisms of the response shift and how this could help our understanding of how people respond to illness or trauma.

FOR DISCUSSION

Consider the last time you felt that your quality of life was reduced. What did this mean to you and would this be addressed by the available measures?

ASSUMPTIONS IN HEALTH PSYCHOLOGY

The measurement of health status highlights some of the assumptions in health psychology:

1   ***The problem of methodology.*** It is assumed that methodology is separate to the data being collected. Accordingly, it is assumed that subjects experience factors as important to their quality of life even before they have been asked about them. It is possible that items relating to family life, physical fitness and work may only become important once the individual has been asked to rate them.

2   ***The problem of the mind–body split.*** Although much outcome research examines both mortality and quality of life, it is often assumed that these two factors are separate. Therefore research explores the impact of an intervention either on an individual's quality of life or on their longevity. Very little research assesses the impact of quality of life itself on longevity. Therefore factors influencing the mind are deemed to be separate to those influencing the body.

3   ***The problem of progress.*** Mortality rates were very much in vogue at the beginning of the last century whereas quality of life measures are in vogue today. This shift is mainly regarded as an improvement in the way in which we understand health status. However, rather than being an improvement, perhaps it simply reflects a change of the way in which we make sense of what health is.

FURTHER READING

Bowling, A. (2005) *Measuring Health: A Review of Quality of Life Measurement Scales*, 3rd edn. Maidenhead: Open University Press.
This is an extremely comprehensive overview of the different scales that have been developed to assess quality of life. It also includes two interesting chapters on what quality of life is and theories of measurement.

Joyce, C.R.B., O'Boyle, C.A. and McGee, H.M. (eds) (1999) *Individual Quality of Life*. London: Harwood.
This edited book provides details on the conceptual and methodological principles of quality of life and focuses on individual measures. It then provides some examples of using these measures, together with some ideas for future directions.

Rapkin, B.D. and Schwartz, C.E. (2004) Towards a theoretical model of quality of life appraisal: implications of findings from studies of response shift, *Health and Quality of Life Outcomes*, 2: 14.
This is an excellent paper that describes the notion of the response shift and outlines the mechanisms that might be involved in this process of change and adaptation.

 Visit the website at www.openup.co.uk/ogden for additional resources on Chapter 18 to help you with your study, such as multiple choice questions, weblinks and a searchable online glossary.

© Jason Verschoor/iStock

PART FIVE

Reflecting on Health Psychology

19 Critical Health Psychology

© Jacob Wackerhausen/iStock

CHAPTER OVERVIEW

Many lecturers encourage their students to be more critical in their thinking and writing. But often students don't really know how to do this and as academics we find it hard to explain what 'being critical' actually means. This chapter outlines a more critical approach to health psychology and highlights the kinds of questions that can be asked to encourage a more critical way of thinking. In particular, it highlights how to be critical in terms of theories, methods, measurement and the very nature of the discipline itself. This book has offered specific forms of criticism in the boxes entitled 'Some problems with . . .'. It has also highlighted a range of assumptions within health psychology. This chapter draws together these problems and assumptions and outlines how they can inform a more critical approach.

LEARNING TO BE CRITICAL

What does 'being critical' mean? When an article is published and presented in columns, with an 'academic'-looking font, complex tables and figures, a long list of references and a number of senior-sounding authors, it is easy to accept it as a 'truth', to be swayed by its arguments and convinced by its data. Becoming critical is about developing the confidence to question and scrutinize a paper to see whether it really makes sense and whether the conclusions are justified. At one level being critical may be quite simple in terms of exploring issues such as sample size (is it representative?), the measures used (are they valid?), the statistical tests employed (are they the right ones?) or the chosen research design (can they make causal conclusions from a qualitative study?). But at a more sophisticated level, being critical also means thinking about the theories being tested (do they make sense?), the constructs used (are they different from each other?) and whether the arguments are coherent (what are they really saying?). Furthermore, being critical may also highlight some fundamental flaws in a discipline if we start to ask about an author's underlying assumptions (do people really have a consistent personality?; is what people say they think what they really think?), or what a discipline chooses to focus on and chooses to ignore (why do psychologists focus on behaviour while sociologists focus on society-level variables such as social class, education, social capital, economic stability, etc.?). And finally, being critical involves learning to trust the feeling that something 'isn't quite right' or 'doesn't quite make sense' or 'is so obvious that it's not interesting'.

BEING CRITICAL OF THEORY

Health psychology uses theories such as the stages of change model (SOC) or the theory of planned behaviour (TPB). It also uses constructs such as self-efficacy, behavioural intentions, illness cognitions and coping. Some theories are based on stages and see their components as leading from one to the other in a linear progression. Other theories are more dynamic as describe their components as being interrelated. Being critical of theory involves learning to ask questions such as the following.

CONSTRUCTS

Health psychology uses a wide range of constructs such as coping, illness beliefs, perceived control, quality of life, depression and anxiety. We need to ask whether these constructs are meaningful and discrete. For example:

- Is 'I feel depressed' an emotion or a cognition?
- Can depression cause poor quality of life or is it part of quality of life?
- Can poor health status lead to poor quality of life or is health status part of quality of life?

- Is the illness belief 'my illness won't last a long time' an illness belief or a coping mechanism?
- Are different personality types mutually exclusive to each other (can I be extrovert and introvert?)?

STAGE MODELS

Health psychology uses a number of stage models such as the SOC. We need to ask:

- Are the different stages qualitatively separate from each other?
- Are stages real or a products of statistics (i.e. if I ask if people across stages are different, will I then find that they are different, because I am imposing difference on the data?)?
- Are stages an artefact of labelling them as such?

FINDING ASSOCIATIONS IN OUR THEORIES

Many of our theories argue that different constructs are associated with each other (e.g. self-efficacy predicts behavioural intentions; control-related illness cognitions predict coping). We need to ask:

- Are these associations true by definition (e.g. control cognitions relate to coping *only* because control cognitions are part of the definition of coping)?
- Are the associations true by observation (e.g. smoking causes cancer because smoking is separate to cancer but then causes cancer to occur)?

FINDING DIFFERENCES IN OUR THEORIES

Many theories also look for differences between populations (e.g. men versus women; old versus young; doctor versus patient). We need to ask:

- Are these differences artefacts of the statistics we use (e.g. if we ask a differences-based question we can find a difference, but if we ask an association-based question we can find an association)? A good example of this is that daughters have higher body dissatisfaction than their mothers (i.e. they are different) *but* daughter body dissatisfaction is correlated with their mothers (i.e. they are associated). The answer depends on the question asked and the statistical test used.
- Are the variables that we use to explore differences (men versus women; old versus young) really dichotomous variables or artificially created as binary variables (what about all the people who fall somewhere between?)?

CAN THEORIES BE TESTED?

Much research in health psychology aims to test a theory. We need to ask:

- Can the theory ever be rejected (e.g. it didn't work but it was the fault of the sample/measures/confounding variables – let's keep the theory)?
- Can the theory ever be accepted (statistics are based on probabilities; our results are never true all the time but true within an accepted level of probability)?

We can therefore learn to be more critical of theories in terms of the constructs we use and the ways in which we explore whether or not these constructs are related to each other. I visualize this as a form of dividing up the soup.

DIVIDING UP THE SOUP

Beliefs (risk perception, outcome expectancies, costs and benefits, intentions, implementation intentions, illness cognitions, coping), emotions (fear, depression, anxiety) and behaviours (smoking, drinking, eating, screening) are conceptualized as separate and discrete. Health psychology then develops models and theories to examine how these variables interrelate. For example, it asks, 'What beliefs predict smoking?', 'What emotions relate to screening?' Therefore it separates out 'the soup' into discrete entities and then tries to put them back together again. However, perhaps these different beliefs, emotions and behaviours were not separate *until* psychology came along. Is there really a difference between all the different beliefs? Is the thought 'I am depressed' a cognition or an emotion? Health psychology assumes differences and then looks for associations. However, perhaps without the original separation there would be nothing to associate!

BEING CRITICAL OF METHOD

In health psychology we use both qualitative and quantitative methods and a range of research designs including cross-sectional studies, experiments and cohort studies. Being critical involves asking questions about all aspects of methodology.

QUANTITATIVE STUDIES

Quantitative studies are the mainstay of more traditional forms of empirical research and involve collecting numerical data through questionnaires, experiments (or trials) or computer tasks. Such quantitative data is often assumed to be more objective and controlled than qualitative data. But being critical involves asking questions such as:

- Is quantitative data really objective and value-free? The researcher chooses what questions to ask, how the data should be coded, what sample to select, what variables to analyse, what tests to use and what story to tell in the final paper. All these processes involve subjective judgements which are value-laden. Many a time have I published papers which have included some but not all of the variables I measured as this tells a clearer story.

QUALITATIVE STUDIES

Health psychology uses a range of qualitative methods such as focus groups and interviews and applies different data analysis approaches such as thematic analysis, interpretative phenomenological analysis (IPA) or narrative analysis. Qualitative researchers are clear about the subjective nature of their data and argue that their findings are neither generalizable nor representative. But we need to ask the following questions:

- If the data analysis is open to subjective interpretation by the researcher, how much of the analysis reflects only what the researcher wants to see and is any of the analysis reflective of what went on in the interview? Is qualitative analysis just the fiction of the researcher?
- Although qualitative findings are not supposed to be generalizable, are we in fact interested to see if they can tell us about people other than those few (just 10 perhaps?) who took part in the study?

THE SAMPLE

Quantitative research requires larger samples that are representative so that the results can be generalized. Qualitative studies involve much smaller samples as generalization is not the aim. But . . .

- Can a sample ever be representative and if so of whom? Samples may well be selected from a school, or a clinic, or even a city or country but can the data ever be representative of all schools, clinics, cities or countries? Yet we assume that data on people with diabetes who took part in the trial can tell us about people with diabetes in general even though the trial population were all under 65 and living in London.

- Qualitative studies use small samples but can a study on seven people really tell us much apart from about those seven people? Are people so consistent that what seven people tell us can inform what we know about other people with a similar condition, illness or behaviour? And if it can't, then why do we only study seven people?

RESEARCH DESIGNS

We have a number of research designs all of which have their strengths and weaknesses. We need to ask:

- How can the authors describe 'cause' or predict anything when a cross-sectional design was used?
- How can the results be generalized when the data were collected in an artificial laboratory setting?
- How can the results be trusted when they were collected in a natural setting with so many uncontrolled potentially confounding variables?

Health psychology uses a range of methods, all of which have their problems. Being critical of methodology involves understanding these problems and making sure that the conclusions from any study are justified. Central to all research is the assumption that data can be collected about the world and that data we separate to the tool that is collecting it. This raises the problem of whether research collects or creates the very things it is trying to measure.

METHODS AS SEPARATE TO DATA

In health psychology we carry out research to collect data about the world. We then analyse these data to find out how the world is, and we assume that our methodologies are separate to the data we are collecting. In line with this, if we ask someone about their implementation intentions, it is assumed that they have such intentions before we ask them. Further, if we ask someone about their anxieties, we assume that they have an emotion called anxiety, regardless of whether or not they are talking to us or answering our questionnaire. However, how do we know that our methods are separate from the data we collect? How do we know that these objects of research (beliefs, emotions and behaviours) exist prior to when we study them? Perhaps by studying the world we are not objectively examining what is really going on but are actually changing and possibly even creating it.

BEING CRITICAL OF MEASUREMENT

Research within health psychology involves using a wide range of measurement tools including subjective questionnaires to detect 'caseness' or variables on a continuum, interview schedules, computer tasks and objective measures of factors such as adherence (blood levels of the drug), smoking (blood levels of nicotine) or stress (measured cortisol). These all have their problems and the following questions can be asked.

SUBJECTIVE MEASURES

It is acknowledged that self-report measures such as questionnaires and interviews are subjective. This raises problems such as:

- Are participants just saying what they believe the researcher wants them to say?
- Does the participant have the language and insight to express what they really feel?
- Can people really differentiate their feelings, beliefs or behaviours into the level of detail expected by numerical scales with 5 or 7 or even 100 options?

OBJECTIVE MEASURES

Some measures are more objective but these also have their problems:

- Most measures still involve the possibility of human error or bias through coding, choosing what to measure and when, and deciding how the data should be analysed.
- An objective measure of a psychological construct may miss the important part of that construct (e.g. is cortisol really a reflection of stress or just one component of it?).

A LEAP OF FAITH

Throughout the different areas of health psychology, researchers develop research tools to assess quality of life, pain, stress, beliefs and behaviours. These tools are then used by the researchers to examine how the subjects in the research feel/think/behave. However, this process involves an enormous leap of faith – that our measurement tool actually measures something *out there*. How do we know this? Perhaps what the tool measures is simply what the tool measures. A depression scale may not assess 'depression' but only the score on the scale. Likewise, a quality of life scale may not assess quality of life but simply how someone completes the questionnaire.

BEING CRITICAL OF A DISCIPLINE

Finally, being critical also involves analysing and criticizing the discipline of health psychology itself in terms of its key perspective and core assumptions. Health psychology positions itself as a discrete discipline separate to other related disciplines such as medicine and medical sociology. It has some core underlying approaches which were outlined in Chapter 1, such as emphasizing a biopsychosocial approach and highlighting a more holistic understanding of health and illness. Furthermore, it is founded on the belief that research will help us to understand health and illness and that the more we research our beliefs and behaviour, the better our understanding will be. These are explored here in terms of the mind–body split, how the individual is integrated into their social context and the notion of progression.

THE MIND–BODY SPLIT

Health psychology sets out to provide an integrated model of the individual by establishing a holistic approach to health. Therefore it challenges the traditional medical model of the mind–body split and provides theories and research to support the notion of a mind and body that are one. For example, it suggests that beliefs influence behaviour, which in turn influences health; that stress can cause illness and that pain is a perception rather than a sensation. In addition, it argues that illness cognitions relate to recovery from illness and coping relates to longevity. However, does this approach really represent an integrated individual? Although all these perspectives and the research that has been carried out in their support indicate that the mind and the body interact, they are still defined as separate. The mind reflects the individual's psychological states (i.e. their beliefs, cognitions, perceptions), which influence but are *separate from* their bodies (i.e. the illness, the body, the body's systems).

INTEGRATING THE INDIVIDUAL WITH THEIR SOCIAL CONTEXT

Psychology is traditionally the study of the individual. Sociology is traditionally the study of the social context. Recently, however, health psychologists have made moves to integrate this individual with their social world. To do this they have turned to social epidemiology (i.e. the exploration of class, gender and ethnicity), social psychology (i.e. subjective norms) or social constructionism (i.e. qualitative methods). Therefore health psychologists access either the individual's location within their social world via their demographic factors or ask individuals for their beliefs about the social world. However, does this really integrate the individual with the social world? A belief about the social context is still an individual's belief. Can psychology really succeed with this integration? Would it still be psychology if it did?

THE PROBLEM OF PROGRESSION

This book has illustrated how theories, such as those relating to addictions, stress and screening, have changed over time. In addition, it presents new developments in the areas of social cognition models and psychoneuroimmunology (PNI). For example, early models of stress focused on a simple stimulus–response approach; nowadays we focus on appraisal. Nineteenth-century models of addiction believed that it was the fault of the drug; in the early twenty-first century we see addiction as being a product of learning. Health psychology assumes that these shifts in theory represent improvements in our knowledge about the world. We know more than we did 100 years ago and our theories are more accurate. However, perhaps such changes indicate *different*, not *better*, ways of viewing the world. Perhaps these theories tell us more about how we see the world now compared with then, rather than simply that we have got better at seeing the world.

Health psychology uses a number of theories, methods and measurement tools. Being critical involves developing the confidence to evaluate and assess any paper (or book) in terms of all of these dimensions and learning to question whether a conclusion is justified, whether a theory makes sense or whether the underlying assumptions which form the basis of any piece of work are clear and transparent.

CRITICAL HEALTH PSYCHOLOGY

Over the past few years a subsection of health psychology has developed which has become known as 'critical health psychology'. Researchers within this area emphasize the qualitative, critical and alternative approaches to understanding health and illness. Further, they highlight the role of the social context and the political dimensions to health. Some of the assumptions addressed in this chapter are also addressed within the domain of critical health psychology.

FURTHER READING

Below are some of my own papers that have attempted to take a more critical stance on health psychology. Read if you are interested!

Ogden, J. (1995) Changing the subject of health psychology, *Psychology and Health*, 10: 257–65.
This paper addresses some of the assumptions in health psychology and discusses the interrelationship between theory, methodology and the psychological individual.

Ogden, J. (1995) Psychosocial theory and the creation of the risky self, *Social Science and Medicine*, 40: 409–15.
This paper examines the changes in psychological theory during the twentieth century and relates them to discussions about risk and responsibility for health and illness.

Ogden, J. (1997) The rhetoric and reality of psychosocial theories: a challenge to biomedicine? *Journal of Health Psychology*, 2: 21–9.
This paper explores health psychology's apparent challenge to biomedicine.

Ogden, J. (2002) *Health and the Construction of the Individual*. London: Routledge.
This book explores how both psychological and sociological theories construct the individual through an exploration of methodology, measurement, theory and the construction of boundaries.

Ogden, J. (2003) Some problems with social cognition models: a pragmatic and conceptual analysis, *Health Psychology*, 22: 424–8.
This paper provides a critique of social cognition models but is also of relevance to other theoretical perspectives used in health psychology. In particular, it questions whether measuring beliefs accesses them or changes (or even creates) them and whether our theories are tautological.

Ogden, J. and Lo, J. (forthcoming) How meaningful is data from Likert scales? An evaluation of how ratings are made and the role of the response shift in the socially disadvantaged. *International Journal of Health Psychology*.
This paper explores some of the fundamental problems with using quantitative measures to explore between-group differences and questions why quantitative and qualitative methods can often produce very contradictory results.

Other useful texts on critical health psychology include the following:

Crossley, M. (2000) *Rethinking Health Psychology*. Buckingham: Open University Press.
This book argues that 'mainstream' health psychology neglects some of the contextual factors that impact upon health and is over-reliant upon quantitative methodologies.

Hardey, M. (1998) *The Social Context of Health*. Buckingham: Open University Press.
This book explores the role of a range of social factors that contribute both to our understanding of health and to the decisions we make about how to behave.

Marks, D.F. (2002) Freedom, responsibility and power: contrasting approaches to health psychology, *Journal of Health Psychology*, 7, 5–14.
David Marks often writes interesting and thought-provoking editorials and articles in this journal. This one encourages researchers to think more widely about what we do.

Visit the website at www.openup.co.uk/ogden for additional resources on Chapter 19 to help you with your study, such as multiple choice questions, weblinks and a searchable online glossary.

Methodology glossary

B

Between-subjects design: this involves making comparisons between different groups of subjects; for example, males versus females, those who have been offered a health-related intervention versus those who have not.

C

Case-control design: this involves taking a group of subjects who show a particular characteristic (e.g. lung cancer – the dependent variable), selecting a control group without the characteristic (e.g. no lung cancer) and retrospectively examining these two groups for the factors that may have caused this characteristic (e.g. did those with lung cancer smoke more than those without?).

Condition: experimental studies often involve allocating subjects to different conditions; for example, information versus no information, relaxation versus no relaxation, active drug versus placebo versus control condition.

Cross-sectional design: a study is described as being cross-sectional if the different variables are measured at the same time as each other.

D

Dependent variable: the characteristic that appears to change as a result of the independent variable; for example, changing behavioural intentions (the independent variable) causes a change in behaviour (the dependent variable).

E

Experimental design: this involves a controlled study in which variables are manipulated in order to specifically examine the relationship between the independent variable (the cause) and the dependent variable (the effect); for example, does experimentally induced anxiety change pain perception?

I

Independent variable: the characteristic that appears to cause a change in the dependent variable; for example, smoking (the independent variable) causes lung cancer (the dependent variable).

L

Likert scale: variables can be measured on a scale marked by numbers (e.g. 1 to 5) or terms (e.g. never/seldom/sometimes/often/very often). The subject is asked to mark the appropriate point.

Longitudinal design: this involves measuring variables at a baseline and then following up the subjects at a later point in time (sometimes called prospective or cohort design).

P

Prospective design: this involves following up subjects over a period of time (sometimes called longitudinal or cohort design).

Q

Qualitative study: this involves methodologies such as interviews in order to collect data from subjects. Qualitative data is a way of describing the variety of beliefs, interpretations and behaviours from a heterogenous subject group without making generalizations to the population as a whole. It is believed that qualitative studies are more able to access the subjects' beliefs without contaminating the data with the researcher's own expectations. Qualitative data are described in terms of themes and categories.

Quantitative study: this involves collecting data in the form of numbers using methodologies such as questionnaires and experiments. Quantitative data are a way of describing the beliefs, interpretations and behaviours of a large population and generalizations are made about the population as a whole. Quantitative data are described in terms of frequencies, means and statistically significant differences and correlations.

R

Randomly allocated: subjects are randomly allocated to different conditions in order to minimize the effects of any individual differences; for example, to ensure that subjects who receive the drug versus the placebo versus nothing are equivalent in age and sex. If all the subjects who received the placebo happened to be female, this would obviously influence the results.

Repeated-measures design: this involves asking subjects to complete the same set of measures more than once; for example, before and after reading a health information leaflet.

S

Subjects: these are the individuals who are involved in the study. They may also be referred to as participants, clients, respondents or cases.

V

Variable: a characteristic that can be measured (e.g. age, beliefs, fitness).

Visual analogue scale: variables such as beliefs are sometimes measured using a 100mm line with anchor points at each end (such as not at all confident/extremely confident). The subject is asked to place a cross on the line at the appropriate point.

W

Within-subjects design: this involves making comparisons within the same group of subjects. How do subjects respond to receiving an invitation to attend a screening programme? How does a belief about smoking relate to the subjects' smoking behaviour?

References

Aaronson, N.K., Ahmedzai, S. and Bergman, B. et al. (1993) The European Organisation for Research and Treatment of Cancer, QLQ-C30: a quality of life instrument for use in international clinical trials in oncology, *Journal for the National Cancer Institute*, **85**: 365–76.

Aarts, H., Verplanken, B. and van Knippenberg, A. (1998) Predicting behaviour from actions in the past: repeated decision making or matter of habit? *Journal of Applied Social Psychology*, **28**: 1355–74.

Abbey, J.G., Rosenfeld, B., Pessin, H. and Breitbart, W. (2006) Hopelessness at the end of life: the utility of the hopelessness scale with terminally ill cancer patients, *British Journal of Health Psychology*, **11**: 173–83.

Abbott, S. and Freeth, D. (2008) Social capital and health: starting to make sense of the role of generalized trust and reciprocity, *Journal of Health Psychology*, **13**(7): 874–83.

Abortion Law Reform Association (1997) *A Report on NHS Abortion Services*. London: ALRA.

Abraham, C. and Michie, S. (2008) A taxonomy of behaviour change techniques used in interventions, *Health Psychology*, **27**: 379–87.

Abraham, C. and Sheeran, P. (1993) In search of a psychology of safer-sex promotion: beyond beliefs and text, *Health Education Research: Theory and Practice*, **8**: 245–54.

Abraham, C. and Sheeran, P. (2005) The health belief model, in M. Conner and P. Norman (eds) *Predicting Health Behaviour*, 2nd edn. Maidenhead: Open University Press.

Abraham, C., Krahé, B., Dominic, R. and Fritsche, I. (2002) Do health promotion messages target cognitive and behavioural correlates of condom use? A content analysis of safer sex promotion leaflets in two countries, *British Journal of Health Psychology*, **7**: 227–46.

Abraham, S., Perz, J., Clarkson, R. and Llewellyn-Jones, D. (1995) Australian women's perceptions of hormone replacement therapy over 10 years, *Maturitas*, **21**: 91–5.

Abraham, S., Sheeran, P., Abrams, D. and Spears, R. (1996) Health beliefs and teenage condom use: a prospective study, *Psychology and Health*, **11**: 641–55.

Abrams, D., Abraham, C., Spears, R. and Marks, D. (1990) AIDS invulnerability: relationships, sexual behaviour and attitudes among 16–19-year-olds, in P. Aggleton, P. Davies and G. Hart (eds) *AIDS: Individual, Cultural and Policy Dimensions*. London: Falmer Press.

Adam, B.D., Husbands, W., Murray, J. and Maxwell, J. (2005) AIDS optimism, condom fatigue, or self-esteem? Explaining unsafe sex among gay and bisexual men, *Journal of Sex Research*, **42**(3): 238–48.

Ader, R. and Cohen, N. (1975) Behaviourally conditioned immuno suppression, *Psychosomatic Medicine*, **37**: 333–40.

Ader, R. and Cohen, N. (1981) Conditioned immunopharmacologic responses, in R. Ader (ed.) *Psychoneuroimmunology*. New York: Academic Press.

Alder, N., David, H., Major, B.N. et al. (1990) Psychological responses after abortion, *Science*, **248**: 41–4.

Adler, N.E., Boyce, T., Chesney, M.A. et al. (1993) Socioeconomic inequalities in health: no easy solution, *Journal of the American Medical Association*, **269**: 3140–5.

Aggleton, P. (1989) HIV/AIDS education in schools: constraints and possibilities, *Health Education Journal*, **48**: 167–71.

Aggleton, P. and Homans, H. (1988) *Social Aspects of AIDS*. London: Falmer Press.

Ahto, M., Isoaho, R., Puolijoki, H. et al. (2007) Stronger symptoms of depression predict high coronary heart disease mortality in older men and women, *International Journal of Geriatric Psychiatry*, **22**(8): 757–63.

Ainsworth, M.D.S., Blehar, M.C., Waters, E. and Wall, S. (1978) *Patterns of Attachment: A Study of the Strange Situation*. Hillsdale, NJ: Erlbaum.

Ajzen, I. (1988) *Attitudes, Personality and Behavior*. Chicago, IL: Dorsey Press.

Ajzen, I. and Madden, T.J. (1986) Prediction of goal-directed behavior: attitudes, intentions, and perceived behavioral control, *Journal of Experimental Social Psychology*, **22**: 453–74.

Albarracín D., Johnson, B. T., Fishbein, M. & Muellerleile, P.A. (2001) Theories of reasoned action and planned behaviour as models of condom use: a meta-analysis. *Psychological Bulletin*, **127**: 142–61.

Albrecht, G.L. (1994) Subjective health status, in C. Jenkinson (ed.) *Measuring Health and Medical Outcomes*. London: UCL Press.

Alderson, T. and Ogden, J. (1999) What mothers feed their children and why, *Health Education Research: Theory and Practice*, **14**: 717–27.

Alex, L. and Hammarström, A. (2004) Women's experiences in connection with induced abortion: a feminist perspective, *Scandinavian Journal of Caring Sciences*, **18**: 160–8.

Allen, I. (1991) *Family Planning and Pregnancy Counseling Projects for Young People*. London: Policy Studies Institute.

Allender, S., Peto, V., Scarborough, P. et al. (2008a) *Coronary heart Disease Statistics*. London: British Heart Foundation.

Allender, S., Scarborough, P., Peto, V. et al. (2008b) *European Cardiovascular Disease Statistics.* Brussels: European Heart Network.

Almedon, A.M. (2005) Social capital and mental health: an interdisciplinary review of primary evidence, *Social Science and Medicine*, **61**: 943–64.

Almqvist, E.W., Brinkman, R.R., Wiggins, S. et al. (2003) Psychological consequences and predictors of adverse events in the first 5 years after predictive testing for Huntington disease, *Clinical Genetics*, **64**: 300–9.

Alonso, J., Black, C., Norregaard, J.C. et al. (1998) Cross-cultural differences in the reporting of global functional capacity: an example in cataract patients, *Medical Care*, **36**: 868–78.

Amelang, M. and Schmidt-Rathjens, C. (1996) Personality, cancer and coronary heart disease: further evidence on a controversial issue, *British Journal of Health Psychology*, **1**: 191–205.

American Lung Association (2002a) *Adolescent Smoking Statistics*, www.lungusa.org/press/tobacco/not_stats.html.

American Lung Association. (2002b) *Trends in Tobacco Use*, www.lungusa.orgdata/smoke/smoke1.pdf.

Anastasiades, P., Clark, D.M., Salkovskis, P.M. et al. (1990) Psychophysiological responses in panic and stress, *Journal of Psychophysiology*, **27**: 34–44.

Andersen, R.E., Franckowiak, S.C., Snyder, J. et al. (1998) Physical activity promotion by the encouraged use of stairs, *Annals of Internal Medicine*, **129**: 363–9.

Anderson, H.R., Freeling, P. and Patel, S.P. (1983) Decision making in acute asthma, *Journal of the Royal College of General Practitioners*, **33**: 105–8.

Annas, G.J. (1990) Quality of life in the courts: early spring in fantasyland, in J.J. Walter and T.A. Shannon (eds) *Quality of Life: The New Medical Dilemma*. New York: Paulist Press.

Antoni, M.H., Carrico, A.W., Durán, R.E. et al. (2006) Randomized clinical trial of cognitive behavioral stress management on human immunodeficiency virus viral load in gay men treated with highly active antiretroviral therapy, *Psychosomatic Medicine*, **68**(1): 143–51.

Antoni, M.H., Cruess, D.G., Cruess, S. et al. (2000) Cognitive–behavioral stress management intervention effects on anxiety, 24-hr urinary norepinephrine output and T-cytotoxic/suppressor cells over time among symptomatic HIV-infected gay men, *Journal of Consulting and Clinical Psychology*, **68**(1): 31–45.

Antoni, M.H., Cruess, D.G., Klimas, N. et al. (2002) Stress management and immune system reconstitution in symptomatic HIV-infected gay men over time: effects on transitional naive T cells (CD4+CD45RA+CD29+), *American Journal of Psychiatry*, **159**(1): 143–5.

Antoni, M.H., Cruess, D.G., Klimas, N. et al. (2005) Increases in marker of immune system reconstitution are predated by decreases in 24-hr urinary cortisol output depressed mood during a 10-week stress management intervention in symptomatic HIV-infected men, *Journal of Psychosomatic Research*, **58**(1): 3–13.

Antoni, M.H., Lehman, J.M., Klibourn, K.M. et al. (2001) Cognitive-behavioral stress management intervention decreases the prevalence of depression and enhances benefit finding among women under treatment for early-stage breast cancer, *Health Psychology*, **20**(1): 20–32.

Anzman, S.L., Rollins, B.Y. and Birch, L.L. (2010) Parental influence on children's early eating environments and obesity risk: implications for prevention, *International Journal of Obesity*, **34**: 1116–24.

Appels, A. and Mulder, P. (1989) Fatigue and heart disease: the association between vital exhaustion and past, present and future coronary heart disease, *Journal of Psychosomatic Research*, **33**: 727–38.

Appels, A., Golombeck, B., Gorgels, A. et al. (2002) Psychological risk factors of sudden cardiac arrest, *Psychology and Health*, **17**: 773–81.

Appleton, P.L. and Pharoah, P.O.D. (1998) Partner smoking behaviour change is associated with women's smoking reduction and cessation during pregnancy, *British Journal of Health Psychology*, **3**: 361–74.

Armitage, C.J. (2004) Evidence that implementation intentions reduce dietary fat intake: a randomized trial, *Health Psychology*, **23**(3): 319–23.

Armitage, C.J. (2005) Can the theory of planned behaviour predict the maintenance of physical activity? *Health Psychology*, **24**(3): 235–45.

Armitage, C.J. (2007a) Effects of an implementation intention-based intervention on fruit consumption, *Psychology & Health*, **22**(8): 917–28.

Armitage, C.J. (2007b) Efficacy of a brief worksite intervention to reduce smoking: the roles of behavioural and implementation intentions, *Journal of Occupational Health Psychology*, **12**: 376–90.

Armitage, C.J. (2008) A volitional help sheet to encourage smoking cessation: a randomized exploratory trial, *Health Psychology*, **27**(5): 557–66.

Armitage, C.J. (2009a) Effectiveness of experimenter-provided and self-generated implementation intentions to reduce alcohol consumption in a sample of the general population: a randomized exploratory trial, *Health Psychology*, **28**(5): 543–53.

Armitage, C.J. (2009b) Is there utility in the transtheoretical model? *British Journal of Health Psychology*, **14**(2): 195–210.

Armitage, C.J. and Conner, M. (2000) Social cognition models and health behaviour: a structured review, *Psychology and Health*, **15**: 173–89.

Armitage, C.J. and Conner, M. (2001) Efficacy of the theory of planned behaviour: a meta-analytic review, *British Journal of Social Psychology*, **40**: 471–99.

Armitage, C.J. and Harris, P.R. (2006) The influence of adult attachment on symptom reporting: testing a meditational model in a sample of the general population, *Psychology and Health*, **21**(3): 351–66.

Armitage, C.J., Harris, P.R., Hepton, G. and Napper, L. (2008) Self-affirmation increases acceptance of health-risk information among UK adult smokers with low socioeconomic status, *Psychology of Addictive Behaviours*, **22**(1): 88–95.

Armstrong, D. (1995) The rise of surveillance medicine, *Sociology of Health and Illness*, **17**: 393–404.

Arnetz, B.B., Wasserman, J., Petrini, B. et al. (1987) Immune function in unemployed women, *Psychosomatic Medicine*, **49**: 3–12.

Arvola, A., Vassallo, M., Dean, M. et al. (2008) Predicting intentions to purchase organic food: the role of affective and moral attitudes in the theory of planned behaviour, *Appetite*, **50**: 443–54.

Ashton, W., Nanchahal, K. and Wood, D. (2001) Body mass index and metabolic risk factors for coronary heart disease in women, *European Heart Journal*, **22**: 46–55.

Athey, J. and Spielvogel, A. (2000) Risk factors and interventions for psychological sequelae in women after miscarriage, *Primary Care Update for Obstetrics and Gynaecology*, **7**: 64–9.

Attie, I. and Brooks-Gunn, J. (1989) Development of eating problems in adolescent girls: a longitudinal study, *Developmental Psychology*, **25**: 70–9.

Aucott, L.S. (2008) Influences of weight loss on long-term diabetes outcomes, *Proceedings of the Nutrition Society*, **67**(1): 54–9.

Autorengruppe Nationales Forschungsprogramm (1984) *Wirksamkeit der Gemeindeorientierten Prävention Kardiovascularer Krankheiten (Effectiveness of community-orientated prevention of cardiovascular diseases)*. Bern: Hans Huber.

Aveyard, P., Lawrence, T., Cheng, K.K. et al. (2006) A randomized controlled trial of smoking cessation for pregnant women to test the effect of a transtheoretical model-based intervention on movement in stage and interaction with baseline stage, *British Journal of Health Psychology*, **11**: 263–78.

Axelson, M.L., Brinberg, D. and Durand, J.H. (1983) Eating at a fast-food restaurant: a social psychological analysis, *Journal of Nutrition Education*, **15**: 94–8.

Bachrach, L.L. (1975) *Marital Status and Mental Disorder: An Analytic Review*. Washington, DC: US Printing Office.

Bagozzi, R.P. (1993) On the neglect of volition in consumer research: a critique and proposal, *Psychology and Marketing*, **10**: 215–37.

Baillie, C., Smith, J., Hewison, J. and Mason, G. (2000) Ultrasound screening for chromosomal abnormality: women's reactions to false positive results, *British Journal of Health Psychology*, **5**: 377–94.

Bain, D.J.G. (1977) Patient knowledge and the content of the consultation in general practice, *Medical Education*, **11**: 347–50.

Ballard, K. (2002) Understanding risk: women's perceived risk of menopause-related disease and the value they place on preventive hormone replacement therapy, *Family Practice*, **19**(6): 591–5.

Ballard, K. (2003) *Understanding Menopause*. Chichester: John Wiley.

Ballard, K., Kuh, D.J. and Wadsworth, M.E.J. (2001) The role of the menopause in women's experiences of the 'changes of life', *Sociology of Health and Illness*, **23**(4): 397–424.

Ballenger, J.C., Davidson, J.R., Lecrubier, Y. et al. (2001) Consensus statement on transcultural issues in depression and anxiety from the International Consensus Group on Depression and Anxiety, *Journal of Clinical Psychiatry*, **62**(Suppl. 13): 47–55.

Bandura, A. (1977) Self efficacy: toward a unifying theory of behavior change, *Psychological Review*, **84**: 191–215.

Bandura, A. (1986) *Social Foundations of Thought and Action*. Englewood Cliffs, NJ: Prentice Hall.

Bandura, A., Cio, D., Taylor, C.B. and Brouillard, M.E. (1988) Perceived self-efficacy in coping with cognitive stressors and opioid activation, *Journal of Personality and Social Psychology*, **55**: 479–88.

Bansen, S. and Stevens, H.A. (1992) Women's experiences of miscarriage in early pregnancy, *Journal of Nurse-Midwifery*, **37**: 84–90.

Barraclough, J., Pinder, P., Cruddas, M. et al. (1992) Life events and breast cancer prognosis, *British Medical Journal*, **304**: 1078–81.

Barth, J., Schumacher, M. and Herrmann-Lingen, C. (2004) Depression as a risk factor for mortality in patients with coronary heart disease: a meta-analysis, *Psychosomatic Medicine*, **66**(6): 802–13.

Barthomeuf, L., Rousset, S., and Droit-Volet, S. (2007) Emotion and food: do the emotions expressed on other people's faces affect the desire to eat liked and disliked food products? *Appetite*, **48**: 211–17.

Baucom, D.H. and Aiken, P.A. (1981) Effect of depressed mood on eating among obese and nonobese dieting and nondieting persons, *Journal of Personality and Social Psychology*, **41**: 577–85.

Baum, A., Fisher, J.D. and Solomon, S. (1981) Type of information, familiarity and the reduction of crowding stress, *Journal of Personality and Social Psychology*, **40**: 11–23.

Bayram, C., Britt, H., Kelly, Z. and Valenti, L. (2003) *Male Consultations in General Practice in Australia 1999–00: General Practice Series No. 11*. Canberra: Australian Institute of Health and Welfare.

Beck, A.T., Mendelson, M., Mock, J. et al. (1961) Inventory for measuring depression, *Archives of General Psychiatry*, **4**: 561–71.

Beck, F., Gillison, F. and Standage, M. (2010) A theoretical investigation of the development of physical activity habits in retirement, *British Journal of Health Psychology*, **15**(3): 663–79.

Beck, K.H. and Lund, A.K. (1981) The effects of health threat seriousness and personal efficacy upon intentions and behaviour, *Journal of Applied Social Psychology*, **11**: 401–15.

Becker, M.H. (ed.) (1974) The health belief model and personal health behavior, *Health Education Monographs*, **2**: 324–508.

Becker, M.H. and Rosenstock, I.M. (1984) Compliance with medical advice, in A. Steptoe and A. Mathews (eds) *Health Care and Human Behaviour*. London: Academic Press.

Becker, M.H. and Rosenstock, I.M. (1987) Comparing social learning theory and the health belief model, in W.B. Ward (ed.) *Advances in Health Education and Promotion*. Greenwich, CT: JAI Press.

Beecher, H.K. (1955) The powerful placebo, *Journal of the American Medical Association*, **159**: 1602–6.

Beecher, H.K. (1956) Relationship of significance of wound to the pain experienced, *Journal of the American Medical Association*, **161**: 1609–13.

Bekker, H. (2003) Genetic testing: facilitating informed choices, *Encyclopedia of the Human Genome*. London: Macmillan, www.ehgonline.net.

Belar, C.D. and Deardorff, W.W. (1995) *Clinical Health Psychology in Medical Settings: A Practitioner's Guidebook*. Hyattsville, MD: APA.

Bell, N.S., Amoroso, P.J., Yore, M.M. et al. (2000) Self-reported risk-taking behaviors and hospitalization for motor vehicle injury among active duty army personnel, *American Journal of Preventive Medicine*, **18**(Suppl. 3): 85–95.

Bellack, A.S. and DiClemente, C.C. (1999) Treating substance abuse among patients with schizophrenia. *Psychiatric Services*, **50**(1): 75–80.

Belloc, N.B. and Breslow, L. (1972) Relationship of physical health status and health practices, *Preventative Medicine*, **1**: 409–21.

Belsky, J. and Rovine, M. (1990) Patterns of marital change across the transition to parenthood: pregnancy to three years postpartum, *Journal of Marriage and the Family*, **52**: 5–19.

Bentley, R, Kavanagh, A. and Smith, A. (2009) Area disadvantage, socioeconomic position and women's contraception use: a multilevel study in the UK, *The Journal of Family Planning and Reproductive Health Care*, **35**(4): 221–6.

Beral, V., Reeves, G. and Banks, E. (2005) Current evidence about the effect of hormone replacement therapy on the incidence of major conditions in postmenopausal women, *BJOG: An International Journal of Obstetrics and Gynaecology*, **112**(6): 692–5.

Berg, C., Lappas, G., Wolk, A. et al. (2009) Eating patterns and portion size associated with obesity in a Swedish population, *Appetite*, **52**(1): 21–6.

Bergner, M., Bobbitt, R.A., Carter, W.B. and Gilson, D. (1981) The sickness impact profile: development and final revision of a health status measure, *Medical Care*, **19**: 787–805.

Berkman, L.F. and Syme, S.L. (1979) Social networks, lost resistance and mortality: a nine year follow up study of Alameda County residents, *American Journal of Epidemiology*, **109**: 186–204.

Berry, D.C. (2004) *Risk Communication and Health Psychology*. New York: Open University Press.

Berry, D.C., Michas, I.C. and Bersellini, E. (2003) Communicating information about medication: the benefits of making it personal, *Psychology and Health*, **18**(1): 127–39.

Berry, D.C., Michas, I.C., Gillie, T. and Forster, M. (1997) What do patients want to know about their medicines, and what do doctors want to tell them? A comparative study, *Psychology and Health*, **12**: 467–80.

Beta-blocker Heart Attack Trial Research Group (BHAT) (1982) A randomized trial of propranolol in patients with acute myocardial infarction: I–mortality results, *Journal of the American Medical Association*, **247**: 1707–14.

Beutel, M., Deckhardt, R., von Rad, M. and Weiner, H. (1995) Grief and depression after miscarriage: their separation, antecedents and course, *Psychosomatic Medicine*, **57**: 517–26.

Bieliauskas, L.A. (1980) Life stress and aid seeking, *Journal of Human Stress*, **6**: 28–36.

Biener, L., Abrams, D.B., Follick, M.J. and Dean, L. (1989) A comparative evaluation of a restrictive smoking policy in a general hospital, *American Journal of Public Health*, **79**: 192–5.

Birch, L.L. (1980) Effects of peer models' food choices and eating behaviors on preschoolers' food preferences, *Child Development*, **51**: 489–96.

Birch, L.L. (1989) Developmental aspects of eating, in R. Shepherd (ed.) *Handbook of the Psychophysiology of Human Eating*, pp. 179–203. Chichester: Wiley.

Birch, L.L. (1999) Development of food preferences, *Annual Review of Nutrition*, **19**: 41–62.

Birch, L.L. and Anzman, S.L. (2010) Learning to eat in an obesogenic environment: a developmental systems perspective on childhood obesity, *Child Development Perspectives*, **4**: 138–43.

Birch, L.L. and Deysher, M. (1986) Caloric compensation and sensory specific satiety: evidence for self-regulation of food intake by young children, *Appetite*, **7**: 323–31.

Birch, L.L. and Fisher, J.O. (2000) Mothers' child-feeding practices influence daughters' eating and weight, *American Journal of Clinical Nutrition*, **71**: 1054–61.

Birch, L.L. and Marlin, D.W. (1982) I don't like it; I never tried it: effects of exposure on two-year-old children's food preferences, *Appetite*, **23**: 353–60.

Birch, L.L., Zimmerman, S. and Hind, H. (1980) The influence of social affective context on preschool children's food preferences, *Child Development*, **51**: 856–61.

Birch, L.L., Birch, D., Marlin, D. and Kramer, L. (1982) Effects of instrumental eating on children's food preferences, *Appetite*, **3**: 125–34.

Birch, L.L., McPhee, L., Shoba, B.C. et al. (1987) What kind of exposure reduces children's food neophobia? Looking vs tasting, *Appetite*, **9**: 171–8.

Birch, L.L., Fisher, J.O., Grimm-Thomas, K. et al. (2001) Confirmatory factor analysis of the Child Feeding Questionnaire: a measure of parental attitudes, beliefs and practices about child feeding and obesity proneness, *Appetite*, **36**: 201–10.

Birch, L.L., Gunder, L., Grimm-Thomas, K. and Laing, D.G. (1998) Infant's consumption of a new food enhances acceptance of similar foods, *Appetite*, **30**: 283–95.

Bish, A., Sutton, S. and Golombok, S. (2000) Predicting uptake of a routine cervical smear test: a comparison of the health belief model and the theory of planned behaviour, *Psychology and Health*, **15**: 35–50.

Bishop, F.L., Yardley, L. and Lewith, G.T. (2007) A systematic review of beliefs involved in the use of complementary and alternative medicine, *Journal of Health Psychology*, **12**(6): 851–67.

Bishop, G.D. and Converse, S.A. (1986) Illness representations: a prototype approach, *Health Psychology*, **5**: 95–114.

Black, R.B. (1989) A 1 and 16 month follow up of prenatal diagnosis patients who lost pregnancies, *Prenatal Diagnosis*, **9**: 795–804.

Blair, S.N. (1993) Evidence for success of exercise in weight loss and control, *Annals of Internal Medicine*, **199**: 702–6.

Blair, S.N., Kampert, J.B., Kohl, H.W. et al. (1996) Influences of cardiorespiratory fitness and other precursors on cardiovascular disease and all-cause mortality in men and women, *Journal of the American Medical Association*, **276**: 205–10.

Blair, S.N., Kohl, H.W., Paffenbarger, R.S. et al. (1989) Physical fitness and all-cause mortality: a prospective study of healthy men and women, *Journal of the American Medical Association*, **262**: 2395–401.

Blair, S.N., Kohl, H.W., Gordon, N.F. and Paffenbarger, R.S. (1992) How much physical activity is good for health? *Annual Review of Public Health*, **13**: 99–126.

Blaxter, M. (1990) *Health and Lifestyles*. London: Routledge.

Bloom, J.R. (1983) Social support, accommodation to stress and adjustment to breast cancer, *Social Science and Medicine*, **16**: 1329–38.

Blundell, J. and Macdiarmid, J. (1997) Fat as a risk factor for over-consumption: satiation, satiety and patterns of eating, *Journal of the American Dietetic Association*, **97**: S63–9.

Blundell, J.E., Lawton, C.L., Cotton, J.R. and Macdiarmid, J.I. (1996) Control of human appetite: implications for the intake of dietary fat, *Annual Review of Nutrition*, **16**: 285–319.

Bocchieri, L.E., Meana, M. and Fisher, B.L. (2002) A review of psychosocial outcomes of surgery for morbid obesity, *Journal of Psychosomatic Research*, **52**: 155–65.

Boersma, S.N., Maes, S. and Elderen, T. (2005) Goal disturbance predicts health-related quality of life and depression 4 months after myocardial infarction, *British Journal of Health Psychology*, **10**(4): 615–30.

Bogg, T. and Roberts, B.W. (2004) Conscientiousness and health-related behaviours: a meta-analysis of the leading behavioural contributors to mortality, *Psychological Bulletin*, **130**: 887–919.

Boldero, J., Moore, S. and Rosenthal, D. (1992) Intention, context, and safe sex: Australian adolescents' responses to AIDS, *Journal of Applied Social Psychology*, **22**: 1374–98.

Bolton-Smith, C. and Woodward, M. (1994) Dietary composition and fat to sugar ratios in relation to obesity, *International Journal of Obesity*, **18**: 820–8.

Bonetti, D. and Johnston, M. (2008) Perceived control predicting the recovery of individual-specific walking behaviours following stroke: testing psychological models and constructs, *British Journal of Health Psychology*, **13**(3): 463–78.

Bongaarts, J., Pelletier, F. and Gerland, P. (2009) Global trends in AIDS mortality, *Poverty, Gender, and Youth*, working paper no. 16, www.popcouncil.org/pdfs/wp/pgy/016.pdf.

Boon, B., Stroebe, W., Schut, H. and Ijntema, R. (2002) Ironic processes in eating behaviour of restrained eaters, *British Journal of Health Psychology*, **7**: 1–10.

Booth, R.J., Petrie, K.J. and Pennebaker, J.W. (1997) Changes in circulating lymphocyte numbers following emotional disclosure: evidence of buffering? *Stress Medicine*, **13**: 23–9.

Boreham, C.A., Wallace, W.F. and Nevill, A. (2000) Training effects of accumulated daily stairclimbing exercise in previously sedentary young women, *Preventive Medicine*, **30**: 277–81.

Borg, S. and Lasker, J. (1982) *When Pregnancy Fails: Coping with Miscarriage, Stillbirth and Infant Death*. London: Routledge & Kegan Paul.

Borland, R., Owens, N., Hill, D. and Chapman, S. (1990) Changes in acceptance of workplace smoking bans following their implementation: a prospective study, *Preventative Medicine*, **19**: 314–22.

Borland, R., Owens, N. and Hocking, B. (1991) Changes in smoking behaviour after a total work place ban, *Australian Journal of Public Health*, **15**: 130–4.

Borrayo, E. and Jenkins, S. (2001) Feeling indecent: breast cancer-screening resistance of Mexican descent women, *Journal of Health Psychology*, **6**(5): 537–49.

Bortner, R.W. (1969) A short rating scale as a potential measure of pattern A behaviour, *Journal of Chronic Disease*, **22**: 87–91.

Bosworth, H.B., Siegler, I.C., Olsen, M.K. et al. (2001) Social support and quality of life in patients with coronary heart disease, *Quality of Life Research*, **9**: 829–39.

Bouchard, C., Trembley, A., Despres, J.P. et al. (1990) The response to long term overfeeding in identical twins, *New England Journal of Medicine*, **322**: 1477–82.

Boulton, M., Schramm Evans, Z., Fitzpatrick, R. and Hart, G. (1991) Bisexual men: women, safer sex, and HIV infection, in P. Aggleton, P.M. Davies and G. Hart (eds) *AIDS: Responses, Policy and Care*. London: Falmer Press.

Bower, J.E., Kemeny, M.E., Taylor, S.E. et al. (1998) Cognitive processing, discovery of meaning, CD 4 decline, and AIDS-related mortality among bereaved HIV seropositive men, *Journal of Consulting and Clinical Psychology*, **66**: 979–86.

Bowlby, J. (1973). *Attachment and Loss: Vol. II. Separation: Anxiety and Anger.* New York: Basic Books.

Boyce, W.T., Alkon, A., Tschann, J.M. et al. (1995) Dimensions of psychobiologic reactivity: cardiovascular responses to laboratory stressors in preschool children, *Annals of Behavioural Medicine*, **17**: 315–23.

Boyle, C.M. (1970) Differences between patients' and doctors' interpretations of common medical terms, *British Medical Journal*, **2**: 286–9.

Bradley, C. (1985) Psychological aspects of diabetes, in D.G.M.M. Alberti and L.P. Drall (eds) *Diabetes Annual*. Amsterdam: Elsevier.

Bradley, C. (1997) Design of renal-dependent individualized quality of life questionnaire, *Advances in Peritoneal Dialysis*, **13**: 116–20.

Bradley, C. (2001) Importance of differentiating health status from quality of life, *Lancet*, **357**(9249): 7–8.

Bradley, C., Todd, C., Symonds, E. et al. (1999) The development of an individualized questionnaire measure of perceived impact of diabetes on quality of life: the ADDQoL, *Quality of Life Research*, **8**: 79–91.

Breckler, S.J. (1994) A comparison of numerical indexes for measuring attitude ambivalence, *Educational and Psychological Measurement*, **54**: 350–65.

Breslow, L. and Enstrom, J. (1980) Persistence of health habits and their relationship to mortality, *Preventive Medicine*, **9**: 469–83.

Brewer, N.T., Chapman, G.B., Brownlee, S. and Leventhal, E.A. (2002) Cholesterol control, medication adherence and illness cognition, *British Journal of Health Psychology*, **7**: 433–47.

Brickell, T.A., Chatzisarantis, N.L. and Pretty, G.M. (2006) Using past behaviour and spontaneous implementation intentions to enhance the utility of the theory of planned behaviour in predicting exercise, *British Journal of Health Psychology*, **11**(2): 249–62.

Brickman, P., Rabinowitz, V.C., Karuza, J. et al. (1982) Models of helping and coping, *American Psychologist*, **37**: 368–84.

Broadbent, E., Ellis, C.J., Thomas, J. et al. (2009) Can an illness perception intervention reduce illness anxiety in spouses on myocardial infarction patients? A randomised controlled trial, *Journal of Psychosomatic Research*, **67**: 17–23.

Broadbent, E., Petrie, K.J., Ellis, C.J. et al. (2004) A picture of health–myocardial infarction patients' drawings of their hearts and subsequent disability: a longitudinal study, *Journal of Psychosomatic Research*, **57**(6): 583–7.

Broadbent, E., Petrie, K.J., Main, J. and Weinman, J. (2006) The brief illness perception questionnaire, *Journal of Psychosomatic Research*, **60**(6): 631–7.

Broadstock, M., Michie, S. and Marteau, T.M. (2000) Psychological consequences of predictive genetic testing: a systematic review, *European Journal of Human Genetics*, **8**: 731–8.

Brodie, D.A., Slade, P.D. and Rose, H. (1989) Reliability measures in disturbing body image, *Perceptual and Motor Skills*, **69**: 723–32.

Brody, L.R. (1999) *Gender, Emotion, and the Family.* Cambridge, MA: Harvard University Press.

Bromet, E. J., Gluzman, S., Schwartz, J. E. and Goldgaber, D. (2002) Somatic symptoms in women 11 years after the Chornobyl accident: prevalence and risk factors, *Environmental Health Perspectives*, **110**(Suppl. 4): 625–9.

Broom, A. (2004) Prostate cancer and masculinity in Australian society: a case of stolen identity? *International Journal of Men's health*, **3**: 73–91.

Broom, A. (2010) Prostate cancer and masculinities in Australia, in B. Gough., and S. Robertson (eds) *Men, Masculinities and Health: Critical Perspectives.* Basingstoke: Palgrave Macmillan.

Broquet, K. (1999) Psychological reactions to pregnancy loss, *Primary Care Update for Obstetrics and Gynecology*, **6**: 12–16.

Brosschot, J.F. and Van der Doef, M.P. (2006) Daily worrying and somatic health complaints: testing the effectiveness of a simple worry reduction intervention, *Psychology and Health*, **21**: 19–31.

Brotherstone, H. Miles, A.K.A., Atkin, W. and Wardle, J. (2006) The impact of illustrations on public understanding of the aim of cancer screening, *Patient Education and Counseling*, **63**: 328–35.

Brown, G.W. and Harris, T.O. (1978) *Social Origins of Depression.* London: Tavistock.

Brown, K., Ogden, J., Gibson, L. and Vogele, C. (2008) The role of parental control practices in explaining children's diet and BMI, *Appetite*, **50**: 252–9.

Brown, R. and Ogden, J. (2004) Children's eating attitudes and behaviour: a study of the modelling and control theories of parental influence, *Health Education and Research*, **19**(3): 261–71.

Brown, R.A., Lichtenstein, E., McIntyre, K. and Harrington-Kostur, J. (1984) Effects of nicotine fading and relapse prevention on smoking cessation, *Journal of Consulting and Clinical Psychology*, **52**: 307–8.

Brown, T.A., Cash, T.F. and Mikulka, P.J. (1990) Attitudinal body-image assessment: factor analysis of the body self relations questionnaire, *Journal of Personality Assessment*, **55**: 135–44.

Browne, J.P., McGee, H.M. and O'Boyle, C.A. (1997) Conceptual approaches to the assessment of quality of life, *Psychology and Health*, **12**: 737–51.

Brownell, K.D. (1989) Weight control and your health, in *World Book Encyclopedia.* Chicago: World Book.

Brownell, K.D. and Steen, S.N. (1987) Modern methods for weight control: the physiology and psychology of dieting, *The Physician and Sports Medicine*, **15**: 122–37.

Brownell, K.D. and Wadden, T.A. (1991) The heterogeneity of obesity: fitting treatments to individuals, *Behaviour Therapy*, **22**: 153–77.

Brownell, K.D. and Wadden, T.A. (1992) Etiology and treatment of obesity: understanding a serious, prevalent and refractory disorder, *Journal of Consulting and Clinical Psychology*, **60**: 435–42.

Brownell, K.D., Greenwood, M.R.C., Stellar, E. and Shrager, E.E. (1986a) The effects of repeated cycles of weight loss and regain in rats, *Physiology and Behaviour*, **38**: 459–64.

Brownell, K.D., Marlatt, G.A., Lichtenstein, E. and Wilson, G.T. (1986b) Understanding and preventing relapse, *American Psychologist*, **41**: 765–82.

Brownell, K.D., Steen, S.N. and Wilmore, J.H. (1989) Weight regulation practices in athletes: analysis of metabolic and health effects, *Medical Science and Sports Exercise*, **7**: 125–32.

Bruch, H. (1974) *Eating Disorders: Obesity, Anorexia and the Person Within.* New York: Basic Books.

Bryant, K.D. (2009). Contraceptive use and attitudes among female college students, *The ABNF Journal: Official Journal of the Association of Black Nursing Faculty in Higher Education Inc.*, **20**(1): 12–16.

Bucci, W. (1995) The power of the narrative: a multiple code account, in J.W. Pennebaker (ed.) *Emotion, Disclosure, and Health.* Washington, DC: American Psychological Association.

Buchi, S.T., Villiger, B., Sensky, T. et al. (1997) Psychosocial predictors of long term success in patient pulmonary rehabilitation of patients with COPD, *European Respiratory Journal*, **10**: 1272–7.

Bucknall, C.A., Morris, G.K. and Mitchell, J.R.A. (1986) Physicians' attitudes to four common problems: hypertension, atrial fibrillation, transient ischaemic attacks, and angina pectoris, *British Medical Journal*, **293**: 739–42.

Buick, D.L., Crook, D. and Horne, R. (2005) Women's perceptions of hormone replacement therapy: risks and benefits (1980–2002) – a literature review, *Climacteric*, **8**(1): 24–35.

Bullen, B.A., Reed, R.B. and Mayer, J. (1964) Physical activity of obese and non-obese adolescent girls appraised by motion picture sampling, *American Journal of Clinical Nutrition*, **4**: 211–33.

Bundy, C., Carroll, D., Wallace, L. and Nagle, R. (1998) Stress management and exercise training in chronic stable angina pectoris, *Psychology and Health*, **13**: 147–55.

Burish, T.G., Carey, M.P., Krozely, M.G. and Greco, F.F. (1987) Conditioned side-effects induced by cancer chemotherapy: prevention through behavioral treatment, *Journal of Consulting and Clinical Psychology*, **55**: 42–8.

Burnett, J. (1989) *Plenty and Want: A Social History of Food in England from 1815 to the Present Day*, 3rd edn. London: Routledge.

Bury, M. (1982) Chronic illness as biographical disruption, *Sociology of Health and Illness*, **4**: 167–82.

Busick, D.B., Brooks, J., Pernecky, S. et al. (2008) Parent food purchases as a measure of exposure and preschool-aged children's willingness to identify and taste fruit and vegetables, *Appetite*, **51**: 468–73.

Butler, C. and Llanedeyrn, M. (1996) Late psychological sequelae of abortion: questions from a primary care perspective, *The Journal of Family Practice*, **43**: 396–401.

Butler, C. and Steptoe, A. (1986) Placebo responses: an experimental study of psychophysiological processes in asthmatic volunteers, *British Journal of Clinical Psychology*, **25**: 173–83.

Byrne, D., Kazwinski, C., DeNinno, J.A. and Fisher, W.A. (1977) Negative sexual attitudes and contraception, in
D. Byrne and L.A. Byrne (eds) *Exploring Human Sexuality*. New York: Crowell.

Byrne, G.J.A., Raphael, B. and Arnold, E. (1999) Alcohol consumption and psychological distress in recently widowed older men, *Australian and New Zealand Journal of Psychiatry*, **33**: 740–7.

Byrne, P.S. and Long, B.E.L. (1976) *Doctor Talking to Patient*. London: HMSO.

Calnan, M. (1987) *Health and Illness: The Lay Perspective*. London: Tavistock.

Cameron, L.D. (2008) Illness risk representations and motivations to engage in protective behavior: the case of skin cancer risk, *Psychology & Health*, **23**(1): 91–112.

Cameron, L.D. (2009) Can our health behaviour models handle imagery-based processes and communications? *The European Health Psychologist*, Keynote Article 1.

Cameron, L.D. and Chan, C.K.Y. (2008) Designing health communications: harnessing the power of affect, imagery, and self-regulation, *Social and Personality Psychology Compass*, **2**(1): 262–82.

Cancer Research Campaign (1991) *Smoking Policy and Prevalence Among 16–19 Year Olds*. London: HMSO.

Cancer Research UK (2006) UK prostate cancer incidence statistics, info.cancerresearchuk.org.8000/cancerstats/types/
prostate/incidence/.

Cancer Research UK (2009) http://info.cancerresearchuk.org/prod_consump/groups/cr_common/@nre/@sta/documents/generalcontent/018070.pdf.

Canetto, S.S. (1997) Meanings of gender and suicidal behavior among adolescents, *Suicide and Life-Threatening Behavior*, **27**: 339–51.

Cannon, W.B. (1932) *The Wisdom of the Body*. New York: Norton.

Cappell, H. and Greeley, J. (1987) Alcohol and tnsion reduction: an update on research and theory, in H.T. Blane and K.E. Leonard (eds) *Psychological Theories of Drinking and Alcoholism*. New York: Guilford Press.

Cappuccio, F.P., Cooper, D., D'Elia, L. et al. (2011) Sleep duration predicts cardiovascular outcomes: a systematic review and meta-analysis of prospective studies, *European Heart Journal*, advance online publication. 0195–668x.

Carey, M.P., Kalra, D.L., Carey, K.B. et al. (1993) Stress and unaided smoking cessation: a prospective investigation, *Journal of Consulting and Clinical Psychology*, **61**: 831–8.

Carlisle, A.C.S., John, A.M.H., Fife-Shaw, C. and Lloyd, M. (2005) The self-regulatory model in women with rheumatoid arthritis: relationships between illness representations, coping strategies, and illness outcome, *British Journal of Health Psychology*, **10**: 571–87.

Carmack, M. and Martens, R. (1979) Measuring commitment to running, a survey of runners' attitudes and mental states, *Journal of Sports Psychology*, **1**: 25–42.

Carrigan, T., Connell., R.W. and Lee, J. (1985) Hard and heavy: toward a new sociology of masculinity, *Theory and Society*, **14**: 551–603.

Carroll, K.M., Libby, B., Sheehan, J. and Hyland, N. (2001) Motivational interviewing to enhance treatment initiation in substance abusers: an effectiveness study, *The American Journal on Addictions*, **10**(4): 335–9.

Carson, J.W., Keefe, F.J., Affleck, G. et al. (2006) A comparison of conventional pain coping skills training and pain coping skills training with a maintenance training component: a daily diary analysis of short and long-term treatment effects, *The Journal of Pain*, **7**(9): 615–25.

Cartwright, A., Hockey, L. and Anderson, J.L. (1973) *Life Before Death*. London: Routledge.

Carver, C.S. and Scheier, M.F. (1999) Stress, coping, and self-regulatory processes, in L. A. Pervin and J.P. Oliver (eds) *Handbook of Personality Theory and Research*. New York: Guildford Press.

Carver, C.S., Scheier, M.F. and Weintraub, J.K. (1989) Assessing coping strategies: a theoretically based approach, *Journal of Personality and Social Psychology*, **56**: 267–83.

Casey, R. and Rozin, P. (1989) Changing children's food preferences: parents' opinions, *Appetite*, **12**: 171–82.

Cash, T., Winstead, B., and Janda, L. (1986) The great American shape-up: body image survey report, *Psychology Today*, **20**: 30–7.

Caspersen, C.J., Powell, K.E. and Christenson, G.M. (1985) Physical activity, exercise, and physical fitness: definitions and distinctions for health-related research, *Public Health Reports*, **100**: 126–31.

Castle, C.M., Skinner, T.C. and Hampson, S. (1999) Young women and suntanning: an evaluation of a health education leaflet, *Psychology and Health*, **14**: 517–27.

Center for Disease Control (2008) Smoking-attributable mortality, years of potential life lost, and productivity losses United States, 2000–2004, *Morbidity and Mortality Weekly Reports*, **57**: 1226–8.

Chafin, S., Roy, M., Gerin, W. and Christenfeld, N. (2004) Music can facilitate blood pressure recovery from stress, *British Journal of Health Psychology*, **9**(3): 393–403.

Chalmers, J., Catalan, J., Day, A. and Fairburn, C. (1985) Anorexia nervosa presenting as morbid exercising, *Lancet*, **1**: 286–7.

Chambers, L.W., McDonald, L.A., Tugwell, P. et al. (1982) The McMaster Health Index Questionnaire as a measure of quality of life for patients with rheumatoid arthritis, *Journal of Rheumatology*, **9**: 780–4.

Champion, V.L. (1990) Breast self-examination in women 35 and older: a prospective study, *Journal of Behavioural Medicine*, **13**: 523–38.

Chan, I.W.S., Lai, J.C.L. and Wong, K.W.N. (2006) Resilience is associated with better recovery in Chinese people diagnosed with coronary heart disease, *Psychology and Health*, **21**(3): 335–49.

Chan, J.M., Rimm, E.B., Colditz, G.A. et al. (1994) Obesity, fat distribution and weight gain as risk factors for clinical diabetes in men, *Diabetes Care*, **17**: 961–9.

Chapman, C.L. and de Castro, J. (1990) Running addiction: measurement and associated psychological characteristics, *The Journal of Sports Medicine and Physical Fitness*, **30**: 283–90.

Chapman, S. and Martin, M. (2010) Attention to pain words in irritable bowel syndrome: increased orienting and speeded engagement, *British Journal of Health Psychology*, **16**: 47–60.

Charles, S.T. and Almeida, D.M. (2006) Daily reports of symptoms and negative affect: not all symptoms are the same, *Psychology and Health*, **21**: 1–17.

Charlton, A. (1984) Children's opinion about smoking, *Journal of the Royal College of General Practitioners*, **34**: 483–7.

Charlton, A. (1992) Children and tobacco, *British Journal of Cancer*, **66**: 1–4.

Charlton, A. and Blair, V. (1989) Predicting the onset of smoking in boys and girls, *Social Science and Medicine*, **29**: 813–18.

Charmaz, K. (1995) Identity dilemmas of chronically ill men, in D. Sabo and D.F. Gordon (eds) *Men's Health and Illness: Gender, Power and the Body*. Thousand Oaks, CA: Sage.

Chassin, L., Presson, C.C., Sherman, S.J. and Edwards, D.A. (1990) The natural history of cigarette smoking: predicting young adult smoking outcomes from adolescent smoking patterns, *Health Psychology*, **9**: 701–16.

Chinn, S. and Rona, R.J. (2001) Prevalence and trends in overweight and obesity in three cross-sectional studies of British children, 1974–94, *British Medical Journal*, **322**: 24–6.

Christensen, A.J., Edwards, D.L., Wiebe, J.S. et al. (1996) Effect of verbal self-disclosure on natural killer cell activity: moderation influence on cynical hostility, *Psychosomatic Medicine*, **58**: 150–5.

Clarke, L., Farrell, C. and Beaumont, B. (1983) *Camden Abortion Study*. London: BPAS.

Coates, T.J., Jeffrey, R.W. and Wing, R.R. (1978) The relationship between a person's relative body weight and the quality and quantity of food stored in their homes, *Addictive Behaviours*, **3**: 179–84.

Cobb, S. and Rose, R. (1973) Hypertension, peptic ulcer and diabetes in air traffic controllers, *Journal of the American Medical Association*, **224**: 489–92.

Cockburn, J., Staples, M., Hurley, S.F. and DeLuise, T. (1994) Psychological consequences of screening mammography, *Journal of Medical Screening*, **1**: 7–12.

Coen, S.P. and Ogles, B.M. (1993) Psychological characteristics of the obligatory runner: a critical examination of the anorexic analogue hypothesis, *Journal of Sport and Exercise Psychology*, **15**: 338–54.

Cohen, F. and Lazarus, R.S. (1979) Coping with the stresses of illness, in G.C. Stone, F. Cohen and N.E. Adler (eds) *Health Psychology: A Handbook*. San Francisco, CA: Jossey-Bass.

Cohen, S. and Lichtenstein, E. (1990) Partner behaviours that support quitting smoking, *Journal of Consulting and Clinical Psychology*, **58**: 304–9.

Cohen, S., Kamarck, T. and Mermelstein, R. (1983) A global measure of perceived stress, *Journal of Health and Social Behaviour*, **24**: 385–96.

Cohen, S., Tyrell, A.J. and Smith, A.P. (1991) Psychological stress and susceptibility to the common cold, *New England Journal of Medicine*, **325**: 606–12.

Cohen, S., Mermelstein, R., Kamarck, T. and Hoberman, N.H. (1985) Measuring the functional components of social support, in I. Sarason and B. Sarason (eds)

Social Support: Theory, Research, and Applications, pp. 73–94. Dordrecht: Martinus Nijhoff.

Cole, B.S., Hopkins, C.M., Tisak, J. et al. (2008) Assessing spiritual growth and spiritual decline following a diagnosis of cancer: reliability and validity of the spiritual transformation scale, *Psycho-Oncology*, **17**: 112–21.

Coleman, L. and Ingham, R. (1998) Attenders at young people's clinics in Southampton: variations in contraceptive use, *British Journal of Family Planning*, **24**: 101–4.

Coleman, P.K., Reardon, D.C., Strahan, T. and Cougle, J.R. (2005) The psychology of abortion: a review and suggestions for future research, *Psychology and Health*, **20**: 237–71.

Collijn, D.H., Appels, A.D. and Nijhuis, F. (1996) Are multiple roles a risk factor for myocardial infarction in women? *Journal of Psychosomatic Research*, **40**: 271–9.

Collins, R.E., Lopez, L.M. and Martheau, T.M. (2011a) Emotional impact of screening: a systematic review and meta-analysis, *BMC Public Health*, **11**: 603.

Collins, R.E., Wright, A.J. and Marteau, T.M. (2011b) Impact of communicating personalized genetic risk information on perceived control over risk: a systematic review, *British Medical Journal*, 342.

Collins, R.L., Taylor, S.E. and Skokan, L.A. (1990) A better world or a shattered vision? Changes in life perspective following victimization, *Social Cognition*, **8**: 263–85.

Colvin, R.H. and Olson, S.B. (1983) A descriptive analysis of men and women who have lost significant weight and are highly successful at maintaining the loss, *Addictive Behaviours*, **8**: 287–95.

Compas, B.E., Barnez, G.A., Malcarne, V. and Worshame, N. (1991) Perceived control and coping with stress: a developmental perspective, *Journal of Social Issue*, **47**: 23–34.

Conklin, M.P. and O'Connor, B.P. (1995) Beliefs about the foetus as a moderator of post-abortion psychological well-being, *Journal of Social and Clinical Psychology*, **14**: 76–95.

Conner, M. and Armitage, C.J. (1998) Extending the theory of planned behaviour: a review and avenues for further research, *Journal of Applied Social Psychology*, **28**: 1429–64.

Connor, M. and Higgins, A. R. (2010) Long-term effects of implementation intentions on prevention of smoking uptake among adolescents: a cluster randomized controlled trial, *Health Psychology*, **29**(5): 529–38.

Conner, M. and Norman, P. (eds) (2005) *Predicting Health Behavior*, 2nd edn. Maidenhead: Open University Press.

Conner, M. and Sparks, P. (2005) Theory of planned behaviour and health behaviour, in M. Conner, and P. Norman (eds) *Predicting Health Behaviour*, 2nd edn. Maidenhead: Open University Press.

Conner, M., Fitter, M. and Fletcher, W. (1999) Stress and snacking: a diary study of daily hassles and between-meal snacking, *Psychology and Health*, **14**: 51–63.

Connor, M., Sandberg, T. and Norman, P. (2010) Using action planning to promote exercise behaviour, *Annual Behavioural Medicine*, **40**: 60–76.

Conner, M., Lawton, R., Parker, D. et al. (2007) Application of the theory of planned behaviour to the prediction of objectively assessed breaking of posted speed limits, *British Journal of Psychology*, **98**: 428–53.

Conner, M., Sandberg, T., McMillan, B. and Higgins, A. (2006) Role of anticipated regret, intentions and intention stability in adolescent smoking initiation, *British Journal of Health Psychology*, **11**: 85–101.

Conner, M., Rhodes, R.E., Morris, B., McEachan, R. and Lawton, R. (2011) Changing exercise through targeting affective or cognitive attitudes, *Psychology & Health*, **26**(2): 133–49.

Constanzo, P.R. and Woody, E.Z. (1985) Domain specific parenting styles and their impact on the child's development of particular deviance: the example of obesity proneness, *Journal of Social and Clinical Psychology*, **4**: 425–45.

Contento, I.R., Basch, C., Shea, S. et al. (1993) Relationship of mothers' food choice criteria to food intake of pre-school children: identification of family subgroups, *Health Education Quarterly*, **20**: 243–59.

Cook, W.W. and Medley, D.M. (1954) Proposed hostility and pharasaic virtue scales for the MMPI, *Journal of Applied Psychology*, **38**: 414–18.

Cools, J., Schotte, D.E. and McNally, R.J. (1992) Emotional arousal and overeating in restrained eaters, *Journal of Abnormal Psychology*, **101**: 348–51.

Cooper, A.F., Jackson, G., Weinman, J. and Horne, R. (2002) Factors associated with cardiac rehabilitation attendance: a systematic review of the literature, *Clinical Rehabilitation*, **16**: 541–52.

Cooper, M.L. (2002) Alcohol use and risky sexual behavior among college students and youth, *Journal of Studies on Alcohol*, **14**(suppl.): 101–17.

Cooper, P.J., Taylor, M.J., Cooper, Z. and Fairburn, C.G. (1987) The development and validation of the body shape questionnaire, *International Journal of Eating Disorders*, **6**: 485–94.

Cooper, V., Buick, D., Horne, R. et al. (2002) Perceptions of HAART among gay men who declined a treatment offer: preliminary results from an interview-based study, *AIDS Care*, **14**: 319–28.

Coopersmith, S. (1967) *The Antecedents of Self-esteem.* San Francisco, CA: WH Freeman.

Corah, W.L. and Boffa, J. (1970) Perceived control, self-observation and responses to aversive stimulation, *Journal of Personality and Social Psychology*, **16**: 1–4.

Corbin, W.R. and Fromme, K. (2002) Alcohol use and serial monogamy as risks for sexually transmitted diseases in young adults, *Health Psychology*, **21**: 229–36.

Cordova, M.J., Cunningham, L.L.C, Carlson, C.R. and Andrykowski, M.A. (2001) Posttraumatic growth following breast cancer: a controlled comparison study, *Health Psychology*, **20**(3): 176–85.

Coulter, A. (1999) Paternalism or partnership? Patients have grown up and there's no going back, *British Medical Journal*, **319**: 719–20.

Courtenay, W.H. (2000a) Engendering health: a social constructionist examination of men's health beliefs and behaviors, *Psychology of Men and Masculinity*, **1**: 4–15.

Courtenay, W.H. (2000b) Behavioral factors associated with disease, injury, and death among men: Evidence and implications for prevention, *The Journal of Men's Studies*, **9**:81–142.

Courtenay, W.H., McCreary, D.R. and Merighi, J.R. (2002) Gender and ethnic differences in health beliefs and behaviors, *Journal of Health Psychology*, **7**(3): 219–31.

Cox, K.L., Gorely, T.J., Puddey, I.B. et al. (2003) Exercise behaviour change in 40 to 65-year-old women: the SWEAT study (Sedentary Women Exercise Adherence Trial), *British Journal of Health Psychology*, **8**(4): 477–95.

Crago, M.A. (1972) Psychopathology in marital couples, *Psychological Bulletin*, **77**: 114–28.

Crichton, E.F., Smith, D.L. and Demanuele, F. (1978) Patients' recall of medication information, *Drug Intelligence and Clinical Pharmacy*, **12**: 591–9.

Crisp, A.H., Hsu, L., Harding, B. and Hartshorn, J. (1980) Clinical features of anorexia: a study of consecutive series of 102 female patients, *Journal of Psychosomatic Research*, **24**: 179–91.

Crombez, G., Bijttebier, P., Eccleston, C. et al. (2003) The child version of the pain catastrophizing scale (PCS-C): a preliminary validation, *Pain*, **104**(3): 639–46.

Crombez, G., Eccleston, C., Baeyens, F. et al. (1999) Attention to chronic pain is dependent upon pain-related fear, *Journal of Psychosomatic Research*, **47**(5): 403–10.

Crombez, G., Eccleston, C., Baeyens, F. and Eelen, P. (1998a) Attentional disruption is enhanced by threat of pain, *Behaviour Research and Therapy*, **36**: 195–204.

Crombez, G., Eccleston, C., Baeyens, F. and Eelen, P. (1998b) When somatic information threatens, catastrophic thinking enhances attentional interference, *Pain*, **75**(2–3): 187–98.

Cropley, M. and Millward Purvis, L.J. (2003) Job strain and rumination about work issues during leisure time: a diary study, *European Journal of Work and Organizational Psychology*, **12**(3): 195–207.

Cropley, M. and Steptoe, A. (2005) Social support, life events and physical symptoms: a prospective study of chronic and recent life stress in men and women, *Psychology, Health & Medicine*, **10**(4): 317–25.

Cropley, M., Ayers, S. and Nokes, L. (2003) People don't exercise because they can't think of reasons to exercise: an examination of causal reasoning within the transtheoretical model, *Psychology, Health & Medicine*, **8**(4): 409–14.

Cropley, M., Steptoe, A. and Joekes, K. (1999b) Job strain and psychiatric morbidity, *Psychological Medicine*, **29**: 1411–16.

Cvetkovich, G. and Grote, B. (1981) Psychosocial maturity and teenage contraceptive use: an investigation of decision-making and communication skills, *Population and Environment*, **4**: 211–26.

DAFNE Study Group (2002) Training in flexible, intensive insulin management to enable dietary freedom in people with type I diabetes: dose adjustment for normal eating (DAFNE) randomised controlled trial, *British Medical Journal*, **325**: 1–6.

Danaher, B.G. (1977) Rapid smoking and self-control in the modification of smoking behaviour, *Journal of Consulting and Clinical Psychology*, **45**: 1068–75.

Daniel, J.Z., Cropley, M. and Fife-Schaw, C. (2006) The effect of exercise in reducing desire to smoke and cigarette withdrawal symptoms is not caused by distraction, *Addiction*, **101**(8): 1187–92.

Danoff-Burg, S., Agee, J.D., Romanoff, N.R. et al. (2006). Benefit finding and expressive writing in adults with lupus or rheumatoid arthritis, *Psychology and Health*, **21**(5): 651–65.

Darker, C.D. and French, D.P. (2009) What sense do people make of a theory of planned behaviour questionnaire? A think-aloud study, *Journal of Health Psychology*, **14**(7): 861–71.

Davies, D.L. (1962) Normal drinking in recovered alcohol addicts, *Quarterly Journal of Studies on Alcohol*, **23**: 94–104.

Davies, MJ., Heller, S., Skinner, TC. et al. (2009) Effectiveness of the diabetes education and self-management for ongoing and newly diagnosed (DESMOND) programme for people with newly diagnosed type 2 diabetes, cluster randomised controlled trial, *British Medical Journal*, **336**: 491–5.

Davis, C. (1928) Self-selection of diets by newly weaned infants, *American Journal of Disease of Children*, **36**: 651–79.

de Gonzalez, A., Hartge P., Cerhan, J.R. et al. (2010) Body-mass index and mortality among 1.46 million white adults, *New England Journal of Medicine*, **363**: 2211–19.

de Ridder, D., Schreurs, K.M.G. and Kuijer, R.G. (2005) Is spousal support always helpful to patients with asthma or diabetes? A prospective study, *Psychology and Health*, **20**(4): 497–508.

de Ridder, D., Geenen, R., Kuijer, R. and van Midden-dorp, H. (2008) Psychological adjustment to chronic disease, *The Lancet*, **372**(9634): 246–55.

De Zwann, M., Lancaster, K.L., Mitchell, J.E. et al. (2002) Health related quality of life in morbidly obese patients: effect of gastric bypass surgery, *Obesity Surgery*, **12**: 773–80.

Dean, C. (1987) Psychiatric morbidity following mastectomy: preoperative predictors and types of illness, *Journal of Psychosomatic Research*, **31**: 385–92.

Dean, C., Roberts, M.M., French, K. and Robinson, S. (1984) Psychiatric morbidity after screening for breast cancer, *Journal of Epidemiology and Community Health*, **40**: 71–5.

Deary, V. (2008) A precarious balance: Using a self-regulation model to conceptualize and treat chronic fatigue syndrome, *British Journal of Health Psychology*, **13**(2): 231–6.

Deary, V., Chalder, T. and Sharpe, M. (2007) The cognitive behavioural model of medically unexplained symptoms: a theoretical and empirical review, *Clinical Psychology Review*, **27**: 781–97.

Debro, S.C., Campbell, S.M. and Peplau, L.A. (1994) Influencing a partner to use a condom: characteristics of the situation are more important than characteristics of the individual, *Psychology, Health and Medicine*, **4**: 265–79.

Deci, E.L. and Ryan, R.M. (1985) *Intrinsic Motivation and Self-determination in Human Behavior*. New York: Plenum.

Deci, E.L. and Ryan, R.M. (2000) The 'what' and 'why' of goal pursuits: human needs and the self-determination of behavior, *Psychological Inquiry: An International Journal for the Advancement of Psychological Theory*, **11**(4): 227–68.

deHaes, J.C.J.M., van Knippenberg, F.C. and Neigt, J.P. (1990) Measuring psychological and physical distress in cancer patients: structure and application of the Rotterdam symptom checklist, *British Journal of Cancer*, **62**: 1034–8.

Dekker, F.W., Kaptein, A.A., van der Waart, M.A.C. and Gill, K. (1992) Quality of self-care of patients with asthma, *Journal of Asthma*, **29**: 203–8.

Dempster, M., Carney, R. and McClements, R. (2010) Response shift in the assessment of quality of life among people attending cardiac rehabilitation, *British Journal of Health Psychology*, **15**: 307–19.

Despres, J-P., Lemieux, I. and Prudhomme, D. (2001) Treatment of obesity: need to focus on high risk abdominally obese patients, *British Medical Journal*, **322**: 716–20.

DH (Department of Health) (1980) *The Black Report*. London: HMSO, www.sochealth.co.uk/Black/black.htm.

DH (Department of Health) (1991) *Dietary Reference Values for Food Energy and Nutrients for the United Kingdom, Report on Health and Social Subjects No. 41*. London: HMSO.

DH (Department of Health (1995) *Obesity: Reversing the Increasing Problem of Obesity in England: A Report from the Nutrition and Physical Activity Task Forces*. London: HMSO.

DH (Department of Health) (2001) *Hospital Inpatient Statistics*, www.doh.gov.uk/HPSSS/TBL.

DH (Department of Health) (2004) *At Least Five a Week: Evidence on the Impact of Physical Activity and its Relationship to Health. A Report From the Chief Medical Officer*. London: DH.

DH (Department of Health) (2005) *Maternity Statistics 2003–2004*. London: OPCS.

Diamond, E.G., Kittle, C.F. and Crockett, J.F. (1960) Comparison of internal mammary artery ligation and sham operation for angina pectoris, *American Journal of Cardiology*, **5**: 483–6.

DiClemente, C.C. and Hughes, S.O. (1990) Stages of change profiles in outpatient alcoholism treatment, *Journal of Substance Abuse*, **2**: 217–35.

DiClemente, C.C. and Prochaska, J.O. (1982) Self-change and therapy change of smoking behavior: a comparison of processes of change in cessation and maintenance, *Addictive Behaviours*, **7**: 133–42.

DiClemente, C.C. and Prochaska, J.O. (1985) Processes and stages of change: coping and competence in smoking behavior change, in F. Shiffman and T.A. Wills (eds) *Coping and Substance Abuse*. New York: Academic Press.

DiClemente, C.C., Prochaska, J.O. and Gilbertini, M. (1985) Self-efficacy and the stages of self-change of smoking, *Cognitive Therapy and Research*, **9**: 181–200.

DiClemente, C.C., Prochaska, J.O., Fairhurst, S.K. et al. (1991) The process of smoking cessation: an analysis of precontemplation, contemplation, and preparation stages of change, *Journal of Consulting and Clinical Psychology*, **59**: 295–304.

Diederiks, J.P., Bar, F.W., Hopponer, P. et al. (1991) Predictors of return to former leisure and social activities in

MI patients, *Journal of Psychosomatic Research*, **35**: 687–96.

DiMatteo, M.R., Giordani, P.J., Lepper, H.S. and Croghan, T.W. (2002) Patient adherence and medical treatment outcomes: a meta-analysis, *Medical Care*, **40**(9): 794–811.

Diner, E., Emmons, R.A., Larson, R.J. and Griffen, S. (1985) The satisfaction with life scale, *Journal of Personality Assessment*, **49**: 71–6.

Dishman, R.K. (1982) Compliance/adherence in health-related exercise, *Health Psychology*, **1**: 237–67.

Dishman, R.K. and Gettman, L.R. (1980) Psychobiologic influences on exercise adherence, *Journal of Sport Psychology*, **2**: 295–310.

Dishman, R.K., Sallis, J.F. and Orenstein, D.M. (1985) The determinants of physical activity and exercise, *Public Health Reports*, **100**: 158–72.

Dishman, R.K., Oldenburg, B., O'Neal, H. and Shephard, R. J. (1998) Worksite physical activity interventions, *American Journal of Preventive Medicine*, **15**(4): 344–61.

Doll, R. and Hill, A.B. (1954) The mortality of doctors in relation to their smoking habits: a preliminary report, *British Medical Journal*, **1**: 1451–5.

Doll, R. and Peto, R. (1981) *The Causes of Cancer*. New York: Oxford University Press.

Donnelly, D.A. and Murray, E.J. (1991) Cognitive and emotional changes in written essays and therapy interviews, *Journal of Social and Clinical Psychology*, **10**: 334–50.

Dormandy, E., Hankins, M. and Marteau, T.M. (2006) Attitudes and uptake of a screening test: the moderating role of ambivalence, *Psychology and Health*, **21**: 499–511.

Dowey, A.J. (1996) Psychological determinants of children's food preferences, unpublished doctoral dissertation, University of Wales, Bangor.

Downing, R.W. and Rickels, K. (1983) Physician prognosis in relation to drug and placebo response in anxious and depressed psychiatric outpatients, *The Journal of Nervous and Mental Disease*, **171**: 182–5.

Doyal, L. (1985) Women and the National Health Service: the carers and the careless, in E. Lewin and V. Olesen (eds) *Women, Health and Healing: Toward a New Perspective*. London: Tavistock.

Doyal, L. (1994) Changing medicine? Gender and the politics of health care, in J. Gabe, D. Kelleher and G. Williams (eds) *Challenging Medicine*. London: Routledge.

Doyal, L. (2001) Sex, gender and health: the need for a new approach, *British Medical Journal*, **323**: 1061–3.

Dubbert, P. and Martin, J. (1988) Exercise, in E.A. Blechman and K.D. Brownel (eds) *Handbook of Behavioral Medicine for Women*. New York: Pergamon.

Duncker, K. (1938) Experimental modification of children's food preferences through social suggestion, *Journal of Abnormal Social Psychology*, **33**: 489–507.

Dunn, A.L., Andersen, R.E. and Jakicic, J.M. (1998) Lifestyle physical activity interventions: history, short and long-term effects and recommendation, *American Journal of Preventive Medicine*, **15**: 398–412.

Dunn, C., Deroo, L. and Rivara, F.P. (2001) The use of brief interventions adapted from motivational interviewing across behavioral domains: a systematic review, *Addiction*, **96**(12): 1725–42.

Dunn, J., Occhipinti, S., Campbell, A. et al. (2011) Benefit finding after cancer: the role of optimism, intrusive thinking and social environment, *Journal of Health Psychology*, **16**(1): 169–77.

Durnin, J.V.G.A., Lonergan, M.E., Good, J. and Ewan, A. (1974) A cross-sectional nutritional and anthropometric study with an interval of 7 years on 611 young adolescent school children, *British Journal of Nutrition*, **32**: 169–79.

Dusseldorp, E., van Elderen, T., Maes, S. et al. (1999) A meta-analysis of psychoeducational programmes for coronary heart disease patients, *Health Psychology*, **18**: 506–19.

Eakin, E.G., Lawler, S.P., Vandelanotte, C. and Owen, N. (2007) Telephone interventions for physical activity and dietary behavior change: a systematic review, *American Journal of Preventive Medicine*, **32**(5): 419–34.

East Ayrshire Council (2011) Pupils earn just reward for healthy eating, www.eastayrshireschoolmeals.com/p/pupils-earn-just-reward-for-healthy-eating.

Ebrecht, M., Hextall, J., Kirtley, L.G. et al. (2004) Perceived stress and cortisol levels predict speed of wound healing in healthy male adults, *Psychoneuroendocrinology*, **29**: 798–809.

Eccleston, C. (1994) Chronic pain and attention: a cognitive approach, *British Journal of Clinical Psychology*, **33**(4): 535–47.

Eccleston, C. and Crombez, G. (1999) Pain demands attention: a cognitive-affective model of the interruptive function of pain, *Psychological Bulletin*, **125**(3): 356–66.

Eccleston, C., Williams, A.C.D.C. and Morely, S. (2009b) Psychological therapies for the management of chronic pain (excluding headache) in aults, *Cochrane Database of Systematic Reviews 2009*, 2., art. no. CD007407.

Eccleston, C., Moore, R.A., Derry, S. et al. (2010) Improving the quality and reporting of systematic reviews, *European Journal of Pain*, **14**: 667–9.

Eccleston, C., Palermo, T.M., Williams, A.C.D.C. et al. (2009a) Psychological therapies for the management of chronic and recurrent pain in children and adolescents, *Cochrane Database of Systematic Reviews 2009*, 2, art. no. CD003968.

Eccleston, C., Crombez, G., Aldrich, S. and Stannard, C. (2001) Worry and chronic pain patients: a description and analysis of individual differences, *European Journal of Pain*, 5(3): 309–18.

Edwards, N. (1954) The theory of decision making, *Psychological Bulletin*, 51: 380–417.

Egger, G., Fitzgerald, W., Frape, G. et al. (1983) Result of a large scale media antismoking campaign in Australia: North Coast 'Quit For Life' Programme, *British Medical Journal*, 286: 1125–8.

Eiser, J.R. (2000) The influence of question framing on symptom report and perceived health status, *Psychology and Health*, 15: 13–20.

Eiser, J.R. and Cole, N. (2002) Participation in cervical screening as a function of perceived risk, barriers and need for cognitive closure, *Journal of Health Psychology*, 7(1): 99–105.

Eisler, R.M., Skidmore, J.R. and Ward, C.H. (1988) Masculine gender-role stress: predictor of anger, anxiety and health-risk behaviour, *Journal of Personality Assessment*, 5: 133–41.

Elliott, M.A., and Armitage, C.J. (2009) Promoting drivers' compliance with speed limits: testing an intervention based on the theory of planned behaviour, *British Journal of Psychology*, 100(1): 111–32.

Elliott, M.A., Armitage, C. J. and Baughan, C.J. (2005) Exploring the beliefs underpinning drivers' intentions to comply with speed limits, *Transportation Research Part F: Traffic Psychology and Behaviour*, 8(6): 459–79.

Elwyn, G., Edwards, A. and Kinnersley, P. (1999) Shared decision making: the neglected second half of the consultation, *British Journal of General Practice*, 49: 477–82.

Eminson, D. M. (2007) Medically unexplained symptoms in children and adolescents, *Clinical Psychology Review*, 27: 855–71.

Emmons, R.A. (1996) Strivings and feeling: personal goals and subjective well-being, in P.M. Gollwitzer and J.A. Bargh (eds), *The Psychology of Action: Linking Cognition and Motivation to Behavior*, pp. 313–37. New York: Guilford.

Engbers, L.H., van Poppel, M.N.M., Chin, A. et al. (2005) Worksite health promotion programs with environmental changes: a systematic review, *American Journal of Preventative Medicine*, 29: 61–70.

Engel, C.C., Jr., Adkins, J.A. and Cowan, D.N. (2002) Caring for medically unexplained physical symptoms after toxic environmental exposures: effects of contested causation, *Environmental Health Perspectives*, 111(suppl. 4), 641–7.

Engel, G.L. (1977) The need for a new medical model: a challenge for biomedicine, *Science*, 196: 129–35.

Engel, G.L. (1980) The clinical application of the biopsychosocial model, *American Journal of Psychiatry*, 137: 535–44.

Eriksen, P.S. and Rasmussen, H. (1992) Low dose 17-β oestradiol vaginal tablets in the treatment of atrophic vaginitis: a double-blind placebo controlled study, *European Journal of Obstetrics & Gynaecology and Reproductive Biology*, 44: 137–44.

Esterling, B.A., Kiecolt-Glaser, J.K., Bodnar, J.C. and Glaser, R. (1994) Chronic stress, social support and persistent alterations in the natural killer cell response to cytokines in older adults, *Health Psychology*, 13: 291–8.

Eurostat (2007) *GP Utilisation*, www.euphix.org.

Everson, S.A., Lynch, J.W., Chesney, M.A. et al. (1997) Interaction of workplace demands and cardiovascular reactivity in progression of carotid atherosclerosis: population-based study, *British Medical Journal*, 314: 553–8.

Eysenck, H.J. (1990) The prediction of death from cancer by means of personality/stress questionnaire: too good to be true? *Perceptual Motor Skills*, 71: 216–18.

Eysenck, H.J. and Grossarth-Maticek, R. (1991) Creative movation behaviour therapy as a prophylactic treatment for cancer and coronary heart disease, Part II – effects of treatment, *Behaviour Research and Therapy*, 29: 17–31.

Eyton, A. (1982) *The F Plan Diet*. London: Bantam Press.

Fabricatore, A.N. and Wadden, T.A. (2006) Obesity, *Annual Review of Clinical Psychology*, 2, http://ssrn.com/abstract=1081451.

Fallon, A. and Rozin, P. (1985) Sex differences in perceptions of desirable body shape, *Journal of Abnormal Psychology*, 94: 102–5.

Fallowfield, L. (1990) *The Quality of Life: The Missing Measurement in Health Care*. London: Souvenir Press.

Fallowfield, L.J., Rodway, A. and Baum, M. (1990) What are the psychological factors influencing attendance, non-attendance and re-attendance at a breast screening centre? *Journal of the Royal Society of Medicine*, 83: 547–51.

Fang, C.Y., Daly, M.B., Miller, S.M. et al. (2006) Coping with ovarian cancer risk: the moderating effects of perceived control on coping and adjustment, *Journal of Health Psychology*, 11: 561–80.

Farooqi, I.S., Jebb, S.A., Cook, G. et al. (1999) Effects of recombinant leptin therapy in a child with leptin deficiency, *New England Journal of Medicine*, 16: 879–84.

Farquhar, J.W., Fortmann, S.P., Flora, J.A. et al. (1990) Effects of communitywide education on cardiovascular disease risk factors: the Stanford Five-City Project, *Journal of the American Medical Association*, **264**: 359–65.

Fernbach, M. (2002) The impact of a media campaign on cervical screening knowledge and self-efficacy, *Journal of Health Psychology*, **7**(1): 85–97.

Ferster, C.B., Nurnberger, J.I. and Levitt, E.B. (1962) The control of eating, *Journal of Mathetics*, **1**: 87–109.

Festinger, L. (1957) *A Theory of Cognitive Dissonance*. Evanston, IL: Row, Peterson.

Feuerstein, M., Carter, R.L. and Papciak, A.S. (1987) A prospective analysis of stress and fatigue in recurrent low back pain, *Pain*, **31**: 333–44.

Field, A.E., Cheung, L., Wolf, A.M. et al. (1999) Exposure to the mass media and weight concerns among girls. *Pediatrics,* **103**(3): e36.

Fife-Schaw, C.R. and Breakwell, G.M. (1992) Estimating sexual behaviour parameters in the light of AIDS: a review of recent UK studies of young people, *Aids Care*, **4**: 187–201.

Figueiras, M.J. and Alves, N.C. (2007) Lay perceptions of serious illness: an adapted version of the Revised Illness Perception Questionnaire (IPQ-R) for healthly people, *Psychology and Health*, **22**(2): 143–58.

Figueiras, M.J. and Weinman, J. (2003) Do similar patient and spouse perceptions of myocardial infarction predict recovery? *Psychology and Health*, **18**(2): 201–16.

Finer, N. (2002) Pharmacotherapy of obesity, *Best Practice and Research Clinical Endocrinology and Metabolism*, **16**: 717–42.

Finlay, S. J. and Faulkner, G. (2005) Physical activity promotion through the mass media: inception, production, transmission and consumption, *Preventive Medicine*, **40**(2): 121–30.

Fiore, M.C., Novotny, T.F., Pierce, J.P. et al. (1990) Methods used to quit smoking in the United States: do cessation programs help? *Journal of the American Medical Association*, **263**: 2760–5.

Fishbein, M. (ed.) (1967) *Readings in Attitude Theory and Measurement*. New York: Wiley.

Fishbein, M. and Ajzen, I. (1975) *Belief, Attitude, Intention, and Behavior: An Introduction to Theory and Research*. Reading, MA: Addison-Wesley.

Fishbein, M. and Middlestadt, S.E. (1989) Using theory of reasoned action as a framework for understanding and changing AIDS-related behaviours, in V.M. Mays, J. Albee and S.F. Schneider (eds) *Primary Prevention for AIDS: Psychological Approaches*. Newbury Park, CA: Sage.

Fishbein, M., Hennessy, M., Kamb, M. et al. (2001) Project Respect Study Group: using intervention theory to model factors influencing behavior change, Project RESPECT, *Evaluation and the Health Professions*, **24**(4): 363–84.

Fisher, J.D. and Fisher, W.A. (1992) Changing AIDS-risk behaviour, *Psychological Bulletin*, **111**: 455–74.

Fisher, J.O. and Birch, L.L. (1999) Restricting access to a palatable food affects children's behavioral response, food selection and intake, *American Journal of Clinical Nutrition*, **69**: 1264–72.

Fisher, J.O., Birch, L.L., Smiciklas-Wright, H. and Piocciano, M.F. (2000) Breastfeeding through the first year predicts maternal control in feeding and subsequent toddler energy intakes, *Journal of the American Dietician Association*, **100**: 641–6.

Fisher, W.A. (1984) Predicting contraceptive behavior among university men: the role of emotions and behavioral intentions, *Journal of Applied Social Psychology*, **14**: 104–23.

Flay, B.R. (1985) Psychosocial approaches to smoking prevention: a review of findings, *Health Psychology*, **4**: 449–88.

Flowers, P., Smith, J.A., Sheeran, P. and Beail, N. (1997) Health and romance: understanding unprotected sex in relationships between gay men, *British Journal of Health Psychology*, **2**: 73–86.

Flowers, P., Smith, J. A., Sheeran, P. and Beail, N. (1998) 'Coming out' and sexual debut: understanding the social context of HIV risk-related behaviour, *Journal of Community & Applied Social Psychology*, **8**(6): 409–21.

Flynn, J., Slovic, P. and Mertz, C.K. (1994) Gender, race, and perception of environmental health risks, *Risk Analysis*, **14**(6): 1101–8.

Folkman, S. and Lazarus, R.S. (1988) *Manual for the Ways of Coping Questionnaire*. Palo Alto, CA: Consulting Psychologist Press.

Folkman, S. and Moskowitz, J.T. (2000) Positive affect and the other side of coping, *American Psychologist*, **55**: 647–54.

Folkman, S., Lazarus, R.S., Pimley, S. and Novacek, J. (1987) Age differences in stress and coping processes, *Psychology and Ageing*, **2**: 171–84.

Ford, E., Williamson, D. and Liu, S. (1997) Weight change and diabetes incidence: findings from a national cohort of US adults, *American Journal of Epidemiology*, **146**: 214–22.

Fordyce, W.E. and Steger, J.C. (1979) Chronic pain, in O.F. Pomerleau and J.P. Brady (eds) *Behavioral Medicine: Theory and Practice*. Baltimore, MD: Williams & Wilkins.

Formon, S.J. (1974) *Infant Nutrition*, 2nd edn. Philadelphia, PA: WB Saunders.

Francis, M.E and Pennebaker, J.W. (1992) Putting stress into words: writing about personal upheavals and health, *American Journal of Health Promotion*, **6**: 280–7.

Fredrickson, B.L., Robson, A. and Ljungdell, T. (1991) Ambulatory and laboratory blood pressure in individuals with negative and positive family history of hypertension, *Health Psychology*, **10**: 371–7.

Fredrickson, B.L., Maynard, K.E., Helms, M.J. et al. (2000) Hostility predicts magnitude and duration of blood pressure response to anger, *Journal of Behavioural Medicine*, **23**: 229–43.

Free, C. and Ogden, J. (2005) Emergency contraception use and non-use in young women: the application of a contextual and dynamic model, *British Journal of Health Psychology*, **10**(2): 237–53.

Freeman, C. (1995) Cognitive therapy, in G. Szmukler, C. Dare and J. Treasure (eds) *Handbook of Eating Disorders: Theory, Treatment and Research*. London: Wiley.

Freeman, E.W. and Rickels, K. (1993) *Early Childbearing: Perspectives of Black Adolescents on Pregnancy, Abortion, and Contraception*. Newbury Park, CA: Sage.

Freeman, R.F., Thomas, C.D., Solyom, L. and Hunter, M.A. (1984) A modified video camera for measuring body image distortion: technical description and reliability, *Psychological Medicine*, **14**: 411–16.

Freidson, E. (1970) *Profession of Medicine*. New York: Dodds Mead.

French, D. and Weinman, J. (2008) Assessing illness perceptions: beyond the IPQ, *Psychology and Health*, **23**: 5–9.

French, D.P. and Hankins, M. (2003) The expectancy-value muddle in the theory of planned behaviour and some proposed solutions, *British Journal of Health Psychology*, **8**: 37–55.

French, D.P. and Sutton, S. (2010) Reactivity of measurement in health psychology: how much of a problem is it? What can be done about it? *British Journal of Health Psychology*, **15**: 453–68.

French, D.P., Cooper, A. and Weinman, J. (2006a) Illness perceptions predict attendance at cardiac rehabilitation following acute myocardial infarction: a systematic review with meta-analysis, *Journal of Psychosomatic Research*, **61**(6): 757–67.

French, D.P., Maissi, E. and Marteau, T.M. (2004) Psychological costs of inadequate cervical smear test results, *British Journal of Cancer*, **91**: 1887–92.

French, D.P., Maissi, E. and Marteau, T.M. (2005a) The purpose of attributing cause: beliefs about the causes of myocardial infarction, *Social Science & Medicine*, **60**: 1411–21.

French, D.P., Maissi, E. and Marteau, T.M. (2006b) The psychological costs of inadequate cervical smear test results: three-month follow-up, *Psycho-oncology*, **15**: 498–508.

French, D.P., Marteau, T., Senior, V. and Weinman, J. (2002a) The structure of belief about the causes of heart attacks: a network analysis, *British Journal of Health Psychology*, **7**: 463–79.

French, D.P., Marteau, T.M., Senior, V. and Weinman, J. (2005b) How valid are measures of beliefs about the causes of illness? The example of myocardial infarction, *Psychology and Health*, **20**(5): 615–35.

French, D.P., Senior, V., Weinman, J. and Marteau, T.M. (2001) Causal attributions for heart disease: a systematic review, *Psychology and Health*, **16**: 77–98.

French, D.P, Senior, V., Weinman, J. and Marteau, T.M. (2002b) Elicit causal beliefs about heart attacks: a comparison of implicit and explicit methods, *Journal of Health Psychology*, **7**(4): 433–44.

French, S.A. and Jeffrey, R.W. (1997) Current dieting, weight loss history and weight suppression: behavioural correlates of three dimensions of dieting, *Addictive Behaviours*, **22**: 31–44.

Friedman, L.A. and Kimball, A.W. (1986) Coronary heart disease mortality and alcohol consumption in Framingham, *American Journal of Epidemiology*, **124**: 481–9.

Friedman, M. and Rosenman, R.H. (1959) Association of specific overt behavior pattern with blood and cardiovascular findings, *Journal of the American Medical Association*, **169**: 1286–97.

Friedman, M., Thoresen, C., Gill, J. et al. (1986) Alteration of Type A behavior and its effects on cardiac recurrences in post myocardial infarction patients: summary results of the recurrent coronary prevention project, *American Heart Journal*, **112**: 653–65.

Friedman, T. and Gath, D. (1989) The psychiatric consequences of spontaneous abortion, *British Journal of Psychiatry*, **155**: 810–13.

Frith, H., Harcourt, D. and Fussell, A. (2007) Anticipating an altered appearance: women undergoing chemotherapy treatment for breast cancer, *European Journal of Oncology Nursing*, **11**: 385–91.

Fuller, E. (2009) *Smoking, Drinking and Drug Use Among Young People in England in 2008*. London: Health and Social Care Information Centre.

Furnham, A. and Greaves, N. (1994) Gender and locus of control correlates of body image dissatisfaction, *European Journal of Personality*, **8**: 183–200.

Furnham, A. and Kirkcaldy, B. (1997) Age and sex differences in health beliefs and behaviors, *Psychological Reports*, **80**(1): 63–6.

Futterman, A.D., Kemeny, M.E., Shapiro, D. et al. (1992) Immunological variability associated with experimentally-induced positive and negative affective states, *Psychological Medicine*, **22**: 231–8.

Gabhainn, S.N., Kelleher, C.C., Naughton, A.M. et al. (1999) Socio-demographic variations in perspectives on cardiovascular disease and associated risk factors, *Health Education Research*, **14**(5): 619–28.

Gallacher, J.E.J., Hopkinson, C.A., Bennett, P. et al. (1997) Effect of stress management on angina, *Psychology and Health*, **12**: 523–32.

Garber, J., Walker, L.S. and Zeman, J. (1991) Somatization symptoms in a community sample of children and adolescents: further validation of the children's somatization inventory, *Psychological Assessment: A Journal of Consulting and Clinical Psychology*, **3**(4): 588–95

Garcia, J., Hankins, W.G. and Rusiniak, K. (1974) Behavioral regulation of the milieu intern in man and rat, *Science*, **185**: 824–31.

Garn, S.M., Bailey, S.M., Solomon, M.A. and Hopkins, P.J. (1981) Effects of remaining family members on fatness prediction, *American Journal of Clinical Nutrition*, **34**: 148–53.

Garner, D.M. (1991) *EDI-2: Professional Manual*. Odessa, FL: Psychological Assessment Resources Inc.

Garrow, J. (1984) *Energy Balance and Obesity in Man*. New York: Elsevier.

Garrow, J. (1997) Treatment of obesity IV: surgical treatments, in J. Garrow, *Obesity*. Blackwell: British Nutrition Foundation.

Garrow, J.S. (1987) Morbid obesity: medical or surgical treatment? The case for medical treatment, *International Journal of Obesity*, **11**(suppl. 3): 1–4.

Garrow, J.S. and Webster, J.D. (1985) Are pre-obese people energy thrifty? *Lancet*, **2**: 670–1.

Gavey, N. (2005) *Just Sex? The Cultural Scaffolding of Rape*. London: Routledge.

Gavey, N., Schmidt, J., Braun, V. et al. (2009) Unsafe, unwanted: sexual coercion as a barrier to safer sex among men who have sex with men, *Journal of Health Psychology*, **14**(7): 1021–6.

Gellaitry, G., Cooper, V., Davis, C. et al. (2005) Patients' perception of information about HAART: impact on treatment decisions, *AIDS Care*, **7**(3): 367–76.

George, W.H. and Marlatt, G.A. (1983) Alcoholism: the evolution of a behavioral perspective, in M. Galanter (ed.) *Recent Developments in Alcoholism*, New York: Plenum Press.

Germain, D., Wakefield, M.A. and Durkin, S.J. (2010) Adolescents' perceptions of cigarette brand image: does plain packaging make a difference? *Journal of Adolescent Health*, **46**: 385–92.

Gerrard, M., Gibbons, F.X., Benthin, A.C. and Hessling, R.M. (1996) A longitudinal study of the reciprocal nature of risk behaviors and cognitions in adolescents: what you do shapes what you think and vice versa, *Health Psychology*, **15**: 344–54.

Giannetti, V.J., Reynolds, J. and Rihen, T. (1985) Factors which differentiate smokers from ex-smokers among cardiovascular patients: a discriminant analysis, *Social Science and Medicine*, **20**: 241–5.

Gibson, B. (2008) Can evaluative conditioning change attitudes towards mature brands? New evidence from the implicit association test, *Journal of Consumer Research*, **35**: 178–88.

Gidron, Y., Magen, R. and Ariad, S. (2001) The relation between hopelessness and psychological and serological outcomes in Israeli women with breast-cancer, *Psychology and Health*, **16**: 289–96.

Gijsbers van Wijk, C.M. and Kolk, A.M. (1997) Sex differences in physical symptoms: the contribution of symptom perception theory, *Social Science and Medicine*, **45**: 231–46.

Gijsbers van Wijk, C.M., Huisman, H. and Kolk, A.M. (1999) Gender differences in physical symptoms and illness behaviour: a health diary study, *Social Science and Medicine*, **49**: 1061–74.

Gil, K.M., Anthony, K.K., Carson, J.W. et al. (2001) Daily coping practice predicts treatment effects in children with sickle cell disease, *Journal of Pediatric Psychology*, **26**(3): 163–73.

Gilbert, D.G. and Spielberger, C.D. (1987) Effects of smoking on heart rate, anxiety, and feelings of success during social interaction, *Journal of Behavioral Medicine*, **10**: 629–38.

Gill, J.J., Price, V.A. and Friedman, M. (1985) Reduction of type A behavior in healthy middle-aged American military officers, *American Heart Journal*, **110**: 503–14.

Gillibrand, R. and Stevenson, J. (2006) The extended health belief model applied to the experience of diabetes in young people, *British Journal of Health Psychology*, **11**: 155–69.

Gillies, P.A. and Galt, M. (1990) Teenage smoking – fun or coping? in J.A.M. Wimbust and S. Maes (eds) *Lifestyles and Health: New Developments in Health Psychology*. Leiden: DSWO/Leiden University Press.

Gillon, R. (2001) Is there a 'new ethics of abortion'? *Journal of Medical Ethics*, **27**(suppl. II): ii5–9.

Glass, D.C. and Singer, J.E. (1972) *Urban Stress*. New York: Academic Press.

Gleghorn, A.A., Penner, L.A., Powers, P.S. and Schulman, R. (1987) The psychometric properties of several measures of body image, *Journal of Psychopathology and Behavioral Assessment*, **9**: 203–18.

Glenn, N.D. and Weaver, C.N. (1981) The contribution of marital happiness to global happiness, *Journal of Marriage and the Family*, **43**: 161–8.

Goddard, E. (1990) *Why Children Start Smoking*. London: HMSO.

Godin, G., Conner, M. and Sheeran, P. (2005) Bridging the intention–behaviour 'gap': the role of moral norm, *British Journal of Social Psychology*, **44**: 497–512.

Godin, G., Conner, M., Sheeran, P. et al. (2007) Determinants of repeated blood donation among new and experienced blood donors, *Transfusion*, **47**(9): 1607–15.

Godin, G., Sheeran, P., Conner, M. et al. (2010) Which survey questions change behavior? Randomized controlled trial of mere measurement interventions, *Health Psychololgy*, **29**(6): 636–44.

Godin, G., Belanger-Gravel, A., Gagne, C. and Blondeau, D. (2008a) Factors predictive of signed consent for posthumous organ donation, *Progress in Transplantation*, **18**(2): 109–17.

Godin, G., Sheeran, P., Conner, M. and Germain, M. (2008b) Asking questions changes behavior: mere measurement effects on frequency of blood donation, *Health Psychology*, **27**: 179–84.

Godin, G., Valois, P., Lepage, L. and Desharnais, R. (1992) Predictors of smoking behaviour: an application of Ajzen's theory of planned behaviour, *British Journal of Addiction*, **87**: 1335–43.

Goldberg, D.P. (1978) *Manual of the General Health Questionnaire*. Windsor: NFER-Nelson.

Goldberg, I.R. (1999) A broad-bandwidth, public-domain, personality inventory measuring the lower-level facets of several five-factor models, in I. Merveilde, I. Deary, F. De Fryt and F. Ostendorf (eds) *Personality Psychology in Europe: Vol. 7*. Tilburg: Tilburg University Press.

Goldschneider, A. (1920) *Das Schmerz Problem*. Berlin: Springer.

Gollwitzer, P.M. (1993) Goal achievement: the role of intentions, *European Review of Social Psychology*, **4**: 141–85.

Gollwitzer, P.M. and Sheeran, P. (2006) Implementation intentions and goal achievement: a meta-analysis of effects and processes, *Advances in Experimental Social Psychology*, **38**: 69–119.

Gomel, M., Oldenburg, B., Lemon, J. et al. (1993) Pilot study of the effects of a workplace smoking ban on indices of smoking, cigarette craving, stress and other health behaviours, *Psychology and Health*, **8**: 223–9.

Good, G.E., Dell, D.M., and Mintz, L.B. (1989) Male role and gender role conflict: relations to help seeking in men, *Journal of Counselling Psychology*, **36**: 295–300.

Goodwin, P., and Ogden, J. (2007) Women's reflections about their past abortions: an exploration of how emotional reactions change over time, *Psychology and Health*, **22**: 231–48.

Gordon, D.F. (1995) Testicular cancer and masculinity, in D. Sabo and D.F. Gordon (eds) *Men's Health and Illness: Gender, Power and the Body*. Thousand Oaks, CA: Sage.

Gottschalk, L.A. and Gleser, G.C. (1969) *The Measurement of Psychological States Through the Content Analysis of Verbal Behavior*. Berkeley, CA: University of California Press.

Gøtzsche P.C., Nielsen M. (2011) Screening for breast cancer with mammography, *Cochrane Database Syst. Rev.* 2011 Jan 19:(1):CD001877. Review. PubMed PMID: 21249649.

Gough, B. and Robertson, S. (eds) (2010) *Men, Masculinities and Health: Critical Perspectives*. Basingstoke: Palgrave Macmillan.

Gracely, R.H., Dubner, R., Deeter, W.R. and Wolskee, P.J. (1985) Clinical expectations influence placebo analgesia, *Lancet*, **i**: 43.

Graham, H. (1987) Women's smoking and family health, *Social Science and Medicine*, **25**: 47–56.

Grant, A. and Elbourne, D. (1989) Fetal movement counting to assess fetal well-being, in I. Chalmers, M. Enkin and M.J.N.C. Keirse (eds) *Effective Care in Pregnancy and Childbirth*. Oxford: Oxford University Press.

Grant, M., Padilla, G.V., Ferrell, B.R. and Rhiner, M. (1990) Assessment of quality of life with a single instrument, *Seminars in Oncology Nursing*, **6**: 260–70.

Gratton, L., Povey, R. and Clark-Carter, D. (2007) Promoting children's fruit and vegetable consumption: interventions using the theory of planned behaviour as a framework, *British Journal of Health Psychology*, **12**: 639–50.

Graybeal, A., Sexton, J.D. and Pennebaker, J.W. (2002) The role of story making in disclosure writing: the psychometrics of narrative, *Psychology and Health*, **17**: 571–81.

Green, E., Griffiths, F. and Thompson, D. (2006) 'Are my bones normal, doctor?' The role of technology in understanding and communicating health risks for midlife women, *Sociological Research Online*, **11**(4).

Greenberg, M.A. and Stone, A.A. (1992) Writing about disclosed versus undisclosed traumas: immediate and long term effects on mood and health, *Journal of Personality and Social Psychology*, **63**: 75–84.

Greeno, C.G. and Wing, R.R. (1994) Stress-induced eating, *Psychological Bulletin*, **115**: 444–64.

Greenwood, J. (2001) The new ethics of abortion, *Journal of Medical Ethics*, **27**(suppl. II): ii2–4.

Greer, S., Morris, T.E. and Pettingale, K.W. (1979) Psychological responses to breast cancer: effect on outcome, *Lancet*, **2**: 785–7.

Greer, S., Moorey, S., Baruch, J.D.R. et al. (1992) Adjuvant psychological therapy for patients with cancer: a prospective randomised trial, *British Medical Journal*, **304**: 675–80.

Grey, M., Boland, E.A., Davidson, M. et al. (2000) Coping skills training for youth with diabetes mellitus has long-lasting effects on metabolic control and quality of life, *The Journal of Pediatrics*, **137**(1): 107–13.

Grimes, D.S. (1988) Value of a negative cervical smear, *British Medical Journal*, **296**: 1363.

Groesz, L.M., Levine, M.P. and Murnen, S.K. (2002) The effect of experimental presentation of thin media images on body satisfaction: a meta-analytical review, *International Journal of Eating Disorders*, **31**: 1–16.

Grogan, S. (2008) *Body Image: Understanding Body Dissatisfaction in Men, Women and Children*, 2nd edn. London: Routledge.

Gross, J. and Levenson, R.W. (1997) Hiding feelings: the acute effects of inhibiting negative and positive emotion, *Journal of Abnormal Psychology*, **106**: 95–103.

Grunfeld, E., Mant, D., Yudkin, P. et al. (1996) Routine follow up of breast cancer in primary care: randomised trial, *British Medical Journal*, **313**: 665–9.

Guadagnoli, E. and Ward, P. (1998) Patient participation on decision making, *Social Science and Medicine*, **47**: 329–39.

Gudmundsdottir, H., Johnston, M., Johnston, D. and Foulkes, J. (2001) Spontaneous, elicited and cued casual attribution in the year following a first myocardial infarction, *British Journal of Health Psychology*, **6**: 81–96.

Gum, A., Snyder, C.R. and Duncan, P.W. (2006) Hopeful thinking, participation, and depressive symptoms three months after stroke, *Psychology & Health*, **21**(3): 319–34.

Gureje, O., Simon, G.E., Ustun, T.B. and Goldberg, D.P. (1997) Somatisation in cross-cultural perspective: a World Health Organization study in primary care, *American Journal of Psychiatry*, **154**: 989–95.

Gustafson, P.E. (1998) Gender differences in risk perception: theoretical and methodological perspectives, *Risk Analysis*, **18**(6): 805–11.

Guyll, M. and Contrada, R.J. (1998) Trait hostility and ambulatory cardiovascular activity: response to social interaction, *Health Psychology*, **17**: 30–9.

Haas, H., Fink, H. and Hartfelder, G. (1959) Das Placebo-problem, *Fortschritte der Arzneimittelforschung*, **1**: 279–354.

Hadley, J. (1996) *Abortion: Between Freedom and Necessity*. London: Virago.

Hagger, M.S. and Chatzisarantis, N.L.D. (2009) Integrating the theory of planned behaviour and self-determination theory in health behaviour: a meta-analysis, *British Journal of Health Psychology*, **14**(2): 275–302.

Hagger, M.S. and Orbell, S. (2003) A meta-analytic review of the common-sense model of illness representations, *Psychology and Health*, **18**(2): 141–84.

Hale, S., Grogan, S. and Willot, S. (2007) Patterns of self-referral in men with symptoms of prostate disease, *British Journal of Health Psychology*, **12**: 403–19.

Hale, S., Grogan, S. and Willott, S. (2010) Male GPs' views on men seeking medical help: A qualitative study, *British Journal of Health Psychology*, **15**: 697–713.

Halford, J.C., Gillespie, J., Brown, V. et al. (2004) Effect on television advertisements for foods on food consumption in children, *Appetite*, **42**(2): 221–5.

Hall, A. and Brown, L.B. (1982) A comparison of the attitudes of young anorexia nervosa patients and non-patients with those of their mothers, *British Journal of Psychology*, **56**: 39–48.

Hall, E.E., Ekkekakis, P. and Petruzzello, S.J. (2002) The affective beneficence of vigorous exercise, *British Journal of Health Psychology*, **7**: 47–66.

Hall, J.A., Epstein, A.M. and McNeil, B.J. (1989) Multidimensionality of health status in an elderly population: construct validity of a measurement battery, *Medical Care*, **27**: 168–77.

Hall, S., Weinman, J. and Marteau, T.M. (2004) The motivating impact of informing women smokers of a link between smoking and cervical cancer: the role of coherence, *Health Psychology*, **23**(4): 419–24.

Hall, S.M., Hall, R.G. and Ginsberg, D. (1990) Cigarette dependence, in A.S. Bellack, M. Hersen and A.E. Kazdin (eds) *International Handbook of Behavior Modification and Therapy*, 2nd edn. New York: Plenum Press.

Halliwell, E. and Dittmar, H. (2004) Does size matter? The impact of model's body size on women's body-focused anxiety and advertising effectiveness, *Journal of Social and Clinical Psychology*, **23**(1): 104–22.

Halm, E.A., Mora, P. and Leventhal, H. (2006) No symptoms, no asthma: the acute episodic disease belief is associated with poor self-management among inner-city adults with persistent asthma, *Chest*, **129**: 573–80.

Halmi, K.A., Stunkard, A.J. and Mason, E.E. (1980) Emotional responses to weight reduction by three methods: diet, jejunoileal bypass, and gastric, *American Journal of Clinical Nutrition*, **33**: 446–51.

Hamilton, K. and Waller, G. (1993) Media influences on body size estimation in anorexia and bulimia: an experimental study, *British Journal of Psychiatry*, **162**: 837–40.

Hamm, P.B., Shekelle, R.B. and Stamler, J. (1989) Large fluctuations in body weight during young adulthood and twenty-five year risk of coronary death in men, *American Journal of Epidemiology*, **129**: 312–18.

Hammond, D., Fong, G.T., McDonald, P.W. et al. (2003) Impact of the graphic Canadian warning labels on adult smoking behaviour, *Tobacco Control*, **12**: 391–5.

Han, T.S., Richmond, P., Avenell, A. and Lean, M.E.J. (1997) Waist circumference reduction and cardiovascular benefits during weight loss in women, *International Journal of Obesity*, **21**: 127–34.

Hanbury, A., Wallace, L. and Clark, M. (2009) Use of a time series design to test effectiveness of a theory-based intervention targeting adherence of health professionals to a clinical guideline, *British Journal of Health Psychology*, **14**(3): 505–18.

Hankins, M., French, D. and Horne, R. (2000) Statistical guidelines for studies of theory of reasoned action and the theory of planned behaviour, *Psychology and Health*, **15**: 151–61.

Harcourt, D. and Frith, H. (2008) Women's experience of an altered appearance during chemotherapy: an indication of cancer status, *Journal of Health Psychology*, **13**(5): 597–606.

Hardeman, W., Johnston, M., Johnston, D.W. et al. (2002) Application of the theory of planned behaviour in behaviour change interventions: a systematic review, *Psychology and Health*, **17**(2): 123–58.

Hardeman, W., Sutton, S., Griffin, S. et al. (2005) A causal modeling approach to the development of theory-based behavior change programmes for trial evaluation, *Health Education Research Theory and Practice*, **20**(6): 676–87.

Hardeman, W., Kinmonth, A.L., Michie, S. and Sutton, S. (2011) Theory of planned behaviour cognitions do not predict self-reported or objective physical activity levels or change in the ProActive trial, *British Journal of Health Psychology*, **16**: 135–50.

Harden, A. and Ogden, J. (1999a) Young women's experiences of arranging and having abortions, *Sociology of Health and Illness*, **21**: 426–44.

Harden, A., and Ogden, J. (1999b) 16–19 year olds' beliefs about contraceptive services and the intentions to use contraception, *British Journal of Family Planning*, **24**: 135–41.

Hardy, S. and Grogan, S. (2009) Preventing disability through exercise: investigating older adults' influences and motivations to engage in physical activity, *Journal of Health Psychology*, **14**(7): 1036–46.

Harland, J., White, M., Drinkwater, C. et al. (1999) The Newcastle exercise project: a randomised controlled trial of methods to promote physical activity in primary care, *British Medical Journal* (clinical research edn.), **319**(7213): 828–32.

Harnish, J.D., Aseltine, R.H. and Gore, S. (2000) Resolution of stressful experiences as an indicator of coping effectiveness in young adults: an event history analysis, *Journal of Health and Social Behaviour*, **41**: 121–36.

Harris, A.A. (2004) Supportive counselling before and after elective pregnancy termination, *Journal of Midwifery and Women's Health*, **49**: 105–12.

Harris, P.R. and Epton, T. (2009) The impact of self-affirmation on health cognition, health behaviour and other health-related responses: a narrative review, *Social and Personality Psychology Compass*, **3**(6): 962–78.

Harris, P.R. and Napper, L. (2005) Self-affirmation and the biased processing of threatening health risk information, *Personality and Social Psychology Bulletin*, **31**(9): 1250–63.

Harris, P.R. and Smith, V. (2005) When the risks are low: the impact of absolute and comparative information on disturbance and understanding in US and UK samples, *Psychology and Health*, **20**(3): 319–30.

Harris, P.R., Mayle, K., Mabbott, L. and Napper, L. (2006) Self-affirmation and graphic warning labels, *Health Psychology*, **26**: 434–46.

Harris, P.R., Mayle, K., Mabbott, L. and Napper, L. (2007) Self-affirmation reduces smokers' defensiveness to graphic on-pack cigarette warning labels, *Health Psychology*, **26**: 434–46.

Harrison, J.A., Mullen, P.D. and Green, L.W. (1992) A meta-analysis of studies of the health belief model with adults, *Health Education Research: Theory and Practice*, **7**: 107–16.

Harrison, K. and Cantor, J. (1997) The relationship between media consumption and eating disorders, *Journal of Communication*, **47**(1): 40–67.

Harrow, A., Wells, M., Humphries, G. et al. (2008) 'Seeing is believing, and believing is seeing': an exploration of the meaning and impact of women's mental images of breast cancer and their origin in health care communications, *Patient Education and Counseling*, **73**(2): 339–46.

Hart, J.T. (1987) *Hypertension*, 2nd edn. Edinburgh: Churchill Livingstone.

Harvey, J.H., Barnett, K. and Overstreet, A. (2004) Trauma growth and other outcomes attendant to loss, *Psychological Inquiry*, **15**: 26–9.

Hatherall, B., Ingham, R., Stone, N. and McEachran, J. (2006) How, not just if, condoms are used: the timing of condom application and removal during vaginal sex among young people in England, *Sexually Transmitted Infections*, **83**(1): 68–70.

Hausenblas, H.A. and Downs, D.S. (2004) Prospective examination of the theory of planned behavior applied to exercise behavior during women's first trimester of pregnancy, *Journal of Reproductive and Infant Psychology*, **22**(3): 199–210.

Hausenblas, H.A. and Fallon, E.A. (2006) Exercise and body image: a meta-analysis, *Psychology & Health*, **21**(1): 33–47.

Hausenblas, H.A., Nigg, C.R., Dannecker, E.A. et al. (2001) A missing piece of transtheoretical model applied to exercise: development and validation of the temptation to not exercise scale, *Psychology and Health*, **16**: 381–90.

Havelock, C., Edwards, R., Cuzlick, J. and Chamberlain, J. (1988) The organisation of cervical screening in general practice, *Journal of the Royal College of General Practitioners*, **38**: 207–11.

Haynes, R.B. (1982) Improving patient compliance: an empirical review, in R.B. Stuart (ed.) *Adherence, Compliance and Generalisation in Behavioral Medicine*. New York: Brunner/Mazel.

Haynes, R.B., Sackett, D.L. and Taylor, D.W. (eds) (1979) *Compliance in Health Care*. Baltimore, MD: Johns Hopkins University Press.

Haynes, R.B., Yao, X., Degani, A. et al. (2002) Interventions to enhance medication adherence, *Cochrane Database Library*, CD000011.

Haynes, S.G., Feinleib, M. and Kannel, W.B. (1980) The relationship of psychosocial factors to coronary heart disease in the Framingham study. III: eight year incidence of coronary heart disease, *American Journal of Epidemiology*, **111**: 37–58.

Health Protection Agency (2010) *HIV in the United Kingdom: 2010 Report*. London: Health Protection Agency.

Heatherton, T.F., Herman, C.P., Polivy, J.A. et al. (1988) The (mis)measurement of restraint: an analysis of conceptual and psychometric issues, *Journal of Abnormal Psychology*, **97**: 19–28.

Heatherton, T.F., Polivy, J. and Herman, C.P. (1991) Restraint, weight loss and variability of body weight, *Journal of Abnormal Psychology*, **100**: 78–83.

Hefferon, K., Greay, M. and Mutrie, N. (2009) Post-traumatic growth and life threatening physical illness: a systematic review of the qualitative literature, *British Journal of Health Psychology*, **14**: 343–78.

Heider, F. (1958) *The Psychology of Interpersonal Relations*. New York: John Wiley.

Heijmans, M., Foets, M. and Rijken, M. (2001) Stress in chronic disease: do the perceptions of patients and their general practitioners match? *British Journal of Health Psychology*, **6**: 229–42.

Heitmann, B.L. and Lissner, L. (1995) Dietary underreporting by obese individuals: is it specific or non-specific? *British Medical Journal*, **311**: 986–9.

Helgeson, V.S. (1994) Relations of agency and communion to well-being: evidence and potential explanations, *Psychological Bulletin*, **116**: 412–28.

Helweg-Larsen, M., Tobias, M.R. and Cerban, B.M. (2010) Risk perception and moralization among smokers in the USA and Denmark: a qualitative approach, *British Journal of Health Psychology*, **15**: 871–66.

Hendy, H.M., Williams, K.E., and Camise, T.S. (2005) 'Kid's choice' school lunch program increases children's fruit and vegetable acceptance, *Appetite*, **45**(3): 250–63.

Henningsen, P., Zimmerman, T. and Sattel, H. (2003) Medically unexplained physical symptoms, anxiety, and depression: a meta-analytic review, *Psychosomatic Medicine*, **65**: 528–33.

Herbert, T.B. and Cohen, S. (1993) Stress and immunity in humans: a meta-analytic review, *Psychosomatic Medicine*, **55**(4): 364–79.

Herlitz, A., Nilsson, L.-G. and Backman, L. (1997) Gender differences in episodic memory, *Memory and Cognition*, **25**: 801–11.

Herman, C.P. and Polivy, J.A. (1984) A boundary model for the regulation of eating, in A.J. Stunkard and E. Stellar (eds) *Eating and its Disorders*. New York: Raven Press.

Herman C.P. and Polivy, J.A. (1988) Restraint and excess in dieters and bulimics, in K.M. Pirke, W. Vandereycken and D. Ploog (eds) *The Psychobiology of Bulimia Nervosa*. Berlin: Springer Verlag.

Herman, P. and Mack, D. (1975) Restrained and unrestrained eating, *Journal of Personality*, **43**: 646–60.

Herold, D.M. and Conlon, E.J. (1981) Work factors as potential causal agents of alcohol abuse, *Journal of Drug Issues*, **11**: 337–56.

Herold, E.S. (1981) Contraceptive embarrassment and contraceptive behaviour among young single women, *Journal of Youth and Adolescence*, **10**: 233–42.

Herold, E.S. and McNamee, J.E. (1982) An explanatory model of contraceptive use among young women, *Journal of Sex Research*, **18**: 289–304.

Heron, K.E. and Smyth, J.M. (2010) Ecological momentary interventions: incorporating mobile technology into psychosocial and health behaviour treatments, *British Journal of Health Psychology*, **15**(1): 1–39.

Herz, E. (1984) Psychological repercussions of pregnancy loss, *Psychiatric Annals*, **14**: 454–7.

Herzlich, C. (1973) *Health and Illness*. London: Academic Press.

Heslop, P., Smith, G.D., Carroll, D. et al. (2001) Perceived stress and coronary heart disease risk factors: the contribution of socio-economic position, *British Journal of Health Psychology*, **6**: 167–78.

Hewson-Bower, B. and Drummond, P.D. (2001) Psychological treatment for recurrent symptoms of colds and flu in children, *Journal of Psychosomatic Research*, **51**(1): 369–77.

Higgins, A. and Conner, M. (2003) Understanding adolescent smoking: the role of the theory of planned behaviour and implementation intentions, *Psychology, Health & Medicine*, **8**(2): 173–86.

Hill, A.J., Draper, E., and Stack, J. (1994) A weight on children's minds: body shape dissatisfactions at 9 years old, *International Journal of Obesity*, **18**: 383–9.

Hill, J.O., and Peters, J.C. (1998) Environmental contributions to the obesity epidemic, *Science*, **280**(5368): 1371–4.

Hite, S. (1976) *The Hite Report*. New York: Macmillan.

Hite, S. (1981) *The Hite Report on Male Sexuality*. New York: A.A. Knopf.

Hite, S. (1987) *The Hite Report on Women and Love*. London: Penguin.

Hodgkins, S. and Orbell, S. (1998) Can protection motivation theory predict behaviour? A longitudinal study exploring the role of previous behaviour, *Psychology and Health*, **13**: 237–50.

Hoiberg, A., Berard, S., Watten, R.H. and Caine, C. (1994) Correlates of weight loss in treatment and at follow up, *International Journal of Obesity*, **8**: 457–65.

Holahan, C.J. and Moos, R.H. (1986) Personality, coping, and family resources in stress resistance: a longitudinal analysis, *Journal of Personality and Social Psychology*, **51**(2): 389–95.

Holahan, C.J. and Moos, R.H. (1990) Life stressors, resistance factors and improved psychological functioning: an extension of the stress resistance paradigm, *Journal of Personality and Social Psychology*, **58**: 909–17.

Holahan, C.J., Moerkbak, M. and Suzuki, R. (2006) Social support, coping, and depressive symptoms in cardiac illness among Hispanic and non-Hispanic white cardiac patients, *Psychology & Health*, **21**(5): 615–31.

Holahan, C.J., Moos, R.H. and Schaefer, J.A. (1996) Coping, stress resistance and growth: conceptualising adaptive functioning, in M. Zeidner and N.S. Endler (eds) *Handbook of Coping*. New York: Wiley.

Holland, J., Ramazanoglu, C. and Scott, S. (1990a) Managing risk and experiencing danger: tensions between government AIDS health education policy and young women's sexuality, *Gender and Education*, **2**: 125–46.

Holland, J., Ramazanoglu, C., Scott, S. et al. (1990b) Sex, gender and power: young women's sexuality in the shadow of AIDS, *Sociology of Health and Illness*, **12**: 336–50.

Holland, K.D. and Holahan, C.K. (2003) The relation of social support and coping to positive adaptation to breast cancer, *Psychology and Health*, **18**(1): 15–29.

Hollands, G.J., Hankins, M. and Marteau, T.M. (2010) Visual feedback of individuals' medical imaging results

for changing health behaviour, *Cochrane Database of Systematic Reviews*, **1**: 1–56.

Hollands, G.J., Prestwich, A. and Marteau, T.M. (2011) Using aversive images to enhance healthy food choices, *Health Psychology*, **30**(2): 195–203.

Holmes, T.H. and Rahe, R.H. (1967) The social readjustment rating scale, *Journal of Psychosomatic Research*, **11**: 213–18.

Honkanen, P., Olsen, S.O., and Verplanken, B. (2005) Intention to consume seafood: the importance of habit, *Appetite*, **45**(2): 161–8.

Hope, S., Wager, E. and Rees, M. (1998) Survey of British women's views on the menopause and HRT, *Journal of the British Menopause Society*, **4**(1): 33–6.

Hoppe, R. and Ogden, J. (1996) The effect of selectively reviewing behavioural risk factors on HIV risk perception, *Psychology and Health*, **11**: 757–64.

Hoppe, R. and Ogden, J. (1997) Practice nurses' beliefs about obesity and weight related interventions in primary care, *International Journal of Obesity*, **21**: 141–6.

Horne, R. (1997) Representations of medication and treatment: advances in theory and measurement, in K.J. Petrie and J.A. Weinman (eds) *Perceptions of Health and Illness: Current Research and Applications*. London: Harwood Academic Press.

Horne, R. (2001) Compliance, adherence and concordance, in K. Taylor and G. Harding (eds) *Pharmacy Practice*. London: Taylor & Francis.

Horne, R. (2006) Compliance, adherence, and concordance: implications for asthma treatment, *Chest*, **130**(1): 65–72S.

Horne, R. and Clatworthy, J. (2010) Adherence to advice and treatment, in D.P. French, K., Vedhara, A.A. Kaptein. and J. Weinman (eds) *Health Psychology*, 2nd edn. Oxford: Blackwell.

Horne, R. and Weinman, J. (1999) Patients' beliefs about prescribed medicines and their role in adherence to treatment in chronic physical illness, *Journal of Psychosomatic Research*, **47**(6): 555–67.

Horne, R. and Weinman, J. (2002) Self-regulation and self-management in asthma: exploring the role of illness perceptions and treatment beliefs in explaining non-adherence to preventer medication, *Psychology & Health*, **17**(1): 17–32.

Horne, R., Weinman, J. and Hankins, M. (1999) The beliefs about medicines questionnaire: the development and evaluation of a new method for assessing the cognitive representation of medication, *Psychology and Health*, **14**: 1–24.

Horne, R., Buick, D., Fisher, M. et al. (2004) Doubts about necessity and concerns about adverse effects: identifying the types of beliefs that are associated with non-adherence to HAART, *International Journal of STD & AIDS*, **15**(1): 38–44.

Horne, R., Cooper, V., Gellaitry, G. et al. (2007) Patients' perceptions of highly active antiretroviral therapy in relation to treatment uptake and adherence: the utility of the necessity-concerns framework, *Journal of Acquired Immune Deficiency Syndromes*, **45**(3): 334–41.

Horwitz, R.I. and Horwitz, S.M. (1993) Adherence to treatment and health outcome, *Archives of International Medicine*, **153**: 1863–8.

Horwitz, R.I., Viscoli, C.M., Berkman, L. et al. (1990) Treatment adherence and risk of death after a myocardial infarction, *Lancet*, **336**(8714): 542–5.

House of Commons Special Select Committee (2002) www.publications.parliament.uk/pa/cm200304/cmselect/cmhealth/23/23.pdf.

Houston, B.H. and Vavak, C.R. (1991) Cynical hostility: developmental factors, psychosocial correlates and health behaviours, *Health Psychology*, **10**: 9–17.

Howie, F.L., Henshaw, R.C., Naji, S.A. et al. (1997) Medical abortion or vacuum aspiration? Two year follow up of a patient preference trial, *British Journal of Obstetrics and Gynaecology*, **104**(7): 829–33.

Hughes, B.M. (2007) Social support in ordinary life and laboratory measures of cardiovascular reactivity: gender differences in habituation-sensitization, *Annals of Behavioral Medicine*, **34**: 166–76.

Hughes, B.M. and Curtis, R. (2000) Quality and quantity of social support as differential predictors of cardiovascular reactivity, *Irish Journal of Psychology*, **21**: 16–31.

Hughson, A., Cooper, A., McArdle, C. and Smith, D. (1986) Psychological impact of adjuvant chemotherapy in the first two years after mastectomy, *British Medical Journal*, **293**: 1268–72.

Hughson, A., Cooper, A., McArdle, C. and Smith, D. (1987) Psychosocial effects of radiotherapy after mastectomy, *British Medical Journal*, **294**: 1515–16.

Hulse, G.K. and Tait, R.J. (2002) Six-month outcomes associated with a brief alcohol intervention for adult inpatients with psychiatric disorders, *Drug and Alcohol Review* **21**(2): 105–12.

Humphris, G. and Ozakinci, G. (2008) The AFTER intervention: a structured psychological approach to reduce fears of recurrence in patients with head and neck cancer, *British Journal of Health Psychology*, **13**: 223–30.

Hunt, S.M., McEwen, J. and McKenna, S.P. (1986) *Measuring Health Status*. Beckenham: Croom Helm.

Hursti, U.K.K. and Sjoden, P.O. (1997) Food and general neophobia and their relationship with self-reported food choice: familial resemblance in Swedish families with children of ages 7–17 years, *Appetite*, **29**: 89–103.

Huston, S.A.; Bagozzi, R.P. and Kirking, D.M. (2010) Decision-making about the use of hormone therapy among perimenopausal women, *British Journal of Health Psychology*, **15**(2): 231–51.

Hutti, M.H. (1986) An exploratory study of the miscarriage experience, *Health Care for Women International*, **7**: 371–89.

Huttunen-Lenz, M., Song, F. and Poland, F. (2010) Are psychoeducational smoking cessation interventions for coronary heart disease patients effective? Meta-analysis of interventions, *British Journal of Health Psychology*, **15**: 749–77.

Idler, E.L. and Benyamini, Y. (1997) Self-rated health and mortality: a review of twenty-seven community studies, *Journal of Health and Social Behaviour*, **38**: 21–37.

Idler, E.L. and Kasl, S.V. (1995) Self-ratings of health: do they predict change in function as ability? *Journal of Gerontology Series B – Psychological Sciences and Social Sciences*, **50B**: S344–53.

Illich, I. (1974) *Medical Nemesis*. London: Caldar Boyars.

Ingham, R. (2005) 'We didn't cover that at school': education *against* pleasure or education *for* pleasure? *Sex Education*, **5**(4): 375–88.

Ingham, R., Woodcock, A. and Stenner, K. (1991) Getting to know you . . . young people's knowledge of their partners at first intercourse, *Journal of Community and Applied Social Psychology*, **1**: 117–32.

Ingledew, D.K. and Ferguson, E. (2007) Personality and riskier sexual behaviour: motivational mediators, *Psychology & Health*, **22**(3): 291–315.

Ingledew, D.K., Markland, D. and Medley, A.R. (1998) Exercise motives and stages of change, *Journal of Health Psychology*, **3**(4): 477–89.

Institute of Medicine (1995) Committee to develop criteria for evaluating the outcomes of approaches to prevent and treat obesity, in *Weighing the Options: Criteria for Evaluating Weight Management Programs*, www.iom.edu.

Isen, A.M., Rosenzweig, A.S. and Young, M.J. (1991) The influence of positive affect on clinical problem solving, *Medical Decision Making*, **11**: 221–7.

Jacks, J.Z. and Cameron, K.A. (2003) Strategies for resisting persuasion, *Basic and Applied Social Psychology*, **25**: 145–61.

Jacobs, N., Hagger, M.S., Streukens, S. et al. (2011) Testing an integrated model of the theory of planned behaviour and self-determination theory for different energy balance-related behaviours and intervention intensities, *British Journal of Health Psychology*, **16**: 113–34.

Jacobs, T.J. and Charles, E. (1980) Life events and the occurrence of cancer in children, *Psychosomatic Medicine*, **42**: 11–24.

James, J.E. (1997) *Understanding Caffeine: A Biobehavioral Analysis*. Thousand Oaks, CA: Sage.

James, J.E. (2004) Critical review of dietary caffeine and blood pressure: a relationship that should be taken more seriously, *Psychosomatic Medicine*, **66**: 63–71.

James, J.E. (2010) Caffeine, in B.A. Johnson (ed.) *Addiction Medicine*, DOI 10.1007/978-1-4419-0338-9_26.

James, J.E. (2011) Editorial: a new journal to advance caffeine research, *Journal of Caffeine Research*, **1**: 1–3.

James, J.E. and Hardardottir, D. (2002) Influence of attention focus and trait anxiety on tolerance of acute pain, *British Journal of Health Psychology*, **7**: 149–62.

James, J.E. and Keane, M.A. (2007) Caffeine, sleep and wakefulness: implications of new understanding about withdrawal reversal, *Human Psychopharmacology*, **22**(8): 549–58.

James, J.E. and Rogers, P.J. (2005) Effects of caffeine on performance and mood: withdrawal reversal is the most plausible explanation, *Psychopharmacology*, **182**: 1–8.

James, J.E., Gregg, M.E., Kane M., Harte, F. (2005) Dietary caffeine, performance and mood: enhancing and restorative effects after controlling for withdrawal relief, *Neuropsychobiology*, **52**: 1–10.

James, J.E., Kristjánsson, Á.L. and Sigfúsdóttir, I.D. (2010) Adolescent substance use, sleep, and academic achievement: evidence of harm due to caffeine, *Journal of Adolescence*, 10.1016/j.adolescence.2010.09.006.

Jamner, L.D. and Tursky, B. (1987) Syndrome-specific descriptor profiling: a psychophysiological and psychophysical approach, *Health Psychology*, **6**: 417–30.

Janis, I.L. (1967) Effects of fear arousal on attitude change: recent developments in theory and experimental research, in L. Berkowitz (ed.) *Advances in Experimental Social Psychology*. San Diego, CA: Academic Press.

Janoff-Bulman, R. (2004) Posttraumatic growth: three explanatory models, *Psychological Inquiry*, **15**: 30–4

Jebb, S.A., Prentice, A.M., Goldberg, G.R. et al. (1996) Changes in macronutrient balance during over feeding and under feeding assessed by 12 day continuous whole body calorimetry, *American Journal of Clinical Nutrition*, **64**: 259–66.

Jeffery, R.W., Drewnowski, A., Epstein, L.H. et al. (2000) Long-term maintenance of weight loss: current status, *Health Psychology*, **19**: 5–16.

Jessop, D.C. and Wade, J. (2008) Fear appeals and binge drinking: a terror management theory perspective, *British Journal of Health Psychology*, **13**: 773–88.

Jessop, D.C., Simmonds, L.V. and Sparks, P. (2009) Motivational and behavioral consequences of self-affirmation interventions: a study of sunscreen use among women, *Psychology and Health*, **24**: 529–44.

Jim, H.S. and Andersen, B.L. (2007) Meaning in life mediates the relationship between social and physical functioning and distress in cancer survivors, *British Journal of Health Psychology*, **12**(3): 363–81.

Jirojanakul, P. and Skevington, S. (2000) Developing a quality of life measure for children aged 5–8 years, *British Journal of Health Psychology*, **5**: 299–321.

Joekes, K., Maes, S. and Warrens, M. (2007) Predicting quality of life and self-management from dyadic support and overprotection after myocardial infarction, *British Journal of Health Psychology*, **12**(4): 473–89.

Johnson, J.H. (1986) *Life Events as Stressors in Childhood and Adolescence*. Newbury Park, CA: Sage.

Johnston, D.W. (1989) Will stress management prevent coronary heart disease? *The Psychologist: Bulletin of British Psychological Society*, **7**: 275–8.

Johnston, D.W. (1992) The management of stress in the prevention of coronary heart disease, in S. Maes, H. Leventhal and M. Johnston (eds) *International Review of Health Psychology*. Chichester: Wiley.

Johnston, D.W. (2002) Acute and chronic psychological processes in cardiovascular disease, in K.W. Schaie, H. Leventhal and S.L. Willis (eds) *Effective Health Behaviour in Older Adults*. New York: Springer.

Johnston, D.W., Anastasiades, P. and Wood, C. (1990) The relationship between cardiovascular responses in a laboratory and in the field, *Psychophysiology*, **4**: 331–9.

Johnston, D.W., Beedie, A. and Jones, M.C. (2006) Using computerized ambulatory diaries for the assessment of job characteristics and work-related stress in nurses, *Work & Stress*, **20**(2): 163–72.

Johnston, D.W., Cook, D.G. and Shaper, A.G. (1987) Type A behaviour and ischaemic heart disease in middle-aged British men, *British Medical Journal*, **295**: 86–9.

Johnston, D.W., Gold, A., Kentish, J. et al. (1993) Effect of stress management on blood pressure in mild primary hypertension, *British Medical Journal*, **306**: 963–6.

Johnston, D.W., Schmidt, T.F.H., Albus, C. et al. (1994) The relationship between cardiovascular reactivity in the laboratory and heart rate response in real life: active coping and beta blockade, *Psychosomatic Medicine*, **56**: 369–76.

Johnston, K.L. and White, K.M. (2003) Binge-drinking: a test of the role of group norms in the theory of planned behaviour, *Psychology and Health*, **18**(1): 63–77.

Johnston, M., Bonetti, D., Joice, S. et al. (2006) Recovery from disability after stroke as a target behavioural intervention: results of a randomized controlled trial, *Disability & Rehabilitation*, **29**(14): 1117–27.

Johnston, M., Earll, L., Giles, M. et al. (1999a) Mood as a predictor of disability and survival in patients newly diagnosed with ALS/MND, *British Journal of Health Psychology*, **4**: 127–36.

Johnston, M., Pollard, B., Morrison, V and Macwalter, R. (2004) Functional limitations of survival following stroke: psychological and clinical predictors of 3-year outcome, *International Journal of Behavioral Medicine*, **11**(4): 187–96.

Johnston, M., Foulkes, J., Johnston, D.W., Pollard, B. and Gudmundsdottir, H. (1999b) Impact on patient and partners of inpatient and extended cardiac counselling and rehabilitation: a controlled trial, *Psychosomatic Medicine*, **61**: 225–33.

Jonas, K., Stroebe, W. and Eagly, A. (1993) Adherence to an exercise program, unpublished manuscript, University of Tübingen.

Jones, H., Hodgins-Vermaas, R., McCartney, H. et al. (2002) Post-combat syndromes from the Boer War to the Gulf War: a cluster analysis of their nature and attribution, *British Medical Journal*, **324**(7333): 321–4.

Jones, R. (1992) Gastrointestinal disorders, in C.R. Hart and P. Burke (eds) *Screening and Surveillance in General Practice*. London: Churchill Livingstone.

Jones, R.K., Purcell, A., Singh, S. and Finer, L.B. (2005) Adolescents' reports of parental knowledge of adolescents' use of sexual health services and their reactions to mandated parental notification for prescription contraception, *Journal of the American Medical Association*, **293**(3): 340–8.

Joo, N.-S. and Kim, B.-T. (2007) Mobile phone short message service messaging for behaviour modification in a community-based weight control programme in Korea, *Journal of Telemedicine and Telecare*, **13**(8): 416–20.

Kahn, E., Ramsey, L.T., Brownson R.C. et al. (2002) The effectiveness of interventions to increase physical activity: a systematic review. *American Journal of Preventive Medicine*, **22**(4S): 73–107.

Kalat, J.W. and Rozin, P. (1973) 'Learned safety' as a mechanism in long-delay taste-aversion learning in rats, *Journal of Comparative and Physiological Psychology*, **83**(2): 198–207.

Kaluza, G. (2000) Changing unbalanced coping profiles: a prospective controlled intervention trial in worksite health promotion, *Psychology and Health*, **15**: 423–33.

Kamen, L.P. and Seligman, M.E.P. (1987) Explanatory style and health, *Current Psychological Research and Reviews*, **6**: 207–18.

Kanner, A.D., Coyne, J.C., Schaeffer, C. and Lazarus, R.S. (1981) Comparison of two modes of stress measurement: daily hassles and uplifts versus major life events, *Journal of Behavioural Medicine*, **4**: 1–39.

Kaplan, J.R., Manuck, S.B., Clarkson, T.B. et al. (1983) Social stress and atherosclerosis in normocholesterolemic monkeys, *Science*, **220**: 733–5.

Karamanidou, C., Weinman, J. and Horne, R. (2008) Improving haemodialysis patients' understanding of phosphate-binding medication: a pilot study of a psycho-educational intervention designed to change patients' perceptions of the problem and treatment, *British Journal of Health Psychology*, **13**: 205–14.

Karasek, R. and Theorell, T. (1990) *Healthy Work: Stress, Productivity and the Reconstruction of Working Life*. New York: Basic Books.

Karasek, R.A., Baker, D., Marxer, F. (1981) Job decision latitude, job demands and cardiovascular disease: a prospective study of Swedish men, *American Journal of Public Health*, **71**: 694–705.

Kasl, S.V. and Cobb, S. (1966) Health behaviour, illness behaviour, and sick role behaviour: II. Sick role behaviour, *Archives of Environmental Health*, **12**: 531–41.

Katz, S., Downs, T.D., Cash, H.R. and Grotz, R.C. (1970) Progress in development of the index of ADL, *Gerontology*, **10**: 20–30.

Kauffman, S.E., Silver, P. and Poulin, J. (1997) Gender differences in attitudes toward alcohol, tobacco, and other drugs, *Social Work*, **42**(3): 231–41.

Keefe, F.J., Lefebvre, J.C., Egert, J.R. et al. (2000) The relationship of gender to pain, pain behaviour and disability in osteoarthritis patients: the role of catastrophizing, *Pain*, **87**: 325–34.

Keller, I. and Abraham, C. (2005) Randomized controlled trial of a brief research-based intervention promoting fruit and vegetable consumption, *British Journal of Health Psychology*, **10**: 543–58.

Kelley, H.H. (1967) Attribution theory in social psychology, in D. Levine (ed.) *Nebraska Symposium on Motivation*. Lincoln, NE: University of Nebraska Press.

Kelley, H.H. (1971) *Attribution: Perceiving the Causes of Behaviour*. New York: General Learning Press.

Kemp, S., Morley, S. and Anderson, E. (1999) Coping with epilepsy: do illness representations play a role? *British Journal of Clinical Psychology*, **38**: 43–58.

Kennedy, P., Lude, P., Elfström, M.L. and Smithson, E. (2010) Sense of coherence and psychological outcomes in people with spinal cord injury: appraisals and behavioural responses, *British Journal of Health Psychology*, **15**(3): 611–21.

Kero, A., Högberg, U. and Lalos, A. (2004) Wellbeing and mental growth: long-term effects of legal abortion, *Social Science and Medicine*, **58**: 2559–69.

Kerr, J., Eves, F.F. and Carroll, D. (2001) The influence of poster prompts on stair use: the effects of setting, poster size and content, *British Journal of Health Psychology*, **6**: 397–405.

Ketonen, M., Pajunen, P., Koukkunen, H. et al. (2008) Long-term prognosis after coronary artery bypass surgery, *International Journal of Cardiology*, **124**(1): 72–9.

Keys, A., Brozek, J., Henscel, A. et al. (1950) *The Biology of Human Starvation*. Minneapolis, MN: University of Minnesota Press.

Keys, A., Taylor, H.L., Blackburn, H. et al. (1971) Mortality and coronary heart disease among men studied for 23 years, *Archives of Internal Medicine*, **128**: 201–14.

Khaw, K.T., Wareham, N. Bingham, S. et al. (2008) Combined impact of health behaviours and mortality in men and women: the EPIC-Norfolk prospective population study, *PLos Medicine*, **5**(12).

Kidd, T. and Sheffield, D. (2005) Attachment style and symptom reporting: examining the mediating effects of anger and social support, *British Journal of Health Psychology*, **10**: 531–41.

Kiebert, G., de Haes, J. and van der Velde, C. (1991) The impact of breast conserving treatment and mastectomy on the quality of life of early stage breast cancer patients: a review, *Journal of Clinical Oncology*, **9**: 1059–70.

Kiecolt-Glaser, J.K. and Glaser, R. (1986) Psychological influences on immunity, *Psychosomatics*, **27**: 621–4.

Kiecolt-Glaser, J.K., Fisher, L.D., Ogrocki, P. et al. (1987) Marital quality, marital disruption and immune function, *Psychosomatic Medicine*, **49**(1): 13–34.

Kiecolt-Glaser, J.K., Marucha, P.T., Malarkey, W.B. et al. (1995) Slowing wound healing by psychosocial stress, *Lancet*, **4**: 1194–6.

Kiecolt-Glaser, J.K., Bane, C., Glaser, R. and Malarkey, W.B. (2003) Love, marriage, and divorce: newlyweds' stress hormones foreshadow relationship changes, *Journal of Consulting and Clinical Psychology*, **71**: 176–88.

Kiernan, M., King, A.C., Kraemer, H.C. et al. (1998) Characteristics of successful and unsuccessful dieters: an application of signal detection methodology, *Annals of Behavioral Medicine*, **20**: 1–6.

Killen, J.D., Maccoby, N. and Taylor, C.B. (1984) Nicotine gum and self-regulation training in smoking relapse prevention, *Behaviour Therapy*, **15**: 234–8.

Killick, S. and Allen, C. (1997) 'Shifting the balance': motivational interviewing to help behaviour change in people with bulimia nervosa, *European Eating Disorders Review*, **5**(1): 33–41.

King, A.C., Ahn, D.K. Oliveira, B.M. et al. (2008) Promoting physical activity through hand-held computer technology, *American Journal of Preventive Medicine*, **34**(2): 138–42.

King, A.C., Blair, S.N., Bild, D.E. et al. (1992) Determinants of physical activity and interventions in adults, *Medicine and Science in Sports and Exercise*, **24**: S221–37.

King, L. and Hill, A.J. (2008) Magazine adverts for healthy and less healthy foods: effects on recall but not hunger or food choice by pre-adolescent children, *Appetite*, **51**(1): 194–7.

Kinlay, S. (1988) High cholesterol levels: is screening the best option? *Medical Journal of Australia*, **148**: 635–7.

Kinsey, A., Pomeroy, W. and Martin, C. (1948) *Sexual Behaviour in the Human Male*. London: Saunders.

Kissen, D.M. (1966) The significance of personality in lung cancer in men, *Annals of the New York Academy of Sciences*, **125**: 820–6.

Kivimaki, M., Leino-Arjas, P., Luukkonem, R. et al. (2002) Work stress and risk of cardiovascular mortality: prospective cohort study of industrial employees, *British Medical Journal*, **325**: 857–60.

Klassen, A., Fitzpatrick, R., Jenkinson, C. and Goodacre, T. (1996) Should breast reduction surgery be rationed? A comparison of the health status of patients before and after treatment: postal questionnaire survey, *British Medical Journal*, **313**: 454–7.

Klem, M.L., Wing, R.R., McGuire, M.T. et al. (1997) A descriptive study of individuals successful at long term maintenance of substantial weight loss, *American Journal of Clinical Nutrition*, **66**: 239–46.

Klesges, R.C. and Klesges, L. (1988) Cigarette smoking as a dieting strategy in a university population, *International Journal of Eating Disorders*, **7**: 413–19.

Klesges, R.C., Stein, R.J., Eck, L.H. et al. (1991) Parental influences on food selection in young children and its relationships to childhood obesity, *American Journal of Clinical Nutrition*, **53**: 859–64.

Klier, C.M., Geller, P.A. and Neugebauer, R. (2000) Minor depressive disorder in the context of miscarriage, *Journal of Affective Disorders*, **59**: 13–21.

Kneebone, I.I. and Martin, P.R. (2003) Coping and caregivers of people with dementia, *British Journal of Health Psychology*, **8**: 1–17.

Knight, K.M., McGowan, L., Dickens, C. and Bundy, C. (2006) A systematic review of motivational interviewing in physical health care settings, *British Journal of Health Psychology*, **11**: 319–32.

Kobasa, S.C., Maddi, S.R. and Puccetti, M.C. (1982) Personality and exercise as buffers in the stress–illness relationship, *Journal of Behavioral Medicine*, **5**: 391–404.

Kohlmann, C.W., Ring, C., Carroll, D. et al. (2001) Cardiac coping style, heartbeat detection, and the interpretation of cardiac events, *British Journal of Health Psychology*, **6**: 285–301.

Kolakowsky-Hayner, S.A., Gourley, E.V., Kreuter, J.S. et al. (1999) Pre-injury substance abuse among persons with brain injury and person with spinal cord injury, *Brain Injury*, **13**: 571–81.

Kopelman, P. (1999) Treatment of obesity V: pharmacotherapy for obesity, in *Obesity: The Report of the British Nutrition Foundation Task Force*. Oxford: Blackwell Science.

Kposowa, A.J. (2000) Marital status and suicide in the National Longitudinal Mortality Study, *Journal of Epidemiology and Community Health*, **54**: 254–61.

Kral, J.G. (1995) Surgical interventions for obesity, in K.D. Brownell and C.G. Fairburn (eds) *Eating Disorders and Obesity*. New York: Guilford Press.

Krantz, D.S., Glass, D.C., Contrada, R. and Miller, N.E. (1981) *Behavior and Health: National Science Foundation's Second Five Year Outlook on Science and Technology*. Washington, DC: US Government Printing Office.

Kripalini, S. et al. (2007) Interventions to enhance medication adherence in chronic medical consultations: a systematic review, *Archives of Internal Medicine*, **167**: 540–50.

Kuh, D.J., Hardy, R. and Wadsworth, M.E.J. (2000) Social and behavioural influences on the uptake of hormone replacement therapy among younger women, *BJOG: An International Journal of Obstetrics and Gynaecology*, **107**(6): 731–9.

Kuijer, R.G. and DeRidder, D.T.D. (2003) Discrepancy in illness-related goals and quality of life in chronically ill patients: the role of self efficacy, *Psychology and Health*, **18**(3): 313–30.

Kumar, R. and Robson, K. (1987) Previous induced abortion and ante-natal depression in primiparae: preliminary report of a survey of mental health in pregnancy, *Psychological Medicine*, **8**: 711–15.

Kune, G.A., Kune, S., Watson, L.F. and Bahnson, C.B. (1991) Personality as a risk factor in large bowel cancer: data from the Melbourne Colorectal Cancer Study, *Psychological Medicine*, **21**: 29–41.

Kunkel, E., Bakker, J., Myers, R. et al. (2000) Biopsychosocial aspects of prostate cancer, *Psychosomatics*, **41**: 85–94.

Kwon, H.-S.; Cho, J.-H.; Kim, H.-S. et al. (2004) Development of web-based diabetic patient management system using short message service (SMS), *Diabetes Rresearch and Clinical Practice*, **66**(suppl. 1): S133–7.

Lader, D. and Matheson, J. (1991) *Smoking Among Secondary School Children in England (1990): An Enquiry Carried out by the Social Survey Division of OPCS*. London: HMSO.

Laerum, E., Johnsen, N., Smith, P. and Larsen, S. (1988) Myocardial infarction can induce positive changes in lifestyle and in the quality of life, *Scandinavian Journal of Primary Health Care*, **6**: 67–71.

Laessle, R.G., Lehrke, S., and Dückers, S. (2007) Laboratory eating behavior in obesity, *Appetite*, **49**: 399–404.

Lam, L.T., Ross, F.I. and Cass, D.T. (1999) Children at play: the death and injury pattern in New South Wales, Australia, July 1990–June 1994, *Journal of Paediatrics and Child Health*, **35**: 572–7.

Lancet (1985) Cancer of the cervix – death by incompetence (editorial), *Lancet*, **2**: 363–4.

Lando, H.A. (1977) Successful treatment of smokers with a broad-spectrum behavioral approach, *Journal of Consulting and Clinical Psychology*, **45**: 361–6.

Lando, H.A. and McGovern, P.G. (1982) Three-year data on a behavioural treatment for smoking: a follow-up note, *Addictive Behaviours*, **7**: 177–81.

Lane, D., Carroll, D., Ring, C. et al. (2000) Effects of depression and anxiety on mortality and quality of life 4 months after myocardial infarction, *Journal of Psychosomatic Research*, **49**: 229–38.

Lane, D., Carroll, D., Ring, C. et al. (2002) The prevalence and persistence of depression and anxiety following myocardial infarction, *British Journal of Health Psychology*, **7**: 11–21.

Lang, A.R. and Marlatt, G.A. (1982) Problem drinking: a social learning perspective, in R.J. Gatchel, A. Baum and J.E. Singer (eds) *Handbook of Psychology and Health, Vol. 1, Clinical Psychology and Behavioral Medicine: Overlapping Disciplines*. Hillsdale, NJ: Erlbaum.

Larsson, G., Spangberg, L., Lindgren, S. and Bohlin, A.B. (1990) Screening for HIV in pregnant women: a study of maternal opinion, *AIDS Care*, **2**: 223–8.

Lashley, M.E. (1987) Predictors of breast self-examination practice among elderly women, *Advances in Nursing Science*, **9**: 25–34.

Lau, R. (1995) Cognitive representations of health and illness, in D. Gochman (ed.) *Handbook of Health Behavior Research*, vol. I. New York: Plenum.

Lau, R., Bernard, J.M. and Hartman, K.A. (1989) Further explanations of common sense representations of common illnesses, *Health Psychology*, **8**: 195–219.

Laudenslager, M.L., Ryan, S.M., Drugan, R.C. et al. (1983) Coping and immunosuppression: inescapable but not escapable shock suppresses lymphocyte proliferation, *Science*, **221**: 568–70.

Lawson, V.L., Lyne, P.A., Bundy, C. and Harvey, J.N. (2007) The role of illness perceptions, coping and evaluation in care-seeking among people with type 1 diabetes, *Psychology and Health*, **22**(2): 175–91.

Lawton, M.P., Moss, M. and Glicksman, A. (1990) The quality of life in the last year of life of older persons, *The Millbank Quarterly*, **68**: 1–28.

Lawton, R., Conner, M. and McEachan, R. (2009) Desire or reason: predicting health behaviors from affective and cognitive attitudes, *Health Psychology*, **28**(1): 56–65.

Lawton, R., Conner, M. and Parker, D. (2006) Beyond cognition: predicting health risk behaviours from instrumental and affective beliefs, *Health Psychology*, **26**(3): 259–67.

Lazane G. (2005) Abortion in Europe: Ten years after Cairo. *Entre nous The European magazine for sexual and reproductive health*, **59**: 4–6.

Lazarus, R.S. (1975) A cognitively oriented psychologist looks at biofeedback, *American Psychologist*, **30**: 553–61.

Lazarus, R.S. and Cohen, F. (1973) Active coping processes, coping dispositions, and recovery from surgery, *Psychosomatic Medicine*, **35**: 375–89.

Lazarus, R.S. and Folkman, S. (1987) Transactional theory and research on emotions and coping, *European Journal of Personality*, **1**: 141–70.

Lazarus, R.S. and Launier, R. (1978) Stress-related transactions between person and environment, in L.A. Pervin and M. Lewis (eds) *Perspectives in International Psychology*. New York: Plenum.

Lean, M. (1997) Sibutramine: a review of clinical efficacy, *International Journal of Obesity*, **21**(Suppl. 1): S30–6.

Lean, M.E.J., Han, T.S. and Morrison, C.E. (1995) Waist circumference as a measure for indicating need for weight management, *British Medical Journal*, **311**: 158–61.

Leary, M.R., Rapp, S.R., Herbst, K.C. et al. (1998) Interpersonal concerns and psychological difficulties of psoriasis patients: effects of disease severity and fear of negative evaluation, *Health Psychology*, **17**: 530–6.

Leck, I. (1986) An epidemiological assessment of neonatal screening for the dislocation of the hip, *Journal of the Royal College of Physicians*, **20**: 56–62.

Lee, C. and Glynn Owens, R. (2002) *The Psychology of Men's Health*. Maidenhead: Open University Press.

Lee, C.J., Collins, K.A. and Burgess, S.E. (1999) Suicide under the age of eighteen: a 10-year retrospective study, *American Journal of Forensic Medicine and Pathology*, **20**: 27–30.

Lee, E. (2003) Tensions in the regulation of abortion in Britain, *Journal of Law and Society*, **30**: 532–53.

Lee, E., Clements, S., Ingham, R. and Stone, N. (2004) *A Matter of Choice? Explaining National Variations in Teenage Abortion and Motherhood*. York: Joseph Rowntree Foundation.

Lee, T.J., Cameron, L.D., Wünsche, B. and Stevens, C. (2011) A randomized trial of computer-based communications using imagery and text information to alter representations of heart disease risk and motivate protective behaviour, *British Journal of Health Psychology*, **16**(1): 72–91.

Leforge, R.G., Velicer, W.F., Richmond, R.L. and Owen, N. (1999) Stage distributions for five health behaviours in the United States and Australia, *Preventive Medicine*, **28**: 61–74.

Lepore, S.J. (1998) Problems and prospects for the social support-reactivity hypothesis, *Annals of Behavioral Medicine*, **20**: 257–69.

Lepore, S.J., Allen, K.A., Evans, G.W. (1993) Social support lowers cardiovascular reactivity to an acute stressor, *Psychosomatic Medicine*, **6**: 518–24.

Lepper, M., Sagotsky, G., Dafoe, J.L. and Greene, D. (1982) Consequences of superfluous social constraints: effects on young children's social inferences and subsequent intrinsic interest, *Journal of Personality and Social Psychology*, **42**: 51–65.

Lerman, C., Hughes, C., Croyle, R.T. et al. (2000) Prophylactic surgery and surveillance practices one year following BRCA1/2 genetic testing, *Preventative Medicine*, **1**: 75–80.

Lett, H.S., Blumenthal, J.A., Babyak, M.A. et al. (2005) Social support and coronary heart disease: epidemiological evidence and implications for treatment, *Psychosomatic Medicine*, **67**: 869–78.

Levenstein, J.H., McCracken, E.C., McWhinney, I.R. et al. (1986) The patient centred clinical method, part 1: a model for the doctor–patient interaction in family medicine, *Family Practice*, **3**: 24–30.

Leventhal, H. and Nerenz, D. (1985) The assessment of illness cognition, in P. Karoly (ed.) *Measurement Strategies in Health Psychology*. New York: Wiley.

Leventhal, H., Benyamini, Y. and Shafer, C. (2007b) Lay beliefs about health and illness, in S. Ayers (ed.) *Cambridge Handbook of Psychology, Health and Medicine*. Cambridge: Cambridge University Press.

Leventhal, H., Meyer, D. and Nerenz, D. (1980) The common sense representation of illness danger, *Medical Psychology*, **2**: 7–30.

Leventhal, H., Prohaska, T.R. and Hirschman, R.S. (1985) Preventive health behavior across the life span, in J.C. Rosen and L.J. Solomon (eds) *Prevention in Health Psychology*. Hanover, NH: University Press of New England.

Leventhal, H., Benyamini, Y., Brownlee, S. et al. (1997) Illness representations: theoretical foundations, in K.J. Petrie and J.A. Weinman (eds) *Perceptions of Health and Illness*. Amsterdam: Harwood.

Leventhal, H., Weinman, J., Leventhal, E.A. and Phillips, L.A. (2007a) Health psychology: the search for pathways between behaviour and health, *Annual Review of Psychology*, **59**: 8.1–29.

Levi, L. (1974) Psychosocial stress and disease: a conceptual model, in E.K. Gunderson and R.H. Rahe (eds) *Life Stress and Illness*. Springfield, IL: Thomas.

Levine, J.D., Gordon, N.C. and Fields, H.L. (1978) The mechanism of placebo analgesia, *Lancet*, 2: 654–7.

Ley, P. (1988) *Communicating with Patients*. London: Croom Helm.

Ley, P. (1989) Improving patients' understanding, recall, satisfaction and compliance, in A. Broome (ed.) *Health Psychology*. London: Chapman & Hall.

Ley, P. and Morris, L.A. (1984) Psychological aspects of written information for patients, in S. Rachman (ed.) *Contributions to Medical Psychology*. Oxford: Pergamon Press.

Lichtenstein, E. and Brown, R.A. (1983) Current trends in the modification of cigarette dependence, in A.S. Bellack, M. Hersen and A.E. Kazdin (eds) *International Handbook of Behavior Modification and Therapy*. New York: Plenum.

Lichtenstein, E. and Glasgow, R. (1992) Smoking cessation: what have we learnt over the past decade? *Journal of Consulting and Clinical Psychology*, 60: 518–27.

Lichtenstein, E., Weiss, S.M., Hitchcock, J.L. et al. (1986) Task force 3: patterns of smoking relapse, *Health Psychology*, 5: 29–40.

Lifson, A., Hessol, N., Rutherford, G.W. et al. (1989) The natural history of HIV infection in a cohort of homosexual and bisexual men: clinical manifestations, 1978–1989. Paper presented to the 5th International Conference on AIDS, Montreal, September.

Lind, E., Ekkekakis, P. and Vazou, S. (2008) The affective impact of exercise intensity that slightly exceeds the preferred level, *Journal of Health Psychology*, 13(4): 464–8.

Lindemann, C. (1977) Factors affecting the use of contraception in the nonmarital context, in R. Gemme and C.C. Wheeler (eds) *Progress in Sexology*. New York: Plenum.

Linton, S.J., Buer, N., Vlaeyen, J. and Hellising, A. (2000) Are fear-avoidance beliefs related to the inception of an episode of back pain? A prospective study, *Psychology and Health*, 14: 1051–9.

Lipkus, I.M., Barefoot, J.C., Williams, R.B. and Siegler, I.C. (1994) Personality measures as predictors of smoking initiation and cessation in the UNC Alumni Heart study, *Health Psychology*, 13: 149–55.

Lippke, S. and Plotnikoff, R.C. (2009) The protection motivation theory within the stages of the transtheoretical model–stage-specific interplay of variables and prediction of exercise stage transitions, *British Journal of Health Psychology*, 14(2): 211–29.

Lissner, L., Odell, P.M., D'Agostino, R.B. et al. (1991) Variability of body weight and health outcomes in the Framingham population, *New England Journal of Medicine*, 324: 1839–44.

Little, P. and Byrne, C.D. (2001) Abdominal obesity and the hypertriglyceridaemic waist phenotype, *British Medical Journal*, 322: 687–9.

Little, P., Griffin, S., Kelly, J. et al. (1998) Effect of educational leaflets and questions on knowledge of contraception in women taking the combined contraceptive pill: randomised control trial, *British Medical Journal*, 316(7149): 1948–52.

Llewellyn, C.D., Miners, A.H., Lee, C.A. et al. (2003) The illness perceptions and treatment beliefs of individuals with severe haemophilia and their role in adherence to home treatment, *Psychology and Health*, 18: 185–200.

Lohan, M. (2010) Developing a critical men's health debate in academic scholarship, in B. Gough and S. Robertson (eds) *Men, Masculinities and Health, Critical Perspectives*. Basingstoke: Palgrave Macmillan.

Lohaus, A., Klein-Hebling, J., Vogele, C. and Kuhn-Hennighausen, C. (2001) Psychophysiological effects of relaxation training in children, *Psychology and Health*, 6: 197–206.

Loro, A.D. and Orleans, C.S. (1981) Binge eating in obesity: preliminary findings and guidelines for behavioural analysis and treatment, *Addictive Behaviours*, 7: 155–66.

Lowe, C.F., Dowey, A. and Horne, P. (1998) Changing what children eat, in A. Murcott (ed.) *The Nation's Diet: The Social Science of Food Choice*. Harlow: Addison-Wesley Longman.

Lowe, C.S. and Radius, S.M. (1982) Young adults' contraceptive practices: an investigation of influences, *Adolescence*, 22: 291–304.

Lowenstein, L., Deutsch, M., Gruberg, R. et al. (2006) Psychological distress symptoms in women undergoing medical vs. surgical termination of pregnancy, *General Hospital Psychiatry*, 28(1): 43–7.

Lucas, R.E. and Gohm, C.L. (2000) Age and sex differences in subjective well-being across cultures, in E. Diner and E.M. Suh (eds) *Culture and Subjective Well-being*. Cambridge, MA: MIT Press.

Luise, C., Jermy, K., May, C. et al. (2002) Outcomes of expectant management of spontaneous first trimester miscarriage: observational study, *British Medical Journal*, 324: 873–5.

Luker, K. (1975) *Taking Chances: Abortion and the Decision Not to Contracept*. Berkeley, CA: University of California Press.

Lupton, D. (1998) *The Emotional Self: A Sociocultural Exploration*. London: Sage.

Luszczynska, A. and Schwarzer, R. (2003) Planning and self-efficacy in the adoption and maintenance of breast self-examination: a longitudinal study on self-regulatory cognitions, *Psychology and Health*, 18(1): 93–108.

Luszczynska, A., Goc, G., Scholz, U. et al. (2010) Enhancing intentions to attend cervical cancer screening with a stage-matched intervention, *British Journal of Health Psychology*, **16**: 33–46.

Lynch, J. (1977) *The Broken Heart: The Medical Consequences of Loneliness*. New York: Basic Books.

Lynch J. and Davey Smith, A. (2002) Commentary: income inequality and health: the end of the story? *International Journal of Epidemiology*, **31**(3): 549–51.

Lynch J., Smith G.D., Harper S. et al. (2004) Is income inequality a determinant of population health? Part 1: a systematic review, *Millbank Quarterly*, **82**(1): 5–99.

Lyndon, J., Dunkel-Schetter, C., Cohan, C.L. and Pierce, T. (1996) Pregnancy decision making as a significant life event: a commitment approach, *Journal of Personality and Social Psychology*, **71**: 141–51.

MacDonald, D., Grant, A., Sheridan-Pereira, M. et al. (1985) The Dublin randomised trial of intrapartum fetal heart rate monitoring, *American Journal of Obstetrics and Gynaecology*, **25**: 33–8.

MacIntyre, S. (1977) *Single and Pregnant*. London: Croom Helm.

MacIntyre, S., Hunt, K. and Sweeting, H. (1996) Gender differences in health: are things really as simple as they seem?, *Social Science & Medicine*, **42**(4): 617–24.

MacKenzie, I. (1965) Breast cancer following multiple fluoroscopies, *British Journal of Cancer*, **19**: 1–18.

MacLean, U., Sinfield, D., Klein, S. and Harnden, B. (1984) Women who decline breast screening, *Journal of Epidemiology and Community Health*, **24**: 278–83.

MacNicol, S.A.M., Murray, S.M. and Austin, E.J. (2003) Relationships between personality, attitudes and dietary behaviour in a group of Scottish adolescents, *Personality and Individual Differences*, **35**: 1753–64.

MacWhinney, D.R. (1973) Problem solving and decision making in primary medical practice, *Proceeds of the Royal Society of Medicine*, **65**: 934–8.

Madden, M.E. (1988) Internal and external attributions following miscarriage, *Journal of Social and Clinical Psychology*, **7**: 113–21.

Maddi, S. and Kobasa, S.G. (1984) *The Hardy Executive: Health Under Stress*. Homewood, IL: Dow Jones-Irwin.

Maeland, J.G. and Havik, O.E. (1987) Psychological predictors for return for work after a myocardial infarction, *Journal of Psychosomatic Research*, **31**: 471–81.

Maes, H.H., Neale, M.C. and Eaves, L.J. (1997) Genetic and environmental factors in relative body weight and human adiposity, *Behavior Genetics*, **27**(4): 325–51.

Mahler, H.I.M., Kulik, J.A., Gibbons, F.X. et al. (2003) Effects of appearance-based interventions on sun protection intentions and self-reported behaviors, *Health Psychology*, **22**: 199–209.

Mahler, H.I.M., Kulik, J.A., Gerrard, M. and Gibbons, F.X. (2007) Long-term effects of appearance-based interventions on sun protection behaviors, *Health Psychology*, **26**: 350–60.

Major, B. and Gramzow, R.H. (1999) Abortion as stigma: cognitive and emotional implications of concealment, *Journal of Personality and Social Psychology*, **77**: 735–45.

Major, B., Cozzarelli, C., Cooper, M.L. et al. (2000) Psychological responses of women after first-trimester abortion, *Archives of General Psychiatry*, **57**: 777–84.

Maker, C. and Ogden, J. (2003) The miscarriage experience: more than just a trigger to psychological morbidity, *Psychology and Health*, **18**(3): 403–25.

Mann, J.M., Chin, J., Piot, P. and Quinn, T. (1988) The international epidemiology of AIDS, in *The Science of AIDS*, readings from *Scientfic American*, pp. 51–61. New York: W.H. Freeman.

Manne, S.L. and Zautra, A.J. (1992) Coping with arthritis: current status and critique, *Arthritis & Rheumatism*, **35**: 1273–80.

Manning, M.M. and Wright, T.L. (1983) Self-efficacy expectancies, outcome expectancies and the persistence of pain control in child birth, *Journal of Personality and Social Psychology*, **45**: 421–31.

Manstead, A.S.R. and Parker, D. (1995) Evaluating and extending the theory of planned behaviour, *European Review of Social Psychology*, **6**: 69–95.

Manuck, S.B., Kaplan, J.R. and Matthews, K.A. (1986) Behavioural antecedents of coronary heart disease and atherosclerosis, *Arteriosclerosis*, **6**: 1–14.

Mapes, R. (ed.) (1980) *Prescribing Practice and Drug Usage*. London: Croom Helm.

Marcus, B.H., Ciccola, J.T. and Sciamanna, C.N. (2009) Using electronic/computer interventions to promote physical activity, *British Journal of Sports Medicine*, **43**:102–5.

Marcus, B.H., Rakowski, W. and Rossi, J.S. (1992) Assessing motivational readiness and decision making for exercise, *Health Psychology*, **22**: 3–16.

Marcus, B.H., Owen, N., Forsyth, L.A.H. et al. (1998) Physical activity interventions using mass media, print media, and information technology, *American Journal of Preventive Medicine*, **15**(4): 362–78.

Marks, D.F., Brucher-Albers, N.C., Donker, F.J.S. et al. (1998) Health psychology 2000: the development of professional health psychology, *Journal of Health Psychology*, **3**: 149–60.

Marlatt, G.A. and Gordon, J.R. (1985) *Relapse Prevention*. New York: Guilford Press.

Marmot, M. (1998) Improvement of social environment to improve health, *Lancet*, **331**: 57–60.

Marmot, M. and Wilkinson, R. (2005) *Social Determinants of Health*, 2nd edn. Oxford: Oxford University Press.

Marshall, S.J. and Biddle, S.J.H. (2001) The transtheortical model of behaviour change: a meta-analysis of applications to physical activity and exercise, *Annals of Behavioural Medicine*, **23**: 229–46.

Marteau, T.M. (1993) Health related screening: psychological predictors of uptake and impact, in S. Marteau, and Baum, J.D. (1984) Doctors' views on diabetes, *Archives of Disease in Childhood*, **56**: 566–70.

Marteau, T.M. and Baum, J.D. (1984) Doctors' views on diabetes, *Archives of Disease in Childhood*, **56**: 566–70.

Marteau, T.M. and Riordan, D.C. (1992) Staff attitudes to patients: the influence of causal attributions for illness, *British Journal of Clinical Psychology*, **31**: 107–10.

Marteau, T.M., Ashcroft, R. and Oliver, A. (2009) Using financial incentives to achieve healthy behaviour, *British Medical Journal*, **338**: 983–5.

Marteau, T.M., Dormandy, E. and Michie, S. (2001) A measure of informed choice, *Health Expectations*, **4**: 99–108.

Marteau, T.M., Senior, V. and Sasieni, P. (2006) Women's understanding of a 'normal smear test result': experimental questionnaire based study, *British Medical Journal*, **322**(7285): 526–8.

Marteau, T.M., French, D.P., Griffin, S.J. et al. (2010) Effects of communicating DNA-based disease risk estimates on risk-reducing behaviours (review), *The Cochrane Library*, 10, CD007275.

Marteau, T.M., Senior, V., Humphries, S.E. et al. (2004) Psychological impact of genetic testing for familial hypercholesterolemia within a previously aware population: a randomized controlled trial, *American Journal of Medical Genetics*, **128**A: 285–93.

Martikainen, P. and Valkonen, T. (1996) Mortality after death of spouse in relation to duration of bereavement in Finland, *Journal of Epidemiology Community Health*, **50**(3): 264–8.

Martin, J.I. (2006) Transcendence among gay men: implications for HIV prevention, *Sexualities*, **9**(2): 214–35.

Martin, M.C. and Kennedy, P.F. (1993) Advertising and social comparison: consequences for female preadolescents and adolescents, *Psychology & Marketing*, **10**(6): 513–30.

Marucha, P.T., Kiecolt-Glaser, J.K. and Favagehi, M. (1998) Mucosal wound healing is impaired by examination stress, *Psychosomatic Medicine*, **60**: 362–5.

Mason, J.W. (1975) A historical view of the stress field, *Journal of Human Stress*, **1**: 22–36.

Mason, T.E. and White, K.W. (2008) Applying an extended model in the theory of planned behaviour to breast self-examination, *Journal of Health Psychology*, **13**(7): 946–55.

Masters, W. and Johnson, V. (1966) *Human Sexual Response*. Boston, MA: Little Brown.

Matarazzo, J.D. (1980) Behavioral health and behavioral medicine: frontiers for a new health psychology, *American Psychologist*, **35**: 807–17.

Matarazzo, J.D. (1984) Behavioral health: a 1990 challenge for the health sciences professions, in J.D. Matarazzo, N.E. Miller, S.M. Weiss et al. (eds) *Behavioral Health: A Handbook of Health Enhancement and Disease Prevention*. New York: Wiley.

Matthews, K.A., Manuck, S.B. and Saab, P.G. (1986) Cardiovascular responses of adolescents during a naturally occurring stressor and their behavioural and psychophysiological predictors, *Psychophysiology*, **23**: 198–209.

Matthews, K.A., Owens, J.F., Allen, M.T. and Stoney, C.M. (1992) Do cardiovascular responses to laboratory stress relate to ambulatory blood pressure levels? Yes in some of the people some of the time, *Psychosomatic Medicine*, **54**: 686–97.

Matthews, K.A., Woodall, K.L., Kenyon, K. and Jacob, T. (1996) Negative family environment as a predictor of boys' future status on measures of hostile attitudes, interview behaviour and anger expression, *Health Psychology*, **15**: 30–7.

McCabe, M.P. and Ricciardelli, L.A. (2001) Parent, peer and media influences on body images and strategies to both increase and decrease body size among adolescent boys and girls, *Adolescence*, **36**(142): 225–40.

McCann, I.L. and Holmes, D.S. (1984) Influence of aerobics on depression, *Journal of Personality and Social Psychology*, **46**: 1142–7.

McClendon, B.T. and Prentice-Dunn, S. (2001) Reducing skin cancer risk: an intervention based on protection motivation theory, *Journal of Health Psychology*, **6**(3): 321–8.

McCormick, N., Izzo, A. and Folcik, J. (1985) Adolescents' values, sexuality, and contraception in a rural New York county, *Adolescence*, **20**: 385–95.

McCracken, L.M. and Eccleston, C. (2003) Coping or acceptance: what to do about chronic pain? *Pain*, **105**(1–2): 197–204.

McCusker, J., Stoddard, J.G., Zapka, M.Z. and Meyer, K.H. (1989) Predictors of AIDS preventive behaviour among homosexually active men: a longitudinal study, *AIDS*, **3**: 443–6.

McDermott, M.R., Ramsay, J.M. and Bray, C. (2001) Components of the anger-hostility complex as a risk factor for coronary artery disease severity: a multi-measure study, *Journal of Health Psychology*, **6**(3): 309–19.

McDonald, D.G. and Hodgdon, J.A. (1991) *Psychological Effects of Aerobic Fitness Training: Research and Theory*. New York: Springer.

McEwan, B.S. and Stellar, E. (1993) Stress and the individual: mechanisms leading to disease. *Archives of Internal Medicine*, **153**: 2093–101.

McGee, H.M., O'Boyle, C.A., Hickey, A. et al. (1991) Assessing the quality of life of the individual: the SEIQoL with a healthy and a gastroenterology unit population, *Psychological Medicine*, **21**: 749–59.

McGee, H.M., Rushe, H., Sheil, K. and Keogh, B. (1998) Association of psychosocial factors and dietary compliance in haemodialysis patients, *British Journal of Health Psychology*, **3**: 97–109.

McGowan, L., Luker, K., Creed, F. and Chew-Graham, C.A. (2007) 'How do you explain a pain that can't be seen?': the narratives of women with chronic pelvic pain and their disengagement with the diagnostic cycle, *British Journal of Health Psychology*, **12**: 261–74.

McGowan, L.P.A., Clarke-Carter, D.D. and Pitts, M.K. (1998) Chronic pelvic pain: a meta-analytic review, *Psychology and Health*, **13**: 937–51.

McGuire, M.T., Wing, R.R., Klem, M.L. and Hill, J.O. (1999) Behavioral strategies of individuals who have maintained long term weight losses, *Obesity Research*, **7**: 334–41.

McKee, K.J., Houston, D.M. and Barnes, S. (2002) Methods for assessing quality of life and wellbeing in frail older people, *Psychology and Health*, **17**(6): 737–51.

McKeown, T. (1979) *The Role of Medicine*. Oxford: Blackwell.

McKinlay, E. (2005) *Men and Health: A Literature Review*. Wellington: Wellington School of Medicine and Health Sciences, University of Otago.

McMillen, J.C. (2004) Posttraumatic growth: what's it all about? *Psychological Inquiry*, **15**(1): 48–52.

McMillen, J.C., Smith, E.M. and Fisher, R.H. (1997) Perceived benefit and mental health after three types of disaster, *Journal of Consulting and Clinical Psychology*, **65**(5): 733–9.

McNair, D., Lorr, M. and Droppleman, L. (1971) *Manual for the Profile of Mood States*. San Diego, CA: Educational and Industrial Testing Service.

McNeil, A.D., Jarvis, M.J., Stapleton, J.A. et al. (1988) Prospective study of factors predicting uptake of smoking in adolescents, *Journal of Epidemiology and Community Health*, **43**: 72–8.

McNeil, B.J., Pauker, S.G., Sox, H.C. and Tversky, A. (1982) On the elicitation of preferences for alternative therapies, *New England Journal of Medicine*, **306**: 1259–62.

McWhinney, I.R. (1995) Why we need a new clinical method, in M. Stewart, B.B. Brown, W.W. Weston et al. (eds) *Patient Centred Medicine: Transforming the Clinical Method*. London: Sage.

Mead, N. and Bower, P. (2000) Patient centredness: a conceptual framework and review of empirical literature, *Social Science and Medicine*, **51**: 1087–110.

Meadows, J., Jenkinson, S., Catalan, J. and Gazzard, B. (1990) Voluntary HIV testing in the antenatal clinic: differing uptake rates for individual counselling midwives, *AIDS Care*, **2**: 229–33.

Mechanic, D. (1962) *Students Under Stress: A Study in the Social Psychology of Adaptation*. Glencoe, IL: Free Press of Glencoe.

Meenan, R.F., Gertman, P.M. and Mason, J.H. (1980) Measuring health status in arthritis: the arthritis impact measurement scales, *Arthritis & Rheumatology*, **23**: 146–52.

Melzack, R. (1975) The McGill Pain Questionnaire: major properties and scoring methods, *Pain*, **1**: 277–99.

Melzack, R. and Wall, P.D. (1965) Pain mechanisms: a new theory, *Science*, **150**: 971–9.

Mercken, L., Candel, M., van Osch, L. and de Vries, H. (2011) No smoke without fire: the impact of future friends on adolescent smoking behaviour, *British Journal of Health Psychology*, **16**: 170–88.

Metcalfe, C., Smith, G.D, Wadsworth, E. et al. (2003) A contemporary validation of the Reeder Stress Inventory, *British Journal of Health Psychology*, **8**: 83–94.

Metler, F.A., Hempelmann, L.H. and Dutton, A.M. (1969) Breast neoplasias in women treated with X-rays for acute postpartum mastitis, *Journal of the National Cancer Institute*, **43**: 803–22.

Meyer, D., Leventhal, H. and Guttman, M. (1985) Common-sense models of illness: the example of hypertension, *Health Psychology*, **4**: 115–35.

Michaud, C., Kahn, J.P., Musse, N. et al. (1990) Relationships between a critical life event and eating behaviour in high school students, *Stress Medicine*, **6**: 57–64.

Michel, G. (2006) A multi-level decomposition of variance in somatic symptom reporting in families with adolescent children, *British Journal of Health Psychology*, **11**(2): 345–55.

Michel, G. (2007) Daily patterns of symptom reporting in families with adolescent children, *British Journal of Health Psychology*, **12**: 245–60.

Michie, S., Ashford, S., Sniehotta, F. et al. (2011) A refined taxonomy of behaviour change techniques to help people change their physical activity and healthy eating behaviours—the CALO-RE taxonomy, *Psychology and Health*, 28 June.

Michie, S., Weinman, J., Miller, J. et al. (2002) Predictive genetic testing: high risk expectations in the face of low risk information, *Journal of Behavioural Medicine*, **25**: 33–50.

Michie, S., Fixsen, D., Grimshaw, J. and Eccles, M. (2009) Specifying and reporting complex behaviour change interventions: the need for a scientific method, *Implementation Science*, **4**(1): 40.

Michie, S., Smith, J.A., Heaversedge, J. and Read, S. (1999) Genetic counselling: clinical genetics views, *Journal of Genetic Counselling*, **8**(5): 275–87.

Michie, S., Smith, J.A., Senior, V. and Marteau, T.M. (2003) Understanding why negative genetic test results sometimes fail to reassure, *American Journal of Medical Genetics*, **119**(A): 340–7.

Milam, J. (2006) Posttraumatic growth and HIV disease progression, *Journal of Consulting and Clinical Psychology*, **74**(5): 817–27.

Miller, P. (1975) A behavioral intervention program for chronic public drunkenness offenders, *Archives of General Psychiatry*, **32**: 915–18.

Miller, S.M., Brody, D.S. and Summerton, J. (1987) Styles of coping with threat: implications for health, *Journal of Personality and Social Psychology*, **54**: 142–8.

Miller, T.Q., Smith, T.W., Turner, C.W. et al. (1996) A meta-analytic review of research on hostility and physical health, *Psychological Bulletin*, **119**: 322–48.

Miller, W. and Rollnick, S. (2002) *Motivational Interviewing: Preparing People to Change Addictive Behaviour*. New York: Guilford Press.

Miller, W.R. and Wilbourne, P.L. (2002) Mesa Grande: a methodological analysis of clinical trials of treatments for alcohol use disorders, *Addiction*, **97**(3): 265–77.

Minsky, S., Vega, W., Miskimen, T. et al. (2003) Diagnostic patterns in Latino, African American and European American psychiatric patients, *Archives of General Psychiatry*, **60**: 637–44.

Mintel (1990) *Eggs. Market Intelligence*. London: Mintel.

Minuchin, S., Rosman, B.L. and Baker, L. (1978) *The Anorectic Family in Psychosomatic Families: Anorexia Nervosa in Context*. London: Harvard University Press.

Misselbrook, D. and Armstrong, D. (2000) How do patients respond to presentation of risk information? A survey in general practice of willingness to accept treatment for hypertension, *British Journal of General Practice*, **51**: 276–9.

Moatti, J.-P., Le Gales, C., Seror, J. et al. (1990) Social acceptability of HIV screening among pregnant women, *AIDS Care*, **2**: 213–22.

Moatti, J.P., Carrieri, M.P., Spire, B., Gastaut, J.A., Cassuto, J.P., & Moreau, J. (2000) Adherence to HAART in French HIV-infected injecting drug users: the contribution of buprenorphine drug maintenance treatment. The Manif 2000 study group. *AIDS*, **14**, 151–5.

Mocroft, A., Vella, S., Benfield, T.L. et al. (1998) Changing patterns of mortality across Europe inpatients infected with HIV-1, EuroSIDA Study Group, *Lancet*, **352**(9142): 1725–30.

Moen, P. (1998) Women's roles and health: a life-course approach, in K. Orth-Gomér, M. Chesney and N.K. Wenger (eds) *Women, Stress, and Heart Disease*. Mahwah, NJ: Erlbaum.

Mokdad, A.H., Marks, J.S., Stroup, D.F. and Gerberding, J.L. (2004) Actual causes of death in the United States, *Journal of the American Medical Association*, **10**(29): 1238–45.

Moller, J., Hallqvist, J., Diderichensen, F. et al. (1999) Do episodes of anger trigger myocardial infarction? A case-crossover analysis in the Stockholm heart epidemiology program (SHEEP), *Psychosomatic Medicine*, **61**: 842–9.

Molloy, G.J., Dixon, D., Hamer, M. and Sniehotta, F.F. (2010) Social support and regular physical activity: does planning mediate this link? *British Journal of Health Psychology*, **15**: 859–970.

Montague, C.T., Farooqi, I.S., Whitehead, J.P. et al. (1997) Congenital leptin deficiency is associated with severe early onset obesity in humans, *Nature*, **387**: 903–8.

Moore, R.A., Eccleston, C., Derry, S. et al. (2010) 'Evidence' in chronic pain – establishing best practice in the reporting of systematic reviews, *PAIN*, **150**: 386–9.

Moore, S.C., Mayne, S.T., Graubard, B.I. et al. (2008) Past body mass index and risk of mortality among women, *International Journal of Obesity*, **32**(5): 730–9.

Moorhead, J. (1997) *New Generations: 40 Years of Birth in Britain* (National Childbirth Trust Guides). London: The Stationery Office.

Moos, R.H. and Schaefer, J.A. (1984) The crisis of physical illness: an overview and conceptual approach, in R.H. Moos (ed.) *Coping with Physical Illness: New Perspectives, 2*. New York: Plenum.

Moos, R.H. and Swindle, R.W. Jr (1990) Stressful life circumstances: concepts and measures, *Stress Medicine*, **6**: 171–8.

Mora, P.A., Halm, E., Leventhal, H. and Ceric, F. (2007) Elucidating the relationship between negative affectivity and symptoms: the role of illness specific affective responses, *Annals of Behavioural Medicine*, **34**(1): 77–86.

Morgan, W.P. and O'Connor, P.J. (1988) Exercise and mental health, in R.K. Dishman (ed.) *Exercise Adherence: Its Impact on Public Health*. Champaign, IL: Human Kinetics.

MORI (1984) *Public Attitudes Towards Fitness: Research Study Conducted for Fitness Magazine*. London: MORI.

Morison, L.A., Cozzolino, P.J. and Orbell, S. (2010) Temporal perspective and parental intention to accept the human papillomaviris vaccination for their daughter, *British Journal of Health Psychology*, **15**: 151–65.

Morrison, D.M. (1985) Adolescent contraceptive behaviour: a review, *Psychological Bulletin*, **98**: 538–68.

Mosbach, P. and Leventhal, H. (1988) Peer group identification and smoking: implications for intervention, *Journal of Abnormal Psychology*, **97**: 238–45.

Mosher, W., Martinez, G., Chandra, A. et al. (2004) Use of contraception and use of family planning services in the United States, 1982–2002, *Advance Data*, **350** (December).

Moss-Morris, R., Weinman, J., Petrie, K.J. et al. (2002) The revised illness perception questionnaire (IPQ-R), *Psychology and Health*, **17**: 1–16.

Moss-Morris, R., Humphrey, K., Johnson, M.H. and Petrie, K.J. (2007) Patients' perceptions of their pain condition across a multidisciplinary pain management programme: do they change and if so does it matter? *Clinical Journal of Pain*, **23**: 558–64.

Moyer, A. (1997) Psychosocial outcomes of breast conserving surgery versus mastectomy: a meta analytic review, *Health Pysychology*, **16**: 284–98.

Moynihan, J.A. and Ader, R. (1996) Psychoneuroimmunology: animal models of disease, *Psychosomatic Medicine*, **58**: 546–58.

Mrdjenovic, G., and Levitsky, D.A. (2005) Children eat what they are served: the imprecise regulation of energy intake, *Appetite*, **44**(3): 273–82.

Muir, J., Mant, D., Jones, L. and Yudkin, P. (1994) Effectiveness of health checks conducted by nurses in primary care: results of the OXCHECK study after one year, *British Medical Journal*, **308**: 308–12.

Muldoon, M.F., Barger, S.D., Flory, J.D. and Manuck, S.B. (1998) What are quality of life measurements measuring? *British Medical Journal*, **316**: 542–5.

Mullen, P.D., Green, L.W. and Persinger, G.S. (1985) Clinical trials of patient education for chronic conditions: a comparative meta-analysis of intervention types, *Preventive Medicine*, **14**: 753–81.

Muller, J.E., Abela, G.S., Nesto, R.W. and Tofler, G.H. (1994) Triggers, acute risk factors and vulnerable

plaques: the lexicon of a new frontier, *Journal of American College of Cardiology*, **23**: 809–13.

Muñoz-Silva, A., Sanchez-Garcia, M., Nunes, C. and Martins, A. (2007) Gender differences in condom use prediction with theory of reasoned action and planned behaviour: the role of self-efficacy and control, *AIDS Care*, **19**: 1177–81.

Murgio, A., Fernandez Mila, J., Manolio, A. et al. (1999) Minor head injury at paediatric age in Argentina, *Journal of Neurosurgical Sciences*, **43**: 15–23.

Murray, M., Swan, A.V., Bewley, B.R. and Johnson, M.R.D. (1984) The development of smoking during adolescence: the MRC/Derbyshire smoking study, *International Journal of Epidemiology*, **12**: 185–92.

Myers, L.B. (2000) Identifying repressors: a methodological issue for health psychology, *Psychology and Health*, **15**: 205–14.

Nanton, V., Docherty, A., Meystre, C. and Dale, J. (2009) Finding a pathway: information and uncertainty along the prostate cancer patient journey, *British Journal of Health Psychology*, 14: 437–58.

Napper, L., Harris, P.R. and Epton, T. (2009) Developing and testing a self-affirmation manipulation, *Self and Identity*, **8**: 45–62.

Nash, H.L. (1987) Do compulsive runners and anorectic patients share common bonds? *The Physician and Sportsmedicine*, **15**(12): 163–7.

National Center for Health Statistics (2009) *Health, United States, 2008*. Hyattsville, MD: National Center for Health Statistics.

National Institutes of Health (1998) Clinical guidelines on the identification, evaluation, and treatment of overweight and obesity in adults: the evidence report, *Obesity Research*, **6**(suppl. 2): 51–209S.

National Statistics (2005) www.statistics.gov.uk.

National Statistics Online (2006) *GP Consultations*.

Neame, R. and Hammond, A. (2005) Beliefs about medications: a questionnaire survey of people with rheumatoid arthritis, *Rheumatology*, **44**: 762–7.

Neighbour, R. (1987) *The Inner Consultation*. London: Petroc Press.

Neilson, S. and Hahlin, M. (1985) Expectant management of first trimester miscarriage, *Lancet*, **345**: 84–6.

Newell, A. and Simon, H.A. (1972) *Human Problem Solving*. Englewood Cliffs, NJ: Prentice Hall.

Newman, E., O'Connor, D.B., Conner, M. (2007) Daily hassles and snack intake: the role of cortisol reactivity status, *Psychoneuroendocrinology*, **32**: 125–32.

Newman, M.G. and Stone, A.A. (1996) Does humour moderate the effects of experimentally induced stress? *Annals of Behavioural Medicine*, **18**: 101–9.

Newman, S., Fitzpatrick, R., Revenson, T.A. et al. (1996) *Understanding Rheumatoid Arthritis*. London: Routledge.

NHS Centre for Reviews and Dissemination (1997) *Systematic Review of Interventions in the Treatment and Prevention of Obesity*. York: University of York.

NICE (National Institute for Health and Clinical Excellence) (2009) *Costing Statement: Medicines Adherence: Involving Patients in Decisions About Prescribed Medicines and Supporting Adherence*. London: NICE.

Noar, S.M., Moroko., P.J. and Harlow, L.L. (2002) Condom negotiation in heterosexually active men and women: development and validation of a condom influence strategy questionnaire, *Psychology and Health*, **17**(6): 711–35.

Norman, P. and Bennett, P. (1995) Health locus of control and health behaviours, in M. Conner and P. Norman (eds) *Predicting Health Behaviour: Research and Practice with Social Cognition Models*. Buckingham: Open University Press.

Norman, P. and Conner, M. (1993) The role of social cognition models in predicting attendance at health checks, *Psychology and Health*, **8**: 447–62.

Norman, P. and Conner, M. (1996) The role of social cognition models in predicting health behaviours: future directions, in M. Conner and P. Norman (eds) *Predicting Health Behaviour: Research and Practice with Social Cognition Models*. Buckingham: Open University Press.

Norman, P. and Conner, M. (2006) The role of social cognition models in predicting health behaviours: future directions, in M. Conner and P. Norman (eds) *Predicting Health Behaviour: Research and Practice with Social Cognition Models*, 2nd edn. Maidenhead: Open University Press.

Norman, P. and Fitter, M. (1989) Intention to attend a health screening appointment: some implications for general practice, *Counselling Psychology Quarterly*, **2**: 261–72.

Norman, P. and Smith, L. (1995) The theory of planned behaviour and exercise: an investigation into the role of prior behaviour, behavioural intentions and attitude variability, *European Journal of Social Psychology*, **25**: 403–15.

Norman, P., Conner, M. and Bell, R. (1999) The theory of planned behavior and smoking cessation, *Health Psychology*, **18**: 89–94.

Norman, P., Searle, A., Harrad, R. and Vedhara, K. (2003) Predicting adherence to eye patching in children with amblyopia: an application of protection motivation theory, *British Journal of Health Psychology*, **8**: 67–82.

North, C.S. (2002) Somatization in survivors of catastrophic trauma: a methodological review, *Environmental Health Perspectives*, **110**(suppl. 4): 637–40.

North East Essex NHS Trust (2009) Food vouchers incentives to pregnant smokers, press release, 21 January, www.northeastessexpct.nhs.uk/news/newsitem.asp?news_id=272.

Nyklíček, I., Vingerhoets, A.D. and Denollett, J. (2002) Emotional (non-)expression and health: data, questions and challenges, *Psychology and Health*, **17**(5): 517–28.

O'Boyle, C., McGee, H., Hickey, A. et al. (1992) Individual quality of life in patients undergoing hip replacements, *Lancet*, **339**: 1088–91.

O'Brien, S. and Lee, L. (1990) Effects of videotape intervention on pap smear knowledge, attitudes and behavior, special issue: *Behavioural Research in Cancer*, *Behaviour Changes*, **7**: 143–50.

O'Connor, A. and O'Brien-Pallas L.L. (1989) Decisional conflict, in G.K. Mcfarlane and E.A. Mcfarlane (eds) *Nursing Diagnosis and Intervention*. Toronto: Mosby.

O'Connor, D.B., Conner, M., Jones, F. et al. (2009) Exploring the benefits of conscientiousness: an investigation of the role of daily stressors and health behaviors, *Annals of Behavioral Medicine*, **37**: 184–96.

O'Conner, D.B., Jones, F., Conner, M. et al. (2008) Effects of daily hassles and eating style on eating behaviour, *Health Psychology*, **27**(1): S2–31.

O'Donnell, L., Stueve, A., Duran, R. et al. (2008) Parenting practices, parents' underestimation of daughters' risks, and alcohol and sexual behaviors of urban girls, *Journal of Adolescent Health*, **42**(5): 496–502.

O'Donovan, A. and Hughes, B.M. (2008) Access to social support in life and in the laboratory, *Journal of Health Psychology*, **13**(8): 1147–56.

O'Neil, J.M., Good, G.E. and Holmes, S. (1995) Fifteen years of theory and research on men's gender role conflict: new paradigms for empirical research, in R.F. Levant, and W.S. Pollack (eds) *A New Psychology of Men*. New York: Basic Books.

Oakley, A. (1984) *The Captured Womb*. Oxford: Blackwell.

Oakley, A. (1992) *Social Support and Motherhood*. Oxford: Blackwell.

Oakley, A., Fullerton, D., Holland, J. et al. (1995) Sexual health education interventions for young people: a methodological review, *British Medical Journal*, **310**: 158–62.

Office for National Statistics Population and Health Monitors (1995) www.statistics.gov.uk.

Ogden, C.L., Carroll, M.D., McDowell, M.A., and Flegal, K.M. (2007) Obesity among adults in the United States:

no statistically significant change since 2003–2004, *NCHS Data Brief*, November, (1): 1–8.

Ogden, J. (1993) The measurement of restraint: confounding success and failure? *International Journal of Eating Disorders*, **13**: 69–76.

Ogden, J. (1995) Cognitive and motivational consequence of dieting, *European Eating Disorders Review*, **24**: 228–41.

Ogden, J. (2000) The correlates of long-term weight loss: a group comparison study of obesity, *International Journal of Obesity*, **24**: 1018–25.

Ogden, J. (2003) Some problems with social cognition models: a pragmatic and conceptual analysis, *Health Psychology*, **22**(4): 424–8.

Ogden, J. (2010) *The Psychology of Eating: From Healthy to Disordered Behaviour*. Chichester: Wiley-Blackwell.

Ogden, J. and Clementi, C. (2011) The experience of being obese and the many consequences of stigma, *Journal of Obesity*, 429098, open access.

Ogden, J. and Elder, C. (1998) The role of family status and ethnic group on body image and eating behaviour, *International Journal of Eating Disorders*, **23**: 309–15.

Ogden, J. and Greville, L. (1993) Cognitive changes to preloading in restrained and unrestrained eaters as measured by the Stroop task, *International Journal of Eating Disorders*, **14**: 185–95.

Ogden, J. and Hills, L. (2008) Understanding sustained changes in behaviour: the role of life events and the process of reinvention, *Health: An International Journal*, **12**: 419–37.

Ogden, J. and Maker, C. (2004) Expectant or surgical management: a qualitative study of miscarriage, *British Journal of Obstetrics and Gynaecology*, **111**: 463–7.

Ogden, J. and Mtandabari, T. (1997) Examination stress and changes in mood and health related behaviours, *Psychology and Health*, **12**: 289–99.

Ogden, J. and Mundray, K. (1996) The effect of the media on body satisfaction: the role of gender and size, *European Eating Disorders Review*, **4**: 171–82.

Ogden, J. and Sherwood, F. (2008) Reducing the impact of media images: an evaluation of the effectiveness of an air-brushing educational intervention on body dissatisfaction, *Health Education*, **108**(6): 489–500.

Ogden, J. and Sidhu, S. (2006) Adherence, behaviour change and visualisation: a qualitative study of patients' experiences of obesity medication, *The Journal of Psychosomatic Research*, **62**: 545–52.

Ogden, J. and Steward, J. (2000) The role of the mother–daughter relationship in explaining weight concern, *International Journal of Eating Disorders*, **28**: 78–83.

Ogden, J., and Taylor, C. (2000) Body size evaluation and body dissatisfaction within couples, *International Journal of Health Psychology*, **5**: 25–32.

Ogden, J. and Wardle, J. (1990) Control of eating and attributional style, *British Journal of Clinical Psychology*, **29**: 445–6.

Ogden, J. and Wardle, J. (1991) Cognitive and emotional responses to food, *International Journal of Eating Disorders*, **10**: 297–311.

Ogden, J. and Zoukas, S. (2009) Generating physical symptoms from visual cues: an experimental study, *Psychology, Health and Medicine*, **14**: 695–704.

Ogden, J., Veale, D., Summers, Z. (1997) The development and validation of the Exercise Dependence Questionnaire, *Addiction Research*, **5**: 343–56.

Ogden, J., Clementi, C., and Aylwin, S. (2006a) Having obesity surgery: a qualitative study and the paradox of control, *Psychology and Health*, **21**: 273–93.

Ogden, J., Reynolds, R. and Smith, A. (2006b) Expanding the concept of parental control: a role for overt and covert control in children's snacking behaviour? *Appetite*, **47**: 100–6.

Ogden, J., Ambrose, L., Khadra, A. et al. (2002) A questionnaire study of GPs' and patients' belief about the different components of patient centredness, *Patient Education and Counselling*, **47**: 223–7.

Ogden, J., Baig, S., Earnshaw, G. et al. (2001a) What is health? Where GPs' and patients' worlds collide, *Patient Education and Counselling*, **45**: 265–9.

Ogden, J., Bandara, I., Cohen, H. et al. (2001b) GPs' and patients' models of obesity: whose problem is it anyway? *Patient Education and Counselling*, **40**: 227–33.

Ogden, J., Boden, J., Caird, R. et al. (1999) You're depressed; no I'm not: GPs' and patients' different models of depression, *British Journal of General Practice*, **49**: 123–4.

Ogden, J., Branson, R., Bryett, A. et al. (2003) What's in a name? An experimental study of patients' view of the impact and function of a diagnosis, *Family Practice*, **20**(3): 248–53.

Ogden, J., Heinrich, J, Potter, J. et al. (2009) The impact of viewing a hysteroscopy on a screen on the patient's experience: a randomised trial, *BJOG*, **116**: 286–92.

Ogden, J., Clementi, C., Aylwin, S. and Patel, A. (2005) Exploring the impact of obesity surgery on patients' health status: a quantitative and qualitative study, *Obesity Surgery*, **15**: 266–72.

Ohlin, A. and Rossner, S. (1990) Maternal body weight development after pregnancy, *International Journal of Obesity*, **14**: 159–73.

Oldridge, N.B., Guyatt, G.H., Fischer, M.E. and Rimm, A.A. (1988) Cardiac rehabilitation after myocardial infarction: combined experience of randomised clinical trials, *Journal of the American Medical Association*, **260**(7): 945–50.

Oliver, K.L. (2001) Images of the body from popular culture: engaging adolescent girls in critical inquiry, *Sport, Education and Society*, **6**: 143–64.

Olivera, S.A., Ellison, R.C., Moore, L.L. et al. (1992) Parent–child relationships in nutrient intake: the Framingham Children's Study, *American Journal of Clinical Nutrition*, **56**: 593–8.

OPCS (Office of Population, Censuses and Surveys) (1992) *General Household Survey*. London: OPCS.

OPCS (Office of Population, Censuses and Surveys) (1994) *General Household Survey*. London: OPCS.

OPCS (Office of Population, Censuses and Surveys) (2004) *General Household Survey*. London: OPCS.

Orford, J. (2001) Addiction as excessive appetite, *Addiction*, **96**(1): 15–31.

Orford, J. (2002) *Excessive Appetites: A Psychological View of Addictions*, 2nd edn. Chichester: Wiley.

Orford, J. and Velleman, R. (1991) The environmental intergenerational transmission of alcohol problems: a comparison of two hypotheses, *British Journal of Medical Psychology*, **64**: 189–200.

Orton, M., Fitzpatrick, R., Fuller, A. et al. (1991) Factors affecting women's responses to an invitation to attend for a second breast cancer screening examination, *British Journal of General Practice*, **41**: 320–3.

Osborn, M. and Smith, J.A. (1998) The professional experience of chronic benign lower back pain: an interpretative phenomenological analysis, *Journal of Health Psychology*, **3**: 65–83.

Ouellette, J. and Wood, W. (1998) Habit and intention in everyday life: the multiple processes by which past behaviour predicts future behaviour, *Psychological Bulletin*, **124**: 54–74.

Owens, R.G., Daly, J., Heron, K. and Leinster, S.J. (1987) Psychological and social characteristics of attenders for breast screening, *Psychology and Health*, **1**: 320–3.

Paffenbarger, R.S. and Hale, W.E. (1975) Work activity and coronary heart mortality, *New England Journal of Medicine*, **292**: 545–50.

Paffenbarger, R.S., Hyde, R.T., Wing, A.L. and Hsieh, C.C. (1986) Physical activity, all-cause mortality, and longevity of college alumni, *New England Journal of Medicine*, **314**: 605–13.

Pakenham, K., Pruss, M. and Clutton, S. (2000) The utility of socio-demographics, knowledge and health belief model variables in predicting reattendance for mammography screening: a brief report, *Psychology and Health*, **15**: 585–91.

Panagiotakos, D.B., Pitsavos, C.H., Chrysohoou, C. et al. (2003) Status and management of hypertension in Greece; role of the adoption of a Mediterranean diet: the Attica study, *Journal of Hypertension*, **21**: 1483–9.

Parfitt, G., Rose, E.A. and Burgess, W.M. (2006) The psychological and physiological responses of sedentary individuals to prescribed and preferred intensity exercise, *British Journal of Health Psychology*, **11**: 39–53.

Park, C.J. (2004) The notion of growth following stressful life experiences: problems and prospects, *Psychological Inquiry*, **15**(1): 69–76.

Park, C.L. and Folkman, S. (1997) The role of meaning in the context of stress and coping, *General Review of Psychology*, **2**: 115–44.

Park, C.L., Cohen, L.H. and Murch, R.L. (1996) Assessment and prediction of stress-related growth, *Journal of Personality*, **64**: 71–105.

Park, C.L., Edmonson, D., Fenster, J.A. and Blank, T.O. (2008) Positive and negative health behavior changes in cancer survivors: a stress and coping perspective, *Journal of Health Psychology*, **13**(8): 1198–206.

Park, L.C. and Covi, L. (1965) Non-blind placebo trial: an exploration of neurotic patients' responses to placebo when its inert content is disclosed, *Archives of General Psychiatry*, **12**: 336–45.

Parkes, K.R. (2006) Physical activity and self-rated health: interactive effects of activity in work and leisure domains, *British Journal of Health Psychology*, **11**: 533–50.

Parsons, T. (1951) *The Social System*. New York: The Free Press.

Partridge, C.J. and Johnston, M. (1989) Perceived control and recovery from physical disability, *British Journal of Clinical Psychology*, **28**: 53–60.

Pasman, L. and Thompson, J.K. (1988) Body image and eating disturbance in obligatory runners, obligatory weightlifters and sedentary individuals, *International Journal of Eating Disorders*, **7**: 759–69.

Patrick, D.L. and Ericson, P.E. (1993) *Health Status and Health Policy: Allocating Resources to Health Care*. Oxford: Oxford University Press.

Paxton, S.J., Browning, C.J. and O'Connell, G. (1997) Predictors of exercise program participation in older women, *Psychology and Health*, **12**: 543–52.

Pearson, N., Biddle, S.J., and Gorely, T. (2009) Family correlates of breakfast consumption among children and adolescents: a systematic review, *Appetite*, **52**(1): 1–7.

Pearte, C.A., Furberg, C.D., O'Meara, E. S. et al. (2006) Characteristics and baseline clinical predictors of future fatal versus nonfatal coronary heart disease events in older adults: the Cardiovascular Health Study, *Circulation*, **113**(18): 2177–85.

Pendleton, D., Schofield, T., Tate, P. and Havelock, P. (1984) *The Consultation: An Approach to Learning and Teaching*. Oxford: Oxford Medical Publications.

Pennebaker, J.W. (1982) *The Psychology of Physical Symptoms*. New York: Springer-Verlag.

Pennebaker, J.W. (1983) Accuracy of symptom perception, in A. Baum, S.E. Taylor and J. Singer (eds) *Handbook of Psychology and Health*, vol. 4. Hillsdale, NJ: Erlbaum.

Pennebaker, J.W. (1993) Social mechanisms of constraint, in D.M. Wegner and J.W. Pennebaker (eds) *Handbook of Mental Control*. Englewood Cliffs, NJ: Prentice Hall.

Pennebaker, J.W. (1997) Writing about emotional experiences as a therapeutic process, *Psychological Science*, 8(3): 162–6.

Pennebaker, J.W. and Beall, S.K. (1986) Confronting a traumatic event: toward an understanding of inhibition and disease, *Journal of Abnormal Psychology*, 95: 274–82.

Pennebaker, J.W., Francis, M.E. and Booth, R.J. (2001) *Linguistic Inquiry and Word Count: LIWC 2001*. Mahwah, NJ: Erlbaum.

Pennebaker, J.W., Kiecolt-Glasser, J.K. and Glaser, R. (1988) Disclosure of trauma and immune function: health implications for psychotherapy, *Journal of Consulting and Clinical Psychology*, 56: 239–45.

Pennebaker, J.W., Mayne, T.J. and Francis, M.E. (1997) Linguistic predictors of adaptive bereavement, *Journal of Personality and Social Psychology*, 72: 863–71.

Pereira, D.B., Antoni, M.H., Danielson, A. et al. (2003) Life stress and cervical squamous intraepithelial lesions in women with human papillomavirus and human immunodeficiency virus, *Psychosomatic Medicine*, 65(1): 1–8.

Perkins, K.A., Grobe, J.E., Stiller, R.L. et al. (1992) Nasal spray nicotine replacement suppresses cigarette smoking desire and behaviour, *Clinical Pharmacology and Therapeutics*, 52: 627–34.

Perna, F.M. and McDowell, S.L. (1995) Role of psychological stress in cortisol recovery from exhaustive exercise among elite athletes, *International Journal of Behavioural Medicine*, 2: 13–26.

Perquin, B., Baillet, F. and Wilson, J.F. (1976) Radiation therapy in the management of primary breast cancer, *American Journal of Roentgenology*, 127: 645–8.

Perquin, C.W., Hazebroek-Kampschreur A.A., Hunfeld, J.A.M. et al. (2000) Pain in children and adolescents: a common experience, *Pain*, 87: 51–8.

Petersen, A. (1998) *Unmasking the Masculine: 'Men' and 'Identity' in a Sceptical Age*. London: Sage.

Peto, R., Lopez, A.D., Boreham, J. et al. (1994) *Mortality from Smoking in Developed Countries 1950–2000*. Oxford: Oxford University Press.

Petrie, K.J., Booth, R.J. and Pennebaker, J.W. (1998) The immunological effects of thought suppression, *Journal of Personality and Social Psychology*, 75: 1264–72.

Petrie, K.J., Booth, R.J., Pennebaker, J.W. et al. (1995) Disclosure of trauma and immune response to a hepatitis B vaccination program, *Journal of Consulting and Clinical Psychology*, 63: 787–92.

Petrie, K.J., Cameron, L.D., Ellis, C.J. et al. (2002) Changing illness perceptions after myocardial infarction: an early intervention randomized controlled trial, *Psychosomatic Medicine*, 64: 580–6.

Petrie, K.J., Weinman, J.A., Sharpe, N. and Buckley, J. (1996) Role of patients' view of their illness in predicting return to work and functioning after myocardial infarction: longitudinal study, *British Medical Journal*, 312: 1191–4.

Petronis, V.M., Carver, C.S., Antoni, M.H. and Weiss, S. (2003) Investment in body image and psychosocial well-being among women treated for early stage breast cancer: partial replication and extension, *Psychology and Health*, 18(1): 1–13.

Petticrew, M., Fraser, J.M. and Regan, M. (1999) Adverse life-events and risk of breast cancer: a meta-analysis, *British Journal of Health Psychology*, 4: 1–17.

Petty, R.E. and Cacioppo, J.T. (1986) The elaboration likelihood model of persuasion, in L. Berkowitz (ed.) *Advances in Experimental Social Psychology*, vol. 19. New York: Academic Press.

Phillips, A.C., Der, G. and Carroll, D. (2008) Stressful life-events exposure is associated with 17-year mortality, but it is health-related events that prove predictive, *British Journal of Health Psychology*, 13(4): 647–57.

Phillips, A.C., Der, G. and Carroll, D. (2010) Self-reported health, self-reported fitness and all-cause mortality: prospective cohort study, *British Journal of Health Psychology*, 15: 337–46.

Piccinelli, M. and Simon, G. (1997) Gender and cross-cultural differences in somatic symptoms associated with emotion distress: an international study in primary care, *Psychological Medicine*, 27(2): 433–44.

Pike, J., Smith, T., Hauger, R. et al. (1997) Chronic life stress alters sympathetic, neuroendocrine and immune responsivity to an acute psychological stressor in humans, *Psychosomatic Medicine*, 59: 447–57.

Pilkonis, P.A., Imler, S.D. and Rubinsky, P. (1985) Dimensions of life stress in psychiatric patients, *Journal of Human Stress*, 11: 5–10.

Pinder, K.L., Ramierz, A.J., Black, M.E. et al. (1993) Psychiatric disorder in patients with advanced breast cancer: prevalence and associated factors, *European Journal of Cancer*, 29A: 524–7.

Platek, S.M., Mohamed, F.B. and Gallup Jr., G.G. (2005) Contagious yawning and the brain, *Cognitive Brain Research*, **23**: 448–52.

Pliner, P. and Loewen, E.R. (1997) Temperament and food neophobia in children and their mothers, *Appetite*, **28**: 239–54.

Plotnikoff, R.C., Rhodes, R.E. and Trinh, L. (2009) Protection motivation theory and physical activity: a longitudinal test among a representative population sample of Canadian adults, *Journal of Health Psychology*, **14**(8): 1119–34.

Plotnikoff, R.C., Lippke, S., Trinh, L. et al. (2010) Protection motivation theory and the prediction of physical activity among adults with type 1 or type 2 diabetes in a large population sample, *British Journal of Health Psychology*, **15**(3): 643–61.

Polivy, J. and Herman, C.P. (1983) *Breaking the Diet Habit*. New York: Basic Books.

Polivy, J. and Herman, C.P. (1999) Distress and eating: why do dieters overeat? *International Journal of Eating Disorders*, **26**(2): 153–64.

Polivy, J., Herman, C.P. and McFarlane, T. (1994) Effects of anxiety on eating: does palatability moderate distress-induced overeating in dieters? *Journal of Abnormal Psychology*, **103**(3): 505–10.

Pollard, C., and Kennedy, P. (2007) A longitudinal analysis of emotional impact, coping strategies and post-traumatic psychological growth following spinal cord injury: a 10-year review, *British Journal of Health Psychology*, **12**: 347–62.

Pomerleau, O.F. and Brady, J.P. (1979) *Behavioral Medicine: Theory and Practice*. Baltimore, MD: Williams & Wilkins.

Posavac, S.S. and Posavac, H.D. (2002) Predictors of women's concern with body weight: the roles of perceived self-media ideal discrepancies and self-esteem, *Eating Disorders*, **10**(2): 153–60.

Povey, R., Conner, M., Sparks, P. et al. (2000) The theory of planned behaviour and healthy eating: examining additive and moderating effects of social influence variables, *Psychology and Health*, **14**: 991–1006.

Prentice, A. (1999) Aetiology of obesity I: Introduction, in *Obesity: The Report of the British Nutrition Foundation Task Force*. Oxford: Blackwell Science.

Prentice, A.M. (1995) Are all calories equal? in R. Cottrell (ed.) *Weight Control: The Current Perspective*. London: Chapman & Hall.

Prentice, A.M. and Jebb, S.A. (1995) Obesity in Britain: gluttony or sloth? *British Medical Journal*, **311**: 437–9.

Prentice, A.M., Black, A.E., Goldberg, G.R. et al. (1986) High levels of energy expenditure in obese women, *British Medical Journal*, **292**: 983–7.

Prentice, A.M., Black, A.E., Murgatroyd, P.R. et al. (1989) Metabolism or appetite: questions of energy balance with particular reference to obesity, *Journal of Human Nutrition and Dietetics*, **2**: 95–104.

Prettyman, R.J., Cordle, C.J. and Cook, G.D. (1993) A three-month follow-up of psychological morbidity after early miscarriage, *British Journal of Medical Psychology*, **66**: 363–72.

Pro-choice Alliance (1993) *A Survey of Abortion Patients*. London: Pro-choice Alliance.

Prochaska, J.O. and DiClemente, C.C. (1982) Transtheoretical therapy: toward a more integrative model of change, *Psychotherapy: Theory Research and Practice*, **19**: 276–88.

Prochaska, J.O. and DiClemente, C.C. (1984) *The Transtheoretical Approach: Crossing Traditional Boundaries of Therapy*. Homewood, IL: Dow Jones Irwin.

Prochaska, J.O. and Velicer, W.F. (1997) The transtheoretical model of health behaviour change, *American Journal of Health Promotion*, **12**: 38–48.

Prugger, C., Wellman, J., Heidrich, J. et al. (2008) Cardiovascular risk factors and mortality in patients with coronary heart disease, *European Journal of Epidemiology*, **23**(11): 731–7.

Puntillo, K. and Weiss, S.J. (1994) Pain: its mediators and associated morbidity in critically ill cardiovascular surgical patients, *Nursing Research*, **43**: 31–6.

Puska, P., Nissinen, A., Tuomilehto, J. et al. (1985) The community-based strategy to prevent coronary heart disease: conclusions from ten years of the North Karelia Project, in L. Breslow, J.E. Fielding and L.B. Lave (eds) *Annual Review of Public Health*, vol. 6. Palo Alto, CA: Annual Reviews Inc.

Putnam, R.D. (1993) The prosperous community: social capital and public life, *American Prospect*, **4**: 13.

Quine, L., Rutter, D.R. and Arnold, L. (1998) Predicting safety helmet use among schoolboy cyclists: a comparison of the theory of planned behaviour and the health belief model, *Psychology and Health*, **13**: 251–69.

Quine, L., Rutter, D.R. and Arnold, L. (2001) Persuading school-age cyclists to use safety helmets: effectiveness of an intervention based on the theory of planned behaviour, *British Journal of Health Psychology*, **6**: 327–45.

Raats, M.M., Shepherd, R. and Sparks, P. (1995) Including moral dimensions of choice within the structure of the theory of planned behavior, *Journal of Applied Social Psychology*, **25**: 484–94.

Rabiau, M., Knäuper, B. and Miquelon, P. (2006) The eternal quest for optimal balance between maximizing pleasure and minimizing harm: the compensatory health benefits model, *British Journal of Health Psychology*, **11**: 139–53.

Radley, A. (1984) The embodiment of social relation in coronary heart disease, *Social Science and Medicine*, **19**: 1227–34.

Radley, A. (1989) *Prospects of Heart Surgery: Psychological Adjustment to Coronary Bypass Grafting.* New York: Springer Verlag.

Radnitz, C., Byrne, S., Goldman, R. et al. (2009) Food cues in children's television programs, *Appetite*, **52**(1): 230–3.

Radtke, T., Scholz, U., Keller, R. et al. (2011) Smoking-specific compensatory health beliefs and the readiness to stop smoking in adolescents, *British Journal of Health Psychology*, 16, 610–625.

Rains, P. (1971) *Becoming an Unwed Mother.* Chicago: Aldine.

Raistrick, D., Heather, N. and Godfrey, C. (2006) *Review of the Effectiveness of Treatment for Alcohol Problems.* London: National Treatment Agency for Substance Misuse.

Rakowski, W. (1986) Personal health practices, health status, and expected control over future health, *Journal of Community Health*, **11**(3): 189–203.

Ramirez, A.J., Craig, T.J.K., Watson, J.P. et al. (1989) Stress and relapse of breast cancer, *British Medical Journal*, **298**: 291–3.

Ramirez, A.J., Watson, J.P., Richards, M.A. et al. (1992) Life events and breast cancer prognosis: letter to the editor, *British Medical Journal*, **304**: 1632.

Ramsay, J.M., McDermott, M.R. and Bray, C. (2001) Components of anger-hostility complex and symptom reporting in patient with coronary artery disease: a multimeasure study, *Journal of Health Psychology*, **6**(6): 713–29.

Rand, C.S.W. and MacGregor, A.M.C. (1991) Successful weight loss following obesity surgery and the perceived liability of morbid obesity, *International Journal of Obesity*, **15**: 577–9.

Rapkin, B.D. and Schwartz, C.E. (2004) Towards a theoretical model of quality of life appraisal: implications of findings from studies of response shift., *Health and Quality of Life Outcomes*, **2**: 14.

Ratner, P.A., Johnson, J.L., Shoveller, J.A. et al. (2003) Non-consensual sex experienced by men who have sex with men: prevalence and association with mental health, *Patient Education and Counseling*, **49**(1): 67–74.

Ravussin, E. and Bogardus, C. (1989) Relationship of genetics, age and physical activity to daily energy expenditure and fuel utilisation, *American Journal of Clinical Nutrition*, **49**: 968–75.

Ravussin, E., Lilioja, S., Knowler, W.C. et al. (1988) Reduced rate of energy expenditure as a risk factor for body-weight gain, *New England Journal of Medicine*, **318**: 467–72.

Rector, T.S., Kubo, S.H. and Cohn, J.N. (1993) Validity of the Minnesota Living with Heart Failure Questionnaire as a measure of therapeutic response: effects of enalapril and placebo, *American Journal of Cardiology*, **71**: 1006–7.

Redd, W.H. (1982) Behavioural analysis and control of psychosomatic symptoms in patients receiving intensive cancer treatment, *British Journal of Clinical Psychology*, **21**: 351–8.

Reed, G.M., Kemeny, M.E., Taylor, S.E. et al. (1994) Realistic acceptance as a predictor of decreased survival time in gay men with AIDS, *Health Psychology*, **13**: 299–307.

Reed, G.M., Kemeny, M.E., Taylor, S.E. and Visscher, B.R. (1999) Negative HIV-specific expectancies and AIDS-related bereavement as predictors of symptom onset in asymptomatic HIVpositive gay men, *Health Psychology*, **18**: 354–63.

Rees, K., Bennett, P., West, R. et al. (2004). Psychological interventions for coronary heary disease, *Cochrane Database of Systematic Reviews*, 2, art no. CD002902.

Reime, B., Novak, P., Born, J. et al. (2000) Eating habits, health status and concern about health: a study among 1641 employees in the German metal industry, *Preventive Medicine*, **30**: 295–301.

Reiss, I.L. and Leik, R.K. (1989) Evaluating strategies to avoid AIDS: numbers of partners versus use of condoms, *Journal of Sex Research*, **26**: 411–33.

Repetti, R.L. (1993) Short-term effects of occupational stressors on daily mood and health complaints, *Health Psychology*, **12**: 125–31.

Resnicow, K., Jackson, A., Wang, T. et al. (2001). A motivational interviewing intervention to increase fruit and vegetable intake through black churches: results of the Eat for Life trial, *American Journal of Public Health*, **91**(10): 1686–93.

Rhodes, R.E., Fiala, B. and Conner, M. (2009) A review and meta-analysis of affective judgments and physical activity in adult populations, *Annals of Behavioral Medicine*, **38**(3): 180–204.

Richard, R. and van der Pligt, J. (1991) Factors affecting condom use among adolescents, *Journal of Community and Applied Social Psychology*, **1**: 105–16.

Riddle, P.K. (1980) Attitudes, beliefs, intentions, and behaviours of men and women toward regular jogging, *Research Quarterly for Exercise and Sport*, **51**: 663–74.

Ridge, D. T. (2004) 'It was an incredible thrill': the social meanings and dynamics of younger gay men's experiences of barebacking in Melbourne, *Sexualities*, **7**(3): 259–79.

Rief, W. and Broadbent, E. (2007) Explaining medically unexplained symptoms-models and mechanisms, *Clinical Psychology Review*, **27**(7): 821–41.

Riegel, B.J. (1993) Contributions to cardiac invalidism after acute myocardial infarction, *Coronary Artery Disease*, **4**: 569–78.

Rimer, B.K., Trock, B., Lermon, C. et al. (1991) Why do some women get regular mammograms? *American Journal of Preventative Medicine*, **7**: 69–74.

Rippetoe, P.A. and Rogers, R.W. (1987) Effects of components of protection-motivation theory on adaptive and maladaptive coping with a health threat, *Journal of Personality and Social Psychology*, **52**: 596–604.

Risdon, A., Eccleston, C., Crombez, G. and McCracken, L. (2003) How can we learn to live with pain? A Q-methodological analysis of the diverse understandings of acceptance of chronic pain, *Social Science and Medicine*, **56**(2): 375–86.

Rise, J., Kovac, V., Kraft, P. and Moan, I.S. (2008) Predicting the intention to quit smoking and quitting behaviour: extending the theory of planned behaviour, *British Journal of Health Psychology*, **13**: 291–310.

Rissanen, A.M., Heliovaara, M., Knekt, P. et al. (1991) Determinants of weight gain and overweight in adult Finns, *European Journal of Clinical Nutrition*, **45**: 419–30.

Robertson, S. (2007) The current context of men's health and the role of masculinities, in S. Robertson, *Understanding Men and Health: Masculinities, Identity and Well-being*. Maidenhead: Open University Press.

Robertson S. and Williamson P. (2005) Men and health promotion in the UK: ten years further on? *Health Education Journal*, **64**: 293–301.

Robinson, B.B.E., Bockting, W.O., Rosser, B.R.S. et al. (2002) The sexual health model: application of a sexological approach to HIV prevention, *Health Education Research*, **17**(1): 43–57.

Rodgers, A., Corbett, T., Bramley, D. et al. (2005) 'Do u smoke after txt?' Results of a randomised trial of smoking cessation using mobile phone text messaging, *Tobacco Control*, **14**(4): 255–61.

Rodin, J., Bray, G.A., Atkinson, R.L. et al. (1977) Predictors of successful weight loss in an outpatient obesity clinic, *International Journal of Obesity*, **1**: 79–87.

Rogers, E. (1983) *Diffusion of Innovations*. New York: Free Press.

Rogers, R.W. (1975) A protection motivation theory of fear appeals and attitude change, *Journal of Psychology*, **91**: 93–114.

Rogers, R.W. (1985) Attitude change and information integration in fear appeals, *Psychological Reports*, **56**: 179–82.

Romero-Corral, A.R., Montori, V.M., Somers, V.K. et al. (2006) Association of body weight with total mortality and with cardiovascular events in coronary artery disease: a systematic review of cohort studies, *Lancet*, **368**: 666–78.

Rook, K.S., Dooley, D. and Catalano, R. (1991) Stress transmission: the effects of husbands' job stressors on the emotional health of their wives, *Journal of Marriage and the Family*, **53**: 165–77.

Rooney, B., Smalley, K., Larson, J. and Havens, S. (2003) Is knowing enough? Increasing physical activity by wearing a pedometer, *Wisconsin Medical Journal*, **102**(4): 31–6.

Rosen, C.S. (2000) Is the sequencing of change processes by stage consistent across health problems? A meta-analysis, *Health Psychology*, **19**: 593–604.

Rosenberg, M. (1965) *Society and the Adolescent Self-image*. Princeton, NJ: Princeton University Press.

Rosenfeld, J.A. (1992) Emotional responses to therapeutic abortion, *American Family Physician*, **45**: 137–40.

Rosenman, R.H. (1978) Role of type A pattern in the pathogenesis of ischaemic heart disease and modification for prevention, *Advances in Cardiology*, **25**: 34–46.

Rosenman, R.H., Brand, R.J., Jenkins, C.D. et al. (1975) Coronary heart disease in the western collaborative heart study: final follow-up experience of 8½ years, *Journal of the American Medical Association*, **233**: 872–7.

Rosenstock, I.M. (1966) Why people use health services, *Millbank Memorial Fund Quarterly*, **44**: 94–124.

Roske, K., Schumann, A., Hannover, W. et al. (2008) Postpartum smoking cessation and relapse prevention intervention: a structural equation modelling application to behavioural and non-behavioural outcomes of a randomized controlled trial, *Journal of Health Psychology*, **13**(4), 556–8.

Roskies, E., Seraganian, P., Oseasohn, R. et al. (1986) The Montreal type A intervention project: major findings, *Health Psychology*, **5**: 45–69.

Ross, C.E. (1994) Overweight and depression, *Journal of Health and Social Behaviour*, **35**: 63–78.

Ross, C.E., and Bird, C.E. (1994) Sex stratification and health lifestyle: consequences of men's and women's perceived health, *Journal of Health and Social Behavior*, **35**: 161–78.

Ross, M. and Olson, J.M. (1981) An expectancy attribution model of the effects of placebos, *Psychological Review*, **88**: 408–37.

Rosser, B.A., Vowels, K.E., Keogh, E. et al. (2009) Technologically-assisted behaviour change: a systematic review of studies of novel technologies for the management of chronic illness, *Journal of Telemedicine and Telecare*, **15**: 327–38.

Rossner, S., Sjostrom, L., Noak, R. et al. (2000) Weight loss, weight maintenance and improved cardiovascular risk factors after 2 years' treatment with Orlistat for obesity, *Obesity Research*, **8**: 49–61.

Roter, D.L., Steward, M., Putnam, S.M. et al. (1997) Communication pattern of primary care physicians, *Journal of the American Medical Association*, **277**: 350–6.

Roth, S. and Cohen, L.J. (1986) Approach avoidance and coping with stress, *American Psychologist*, **41**: 813–19.

Rozin, P. (1976) *The Selection of Foods by Rats, Humans, and Other Animas: Advances in the Study of Behavior.* New York: Academic Press.

Rubak, S., Sandbæk, A., Lauritzen, T. and Christensen, B. (2005) Motivational interviewing: a systematic review and meta-analysis, *The British Journal of General Practice*, **55**(513): 305–12.

Rubin, R. and Quine, L. (1995) Women's attitudes to the menopause and the use of hormone replacement therapy. Paper presented at the conference of the British Psychological Society, London.

Ruble, D.N. (1977) Premenstrual symptoms: a reinterpretation, *Science*, **197**: 291–2.

Ruiter, R.A.C., Abraham, C. and Kok, G. (2001) Scary warnings and rational precautions: a review of the psychology of fear appeals, *Psychology & Health*, **16**(6): 613–30.

Russell, M.A.H., Wilson, C., Taylor, C. and Baker, C.D. (1979) Effect of general practitioners' advice against smoking, *British Medical Journal*, **2**: 231–5.

Russo, N.F. and Zierk, K.I. (1992) Abortion, childbearing, and women's well-being, *Professional Psychology: Research and Practice*, **23**: 269–80.

Ryan, L., Ripper, M. and Buttfield, B. (1994) *We Women Decide: Women's Experience of Seeking Abortion in Queensland, South Australia and Tasmania 1985–1992.* Adelaide: Flinders University.

Rymer, J., Wilson, R. and Ballard, K. (2003) Making decisions about hormone replacement therapy, *British Medical Journal*, **326**(7384): 322–6.

Sable, M.R., Libbus, M.K. and Chiu, J.E. (2000) Factors affecting contraceptive use in women seeking pregnancy tests: Missouri, 1997, *Family Planning Perspectives*, **32**(3):124–31.

Sairam, S., Khare, M., Michailidis, G. and Thilaganathan, B. (2001) The role of ultrasound in the expectant management of early pregnancy loss, *Ultrasound in Obstetrics and Gynecology*, **17**: 506–9.

Sala, F., Krupat, E. and Rother, D. (2002) Satisfaction and the use of humour by physicians and patients, *Psychology and Health*, **17**: 269–80.

Sallis, J.F., Haskell, W.L., Fortmann, S.P. et al. (1986) Predictors of adoption and maintenance of physical activity in a community sample, *Preventive Medicine*, **15**: 331–41.

Salvy, S.J., Romero, N., Paluch, R., and Epstein, L.H. (2007) Peer influence on pre-adolescent girls' snack intake: effects on weight status, *Appetite*, **49**(1): 177–82.

Salvy, S.J., Vartanian, L.R., Coelho, J.S. et al. (2008) The role of familiarity on modeling of eating and food consumption in children, *Appetite*, **50**: 514–18.

Samwel, H.J.A., Kraaimaat, F.W., Crul, B.J.P. et al. (2009) Multidisciplinary allocation of chronic pain treatment: effects and cognitive-behavioural predictors of outcome, *British Journal of Health Psychology*, **14**(3): 405–21.

Sandberg, T. and Conner, M. (2009) A mere measurement effect for anticipated regret: impacts on cervical screening attendance, *British Journal of Social Psychology*, **48**: 221–36.

Sanders, C., Egger, M., Donovan, J. et al. (1998) Reporting on quality of life in randomised controlled trials: bibliographic study, *British Medical Journal*, **317**: 1191–4.

Sanderson, C.A. and Yopyk, D.J.A. (2007) Improving condom use intentions and behavior by changing perceived partner norms: an evaluation of condom promotion videos for college students, *Health Psychology*, **26**(4): 481–7.

Santi, S., Best, J.A., Brown, K.S. and Cargo, M. (1991) Social environment and smoking initiation, *International Journal of the Addictions*, **25**: 881–903.

Sarason, I.G., Levine, H.M., Basham, R.B. et al. (1983) Assessing social support: the social support questionnaire, *Journal of Personality and Social Psychology*, **44**: 127–39.

Sarason, I.G., Sarason, B.R., Shearin, E.N. and Pierce, G.R. (1987) A brief measure of social support: practical and theoretical implications, *Journal of Social and Personal Relationships*, **4**: 497–510.

Savage, I. (1993) Demographic influences on risk perceptions, *Risk Analysis*, **13**: 413–20.

Savage, R. and Armstrong, D. (1990) Effect of a general practitioner's consulting style on patients' satisfaction: a controlled study, *British Medical Journal*, **301**: 968–70.

Scambler, A., Scambler, G. and Craig, D. (1981) Kinship and friendship networks and women's demands for primary care, *Journal of the Royal College of General Practice*, **26**: 746–50.

Schachter, S. and Gross, L. (1968) Manipulated time and eating behaviour, *Journal of Personality and Social Psychology*, **10**: 98–106.

Schachter, S. and Rodin, J. (1974) *Obese Humans and Rats.* Potomac, MD: Erlbaum.

Schaefer, C., Quesenberry, C.P. Jr and Wi, S. (1995) Mortality following conjugal bereavement and the effects of a shared environment, *American Journal of Epidemiology*, **141**: 1142–52.

Schappert, S.M. (1999) Ambulatory care visits to physician offices, hospital out-patient departments, and emergency departments: United States 1997, *Vital and Health Statistics – Series 13: Data from the National Health Survey*, November: 1–39.

Schmidt, L.R. and Frohling, H. (2000) Lay concepts of health and illness from a developmental perspective, *Psychology and Health*, **15**: 229–38.

Schnurr, P.P. and Green, B.L. (eds) (2004) *Trauma and Health: Physical Health Consequences of Exposure to Extreme Stress*. Washington, DC: American Psychological Association.

Scholz, U., Schüz, B., Ziegelmann, J.P. et al. (2008) Beyond behavioural intentions: planning mediates between intentions and physical activity, *British Journal of Health Psychology*, **13**(3): 479–94.

Schurman, M., Hesse, M.D., Stephan, K.E. et al. (2005) Yearning to yawn: the neural basis of contagious yawning. *Neuro Image*, **24**: 1260–4.

Schwartz, G.E. and Weiss, S.M. (1977) *Yale Conference on Behavioral Medicine*. Washington, DC: Department of Health, Education and Welfare; National Heart, Lung, and Blood Institute.

Schwartz, J.L. (1987) *Review and Evaluation of Smoking Cessation Methods: The United States and Canada, 1978–1985*, NIH pub. no. 87–2940. Washington, DC: National Cancer Institute.

Schwarzer, R. (ed.) (1992) *Self Efficacy: Thought Control of Action*. Washington, DC: Hemisphere.

Scott, E.J., Eves, F.F., French, D.P. and Hoppe, R. (2007) The theory of planned behaviour predicts self-reports of walking, but does not predict step count, *British Journal of Health Psychology*, **12**: 601–20.

Scott, S.E., Grunfeld, E.A., Auyeung, V. and McGurk, M. (2009) Barriers and triggers to seeking help for potentially malignant oral symptoms: implications for interventions, *Journal of Public Health Dentistry*, **69**(1): 34–40.

Searle, A., Norman, P., Thompson, R. and Vedhara, K. (2007) A prospective examination of illness beliefs and coping in patients with type 2 diabetes, *British Journal of Health Psychology*, **12**(4): 621–38.

Sebregts, E.H.W.J., Falger, P.R.J. and Bar, F.W.H.M. (2000) Risk factor modification through nonpharmacological interventions in patients with coronary heart disease, *Journal of Psychosomatic Research*, **48**: 425–41.

Segal, L. (1994) *Straight Sex: The Politics of Pleasure*. London: Virago.

Seligman, M.E.P. and Csikszentmihalyi, M. (2000) Positive psychology: an introduction, *American Psychology*, **55**: 5–14.

Seligman, M.E.P. and Visintainer, M.A. (1985) Turnout rejection and early experience of uncontrollable shock in the rat, in F.R. Brush and J.B. Overmier (eds) *Affect Conditioning and Cognition: Essays on the Determinants of Behavior*. Hillsdale, NJ: Erlbaum.

Seligman, M.E.P., Peterson, C. and Vaillant, G.E. (1988) Pessimistic explanatory style is a risk factor for illness: a 35-year longitudinal study, *Journal of Personality and Social Psychology*, **55**: 23–7.

Selye, H. (1956) *The Stress of Life*. New York: McGraw-Hill.

Senior, V., Marteau, T.M. and Weinman, J. (2000) Impact of genetic testing on causal models of heart disease and arthritis: an analogue study, *Psychology and Health*, **14**: 1077–88.

Seydel, E., Taal, E. and Wiegman, O. (1990) Risk appraisal, outcome and self efficacy expectancies: cognitive factors in preventative behaviour related to cancer, *Psychology and Health*, **4**: 99–109.

Shaffer, J.W., Graves, P.L., Swank, R.T. and Pearson, T.A. (1987) Clustering of personality traits in youth and the subsequent development of cancer among physicians, *Journal of Behavioural Medicine*, **10**: 441–7.

Shahab, L. and Fidler, J. (2010) Tobacco-related disorders, in P. Sturney and M. Hersen (eds) *Handbook of Evidence-based Practice in Clinical Psychology, Vol. 11: Adult Disorders*. New York: Wiley.

Shahab, L. and McEwen, A. (2009) Online support for smoking cessation: a systematic review of the literature. *Addiction*, **104**: 1792–804.

Shahab, L., Hall, S. and Marteau, T.M. (2007) Showing smokers with vascular disease images of their arteries to motivate cessation: a pilot study, *British Journal of Health Psychology*, **12**: 275–83.

Shea, S., Basch, C.E., Lantigua, R. and Wechsler, H. (1992) The Washington Heights-Inwood Healthy Heart Program: a third generation community-based cardiovascular disease prevention program in a disadvantaged urban setting, *Preventive Medicine*, **21**: 201–17.

Sheeran, P. (2002) Intention-behaviour relations: a conceptual and empirical review, *European Review of Social Psychology*, **12**: 1–36.

Sheeran, P. and Orbell, S. (1998) Implementation intentions and repeated behaviour: augmenting the predictive validity of the theory of planned behaviour, *European Journal of Social Psychology*, **28**: 1–21.

Sheeran, P. and Orbell, S. (2000) Using implementation intentions to increase attendance for cervical cancer screening, *Health Psychology*, **19**: 283–9.

Sheeran, P., Abraham, C. and Orbell, S. (1999) Psychosocial correlates of heterosexual condom use: a meta-analysis, *Psychological Bulletin*, **125**(1): 90–132.

Sheeran, P., White, D. and Phillips, K. (1991) Premarital contraceptive use: a review of the psychological literature, *Journal of Reproductive and Infant Psychology*, **9**: 253–69.

Sheldrick, R., Tarrier, N., Berry, E. and Kincey, J. (2006) Post-traumatic stress disorder and illness perceptions over time following myocardial infarction and subarachnoid haemorrhage, *British Journal of Health Psychology*, **11**: 387–400.

Shenassa, E.D., Frye, M., Braubach, M., and Daskalakis, C. (2008) Routine stair climbing in place of residence and body mass index: a pan-European population based study, *International Journal of Obesity*, **32**(3): 490–4.

Shepherd, R. (1988) Belief structure in relation to low-fat milk consumption, *Journal of Human Nutrition and Dietetics*, **1**: 421–8.

Shepherd, R. and Farleigh, C.A. (1986) Attitudes and personality related to salt intake, *Appetite*, **7**: 343–54.

Shepherd, R. and Stockley, L. (1985) Fat consumption and attitudes towards food with a high fat content, *Human Nutrition: Applied Nutrition*, **39A**: 431–42.

Shepperd, S., Harwood, D., Jenkinson, C. et al. (1998) Randomised controlled trial comparing hospital at home care with inpatient hospital care. I: three-month follow-up of health outcomes, *British Medical Journal*, **316**: 1786–91.

Sherman, D.A.K., Nelson, L.D. and Steele, C.M. (2000) Do messages about health risks threaten the self? Increasing the acceptance of threatening health messages via self-affirmation, *Personality and Social Psychology Bulletin*, **26**: 1046–58.

Shiloh, S., Vinter, M. and Barak, A. (1997) Correlates of health screening utilisation: the roles of health beliefs and self-regulation motivation, *Psychology and Health*, **12**: 301–17.

Shinar, D., Schechtman, E. and Compton, R. (1999) Trends in safe driving behaviors and in relation to trends in health maintenance behaviors in the USA: 1985–1995, *Accident: Analysis and Prevention*, **31**(5): 497–503.

Shy, K.K., Luthy, D.A., Whitfield, M. et al. (1990) Effects of electronic fetal-heart-rate monitoring, as compared with periodic auscultation, on the neurologic development of premature infants, *New England Journal of Medicine*, **322**: 588–93.

Siegel, K., Raveis, V.H., Krauss, J. et al. (1992) Factors associated with gay men's treatment initiation decisions for HIV-infection, *AIDS Education and Prevention*, **4**(2): 135–42.

Siegman, A.W. and Snow, S.C. (1997) The outward expression of anger, the inward experience of anger and CVR: the role of vocal expression, *Journal of Behavioural Medicine*, **20**: 29–46.

Siegman, A.W., Townsend, S.T., Civelek, A.C. and Blumenthal, R.S. (2000) Antagonistic behaviour, dominance, hostility and coronary heart disease, *Psychosomatic Medicine*, **62**: 248–57.

Simon, G.E., Von Korff, M., Saunders, K. et al. (2006) Association between obesity and psychiatric disorders in the US adult population, *Archives of General Psychiatry*, **63**: 824–30.

Simon, N. (1977) Breast cancer induced by radiation, *Journal of the American Medical Association*, **237**: 789–90.

Simpson, S.H., Eurich, D.T., Majumdar, S.R. et al. (2006) A meta-analysis of the association between adherence to drug therapy and mortality, *British Medical Journal*, **333**(7557): 15.

Simpson, W.M., Johnston, M. and McEwan, S.R. (1997) Screening for risk factors for cardiovascular disease: a psychological perspective, *Scottish Medical Journal*, **42**: 178–81.

Sirriyeh, R., Lawton, R. and Ward, J. (2010) Physical activity and adolescents: an exploratory randomized controlled trial investigating the influence of affective and instrumental text messages, *British Journal of Health Psychology*, **15**(4): 825–40.

Sjostrom, L., Rissanen, A., Andersen, T. et al. (1998) Randomised placebo controlled trial of orlistat for weight loss and prevention of weight regain in obese patients, *Lancet*, **352**: 167–72.

Skar, S., Sniehotta, F.F., Araujo-Soares, V. and Molloy, G.J. (2008) Prediction of behaviour vs. prediction of behaviour change: the role of motivational moderators in the theory of planned behaviour, *Applied Psychology: An International Review*, **57**: 609–27.

Skelton, J.A. and Pennebaker, J.W. (1982) The psychology of physical symptoms and sensations, in G.S. Sanders and J. Suls (eds) *Social Psychology of Health and Illness*. Hillsdale, NJ: Erlbaum.

Skevington, S. and O'Connell, K. (2003) Measuring quality of life in HIV and AIDS: a review of the recent literature, *Psychology and Health*, **18**(3): 331–50.

Skevington, S., O'Connell, K.A. and the WHOQoL Group (2004a) Can we identify the poorest quality of life? Assessing the importance of quality of life using the WHOQoL-100, *Quality of Life Research*, **13**: 23–34.

Skevington, S., Sortarius, N., Amir, M. and the WHOQoL Group (2004b) Developing methods for assessing quality of life in different cultural settings, *Social Psychiatry and Psychiatric Epidemiology*, **39**: 1–8.

Skinner, T.C., Carey, M.E., Cradock, S. et al (2006) Diabetes education and self-management for ongoing and newly diagnosed (DESOND): process modelling of pilot study, *Patient Education and Counselling*, **64**: 369–77.

Sklar, S.L. and Anisman, H. (1981) Stress and cancer, *Psychological Bulletin*, **89**(3): 369–406.

Skrabanek, P. (1988) The physician's responsibility to the patient, *Lancet*, **1**: 1155–7.

Slade, P. and Russell, G.F.M. (1973) Awareness of body dimensions in anorexia nervosa: cross-sectional and longitudinal studies, *Psychological Medicine*, **3**: 188–99.

Slade, P., Heke, S., Fletcher, J. and Stewart, P. (1998) A comparison of medical and surgical termination of pregnancy: choice, emotional impact and satisfaction with care, *British Journal of Obstetrics and Gynaecology*, **105**(12): 1288–95.

Slottje, P., Witteveen, A.B., Twisk, J.W.R. et al. (2008) Post-disaster physical symptoms of firefighters and police officers: role of types of exposure and post-traumatic stress symptoms, *British Journal of Health Psychology*, **13**: 327–42.

Smart, L. and Wegner, D.M. (1999) Covering up what can't be seen: concealable stigma and mental control, *Journal of Personality and Social Psychology*, **77**: 474–86.

Smedslund, G. (2000) A pragmatic basis for judging models and theories in health psychology: the axiomatic method, *Journal of Health Psychology*, **5**: 133–49.

Smith, A. and Chamberlain, J. (1987) Managing cervical screening, in *Institute of Health Service Management: Information Technology in Health Care*. London: Kluwer Academic.

Smith, J.A. (1996) Beyond the divide between cognition and discourse: using interpretative phenomenological analysis in health psychology, *Psychology & Health*, **11**: 261–71.

Smith, J.A. and Osborn, M. (2003) Interpretative phenomenological analysis, in J.A. Smith (ed.) *Qualitative Psychology*. London: Sage.

Smith, J.A. and Osborn, M. (2007) Pain as an assault on the self: an interpretative phenomenological analysis of the psychological impact of chronic benign low back pain, *Psychology and Health*, **22**: 517–34.

Smith, J.A., Michie, S., Stephenson, M. and Quarrell, O. (2002) Risk perception and decision-making processes in candidates for genetic testing for Huntington's disease: an interpretative phenomenological analysis, *Journal of Health Psychology*, **7**(3): 131–44.

Smith, L.M., Mullis, R.L. and Hill, W.E. (1995) Identity strivings within the mother–daughter relationship, *Psychological Reports*, **76**: 495–503.

Smith, R.A., Williams, D.K., Silbert, J.R. and Harper, P.S. (1990) Attitudes of mothers to neonatal screening for Duchenne muscular dystrophy, *British Medical Journal*, **300**: 1112.

Smyth, J.M. (1998) Written emotional expression: effect sizes, outcome types and moderating variables, *Journal of Consulting and Clinical Psychology*, **66**: 174–84.

Smyth, J.M. and Pennebaker, J.W. (2008) Exploring the boundary conditions of expressive writing: in search of the right recipe, *British Journal of Health Psychology*, **13**(1): 1–7.

Snedecor, M.R., Boudreau, C.F., Ellis, B.E. et al. (2000) U.S. air force recruit injury and health study, *American Journal of Preventive Medicine*, **18**(3, suppl.): 129–40.

Sniehotta, F.F. (2009) Towards a theory of intentional behaviour change: plans, planning, and self-regulation, *British Journal of Health Psychology*, **14**(2): 261–73.

Sniehotta, F.F., Scholz, U. and Schwarzer, R. (2005) Bridging the intention-behaviour gap: planning, self-efficacy, and action control in the adoption and maintenance of physical exercise, *Psychology and Health*, **20**(2): 143–60.

Sniehotta, F.F., Scholz, U. and Schwarzer, R. (2006) Action plans and coping plans for physical exercise: a longitudinal intervention study in cardiac rehabilitation, *British Journal of Health Psychology*, **11**: 23–37.

Snoek, H.M., Engels, R.C., Janssens, J.M., and van Strien, T. (200) Parental behaviour and adolescents' emotional eating, *Appetite*, **49**(1): 223–30.

Sobel, M.B. and Sobel, L.C. (1978) *Behavioral Treatment of Alcohol Problems*. New York: Plenum.

Söderberg, H., Janzon, L. and Sjöberg, N.O. (1998) Emotional distress following induced abortion: a study of its incidence and determinants among abortees in Malmö, Sweden, *European Journal of Obstetrics and Gynecology, and Reproductive Biology*, **79**: 173–8.

Sodergren, S.C., Hyland, M.E., Singh, S.J. and Sewell, L. (2002) The effect of rehabilitation on positive interpretations of illness, *Psychology and Health*, **17**(6): 753–60.

Sodroski, J.G., Rosen, C.A. and Haseltine, W.A. (1984) Transacting transcription of the long terminal repeat of human T lymphocyte viruses in infected cells, *Science*, **225**: 381–5.

Soetens, B., Braet, C., Dejonckheere, P. and Roets, A. (2006) When suppression backfires: the ironic effects of suppressing eating-related thoughts, *Journal of Health Psychology*, **11**(5): 655–68.

Solano, L., Costa, M., Temoshok, L. et al. (2002) An emotionally inexpressive (type C) coping style influences HIV disease progression at six and twelve month follow-up, *Psychology and Health*, **17**(5): 641–55.

Solano, L., Montella, F., Salvati, S. et al. (2001) Expression and processing of emotions: relationship with CD4+ levels in 42 HIV-positive asymptomatic individuals, *Psychology and Health*, **16**: 689–98.

Solomon, G.F. and Temoshok, L. (1987) A psychoneuro-immunologic perspective on AIDS research: questions, preliminary findings, and suggestions, *Journal of Applied Social Psychology*, **17**: 286–308.

Solomon, G.F., Temoshok, L., O'Leary, A. and Zich, J.A. (1987) An intensive psychoimmunologic study of long-surviving persons with AIDS: pilot work background studies, hypotheses, and methods, *Annals of the New York Academy of Sciences*, **46**: 647–55.

Sparks, P., Hedderley, D. and Shepherd, R. (1992) An investigation into the relationship between perceived control, attitude variability and the consumption of two common foods, *European Journal of Social Psychology*, **22**: 55–71.

Sparks, P., Conner, M., James, R., et al. (2001) Ambivalence about health-related behaviours: an exploration in the domain of food choice, *British Journal of Health Psychology*, **6**: 53–68.

Speisman, J.C., Lazarus, R.S., Mordko, A. and Davison, L. (1964) Experimental reduction of stress based on ego defense theory, *Journal of Abnormal and Social Psychology*, **68**: 367–80.

Spera, S.P., Buhrfeind, E.D. and Pennebaker, J.W. (1994) Expressive writing and coping with job loss, *Academy of Management Journal*, **37**: 722–33.

Spitzer, L. and Rodin, J. (1981) Human eating behaviour: a critical review of studies in normal weight and overweight individuals, *Appetite*, **2**: 293–329.

Stead, M., Hastings, G. and Eadie, D. (2002) The challenge of evaluating complex interventions: a framework for evaluating media advocacy, *Health Education Research*, **17**(3): 351–64.

Steele, C.M. (1988) The psychology of self-affirmation: sustaining the integrity of the self, in L. Berkowitz (ed.) *Advances in Experimental Social Psychology*. New York: Academic Press.

Steer, C., Campbell, S., Davies, M. et al. (1989) Spontaneous abortion rates after natural and assisted conception, *British Medical Journal*, **299**: 1317–18.

Stegen, K., Van Diest, I., Van De Woestijne, K.P. and Van Den Berch, O. (2000) Negative affectivity and bodily sensations induced by 5.5% CO_2 enriched air inhalation: is there a bias to interpret bodily sensations negatively in persons with negative affect? *Psychology and Health*, **15**: 513–25.

Steiger, H., Stotland, S., Ghadirian, A.M. and Whitehead, V. (1994) Controlled study of eating concerns and psychopathological traits in relatives of eating-disordered probands: do familial traits exist? *International Journal of Eating Disorders*, **18**: 107–18.

Steinberg, J. (2001) Many undertreated HIV-infected patients decline potent antiretroviral therapy, *AIDS Patient Care*, **15**: 185–91.

Steptoe, A., Kearsley, N. and Walters, N. (1993) Acute mood responses to maximal and submaximal exercise in active and inactive men, *Psychology and Health*, **8**: 89–99.

Steptoe, A., Lundwall, K. and Cropley, M. (2000) Gender, family structure and cardiovascular activity during the working day and evening, *Social Science and Medicine*, **50**: 531–9.

Stern, J.S. (1984) Is obesity a disease of inactivity? in A.J. Stunkard and E. Stellar (eds) *Eating and Its Disorders*. New York: Raven Press.

Stewart, A.L. and Ware, J.E. (eds) (1992) *Measuring Functioning and Well Being: The Medical Outcomes Study Approach*. Durham, NC: Duke University Press.

Stewart, W.F., Lipton, R.B. and Liberman, J. (1996) Variation in migraine prevalence by race, *Neurology*, **47**: 52–9.

Stice, E., Schupak-Neuberg, E., Shaw, H.E. and Stein, R.L. (1994) Relation of media exposure to eating disorders symptomatology: an examination of mediation mechanisms, *Journal of Abnormal Psychology*, **103**: 836–40.

Stiles, W.B. (1978) Verbal response models and dimensions of interpersonal roles: a method of discourse analysis, *Journal of Personality and Social Psychology*, **36**: 693–703.

Stoate, H. (1989) Can health screening damage your health? *Journal of the Royal College of General Practitioners*, **39**: 193–5.

Stokes, J. and Rigotti, N. (1988) The health consequences of cigarette smoking and the internist's role in smoking cessation, *Annals of Internal Medicine*, **33**: 431–60.

Stone, A.A. and Brownell, K.D. (1994) The stress-eating paradox: multiple daily measurements in adult males and females, *Psychology and Health*, **9**: 425–36.

Stone, A.A. and Neale, J.M. (1984) New measure of daily coping: development and preliminary results, *Journal of Personality and Social Psychology*, **46**: 892–906.

Stone, A.A., Cox, D.S., Valdimarsdottir, H. et al. (1987) Evidence that secretory IgA antibody is associated with daily mood, *Journal of Personality and Social Psychology*, **52**: 988–93.

Stone, K.E. Lamphear, B.P., Pomerantz, W.J. and Khoury, J. (2000) Childhood injuries and deaths due to falls from windows, *Journal of Urban Health*, **77**: 26–33.

Stone, N. and Ingham, R. (2000) *Young People's Sex Advice Services: Delays, Triggers and Contraceptive Use*. London: Brook Publications.

Stone, N. and Ingham, R. (2002) Factors affecting British teenagers' contraceptive use at first intercourse: the importance of partner communication, *Perspectives on Sexual and Reproductive Health*, **34**(4): 191–7.

Stone, N. and Ingham, R. (2003) When and why do young people in the United Kingdom first use sexual health services? *Perspectives on Sexual and Reproductive Health*, **35**(3): 114–20.

Stone, N., Hatherall, B., Ingham, R. and McEachran, J. (2006) Oral sex and condom use among young people in the United Kingdom, *Perspectives on Sexual and Reproductive Health*, **38**(1): 6–12.

Stoney, C.M. and Finney, M.L. (2000) Social support and stress: influences on lipid reactivity, *International Journal of Behavioural Medicine*, **7**: 111–26.

Stoney, C.M., Mathews, K.A., McDonald, R.H. and Johnson, C.A. (1990) Sex differences in acute stress response: lipid, lipoprotein, cardiovascular and neuroendocrine adjustments, *Psychophysiology*, **12**: 52–61.

Stormer, S.M. and Thompson, J.K. (1996) Explanations of body-image disturbances: a test of maturational status, negative verbal commentary, social comparison, and sociocultural hypotheses, *International Journal of Eating Disorders*, **19**(2): 193–202.

Stovitz, S.D., VanWormer, J.J., Center, B.A. and Bremer, K.L. (2005) Pedometers as a means to increase ambulatory activity for patients seen at a family medicine clinic, *The Journal of the American Board of Family Medicine*, **18**(5): 335–43.

Stratton, G., Fairclough, S.J. and Ridgers, N.D. (2008) Physical activity levels during the school day, in A.L. Smith and S.J.H. Biddle (eds) *Youth Physical Activity and Sedentary Behaviour: Challenges and Solutions*. Champaign, IL: Human Kinetics.

Strax, P. (1978) Evaluation of screening programs for the early diagnosis of breast cancer, *Surgical Clinics of North America*, **58**: 667–79.

Stronegger, W.J., Freidl, W. and Rasky, E. (1997) Health behaviour and risk behaviour: socioeconomic differences in an Austrian rural county, *Social Science and Medicine*, **44**: 423–6.

Stroop, J.R. (1935) Studies of interference in serial verbal reactions, *Journal of Experimental Psychology*, **18**: 643–62.

Stuart, R.B. and Davis, B. (1972) *Slim Chance in a Fat World: Behavioral Control of Obesity*. Champaign, IL: Research Press.

Stunkard, A.J. (1958) The management of obesity, *New York State Journal of Medicine*, **58**: 79–87.

Stunkard, A.J. (1984) The current status of treatment for obesity in adults, in A.J. Stunkard and E. Stellar (eds) *Eating and its Disorders*. New York: Raven Press.

Stunkard, A.J. and Messick, S. (1985) The three factor eating questionnaire to measure dietary restraint, disinhibition and hunger, *Journal of Psychosomatic Research*, **29**: 71–8.

Stunkard, A.J., Sorenson, T.I.A., Hanis, C. et al. (1986) An adoption study of human obesity, *New England Journal of Medicine*, **314**: 193–8.

Stunkard, A.J., Harris, J.R., Pedersen, N.L. and McClearn, G.E. (1990) A separated twin study of body mass index, *New England Journal of Medicine*, **322**: 1483–7.

Suarez, E.C, Williams, R.B., Kuhn, C.M. et al. (1991) Biobehavioural basis of coronary-prone behaviour in middle-aged men: part II, serum cholesterol, the type A behaviour pattern and hostility as interactive modulators of physiological reactivity, *Psychosomatic Medicine*, **53**: 528–37.

Sullivan, M.J.L., Thorn, B., Haythornthwaite, J.A. et al. (2001) Theoretical perspectives on the relation between catastrophising and pain, *Clinical Journal of Pain*, **17**: 53–61.

Sussman, S., Dent, C., Stacy, A.W. et al. (1990) Peer group association and adolescent tobacco use, *Journal of Abnormal Psychology*, **99**: 349–52.

Sutherland, K., Christianson, J.B. abd Leatherman, S. (2008) Impact of targeted financial incentives on personal health behaviour: a review of literature. *Medical Care Research and Review*, **65**: 36–78S.

Sutton, S. (1998a) Predicting and explaining intentions and behavior: how well are we doing? *Journal of Applied Social Psychology*, **28**: 1317–38.

Sutton, S. (1998b) How ordinary people in Great Britain perceive the health risks of smoking, *Journal of Epidemiological Community Health*, **52**: 338–9.

Sutton, S. (1999) The psychological costs of screening, in J.S. Tobias and I.C. Henderson (eds) *New Horizons in Breast Cancer: Current Controversies, Future Directions*. London: Chapman & Hall.

Sutton, S. (2000) Interpreting cross-sectional data on stages of change, *Psychology and Health*, **15**: 163–71.

Sutton, S. (2002a) Testing attitude-behaviour theories using non-experimental data: an examination of some hidden assumptions, *European Review of Social Psychology*, **13**: 293–323.

Sutton, S. (2002b) Using social cognition models to develop health behaviour interventions: problems and assumptions, in D. Rutter and L. Quine (eds) *Changing Health Behaviour: Intervention and Research with Social Cognition Models*. Maidenhead: Open University Press.

Sutton, S. (2005) Stage theories of health behaviour., in M. Conner and P. Norman (eds) *Predicting Health Behaviour*, 2nd edn. Maidenhead: Open University Press.

Sutton, S. (2010) Using social cognition models to develop health behavior interventions: the theory of planned behavior as an example, in D. French, K. Vedhara, A. Kaptein and J. Weinman (eds) *Health Psychology*, 2nd edn. Oxford: Blackwell.

Sutton, S.R. and Hallett, R. (1989) Understanding the effect of fear-arousing communications: the role of cognitive factors and amount of fear aroused, *Journal of Behavioral Medicine*, **11**: 353–60.

Sutton, S., McVey, D. and Glanz, A. (1999) A comparative test of the theory of reasoned action and the theory of planned behaviour in the prediction of condom use intentions in a national sample of English young people, *Health Psychology*, **18**: 72–81.

Sutton, S., Wardle, J., Taylor, T. et al. (2000) Predictors of attendance in United Kingdom flexible sigmoidoscopy screening trial, *Journal of Medical Screening*, **7**: 99–104.

Sutton, S., Saidi, G., Bickler, G. and Hunter, J. (1995) Does routine screening for breast cancer raise anxiety? Results from a three wave prospective study in England, *Journal of Epidemiology and Community Health*, **49**: 413–18.

Swindle, R.E. Jr and Moos, R.H. (1992) Life domains in stressors, coping and adjustment, in W.B. Walsh, R. Price and K.B. Crack (eds) *Person Environment Psychology: Models and Perspectoves*. Mahwah, NJ: Erlbaum.

Sysko, R., Walsh, T.B., and Wilson, G.T. (2007) Expectancies, dietary restraint, and test meal intake among undergraduate women, *Appetite*, **49**: 30–7.

Szasz, T. (1961) *The Myth of Mental Illness*. New York: Harper & Row.

Tardy, C.H. (1985) Social support measurement. *American Journal of Community Psychology*, **13**: 187–203.

Tataranni, P.A., Harper, I.T., Snitker, S. et al. (2003) Body weight gain in free-living Pima indians: effect of energy intake vs expenditure, *International Journal of Obesity*, **27**: 1578–83.

Tayler, M. and Ogden, J. (2005) Doctors' use of euphemisms and their impact on patients' beliefs about their illness, *Patient Education and Counselling*, **57**: 321–6.

Taylor, R., Morrell, S., Slaytor, E. and Ford, P. (1998) Suicide in urban New South Wales, Australia 1985–1994: socio-economic and migrant interactions, *Social Science and Medicine*, **47**: 1677–86.

Taylor, R.E., Mann, A.H., White, N.J. and Goldberg, D.P. (2000) Attachment style in patients with medically unexplained physical complaints, *Psychological Medicine*, **30**: 931–41.

Taylor, S., Kemeny, M., Reed, G. and Bower, J. (1998) Psychosocial influence on course of disease: predictors of HIV progression, *Health Psychology Update*, **34**: 7–12.

Taylor, S.E. (1983) Adjustment to threatening events: a theory of cognitive adaptation, *American Psychologist*, **38**: 1161–73.

Taylor, S.E., Lichtman, R.R. and Wood, J.V. (1984) Attributions, beliefs about control, and adjustment to breast cancer, *Journal of Personality and Social Psychology*, **46**: 489–502.

Tedeschi, R.D. and Calhoun, L.G. (2004) Posttraumatic growth: conceptual foundations and empirical evidence, *Psychological Inquiry*, **15**(1): 1–18.

Tedeschi, R.D. and Calhoun, L.G. (2006) Foundations of post traumatic growth, in R.G. Tedeschi and L.G. Calhoun (eds) *Handbook of Post Traumatic Growth*. Hillsdale, NJ: Erlbaum.

Temoshok, L. and Fox, B.H. (1984) Coping styles and other psychosocial factors related to medical status and to prognosis in patients with cutaneous malignant melanoma, in B.H. Fox and B.H. Newberry (eds) *Impact of Psychoendocrine Systems in Cancer and Immunity*. Toronto: C.J. Hogrefe.

Temoshok, L., Sweet, D.M. and Zich, J.A. (1987) A three city comparison of the public's knowledge and attitudes about AIDS, *Psychology and Health*, **1**: 43–60.

Tennen, H. and Affleck, G. (1999) Finding benefits in adversity, in C.R. Snyder (ed.) *Coping: The Psychology of What Works*. New York: Oxford University Press.

Tennen, H., Affleck, G., Armeli, S. and Carney, M.A. (2000) A daily process approach to coping: linking theory, research and practice, *American Psychologist*, **55**: 626–36.

Thapar, A.K. and Thapar, A. (1992) Psychological sequelae of miscarriage: a controlled study using the general health questionnaire and hospital anxiety and depression scale, *British Journal of General Practice*, **42**: 94–6.

The Henry J. Kaiser Foundation (2005) http://www.kff.org.

Theadom, A. and Cropley, M. (2006) Effects of preoperative smoking cessation on the incidence and risk of intraoperative and postoperative complications in adult smokers: a systematic review, *Tobacco Control*, **15**: 352–8.

Thompson, J.K. and Heinberg, L.J. (1999) The media's influence on body image disturbance and eating disorders: we've reviled them, now we can rehabilitate them? *Journal of Social Issues*, **55**(2): 339–53.

Thompson, J.P., Palmer, R.L. and Petersen, S.A. (1988) Is there a metabolic component to counter-regulation? *International Journal of Eating Disorders*, **7**: 307–19.

Thompson, M., Zanna, M. and Griffin, D. (1995) Let's not be indifferent about (attitudinal) ambivalence, in R.E. Perry and J.A. Krosnick (eds), *Attitude Strength: Antecedents and Consequences*, pp. 361–86. Hillsdale, NJ: Erlbaum.

Thompson, S.C. (1986) Will it hurt less if I can control it? A complex answer to a simple question, *Psychological Bulletin*, **90**: 89–101.

Tiggemann, M. and McGill, B. (2004) The role of social comparison in the effect of magazine advertisements on women's mood and body dissatisfaction, *Journal of Social and Clinical Psychology*, **23**(1): 23–44.

Tiggemann, M., and Pennington, B. (1990) The development of gender differences in body-size dissatisfaction, *Australian Psychologist*, **25**: 306–13.

Tiggemann, M., Martins, Y. and Churchett, L. (2008) Beyond muscles: unexplored parts of men's body image, *Journal of Health Psychology*, **13**(8): 1163–72.

Timio, M., Verdecchia, P., Venanzi, S. et al. (1988) Age and blood pressure changes: a 20-year follow-up study in nuns in a secluded order, *Hypertension*, **12**: 457–61.

Torgerson, J.S. and Sjostrom, L. (2001) The Swedish Obese Subjects (SOS) study: rationale and results, *International Journal of Obesity*, May **25**(suppl. 1): S2–4.

Totman, R.G. (1987) *The Social Causes of Illness*. London: Souvenir Press.

Trafimow, D. (2000) Habit as both a direct cause of intention to use a condom and as a moderator of the attitude-intention and subjective norm intention relations, *Psychology and Health*, **15**: 383–93.

Trafimow, D., Sheeran, P., Conner, M. and Finlay, K.A. (2002) Evidence that perceived behavioural control is a multidimensional construct: perceived control and perceived difficulty, *British Journal of Social Psychology*, **41**: 101–21.

Treiber, F.A., Kamarck, T., Schneiderman, N. et al. (2003) Cardiovascular reactivity and development of pre-clinical and clinical disease states, *Psychosomatic Medicine*, **65**(1): 46–62.

Trostle, J.A. (1988) Medical compliance as an ideology, *Social Science and Medicine*, **27**: 1299–308.

Tsutsumi, A., Tsutsumi, K., Kayaba, K. et al. (1998) Job strain and biological coronary risk factors: a cross-sectional study of male and female workers in a Japanese rural district, *International Journal of Behavioural Medicine*, **5**: 295–311.

Tuckett, D., Boulton, M., Olson, C. and Williams, A. (1985) *Meetings Between Experts*. London: Tavistock.

Tudor-Locke, C., Ainsworth, B. E. and Popkin, B. M. (2001) Active commuting to school: an overlooked source of children's physical activity? *Sports Medicine*, **31**(5): 309–13.

Tunaley, J.R., Slade, P. and Duncan, S. (1993) Cognitive processes in psychological adaptation to miscarriage: a preliminary report, *Psychology and Health*, **9**: 369–81.

Turk, D.C. and Rennert, K. (1981) Pain and the terminally ill cancer patient: a cognitive social learning perspective, in H. Sobel (ed.) *Behavior Therapy in Terminal Care*. New York: Ballinger.

Turk, D.C., Meichenbaum, D. and Genest, M. (1983) *Pain and Behavioral Medicine*. New York: Guilford Press.

Turk, D.C., Wack, J.T. and Kerns, R.D. (1985) An empirical examination of the 'pain-behaviour' construct, *Journal of Behavioral Medicine*, **8**: 119–30.

Turner, J.R. and Carroll, D. (1985) The relationship between laboratory and 'real world' heart rate reactivity: an exploratory study, in J.F. Orlebeke, G. Mulder and J.L.P. Van Doornen (eds) *Psychophysiology of Cardiovascular Control: Models, Methods and Data*. New York, Plenum.

Twigg, L., Moon, G. and Walker, S. (2004) *The Smoking Epidemic in England*. London: Health Development Agency.

Uchino, B.N. and Garvey, T.S. (1997) The availability of social support reduces cardiovascular reactivity to acute psychological stress, *Journal of Behavioral Medicine*, **20**: 15–27.

Uitenbroek, D.G., Kerekovska, A. and Festchieva, N. (1996) Health lifestyle behaviour and socio-demographic characteristics: a study of Varna, Glasgow and Edinburgh, *Social Science and Medicine*, **34**: 907–17.

Unruh, A.M., Ritchie, J. and Merskey, H. (1999) Does gender affect appraisal of pain and pain coping strategies? *Clinical Journal of Pain*, **15**: 31–40.

Upton, A.L., Beebe, G.W., Brown, J.W. et al. (1977) Report of NCI ad hoc working group on the risks associated with mammography in mass screening for the detection of breast cancer, *Journal of the National Cancer Institute*, **59**: 479–93.

US Environmental Protection Agency (1992) *Respiratory Health Effects of Passive Smoking: Lung Cancer and Other Disorders*. Washington, DC: US Environmental Protection Agency.

USDA (1998/1999) *Continuing Survey of Food Intakes by Individuals (1994–6)*, www.ars.usda.gov.

Ussher, M., Nunziata, P. and Cropley, M. (2001) Effect of a short bout of exercise on tobacco withdrawal symptoms and desire to smoke, *Psychopharmacology*, **158**: 66–72.

Utian, W.H., Burry, K.A., Archer, D.F. et al. (1999) Efficacy and safety of low, standard, and high dosages of an estradiol transdermal system (Esclim) compared with placebo on vasomotor symptoms in highly symptomatic menopausal patients: the Esclim Study Group, *American Journal of Obstetrics and Gynecology*, **181**(1): 71–9.

Van Asbeck, F.W.A., Post, M.W.M. and Pangalila, R.F. (2000) An epidemiological description of spinal cord injury in The Netherlands in 1994, *Spinal Cord*, **38**: 420–4.

Van Damme, S., Crombez, G. and Eccleston, C. (2002) Retarded disengagement from pain cues: the effect of pain catastrophizing and pain expectancy, *Pain*, **100**(1–2): 111–18.

van de Pligt, J., Zeelenberg, M., van Dijk, W.W. et al. (1998) Affect, attitudes and decisions: let's be more specific, *European Review of Social Psychology*, **8**: 33–66.

van den Berg, A.E. and Custers, M.H.G. (2011) Gardening promotes neuroendocrine and affective restoration from stress, *Journal of Health Psychology*, **16**(1): 3–11.

van den Berg, H., Manstead, A.S.R., van der Pligt, J. and Wigboldus, D. (2005) The role of affect in attitudes toward organ donation and donar relevant decisions, *Psychology and Health*, **20**: 789–802.

van Elderen, T. and Dusseldorp, E. (2001) Lifestyle effects of group health education for patients with coronary heart disease, *Psychology and Health*, **16**: 327–41.

van Elderen, T., Maes, S. and van den Broek, Y. (1994) Effects of a health education programme with telephone follow-up during cardiac rehabilitation, *British Journal of Clinical Psychology*, **33**: 367–78.

van Griensven, G.J.P., Teilman, R.A.P., Goudsmit, J. et al. (1986) Riskofaktoren en prevalentie van LAV/HTLV III antistoffen bij homoseksuele mannen in Nederland, *Tijdschrift voor Sociale Gezondheidszorg*, **64**: 100–7.

van Strien, T., Frijters, J.E., Bergers, G.P. and Defares, P.B. (1986) Dutch eating behaviour questionnaire for the assessment of restrained, emotional, and external eating behaviour, *International Journal of Eating Disorders*, **5**: 295–315.

van Strien, T., Herman, C.P. and Verheijden, M.W. (2009) Eating style, overeating, and overweight in a representative Dutch sample: does external eating play a role? *Appetite*, **52**(2): 380–7.

van Tulder, M.W., Ostelo, R., Vleeyen, J.W.S. et al. (2000) Behavioural treatment for chronic low back pain, *Spine*, **25**(20): 2688–9.

van Zuuren, F.J. (1998) The effects of information, distraction and coping style on symptom reporting during pre-term labor, *Psychology and Health*, **13**: 49–54.

Vandelanotte, C., Spathonis, K.M., Eakin, E.G. and Owen, N. (2007) Website-delivered physical activity interventions: a review of the literature, *American Journal of Preventive Medicine*, **33**(1): 54–64.

Veale, D. (1987) Exercise dependence, *British Journal of Addiction*, **82**: 735–40.

Veenstra, G. (2000) Social capital, SES and health: an individual-level analysis, *Social Science & Medicine*, **50**(5): 619–29.

Velicer, W.F., DiClemente, C.C., Prochaska, J.O. and Brandenberg, N. (1985) A decisional balance measure for assessing and predicting smoking status, *Journal of Personality and Social Psychology*, **48**: 1279–89.

Venturini, F., Romero, M. and Tognoni, G. (1999) Patterns of practice for acute myocardial infarction in a population from ten countries, *European Journal of Clinical Pharmacology*, **54**(11): 877–86.

Verbeke, W., and Vackier, I. (2005) Individual determinants of fish consumption: application of the theory of planned behaviour, *Appetite*, **44**: 67–82.

Verbrugge, L.M. (1979) Marital status and health, *Journal of Marriage and the Family*, **41**: 267–85.

Verplanken, B. and Aarts, H. (1999) Habit, attitude, and planned behaviour: is habit an empty construct or an interesting case of automaticity? *European Review of Social Psychology*, **10**: 101–34.

Verplanken, B., Aarts, H., van Knippenberg, A. and van Knippenberg, C. (1994) Attitude versus general habit: antecedents of travel mode choice, *Journal of Applied Social Psychology*, **24**: 285–300.

Violanti, J., Marshall, J. and Howe, B. (1983) Police occupational demands, psychological distress and the coping function of alcohol, *Journal of Occupational Medicine*, **25**: 455–8.

Vitaliano, P.P., Maiuro, R.D., Russo, J. et al. (1990) Coping profiles associated with psychiatric, physical health, work and family problems, *Health Psychology*, **9**: 348–76.

Vitaliano, P.P., Russo, J., Bailey, S.L. et al. (1993) Psychosocial factors associated with cardiovascular reactivity in old adults, *Psychosomatic Medicine*, **55**(2): 164–77.

Vlaeyen, J.W.S. and Linton, S. (2000) Fear-avoidance and its consequences in chronic muculoskeletal pain: a state of the art, *Pain*, **85**: 317–32.

Vollrath, M. and Toergensen, S. (2002) Who takes health risks? A probe into eight personality types, *Personality and Individual Differences*, **32**: 1185–97.

Von Frey, M. (1895) *Untersuchungen über die Sinnesfunctionen der menschlichen Haut erste Abhandlung: Druckempfindung und Schmerz*. Leipzig: Hirzel.

Wadden, T.A. (1993) Treatment of obesity by moderate and severe calorie restriction: results of clinical research trials, *Annals of Internal Medicine*, **119**: 688–93.

Wadden, T.A., Stunkard, A.J. and Smoller, W.S. (1986) Dieting and depression: a methodological study, *Journal of Consulting and Clinical Psychology*, **64**: 869–71.

Wadden, T.A., Foster, G.D., Wang, J. et al. (1992) Clinical correlates of short and long term weight loss, *American Journal of Clinical Nutrition*, **56**: S271–74.

Wadsworth, M.E.J. (1991) *The Imprint of Time: Childhood History and Adult Life*. Oxford: Oxford University Press.

Wadsworth, M.E.J. and Kuh, D.J. (1997) Childhood influences on adult health: a review of recent work from the British 1946 National Birth Cohort Study, the MRC National Survey of Health and Development, *Paediatric and Perinatal Epidemiology*, **11**: 2–20.

Walburn, J., Vedhara, K., Hankins, M. et al. (2009) Psychological stress and wound healing in humans: a systematic review and meta-analysis, *Journal of Psychosomatic Research*, **67**(3): 253–71.

Walker, W.B. and Franzini, L.R. (1985) Low-risk aversive group treatments, physiological feedback, and booster sessions for smoking cessation, *Behaviour Therapy*, **16**: 263–74.

Waller, D., Agass, M., Mant, D. et al. (1990) Health checks in general practice: another example of inverse care? *British Medical Journal*, **300**: 1115–18.

Waller, G., Hamilton, K. and Shaw, J. (1992) Media influences on body size estimation in eating disordered and comparison subjects, *British Review of Bulimia and Anorexia Nervosa*, **6**: 81–7.

Waller, K., Kaprio, J., and Kujala, U.M. (2008) Associations between long-term physical activity, waist circumference and weight gain: a 30-year longitudinal twin study, *International Journal of Obesity*, **32**(2): 353–61.

Wallsten, T.S. (1978) Three biases in the cognitive processing of diagnostic information, unpublished paper, Psychometric Laboratory, University of North Carolina, Chapel Hill, NC.

Wallston, B.S., Alagna, S.W., Devellis, B.M. and Devellis, R.F. (1983) Social support and physical illness, *Health Psychology*, **2**: 367–91.

Wallston, K.A. and Wallston, B.S. (1982) Who is responsible for your health? The construct of health locus of control, in G.S. Sanders and J. Suls (eds) *Social Psychology of Health and Illness*. Hillsdale, NJ: Erlbaum.

Walton, A.J. and Eves, F. (2001) Exploring drug users' illness representations of HIV, hepatitis B and hepatitis C using repertory grids, *Psychology and Health*, **16**: 489–500.

Wanebo, C.K., Johnson, K.G., Sato, K. and Thorslind, T.W. (1968) Breast cancer after the exposure to the atomic bombings of Hiroshima and Nagasaki, *New England Journal of Medicine*, **279**: 667–71.

Wang, S.J., Liu, H.C., Fuh, J.L. et al. (1997) Prevalence of headaches in a Chinese elderly population in Kinmen: age and gender effect and cross-cultural comparisons, *Neurology*, **49**: 195–200.

Wardle, J. (1980) Dietary restraint and binge eating, *Behaviour Analysis and Modification*, **4**: 201–9.

Wardle, J. (1995) Parental influences on children's diets, *Proceedings of the Nutrition Society*, **54**: 747–58.

Wardle, J. and Beales, S. (1988) Control and loss of control over eating: an experimental investigation, *Journal of Abnormal Psychology*, **97**: 35–40.

Wardle, J., Cooke, L.J., Gibson, E.L. et al. (2003) Increasing children's acceptance of vegetables: a randomized trial of parent-led exposure, *Appetite*, **40**(2): 155–62.

Wardle, J., Steptoe, A., Bellisle, F. et al. (1997) Health dietary practices among European students, *Health Psychology*, **16**: 443–50.

Wardle, J., Sanderson, S., Guthrie, C.A., Rapoport, L. and Plomin, R. (2002) Parental feeding style and the intergenerational transmission of obesity risk, *Obesity Research*, **10**: 453–62.

Ware, J.E. and Sherbourne, C.D. (1992) The MOS 36-item short form health survey (SF-36): conceptual framework and item selection, *Medical Care*, **30**: 473–83.

Warren, C. and Cooper, P.J. (1988) Psychological effects of dieting, *British Journal of Clinical Psychology*, **27**: 269–70.

Wason, P.C. (1974) The psychology of deceptive problems, *New Scientist*, 15 August: 382–5.

Wathen, C.N. (2006) Alternatives to hormone replacement therapy: a multi-method study of women's experiences, *Complementary Therapies in Medicine*, **14**(3): 185–92.

Watson, J. (2000) *Male Bodies: Health, Culture and Identity*. Buckingham: Open University Press.

Watson, M., Greer, S., Rowden, L. et al. (1991) Relationships between emotional control, adjustment to cancer and depression and anxiety in breast cancer patients, *Psychological Medicine*, **21**: 51–7.

Watson, W.L. and Ozanne-Smith, J. (2000) Injury surveillance in Victoria, Australia: developing comprehensive injury incidence estimates, *Accident Analysis and Prevention*, **32**: 277–86.

Wearden, A. and Peters, S. (2008) Therapeutic techniques for interventions based on Leventhal's common sense model, *British Journal of Health Psychology*, **13**: 189–93.

Wearden, A., Cook, L. and Vaughan-Jones, J. (2003) Adult attachment, alexithymia, symptom reporting, and health related coping, *Journal of Psychosomatic Research*, **55**(4): 341–7.

Weatherall, R., Joshi, H. and Macran, S. (1994) Double burden or double blessing? Employment, motherhood and mortality in the Longitudinal Study of England and Wales, *Social Science and Medicine*, **38**: 285–97.

Weatherburn, P., Hunt, A.J., Davies, P.M. et al. (1991) Condom use in a large cohort of homosexually active men in England and Wales, *AIDS Care*, **3**: 31–41.

Weg, R.B. (1983) Changing physiology of aging, in D.S. Woodruff and J.E. Birren (eds) *Ageing: Scientific Perspectives and Social Issues*, 2nd edn. Monterey, CA: Brooks/Cole.

Wegner, D.M. (1994) Ironic processes of mental control, *Psychological Review*, **101**: 34–52.

Wegner, D.M., Erber, R., and Zanakos, S. (1993) Ironic processes in the mental control of mood and mood related thought, *Journal of Personality and Social Psychology*, **65**: 1093–104.

Wegner, D.M., Schneider, D.J., Cater, S.R. and White, T.L. (1987) Paradoxical effects of thought suppression, *Journal of Personality and Social Psychology*, **53**: 5–13.

Wegner, D.M., Shortt, J.W., Blake, A.W. and Page, M.S. (1999) The suppression of exciting thoughts, *Journal of Personality and Social Psychology*, **58**: 409–18.

Weidner, G., Rice, T., Knox, S.S. et al. (2000) Familiar resemblance for hostility: the National Heart, Lung, and Blood Institute Family Heart Study, *Psychosomatic Medicine*, **62**: 197–204.

Weiner, B. (1986) *An Attributional Theory of Motivation and Emotion*. New York: Springer-Verlag.

Weinman, J., Ebrecht, M., Scott, S. et al. (2008) Enhanced wound healing after an emotional disclosure intervention, *British Journal of Health Psychology*, **13**: 95–102.

Weinman, J., Yusuf, G., Berks, R. et al. (2009) How accurate is patients' anatomical knowledge: a cross-sectional, questionnaire study of six patient groups and a general public sample, *BMC Family Practice*, **10**: 43.

Weinman, J., Petrie, K.J., Moss-Morris, R. and Horne, R. (1996) The Illness Perception Questionnaire: a new method for assessing the cognitive representation of illness, *Psychology and Health*, **11**: 431–46.

Weinstein, N. (1983) Reducing unrealistic optimism about illness susceptibility, *Health Psychology*, **2**: 11–20.

Weinstein, N., Rothman, A.J. and Sutton, S.R. (1998) Stage theories of health behavior: conceptual and methodological issues, *Health Psychology*, **17**: 290–9.

Weinstock, M.A., Rossi, J.S., Redding, C.A. et al. (2000) Sun protection behaviors and stages of change for the primary prevention of skin cancers among beachgoers in southeastern New England, *Annals of Behavioral Medicine*, **22**(4): 286–93.

Weisman, C.S., Plichta, S., Nathanson, C.A. et al. (1991) Consistency of condom use for disease prevention among adolescent users of oral contraceptives, *Family Planning Perspective*, **23**: 71–4.

Weiss, G.L. and Larson, D.L. (1990) Health value, health locus of control and the prediction of health protective behaviours, *Social Behaviour and Personality*, **18**: 121–36.

Weisse, C.S., Turbiasz, A.A. and Whitney, D.J. (1995) Behavioral training and AIDS risk reduction: overcoming barriers to condom use, *AIDS Education and Prevention*, **7**(1): 50–9.

Weller, S.S. (1984) Cross-cultural concepts of illness: variables and validation, *American Anthropologist*, **86**: 341–51.

Wellings, K., Field, J., Johnson, A.M. and Wadsworth, J. (1994) *Sexual Behaviour in Britain: The National Survey of Sexual Attitudes and Lifestyles*. Harmondsworth: Penguin.

Welton, A., Hepworth, J., Collings, N. et al. (Women's International Study of Long Duration Oestrogen after Menopause (WISDOM) team) (2004) Decision-making about hormone replacement therapy by women in England and Scotland, *Climacteric*, **7**(1): 41–9.

Wenzlaff, R.M. and Wegner, D.M. (2000) Thought suppression, *Annual Review of Psychology*, **51**: 59–91.

West, R. (2006) *Theory of Addiction*. Oxford: Blackwell.

West, R. and Shiffman, S. (2004) *Smoking Cessation*. Oxford: Health Press.

West, R. and Sohal, T. (2006) 'Catastrophic' pathways to smoking cessation: findings from a national survey, *British Medical Journal*, **332**(7539): 458–60.

West, R., and Stapleton, J (2008) Clinical and public health significance of treatments to aid smoking cessation, *European Respiratory Review*, **17**: 199–204.

West, R., Walia, A., Hyder, N. et al. (2010) Behavior change techniques used by the English Stop Smoking Services and their associations with short-term quit outcomes, *Nicotine & Tobacco Research*, **12**(7): 742–7.

Westhaver, R. (2005) 'Coming out of your skin': circuit parties, pleasure and the subject, *Sexualities*, **8**(3): 347–74.

White, I.R., Altmann, D.R. and Nanchahal, K. (2002) Alcohol consumption and mortality: modelling risks for men and women at different ages, *British Medical Journal*, **27**(325): 191.

White, K.M., Robinson, N.G., Young, R.M. et al. (2008) Testing an extended theory of planned behaviour to predict young people's sun safety in a high risk area, *British Journal of Health Psychology*, **13**(3): 435–48.

White, P.D., Goldsmith, K.A., Johnson, A.L. et al. (2011) Comparison of adaptive pacing therapy, cognitive behaviour therapy, graded exercise therapy, and specialist medical care for chronic fatigue syndrome (PACE): a randomised trial, *Lancet*, **377**(9768): 823–36.

Whitley, B.E. and Schofield, J.W. (1986) A meta-analysis of research on adolescent contraceptive use, *Population and Environment*, **8**: 173–203.

WHO (World Health Organization) (1947) *Constitution of the World Health Organization*. Geneva: WHO.

WHO (World Health Organization) (2003) *Adherence to Long-term Therapies: Evidence for Action*. Geneva: WHO.

WHO (World Health Organization) (1996) *Research on the Menopause in the 1990s*. Geneva: WHO.

WHO (World Health Organization) (2006) Obesity and overweight, www.who.int/mediacentre/factsheets/fs311/en/index.html.

WHO (World Health Organization) (2008) *Progress on Drinking-water and Sanitation: Special Focus on Sanitation*, http://www.who.int/water_sanitation_health/monitoring/jmp2008/en/index.html.

WHO (World Health Organization) (2010) *World Health Statistics 2010*, www.who.int/whosis/whostat/EN_WHS10_Full.pdf.

WHO Europe (World Health Organization Europe) (2007) *The Challenge of Obesity in the WHO European Region and the Strategies for Response*, www.euro.who.int/document/E90711.

WHO European Health for All Database (accessed December 2004), http://www.euro.who.int/en/what-we-do/data-and-evidence/databases/european-health-for-all-database-hfa-db2.

WHOQoL Group (1993) *Measuring Quality of Life: The Development of a World Health Organization Quality of Life Instrument (WHOQoL)*. Geneva: WHO.

Wickramasekera, I. (1980) A conditioned response model of the placebo effect: predictions from the model, *Biofeedback and Self Regulation*, **5**: 5–18.

Wiczinski, E., Döring, A., John, J. and von Lengerke, T. (2009) Obesity and health-related quality of life: does social support moderate existing associations? *British Journal of Health Psychology*, **14**: 717–34.

Wiebe, D.J. and McCallum, D.M. (1986) Health practices and hardiness as mediators in the stress–illness relationship, *Health Psychology*, **5**: 425–38.

Wiedenfeld, S.A., O'Leary, A., Bandura, A. et al. (1990) Impact of perceived self-efficacy in coping with stressors on immune function, *Journal of Personality and Social Psychology*, **59**: 1082–94.

Wild, B., Erb, M. and Batels, M. (2001) Are emotions contagious? Evoked emotions while viewing emotionally expressive faces: quality, quantity, time course and gender differences, *Psychiatry Research*, **102**: 109–24.

Wilkinson, A.V., Holahan, C.J. and Drane-Edmundson, E.W. (2002) Predicting safer sex practices: the interactive role of partner cooperation and cognitive factors, *Psychology and Health*, **17**(6): 697–709.

Wilkinson, C., Jones, J.M. and McBride, J. (1990) Anxiety caused by abnormal result of cervical smear test: a controlled trial, *British Medical Journal*, **300**: 440.

Wilkinson, D. and Abraham, C. (2004) Constructing an integrated model of the antecedents of adolescent smoking, *British Journal of Health Psychology*, **9**: 315–33.

Willett, W.C., Manson, J.E., Stampfer, M.J. et al. (1995) Weight, weight change and coronary heart disease in women: risk within the 'normal' weight range, *Journal of the American Medical Association*, **273**: 461–5.

Williams, A.C. (2002) Facial expression of pain: an evolutionary account, *Behaviour and Brain Sciences*, **25**(4): 439–55.

Williams, K.E., Paul, C., Pizzo, B. and Riegel, K (2008) Practice does make perfect: a longitudinal look at repeated taste exposure, *Appetite*, **51**(3): 739–42.

Williams, S., Weinman, J.A., Dale, J. and Newman, S. (1995) Patient expectations: what do primary care patients want from their GP and how far does meeting expectations affect patient satisfaction? *Journal of Family Practice*, **12**: 193–201.

Wills, T.A. (1985) Supportive functions of interpersonal relationships, in S. Cohen and S.L. Syme (eds) *Social Support and Health*. Orlando, FL: Academic Press.

Wilson, D.M., Taylor, M.A., Gilbert, J.R. et al. (1988) A randomised trial of a family physician intervention for smoking cessation, *Journal of the American Medical Association*, **260**: 1570–4.

Wilson, G.T. (1978) Alcoholism and aversion therapy: issues, ethics, and evidence, in G. Marlatt and P. Nathan (eds) *Behavioral Approaches to Alcoholism*. New Brunswick, NJ: Journal of Studies on Alcohol.

Wilson, G.T. (1994) Behavioural treatment of obesity: thirty years and counting, *Advances in Behavioural Research Therapy*, **16**: 31–75.

Wilson, J.M.G. (1965) Screening criteria, in G. Teeling-Smith (ed.) *Surveillance and Early Diagnosis in General Practice*. London: Office of Health Economics.

Winefield, H., Murrell, T., Clifford, J. and Farmer, E. (1996) The search for reliable and valid measures of patient centredness, *Psychology and Health*, **11**: 811–24.

Winfield, E.B. and Whaley, A.L. (2002) A comprehensive test of the health belief model in the prediction of condom use among African American college students, *Journal of Black Psychology*, **28**: 330–46.

Wing, R.R., Koeske, R., Epstein, L.H. et al. (1987) Long term effects of modest weight loss in type II diabetic patients, *Archives of Internal Medicine*, **147**: 1749–53.

Wolf, T.M. and Kissling, G.E. (1984) Changes in life-style characteristics, health, and mood of freshman medical students, *Journal of Medical Education*, **59**: 806–14.

Wong, C.L. and Mullan, B.A. (2009) Predicting breakfast consumption: an application of the theory of planned behaviour and the investigation of past behaviour and executive function, *British Journal of Health Psychology*, **14**: 489–504.

Wong, M. and Kaloupek, D.G. (1986) Coping with dental treatment: the potential impact of situational demands, *Journal of Behavioural Medicine*, **9**: 579–98.

Wong, M.L., Koh, D., Lee, M.H. and Fong, Y.T. (1997) Two-year follow up of a behavioural weight control programme for adolescents in Singapore: predictors of long term weight loss, *Annals of the Academy of Medicine, Singapore*, **26**: 147–53.

Wood, D.A., Kinmouth, A.L., Pyke, S.D.M. and Thompson, S.G. (1994) Randomised controlled trial evaluating cardiovascular screening and intervention in general practice: principal results of British family heart study, *British Medical Journal*, **308**: 313–20.

Woodcock, A., Stenner, K. and Ingham, R. (1992) Young people talking about HIV and AIDS: interpretations of personal risk of infection, *Health Education Research: Theory and Practice*, **7**: 229–47.

Woods, E.R., Lin, Y.G. and Middleman, A. (1997) The associations of suicide attempts in adolescents, *Pediatrics*, **99**: 791–6.

Wooley, S.C. and Wooley, O.W. (1984) Should obesity be treated at all? in A.J. Stunkard and E. Stellar (eds) *Eating and Its Disorders*. New York: Raven Press.

World Bank (2008) World Bank backs anti-AIDS experiment, press reviews 28 April, http://web.worldbank.org/ WBSITE/EXTERNAL/NEWS/0,date:2008-04-28~ menuPK:34461~pagePK:34392~piPK:64256810~theSit ePK:4607,00.html.

Wright, C.E., Ebrecht, M., Mitchell, R. et al. (2005) The effect of psychological stress on symptom severity and perception in patients with gastro-oesophageal reflux, *Journal of Psychosomatic Research*, **59**: 415–24.

Wright, J.A., Weinman, J. and Marteau, T.M. (2003) The impact of learning of a genetic predisposition to nicotine dependence: an analogue study, *Tobacco Control*, **12**: 227–30.

Writing Group for the Women's Health Initiative Investigators (2002) Risks and benefits of oestrogen plus progesterone in healthy post-menopausal women, *Joirnal of the American Medical Association*, **288**(3): 321–33.

Wyper, M.A. (1990) Breast self-examination and health belief model, *Research in Nursing and Health*, **13**: 421–8.

Yip, P.S., Callanan, C. and Yuen, H.P. (2000) Urban/rural and gender differentials in suicide rates: east and west, *Journal of Affective Disorders*, **57**: 99–106.

Yzer, M.C., Siero, F.W. and Buunk, B. (2001) Bringing up condom use and using condoms with new sexual partners: intentional or habitual? *Psychology and Health*, **16**: 409–21.

Ziegler, D.K. (1990) Headache: public health problem, *Neurologic Clinics*, **8**: 781–91.

Zigmond, A.S. and Snaith, R.P. (1983) The Hospital Anxiety and Depression Scale, *Acta Psychiatrica Scandinavica*, **67**: 361–70.

Zola, I.K. (1973). Pathways to the doctor: from person to patient, *Social Science and Medicine*, **7**: 677–89.

Zolese, G. and Blacker, C.V.R. (1992) The psychological complications of therapeutic abortion, *British Journal of Psychiatry*, **160**: 742–9.

Index

Locators shown in *italics* refer to figures, tables, boxes and case studies.

LIBRARY, UNIVERSITY OF CHESTER